VEERING RIGHT

Veering Right

How the Bush Administration Subverts the Law
for Conservative Causes

CHARLES TIEFER

UNIVERSITY OF CALIFORNIA PRESS

Berkeley   Los Angeles   London

University of California Press
Berkeley and Los Angeles, California

University of California Press, Ltd.
London, England

Library of Congress Cataloging-in-Publication Data

Tiefer, Charles.
   Veering right : how the Bush administration subverts the law for conservative causes / Charles Tiefer.
       p.   cm.
   Includes bibliographical references and index.
   ISBN 0-520-24286-6 (cloth : alk. paper).
   1. United States—Politics and government.   2. United States—Social
policy—1993–.   3. Bush, George W. (George Walker), 1946—Political and
social views.   4. Conservatism—United States.   5. Constitutional law—
United States.   6. Law—Political aspects—United States.   7. Political
corruption—United States   I. Title.

E902.T54   2004
320.52'0973'090511—dc22   2004044062

Manufactured in the United States of America
13   12   11   10   09   08   07   06   05   04
10   9   8   7   6   5   4   3   2   1

The paper used in this publication meets the minimum requirements of
ANSI/NISO Z39.48-1992 (R 1997) (Permanence of Paper). ∞

For my perfect trophy wife, Hillary—whom I dreamt of and searched for so long, whose lucky discovery gave me hope of a full life, and who, while I wrote this, juggled the work of three: sustaining me, bearing Roy the bunny boy, and raising Max and him to be wonderful

Contents

Acknowledgments

Doing this real-time analysis of the Bush administration has depended upon extraordinary people generously giving me extraordinary help, particularly to handle the challenge of penetrating the administration's secretiveness. All mentioned here are absolved of all responsibility for what these pages say.

I express special thanks to the scores of journalists who helped, in their funny way. They called me up pretty constantly because I'm a law professor who opines a lot; who served from 1979 to 1995 first in the Senate and then as the solicitor of the House of Representatives in posts that let me be near the action; and whose thousand-page treatise on congressional procedure, with its two thousand footnotes, signifies having lots of opinions about how leaders get things done for their causes in Washington. The press's questions consistently contained more source material, more of the journalists' own comparisons and analysis, and more of the emerging sense of what the administration is up to than is available any other way. I won't name these coworkers individually, apart from their queen, Gwen Ifill, who interviewed me on the *Lehrer NewsHour*. But you would find them on *ABC World News Tonight*, Black Entertainment Television, CBS radio, C-Span, *McLaughlin One-on-One*, MSNBC, *NBC Nightly News*, and NPR; published in the *Baltimore Sun*, *Chicago Tribune*, *Legal Times of Washington*, *Los Angeles Times*, *New York Times*, *Wall Street Journal*, *Washington Post*, and many other domestic print outlets; and in numerous foreign broadcast and print sources as well. Bless them all for calling (or filming) and chatting. Especially bless those whose reaction to my first comments was to snort or to laugh and then to challenge me with their own superior understanding.

I similarly owe huge debts to many congressional and administration staff, and a few members of Congress whom it's probably more discrete not to name. I'll just say that while I filed several Supreme Court and appellate court briefs for the House Democratic leadership and other congressional entities and repeatedly testified before House and Senate committees, in the past few years, the staff and members always give me much more than I give them.

Now, to specific helpers. The list must start with Robert Shepard, muse, strategist, eternal fount of positive thinking, savant of public affairs in his own right, a true gentleman; and, too, when the going got difficult and certain passages I'd researched to death and redone umpteen times still seemed not quite there, someone who could, and would, don his author cap, sit down at the keyboard, and put in his own two cents, which turned out to fit quite nicely. On a piece of paper we signed, it says that Robert Shepard is my agent. But the acuity he brought, the soul he poured into this book, reflect not just a seasoned and superb publishing professional but also a keen observer of national affairs and a gifted writer. I've said only a million times that he's the best.

I thank my colleagues at the University of California Press in Berkeley. Naomi Schneider, my editor, evidently saw inside the rough and crude draft that came in the door that there might be lurking a book like this. Her fresh and elevated vision of the possible book awoke me from dogmatic slumber, and her incisive insights into every chapter then furnished the guidance to try to keep faith with her lead. Above all, she kept the process of lifting the draft to the level of quality and substance on which she insisted zooming along at the appropriate, albeit author-killing, pace. Now that it's out, Naomi, you don't mind if I have a life again, do you? Credit is also due to the indispensable Sierra Filucci.

At the copyediting and production stage—ably managed by Michael Bass—project editor Valentina Pfeil, compositor Linda Marcetti, proofreader Leon Unruh, and Herr's Indexing Service provided remarkable organization, skill, and speed. They had to be—and were—wizards of coordination to handle the extensive revisions made to incorporate late-breaking events and disclosures. The remarkably versatile copy editor, Steven Baker, fluently translated the book's voice from my basic law professor's pattern into a smoother, very different dialect of the King's English. By his patient yet acute queries and his proposal of always superior alternative modes of presentation, he achieved on every page exposition more nuanced and precise yet more clear and concise.

I am thrilled by the cover, designed by the aesthetically gifted Eric Heiman, with text well crafted by Leslie Larson. And Alex Dahne, director of publicity at UC Press, gave my work in progress the kind of royal supportive (and effective) treatment usually reserved for trade presses with high budgets handling already best-selling authors. Producing a scholarly book about the current presidency in real time meant that the manuscript still was being completed when Alex began serving as the gifted seer of readers' demands. No one could provide more sophisticated and acute counsel on how to measure up to those demands. I have published three books before and received help from publishers for each that ranged from good to excellent, but the people who work at, and with, UC Press are in a class by themselves. They gave me their best, and I felt blessed.

Among my scholarly colleagues, Louis Fisher, the renowned author of a whole library of works about the dance of law and politics, conducted multiple close readings of drafts and gave recklessly the fruits of his universal knowledge and balanced, nonpartisan perspicacity. The other munificent lavisher of attention and insights was Michael Glennon, who soars above all mere mortals in his rarified altitudes of the theory of international law—but also happens to know his way around the dark subterranean corridors of the Capitol and Foggy Bottom and can put the high and the low together better than anyone else. Richard Briffault gave me the ultimate tutorial in the reality of campaign finance law in the course of his year preparing the Supreme Court amicus brief we filed in *McConnell v. FEC* (on the winning side, I'm pleased to say).

Jon Cuneo, tireless and ingenious builder of his own compact yet highly respected Capitol Hill law firm, shared precious ideas about key chapters. I published some tentative ideas (and three hundred early footnotes) about the Bush administration in an article entitled "How to Steal a Trillion: The Uses of Laws about Lawmaking in 2001" in the University of Virginia's *Journal of Law and Politics*. At that time, I received help from Elizabeth Garrett and Kate Stith—the two high scholarly priestesses of the cult of the mystical budget process; from Michael J. Graetz and Daniel Shaviro; and from several dozen lively faculty at three locations where we held discussions—the National Law Center at George Washington University, the Dickinson Law School, and the 2004 Legislation Section of the American Association of Law Schools.

At my own University of Baltimore School of Law, the exceptional dean, Gilbert Holmes, took care of me in many key ways—even beyond his focus on his vital school-building efforts—backing me in this project with both personal inspiration and concrete resources. So did our dexterous and diplomatic associate dean, Donald Stone. My colleagues at the school gave unstintingly of their own legal acumen, including Robert Lande and Barbara White on the interplay of law, money, and politics (they prefer the loftier phrase of "law and economics"); Michael Meyerson on political history; Eric Easton on the administration's strategy as to war and as to the press; Michael Higginbotham and Jane Murphy on conservatism as an obstacle to social progress; Tim Sellers on the higher theory of democratic structure; and many others in their own specialties about the interplay of law and politics, led by Kenneth Lasson, Richard Bourne, Audrey McFarlane, and Jonathan Lipson.

Two superb research assistants aided me: Philip J. Sweitzer, a legal investigative "bounty hunter" par excellence who can go in search of anything anywhere and bring it back dead or alive; and Erin Sher, whose comprehensive study of the administration's unilateralism in foreign affairs really deserves publication in its own right. I also thank the students in my classes, many of whom had fresh ideas I've grabbed for use somewhere in these pages. Their youthful vigor and enthusiasm did wonders for many a page that needed the tonic. I receive wondrous support from the law school's library and computer professionals—Will Tress, Harvey Morrell, Jim Gernert, and Sean Farmer—and especially Bob Pool, who has saved my sanity in countless computer crises, as have my ace private consultants, Marty Sutton and Shawn Weed.

I owe everything practical to my part-time legal secretary, Mary I. Heywood-Peterson, who can (and has) climbed computer/manuscript Mt. Everests to produce the technically challenging parts of my books and Supreme Court briefs. The endnotes received inordinate improvement by her; the bibliography came into this world much more from her muse than from mine; and she kept up our morale with tales of her athletic son, Kevin. My secretary at the law school, Barbara Jones, cheerfully patches over all problems and difficulties in squeezing the demands of my book in with those of my teaching schedule.

In Washington, the personal is also political. I owe debts in relation to this book that can never be repaid to many other experts and friends, including Stan Brand, Margarita Cereijido, Kathleen Clark, Bob Cowen, Elizabeth Culbreth, Jim Gelb, Adam Goldberg, Don Goldberg, Richard Goodstein, Sandy Harris, Michael Harrison, Marge Lenane, Chuck Ludlam, Wendy Pachter, Sharon Pohoryles, Ellen Rayner, Mort Rosenberg, Bill Shook, Virginia Sloan, and Stu Weisberg.

Rosalind Tiefer, who taught history for many decades both to her classes and to her son, provided a substantial part of the historic perspective in this book, sometimes indirectly, sometimes directly. Her unflagging devotion to reading and discussion about history and current events, informed by her ever youthful idealism and indignation, render her four-score years and ten simply another source of superb perspective. Dr. Leonore Tiefer, an eminent writer and public speaker, illuminated the issues of contemporary conservative causes from another angle by her own powerful and noble efforts and also provided uniquely precious emotional sustenance. My wife's relatives, notably her grandmother Frida and her brother Howard, also provide much-appreciated encouragement and support.

Notwithstanding the many expert helpers previously noted, particularly challenging and knotty intellectual problems, too hard for anyone else, often had to be referred to the clearest, deepest, and most supportive thinkers I know: Max, born in 1999, and Roy, born in 2002. Because they understand my own limitations, they explain things to me in simple terms, by drawing upon the metaphor of baseball in the backyard (Max) or tossing objects various distances off the table (Roy). Their ingenuity, wisdom, and good cheer far outshines those of anyone else I know. If anything after this book ever gets submitted under my name, it must be when Max and Roy lend me copies of their school homework assignments to turn in as my own. As for Hillary, I have said it in the dedication. She is my beautiful trophy wife. Her ideas, her emotional support, and her ability to take care of everything else while I did this are what made this book possible.

Introduction

He secretly started planning the occupation of Iraq from September 17, 2001, manipulated the issue right before the 2002 congressional race, and kept the public in the dark about the price tag until late 2003. His attorney general, John Ashcroft, would not let the FBI investigate terrorist suspects' gun buys—the NRA wouldn't like that—but sent out the FBI fifty times to demand public-library patron information. In both cases Ashcroft told his trademark give-no-ground yet highly embroidered fables as cover stories. The president rammed trillion-dollar deficit-financed tax cuts for the rich through Congress using statutory power intended only for debt-reducing measures, thereby abusing the law on the nation's highest budget governance. He installed his personal lawyer as an oversight-proof back channel in Riyadh, facilitating the darker aspects of diverting national anger after 9/11 from the implicated Saudis to the nonimplicated Iraqis. All these subversions of the law either were actively concealed or were buried by the White House's restricted, camouflaging, "daily message" system, so the public could barely even guess about its ruler's projects and plans.

All presidents govern by political means, including at least some political uses of the law. In my eleven years (1984–1995) as solicitor of the House of Representatives, representing the House in court and in investigations, I participated in countless inquiries and analyzed from an insider's vantage point the many concealed, devious, but potent ways that presidents have made and might henceforth make such political uses of the law. In foreign affairs modern presidents have extensive legal powers and often act with at least some political considerations in mind. President George H. W. Bush used a secret Presidential Decision Directive to court Saddam Hussein in the late 1980s, inducing in Iraq the false impression that invading Kuwait might be all right, then refused, even after the Gulf War, to let the public read the whole directive to know how it all had happened. President Bill Clinton signed various international agreements he supported, on matters from global warming to the creation of a war crimes court, that a Republican Congress was in no rush to approve and that some considered usurpation of power.

In domestic affairs presidents lack the vast freedom of action they have in foreign affairs, but they can still use law to reward their supporters rather than their opponents. President Ronald Reagan beefed up a tough "regulatory reform" office in order to please his business supporters by squelching regulation, setting back public-interest efforts for the environment and health for a decade. President Clinton conducted sweeping lame-duck actions in his final two months, from widely approved public-land protections to ill-considered pardons.

We expect presidents to use the law in doctrines and strategies that push, and sometimes push very hard, the limits of their political—and legal—powers. But there are legal boundaries we do not expect or condone a president to cross for political reasons. When presidents exceed even the public's broad tolerance for their prerogatives of office, we scrutinize the motivations and implications of their acts for possible abuses of the law. Subversions of the law need not constitute breaking the law; they may just involve straining and manipulating it in a way that causes voters, if fully informed, to shake their heads and say, "That's bad; don't do that." Some actions, though often not criminal, constitute abuses of the law, such as use of the toxic waste Superfund as patronage by Reagan's EPA head, Ann Gorsuch, who then let subordinates shred the evidence rather than come clean; or the patronage-motivated firing by President Clinton of the White House Travel Office employees. But subversions also include enormous national scandals, far-reaching and hard-edged, exposing whole networks of rot and corruption at the top, like Watergate and Iran-contra.

We accept a president's reaching for political power to provide some of what presidential supporters want, but not serving extreme ideological causes in ways that could distort the governance process in a long-term bid to put the extremists in power over the centrist majority. President Reagan had to drop his project to have Ollie North run right-wing foreign affairs projects, from deals to wars, with funds obtained from rich donors or duped "allies" and without even letting Congress know. President Clinton's "creative" new loopholes in campaign financing to fill his 1996 reelection coffers, although not intrinsically ideological, had the potential to give big donors with wish lists in their pocket a major say in the government; disclosure of these abuses in the campaign finance investigations motivated and enabled passage of the McCain-Feingold reform act of 2002.

President George W. Bush entered office eager to accomplish a larger-than-suspected far-right agenda, delivering much more for his conservative bases than their limited political strength would seemingly sustain. Through political uses of the law and under the cloak of secrecy whenever possible, the president delivers for conservative causes in domestic affairs, from environmental rollbacks to the redirection of the judiciary, and in international affairs as well. This all raises the question: how much more of this will a Bush second term bring?

The Bush administration's capacity to advance conservative causes impresses observers all the more because on their own these causes usually lack the strength to overcome centrist resistance. The National Rifle Association, the Christian Coalition, the top 1 percent of wealth holders in the country, and the industries seeking relaxation of environmental protections—each has its own substantial leverage, but none possesses the weight of a majority, or even a decisive plurality, of the electorate. Indeed, these organizations and groups, which are further from the nation's moderate consensus than even President Reagan's constituencies, would encounter difficulty achieving their goals by moving bills through the obstacle course of Congress. Aware of this, the administration uses other means to assist them.

The 2000 and 2002 elections and polls before and throughout Bush's presidency show that his popular support comes mainly from his image, or "character," including his leadership after 9/11. Large majorities reject his conservative stance on issues such as his objections to *Roe v. Wade* and his proposals to drain the Treasury for tax cuts for the wealthy instead of husbanding resources to shore up Social Security, Medicare, and education. In 2000 President Bush's loss of the popular vote, the problematic Florida contest, and his party's loss of six precious Senate seats denied him a real mandate for conservative activism. Even in 2002 his party regained only two Senate seats, a margin much too narrow to push ideological bills past a filibuster. In international affairs his conservative causes have had to swim upstream against increasing international resistance instead of moving with the current of international legal systems. By 2003–2004 his cause of occupying Iraq under the legal framework of a "preemption" doctrine had largely isolated America from world support.

And yet, instead of a presidency constrained by limited election mandates and world support and the limited popularity of his supporters' extreme causes, President Bush proved ready and able to do a great deal for the Republican Party's most conservative social and economic bases. How? Deft ordinary political maneuvering and an element of fate played their roles in enabling Bush to go so far. But this book focuses on a far more important, interesting, and troubling aspect of the Bush administration's effectiveness: its political use and sometimes abuse of the law for conservative political causes.

President Bush's new uses and abuses of law tap power sources independent of democratic political struggle on the floor of Congress. These include administrative, judicial, and foreign-affairs powers, as well as legal mechanisms within Congress that sidestep its normal processes. To maneuver around the absence of centrist support for conservative causes, the president depends on his augmented powers in international and national security matters; his scope for manipulation in domestic affairs, such as environmental regulation and campaign finance law; the support of the Supreme Court's conservative bloc of five, reinforced by an increasingly conservative lower judiciary; legal manipulation of other governance processes, from federalism to budget action; and smokescreens such as the official daily presidential "message," shielding the administration's actions from congressional questioning and other criticism.

Of course, the attacks of September 11, 2001, were not the president's specific fault, nor did he respond to them in a purely partisan way in the short run. Yet they initiated a climate of urgency and secrecy that added powerful new tools and strengthened old ones in the administration's arsenal for accomplishing ideological goals. Taken together, these tools have allowed President Bush to leverage his powers away from the legislative process, which requires coping with Senate rules that enforce moderation, and to act in ways shielded from congressional oversight and criticism. His course of action depends upon keeping the American public unaware of polices it would not fully support, and he has achieved such secrecy.

Rather than seeing President Bush's various tactical maneuvers as scattered and unconnected, this book analyzes his approach as a unified, if flexible, program of the political use of law. I start with an examination of the conditions that gave rise to President Bush's desire and capacity to follow this new course. Two distinct conservative constituencies sought to achieve noncentrist goals: social conservatives sought mainstream legitimacy for their various culturally restrictive and religiously oriented causes, some on the fringes; economic conservatives sought to increase the wealth and power of those in the very top tax brackets and felt that business should be "taken care of," as through a relaxation of environmental, safety, and other regulations. Neither conservative base, however, commanded the strong political support needed to roll over opposition in the open legislative arena, particularly in the Senate. There, the balance and the polarization of post-1990s politics meant that each party had the forces to block ideological legislative proposals and to curb, through criticism and oversight, the more extreme ideological initiatives of the other party's outer wing. Yet the rise of the conservative bloc of five on the Supreme Court, along with developments such as the lapse of the scandal-investigation machinery that had scrutinized Washington from Iran-contra to Monicagate, created the potential for a president with the requisite determination to serve those conservative groups. Finally, the background of the incoming president prepared him for the political uses of law. Even before taking public office in Texas, he used his law firm's connections, set up by the appointments of the senior President Bush, to fend off the SEC's insider trading case against him. As Texas governor, he mastered the art of offering legal favors to conservative business interests in exchange for receipt of massive campaign contributions.

In a critical step for Bush's implementation plans, he chose John Ashcroft to head the Justice Department. Chapter 2 begins with an analysis of Ashcroft's rise in the social conservative movement. Ashcroft used religiosity and race-baiting to build his political career, the latter most blatantly in his derision of a respected African American jurist as "pro-criminal" during a key 1999 Senate battle. Yet after being appointed attorney general in the Bush administration in 2000, Ashcroft's extreme notions were given relatively free reign. His ideological patronage for conservatives included the president's 2004 campaign poster of a late-term abortion statute, manipulated as a tool for undermining Roe v. Wade, and the president's fateful shift in 2004 to a stance of intolerance and manufactured confrontation with the courts on gay rights. Chapter 3 explores Ashcroft's supplication to the NRA on a national personal right to weaponry, even when doing so potentially imperiled national security. His 2003 implementation of the misnamed USA PATRIOT Act turned the most dangerous privacy- and liberty-threatening central government superpowers, intended only for fighting large-scale threats, against mere garden-variety crimes. Invoking his right to surveil library records of books taken out by patrons and

Internet material accessed at libraries, Ashcroft pushed for a further erosion of civil liberties, cavalierly dismissing citizens' rights to personal privacy, one of the nation's most cherished values. Further, he fueled Bush's effort to stack the federal judiciary with lifetime far-right appointments, with enormous future implications for democratic governance.

Chapter 4 takes an in-depth look at how President Bush sought to move domestic policy to the right by using and sometimes abusing the law for political reasons. Bush had no higher goal than to shift the balance between rich and poor by regressive, trillion-dollar top-bracket and estate tax cuts. Ordinarily, the Budget Act facilitates only those presidential proposals paid for by spending cuts, but President Bush abused the law in 2001 and 2003 by using the facilitated track for his program *without* paying for it. Further subversion may occur when, starting in 2005, his program's implementation schedule contrives that an increasingly large alternative tax will fall on middle-class Americans living mainly in the major Democratic-leaning states.

On another key domestic issue, environmental regulation, President Bush implemented a stealth approach. Interior Secretary Gail Norton and her staff of lawyer-lobbyists ran the public's resources and its pollution controls like a candy store for pariah industries. Chapter 5 examines the huge success of Bush's domestic gambits for big money, which paid off in 2004 with a historically large campaign war chest as a quid pro quo for favors rendered. Even the implementation in campaign finance of the McCain-Feingold legislation couldn't prevent Bush's aggressive tactics in "coordinating" the use of huge financial resources to achieve electoral goals. His agenda included the ruthless push for redistricting, most egregiously showcased in DeLay's manipulation of the Texas legislature to create more Republican congressional districts in the state. Bush also presided over a formidable dismantling and weakening of regulatory agencies, with his staff even developing a "tool kit" for using White House legal power against individual legislation.

Chapter 6 discusses international and security affairs. In this context presidents have great scope for initiative and hence for the political use of the law. President Bush's approach started with nullifying international legal regimes, ranging from arms control to global climate control and international tobacco regulation. And he secured, on the most partisan terms, fast-track authority to make trade deals, taking a hard line against environmental, labor, and other social concerns. This means the prospect in his second term, via the Doha Round and talks toward a Free Trade Agreement of the Americas, of establishing powerful global engines that export jobs and serve conservative economic ends. President Bush also cranked up the legal theory of unilateral preemption," the focus of chapter 7. This strategy allowed him to control and time the issue of Iraq to suit his 2002 political agenda at the price of creating the worst international isolation in American memory. His unilateral approach catered symbolically to his party's conservative bases and exacerbated the alienation of world support —support won in the Gulf War by the first President Bush and in Yugo-slavia by President Clinton.

Government secrecy warrants its own discussion in chapter 7. For President Bush to attain conservative goals by the political use of law, he vitally needs to fend off congressional criticism and legal oversight. An early demonstration of the new secrecy came in his lone formal executive privilege claim, which was resolved in the end by a showdown at a House hearing in March 2002 where I had the honor of giving the key testimony on the legal issues. In the international arena, the new secrecy proved essential in letting the president control the homeland security and Iraq issues, so that his own purposes, not those of the public, were served in the runup to the 2002 and 2004 elections. Bush's use of his personal lawyer as envoy to Saudi Arabia provided a channel that, because it was beyond the scrutiny even of his own State and CIA heads, was well adapted to coordinating the redirection of post-9/11 action from Riyadh to Baghdad. Domestically, the secrecy proved equally vital for such efforts as pushing exploitation of public resources.

The final chapter presses the analysis to a conclusion. President Bush has harnessed effective legal means to accomplish conservative goals in ways that leave him much latitude for the future. The road ahead may provide further opportunities for conservatives to achieve previously unimaginable successes. In one scenario President Bush could hit the short-term jackpot by expanding his Senate majority while appointing several conservatives to the Supreme Court. Together these would allow a coordinated multibranch drive to bring major far-right aspirations to fruition. The increasing push to the right could become irreversible through the combination of massive campaign financing by the well-heeled and the increasing conservatism of the courts.

But if the tension increases between the use of the law to serve political and ideological goals and the centrist desires of the electorate, an electoral and congressional backlash could develop. A number of administrations have faced major meltdowns or scandals in their second terms—for example, President Johnson's Vietnam, President Nixon's Watergate, President Reagan's Iran-contra, and President Clinton's Monicagate. These failures reflect a number of factors that trap presidents in their second terms, as their administrations forgo the political discipline previously self-imposed to win reelection while charging forward after election toward even more distant goals. Similar factors could operate during the years after 2005.

And now, first things first. Events leading up to 2001 help explain what happened next. These are the focus of chapter 1.

1   Getting Ready to Veer Right

The Bush administration's approach to governance evolved through three stages in America's two-decade march to the right: the realignment "South" underlying President Reagan, the further realignment "South" underlying the Gingrich-DeLay takeover, and Governor Bush's development in Austin of his own, even further-out program. Basically it all came down to turning right in 1981, turning hard right in 1995, and in Texas altogether rejecting the steering wheel on the driver's side and putting one in, special, to steer from the vehicle's right side. While that account conveys the overall direction, it omits the nuance, particularly the very distinctive groups pushing and sustaining the right turn—the sharp differences between, say, Jerry Falwell's Moral Majority movement and Malcolm Forbes's "Let *me* eat cake" approach. Moreover, it deserves supplementing with an examination of how the right could overcome the big political and legal obstacles that normally keep ideological minorities from beating down centrist majorities. And it calls for some understanding of the quite separate considerations involving how Jesse Helms and others put together a new stance for the right in foreign affairs to fill the gap left by the obsolescence of the hitherto all-important anti-communism issue. After addressing these points, the chapter moves to the foreshadowing of Bush's approach in the 2000 campaign and the Florida election contest.

"STAGGERED REALIGNMENT" RIGHT

For more than three decades national politics has moved through a political paradigm shift called by academics a "staggered realignment." An excellent if chilling account comes from William C. Berman in *America's Right Turn: From Nixon to Clinton.*[1] This realignment began in the ashes of Barry Goldwater's defeat in 1964, when Southern conservatives and the "Party of Lincoln" put aside their century-long animosity to unite Bible Belt conservatives with their Northern ideological cousins. This staggered realignment of Southern conservatives out of the Democratic party and into the Republican party over three decades ushered in an era of polarized politics.[2] Conservatives could begin to dream that through definitive dominance of a single party, they might one day come to control both houses of Congress as well as the presidency, as finally occurred in 2001, and then lock in place a rightist regime change. Yet the realities of American politics and law seemed destined to frustrate this project. Through most of the long period of this staggered realignment, the Democrats still controlled Congress and sometimes the White House. And the system of formal and informal checks and balances seemed to bar an ideological program, even with entry into office, without broad, supermajority support, which could never be forthcoming for such a regime change.

The balance began to shift decidedly in favor of conservatives and the Republican Party they controlled when President Reagan arrived in office with a relatively substantial mandate in 1980. He did not have a majority of the vote, but he had decisively outpolled Carter, and his coattails had brought a new class of Republicans into control of the Senate. Not resting a moment on his laurels, Reagan demanded and got an enormous regressive package of tax and spending cuts in 1981 and made the first in what was to become a great wave of activist conservative appointments to the federal judiciary. For a time Reagan's success despite the seeming impediment of a Democratic-controlled House of Representatives (and Senate, after 1986) seemed to herald a full-scale conservative victory in mastering the reins of governance.[3]

But as it turned out, these conservative thrusts, while important, constituted a high-water mark instead of a beginning. Attorney General Edwin Meese made himself the spokesperson for ideological conservatives and gave them some legitimation but could do little to promote their causes except to start stacking the judiciary. The Reagan administration delivered much for business interests, accelerating deregulation and making a high-profile effort to break the power of labor unions (notably through

Reagan's termination, with extreme prejudice, of the whole echelon of air traffic controllers immediately after he took office in 1981, when they made the mistake of underestimating his determination). But here too the administration encountered limits, as when Interior Secretary James Watt overplayed his anti-environmental hand and left office an object of scorn and ridicule.

Conservatives found themselves even more frustrated with the congressional elections of the 1980s, culminating in the Republican loss of the Senate in 1986. This started a temporary pendulum swing away from conservative revolution, characterized by the first President Bush's staking out what he called "kinder, gentler" positions. The anti-conservative reaction accelerated when the Republican Party underwent a sharp temporary schism in 1991–1992 as the right became highly dissatisfied with their sitting president. The fallout from the fight between "Read my lips" President Bush and the party's right wing, personified by Newt Gingrich, gave the Democrats a leg up. Speaker Tom Foley assumed a cautiously balanced and internally well respected management of the House, enabling Congress to move reform legislation despite Gingrich's tactics. And at the polls, President Clinton scored a decisive victory in the 1992 presidential election, thereby seeming to make major additional progress for conservatives unlikely. Important to note is that most voters, at least for a time, accepted Clinton as a political moderate who staked out business-friendly positions half the time and joined the majority of the populace in a tendency toward very mild social progressivism, like extending health insurance coverage to more Americans, but whose sound fiscal credentials, including his desire to balance the budget, were, ironically, in much better order than the "tax cuts at any cost" Republicans. That he was a churchgoing Southerner probably impressed few on the extreme social and religious right but reassured many voters (especially in the politically critical South and West) that Clinton wouldn't rock the boat. Clinton's election swung the ideological pendulum toward its stable midpoint—not at all that much toward liberalism but rather toward the equilibrium of the political center, where the majority of the population felt most comfortable.

Indeed, in 1993 and 1994 the right suffered some distinct setbacks. The wealthy found their taxes slightly restored by a top-bracket income tax increase, which contained the Reagan-triggered deficit explosion. Congress enacted two significant control measures for Uzis and Saturday night specials, a major statement that the way to control violence was the way most law enforcement professionals, not the NRA, preferred. And

President Clinton won a series of symbolic victories for cultural diversity and tolerance that portended the possible isolation, in impotent unpopularity, of single-sect partisan preachers like Pat Robertson and Jerry Falwell.

But it was in this last area that Clinton overplayed his hand, mostly by undertaking too much too soon. This beginner's error cost the Democrats dearly. Clinton's clumsy attempt to settle the matter of homosexuals serving in the military satisfied no one—not even Clinton's most loyal supporters—but convinced the Christian right that their preachers had indeed seen the Devil in the White House and that Clinton might not be so moderate after all. His legitimate attempt to solve a health insurance crisis (the large percentage of the population without insurance), resulting in an infamously complicated plan promoted by First Lady Hillary Rodham Clinton, allowed the Republicans, generously backed by the insurance-company ad buyers, to bring the main part of his program to grief. Republicans used one symbolic issue after another, from the ambush in Somalia (where Bush senior had made the actual commitment of troops) to the Republicans' meretricious enthusiasm for term limits, to surge in the polls. In the low-turnout election of 1994, the conservative base mobilized vigorously, and the Republicans took control of both chambers of Congress.[4]

In one election, the momentum of the "staggered realignment" was restored and accelerated. Unlike the era before the 1990s, when the parties were not so strongly polarized, ideology began to trump temporizing impulses in both parties.[5] In those former times, the potency of the conservative coalition, holding decisive seniority-determined committee posts and spanning both parties, had prevented strong ideological Democratic Party leadership control except in rare circumstances.[6] Similarly, the once large cadre of centrists in the congressional Republican Party had tended to restrain their own party's leadership.[7] No more. From the mid-1990s on, the staggered realignment reached an advanced stage with the czarlike power of Newt Gingrich (R-Ga.) and Tom DeLay (R-Tex.).[8] (A former pest exterminator and a politician closely tied with the Texas Christian right, DeLay was known in the House as "the Hammer" for what happened to those who didn't obey him.) Their related strengthening of majority leadership control, particularly in the House, strikingly manifested what some political scientists aptly termed "conditional party government." In other words, Gingrich and DeLay held the reins firmly with relatively strong party loyalty, their small moderate wing feeling themselves kept on a short leash.[9]

These House leaders allied with a clique of conservative senators epitomized by the senior figure of Jesse Helms (R-N.C.) but also including a younger star of great promise and some particular skill for polarizing sides and then hanging not-so-nice labels on his targets, Senator John Ashcroft (R-Mo.) (to whom a fair amount of analysis is devoted in chapter 2). Gingrich-DeLay and the Helms group held the necessary legislative reins to manage an ideological congressional program prefiguring many key parts of the post-2000 Bush approach.

There remained one last bump along the way, a centrist backlash in 1995–1996 akin to similar backlashes that had halted both presidents Reagan and Clinton during their first terms. In this case the public—again demonstrating its desire for centrist governance—rejected radical Republican leaders' attempt to hold the White House hostage by shutting down the government during a budget impasse. Constituents lobbied their senators to line up behind presidential vetoes and Democratic filibusters.[10] Anger with Gingrich and his allies led to Clinton's reelection in 1996 and to the Republicans' historically poor showing in the 1998 second-term midterm elections.[11] Another contributing factor was public repugnance for the tactics of Kenneth W. Starr and his staff of right-wing lawyers, working hand in glove with Gingrich and with congressional investigative chairs like Senator Alphonse D'Amato (R-N.Y.) and Representative Dan Burton (R-Ind.). (Burton returns in the chapter on Bush administration secrecy in the unexpected but highly welcome role in 2002 of Bush's unstoppable nemesis, demanding truth about FBI abuses and refusing to take "no" for an answer. It just goes to show that absolutely anyone can turn hero.) Congressional Republicans found the nation curbing their strength, even with all their powers of incumbency and their massive fundraising. By 2000 Republicans found their former strength reduced to a 50–50 standoff in the Senate, which returned, even after the Bush presidency's first two years, to only an anemic 51–49 majority. Extreme goals seemed far out of reach.

THE CHRISTIAN RIGHT AND THE SUPERRICH/CEO CREW

This sequence of events spelled frustration for two conservative constituencies that had effectively taken control within the Republican Party despite their lack of centrist public support. Each base could devote a great deal of its particular political resources to keep their party in power, and each expected fulfillment of its extreme goals. But from 1980 to 2000 each experienced disappointment: the limits encountered during the Reagan administration, neglect by the first President Bush, the pendulum swing toward the center under President Clinton, the congressional leadership's failures during the Gingrich era, and the absence of further electoral gains after the staggered realignment peaked in 1994. Neither group could enact radical, nonconsensus legislation in the 1990s, nor could either expect total, easy fulfillment of its desires by mere presidential fiat after 2000.

Who were these two groups of conservative voters?[12] The first consisted of social conservatives who sought mainstream legitimacy for causes defined on the one hand by religious beliefs and on the other by a desire to rein in what they considered cultural excesses. When they were furthest out on the fringes—which was not infrequently—their exponents evinced tremendous antagonism to cultural and ethnic diversity and supported selective government intolerance toward groups such as immigrants, sexual minorities, non-English-speakers, nonwhites, anyone too "secular" and hence evidently without "real" morality, those afraid of being shot by concealed handguns carried in public places, and even occasionally vegetarians. As I show in the next chapter, religious conservatives of differing religious backgrounds whose cultural outlooks also once differed markedly have managed since the 1970s to come together to champion certain social causes, particularly legal ones. These causes included undoing *Roe v. Wade* and using tax revenues to make patronage payoffs to religious institutions, as well as the nonreligious but culturally correlated cause of establishing a national personal constitutional right to sell and to carry firearms in urban centers (mostly for "sporting" purposes, of course). More generally, social conservatives sought a special brand of moral approval from their government in the form of government disapproval of whole categories of citizens and their behavior. These groups might be tolerated in certain urban metropolitan areas on the coasts, but not elsewhere and not by religious conservatives stirred up by leaders manipulating intolerant anger.[13]

Social conservatives' strength lay in their activist willingness when aroused by the right "messages" from on high to organize, campaign, and turn out at the polls. They could have a big impact in low-turnout races such as Republican primaries and, sometimes, midterm elections. However, in a general national election with a high turnout, they fell far short of a majority or even, for their further-out elements, a decisive national plurality. In the 1990s quest for public support, the social causes subsumed in Gingrich's revolution proved unable to compete with President Clinton's much more popular centrist message about the rights of women, minorities, and the struggling poor and about government tolerantly providing equal respect to all. Hence, social conservatives could not move major legislation through Congress, particularly past Senate filibusters; prevent President Clinton's filling two Supreme Court vacancies with moderates; nor demonstrate a national popular mandate in 1992, 1996, 1998, or for that matter, 2000, and not really in 2002.

The second key Republican constituency consisted of economic conservatives in two distinct major streams: the wealthy and conservative-leaning business heads (referred to here as "pariah businesses" led by the "CEO crew"). First, the Republican Party had become the engine of the wealthy to change the tax system. This mattered particularly because a changing national economy in the last quarter of the twentieth century accentuated top-heavy inequality both in income and even more so in wealth.[14] With the increasing capacity and interest of the wealthy as a group to fund their own political goals,[15] the greed of the wealthy to cut their own taxes, regardless of who paid for this, made them part of a political base of great significance.[16] This group aimed to direct the budgetary system away from the ability-to-pay principle toward the group's own enrichment through enacting repeated regressive rate cuts and creating loopholes in corporate, inheritance, and top-bracket income taxes.[17] This redirection meant that those not in the top bracket would pay for an increasing share of government expenditure through the combination of payroll taxes, fewer tax loopholes than upper brackets enjoyed, and local sales and property taxes. The rich also benefited from policies that undermined secure employment with adequate benefits for middle-income Americans, essential for promoting family savings and community building. Instead the economy moved toward a top-heavy system benefiting owners and managers and visiting pain upon the lower middle class. Government benefits received by the lower class, already slashed, would receive further trims.

Looking at the sequence, President Reagan gave the wealthy their first great feast of income and corporate tax chopping in 1981, accompanied by spending cuts and enduring ceilings directed at the poor. At that time conservatives marshaled various economic theories, albeit of questionable validity, justifying inequality-heightening measures as economic stimuli, but this rationalization forfeited virtually all its support in mainstream economics in ensuing years. After the deficit soared and the economy repeatedly tanked in the 1980s, President Bush had the courage to break his "Read my lips" pledge in 1990 and raise taxes somewhat (and then suffered party schism afterward). Now the wealthy increasingly levered the Republican Party to tax cuts heavily tilted only toward the top brackets and not, in responsible economists' views, seriously likely to pay their way through economic stimulation—top-bracket tax cuts financed, in short, only by deficits. Such drives faced a double obstacle. Intrinsically, they lacked appeal to the centrist majority, which received little and had little reason to accept the rationalizations. More obscure to the public's eyes but significant in terms of getting budget acts passed, the statutory law of the budget process, initiated in the 1970s and strengthened repeatedly down to 1990 by bipartisan anti-deficit centrists, simply was not designed to facilitate national debt explosions set off by unpaid-for tax cuts. The law barred a bare congressional majority, however extreme in its ideology, from enacting such cuts.

The other, overlapping component of the economic-conservative constituency consisted of certain groups of business executives—not all business sectors or all executives but those either intrinsically conservative or capable of being persuaded to conservatism due to the shifting incentives created by the polarizing parties. Some business elements tacked right from a desire to overthrow or restrain government policies protecting the public interest, from environmental protection and securities fraud regulation to occupational health and safety and consumer protection. Certain semipariah industries felt particularly at odds with the national consensus on these matters, notably Big Tobacco, heavy polluters, those wary of health care profit constraint (at different times insurers and drug makers), would-be overexploiters of public lands and resources, firearms marketers, hard-edged anti-labor companies, and others with similar perspectives.

Besides the potentially outcast sectors, much of business as a whole had the capacity to take more or less alternative perspectives, varying from relative willingness to deal sometimes even with Democrats, if they would do an effective and somewhat business-friendly job, to an ideological approach of lining up behind the party that offered more favors but threatened harsher consequences for insufficient loyalty. From 1993 on, the Clinton administration's many elements of business appeal strongly tapped the constituency's willingness to be somewhat bipartisan in its political support: Treasury Secretary Rubin's respected management of domestic economic growth and international economic stability; approval of NAFTA and the Uruguay Round of WTO trade agreements (pushed through by Clinton in the teeth of opposition from angry labor hurt by the exporting of jobs); wooing of specific business sectors, such as information technology, that were put off by the culturally intolerant bedfellows that came with the far right and that possessed nonpariah desires for governmental action like strengthened intellectual property protection; and overall restraint on measures seen by business as unfriendly, both new regulations and pro-labor steps.[18] The expanded soft-money fund-raising in the elections from 1996 on, which temporarily leveled the fund-raising playing field of the two parties, continued somewhat the prior tradition in which some business support went to centrist Democrats rather than solely to a polarized party of the right wing.

Ironically, this moderation spurred conservatives like DeLay even harder toward the approaches that sought to polarize business—foreshadowing Rove and Bush.[19] These conservatives saw bipartisan compromises as effective defeats because passing up opportunities to polarize meant not diminishing sustenance for centrist voices —that is, Democrats and overly moderate Republicans. To oversimplify, conservative Republican leaders felt that they must persuade business to use its funding and other political resources predominantly to support ideologically party-loyal Republicans, not Democrats.[20]

The wealthy together with the conservative or potentially conservative business elements, viewed as a single base of economic conservatives, with its dominant weight in the nation's political funding, could provide an enormous comparative advantage to an ideological party, compensating for its weaker policy appeal to the center. By the 1990s the structure of campaign finance, channeled by law and the party system, involved two massive, expensive ad broadcast streams.[21] One consisted of ads by the candidates and parties themselves funded by contributions of either hard or soft money. The other consisted of well-heeled interests' own powerful political ads, typically bogus "issue ads" permitted by a loophole in the campaign finance laws. For example, later, in 2002, pharmaceutical makers spent $30 million, overwhelmingly for Republicans—some via contributions, some on the industry's own phony issue ads—with potent effect in achieving industry goals (which, if made clear, would have alienated the broad public center), such as defeating the legislative drive to have Medicare increase purchases of effective but lower-profit, generic-label drugs.

The potent ideological thrust, particularly in the 1990s, lay in how carefully directed floods of broadcast advertising funded from the conservative economic base could make up for conservative causes' unpopularity with the centrist public. Loyal conservatives would get the protection of funding floods that buried centrist or progressive candidates in negative advertising on issues of only superficial significance. Conversely, the large comparative advantage that conservatives enjoyed over centrists in access to funding—or more bluntly, the "defunding" of Democrats—would diminish the electorate's effective awareness that party-loyal conservatives did not represent voters' centrist views. Thus, by the double hit of extra-arming conservative candidates and relatively defunding the opposition,[22] the conservative economic base could play a decisive part in a winning ideological movement. This relative campaign fund-raising advantage of the conservative base ultimately depended, to some extent, on a certain campaign finance legal structure. In the final analysis, virtually unknown to the public, this depended upon the fixed bias of the bloc of Supreme Court conservatives—their unwillingness to accept campaign finance regulation that would seriously reduce the awesome plutocratic ability of wealth to buy power.[23] Some political uses of constitutional law just rarely get the public's notice—sometimes even very big ones.

Turning from domestic affairs, from 1991 on, both social and economic conservatives gave less weight to national security and international policy issues. With the Cold War over, a number of different approaches to international and security affairs found support on the right, some of them having nothing more in common, it seemed, than scattershot criticism of President Clinton or his party. Yet both groups did carry certain predilections that could lead them back toward a unified stance on security and international policy issues under some potential conditions. Social conservatives, particularly males (as a large gender gap opened on this issue), resonated even in the 1990s with a chauvinistic stance of unrestrained American use of military force against certain morally "evil" regimes from Havana to Baghdad.[24] They did not especially like how the first President Bush had respected the United Nations (notably in getting the Security Council's authorization for the Persian Gulf War) or how President Clinton had likewise used NATO against the Serbian leader Slobodan Milošević. Economic conservatives favored an international system that would spare them burdensome responsibilities, such as adhering to international environmental and labor standards, while advancing their business interests. Both thus turned away ideologically from what James Lindsay has termed the "apathetic internationalism" of the centrist public.[25]

Nor did the conservative bases join that centrist public in its support—often inattentive and tepid but nevertheless vital—of the United States' role in various international legal regimes, such as those concerning human rights, labor rights, arms control, women's rights, and global warming. These reciprocal undertakings were necessary for the United States as a world leader because they engaged the social democracies of Europe and Japan and secured grudging cooperation from the Third World. However, both conservative bases often disdained these. For example, the two conservative bases reacted, for different reasons, against accords on the spread of unconventional weapons that required developed and developing countries alike to work together in the nuclear, chemical, and biological realms. The chauvinistic social conservatives saw these as "handcuffing" America's own war arsenal. Affected business sectors feared their potential exposure for aggressive efforts to sell such weapons in borderline contexts or opposed interference with hitherto proprietary manufacturing fiefdoms. In a word, both groups had tendencies toward American exceptionalism or unilateralism as to unconventional weapons proliferation in particular and other international legal regimes in general.

DEMOCRATIC CONSTRAINTS

Even with the rise of polarized politics and conditional party government, Congress and the president continued to operate with a system of checks and balances. In three notable respects, even a unified Republican government in January–May 2001 and, again, after January 2003 confronted limits on the success of noncentrist efforts.

These limiting factors consisted of the Senate filibuster; the relatively high standards for a presidential mandate to push ideological measures in the tradition of the New Deal of 1933–1934, the Great Society of 1965–1966, or the Reagan program of 1981; and the limited significance of international security affairs prior to 9/11.[26] Taking each of these in turn, if the two chambers of Congress operated within a system oriented toward bare party majorities possessing unconstrained power, in an era of polarized party government the ideologies of the left and right could take startlingly alternating turns in achieving major successes. Elections in which the Democratic Party did well, such as 1976 or 1992, would produce massive waves of progressive policy making. Conservatives would wait their turn and, after elections like 1952 or 1994, produce their own massive waves of conservative policy making. Yet none of those four years saw a great wave of ideological legislation. Restraints due to the democratic, stable, and deliberative operation of Congress prevented this—among the most prominent from the 1970s on being the procedure of filibuster and cloture, extended delay that the majority party can overcome only by mustering sixty votes.[27]

In 1993–1994 Senate Republicans banded together to prevent passage of President Clinton's economic stimulus bill. They then filibustered to death a string of relatively mild bills otherwise assured of enactment by majority support—campaign finance reform, lobby reform, and reducing striker replacement—for lack of sixty Senate votes.[28] Had it gotten that far, health care reform was expected to fail the same way; many lesser bills died or got compromised to avoid this fate.

The 1993–1994 slaughter of even mildly progressive legislation showed how "conditional party government"—parties unified and strong but polarized because of the Southern conservatives' party switch—made the sixty-vote cloture requirement decisive. The same polarization that led to ideological bills winning a majority of votes from one party's loyal backing led to such bills getting the other party to unify loyally around denying the sixty votes for cloture. The 1993–1994 period showed that ideological propositions backed by one or the other party could not succeed absent centrist support sufficient to provide sixty Senate votes. The final enactment of campaign finance in 2002 completed this proof: the McCain-Feingold bill became law only when compromise provisions were added that so appealed to the Republican party—such as doubling the ceiling on hard-money donations—as to attract enough moderate Republicans to make sixty Senate votes. Only in this way could the bill overcome the Republican conservatives' filibuster under Senator Mitch McConnell (R-Ky.).

A second phenomenon of democratic politics also constrained the enactment of ideological measures: the relatively elevated standard for a presidential mandate to push ideological measures.[29] A president could win the office in a two-way race with just a few more electoral votes than the other candidate; but such a president, while having the minimum powers of the office, would not have the action boost of a "mandate." A president who ran in a polarized race and won big with congressional coattails thereafter had a mandate: certainly Roosevelt in 1932 and Johnson in 1964, and to some extent Reagan in 1980. Conversely, a president who lacked these advantages or who lost vital ground in the midterm congressional election very much lacked the mandate for even minimal movement of ideological measures: Carter after 1978, Reagan after 1986, the first Bush throughout, and Clinton, needless to say, after 1994. For example, President Bush won with a comfortable margin in 1988 but had no coattails: Republican ranks in Congress stayed distinctly in the minority, and he inspired no concern among Democrats that he could cause them to lose reelection. So he could not even get his pet domestic project, a capital gains tax cut, off the ground in the Senate. In foreign affairs Bush's own impressive skills and experience, his well-chosen Cabinet team, and the strong inherent powers of a president in that context enabled him to achieve some great feats, including a smooth end of the Cold War and the building of a global Gulf War coalition. Not so in domestic affairs, which depend upon Congress.

Finally, the Cold War, like national security threats before it, had served as a great augmenter and justifier of presidential power, feeding the "imperial presidency" especially in the Nixon and Reagan administrations.[30] Presidents facing a hostile international environment could launch overseas interventions, reach major international agreements, command public attention with frequency, and push up defense spending. They simply had more power. Even though Congress sometimes fought to constrain this power, presidents had a less constrained share of power in foreign than domestic affairs.[31]

From the Cold War's end until 9/11, international affairs received notably limited public attention. This in itself did not hurt conservatives at all times. Notably, the public let Governor Bush slide in the election of 2000, as it might not at another time, about his ignorance of and boredom with foreign affairs;[32] and even the military-minded Republican primary voters let slide the contrast between his avoidance of the draft by hiding in the special sons-of-the-elite unit of the Texas Air National Guard (thanks to a nice use of law on behalf of his politician father) and Senator McCain's staggering record as a war hero. However, the limited role of international affairs after the Cold War seemed to augur limits to conservatives' hopes immediately after January 2001, because the end of that visible international confrontation shriveled the largest potential power source their president might otherwise tap to make up for a meager mandate at the polls.

These phenomena show the large prescription for further frustration of ideological conservatives' plans starting in the 1990s and continuing after the 2000 election. Conservatives had control of the Republican Party in Congress and presumably, once a Republican became president, a share of his power. But they would certainly not have sixty Senate votes to overcome filibusters of ideological propositions. The Senate after 2001 would presumably demonstrate to conservatives what it had to progressives in 1993–1994: the impotence of ideologues facing a filibuster. Indeed, the Senate did this somewhat when it would not pass items dear to them and President Bush such as school vouchers and opening the Arctic National Wildlife Refuge to drilling. And the close division of the electorate in November 2000, together with international quiescence, meant no electoral mandate and no imperial president.

Moreover, those contemplating an effort on a one-party basis to achieve conservative goals must understand the basic danger of centrist backlash, not just to the immediate goals but to long-term preservation of even the least modicum of control. In 1992 the centrist backlash against social conservative domination of the televised Republican national convention—particularly its shrill denunciations of *Roe v. Wade*—had hurt the party in the presidential race. In 1996 and 1998 the centrist backlash against the unpopular program of House Republicans—perceived as anti-environmental, anti-minority, and oriented toward social causes—had hurt the party in both presidential and congressional races. Public hatred of the patently partisan counsel Ken Starr did not help either. After the November 1998 campaign and election, when numerous Democratic candidates ran well by morphing Gingrich's House colleagues (or potential colleagues) into the image of Gingrich, he himself—although the architect, leader, and central symbol of the party's hitherto triumphant conservatives—resigned, describing his party colleagues as "cannibals."[33]

Also, in 2000 the prospect for 2002 had the characteristics of a traditionally dangerous election, two years after a new president had taken office and, as it turned out, during a year of a disappointing economy. A centrist backlash in 2002 might have the impact of previous setback years—such as 1978, 1982, and 1994—for the party newly installed in the White House. Those with long memories recalled how an environmental backlash in 1982 had played a part in reducing President Reagan's congressional support. When early 2001 brought a powerful stream of negative publicity about Bush's anti-environmentalism, including how he apparently didn't mind a little arsenic in the public's drinking water, it seemed as if the same environmental backlash as in 1982 could occur in 2002.

POTENTIAL LEGAL OPPORTUNITIES

Conversely, some 1990s Washington trends quietly laid the groundwork for the new ways conservatives could overcome these same political constraints, particularly by the political uses of law. During the eight years of the Clinton administration, especially during the six years of congressional control at odds with that administration, conservatives stored up a backlog of strategies and tactics, projects and personnel. To bear fruit, some needed little more than a Republican White House with just enough delicacy to act without awakening the quiescent centrists. Others required more—a very elaborate process with a major legal component, much of it out of public sight.

A great deal depended on the third branch of government, often the key for uses of law: the judiciary. As discussed later in this chapter, a bloc of five conservative Supreme Court justices came together in the late 1990s.

The bloc's role in the 2000 electoral contest could not, of course, have been foreseen. However, the bloc's potential to aid a conservative administration on political issues like striking down wetlands protections, denying a reality-based census procedure that would count all minorities by sampling, allowing extremist Republican redistricting tactics, and upholding vouchers for religious schools could certainly, in general terms, be envisaged.[34]

A related potential strategy that developed during the 1990s lay in the major campaign the Republican Senate mounted to stall hearings, committee reporting, and floor action on confirming judicial nominees. One in ten seats on the federal judiciary became vacant by the end of 1997, and twenty-six remained empty for more than eighteen months.[35] Moreover, the stalling occurred despite President Clinton's preference for nominees with race and gender diversity but with moderate views quite conciliatory to conservative senators.[36] Hence, the successor president, if conservative, could complete the conservative stacking of the lower judiciary.

Quietly, indeed virtually unknown to the outside world, another development brewed for delivering the economic conservatives' main goal by an artifice to circumvent the sixty-vote cloture requirement. In 1993 conservatives filibustered, and defeated for lack of sixty Senate votes, President Clinton's relatively small deficit-stimulus proposal.[37] Seemingly, a conservative president would face the same problem: lack of sixty Senate votes to overcome resistance to debt-increasing tax cuts. However, tax cuts so utterly and completely obsessed Senate conservatives all through the late 1990s that they mounted a legally strained but potentially decisive procedural effort via abuse of the Budget Act.[38] As the Senate Republican ranks shrank from fifty-six in 1999, that legal artifice, which made fifty-one Senators potentially as powerful as sixty for pushing through unpaid-for tax cuts, took on huge significance. I examine this process in much greater detail later.

In another vein, during the 1990s Attorney General Janet Reno had satisfied the centrist public while infuriating social conservatives.[39] Conservative senators like Ashcroft had field-tested a series of proposals for use after the hated Reno left office, such as undermining *Roe v. Wade* by using the issue of the "late term" abortion procedure. A president unleashing an activist conservative attorney general could use such proposals to legitimate a range of far-out social conservative ideas while averting a full-scale centrist backlash. No one could know that Ashcroft would himself be the one to take over the Justice Department, but the proposals lay ready to achieve right-wing goals.[40]

And on international and security matters, congressional conservatives could begin to forge a legal path away from the bipartisan and international consensus they disdained. They set themselves against international legal regimes not just on security matters but across the array of social, environmental, and other multilateral collective efforts. In the 1990s they nurtured several concrete projects: repetition of President Reagan's "Star Wars" in the form of missile defense; a partisan rather than bipartisan approach to trade deals;[41] and a revival of the conflict with Iraq, this time going on to Baghdad.[42] Still, even among conservatives, few if any could imagine how the terrible shock of 9/11 would create the opportunity for unilateralism in full war gear by providing the president the political strength to unleash the legal doctrines of preemptive war even against the Middle Eastern country without funding or nationals involved in 9/11.

One other highly significant legal potential arose in the late 1990s that later proved invaluable for avoiding a centrist backlash against the most extreme manipulations of the law for conservative causes: that of an exceptionally secretive presidency. The long cycle of investigations of the presidency that began with Watergate in 1973–1974 and continued through the era of special prosecutors and potent congressional investigations finally degenerated into dramatically unpopular crusades against President Clinton (especially regarding Whitewater and the Monica Lewinsky affair).[43]

By the Senate impeachment trial of 1999, the public so heartily disliked the political use of the investigations machinery that its attitudes came full circle: it ceased to demand even a modicum of regular, healthy oversight of the president.[44] The public not only allowed but almost demanded that the machinery completely shut down, as the independent counsel statute lapsed and support for congressional resistance against executive privilege largely did.[45] Though few predicted it, a new president in 2001 would find the investigative apparatus in a trough not seen since before Watergate and the other revelations of the 1970s. Public indifference to presidential fending off of press, congressional, and legal scrutiny would allow nearly complete control over information—allowing the president, even without much of a mandate, to manage the course of public affairs with an amazing degree of control over timing and freedom from checks and oversight.

A new president could actually get away with such hitherto taboo actions as having the press secretary deny any report that fell beyond the daily spin message or even tell the press outright untruths; having the vice president pick, and win, a secrecy fight over closed-door lobbying by big energy interests, seemingly an unappealing proposition; telling congressional committees they must do without querying the homeland security czar although the subject was at the top of national interest; and diverting the country's attention from the administration's alleged pre-9/11 negligence, another subject critical to the national interest. Political scientists attuned to the use of media have emphasized the president's power to control what becomes news and what stays hidden.[46] A president serving conservative causes after 2001 would have more power to direct public attention than any predecessor for forty years.

Had all of these political processes taken their course and some other conservative candidate been elected in 2000—say, Senator John McCain—we can only speculate as to what might have transpired next. But it's safe to say that George W. Bush brought with him a separate set of political experiences that worked in tandem with the altered conditions of national politics to produce a unique presidential trajectory. As much as anything else presaging his presidency, Bush's rise through the peculiar crucible of Texas politics gave him the tools he needed to subvert the law for conservative political causes.

BUSH'S OWN EAGERNESS TO STEER RIGHT

Bush himself sedulously encouraged an obscuring myth around his Texas rise. In short, it told of an undisciplined, even self-destructive child of privilege, a sinner redeemed by his good wife and his awakened religious faith whose career training lay in the challenge, and success, of being an entrepreneur in oil and other businesses. Like other myths, this one enlightens more when analyzed for its social purposes than if treated as serious history. Bush's oft quoted parable of vaguely defined sin, religious redemption, and marital fidelity sold well among social conservatives. Likewise, his emphasis of the trials and ultimate successes of entrepreneurship sold well among economic conservatives. It also told them that Bush knew how to present business—even the business of partaking in Arabian Peninsula deals facilitated by his White House connections—in prettified terms and deal with the inevitable charges, given what Bush planned to do, that pariah industries funded him simply so that he would protect and enrich them. As for the rest of the public, the myth aims less at finding any powerful, universally appealing pitch—as in the humble origins of Abe Lincoln, Harry Truman, and Bill Clinton or the honorable battlefield service of Dwight Eisenhower, John F. Kennedy, or Bush's own father—than simply at diverting attention from the truth, with legal patches slapped on the most awkward parts.

Of course George W. Bush came of age having the lush inheritance of an elite political and economic dynasty (well analyzed by Kevin Phillips), extending from his grandfather Senator Prescott Bush (R-Conn.) to his father.[47] He himself had taken his Harvard MBA and made a fortune, but not by means of any personal talent or hard personal effort and risk. His fortune came from his father's connections. After his father's friends first staked him, his big initial boost came when agents of powerful Arabian interests came looking to help him.[48] He made his fortune by greasing an enormous 1989 deal bestowed generously upon his not particularly special Harken Oil firm by the Arabian kingdom of Bahrain. In context, Bahrain's generosity to Bush could have no persuasive explanation other than as baksheesh to his father from Persian Gulf rulers who knew how to use family connection payoffs as a legally correct form of international boodle to politicians.[49] This deal took on special significance later, in the wake of 9/11, when Bush would use his legally enhanced powers in international affairs to divert public attention to Iraq in order to protect the conservative rulers of the Persian Gulf from the American public's fury over their preattack *jihadi* funding role and postattack lack of cooperation.

Another aspect of Bush's personal rise also took on special significance later in the form of a crucial influence reinforcing his willingness to protect his conservative economic base from the 2001–2002 Enron-Worldcom corporate governance legal scandal. Young Bush himself had gotten involved through his energy company in a dizzying string of Enron-style corporate governance capers. These ranged from sweetheart company loans to him for profitable stock purchases, to phony corporate-earnings accounting blessed by the audit committee on which Bush served, to use by his company of a Cayman Islands offshore tax dodge like those that later made "expatriate" companies like Stanley Works infamous. He was caught by authorities on two proofs of insider trading: his profiting handsomely from inside information by selling eight days before serious bad news, and his very late reporting of insider selling and exercise of lucrative stock options—late four different times on a million dollars in transactions.[50]

Then, the Securities and Exchange Commission (SEC) investigated him for several years after 1991. The two instances of the SEC going embarrassingly easy on insider trading and related misconduct—in 1991–1993 as to Bush himself and in 2001–2002 under his presidency as to Enron and Worldcom—fit together neatly. In the early SEC investigation he received kid-glove treatment utterly out of sync with the blatant nature of his legal violations. The key lay in the matchless insider connections of his legal counsel, the Bush family's law firm—Houston's biggest, Baker & Botts (aka Baker Botts LLP).[51] Naturally, the first President Bush put Baker & Botts partners in the posts of chair and general counsel of the SEC.[52] So naturally, his son George W. was represented by another Baker & Botts partner, Robert W. Jordan, who will reappear more than once in this book in discussions of the Florida election contest and as ambassador to Saudi Arabia.[53] Mark him well: he is Bush's personal lawyer for backdoor dealing.

Jordan withheld key evidence of Bush's wrongdoing under an apparently bogus privilege claim until after the inquiry ended and the SEC had given Bush a pass, whereupon the claim was given up.[54] From that point through even the media firestorm in July 2002, Bush refused to let his SEC investigative file be publicly released. And Jordan persuaded the SEC not to interview Bush himself. These many layers of concealment proved vital because Bush badly fumbled his multiple inconsistent explanations of his late insider trading notification. He did so both while running for Texas governor, when he tried the prevarication that the SEC itself had lost his disclosure forms,[55] and again when public indignation over insider sleaze at Enron and Worldcom reawakened interest in this matter in 2002 and President Bush could not handle the press's questions.[56]

To put in context Bush's ten-year quest to distract the public from those SEC insider-trading charges, political scientists and legal scholars often put presidential claims of privilege in one category of study and presidential powers of "going public" to put out a message in another.[57] However, in Washington reality the capacities of presidents to go public with their preferred message and to fend off scrutiny on other matters work together in redirecting public attention. Both, together, depend, not on the abstract or theoretical concepts of public posture and privilege, but on legally constraining access to discrediting material in order to direct public attention instead to the preferred message. Bush's early experience taught him the key political uses of law to accomplish this.

So, during the 2002 corporate governance firestorm, Bush gave full support to his heavily criticized SEC chair, Harvey Pitt. This enabled Pitt to fight hard to keep public attention focused on limited and superficial responsive steps, in order to delay and minimize reforms (e.g., reform of corporate insider stock options) until Pitt, his credibility exhausted, finally resigned at the convenient time, after the 2002 election. As House counsel during a 1980s congressional probe of alleged corporate sleaze, I crossed swords with Pitt and got to know him, as President Bush would presumably have known him, as intensely and lucratively committed to the legal blessing and indulgence (not punishment) of business executives accused of securities and accounting fraud. Bush had learned the political value of lax SEC enforcement in 1991–1993 as it affected himself; he demonstrated that value again for his conservative economic base at the key juncture for that base in 2002.

Bush's political career effectively began when he went to work on his father's 1992 campaign. The president assigned his son the special role of liaison with social conservatives. He saw the damage to his father arising from the alienation of social and economic conservatives and observed the backlash in the 1992 general election against those same social conservatives.

From then on, George W. Bush's own route to power lay through the Texas Republican Party, under the control of extreme social conservatives. In the gubernatorial race of 1993–1994, Bush put himself in Karl Rove's hands and campaigned hard on just a few right-wing themes, like support for carrying concealed firearms, to defeat the very capable incumbent Ann Richards in the Republican sweep of 1994.[58] Thereafter Governor Bush worked for many items on the social conservatives' wish list, as he later did in the White House, finding ways to do so that minimized the centrist backlash. Molly Ivins, the insightful Texas commentator, in 2000 admired Bush's "masterful straddle [for] keeping a moderate face on the Texas Republican Party while keeping the Christian right happy."[59] He did so by putting in far-right judges, reducing abortion rights, signing sheaves of death warrants, letting minorities' economic position languish, visibly branding gays as having no rights, and getting taxpayer funds into religious coffers.[60] To summarize without pausing over the details, Bush accomplished in Texas a version of the political uses of law for ideological causes that conservative congressional leaders contemporaneously envisaged in Washington and that he himself would complete as president after 2001.

As to economic conservatives, his frugal Democratic predecessor in Texas (Richards) bequeathed him, as would a similarly frugal Democratic predecessor in Washington (Clinton), a budget surplus husbanded with difficult effort. As he would in Washington, Governor Bush left urgent needs (mainly educational) unfunded while using funds on regressive tax cuts for his base. His reverse–Robin Hood policy was particularly revealed in his fight to bar poor Texas children from vitally needed, federally purchased health care, something even the other conservative Republican governors would not forgo.[61] It was a cruel use of the governor's legally strategic position to disrupt a child-friendly cooperative federalism program so that he could pose as keeping the "welfare rolls" down.

THE CAMPAIGN

Above all, Governor Bush perfected the basic conservative exchange transaction by engaging in a crucial political use of law: gaming the campaign finance laws to bless the exchange of government favors for business in return for the massive funding needed to win campaigns notwithstanding ultimately noncentrist goals. Bush in 1999–2000 famously used the loophole of releasing himself even from the high legal ceiling on raised funds by declining federal matching funds in the primaries. Even peer candidates with seemingly impressive fund-raising potential of their own—former Senate majority leader Robert Dole (R-Kan.) in 1996, Vice President Al Gore in 2000—would not aspire to that loophole. No one but Governor Bush, other than self-funded rich candidates, so represented the class of wealthy and business donors as to need the sky-is-the-limit loophole used by those flooded with funds even without a match.

His premier fund-raisers, the "Pioneers," raised $113 million in hard-money bundled contributions of no more than $1,000 per donor. This fantastic feat illustrated the approach that made his Texas-based experience parallel to the potential he would have in Washington for serving conservative causes. For example, as documented by Texas public interest groups, particularly environmentalists, millions came in for his easing of restrictions on big Texas polluters producing the worst smog in the country.[62] And only later did it attract attention that Enron's CEO, Kenneth Lay, whom Governor Bush familiarly called "Kenny Boy," served at the very center of his Texas-based fund-raising engine.[63] The excess giving to Governor Bush in 2000 over Dole in 1996, although partly reflecting Bush's better chances, also represented a further evolution in the planned service of conservative causes. Unlike 1992 and 1996, when his party hoped to compete for the center, now the strategy involved greater service from the more extreme conservative economic causes—like the semioutcast industry sectors—in return for unheard-of funding levels sanctioned by the legal loopholes of campaign finance regulation.

Another key to the arranging of mutually supporting far-out conservative causes lay in Governor Bush's obscuring the deals by legally contrived secrecy, foreshadowing the White House strategy discussed in chapter 8. At this stage the layers of such secrecy started with the secret meetings of Bush gubernatorial appointees in which the gratitude-inspiring grandfathering of polluters was arranged, foreshadowing the Cheney energy task force and its court struggle in 2001–2002. The secrecy continued with minimizing what the press and public could learn from the limited requirements of donation disclosure, as press and public access to information would be legally constrained throughout president Bush's tenure.[64] The secrecy represented an important foreshadowing of what would in the Bush presidency continue to make possible the essential exchange of government favors for conservative economic fund-raising support, not just in the 2000 election but also in 2002 and 2004.

Bush's campaign for the 2000 Republican presidential nomination evinced his relation to the two key conservative constituencies. Initially, in Iowa Steve Forbes mounted the principal contest to Bush, proposing as his centerpiece to replace the progressive income tax with a flat tax. So Bush had to outbid Forbes with his own, unrestrained scheme to slash upper-bracket income taxes.[65] Then, when John McCain emerged after the New Hampshire primary as his principal opponent, Bush carried the critical South Carolina primary by signaling that he would satisfy the rightmost portion of the rightmost social conservative electorate in the country. He did this through his appearance at Bob Jones University, his support of flying the Confederate flag, and his campaign's devices for indirectly stirring far-right intolerance for cultural and ethnic diversity against McCain.[66] It was his moment of commitment to what later became the Ashcroft agenda.

In the general election, Bush defined himself most by choosing Dick Cheney as his running mate. Cheney could not have had more impeccable credentials with both social and economic conservatives.[67] Before the rise of Reagan and Gingrich Republicanism, Cheney started as the Rumsfeld protégé who became President Ford's unreconstructed chief of staff,[68] rose to the number-two position in the House Republican Party during its swing right in the late 1980s, served as a hard-line secretary of defense in the first Bush administration, and became CEO of the international oil driller Halliburton. Cheney had generally opposed progressive or even moderate causes, from reform in apartheid South Africa to Head Start and food stamps. As ranking Republican on the House Iran-Contra Committee, for which I was special deputy chief counsel, Cheney had energetically defended President Reagan against charges of lawbreaking in foreign affairs. During the first Bush administration, Cheney had argued hard for launching the Gulf War without asking Congress for authority.[69] Bush's pick had the prominent specialties of conservative ideological intensity on national security and on presidential secrecy.

BUSH VERSUS GORE

Then came the great Florida election contest. The outcome served as a bombshell revelation to the country of the hitherto relatively unnoticed consolidation of the Supreme Court's conservative bloc during the late 1990s. This development warrants analysis of the Court, since nothing shows better than the lead-up to *Bush v. Gore* the way the right could have triumphed, in particular the large role of the political use of law in that triumph.

At the beginning of the 1990s, the Court's rejection of the first Bush administration's efforts to overrule *Roe v. Wade* supported the thesis expressed in the title of the Court study *The Center Holds*.[70] During that period, the three radical-right activists—justices Antonin Scalia and Clarence Thomas and Chief Justice William H. Rehnquist—only sometimes got the support of the two more measured conservatives, justices Sandra Day O'Connor and Anthony Kennedy. President Clinton's two moderate appointments, justices Ruth Bader Ginsburg and Stephen Breyer, linked up with John Paul Stevens and David Souter for a four-justice moderate bloc that could sometimes obtain a kind of split-the-baby cautious outcome from O'Connor or Kennedy. Hence, the Rehnquist Court of the early to mid-1990s ruled conservatively but did not move hyperactively.

However, in a relatively subtle legal development during the late 1990s partly overlooked outside Court-watching circles, Chief Justice Rehnquist changed that earlier dynamic. He forged a bloc of five votes by persuading O'Connor and Kennedy more regularly to join the activist position of the further-out three conservative radicals.[71] The Rehnquist Court did this most noticeably on striking down statutes protecting women, minorities, or those in need, such as civil rights laws, in their applications either to state governments or to an asserted state sphere of activity beyond the reach of federal law. For example, O'Connor joined 5–4 decisions striking down the Violence against Women Act,[72] affirmative action in procurement,[73] and the Americans with Disabilities Act as to states.[74]

The newly consolidated, activist bloc of five gave conservatives many victories they could not have achieved, for lack of centrist support, by legislating. The bloc frustrated Clinton's drive to control cigarette addiction by putting it beyond the FDA's power.[75] It defeated attempts to count every citizen by ruling out census sampling for House apportionment.[76] And it struck down firearms control provisions for not deferring enough to states or respecting their assertedly distinct sphere.[77]

Sometimes, even after the mid-1990s, the Court still seemed to refrain from the full-tilt activism of some of the most extremist lower-court judges appointed by presidents Reagan and Bush. For example, an activist appellate panel invalidated the famous *Miranda* warnings. When House

Republicans rushed to support this ruling, the House Democratic leadership commissioned me to file its brief defending *Miranda*, reflecting the parallel polarities between activists and centrists in the judicial and political worlds.[78] The Court did hold back from overruling *Miranda*, but with an opinion by Chief Justice Rehnquist slyly preventing any reinforcement of *Miranda* against the incremental undermining he regularly indulged.[79]

As for the events that suddenly burst after Election Day 2000, their by-now-universal familiarity allows a compressed treatment. Of course the 2000 presidential election results showed a nation split down the middle, with Bush losing the popular vote to Gore, the electoral count victory hinging upon Florida, and the popular vote count in Florida so close as to start a major legal contest between Bush and Gore. At the start, it seemed Gore might well receive what he needed to have a fair chance at winning— a counting of all the disputed ballots. The Florida Supreme Court should have had exclusive jurisdiction because election contests by states of this kind had not hitherto raised federal court issues. That Florida court had previously established its cardinal rule of insisting election contest outcomes reflect the true will of the electorate.[80]

Election contests require each campaign to assemble instantly a legal-political team, and it merits noting just who Governor Bush fielded. Its core, local counsel aside, consisted again of the giant Houston law firm that had effectively fixed the SEC case against him in 1991–1993, Baker & Botts. James Baker headed the team and used Baker & Botts trial lawyers, including Robert W. Jordan, Bush's personal lawyer in the SEC fix and later ambassador to Saudi Arabia.[81] Non–Baker & Botts lawyers who later became prominent included Baker's former aide Robert Zoellick, later trade representative, and Ted Olson, later Ashcroft's solicitor general. Drawing on its unlimited coffers, the Bush legal team simply swamped the limited capacities of the Gore campaign.[82]

Because Governor Jeb Bush could not himself issue the rulings by which one brother would appoint the other president, he did so through Katherine L. Harris, the state election commissioner.[83] Harris, an unmitigated partisan paid off by her party in November 2002 with a plum safe seat in the U.S. House of Representatives, issued a series of rulings to stymie recount efforts, forcing the Florida Supreme Court to rein her in. She thereby set the Florida court up to attract the indignation of the U.S. Supreme Court's activist bloc, especially the crucial attention of O'Connor. O'Connor's well-known partisan political streak, going back to her days as Republican Party leader in the Arizona state legislature, overwhelmed the

Court's lack of precedented or legitimate reasons to intervene in a case that fell under the Florida court's jurisdiction, not its own.

In its first ruling (the *Palm Beach County* case),[84] the Court maintained, after an initial internal split, a fragile surface unanimity among the moderates in favor of letting the conservative activist bloc intervene without dissent and fire shots across the Florida court's bow.[85] However, in the second judicial round, *Bush v. Gore,*[86] the activists took the gloves off. The Baker & Botts legal team and Harris had stalled the ballot count beyond the Florida Supreme Court's first deadline, so it had ordered an expedited statewide counting of all the ballots under neutral judicial supervision. I can easily recall the moment of that ruling late in the afternoon of Friday, December 8, just after I had filed one of three legal analyses of the election contest in the weekly *Legal Times.* Because the filing had been at the absolute drop-dead deadline for locking up the next issue, when the Florida Supreme Court temporarily reinjected hope into the matter, a complete rewrite had to occur immediately at a don't-look-back pace.[87]

The next day, by a 5–4 vote with an opinion by Justice Scalia, the conservative activists stopped the count.[88] Judges who would stop a count, like judges who would stop citizens or a legislature from voting, disrespect democracy itself in their misplaced activism. That the five-justice bloc shortly ruled for Bush came as no surprise. What did again display far-out activism lay in the bloc's compounding its previous stance by refusing to remand the case, after its decision, to the Florida court to which the Constitution gave the jurisdiction in the matter. This amounted not just to a wrong ruling but to a naked power grab. The separate opinion of justices Breyer and Souter reflected their own extraordinarily conciliatory gesture toward the conservatives, offering to let the five conservatives have their newly counterfeited legal doctrines so Bush could win on condition that the case then go back to the state court of jurisdiction. While this would almost certainly not change the result—approval of Bush as victor—the potential 7–2 compromise offered by Breyer and Souter would have respected the elementary bounds of judicial power. Instead, Kennedy and O'Connor chose the activist position, far out of normal bounds, that gave them alone undiluted, unveiled, unbuffered power directly to appoint their personal choice of president.

When the five activists did this, they opened the country's eyes, at least temporarily, to just how potently the law could serve conservatives in the absence of a cause that could win centrist support in the polls. In hindsight, *Bush v. Gore* told even more. The extreme nature of the majority's fast-paced actions—especially the instant stay of the vote count and the spurning of the Breyer-Souter compromise on a remand—displayed the five having forged a tight activist unit beforehand. More than any of the other potentials created in the 1990s, the bloc's prior formation turned out to facilitate the post-2000 presidential right turn without a mandate from the electorate. Without that special supreme right-wing activist bloc, candidate Bush still probably would have come into office without winning an actual count of the ballots. He would have depended upon the crass politics of the Republican-controlled Florida state legislature and the Republican-controlled U.S. Senate and House, respectively appointing and approving a Bush electoral slate regardless of the actual Florida vote.[89] However, these routes to the office, involving the politicking of fellow party members, would have cost him a sharp diminution in stature. Instead, the bloc's court-cloaked victory, with the ballot count stopped, would let him steer right with the semblance of legitimacy albeit no mandate, veiling the cracks in that legitimacy by the political abuse of law.

I analyze most of what ensued in the chapters to come. But, it is worth mentioning how a few of the themes in this chapter played out in the election year of 2004. For example, as discussed, the financial community emerged relatively unscathed from the Enron-Worldcom firestorm of 2002 largely owing to Bush's use of Pitt to prevent serious reforms on the big-greed matters like oversized CEO stock options. Naturally, come next election, the financial industry generously showered political contributions on him in quantities not seen since the Rockefellers and the Morgans used to buy control of the whole Senate in the early 1900s. Robert W. Jordan, who has often turned up as Bush's own lawyer in this chapter, reaped the rich prize for his firm of his appointment as ambassador to Saudi Arabia. His firm opened an office in Riyadh. Recall how the Bahrainis had paid off the senior Bush with the sweet deal for Bush junior. Likewise, Bush set Jordan up so that the Saudis could expect kid-glove treatment from him— when, after the stunning attack of 9/11, their (presumably unwitting) role in financing and staffing the attack angered the American public. Jordan's undoubted awareness of how green his future, and that of his firm's new Riyadh office, would be if the Saudis saw merit in him no doubt made him strive to be the most Saudi-simpatico ambassador he could be; these too are among the uses of law.

2 "Ashy"

The Social Conservative Agenda

By 2004 Attorney General John Ashcroft had succeeded, to a dreadful extent, in advancing social conservative causes and undermining civil liberties in this country. This chapter focuses on social conservative issues; the next, on civil liberties. Ashcroft had pushed far out on right-wing religious and social causes ranging from depriving women of their abortion rights to creating a national personal right to firearms. This chapter starts with the rise of social conservatism as a key Republican base, Ashcroft's own ascent, and the social issues arising during his tenure. The chapter's heart concerns how Ashcroft undermined *Roe v. Wade* so as to muster political support without overly awakening centrist opposition. The Bush administration's right-wing judge picking and some other prospects also receive attention.

The Burger Court's 1973 abortion rights decision, *Roe v. Wade*,[1] liberated the nation's women in a vital respect, giving them legal control over their bodies, choices about their lives, and an alternative to life- and health-threatening, illegal back-alley abortions. But politically, *Roe v. Wade* brought two levels of opposition. First, the population's acceptance of the decision was mixed. Second, the ruling allowed political figures in the Republican Party, or those helping it, to shape the various ensuing subissues for decades thereafter so as to get support from groups of voters who were otherwise not particularly committed to partisan political action. *Roe* provided the means to whip up a partisan frenzy in some members of

Protestant denominations like Southern Baptists and evangelicals. And it gave the Republican Party one of its few ways of appealing to socially conservative Catholics who traditionally had looked askance at Republican candidates tied to militantly political preachers.

Previously, sectarian differences had more often divided conservative Protestants and Catholics than their common cultural attitudes had united them. Opposition to *Roe* provided a cross-sect conservative religious base to come together for the benefit of the Republican Party.[2] Presidents Reagan and Bush senior picked up sizable support from pledging to support the right wing against abortion rights.[3] The first Bush administration vigorously but unsuccessfully tried to persuade the Supreme Court to overrule *Roe v. Wade* in 1992. However, this visible and radical approach widened a "gender gap" that, along with social conservatives' high visibility, contributed to the party's loss of that year's presidential race.

George W. Bush learned much from this defeat while helping manage his father's reelection campaign, and he began applying the lessons to his own race in Texas two years later.[4] He needed those lessons for his long-term project as well. He stood high among the presidential candidates dependent upon the shift of Southern conservatives to Republican support in presidential elections between 1964 and 1988 and after the 1994 Gingrich-DeLay takeover the House. Obviously, that shift owed partly to a long-term conservative Southern white reaction against the civil rights movement, the Warren Court decisions, and civil rights and anti-poverty laws. But the end of the Cold War and President Clinton's own agenda neutralized or at least temporarily co-opted some legal issues previously important to conservatives, such as the fights against communism, crime, and affirmative action.

Clinton's attorney general, Janet Reno, became the target of social conservatives' rage. Reno enjoyed wide centrist support, as she was herself a serious manager of prosecutors yet one with enough tolerance on issues of morality and diversity to reassure a diverse nation. Social conservatives, however, reviled Reno for being "soft" on Clinton's alleged immorality and crimes, for being "hard" on extremists who had splintered off the right end of the political spectrum (e.g., the violent far-out cult in the siege at Waco), and for upholding constitutional abortion rights.[5]

In the early 1990s, social conservatives served the Republican Party with a burgeoning political apparatus of organizations, media, and message delivery. By 1994 eight in ten fundamentalist Christians, many manipulated by the Republican shill organization known as the Christian

Coalition, voted Republican.[6] For its part, the NRA, generously funded by the gun manufacturers, pulled the strings to make gun enthusiasts into ardent social conservative allies, with 69 percent voting Republican in 1994.[7] By contrast to the Republican loss in 1992, the 1994 elections, including George W. Bush's capture of the Texas governorship, successfully field-tested what later became the Ashcroft agenda of ideological legal patronage.

ASHCROFT: PRESIDENTIAL CANDIDATE

In his own rise, Ashcroft prominently displayed religiosity as part of his campaigning.[8] His legal career started at the University of Chicago law school and continued in early jobs teaching law. These had draft-deferment value at the time; the *Boston Globe* found evidence that his father's connections helped him get out of the draft altogether—not unlike the connections that got George W. Bush, along with other sons of the privileged, into the elite unit of the Texas Air National Guard.[9]

Ashcroft went to work in the Missouri attorney general's office, a stepping-stone into politics. He won two terms as Missouri attorney general in 1976 and 1980 and then two terms as governor in 1984 and 1988. In 1994 Ashcroft won an open U.S. Senate seat from Missouri, defeating a highly respected black congressman, Alan Wheat. In that race Ashcroft displayed his customary skill in taking advantage of the race issue, designing messages on welfare and crime, for example, that voters could view as racial or not, as they chose.[10]

Since Missourians have in some respects allowed their political leaders to champion the anti–*Roe v. Wade* cause, Ashcroft's later description (in 1998) of his crusade on that issue was quite accurate: "Abortion is a cause in which I have been active since my first days in office. I argued *Planned Parenthood v. Ashcroft* [a first assault on *Roe* during the Reagan administration] before the U.S. Supreme Court as Missouri's Attorney General. And, as Missouri's Governor, I fought for and signed into law the enactment which became the basis for *Webster v. Reproductive Health Services* [a second assault on *Roe* during the first Bush administration]."[11] Perhaps no single official at Ashcroft's level could credit himself with a greater lead role in the fight against *Roe*.

In 1995 Senator Ashcroft led congressional modification of the welfare reform law to include the "charitable choice" provision, by which religious social service organizations could obtain federal funding on the same basis as nonsectarian organizations. This approach became the model for what Governor Bush began urging in Texas, and what President Bush later urged in Washington, as "compassionate conservatism."[12] The Ashcroft-Bush approach involved no increase (indeed, often a decrease) in aid to the poor but assured less tolerance of any "sinful" lifestyles amongst them. And it approved more preaching at them as a condition for the limited help they received, notwithstanding that the help was funded by taxpayers most of whom were uninterested in or highly opposed to using their tax dollars to advance the cause of some sect they didn't choose.

Ashcroft had built up sufficient national support among social conservatives to devote much of 1998 to a serious preliminary run for president. His run received little coverage in the general press at the time and not much even after he took over the Justice Department. But he sustained the campaign all year by conducting hearings in the Constitution Subcommittee he chaired of the Senate Judiciary Committee. Ashcroft's role as chair in the hearings foreshadowed much of his attorney generalship. He used the hearings as a laboratory in which to experiment with the complex maneuvers of legitimating hot-button social conservative legal themes at the national level. In January 1998 Ashcroft chaired a hearing to condemn *Roe v. Wade* on its twenty-fifth anniversary.[13] In March a hearing he chaired lambasted Clinton-Reno proposals for increased counterterrorism efforts—prefiguring Attorney General Ashcroft's fateful underestimation, during the first nine months of 2001, of the terrorism threat.[14] And in September he chaired a hearing to expound the theory, contrary to all judicial holdings up to that time, of a national personal constitutional right to firearms.[15]

He capped the campaign with a September address to the national "Road to Victory" Christian Coalition convention, a revealing speech not reported then or since in the general press.[16] At this convention Ashcroft vied with others, such as Steve Forbes and Dan Quayle, for support from arch–social conservatives; conspicuously absent was Governor Bush, for whom this forum was too extreme to attend in person. Afterwards, just as the national electorate frustrated congressional Republicans by disapproving of the Starr-Gingrich arrangements for impeachment of Clinton, so Missouri exit polls in 1998 showed Ashcroft with a feeble 38 percent support in his own state (his name was not on the ballot). Centrist voters had fled him.

Putting aside his national ambitions (for the moment), Ashcroft turned to an active reelection run in Missouri, trying to hold his Senate seat against a spirited conservative Democratic opponent, Governor Mel Carnahan. Here again, Ashcroft skillfully positioned himself to benefit from the race issue, this time from his Senate Judiciary seat. He helped lead resistance to Clinton administration judicial appointments,[17] and while the main Senate Republican strategy on Clinton judicial nominees was to stall them, occasionally a high-visibility, all-out floor battle occurred. In 1999, as a signal to his conservative white Missouri electoral base, Ashcroft famously led one of the biggest Senate floor battles against a judicial nominee, Ronnie White, who was a distinguished black judge then on the Missouri Supreme Court.

In a key floor speech Ashcroft denounced the black nominee as "pro-criminal" based on his having issued one opinion not favoring the death penalty. That was an unusually direct innuendo, a bold polarizing thrust of the sort Ashcroft would use as attorney general. Conservative whites listening in Missouri could, if they wished, hear Ashcroft stereotyping even the most highly respected of moderate black jurists as "pro-criminal." It was a naked playing of the crime card on the race issue, because it did not concern a criminal who happened to be black, but a moderate judge on the highest court of his state who happened to be black. And it was inaccurate because White voted to uphold death penalty convictions forty-one out of fifty-nine times, about as often as did the judge's white colleagues picked by then governor Ashcroft himself.[18]

After Ashcroft's private pleas persuaded his party's moderate senators to defeat White on a party-line vote, they discovered aspects of Ronnie White that Ashcroft had concealed even from his own close colleagues. They felt Ashcroft had deceived them about the part that race played in the matter—an extraordinary feeling for the senator to have engendered.[19] Playing the crime/race card is accepted in some versions as a part, albeit unfortunate, of political rough-and-tumble; but rarely would one Senate Republican descend to leaving his colleagues in the club-within-a-club of the Senate Republican Party feeling deceived about it on a high-visibility matter. Doing so risks losing the trust of one's fellow Republican senators. In the event, with the Senate reelection race coming to a close finish, Carnahan and his son died in October 2000 in a plane crash. Ashcroft lost at the polls to the deceased Carnahan.[20]

ASHCROFT STARTS

Whereas Ashcroft eagerly accepted public identification with the right's social agenda, Bush tried, in his 1990s campaigning in Texas and then nationally, to keep the public from becoming too aware of his courting of social conservatives.[21] Bush had to accept the Texas Republican Party's capture by arch–social conservatives, including installation of a social conservative party chair whom Bush disliked intensely but accepted under heavy pressure.[22] His conservative adviser Karl Rove urged him to play ball with the social conservatives dominating the party. But characteristically, Bush wanted to have his cake and eat it too. He wanted to tell social conservatives constantly about his own religious beliefs, a safe way of bonding with them and distancing himself from the "sinner" President Clinton. Meanwhile he avoided clear pledges on their legal matters, commitments that, made public, would injure his chances of reassuring centrist voters that he was with them too. He might well deliver on privately given pledges, but not with advance warnings that would alienate centrists and only when he could do so safely, by means such as manipulating or even subverting the law.

So in the 1999–2000 Republican primary campaigning, he stayed focused on economic issues until the New Hampshire primary washed out Steve Forbes. Bush tacked right on social issues only when it was necessary to handle the surprisingly powerful challenge from Senator John McCain, as in the South Carolina primary. Even then, Bush made his personal public appeals only by symbolic gestures, such as his support for flying the Confederate flag over the state capitol and his pilgrimage to Bob Jones University. To the outside world, BJU simply meant a bastion of intolerant Christian-right extremism with a record even of rejecting Catholics, tapping a dark side of South Carolina history that included the anti-Catholic Ku Klux Klan. In South Carolina politics, that BJU pilgrimage meant much more: the "Bob Jones contingent" represented the most extreme right wing of the very far right state Republican Party. As the leading political science study on the Christian right notes, "BJU provided a large cadre of skilled activists, who usually backed the most conservative entrant in the GOP primaries."[23]

Bush thus found ways to recruit the very far social right while limiting his personal public embrace of such concerns as an abortion litmus test for judicial nominees that might imperil his ability to sell himself to the moderate national electorate. Rather, Bush delegated to Rove the task of crafting a low pitch to the conservative South Carolina primary voters, which Rove handled artfully in a below-the-radar, no-fingerprints way. Reporters present at Bush events detected Rove's versatility, like a ventriloquist who smilingly and blandly drinks a glass of water while from somewhere a nasty voice is heard—in this case the barrage of racially tinged smears that buried McCain. McCain was a Reaganite on most issues, but his brave personal toleration of diversity rendered him vulnerable in South Carolina, with its Republican primary electorate's unsubtle embrace of racial intolerance.[24] At the key juncture, Bush had Rove smear and beat McCain on the race issue, using ads funded from sources like Big Tobacco.

After the 2000 election contest, Ashcroft represented something more to president-elect Bush than merely a former competitor just repudiated by his home state. Rather, Ashcroft himself occupied a high position as a nationally recognized leader of social conservative legal causes. Bush could use Ashcroft to do the dirty work while he stood above, working on his image as a *compassionate* conservative.

Initially, a month after the election, Bush chose Montana governor Marc Racicot for attorney general. Racicot was a close Bush friend who had just served with distinction as a high-profile spokesman during the Florida vote recount. Nonetheless, his selection elicited virtually the only internal revolt against a Bush cabinet selection.[25] Social conservatives spanning the religious spectrum opposed Racicot for not having fought sufficiently hard against abortion rights and for supporting the extension of hate-crimes law protection to gays. Racicot and Montana had taken that position in reaction to the barbaric 1998 murder of a gay student in next-door Wyoming, evincing his and his state's condemnation of bigotry. But to many in the religious right, that stance was anathema. As the pressure built, president-elect Bush let Rove make the switch, and Racicot withdrew on December 20. Under pressure from his right flank, Bush now turned to Ashcroft, later installing Racicot as chair of the Republican National Committee.[26] Although they had no personal chemistry at first, as Ashcroft began demonstrating his usefulness to President Bush as a lightning rod, Bush assigned him his own nickname: "Ashy."[27]

A month of Washington struggle ensued over the nomination, marking the incoming administration's largest controversy and the most debated attorney general appointment in history.[28] Ashcroft barely eked out that victory, narrow as it was, by pretending how nice, not nasty, he would be on social issues as attorney general.[29] He pledged, for example, not to ask the Supreme Court to overrule *Roe v. Wade*, even if the Court's composition changed to invite this, a promise that soon proved even less reassuring than it sounded.[30]

Ashcroft's Justice Department prepared in certain respects for future right-wing maneuvers, notably by two appointments to high posts. The White House chose Ted Olson as solicitor general, the government's chief advocate in the Supreme Court and head of appellate litigation in the Justice Department.[31] Olson was the prominent senior figure who had argued the *Palm Beach County* and *Bush v. Gore* cases successfully for Bush in the Supreme Court; he was naturally Bush's ambassador to the bloc of five conservatives on the Court. He had become a hero to movement conservatives, in part by authoring shrill attacks on Reno.[32] During his 2001 nomination hearings, Olson got into serious credibility problems over his flat denial under oath of involvement in the "Arkansas Project," a far-right cause that dredged up unsupported sleazy slanders against Clinton.[33]

The other signal appointment was of Viet Dinh as assistant attorney general for the Office of Legal Policy.[34] This position involved a role in both formulating Justice Department proposals and promoting ideological judicial nominations. Dinh liked to describe his origins in a family of Vietnamese refugees from communism—playing the diversity card (which Ashcroft particularly needed) while reassuring the right he was with them. More to the point, Dinh had served as a junior staffer for Senator Alphonse D'Amato's (R-N.Y.) Whitewater Committee—that is, as an anti-Clinton congressional hatchet man. Big Tobacco richly rewarded Dinh with exclusive opportunities to provide expertise on how to exclude damning evidence on nicotine addiction from trials of major tobacco companies.[35]

He proved loyal and useful in office. When, for example, the Bush administration had to explain why its ideological judicial appointments so lacked the racial and gender diversity of Clinton's choices, the honor of giving the lame explanations often fell to Dinh. In 2003 after Dinh left office and Arnold Schwarzenegger won the California gubernatorial recall, Dinh rushed to be photographed beside the new governor, thereby providing at least a faint image of diversity for yet another white male Republican leader not exactly overloaded with support from big-name elected black officials.[36]

Although many officials of the rank of Olson and Dinh occupied nominally powerful posts in the Justice Department, in fact, Ashcroft ran the department through two long-time, highly political senior aides known as "the Davids." David Thompson Ayres had run Ashcroft's 1994 and 2000 Senate campaigns and served as his Senate chief of staff: clearly he was Ashcroft's personal campaign manager.[37] David Israelite, a political lawyer, had worked for Missouri's other Republican senator, "Kit" Bond, and also served as director of political and governmental affairs for the Republican National Committee. Having the Davids run the department was a dramatic change from previous administrations. Reno had no such politico underbosses but dealt directly, often in large-group "open-tent" meetings, with the senior department officials.

By October 2003 Ashcroft's political style, however much he tried to conceal it from the public and even from his own department's top levels, had become so blatant that *Legal Times of Washington* (by no means an administration-critical forum) ran the headline "John Ashcroft's Inner Circle: Critics say that attorney general's management style gives too much power to political aides."[38] Ashcroft held a daily morning meeting with the Davids and his other close personal (political) advisers; he did not include even the hard-right departmental senior officials—this was for the pure pols. As the reporter found from interviewing fifteen current and former Bush administration officials, "access to the attorney general is tightly controlled by political advisers who . . . run the department more like the office of a legislator seeking re-election than an executive branch agency."[39] Meanwhile, Ashcroft's initial effort to staff the Justice Department with a representative number of minority officials did not last; as minorities left, Ashcroft replaced them with whites. By late 2003 eleven out of the twelve most senior officials appointed or nominated at the main Justice Department were white.[40]

ABORTION RIGHTS

At his confirmation hearings, Ashcroft promised that he would not directly ask the Supreme Court to overrule *Roe v. Wade*. Nonetheless, his attorney generalship threatened a mortal campaign against women's abortion rights.[41] In fact, his confirmation hearing statement merely confirmed his understanding of the general tactical redirection his own movement—that of anti-abortion political activists—had made in the 1990s.

Here I should note the delicate political situation that Bush, with Rove as consigliere, took on when he decided to use Ashcroft and others like him as his tools. There are plenty of leaders with sincere anti-abortion views, such as Representative Henry Hyde (R-Ill.), and without agreeing with them, one can respect the sincerity of their views; with sincere leaders, the two sides on the issue can even look for dialogue and for points of agreement amidst the struggle. If unwanted pregnancies can be avoided, without having to be terminated, in ways respectful of women's rights, for example, both sides can feel morally right. If women with advanced unwanted pregnancies can, of their own free will, accept the expected trauma of going to term and then giving up their baby for adoption and can be healed afterward and see their deed as a noble way of helping another family, then both sides can rejoice.

But the search for dialogue and progress could hardly be further from what the manipulating conservative politicos on the issue desire. Such puppet masters as Rove had long gotten the Christian right working for their candidates by playing this issue. The real frontier now lay in maximizing the issue's use in attracting conservative Catholic voters. Traditionally Catholic voters had thrown most of their support and sympathy to the Democratic Party, as reflected in the party's nomination of Al Smith for president in 1928, John Kennedy for president in 1960, and Geraldine Ferraro for vice president in 1984. Of course, in general, there is nothing wrong in the Republican Party finding ways to compete with its Democratic rival for the support of Catholics or any other group, and there is nothing to prevent Republicans from some day nominating a Catholic for president.

But the climate in the 2000s was very different from an open, positive competition for the allegiance of America's lively community of Catholics, with their great diversity of ethnic backgrounds and personal beliefs. For decades, the Vatican had foisted a series of far-right appointees on the American Catholic hierarchy. Then the scandal of priest abuse of children broke, exposing the hierarchy to extreme embarrassment before its community. And Rome would not allow the hierarchy, whatever it wanted to do, to truly reach out. There was no coming to terms with what Church leaders derisively called "Cuomism"—the doctrine perfected by Governor Mario Cuomo of New York in 1984 when he explained how, in the open world of American politics, Catholic leaders could personally oppose abortion yet support the aspirations of their people politically by participating in an inclusive party of progress. There was no coming to terms with the fact that of sixty million Catholics in America, only about one-third (fifteen million to twenty million) are "core" religionists today, down from three-fourths or higher in the 1950s.[42] Manipulators of the abortion-rights issue like Rove could scheme to pick up that one-third of "core" Catholics by aligning with the American Church hierarchy on issues it cared about that wouldn't unduly raise centrist hackles elsewhere, so that at least that portion of the flock, following their shepherds, would move toward the Republican pens for vote shearing.

Accordingly, the Bush administration started to deliver for the anti-abortion activist movement immediately. Rather than put Ashcroft on the spot, President Bush temporarily shifted the locus of action to other points in the government. Domestically, he turned over key posts in the Department of Health and Human Services (HHS) to movement right-to-lifers. These appointments figured in President Bush's famous summer 2001 decision to forbid, except at a very limited level, all fetal stem cell research. In the 2000 election, President Bush had thrown in with the anti–stem cell research cause, a way to align politically with the Catholic hierarchy, as well as the sects that loved Ashcroft, that appeared to pose few risks because the issue did not seem so bluntly to deprive women of rights. When he actually took a serious look at what he had promised, he discovered that on one hand he had taken a position whose defense in an age of widely popular desire to see medical scientific progress was problematic. On the other hand, the political leaders that Bush had embraced on this issue, like Senator Sam Brownback (R-Kan.), compared stem cell research to Nazi medicine.[43]

Therefore, in August 2001, after the media cooperated in the staged drama to portray Bush as the thoughtful healer putting politics aside, sort of a Henry Clay of the twenty-first century, the president struck what he presented as his great compromise. Bush said he would allow research only on existing cell lines, based on the claim that those amounted to "more than sixty"—a seemingly ample amount that, if true, would not slow development overmuch. Thus he achieved the goal of the schemers for recruiting the conservative religious vote. His claim that "more than sixty" cell lines existed, though, was at best nonsense and—considering how conveniently it served his political interests in implementing a terribly anti-science, anti-health position—most likely more than merely accidental nonsense. Many informed sources immediately disputed the president's inflated number, so that it took a substantial HHS misinformation campaign to delay the inevitable exposure of his "compromise."[44] Not until two years later did the fog fully clear; in April 2003 the *New York Times* reported that there were not sixty lines but only eleven, making clear the policy's negative impact on medical science. Bush may have rerun the Scopes Monkey Trial of the 1920s on a vital health research issue of the 2000s and let reaction win, but he had the issue in his pocket for the 2002 and 2004 elections.

Meanwhile, the main line of delivery to the political manipulators of the abortion rights issue (still leaving Ashcroft aside for the moment) occurred in the international realm. On his first workday in the White House, Bush had announced reinstatement of the "Mexico City Policy," developed in the Reagan and first Bush years.[45] The policy not only bans the use of U.S. funds for abortion but also denies funds to organizations that support abortion activities anywhere in the world—even if the organization uses *only* non-U.S. funds for this purpose (and, of course, even when those activities are completely voluntary and legal).

In the era before the Mexico City Policy, the United States had led the world in population control, helping to establish and support (providing almost one-third of the yearly funding) the United Nations Population Fund (UNFPA)—the world's premier collective family planning effort. In 1993 President Clinton, acting on his pro-choice mandate in the 1992 election, had reversed the Mexico City Policy.[46] Now, in 2001, President Bush struck a hard blow by reinstating it.[47] It was punishment for international family-planning organizations, and it attempted to use U.S. funding as a club to beat the rest of the world into line on abortion policy.

This started a complex legal struggle between president and Congress since congressional appropriations fund UNFPA, but it was a struggle in which Bush's anti-abortion activist supporters held most of the high cards. Centrists on this issue found their standard-bearer in Secretary of State Colin Powell, one of the diminishing circle of visible pro-choice figures left high in the Republican Party and nominally, as secretary of state, the administration's own leader of American foreign policy. Powell's relatively tolerant views fit, in this regard, not only U.S. centrist opinion but the predominant world opinion, which bridled at the American right wing's use of legal conditions on aid funding to dictate and throttle world population policy.

The struggle surfaced in many places.[48] At a regional family planning conference in Bangkok in December 2002, the Bush administration threatened to withdraw its support for a 1994 family planning agreement.[49] That 1994 "Cairo conference" agreement involved two major matters for the world women's movement: the Convention on the Elimination of All Forms of Discrimination against Women (CEDAW) and a worldwide goal to raise $17 billion in aid for women in developing nations. Snubbing Powell, President Bush sent John Klink, who had represented the Vatican at international conferences, as the United States' figure at conferences like that in Bangkok. One article described Mr. Klink's position on international women's health issues as "so far right, he has opposed providing the 'morning after' pill to rape victims in refugee camps and decried the use of condoms even to halt the spread of HIV."[50] Following his president's script, in Bangkok Klink helped disrupt the conferences and undermine CEDAW and funding on issues from sex education to fighting AIDS. He did so by insisting all such discussions be back-burnered until world abortion policy fit the Bush administration's desires. Also, President Bush instituted what has been nicknamed the "global gag rule." This prohibits international organizations that receive U.S. funds from providing women even with information about abortion—not services, just facts—even if abortion is legal in the country in which the organization operates.[51]

The Bush administration's approach was not one of the best ways to compete for Catholic support, even in the international arena. It did not bid against the Democratic Party, for example, for support of the Church's world efforts to achieve peace, reduce hunger, establish decent wages, help those in want and need, assist development in Latin American and African nations, and so forth. Doing so would compete with the agenda of maximizing profits for elites and for pariah businesses, his other base. Rather, Bush championed only the particular element that served the social conservative alliance without riling his conservative economic base—namely, fighting worldwide against the women's movement and against international family planning. Powell did not say for the record how he felt about being rebuffed on world women's rights issues. But he is (rightfully) a proud leader. When talk circulated in Washington in 2003 about whether Powell would stay in a second Bush term, memories ran to moments such as this.[52]

As the 2000s went on, the administration continued implementing its approach on the key issue of the appropriations Congress made to UNFPA and the World Health Organization (WHO). The appropriations carried Congress's carefully crafted legal standard on the UNFPA's help for China, a major world issue. China has brought its previously unsupportable population explosion under control by its "one child policy," but the country uses distinctly controversial means, such as forced sterilization in some localities—something the world disapproves. So the Clinton administration had struck the compromise of funding just the UNFPA activities outside China, which roughly reconciled American and world opinions. In the 2000s, Congress's legal standard for letting UNFPA have American support attempted to make it a question of fact whether UNFPA activities inside China not only went on with no American funding but, even with non-American funding, kept well clear of the controversial practices in localities. It was a tough standard but at least a potentially objective one.

Powell tried, albeit futilely, to play the game straight and by the rules. He sent an expert American diplomatic team to investigate in China. The team reported in May 2002 that the UNFPA had, as the rest of the world maintained, succeeded in avoiding the controversial Chinese local practices.[53] However, in September 2002 administration hard-liners overrode Powell and withheld the appropriations anyway, insisting that unless China took known-to-be-unacceptable steps, the United States must defund UNFPA worldwide. Similarly, President Bush wanted to defund the World Health Organization for doing research on the so-called morning-after pill, RU-486.[54] The administration seemed well on the road to insisting the entire world dance on the string of the administration's extreme stances—or else suffer all of its American support being cut. Either way, Bush was well equipped to manipulate the social conservative constituency on these issues.

LATE-TERM ABORTIONS

Domestically, the major element of President Bush and Attorney General Ashcroft's campaign to undermine *Roe v. Wade* concerned the relentless focusing of national attention on one unusual abortion method. Used only at late stages of pregnancy, it is known technically as dilation and extraction (D&X) and popularly (albeit a bit too broadly) as the "late term" method. (Right-to-lifers call it the "partial birth" method, but no part of the medical procedure involves the process of natural childbirth, so that term is for political purposes.)[55] D&X has medical justifications for its limited use in special circumstances, such as a woman's health difficulties that render other procedures dangerous, or nonviable and problematic advanced pregnancies, such as the absence of a brain. Still, when opponents of abortion rights described D&X graphically in isolation from its prescribed medical uses—as they never tired of doing and as the Ashcrofts and Roves of the political world encouraged them to do—they could use what occurs in the medical steps involving the fetus to arouse pity. Polls showed that the usually pro-choice public majority did not care to get deeply into the medical complexities of the issue and that, without making fine distinctions, the public, when asked flat uninformative questions about this procedure in isolation, mostly opposed it. Clever repetition of the phony epithet "abortion on demand," which is simply not what Justice Blackmun wrote about late-term pregnancies in *Roe*, further helped manufacture in the public mind an artificially heightened level of opposition on this subject.

When the 1994 election delivered Congress over to conservative leadership, those leaders immediately steered many aspects of national policy on women's legal hopes toward the right so as to solidify their pact with activist religious sects that placed little value on women's rights.[56] In particular, in the late 1990s they boosted the strategy of picking aspects of the abortion rights issue to push to the right on while not overly stirring up the centrist pro-choice majority. Although the "late-term abortion" method is used in only a tiny fraction of all abortions and hardly warrants a focus to the exclusion of other, important issues, conservative leaders recognized its superior political potential and made it the centerpiece and recurrent focus of their politics. The Republican House and Senate began regularly passing bills against the procedure, timed to exploit the issue by compelling President Clinton to veto them in the election years of 1996 and 1998. As a leading authority on this conservative strategy, William Saletan, observes, in 1996 the issue "wasn't enough to save Dole, but analysts agreed that the issue hurt Democrats in several House and Senate contests."[57]

Senator Ashcroft, fresh from cleverly building his career on this issue as Missouri attorney general and governor, personally led the Senate on this approach. He denounced the D&X procedure during the 1998 hearing he convened in his Senate Judiciary subcommittee to criticize *Roe v. Wade* on its twenty-fifth anniversary. He ran for president on the issue in 1998. Then in 2000, the Clinton administration's final year, the Supreme Court decided *Stenberg v. Carhart*,[58] regarding a Nebraska statute that criminalized "partial-birth abortions." Under Attorney General Reno, the United States positioned itself in this case to defend *Roe v. Wade* and therefore to join in challenging the Nebraska act. A 5–4 majority agreed with Reno and struck down the act, with all five justices in the majority joining the Court's opinion.[59] Besides joining the majority, Justice O'Connor wrote a separate concurring opinion with significant language about what laws on the subject might be upheld.

Bush had shown no particular sign of having personal principles on the matter. His mother is pro-choice, and his father had politically flip-flopped on the issue: where would the principles come from? From Laura Bush? Not likely; she did not put principles in his way as his mother had done to his father. True, when Bush first ran (unsuccessfully) for office in 1978, he made statements indicating a basically pro-choice position.[60] As with his other youthful indiscretions, however—including "partying" with "intoxicants," serving in the Texas Air National Guard rather than going to Vietnam like McCain or even Gore, and coming under SEC investigation for multiple counts of insider trading—he recovered from this revelation in a way that challenged his predecessor Bill Clinton's world championship title as "comeback kid."

When Bush actually began his run for president, first as governor and then as Republican nominee, he had the manipulative line down pat. After all, according to the leading political science study of the Christian right, "in the late 1990s, as Governor Bush prepared his run for the GOP presidential nomination, he brought Ralph Reed on board as an adviser."[61] We have met Ralph Reed before—the Christian Coalition's string puller who became head of the Georgia Republican Party. How wise to enlist him: he could tell Bush just what to say and persuade even the true believers not to hold against Bush his, or his father's or mother's, past pro-choice statements. In Saletan's careful tracing, "Bush continued his Texas Three-Step, paying lip service to an abortion ban [i.e., to overturn *Roe v. Wade* by direct assault] while effectively ruling it out and focusing instead on popular restrictions."[62]

On that last key step of the dance, Bush backed the restrictions especially popular in conservative Texas (where the ultraconservatives had taken over the Republican Party): putting obstacles in the path of desperate teenagers with unwanted pregnancies ("parental control"), allowing public funding for men's medical problems but not for this one of women's ("abolish public funding"), and completely outlawing late-term abortions. It was a politically convenient stance. Democrats steering for centrist support, instead of getting to compete on the issues that mattered the most to women and the poor, like health care and child care, must struggle to find defensible compromise positions on each of those restrictions.

So the volcanic outpouring of conservative propaganda aiding the new type of openly sectarian politicians like Ashcroft had succeeded, in two very different fields, in extending the late-term abortion issue after the 2000 *Stenberg* decision into the pivotal line of combat along which Bush's manipulators waged relentless war against the women's movement. The two contrasting fields for subverting the law were national electoral politics and the Supreme Court. In control of the House and Senate, the strategists of well-funded political conniving had designated for attack the exception to the proposed national federal ban on late-term abortions for preserving the life and health of the pregnant woman. In short, would Congress let stand this pillar of the legal understructure of *Roe*?

In the 2000 presidential debates, Gore said, "On the issue of partial birth or so-called late-term abortion, I would sign a law banning that procedure, provided that doctors have the ability to save a woman's life or to act if her health is severely at risk." Following his Texas Three-Step, Governor Bush said, "We need to ban partial birth abortions. . . . [Doing so] would be a positive step toward reducing the number of abortions in America."[63] Bush's silence in the Texas Three-Step signified that he would not favor any exception to the ban, even when the health of the mother was severely at risk. That was his line of attack for undermining *Roe v. Wade*.

Once President Bush installed Ashcroft, he could turn the issue over to be shaped for exploitation in 2002 and 2004, and Ashcroft did not disappoint him. Ashcroft took an important early in-court position in a state-originated late-term abortion case. His filing warrants some analysis because the news media—preferring to repeat the daily "message" from Bush's press handlers—let that revealing legal move slip by almost unnoticed (though it's right there on the public record). Ohio had enacted a new ban on D&X that attempted feebly to satisfy at least some of O'Connor's criteria in her *Stenberg* concurrence. Notably, it included an exception allowing the method to be used when "necessary" to protect the life or health of the mother. Ohio sought to get this statute, with its stingy concern for women's health, upheld. A stalwart women's clinic challenged Ohio, which defended the case. In *Women's Medical Profession Corp. v. Taft*, the federal district court struck down the state statute, finding that Ohio's exception was too narrow and did not protect against health risks as much as *Stenberg* required.[64] Ohio appealed to the Sixth Circuit.

At that point, in February 2002, Ashcroft's Justice Department filed an amicus curiae brief. In that brief the United States sought to turn back the clock, reminding the Sixth Circuit that during the Reagan and Bush administrations, the United States had defended state laws depriving women of their abortion rights. So much for Ashcroft's disavowal of the hard line; as with the Mexico City Policy, it was déjà vu for the policies of the two Bushes. The brief further noted that the House and Senate had voted for bills in the late 1990s against the late-term method. Ashcroft brushed aside the fact that those bills had not become federal laws;[65] and he particularly brushed aside the formal position the United States had taken in the Supreme Court quite recently, in 2000, when Reno had won *Stenberg*. And this was done neither by surrogate nor indirection nor letter. In the most formal legal way, Ashcroft treated the assault on abortion rights as his personal ideological spoils of victory in 2000, to be manipulated for maximum political profit. He weighed in just as his department had prior to 1993, back when the Reagan and Bush administrations had caused the center of the Supreme Court real pain, with its unabashed demand that the Court treat its own authoritative constitutional precedents (*Roe v. Wade*) as mere weather vane politics. From this position, Ashcroft's brief assailed the district court ruling with a full-length defense of the Ohio statute.

For those who recognized Ashcroft's filing in the Ohio case as his debut as schemer on the issue, it signalled that the Justice Department was circumventing his confirmation-hearing pledge not to mount a frontal attack on *Roe v. Wade* by mounting a flank attack instead. Ashcroft sent the same signal by supporting the Republican House in moving another bill against the late-term method in July 2002, expediently timed, like its predecessors in 1996 and 1998, for the election year. But because Bush had lost his party so many Senate seats in 2000, the Democrats had a majority in 2002. So the bill was a political zero.

When Republicans regained the Senate in 2003, the way was open for Ashcroft to complete his long-term campaign to force the legislation through the Senate to enactment. His party shaped the law to push the Supreme Court very hard—really to punish the Court's fragile uphold-*Roe* majority. Justice O'Connor's concurring opinion in *Stenberg*, expressing concerns about two key points against the Nebraska statute, had offered some standards for subsequent legislation and cases. In particular, O'Connor complained that the Nebraska statute lacked an exception for the preservation of the health of the mother, suggesting possible flexibility on the nature of that exception; and that Nebraska's ban did not clearly single out the D&X method but also had implications for the more common, non-D&X method. The justice, who represented the last best hope of women's rights not only on the Court but maybe in the world, knew she could not let the legislative manipulators push the Constitution down the slippery slope from one method to another. That would betray *Roe*, with its further fundamental pillar that the choice of method used be left in general to a woman and her physician.

Ashcroft's party shaped its legislated prohibition on late-term abortion —essentially its platform for the 2004 election—as a truculent attack on O'Connor's two points of dogged constitutional resistance. Upon inspecting the proposed "Partial-Birth Abortion Ban Act," both protesting minority Democrats and commentators took note of the draft's strange twists— some particularly aggressive political abuses of law. To begin with, the bill avoided defining precisely which method it applied to, notwithstanding all the public and legislative rhetoric about D&X. As the 2002 minority House report on the bill commented, "Nor is it limited to the clearly-defined 'late-term' abortion procedure. To the contrary, the bill's definition of 'partial-birth abortion' is vague, overbroad, and covers the most common type of 2d trimester abortion procedure. In fact, the term 'partial-birth abortion' is not a medical term, but a political one."[66] Democrats and Republicans disputed just what the bill's final version governed, with Republicans insisting they had narrowed somewhat the coverage of methods and Democrats insisting that, like the struck-down Nebraska statute, it could apply to the more common non-D&X method.[67] It was a missile aimed straight at O'Connor.

Moreover, this "Partial-Birth Abortion Ban Act" did not have an exception for the preservation of the health of the mother, O'Connor's other concern. It omitted this despite the strong thread in the line of cases going back to *Roe v. Wade* that curtailed the government's power to dictate medical methods when the mother's health is at issue, the preservation of her health being a matter completely between her and her physician. Thus, the act not only swung at *Stenberg* but also challenged *Roe* itself.

The act also contained pages and pages of purported congressional "findings of fact" that further took an ax to *Roe*. Historically, Congress has had some to make findings that the Supreme Court has felt obliged, to a fluctuating and uncertain degree, to accept in certain kinds of cases regarding the constitutionality of federal statutes. The two sides in deliberations over the act disputed whether the Court, which of late had deferred relatively little to congressional findings in other contexts, would do so in this one.[68]

Congressional enactment of these particular "findings" amounted to conferring on anti-abortion ideologues the use of Congress's muscle for arm-twisting the Court's potentially persuadable justices (current or new ones) as to *Roe*. Congress declared in the findings that the Court's own *Stenberg* finding that the D&X procedure was sometimes necessary for the health of the mother fell afoul of the "great weight of the evidence" and that this congressional finding of fact supersedes the judiciary's.[69] Congress purported to find that the procedure was, not just infrequently or rarely, but *never* necessary for the preservation of the woman's health. This assertion flouted not just the Supreme Court's findings but those of the lower court, all based upon full medical records compiled and studied. In this way Congress wrestled with the Court over (to paraphrase a Groucho Marx line) whom the Court should believe—the conservative voodoo doctors or its own eyes—and warned the Court it better not believe its own eyes.

Ashcroft's party in Congress had thus subverted the Constitution by making powerful strategic use of the minority party's inability to defeat or amend the late-term abortion bill. The Ashcroft approach denied Democrats what they had wanted all along, during Clinton's vetoes of the 1990s, during the 2000 campaign, and during debates on the issue in 2003: a fair chance to enact a bill that would regulate this publicly unpopular but relatively infrequent procedure in a way that would not chop away at the foundations of *Roe*.[70] The tight control that the Ashcroft wing of the party now held contrasted sharply with the ability, not long before, of a Republican such as Barbara Bush to stand by her own, traditional Republican principles on this issue and thus arrest the party's march to the right.

The significance of the play Ashcroft's wing of the party had made with the act became apparent when, in May 2003, Ashcroft privately addressed the Family Research Council, in many ways the successor to the Christian Coalition of Pat Robertson and Ralph Reed as the religious right's leading Republican shill organization.[71] Hoping to escape the press's attention, a gloating Ashcroft told the three hundred activist leaders (the kind he had based his presidential run on in 1998, and might again): "If you don't believe you have an impact in this city, take a look at the vote in the United States Senate yesterday [to adopt the late-term abortion bill] and then go 16 blocks down Pennsylvania Avenue and think about the fact that the president has indicated he will sign that legislation." At that, a witness tells us, "the ballroom erupted in cheers and applause."[72] In subsequent public pronouncements, Ashcroft limited himself to sternly opposing, not Saudi-based hijacking as on 9/11, but the nation's enemies, traitors—whom he seemed frequently to equate with those who dared disagree with him. But in private he still enjoyed being the beloved of social conservative activists, and given a chance to express their appreciation for his politicolegal black magic, they erupted in cheers and applause.

The conservative strategy in the Partial Birth Abortion Ban Act carried multiple implications. To begin with, it kept the issue alive for electoral use by the right not just in 2004 but in years to come. The issue had already helped the conservatives in every election since 1996: thanks to the heavy-handed descriptions of the procedure's grisly details and to well-funded propaganda focused exclusively on the issue, activists and susceptible voters now responded to it almost in automatic fashion. Now, by putting poison-pill "findings" in the federal statute, conservatives seized the legal opportunity to keep the abortion issue enmeshed in this still-unprohibited D&X procedure year after year through the mid- to late 2000s, until either O'Connor buckled under the pressure or, more likely, the Court's lineup changed.

For conservative causes the political stakes could not have been higher. In 2003 anti-abortion activists claimed that the abortion issue had affected the selection of over 40 percent of voters in the 2002 election, with pro-life candidates receiving a 7-percent-point boost over pro-choice candidacies, a material boon to Republican Senate candidates.[73] Probably much of this claim was spin and hype, but the Republican right certainly understood that it benefited from every opportunity to keep the public, especially conservative Catholics, and Congress focused on the D&X issue. Rove had all the money he needed, but to pull the available fraction of the votes in Catholic areas, he needed fired-up ground troops with the same ethnicity as the target population. Given the American Church hierarchy's desire for political distraction from its flubbing of the priest abuse issue, Rove could count on that hierarchy to encourage those ground troops, at the times he needed them, to advocate among Catholic voters the importance of electing a president, senators, and representatives who would protect innocent life. (For Rove, this was mere political hypocrisy. In the Church, it was adherence to the Vatican's pronouncement on a matter of faith. It was the concordance of the timing and intensity of the Church's emphasis with Rove's political maneuvers that was no coincidence.)

After all, what should an American Church ministering to populations such as poor but faithful Mexican Americans dwell upon—how shifting the tax burden from the rich to the working poor made their children's lives worse? That would be—well, Cuomism. Moreover, legally, by this strategy the right's political playmakers insured that whenever, sooner or later, they won their point—either by changing the Court's lineup or O'Connor views—they would win not just big but very big. As one scholarly legal analysis concluded, "How future courts interpret the health exception in statutes banning partial birth abortion . . . will shape future abortion jurisprudence, and will alter the meaning of the right to abortion for future generations of women."[74]

By this approach Ashcroft's party could anticipate over time, if the Court appointments went their way, nudging the Court further and further away from *Roe v. Wade*. Once the Court accepted counterfactual congressional findings on the D&X issue, perhaps it would only take the changed Court of the late 2000s or the early 2010s to accept some more such findings in another case or two. As one anti-abortion activist wrote in the *National Review*, "Pro-lifers should push for more . . . [t]o ban all elective abortions past, say, the twentieth week of pregnancy."[75] Congressional findings in a bill to ban abortions past the twentieth week of pregnancy might argue along lines very similar to those in the late-term act. Ashcroft might testify in favor of such a ban before the congressional judiciary committees in the late 2000s. He would ask for findings concerning viability by means of advancing neonatal intensive care, the asserted responsibility of pregnant women not to "dally" during the first twenty weeks in exercising their abortion rights lest they waive them, the grisliness of any single one of the different medical procedures used for abortion after twenty weeks, the supposedly attractive alternatives to abortion assertedly available these days to women if compelled to remain involuntarily pregnant from week twenty through birth, and so forth. Never mind that the reasons hapless women do not act so fast often stem from obstacles and problems placed in their path by their life circumstances and by previous rounds of anti-abortion politics—and by Ashcroft. Never mind that the women who have the child against their will then face a terrible choice: either the trauma of giving the baby up or keeping him or her but putting the child on the conveyor belt of diminishing life prospects. The likelihood of a husband-father's presence in the household and of the income necessary to afford adequate food, medicine, education, and care is higher for a baby born at an opportune point in the family's life cycle than for an unplanned birth.

Or, Ashcroft might pursue a different avenue for the next round of major federal legislation. He might back up the legal pressures that many states, particularly the strongholds of conservative political activists, have placed on pregnant women. Federal legislation could authorize state legislatures to impose a heightened gamut of legal formalities and obstacles women must run at the harassed and decreasingly tolerated clinics, under the guise of congressional "findings" that these hurdles were not an "undue burden" on *Roe v. Wade* rights. The federal legislation might allow states to put up yet more obstacles after a certain stage in the pregnancy, such as that five-month line; require heightened levels of paternal or (for juveniles) parental consent; or support longer delays with more burdensome "information" requirements, such as mandating that physicians provide this in person on multiple occasions, an increasingly expensive and practically insurmountable requirement in many localities.[76] The forces attacking the clinics on the late-term issue simultaneously attacked them in these other ways.[77]

Of course, Ashcroft's party had many other measures to move in 2003–2004 in order to undercut abortion rights, thanks to agenda control in both the Senate and the House and the leadership of a Bush administration with Rove and Ashcroft at the helm. In response to the infamous April 2003 crime involving the death of the pregnant Laci Peterson of Modesto, California, the DeLay-Frist legislative team hijacked the issue with the "Unborn Victims of Violence Act." Rather than simply stiffening and federalizing the penalties for crimes against pregnant women, the bill's authors enmeshed the law with an assault on *Roe* from a different direction by defining fetuses as individual legal entities.[78] Another bill on the Ashcroft agenda would criminalize relatives' efforts to help pregnant girls travel from their home state to have an abortion in another in order to avoid parental consent laws. Presumably this law would bring the FBI and federal prisons down on, say, a pregnant juvenile's grandmother if she circumvented a hostile father by driving her desperate granddaughter the few miles from Pennsylvania to New York.[79]

Such legislation opened the way to further federal legislative approaches to isolate women in regions hostile to *Roe*. Violence and harassment had already helped to produce an absence of abortion providers in 86 percent of U.S. counties.[80] Congress might step up from criminalizing interstate travel to aid juveniles seeking an abortion to outlawing interstate travel for abortion purposes by *any* women out of *Roe*-hostile areas. By such laws, Ashcroft's FBI might become a kind of fugitive posse for capturing women attempting to cross state lines to exercise their constitutional rights. And woe to the doctors who took their Hippocratic oath too seriously and refused to cooperate with Ashcroft's agents in the fugitive roundup. As with the fugitive slave laws of the antebellum era, the use of national police power to extend the tough rules of the South or other conservative regions to regions like the Northeast or California where people viewed those rights differently portended a supercharged legal struggle, with federal power ranged against individuals treated as having no rights where it counted.

The Ashcroft agenda could also work with the hard edge of the militant anti-abortion strategy traditionally aimed at reducing the availability of doctors, doctor training, and the number of other medical personnel under doctor supervision who might help women. Expanding on existing provisions,[81] conservatives sought to enact legislation that would combine in effect with the informal pressures against abortion they increasingly brought on all medical institutions to lock their doors to desperate women.[82]

One of the provisions of the Partial Birth Abortion Ban Act allowed the big activist anti-abortion organizations—legal powerhouses with the funding and staff to wield powerful legal tools effectively against clinics— to sue doctors performing the procedures covered by the act.[83] (Recall also that, with calculated vagueness preserved several years in a row by hard partisan combat, the act did not limit the ban just to D&X.) All those activist organizations needed was authorization from the husband of the pregnant woman or, if she were under eighteen, her parents—something easy to obtain in the context of a pregnant wife or daughter who, perhaps at odds with an angry spouse or parent, could not (for any of a number of physical or emotional reasons) go to term with the pregnancy. With the angry family member's signature on a legal form, the organization could then turn the federal courts into an engine of destruction against the doctor or clinic. The organization could collect money damages and put the defendant through endless rounds of legal discovery about this patient, other patients, this doctor, other doctors, donor lists, and so forth. Who would interpret and apply this statutorily open-ended invitation to deter, harass, and punish doctors for helping pregnant women in extremis? Ashcroft's appointees to the federal courts, of course, quietly litmus tested in many instances by these same anti-abortion activists.[84]

Legislation of these various kinds created future legal opportunities for Ashcroft's attorneys, particularly Olson, to campaign in the lower courts and in the Supreme Court to move the case law in the direction Rove desired. Ashcroft and Olson could offer the courts and especially the new Supreme Court justices relatively easier ways to erode *Roe* and its progeny. Even just a single, newly appointed justice could join the previous dissenting justices on these decisions, plus the wavering Justice Kennedy, to create a new conservative bloc.[85] Or congressional Republicans could use the issues over and over again, in more elections and other organizational activity, citing any court losses as a reason to further stack the judiciary. Ashcroft's career-long campaign to make political hay out of the misery of the abortion issue appeared to be paying off for him better than ever.

FIREARMS, VOUCHERS, AND ASSISTED SUICIDE

Ashcroft's promotion of a constitutional right to firearms deserves special study since it shows how the Bush administration embarked on a new course of molding constitutional law for political purposes. Not so long ago, the rulings of the nation's high courts had established beyond question the absence of any individual constitutional right to firearms. The Second Amendment of the Constitution declares:

> A well regulated Militia being necessary to the security of a free State,
> the right of the people to keep and bear arms, shall not be infringed.

The amendment's text supports what is termed the classic "collective right" explanation of the Framers' intent. That is, the phrase about the "well regulated Militia" merely prohibits Congress from disarming any state's whole population (the "people" who formed the "Militia" of a "free State" having been very important for "security" in the 1790s), not individual owners of personal firearms. This classic collective interpretation[86] contrasts sharply with the opposing theory, which the NRA has pushed hard in the past three decades, of a national right of individual citizens to firearms for personal use, a notion that ill fits the amendment's words. (Indeed, the Framers' elaborate requirement of a "well regulated Militia" suggests quite the opposite: they no more wanted Saturday night specials and Uzis on the loose than anyone today.)

The 1968 Gun Control Act prompted lawyers who were supported financially by the NRA or allied groups to publish articles and books upholding the individual right theory. In the late 1970s the NRA took an even more partisan turn, becoming increasingly involved with the project of electing conservative-movement Republicans.[87] The NRA and allied groups helped with the 1994 congressional Republican victory.[88] No one used this issue better than George W. Bush. He successfully campaigned in 1994 to unseat incumbent Texas governor Ann Richards, who had vetoed a bill to allow Texans to pack concealed handguns. This he did by loudly and firmly promising he would sign such a bill—a promise, unlike some he would make in 2000 to centrists, that he kept. Richards concluded after the election that "he is governor today because of guns."[89]

After the 1994 election victory, the NRA lost ground in the wake of the 1995 domestic terrorist bombing of the Oklahoma City federal building.[90] Soon after came other difficulties for the NRA's position, such as the national reaction to the shootings at Columbine High School in Littleton, Colorado. But the NRA proved able to fight off congressional efforts to close gun sales loopholes. And a few years later, in September 1998, Ashcroft's Senate subcommittee hearing touting the individual rights theory of the Second Amendment went smoothly, casting Ashcroft as the national legitimator of social conservative legal causes. He had hit his stride. Once Ashcroft took office as attorney general, he could bring this campaign to unprecedented levels.[91] Before Ashcroft the Justice Department's official position had consistently and approvingly followed the judicial rulings against an individual right. Institutionally, the Justice Department had always abhorred undermining both the security of its own law enforcement officers—by potentially arming with heavy weapons those it properly sought to arrest—and the government's legal ability to defend its firearms statutes in court.[92]

On May 17, 2001, Ashcroft answered an April query from the NRA with an official letter that declared, "The Second Amendment clearly protects the right of individuals to keep and bear firearms." The Ashcroft letter cited in a few paragraphs the usual bits and pieces the NRA recites for its view. At the end, Ashcroft concluded, "In light of this vast body of evidence, I believe it is clear that, the Constitution protects the private ownership of firearms for lawful purposes." At the same time, the Justice

Department announced that the May 17 letter "was not [merely] a personal view. The Office of Legal Counsel was consulted." The position was announced as "a change from the aggressive gun-control policies of the Clinton Administration."[93]

Later in 2001 Ashcroft seized an opportunity to reinforce the constitutional maneuvering begun in the letter. In October a panel of the U.S. Court of Appeals for the Fifth Circuit, by a divided 2–1 vote, issued a lengthy opinion discussing the Second Amendment in *United States v. Emerson*.[94] Almost all the discussion by the two-judge majority was legal dictum—that is, statements that are part of the court majority's opinion but carry little weight because they are unnecessary to the actual decision in the case.[95] Nonetheless, the two delivered a lengthy discourse on the asserted individual constitutional right to firearms. They even noted that "none of our sister circuits has subscribed to this model." The third judge sharply commented that the two-judge "majority today departs from . . . sound precepts of judicial restraints" by publishing such dicta and that "since nothing in this case turns on the original meaning of the Second Amendment . . . no court need follow what the majority has said in that regard."[96]

Previous attorneys general would have shrugged off *Emerson*. Ashcroft made it as big a deal as he could. In November he took time out from post-9/11 duties (which, he kept saying, wholly preoccupied him) to instruct all U.S. attorneys' offices to adopt the view of the two judges. Moreover, his memo required that every case raising what were called Second Amendment issues be sent to the Criminal Division at Justice Department headquarters in Washington, D.C., for review.[97] The Criminal Division (also said to be too busy with post-9/11 work to bother with responding to civil liberties groups or congressional oversight) would front for political efforts serving the NRA.

Then Olson filed a brief in the Supreme Court about the *Emerson* case, on the pretext of persuading the Court not to grant the request by the defendant, a firearm purchaser, for full review of the case. Another attorney general might have brushed off the defendant's virtually frivolous petition.[98] Instead, Olson and Ashcroft used the high court as a public advertising space, as part of a plot to overthrow the firm Justice Department position on firearms going back to 1939 and to proclaim what now became the governmental position that an individual right to own potent weaponry exists. It hardly mattered that the case at hand required no such position by the government. Ashcroft had arranged for the government to present his view unceasingly, in a forum in which alternative views would not be similarly pressed. Not long before, the Second Amendment had meant one thing; soon it would mean something else. Ashcroft was altering the meaning of the Constitution. There are few more striking political uses of law.

The voucher issue further showed how the attorney general could influence the Supreme Court's conservative bloc. Ashcroft did what he could to secure perhaps his single largest practical judicial victory of the early 2000s: the Court's decision to hear a case upholding the publicly funded voucher program for Cleveland religious schools, *Zelman v. Simmons-Harris*.[99] Unlike some of Ashcroft's other causes, the school voucher issue was not one that only social conservatives supported; school vouchers had some centrist support too. Still, in terms of what social conservatives wanted, the quest to legitimate school vouchers brought conservative Protestants and Catholics together in support of the Bush administration. Vouchers might promote the movement of children from secular public schools to religiously controlled ones; they would undermine public school teachers' unions, a prime Democratic constituency. All of these voucher-related effects were, to Ashcroft, politically desirable goals. Indeed, the voucher issue had figured in the replacement of Racicot with Ashcroft.[100] Politically, it mattered.

But vouchers had enjoyed only a mixed record in the courts and received major blows during the first six months of the Bush administration.[101] Bush himself had tried and failed to pass a voucher program in Texas, and though he campaigned in 2000 in support of a $1,500 federal voucher for students in failing schools, his party's 2000 election losses in the Senate foreshadowed difficulty in moving the proposal. On June 12, 2001, the Senate defeated the president's voucher proposal, 58–41.[102] That strong Senate anti-voucher vote apparently reflected, among other factors, some centrist wariness of spending federal taxpayer dollars on vouchers for local religious schools.

But the voucher issue still offered President Bush a big political opportunity to serve his conservative religious constituency. And Bush's defeat in the Senate did not foreclose gains in the courts. In July 2001 it was time for the Court to consider whether to include on its crowded docket the appellate decision that had struck down the Cleveland voucher program. Ashcroft's newly confirmed solicitor general, Ted Olson, asked the Supreme Court to take up the case.[103] This was a relatively subtle but crucial political use of law. Barely half a year after *Bush v. Gore*, Olson remained just the right go-between for Bush to persuade the five conservative on the Court to take up a politically useful case.

During the Clinton administration, the Justice Department had not filed a brief in any voucher case, and the Supreme Court had not taken any. Doing so without a Court invitation ranks as a use of the solicitor general's leverage for the president's party, not for the federal government.[104] What the United States was doing in a Cleveland school case would strike a purist nonpolitical analyst of the sophisticated action in the Supreme Court as a legal mystery, given that Congress had enacted no law committing the United States on the question. Olson was reduced in his filing to invoking plain conservative rhetoric in urging the Court to take the case.[105]

The Court did agree to take the Cleveland case. It is an interesting question how much legal weight Ashcroft and Olson swung in that crucial action.[106] This particular case had major drawbacks as a vehicle by which the Court's conservative bloc could uphold vouchers.[107] Cleveland's very large Catholic community meant that 96 percent of the voucher funding went to religious schools and a mere 4 percent to the nonsectarian alternatives.[108] It was difficult for the Court to say with a straight face that the flow of funds in Cleveland only "coincidentally" or "accidentally" worked to publicly fund the establishment of religion.

The 5–4 division on the Court showed clearly during oral argument in February 2002. Olson himself personally argued for the United States, and the conservative justices seemed to get just what they needed from him. And so, when the Court issued its decision in *Zelman v. Simmons-Harris*, the five conservatives handed a resounding victory to voucher proponents. In one of the most important Establishment Clause decisions ever, the Court found no insuperable problem even with 96 percent of a taxpayer-funded program going to religious institutions almost wholly of the sect that is popular in that locale. Justice O'Connor wrote a separate opinion acknowledging at length the severe problem posed by the 96 percent figure, then blinking as Ashcroft and Olson carried off their political prize. The four nonconservative justices dissented on this point with eloquent vigor, but they had as little influence on the outcome as they had had a half year earlier on *Bush v. Gore*.

At that time and throughout the ensuing years, the Bush White House had created an institutional structure supporting a large potential federal effort at taxpayer funding of religious institutions that promised wide-ranging benefits for social conservatives. The White House "faith-based" office had satellites in many cabinet departments and budgeted funds, as in any patronage system, to be dispensed to religious organizations that danced along sufficiently to its political tune. In December 2002, emboldened by the 2002 election results and taking advantage of the inattention to Washington affairs in that season, President Bush promulgated his executive order for federal assistance to "faith-based" community social service programs.[109] In 2003 his party promoted legislation that would back up the executive orders, making federal funds available to religious organizations, but that slyly omitted the most controversial of the orders' express provisions, those bluntly authorizing religious criteria in hiring and firing.[110]

The administration's rhetoric on this issue cloaked an elaborate legal strategy. Even without blunt express authorization to discriminate in employment, the combination of the executive order and the legislation gave much legal room for federal funding of organizations that would then manage to discriminate. Now taxpayer-funded organizations could move, for their gay employees, from "Don't ask, don't tell" toward something like "If you don't conform your private life on Sunday, don't come in Monday."

As to Ashcroft and the assisted suicide issue,[111] the polls show a clear majority of the public would let individuals decide for themselves, with help from a physician and under appropriate safeguards, what they deem "death with dignity" when faced with terminal conditions of progressive debilitation and agonizing pain. But a vocal minority wants the government to enforce its religious views on this subject upon all; sometimes these views are linked with activism against abortion rights. In 1994 Oregon set up what eventually became its confrontation with Ashcroft when, by a popular initiative, it enacted the "Oregon Death with Dignity Act" and thus became the first state to approve physician-assisted suicide.

Social conservatives played a leading role in the ensuing legal and political struggle. On the federal front, the issue became, legally, whether federal law barred state-authorized medical use of drugs for this purpose. A strong tradition of state self-governance on such issues would be displaced if the federal government used its pharmaceutical regulatory powers to dictate what states can permit patients and doctors to do in this regard. That would amount to a national morality directed from Washington in the guise of pharmaceutical regulation. In June 1998 Attorney General Reno decided, much to the dismay of social conservatives, that federal laws for controlled substances did not take away Oregon's ability to decide the matter for itself. Given the political profit in serving the interested religious groups on this issue, the Senate Judiciary Committee, with Senator Ashcroft's support, tried twice to enact legislation on the issue, in 1998 with the "Lethal Drug Abuse and Prevention Act" and again in 1999–2000 with the "Pain Relief Promotion Act."[112] Neither bill reached the Senate floor.

Ashcroft's appointment as attorney general provided an opportunity to revisit the issue and pick up some religious political support without seriously alienating large numbers of centrist voters. To be sure, Ashcroft's direction of such a matter from Washington made hash of the state autonomy that conservatives traditionally venerated. Ever since Goldwater opposed fluoridation of drinking water, conservatives had fought tooth and nail to keep Washington from dictating local medical issues, yet Ashcroft would establish a powerful central system for national control on one of the most important libertarian issues.

With Ashcroft in the saddle, however, apparently the powers of the Justice Departments would get used, on such federalism issues, opportunistically; social conservatives cared much less about celebrating America's diversity and liberty through federalism than about promoting nationally their religiously based views using Ashcroft's powers.[113] In June 2001 a young deputy assistant attorney general, Sheldon Bradshaw, presented an elaborate memo to Ashcroft on how to block the Oregon law. Without any prior public notice, on November 9, 2001, Ashcroft issued a directive implementing the Bradshaw memo and reversing the Reno position. He took time out to pick up again his old 1990s Senate Judiciary political play on the subject, even while maintaining that his total (and, of course, nonpolitical) focus upon his post-9/11 duties kept him too busy to respond to congressional inquiries on civil liberties matters.

The Oregon state attorney general took the brave course of filing suit to challenge the Ashcroft directive in district court, winning a full victory in April 2002. Judge Robert R. Jones had a distinctly conservative Republican reputation and hinted in his opinion at how much he did not personally approve of physician-assisted suicide; however, the good judge pulled no punches in his opinion in excoriating Ashcroft. "To allow an attorney general—an appointed executive whose tenure depends entirely on whatever administration occupies the White House—to determine the legitimacy of a particular medical practice without a specific congressional grant of such authority," Jones wrote, "would be unprecedented and extraordinary."[114] Judges had rarely expounded from the bench so frankly about the political nature of an attorney general's action; Judge Jones apparently picked up a strong scent here of Ashcroft abusing the law for an ideological payoff.

A particularly complex issue for Bush and Ashcroft to navigate consisted of the many aspects of legal tolerance or acceptance of gays. The Supreme Court raised these to high visibility in *Lawrence v. Texas* in 2003, when it struck down Texas's attempt to arrest gays as criminals for private acts within their homes. Observers saw this case as serving President Bush with a potential opportunity to benefit from the issue's prominence.[115] The social conservative community went predictably ballistic over the Court's actually legitimating what they deemed irredeemably immoral. Notably, the issue let social conservative Protestants build bridges to social conservative Catholics, so Ashcroft (from a discrete distance) could pursue his favorite quest of ostensibly structuring neutral legal propositions (e.g., being against Judge Ronnie White because he was "pro-criminal") while benefiting politically from a coalition of the intolerant. Just as President Bush, earlier that year, had guilefully let Senator Rick Santorum (R-Pa.) slime gays without directly commenting himself, so Bush could use Ashcroft and others as his buffering surrogates on this issue.[116]

The conservative game plan unrolled like clockwork in 2003–2004. First, the ideological organizations that serve as sectarian shills for the party caucused privately about strategy before going out to whip up the troops. As with so many of their causes, the groups liked the idea of a constitutional amendment. Either it passed, which showed huge muscle for the movement, or the movement played it a few years and it held the stage; later, conservatives could always go back to do the "delicate" work, like enacting state statutes in conservative states, enacting federal statutes, litmus testing judicial choices, pressuring business groups to get in line, organizing, propagandizing, and always turning out the vote. Meanwhile, conservative members of Congress would translate the "line" into statements that could viably be made in public media like Congress and television. They'd tone down the rhetoric about "sin" and the preoccupation with acts of sex that excited an interest in conservative activist leaders that was hard to distinguish from prurience.

A constitutional amendment, to the extent it did anything other than line up votes for conservative causes, would merely keep loving and stable couples from formalizing their family arrangements and gaining the acceptance of the society around them. So congressional conservatives had a vital function: to give the amendment campaign some kind of policy or general-morals slipcover, rationalizing how a constitutional amendment would work like Wonder Bread and build a strong body politic twelve different ways. Using their control of Congress, they'd crank up the apparatus of hearings, reports, and floor proceedings, especially in Tom DeLay's tightly controlled House. Now legal experts on the conservative payment plan could expound on this issue in depth; the more they talked, the more they were welcome. It might be risking centrist backlash at the polls controversial to move it too close to Bush by bringing Ashcroft front and center before the election. But conservatives knew Ashcroft, knew where he'd stand. Other surrogates for the president could do the job. President Bush himself could stay, without precise comment, ambiguously above the fray. He would present himself to centrists, who might get queasy about any blunt gay bashing coming from him directly, as compassionate and moderate in his silence.[117]

On behalf of Ashcroft conservative legal spokespersons would have an array of opportunities to use the legal aftermath to *Lawrence v. Texas* to send out his coded messages without making President Bush or Attorney General Ashcroft a lightning rod. The decision opened the way for legislative and judicial battles not just about recognition of homosexual partnerships or marriages but also about other legal rights of gays including employment, government benefits, and custody after divorce.[118] In past times states with religious conservative lobbies used their legal powers to make local divorce difficult or impossible and condemned Nevada and Mexico as faraway divorce centers. Now foreign and domestic jurisdictions according rights to homosexual partnerships would fuel the conservative movement's efforts to raise hysteria in antagonistic states controlled by religious lobbies and to use their legal powers to make homosexual partnerships as illegitimate as possible. Those speaking now for Ashcroft, and when the coast was clear, Ashcroft himself, might position him carefully on such an issue by, for example, posing as the defender of the rights of (conservative) states to decide not to respect such partnerships even when formalized elsewhere. Constitutional amendment proposals, statutes, and court cases would all provide occasions for maneuver and struggle. President Bush might get multiple layers of juridical insulation and deniability: his attorney general (not him) would discuss the legal (not moral) issue of merely the rights of a state (not what the United States should do) to "defend" its own internal institution of marriage against the "threat" of such out-of-state counterfeiting. To put it more directly, for a president, having Ashcroft as attorney general means never having to say, for the administration's support of intolerance, that it's sorry.

JUDICIAL NOMINATIONS

Struggles over judicial nominations constitute a prime arena for the political uses of law.[119] Historically, a variety of considerations and approaches have governed the choice of judges. In past eras presidents paid predominant attention in their Supreme Court nominations to geographical balance and political patronage, and only somewhat to ideology.[120] Indeed, once upon a time presidents of both parties used to confer with senators of both parties in selecting judges.

Extreme ideology only later came into fashion as a criterion, and not uniformly. Though presidents Reagan and Bush appointed the conservative justices Scalia and Thomas,[121] they also chose distinct moderates like Justice Souter. Nor did President Clinton try to appoint left-wing ideologues.[122] In sum, ideology played a role in the 1980s and 1990s, but without the single-minded intensity seen after 2001. Against that background President Bush's desire to satisfy social conservatives by his judicial appointments marked more of a new direction than some realized.

Several developments at the heart of the Bush administration's political uses of law raised the stakes and the tensions in judicial nominations. For social conservatives judicial nominations mattered both practically and symbolically. Practically, the situation for social conservatives contrasted with that of economic conservatives, who could achieve most of their goals by legislative and administrative actions like tax cuts and regulatory rollbacks. But conservative social issues such as fighting against the rights of women or gays and promoting school prayer, establishment of taxpayer-funded religion, censorship of adult speech in new and old media, wide-open firearms rights, maximum use of the death penalty (particularly for minorities), and so forth depend heavily upon judicial decisions. Much of what social conservatives asked from President Bush could come to pass only by a rollback of Warren and Burger Court precedents. Winning as to ideological judicial appointments was not just one of the helpful alternatives; it was all-important.

Moreover, ideological judicial appointments provided an enormously important, though not frankly articulated, route for President Bush to deliver results more conservative than he could by ordinary democratic means. The Senate might have a majority for some limited aspects of the anti-abortion rights cause, but it certainly did not have a filibuster-proof *Roe*-repealing supermajority. President Bush could not hope to push through the Senate—with its body of Democrats and Republican moderates and its rules and traditions such as the sixty-vote threshold for cloture—a stream of bills to satisfy social conservatives. But he could appoint judges to rule the way they wanted and thereby deliver for them legally what he could not by ordinary Senate politics. The voucher issue gave a taste as early as 2001–2002 of how he could deliver via the courts (the Dayton decision) even when unable to in the Senate (the 58–41 defeat of his voucher proposal).

But beyond practicality, social conservatives saw judicial appointments in symbolic terms. Judicial pronouncements established the socially approved meaning of liberty and morality. The progressive Warren Court had symbolically legitimated such out-groups as feminists, minorities, members of the underclass who experienced police stops and questions as harassment, and those who sought "forbidden" sexual books or films. Its themes of cultural tolerance opened the door for other groups, such as gays and immigrants, who sought freedom from repression in the era that followed. The Burger Court and even the Rehnquist Court had limited their alteration of this stance to an extent far short of what social conservatives desired.

To social conservatives, the Warren and Burger courts had legitimated the wrong groups, and the Rehnquist Court had been tardy in making up for this. Conservatives reviled even the "fifth conservative," Justice O'Connor, who, for example, would not come through for them in cases to cut back severely on abortion rights. President Bush could appoint, in contrast, conservative judges like Justice Scalia. These would strengthen the status of community and family norms, allow government to return these upstart groups to their appropriately low legal status, and restore local capability to tolerate minimally any lifestyle divergence. Social conservatives would now be the in-group.

Court decisions, though issued as elevated jurisprudential pronouncements, can readily be translated into weekday talk-radio broadcasts and Sunday sermons. Much of the social conservative political apparatus of organizations, media, message manufacturing, and electioneering existed precisely to transform reactions to judicial actions into poll numbers and political organization. That apparatus produced first the nomination and election of President Bush and his handing the baton to Ashcroft and then four years of appointments to move the federal judiciary to the right. The Supreme Court had intervened decisively, and controversially, in *Bush v. Gore* to install the president. How much judicial ideology mattered everyone who had voted for president could assess for themselves.

The Initial Process

In two respects President Bush signalled his pattern of ideological patronage early on. First, his White House counsel, Alberto Gonzales, ended the practice of vetting judicial picks with the American Bar Association before nomination. Second, on March 9, 2001, quite early in his term, President Bush sent his first batch of nominees, eleven predominantly conservative ideologues, to the Senate, with maximum publicity. It was extraordinary for a president to make a statement that his agenda gave early judicial patronage a higher priority than even a fully functioning administration. President Bush not merely anticipated but actually relished instigating a struggle over ideological patronage, giving high-visibility proof of his loyalty to his conservative base. Conflict on the Senate Judiciary Committee between the senior Republican, Orrin Hatch (R-Utah), and the top two Democrats, Patrick Leahy (D-Vt.) and Edward Kennedy (D-Mass.), fostered thematically beneficial communication by the party's leaders with its social conservative base. Just as important, such matters would probably not alienate the centrist public, which might care about the Supreme Court but could not pay attention to the myriad lower-court judgeships typically sitting nowhere near any citizen's own particular locale.

However, before the Senate could act upon the first group, Vermont senator Jim Jeffords's defection from the Republicans to be independent in May 2001 flipped party control in the Senate. For the next year, the White House faced an altered process.[123] On few issues did the change in party control matter more than on judicial confirmations. The minority party cannot bring nominations to the floor if they're bottled up in committee. The Judiciary Committee, chaired by Senator Leahy (D-Vt.), thus had much control over the sequence and timing of consideration of nominees. Senator Charles Schumer's (D-N.Y.) Judiciary subcommittee held high-quality hearings in June and September 2001 on the role of ideology in confirmations and the confirmation process generally.[124]

As the new process took shape, Democrats and Republicans argued for the public about the pace and handling of confirmations. By December 2001 the developing mix of action and inaction allowed each side to make some new arguments. Democrats could tout their steady overall progress, having confirmed twenty-one of thirty-six choices for district courts. Of course, Ashcroft's side just complained about the low rate of confirmations of appellate judges and ignored comparisons showing the Democrats were doing much more for Ashcroft's right-wing picks than the Republican Senate had done in the 1990s for Clinton's moderate nominees. By early 2002 Republican-nominated judges held a majority on seven of the thirteen circuit courts of appeal. If all President Bush's nominees were approved, at that point such judges would have made up a majority on eleven circuit courts and, by the end of 2004, on every circuit court.[125] Hence, Republican appointments to the appellate courts would control the law throughout the country in the vast majority of federal cases, and an increasing percentage of these judges would hold views even further to the right than the bloc of five conservatives on the Supreme Court.

The Fourth Circuit had illustrated how a court could go to the right even of the Supreme Court. A Fourth Circuit panel struck down the *Miranda* warnings that remind those in custody of their right to remain silent, and the Supreme Court took the case for decision in 1999. House Republicans filed an archconservative brief against *Miranda*—putting forth the basic line of Ashcroft's congressional group that steps to effectuate the Bill of Rights just handcuff the police. The House Democratic leadership allowed me the high honor (for which I feel much in its debt) of writing and filing its strong answering brief to uphold *Miranda*, to scotch that nonsense about handcuffing the police and reverse the Fourth Circuit panel. To do so was a pleasure.[126] And making it a double pleasure, the Supreme Court ruled our way, upholding *Miranda* in an opinion written by Chief Justice Rehnquist himself.[127] Of course it was a relief to win that one, but the episode marked how far to the right the Ashcroft congressional group aimed and how far that way much of the lower judiciary had headed even prior to Bush sending his wave of activist conservatives in.

The Struggle for the D.C. Circuit

As expected, when Ashcroft's party retook the Senate for 2003–2004, the parade of conservative picks intensified. His old comrades-in-conservatism on the Senate Judiciary Committee processed the nominees with mass-production techniques, giving little time to expose their ideological extremism and their often dubious credentials. Worse, with the nominations pouring onto the floor, the Democrats got thrown onto the difficult position of having to mount and sustain Senate floor filibusters on each and every unacceptable nominee. Ashcroft had the whip hand on this, and he did not stint in its use.

One particular aspect of the nomination contest captures the overall situation: the struggle for the D.C. Circuit. Of all the federal courts of appeals, the D.C. Circuit is the most important since it handles cases filed in the federal court in Washington, D.C. Having the seat of government means that a sizable fraction of the cases concerning the federal government's powers and responsibilities, both constitutional and statutory, go through that circuit, and the Supreme Court takes up only a very small fraction of them. What the D.C. Circuit decides impacts heavily what the federal government can and cannot do. A quarter century ago, I clerked for the D.C. Circuit. It was an awesome court to watch then, and so it still was in the early 2000s. But watching it in the 2000s means looking a lot more to the right, and fearing how much further right it could yet get tilted. Judge Lawrence Silberman, on the D.C. Circuit, typifies the right-wing tilt of that court that occurred even before Ashcroft got to add his picks. I discuss his service on "Ashcroft's Review Court" in chapter 9.

In 2003 Bush and Ashcroft made two nominations for the D.C. Circuit that sent shivers down the spines of centrist Washington lawyers. Bush nominated Janice Rogers Brown, then serving on the California Supreme Court. When Brown was nominated to that court in 1996, the state bar evaluation committee found her unqualified—an extraordinarily negative judgment. The bar stamped her unfit not only because she was relatively inexperienced but also because she was "prone to inserting conservative political views into her appellate opinions" (on a lower, or intermediate, California appellate court) and complaints had been made that she was "insensitive to established precedent." In other words, she just did not care what the established law is, only what her ultraconservative ideology indicated was right. In speeches Brown has trashed the Supreme Court's modern trend going back to 1937, when—almost three-quarters of a century ago—the New Deal Court allowed modern legal America to emerge with developments like Social Security and minimum wages. In her words the "Revolution of 1937" at the Court was a "disaster" that marked "the triumph of our socialist revolution."[128] Speeches like that make Rehnquist look like *Mother Jones* magazine.

Why did it matter so much that Bush tried to install Brown? Because Brown was not just a far-right judge. She was, at this level of the judiciary, probably the most prominently extreme far-right *black* judge, and Bush and Ashcroft were attempting to place her, like a prime chess piece, exactly on the board where she could be in the group from which Bush would, when a vacancy opened, pick his Supreme Court nominee. The Brown nomination matters in the chess game of administration judge picks for the same reason it matters that Bush nominated Priscilla Owen and Carolyn Kuhl, far-right female judges, to the Fifth and Ninth circuits, respectively; nominated Claude Allen, a far-right black high official, to the Fourth Circuit; and tried to appoint (until he declined the nomination) Miguel Estrada, a far-right Hispanic prominent figure, to the D.C. Circuit. The operative qualifications in these nominations did not consist alone of what would not matter in the chess game: woman, black or other minority, solid Republican—qualifications Bush had looked for in placing Secretary of State Powell or former EPA head Christine Whitman in his cabinet. Quite the opposite: Bush and Ashcroft would lose ground in their chess game to promote conservative causes through abuses of law if they filled these prime vacancies with Republican minorities or women who had moderate views.

In other words, in the Brown group of nominations, Bush and Ashcroft used their 2003–2004 Senate majority to make a squeeze play on the beleaguered Senate Democrats desperately trying to guard the many, many jumping-off places for Supreme Court nominees. When Bush nominated Brown to the D.C. Circuit, he put her "on deck," in baseball terms, for later nomination to the Supreme Court. When he nominated many like Brown, he put Senate Democrats in a dilemma: they could either filibuster a whole string of minority and female nominations, one after another, or, by letting go and voting up a confirmation, they could increase the pool of radical-right potential Supreme Court nominees. Regarding these latter, when the time came, the Republicans would accurately tell the press, "How can the Democrats oppose Brown [or the others] for the high court when they voted in favor of that one for the appellate judgeship?"

The squeeze play had another nice ideological benefit for Bush and Ashcroft: it gave them a huge opening, which they eagerly took, to fill lots of other top judgeships with their conservative activist picks among white males. As analyzed in the *Legal Times of Washington* by Jonathan Groner (possibly the nation's most acute legal analyst of the great game), "Since it's widely believed that the president plans to appoint minorities and women to the high court [an unnamed Republican source told Groner], Democrats are trying to stop high-profile choices such as Estrada and Owen at the appeals court stage. [So] [w]hite males such as [Jeffrey] Sutton, who are deemed less likely [future Supreme Court] picks, get a wider berth."[129] In other words, the beleaguered Senate Democrats felt pressed to let Bush and Ashcroft fill large numbers of terribly significant judgeships with extremist young Tories, as long as these were white males. The rulings from this crew might be delighting the far right for decades to come, but at least they might hand them down "merely" from powerful appellate positions rather than from the high court itself.

Speaking of such nominees, Bush and Ashcroft nominated for another seat on the D.C. Circuit Brett M. Kavanaugh. Recently, Kavanaugh had served as associate White House counsel—next door, so to speak, to Bush himself—pretty clearly the opposite of an independent judge who would dispassionately and disinterestedly weigh arguments for and against the Bush White House. Because of the squeeze play, Senate Democrats would be all but forced to let either Kavanaugh or others like him through. As a Republican Senate Judiciary Committee staffer bluntly told Groner for the *Legal Times*, "If we made a group of four or five and sent them to the floor together, the Democrats would be hard pressed not to let one or two of them through."[130]

ELECTION-YEAR DEVELOPMENTS

By turning hard right against the cleverly conjured threat of gay rights, President Bush energized the social conservative base for the 2004 campaign. Bush kicked this operation off with a passage in his State of the Union message that sent multilevel signals.[131] The dynamic he unleashed went far beyond short-term campaign mobilizing, to sowing what he could later reap as an electoral mandate for an elaborate legal campaign to curb gay rights, not all the way back to the repressive national system of the 1950s, but a significant distance down the road his social conservative base sought.

Congressional conservatives had already established a framework of legal rhetoric and concepts in legislation starting with moves by the Helms wing of the party in the late 1970s and including the Gingrich-DeLay Defense of Marriage Act (DOMA) of 1996, which "protects marriage under federal law as the union of a man and a woman." Social conservatives thereby made their crusade for exclusively heterosexual marriage the legal medium for depicting gay rights advocates as attacking and, indeed, mortally threatening and besieging that fundamental institution. A more apparent challenge for marriage in America was the ever increasing economic pressure on working families, especially those with dependent seniors or children, and increasing economic inequality and the conservative mobilization supporting it. Just as social conservatives had depicted the threat to "life"—not as, say, economic pressures that reduce the affordability of children's day care and health care and other family-sustaining services—but rather as the rare and obscure late-term abortion procedure, so now they depicted the threat to marriage as gay rights, thereby mobilizing their social movement and electoral base to join the other, economic base despite their opposed interests.

In both the 2000 campaign and Bush's first three years in office, he steered clear of any all-out assault on gay rights; the negatives of appearing intolerant to centrists outweighed the benefits of mobilizing the base.

So Bush's decision to make this anti-gay effort a full-volume election campaign theme signaled a major swing toward using the presidency's
national leadership power, dubbed by Theodore Roosevelt the "bully pulpit," to advance social conservatism. Bush's State of the Union passage
moved a step beyond merely embracing DOMA: "Activist judges, however,
have begun redefining marriage by court order." He thereby employed the
tactic that figures like George Wallace had used in the 1960s to subvert
civil rights law. Like Wallace, Bush stood in the doorway, opposing neutral
adjudication of the claims of an out-group to some of the rights accruing to
legitimate members of society. Wallace then and Bush now rallied a conservative base, each wrapping himself in the mantle of the protector of
sacred and threatened ground (racial segregation then, exclusivity of heterosexual marriage now) against activist judges. Like Wallace, Bush accused
the judges of proceeding by undemocratic and "arbitrary" impositions
that had nothing to back them but naked force. "If judges insist on forcing
their arbitrary will upon the people," Bush declared, then "on an issue of
such great consequence, the people's voice must be heard." Wallace had by
a similar device built political bridges between Southern conservatives
defending his region's comprehensive Jim Crow segregation and North-
erners of a totally different background and separate political tradition.
Ironically, Wallace had at least faced federal marshals enforcing injunctive
federal court orders, though they had used no force on the governor's person. In 2004, by contrast, Bush stood in no doorways, faced no contempt
citation: the issue was an advisory one between state courts and state legislatures until he jumped in.

And as with Wallace's racial pitch and, later, the Ashcroft crusade to
undermine *Roe v. Wade,* Bush used this cause to build a wide-span bridge
over which to lead otherwise diverse conservative constituencies to his
support. Ashcroft's own core base—evangelicals with a traditionally moralistic stance against gays—now could ally via Bush's casting of the issue
with the far-right segment of Catholic leaders. Recall the ads suggesting
that sitting senators who dared not support Judge Pryor's appellate nomination were anti-Catholic—Rove's legal gambit to transform a quest for
a far-right judiciary into a cause to recruit Catholics. The "Catholics need
not apply" ads were funded by the Ave Maria List, affiliated with Domino's
Pizza founder Thomas Monahan's Ave Maria Foundation, which supported Rove's social conservative pitch. Pryor had flaunted his intolerance
of gays, making himself the poster child for the conservative Catholic
effort to resolve the strains that scandal had caused in the American
Church—and in 2004, to counter the challenge posed by the Democratic

Party in nominating a Catholic for president—by creating social conservative issues that would mobilize support for Bush.[132]

The mandate Bush would thereby obtain for his second term would allow him to appoint a host of anti-gay activists who would likely take intolerant steps against this asserted threat—just as he had used the mandate from his 2000 campaign position against late-term abortion as a springboard for the host of steps that Ashcroft and his allies took against women's abortion and related rights. Although the centrist public might be told the debate concerned only Bush's support for a DOMA-like constitutional amendment, the asserted mandate would support broad anti-gay appointments. Conservative professors at the law school of the Catholic University of America had drawn up a road map for this agenda in the Marriage Law Project. The proposed constitutional amendment and the nomination of conservative activist justices were just the start.

The full agenda would begin with undermining and circumventing the federal executive order prohibiting federal employment discrimination against gays. Whereas Bush had carefully refrained even from hinting about this step, after the hard-right turn for the campaign, he seemed fully launched on that path. For the previous quarter century, the former policy of threatening to exclude gays from the civil service, enforced most assiduously by J. Edgar Hoover during the Cold War, had very largely relented. But the mandate taken from the 2004 election would make it official policy to eliminate the barriers to anti-gay discrimination, giving social conservatives the open season they had already quietly sought in the first half of 2004.[133] Legally, more than half of federal employees had already lost the backbone of their civil service and collective bargaining rights between Rumsfeld's quietly obtained provisions in the fiscal year 2004 Defense Department authorization and the bill chartering the sprawling Homeland Security Department. If right-wing groups outside the government joined with their ideological comrades within the government in a witch hunt against gays, both groups believing themselves backed by a conservative electoral mandate, there would be little to stop them.

Nor would such a crusade stop with the federal payroll. The aforementioned Marriage Law Project counseled the president on making "marriage-friendly"—in practice translating as "anti-gay"—"interpretations of laws, regulations, and executive orders," including how he "should instruct the Internal Revenue Service" and what he should do with his power "in the International Arena."[134] Few understood how far government right wingers could push this legal strategy in looking for symbolically useful battlegrounds. American states or foreign countries that sanctioned civil unions would naturally expect standard federal tax treatment for such couples' senior or child dependents. Legally, however, an executive order plus White House policy would attack fair treatment for dependents on matters such as the child tax credit or the earned income tax credit.[135] Soon conservatives would have a new spin on the old "welfare queen" label—some new myth about gay couples in civil union states using custodial rights to obtain what they should not from the Treasury through claiming such tax credits. To ferret out such hypothetical cheats, new uses could be devised for IRS regulations, forms, and even agents, tasked to probe personal lifestyles. Down the road lay more IRS controversies when civil unions ended in split-ups—as half of heterosexual marriages do—and the tax issues concerned a former partner's court-ordered support obligations (alimony) and the tax consequences of property divisions.[136] Again, as in federal personnel actions, conservatives would have their victory by defining the delegitimation of alternative lifestyles as the defense of their own lifestyle and by thus manufacturing legal issues to bring lifestyle differences around the country into the realm of usable political controversy. In short, for federal power the watchword might become "Investigate gays, not guns." The leaders of the conservative base would perpetually assail local tolerance as a threat.

The efforts by gays to get justice from the courts would create even more opportunity for social conservatives, who would draw on Ashcroft's and Olson's positioning and advocacy in the ensuing cases, much as they had in the continuing effort to undermine *Roe v. Wade*. The Marriage Law Project already urged something called a principle of interpretation to apply in every context. The volatile combination of the Supreme Court's *Lawrence* decision, the controversy over "defense of marriage," and the clash between state civil union laws and Bush administration policy would give Ashcroft and Olson a wide array of controversies to pick from for political and legal strategy.[137] John Bolton would do the same with the government's muscle in international forums. Bush's hard-right turn in 2004 presaged a fount of ideological patronage for his party's social conservative base.

3 Flouting Civil Liberties

Libraries or Weapons?

In the aftermath of 9/11, Ashcroft's assault on civil liberties came hard and fast, with many denials that it was politically motivated. The historical antecedents of this assault warrant some explanation. For many decades now, elements in the Republican Party have often played on public concerns about crime and security. (Then again, Republicans sometimes respond to this criticism by charging Democrats with fomenting class antagonism when they propose taxes on the rich to support popular programs for other classes.) In 1952 the young Republican candidate for vice president, Richard M. Nixon, hit Democrats hard with the demagogic "C3" theme formula, "Communism, crime, and corruption." The accused Democrats went down like bowling pins, with Nixon, in his role as "basher," helping Eisenhower win not only the White House but the Congress for the first time since 1930. In the same way, Ashcroft may deserve some credit for Bush's retaking the Senate in 2002. The C3 theme formula might be updated (phonetically) to "Qaeda, crime, and the career civil service."

In 1968 Nixon won the presidency by blaming street crime on civil liberties decisions of (Democrat-appointed) justices that "handcuffed the police" (e.g., decisions requiring police to give Miranda warnings to take confessions and to obtain warrants for house searches). In 1988 George H. W. Bush's political hardball strategist Lee Atwater ran the infamous Willie Horton ad—a picture that did the work of a thousand words, framing

Democratic nominee Dukakis as "soft" on black convicts who raped white women.[1] Every student of presidential politics knows these and similar landmarks in the Hall of Fame for security and crime themes. Ashcroft, himself a presidential candidate in 1998 and veteran of numerous hard-fought campaigns on such issues, is hardly a naïf about such strategies.

In the 1990s, conservative Republicans temporarily lost the use of some of the security and crime themes. The Cold War's end meant that (Soviet) communism was no longer an issue, though the Republican Congress did strain to charge the Clinton administration with "softness" on Chinese Communist intelligence (alas, the serious penetrations all apparently dated from Reagan and Bush's tenures, not Clinton's). And Clinton detoxified the crime issue temporarily by calling for federal aid to put "100,000 cops on the beat."

Then, the genuine, awful menace of terrorism against American interests emerged. Ironically, Clinton and Reno clearly got out front in recognizing and combating the threat when it arose, leaving congressional conservatives in the contrasting, undignified stance of sulking hindrances. Clinton and Reno took seriously the Oklahoma City bombing in 1995 and al-Qaeda's embassy bombings in Africa in 1998, the attorney general appealing to Congress "for more than 1,000 new FBI personnel for counterterrorism."[2] Reno's background as a career supervisor of prosecutors in violence-ridden Dade County (Miami) from 1978 to 1992, the era of the machine gun–toting "cocaine cowboys," stood her in good stead. (Ashcroft would have no such experience to draw upon as attorney general.) As the *Washington Post* reported in 1996, "Clinton's attorney general may seem like a social worker.... Behind closed doors at the Justice Department, however, Reno is a stone-cold law enforcer.... In particular, she is a major supporter of wiretapping and electronic surveillance."[3] Reno repeatedly asked the Republican Congress for additional law enforcement authority carefully gauged to counter terrorism.[4]

During those years Ashcroft's group in Congress concentrated on attacking Attorney General Reno's quite limited requests and her measured deployment of authority against armed right-wing militias as persecution of simple, misunderstood heartland folk.[5] This is not dated history. Terrifying anthrax attacks occurring in Washington, D.C., New York, and elsewhere in late 2001 included mailings to the offices of Senate Democratic leader Thomas Daschle and Senator Patrick Leahy, the leading Democrat on the Judiciary Committee but no corresponding members of the other party. As reported in the *Washington Post*, "The FBI emphasized that there was no 'direct or clear' link between the attacks and foreign terrorism";[6] the cover letters and the anthrax itself seemed more the work of a deranged yet sophisticated domestic source than of al-Qaeda. Political leaders had to consider the possibility—at least as likely as an al-Qaeda origin—that the anthrax, like the Oklahoma City bombing, came from violent nuts with attitudes resembling the lunatic far-right fringe. Congressional Republican attitudes in the 1990s about Oklahoma City and Waco may explain why Ashcroft, self-proclaimed zealous "terror-fighter," seemed not to say much about the possible domestic origins of the anthrax attacks. He left that to be said by the lowest-visibility FBI spokespersons while he himself put across his politically preferred message on high-visibility TV. In Reno we had a law enforcement professional. In Ashcroft we were getting another pol-posing-as-prosecutor—another Richard Nixon.

From his key post as chair of the Judiciary subcommittee, Ashcroft led his congressional group to attack Reno as a bigger danger to America than almost anyone else. In particular, the group fought tooth and nail against Reno's requests to legislate more counterterrorism authority.[7] Whenever grudgingly granting any of her requests, as in a 1996 Republican congressional bill inadequately responding to the Oklahoma City bombing, Ashcroft's group used the opportunity to further their own political causes. They particularly demanded that imposition of the death penalty for nonterrorist offenses be facilitated by truncating the few safeguards against its racist misuse.[8] Significantly, in those years, congressional Republicans sharply distinguished the "enemy" Reno, from the "good" Louis Freeh, an FBI head not known for management skills. Not since right-wing congressmen of a generation before had adored the aging, failing J. Edgar Hoover had congressional Republican so coddled such an FBI director. Again, this is not dated history. It may well implicate congressional conservatives in the FBI's inadequate capability to prevent 9/11.[9]

Ashcroft's entering office in 2001 at what proved to be a crucial time, the eleventh hour before 9/11, effectively retarded government efforts to get out front on the security issue. Ideologically, the 2001 Attorney General Ashcroft inherited the 1990s Senator Ashcroft attitude that counterterrorism was partly a Reno bugaboo. Ashcroft dropped Reno's effort to obtain more surveillance authority from Congress, significantly downgraded counterterrorism as a Justice Department priority, and took no steps toward reprioritizing Freeh's FBI.[10] As the *National Journal* dryly reported, "On September 10 [2001]"—the day before 9/11—"Ashcroft refused to endorse the FBI's request for $58 million in counter-terrorism funding and $64 million in state and local counter-terrorism grants."[11] Ashcroft instead devoted the political resources available for counterterrorism to his conservative symbolic priorities.[12]

The devastating terrorist attacks of 9/11, of course, revealed with Pearl Harbor vividness a security enemy vastly more ruthless and a U.S. vulnerability terribly greater than hitherto suspected. America's approach to domestic security had to change, radically, immediately. The call to arms and the bolt-upright awakening into swift and decisive protective reaction would have ensued under any administration—John McCain's or Al Gore's no less than George W. Bush's, in the same way any president and cabinet would have reacted to Pearl Harbor. The attorney general must back a swift and strong law enforcement campaign.

But Ashcroft had personal reasons for throwing many symbolically important concerns into the mix, ones not necessarily having practical helpfulness, ones a McCain or Gore would not necessarily have required of his attorney general. Ashcroft must instantly transform his own image from preoccupied social-cause zealot considered by critics as AWOL on the security issue to the opposite. Indeed, he had to remake the image of his whole congressional Republican group as critics of Reno's counterterrorism efforts in the 1990s; the group had to convert the issue into one of their own. And once energized and in the saddle, Ashcroft would not stop there: politically he would go for broke, adding to his role as his party's polarizing figure on social issues and (a distinct but related priority) judge picking. Just when America most needed someone with both prosecutorial skill and civil liberties insight—like Robert Jackson during World War II, Reno in the 2000s, or the greatest modern attorney general, the Robert F. Kennedy of the 1961–1964 anti-Mafia and pro-civil-rights struggles— instead we got a reincarnation of Nixon.

Right after 9/11, as law enforcement agencies pursued the security program they would have under any attorney general, Ashcroft quickly implemented several maneuvers clearly his own. One of the first steps the FBI took in the wake of 9/11 was a massive detention sweep.[13] This course of action, unwarranted under any other circumstances, was an understandable choice of an FBI caught unawares by the crisis of unknown dimensions created by 9/11 and deprived by the White House of the opportunity to question methodically the bin Ladens and other high Saudis.[14]

But whatever the FBI's desperate situation in 2001, by July 2003 an attorney general had two years to clean up an understandable initial mess and make amends. By that time, with the sense of imminent doom prevalent immediately after 9/11 somewhat relieved, Ashcroft's own Justice Department inspector general—not an outside body nor a Democrat but a Bush-picked figure—issued a blistering report on the FBI-led post-9/11 roundup. Of 762 immigrants studied in the report who were locked up domestically in the weeks and months after the attacks, some for minor immigration violations and more than a few for clumsy law enforcement mistakes, exactly zero were ever charged as terrorists. Most of the people swept up had been denied their most elementary rights, often in a shocking and unnecessary way. Many prisoners had been exposed to abuse, as though a Third World police state had "rounded up the usual suspects."[15] Many officials within even the Justice Department had contemporaneously protested these questionable and ineffective tactics, only to be overruled by those closer in rank to Ashcroft.

In response, did Attorney General Ashcroft promise—at this relatively safe date, two years after 9/11—that he understood the need now to implement the modest reforms his own Bush-picked inspector general had strongly backed? No. Instead, Ashcroft toughed it out, telling a House Judiciary Committee hearing in June 2003 and having his departmental spokespersons tell the press: "We make no apologies."[16] The message this response sent as to the other civil liberties and security issues: give Ashcroft power and he would not hesitate to approve similar abuses again. But now he would have new, unprecedented authority, usable against the civil liberties of full American citizens.

From 2001 through early 2004 Ashcroft provocatively flaunted a disdain for both measured effectiveness and a reasonable balance between governmental power and civil liberties.[17] He championed a series of intrusions on civil liberties, of no generally accepted security benefit, so he could play the polarizing zealot-hero. (Meanwhile the quietly effective FBI director Robert Mueller did the actual work of organizing security activities and cleaning up the organizational problems left by Freeh.) Ashcroft had begun by proposing an order on November 13, 2001, to set up military tribunals for U.S. citizens in areas within the United States where civilian courts were in normal operation and, in the process, to suspend the writ of habeas corpus—powers not exercised so boldly even during the post–Civil War Reconstruction, right after half the country had made war on the other. Appalling even to the professional military-justice officers, Ashcroft's order (probably largely reflecting the ideas of Viet Dinh) would have overthrown not merely the Bill of Rights (which, as it only dates to the 1790s, might be considered still a novelty) but Magna Carta itself, fundamental to Anglo-American civilization since 1215.[18]

Ashcroft himself promoted his new image relentlessly on television. Indeed, in June 2002 he riled even the usually adoring Bush White House when he took the bizarre step of announcing in a live TV appearance from Moscow the apprehension of a low-level "dirty bomb" suspect in Chicago. Even many Republicans saw this disoriented production as sending the public an overblown, alarmist, and (worst, from the White House perspective) credit-stealing message. Conservatives disdained Ashcroft's stance as contrary to their own principles.[19]

But nothing so revealed the political calculations behind Ashcroft's self-described "security first" stance than his eagerness to rank genuine security needs, raised by the professionals, below the political agenda of the NRA.[20] To first provide a bit of statutory background, under the 1993 Brady Law, firearms dealers perform background checks on purchasers using the National Instant Criminal Background Check System (NICS). The Brady Law provides that NICS logs of background checks, which constitute a central national record of recent weapons purchases, be kept temporarily and then destroyed. The FBI established a six-month period of retention of the audit logs.

Those logs became an important point of contention in the 1990s. Law enforcers saw them as a means of tracking down purchasers of firearms, particularly those buying wrongfully, who used the weapons shortly after purchase in crimes or attacks. But the NRA viewed even temporary preservation of such records as official meddling with the sacred rights of cash-and-carry killers to the products of the gun manufacturers, the organization's financial backers. Ashcroft had joined a 1998 Senate majority that voted for an NRA-supported amendment to destroy NICS audit logs promptly. The maneuver was part of that year's posturing by Ashcroft's group in Congress against President Clinton, but lacking political support, the amendment died in conference.[21] On January 22, 2001, the Justice Department, in what may have been a late-Clinton-legacy initiative or just routine bureaucratic slow functioning, finally established a ninety-day retention period, meant as a sensible compromise between immediate destruction and long-term retention. Once Ashcroft took office, however, he repeatedly suspended the rule. As this was an NRA matter, he actively intervened but did not yet go the limit and, as the NRA wanted, order the immediate, twenty-four-hour destruction of those potentially invaluable arms purchase records.[22]

Then came 9/11. Federal law enforcement agencies, including the Bureau of Alcohol, Tobacco, and Firearms (BATF), launched their all-out counterterrorism investigation. They knew the plane hijackers had not used firearms or explosives, but they suspected what a seized al-Qaeda manual later documented: that al-Qaeda teaches its operatives to consider using the wide-open American firearms market (courtesy of the NRA) as their conveniently-near-the-targets arsenal. On September 16 the BATF requested NICS records so it could cross-check a list of 186 names of suspects identified by its counterterrorism investigation. BATF agents would have been worse than Keystone cops not to have reached for this prime resource—and on September 16 they were one fired-up bunch of investigators. Indeed, without revealing names, the officials actually holding the NICS records discovered that two of the BATF's terrorist suspects had sought and received approvals for firearms purchases. At the same time, the BATF's check of another database—one listing firearms used in crimes, not under the NRA-imposed wraps of the NICS logs—turned up thirty-four weapons that had been involved in crimes and that were tied to its suspects.[23]

Under Justice Department and NICS rules effective until September 2001, investigators could use retained records to investigate "violations of criminal or civil law that may come to light during N.I.C.S. operations." Many terrorist suspects fell into the category of those who should not have been allowed to buy a firearm.[24] Indeed, it was revealed almost a year later, in July 2002, that even the Bush administration's own Office of Legal Counsel, headed by a Bush appointee of unimpeachably conservative and loyal credentials, found nothing legally wrong with checking the records.[25] Not to do so with a terrorist suspects list right after 9/11 was unthinkable.

But Ashcroft's handpicked conservative politicolegal operative, Viet Dinh, had other ideas, and the ball got passed to him, perhaps because he was in charge of such NRA-related matters. Dinh secretly reversed the existing rule that hitherto had allowed NICS log checks on recent weapons purchases and simply blocked the investigators from knowing what the firearms purchase records showed about terrorist suspects. In October the FBI, not to be put off by this Ashcroft-backed resistance, demanded to check a smaller list of names, presumably the most alarming suspects. Though the department's own FBI was now knocking, and knocking hard, Dinh still secretly refused. As the *New York Times* later reported, "In what several officials called a reversal of existing procedure, Mr. Dinh ruled that these checks were improper, reasoning that they would *violate the privacy of these foreigners.*"[26]

Dinh's refusals became a central point of confrontation when Ashcroft finally agreed, after a lengthy delay, to come before the Senate Judiciary Committee in December 2001 for oversight of post-9/11 issues. Senator

Edward Kennedy (D-Mass.) questioned Ashcroft about his refusal to let the FBI's counterterrorism investigators look at the firearms purchase background checks. Insisting the firearms statute obliged him to refuse, Ashcroft did not give an inch. As previously noted, this proved contrary to the clear position of the Bush-picked Office of Legal Counsel. Moreover, there was no chance he had simply misinterpreted the statute, for when asked whether he would support revising the statute to allow such investigation, he refused.[27] He held this line in the face of a roar of press and public disapproval. Dinh's decision, and Ashcroft's rigid adherence to it, posed a real puzzle at the time.

It is worth recalling just whose privacy the Ashcroft-Dinh team told the BATF, FBI, Senate, and public it was striving so hard to protect. This was a group whose rights Ashcroft demonstrably did not care about. According to the inspector general's July 2003 report, federal law enforcers subjected the foreigners in detention immediately after 9/11—in large numbers and on the basis of suspicion not nearly so strong as that attaching to the concentrated BATF and FBI lists—to the most brutal deprivations of rights seen in modern federal law enforcement. The detainees faced incarceration for indefinite periods without charges, confinement under rough conditions, sealed nonpublic records of closed hearings, largely incommunicado status as they were effectively cut off even from counsel and their families, the most thorough and intrusive investigation the FBI and BATF could perform, and exposure to harsh physical abuse in the facilities. All this occurred in the historically unprecedented absence of accountability to the press, Congress, or any other external guarantor of elementary human rights. Whether these procedures were right is a separate issue. The point here is that Ashcroft thought them justified—indeed, not just in late 2001 but two years later.

And yet Ashcroft and Dinh told not only outside inquiries but their own BATF and FBI investigators that they refused access to the NICS logs to protect the privacy rights of these terrorist suspects in their weapons purchases—even though the department's own legal counsel office said there was no such requirement. Such transparent nonsense, put forth both internally and externally as the official explanation Ashcroft gave the Senate for blocking perhaps the most serious security investigation in the nation's history only deepened the mystery. The only explanation, it seemed, was one Ashcroft could never even hint at, not to the BATF, nor the FBI, nor the Senate, and not publicly under any circumstances, regardless of how absurd his fig leaf looked.

Solving the mystery, as with most political mysteries of this kind, merely requires asking who benefits from what was done. Recall that Ashcroft made it a high priority—first as senator, then as attorney general—to satisfy the NRA's desire for instant (after twenty-four hours) destruction of the NICS records of firearms purchases. This was more than just a prime long-term NRA goal in itself, because it camouflaged the lethality of the freshly conjured individual right to firearms. Giving investigators access to these records would seriously undermine the NRA project of scotching NICS record retention altogether. From then on, it would be hard to explain why records that had proved valuable to the FBI and the BATF after 9/11 should never be checked or kept again.

More important, destroying such records and thus concealing wrongful firearms sales to terrorism suspects vitally protected the NRA's other goals. What if the BATF and the FBI found what they so hoped they would: leads? Sales of firearms to terrorism suspects would blow the lid right off the NRA's dirty little not-so-secret: just how seriously the threat of terrorism might be linked to America's wide-open firearms market. Indeed, it might become impossible, without Ashcroft appearing to rank the NRA's interests above those of the United States in restricting terrorists' access to firearms, for the NRA and Ashcroft to achieve any of their joint projects. The best way to keep the genie of NICS record retention bottled up lay in staunchly preventing the post-9/11 investigators from seeing those weapons purchase logs. If the BATF and FBI blew the whistle in the *New York Times,* such a disclosure was still not as bad as disappointing the NRA. Excuses, however transparently bogus, must be made and would suffice as long as they did not mention the NRA. But it's hard to take seriously Ashcroft's self-described stance of putting security first or his criticisms of everyone who questioned him as self-evidently soft on terror given that he ranked tracing the weapons purchases of terrorist suspects so low as compared to his political objectives.

Ultimately, in February 2004, Ashcroft won his victory. Meanwhile the evidence continued to accumulate against his position: a study by the General Accounting Office found that the FBI had used the NICS records to initiate 235 actions to retrieve guns wrongfully sold, often to felons, in a sample six-month period. A full 97 percent of those 235 retrievals were records that would have been lost if purged after twenty-four hours. The omnibus appropriation signed into law by President Bush in February 2004 forced BATF to destroy the records after twenty-four hours, so it basically blocked the FBI from getting back those wrongfully sold firearms. Once Ashcroft and Dinh had kept those records out of the one investigation that would reveal guns falling into intolerable hands, the NRA simply waited until the approaching election rallied congressional conservatives.[28] Indeed, the provision kicked off a major election-year thrust by the NRA to put expanded loopholes in the laws on firearm sales to congressional votes and thereby to mobilize the conservative base behind President Bush.[29]

CHILLING LIBERTY

Putting aside for the moment just how Ashcroft maneuvered in October 2001 his pride and joy, the USA PATRIOT Act, toward enactment,[30] as well as the act's initial implementation, while the country was for the most part asleep, I turn to the time of the nation's awakening to Ashcroft's greatest legacy. This did not fully occur until after summer of 2003, in part because Bush and Ashcroft intimidated even the major press, and certainly their sources, with charges that all criticism helped terrorists. Then the failure to find the putative Iraqi arsenal of nuclear weapons revealed the gap between the administration's "intelligence-based" public relations and reality. Partly the awakening started at the grass roots as over a hundred communities across the country adopted measures and resolutions vocalizing their constituents' angry opposition to collaborating with Ashcroft's so-called PATRIOT Act regime. But one of the most remarkable aspects of this grass-roots awakening was a display of toughness, audacity, and sheer in-your-face gall from a source one might not have anticipated: the nation's librarians. (By starting with them I in no way mean to slight the many other vital—and often courageous—resisters who prepared the way for the awakening in preceding months.)[31]

The librarian's sign posted at ten public libraries in Santa Cruz, California, accurately translating the relevant aspects of the PATRIOT Act as to their effect on all American library patrons, said it all:

> Warning: Although the Santa Cruz Library makes every effort to protect your privacy, under the federal USA PATRIOT ACT (Public Law 107-56), records of the books and any other materials you borrow from this library may be obtained by federal agents. That federal law prohibits library workers from informing you if federal agents have obtained records about you. Questions . . . should be directed to Attorney General John Ashcroft.[32]

What was this sign doing in a free society's libraries? Ashcroft tried to deny the sign's accuracy. He had found himself facing, with a special focus on the librarians' issue, one of the biggest national civil liberties firestorms in at least thirty years. The librarians hit him so hard in the national press, month after month, in a very sore spot—claiming that he was Big Brother, watching readers, unseen, everywhere—that he must drop his usually obdurate nondisclosure stance. He said the librarians were "duped," accused them for two days running of "hysteria," and made a very narrowly worded denial that he had unleashed the PATRIOT Act's section 215 specifically against library users. His spokesperson said, "Section 215 has not been used. Period. Zero times."[33] But what exactly did Ashcroft's denial mean had occurred "zero times"? Ashcroft disingenuously beclouded that little point.

His denial raised far more questions than it answered. The national Library Research Center did a poll in 2002—well before the librarians began their protest—and found that federal agents had requested information on patrons under the PATRIOT Act in sixty libraries. In May 2003 Viet Dinh himself admitted to the House Judiciary Committee that libraries had been contacted approximately fifty times in 2002 using the PATRIOT Act.[34] Fifty or sixty seems a bit different than zero.

Presumably, Ashcroft's strangely isolated denial, made in a phone call and not the subject of any full report or explanation, was what is called in Washington a "nondenial denial"—that is, a statement that denies a deadly serious charge by a semantic sidestep concealed in the shaping of the denial. But again, this poses a mystery. How could even Viet Dinh admit the PATRIOT Act had been used fifty times, while Ashcroft said something about "zero"?

This time the answer comes from knowing how Ashcroft's agents use powers like those Ashcroft gave them in section 215. As counsel for the House of Representatives, I gained such knowledge over the years during the FBI's numerous investigations. Bureau agents do not actually need to apply for a Foreign Intelligence Surveillance Court (FISC) warrant, involving all that paperwork and supervision,[35] to employ the vast powers over libraries that Ashcroft unleashed. Anyone who has seen the FBI in action knows that its agents can walk into a public library, flash their big black ID wallets, and just make known to the librarian that such a warrant is coming "if she wants one." As the armed and legally powerful agents, exuding the confidence of righteous pursuers of the nation's enemies, discuss the matter with the librarian, the librarian comes to understand what they say is true. The librarian will invariably give up his or her patrons' rights without mounting an unpatriotic resistance, thereby impeding the FBI by uselessly demanding such paperwork. And it is the paperwork that Ashcroft counted by his "zero."[36] The librarian complies, especially because, as I show below, Ashcroft has made fighting the matter in court about as effective as hitting the agents with a paper bookmark. Ashcroft's agents politely ask the librarians not to resist as, in a sense, they exercise powers that could potentially ravage her library patrons' civil liberties. To paraphrase their stance, the agents simply assure the librarians that their cooperation in the act is their patriotic duty. So instead of asking for the ceremonial FISC warrant on "zero" occasions, the librarians just lay down their rights and comply.

But here the Constitution and Ashcroft's statute need examination, without the distraction of Ashcroft's clumsy nondenial denial: in what sense had the PATRIOT Act actually picked the dragon's locks and stripped the public of its sacred right to read material in public libraries without the government watching, unseen? We start with the classic prose of the Fourth Amendment to the Constitution, part of the Bill of Rights crafted brilliantly by James Madison in the 1790s:

> The right of the people to be secure in their persons, houses, papers, and effects, against unreasonable searches and seizures, shall not be violated, and *no Warrants shall issue, but upon probable cause,* supported by Oath or affirmation, and *particularly describing* the place to be searched, and the persons *or things to be seized.* [emphasis added]

Over two centuries after the United States adopted this amendment as the constitutional constraint upon its central government, the highest law of the land remains fixed and constant in requiring that for the FBI to search for and seize something like library patron records, it needs a search "Warrant." The warrant must issue "upon probable cause," meaning a relatively high standard of proof in advance tying the records to something suspicious. And above all for these purposes, the warrant must "particularly describ[e] . . . the . . . things to be seized," meaning that agents may grab *only* the records described in the writ "particularly" (e.g., which patron's or which books) as the "things to be seized." And of course the information underlying the warrant must be available to those who might follow up on or challenge the warrant in court, or the whole process becomes the government's rigged game of unwatched solitaire, with cheating never caught.

Recent events demonstrate the Fourth Amendment's general centrality to a free society today, and the particular import of its commandments to the protection of libraries and similar places, such as bookstores and video stores. During Justice Clarence Thomas's Senate confirmation hearings about whether he had sexually harassed Anita Hill, a factual question came up between Hill and Thomas. Hill suggested, and Thomas denied, that in talking to (harassing) her, he had alluded to his having viewed X-rated videos (the title *Long Dong Silver* was mentioned), presumably rented from the video rental store he frequented.[37] The Senate Judiciary Committee, as a federal tribunal, could, and typically would, resolve such a practical factual question—helpful in this case in ending the he said–she said dispute between Hill and Thomas—by issuing a subpoena, a legal cousin of the search warrant, for the pertinent records of video stores. However, Thomas told the committee in mutually understood code language that if the committee issued that writ to video stores, he would quit his nomination forthwith and denounce them for "lynching" him by violating the sanctity of his privacy.[38] To the Senate Judiciary Committee, this meant that the day after they sent an agent with such a writ into his video stores, news broadcasters and headlines across the country would scream that the Judiciary Committee had utterly and brazenly disrespected Thomas's right to be secure in his video store records. The committee got the message. It issued no subpoena. Since then, you can find Thomas on the Supreme Court.

In 1998 Ken Starr subpoenaed Monica Lewinsky's bookstore purchase records from the Barnes & Noble in Georgetown and Kramerbooks in Washington, D.C. Starr made sweeping demands and seemed to relish the ensuing high-profile publicity; he said his specific target was a book Lewinsky had bought, the phone-sex novel *Vox*, but he asked for details of at least sixteen purchases.[39] The store owners fought the subpoena in court as a grave infringement on constitutional rights. They argued, with some agreement from the courts, that the Fourth Amendment's strictures apply with extra vigor in the First Amendment (freedom of speech and press) context of prosecutorial demands on bookstores.

Word of this controversy added its own fuel to the centrist public's general disgust with Starr's tactics, many calling Starr by names recalling the police forces of 1930s totalitarian regimes. But to concede Starr his legal due, although his view of the Constitution's spirit when it comes to bookstore subpoenas was, shall we say, not highly libertarian, he did not conduct his search of the bookstore purchase records in the shadows; he asked only for Lewinsky's purchases, albeit sixteen rather than one; the public could debate the matter; the courts carefully balanced the constitutional issues; and in fact and in law, in searching those bookstore records, Starr never claimed to escape the binding letter of the Bill of Rights.

In sum, individual freedom and privacy today depends, perhaps even more than they did in the Framers' era, upon the strict and unyielding application of the Fourth Amendment, strengthened by the First Amendment, to searches by federal government authorities like Starr, the Senate, and Ashcroft of things very much like library patron records.

But since 9/11 the Fourth Amendment has faced an enormous challenge in its application to central government power in the context of the war on terrorism. In fact, ever since World War II Congress has authorized central government investigations (most conducted by the FBI) of espionage and other hostile operations in this country carried out by foreign organizations, including the KGB during the Cold War and, after the Cold War, Communist Chinese intelligence, the violent "Provisional IRA," and al-Qaeda. As foreign wars fought on American soil, they could not be fought by the same exact procedures by which the Fourth Amendment is satisfied, for liberty's sake, in domestic criminal investigations.

So when, starting in 1978 and with subsequent oversight, Congress faced up to this legally knotty problem, it tried to authorize and yet control the uses of search and seizure in these wars by enacting the Foreign Intelligence Surveillance Act (FISA). FISA created a special court, the Foreign Intelligence Surveillance Court (FISC or FISC court).[40] This mysterious "court" exists in a legal twilight zone all its own, halfway between a public court responsible for protecting individual citizens' privacy rights and a judicial partner of the FBI's huge counterintelligence and counterterrorism operations. To fight the war the FBI and hence the FISC court must of course operate with nationwide powers at all times and all locations, transcending the limits of ordinary courts, procedures, state lines, or any other ordinary limits. Pursuant to FISA, the chief justice of the Supreme Court designates judges to serve on the FISC court, which means that, while William Rehnquist has been chief justice, the FISC's judges are not exactly overimbued with an ardent ACLU spirit. And not only does the court meet in secret, but almost everything about it has always been kept as secret as can be.

Although FISA, as applied to records like those of library patrons, could put the Fourth Amendment to considerable strain, a vitally important protection for privacy always remained—until Ashcroft. The statute might still pose a threat to liberty in authorizing the FBI to march into libraries demanding records of some patron it suspected as involved in some nefarious foreign matter; even so, FISA before Ashcroft did not challenge the Fourth Amendment's strict particularity requirement. In a domestic criminal investigation, if Ken Starr asks a bookstore what it sold to Monica

Lewinsky or, even in a FISA matter, if FBI agents want to know whether a suspicious foreigner rented something from Clarence Thomas's video store, the court authorizes grabbing only the particular records Starr or the FBI wants. Starr or the agents grab that, and only that. Meanwhile, if Dr. Ruth Westheimer shops at Monica's bookstore for *The Joy of Sex*, or if Clarence Thomas goes back to his video store to rerent some of his old favorites, the FBI keeps its nose out of it—that is not what they came to the stores to get—and Dr. Ruth's and Thomas's patron records of book and video choices don't go into some enormous federal database.

But as a 2003 study in the *Journal of Legislation* put it,

> The USA PATRIOT Act . . . does not require specificity; the government can use these warrants for the "production of any tangible things." . . . Under the new 2001 legislation, the F.B.I. . . . can go into a public library and ask for the records on everybody who ever used the library. . . . This exposes innocent citizens to invasions of privacy the government has historically justified only for the most criminal of suspects.[41]

To put it bluntly: because of section 215 of the PATRIOT Act, we no longer have the same guarantee of privacy when we go to the library, bookstore, or video store that we used to have.[42] We now have to imagine the FBI there also, looking over our shoulder as we choose our books or videos. Moreover, in the very serious event that the FBI abuses its power, no one—not the store, the library, nor any of us—has a real chance immediately to challenge it, nor can we even compose ourselves sufficiently to accept the forfeiture of our privacy. Section 215 means the FBI and the FISC court leave behind a gag order as they depart the library and the store. Regarding our privacy, libraries and video stores no longer serve only us. Now they serve as surveillance agents for the central government, whenever it asks.

In the meantime Ashcroft's polarizing, left-baiting stance on issues surrounding section 215 prepared the way for Bush's own call, not to rectify or reform the PATRIOT Act, but to make it even more extreme. In September 2003 Bush called for a three-part "PATRIOT II." The two simple and obvious moves in Bush's proposal—more death penalties and a refusal to let neutral judges determine bail based on evidence and facts but instead giving all the incarceration power without check to Ashcroft—require no analysis. They bear the label "campaign platform" and the implicit message "Candidate Bush is hard on terror and anyone else is, by contrast, soft."

The third move, allowing administrative subpoenas without any judicial approval whatever, deserves a longer glance as it bears on libraries.

Senator Lieberman responded to Bush's PATRIOT II, "Is the government snooping through people's library records? Inappropriately searching people's belongings? George W. Bush isn't answering these questions. As usual, he's keeping secrets and fueling suspicions."[43] The senator well understood the proposal regarding administrative subpoenas. By that proposal Bush threw the gauntlet right in the librarians' face. Suppose the librarians get really assertive and, when the FBI asks to grab whole library user databases, demand that the bureau actually fill out the paperwork and get FISC court warrants on its next sixty visits. Bush now came up with a way for the FBI to avoid even the minimal paperwork a FISC judge would ask. He would take the judge out. The FBI could issue the writ itself. And if the FBI committed a few more dozen or hundred abuses—as it has on past occasions, not all of which it confessed to the FISC court—the librarians must no longer even expect the FBI to confess this to a judge—because Bush's PATRIOT II called for there to be no judge.[44]

UNDERCUTTING PRIVACY

When the librarians awakened to the chilling effect of section 215 in 2003–2004, they addressed just the first of several successive unpleasant levels of surprise in Ashcroft's PATRIOT Act kit bag. One might at first take heart that the central government will use its section 215 powers only in terrorism investigations, perhaps a narrow category. But the PATRIOT Act also has section 218.

As part of foreign counterintelligence, for many years the FBI (it is reported in public sources),[45] like the domestic counterintelligence operations of foreign countries, may enter foreign embassies and similar targets to plant bugs and taps. Such government entry into private places used to be called by the cute name "black bag jobs."[46] FISA authorizes bugs, taps, and black bag jobs with FISC Court–issued warrants, but on very different terms than in domestic criminal investigations, much easier for the government to obtain and much more intrusive on the privacy of those targeted. FISA stretched the Fourth Amendment here too.

The pre-Ashcroft FISA confined those FISA superwarrants to what legal commentators since the PATRIOT Act have routinely called "two small words": *primary purpose*. That is, only when the "primary purpose" of the FBI's black bag job or other operation was foreign counterintelligence or counterterrorism could it have that easily issued, extra-intrusive FISA superwarrant. The FBI could not use such powers for its regular domestic crime work, because that would make hash of the normal Fourth Amendment process. It bears mention that the FISA superwarrant business is not some once-in-a-blue-moon affair. Even under President Clinton FISA warrants increased so dramatically that by 1997, 749 FISA search and electronic surveillance orders issued, whereas only 569 similar federal criminal warrants issued for the entirety of domestic federal crime investigations combined.[47] In other words, the FBI stood ready to perform a substantial quantity of superintrusive warrant work—even before its post-9/11 step-up of activity.

With section 218 Ashcroft picked another lock restraining the dragon of central government power, in this case superintrusive bugs, taps, and black bag jobs. He changed FISA's provision that the operation's *"primary* purpose" be to fight foreign intelligence or terrorism to require that one of these be merely *"a* purpose."[48] Now the government's FISA superpowers of surveillance and intrusion could occur, not just in the investigations for which Congress originally intended FISA, but for something perilously close to investigations of mere run-of-the-mill domestic crime hitherto under the regular Fourth Amendment system. If the FBI avowed that even one purchaser from a shoplifter, forger, smuggler, or other such run-of-the-mill criminal might possibly be linked in some attenuated way to the type of target FISA exists for, that might suffice to remove the investigation from the regular Fourth Amendment system.[49] Why should the central government's agents confine themselves by the regular Fourth Amendment when they need only avow a mixed, merely nonprimary purpose and become super-agents?[50]

In March of 2002 Ashcroft really got the ball rolling with a memo, well described by Stephen J. Schulhofer of the New York University School of Law, a leading national expert on this subject: Ashcroft's "memorandum instructed FBI and Justice Department officials that FISA powers could now 'be used primarily for a law enforcement purpose. . . .' and he deleted the previous caveat that barred [ordinary criminal] prosecutors from 'directing or controlling' the scope of FISA surveillance."[51] Schulhofer adds that "we have seen inexcusable opportunism" in this that "has exploited the momentum of 9/11 to expand government power to intrude on privacy in pursuit of wholly unrelated goals."[52]

In May of 2002 the FISC court issued a ruling to keep the genie from getting completely out of the bottle.[53] Apparently, the court was outraged to discover widespread and extensive patterns of FBI abuse of FISA surveillance. In one notification, the government confessed to errors in over seventy-five FISA applications—quite a lot—that were filed and approved.[54] The judge writing this opinion for the FISC court, Royce Lamberth, is well-known in Washington. Having been a career Justice Department senior official before coming to the bench, he has much legitimate sympathy for his former longtime colleagues in the department and the FBI. Yet this time, he wrote a rather scorching opinion for a unanimous group of all seven FISC court judges. It reads as if they were fighting to keep the regular Fourth Amendment on life support in the face of the FISA powers of Ashcroft's agents.

Once again, Ashcroft proved his crusade had no limits (apart, that is, from terrorist suspects' right to privacy in purchasing weapons for prompt use). The Justice Department appealed Judge Lamberth's ruling. Ted Olson himself "argued" the appeal, though for both him and Ashcroft it was like shooting fish in a barrel. Ashcroft invoked a sleight of hand, convening an entity never before called into action called the "United States Foreign Intelligence Surveillance Court of Review," though perhaps "Ashcroft's Review Court" is more apropos. Ashcroft put the court on the map on its first time out—that is, way over on the map's far-right edge.

Ted Olson's "argument" against civil liberties and the Fourth Amendment did not occur in public. But what really stung, Ashcroft's Review Court allowed no one to orally argue the other side. Only Ashcroft's side got heard; the other side could not even get a seat in the room.[55] We have been waiting almost a century for the sequel to Kafka's *The Trial*, and Ashcroft may well have written it; it might be entitled "The Appeal."

Olson did not have all that difficult a time, it seems. The three judges of Ashcroft's Review Court included, as its one well-known powerhouse, the famous Judge Silberman of the D.C. Circuit—a judge of impressive intellect and credentials but with ample sympathies, to put it mildly, for the Bush administration's legal interests in this situation. These three judges reversed the unanimous seven judges of the FISC court and gave Ashcroft what he wanted, along with extra helpings, in a ruling in November 2002.[56] In 2004 Bush chose Silberman to cochair his commission on weapons of mass destruction (like putting Romeo in charge of the "critique Juliet" commission).

Those who think that Ashcroft could never get his agents to do anything untoward with their powers to bug, tap, and do black bag jobs in the name of national security might review how J. Edgar Hoover used to order the bugging of Martin Luther King's hotel rooms (King might be under Communist control, the FBI agents said) and then send the tapes to Coretta Scott King in an attempt to break up their marriage. Those who think it alarmist to worry about the PATRIOT Act because they figure the courts will surely rein it in might review the procedures followed by Ashcroft's three-judge review court in dropping its bombshell on the protesting seven judges of the FISC court.

Even now, though, there is yet a further depth of Ashcroft's work in the so-called PATRIOT Act to explore. Even under sections 215 and 218, some connection must exist, however attenuated, however dicey to check on, with foreign counterintelligence or counterterrorism. The PATRIOT Act contains other sections, however, among which a particular bundle of joy is 213, conferring "sneak and peak" powers. Section 213 allows federal agents to get authorization to sneak into a home while the residents are out and do a real number on it.[57] The agents can examine the home's computer hard drive(s), where many of us store much of our private lives these days. During the covert search, the agents can not only take photos but install in the computer a cutie called a digital "magic lantern" or "sniffer keystroke logger." It creates a record of every stroke made—even in files *not* sent out over the Internet, like the personal first drafts of letters to family intimates not sent in that form, maybe not sent in any form. On another sneak-and-peek search the next time the residents leave, the agents download the information. With these search warrants, unlike those issued under the Fourth Amendment, the FBI repeatedly returns to and scrutinizes the home without even leaving a piece of paper or a calling card to inform the men, women, and/or children living there that their privacy has evaporated courtesy of the federal government. A family might parade down Main Street nude with less of a sense of violated privacy than by Ashcroft's sneak-and-peek jobs, because at least then the members would know they were being exposed.

And now we come to an even deeper layer of Ashcroft's work. Like a number of the PATRIOT Act's other sections, sneak-and-peek requires *no* connection whatsoever to counterterrorism. The authority exists clear of that subject-matter restriction for agents to use in regular domestic criminal investigations that used to occur only under the regular Fourth Amendment system. And when the press confronted Ashcroft starting in late 2003, he coolly confirmed that he did indeed make generous use of his so-called PATRIOT Act superpowers in plain-vanilla crime matters without any connection to the supposed reason for passing the act in the first place. The legally subtle and complex disclosure came out in a September 2003 *New York Times* article entitled "U.S. Uses Terror Law to Pursue Crimes from Drugs to Swindling: Broad Steps Anger Critics of Expanded Powers." Ashcroft provided no numbers, no specifics, no real opportunity for oversight. In the bland words of his departmental spokesperson, "There are many provisions in the Patriot Act that can be used in the general criminal law"—meaning Ashcroft can and will deploy them in investigating what the spokesperson called "garden-variety criminals."[58]

Here finally I connect up Ashcroft's overall long-term strategy. The country got by just fine before him dealing with regular domestic offenses under the regular Fourth Amendment system. Even the Reagan and first Bush administrations avoided Ashcroft's kinds of breaches in the regular Bill of Rights system for garden-variety situations. But the classic polarizing position I described earlier—Richard Nixon's in 1968, for example—consists of arguing that the regular Bill of Rights system "handcuffs the police" in dealing with crime, then blaming the Democrats as "soft" on crime. Before 9/11 and now under many of the provisions of the so-called PATRIOT Act, Ashcroft's stance has never been about counterterrorism at all. That was a Reno concern.

Now we can understand just what Ashcroft did in drafting and pushing through the USA PATRIOT Act in the first place. On September 19, 2001, Dinh himself, under Ashcroft's direction, led a team at the Justice Department to pull together past wish lists for new authority in an omnibus legislative request. Clearly, the team was told to assemble authority not just for fighting terrorism but for, in effect, un-"handcuffing the police" across the board. Then Ashcroft contended, dubiously, that this whole omnibus measure required enactment on a rush timetable, so that the House and Senate Judiciary committees held one day of hearings each to receive Ashcroft's vague testimony, with little response allowed, on September 24 and 25, 2001.

In the House, the Judiciary Committee marked up the bill on October 3, producing bipartisan unanimity on a moderated version, a remarkable achievement considering the thirty-six members spanned the ideological spectrum in Congress from furthest conservative right to progressive left. They came together, drawing on their previous half-dozen years of experience with many of these same proposals, to push the outer limits of what would actually serve counterterrorism while avoiding dangerous incursions on some of the rights essential for democracy.[59]

Ashcroft had discovered that his own congressional group still had not gotten the message about changing the party's stance on central government authority from fear that it could get misused (in the 1990s by Reno) to cheer at release from all limits on it (except those the NRA wanted). Apparently, it enraged Ashcroft that conservative House Judiciary Republicans would still recall the very concerns about misuse of Justice Department powers that Chairman Ashcroft himself had shouted about in the Senate Judiciary Committee just two or three years earlier. While he was helping to defeat Ronnie White's nomination because the black judge, he said, was "pro-criminal," he had induced even Senate Judiciary Republicans, his closest allies, to doubt his trustworthiness; now he induced the same feelings in his closest soul mates, hard-right House Judiciary Republicans.

Just as those conservative Republicans were congratulating themselves on having done something good both for security and for the Constitution, Ashcroft ran a quarterback sneak around them, leaping over their heads for a one-on-one meeting with Speaker Dennis Hastert (R-Ill.).[60] In private, Ashcroft declared that he must have every bit of his version of the bill, apparently bowling Hastert over. That one-time junior high school gym coach apparently did not understand the details of Fourth Amendment procedure the way House Judiciary Republicans did. Ashcroft simply made the hysterical plea that the next terrorist attack could occur at any moment and no one—not even the House Judiciary Committee, run by conservative congressional Republicans with far more depth of experience with these issues than he—understood it like he did. Hastert then made the committee chair ditch the 36–0 committee bill in favor of Dinh's un-"handcuff-the-police" grab bag. This move disgusted even the most reliably conservative House Republicans; House majority leader Dick Armey later commented that Ashcroft was "out of control."[61]

Ashcroft got his way. So, it seems, it was for him throughout 2001–2004 whenever he played the "soft on crime" card. Or to paraphrase how an insightful observer who wishes to remain anonymous explained it to me, "You mean Ashcroft said the FBI could not investigate guns, but only libraries? Well, that makes sense. He would figure that conservatives like guns. But that only liberals like libraries."

After 9/11 Ashcroft ascended in the polls without putting aside more than momentarily his right-wing social agenda.[62] In polling terms Ashcroft's stance particularly appeals to "those most supportive of tightened national security at the expense of individual liberties," which the experts say consists of those "significantly more authoritarian in personality."[63] This is another way of describing Ashcroft's natural constituency. But what went up in 2001 came down in 2003. By August 2003 Harris poll numbers showed the percentage of the public disapproving of his performance—despite all his posturing about the war on terrorism—had climbed to nearly 40 percent. No one may ever beat his record as a public official who, while insisting he was fighting (in terrorism) the most irredeemable and unpopular of enemies, engendered such intense levels of centrist unpopularity and, among leaders of his own party who had seen him in action up close, wary and suspicious distrust. That is except perhaps Richard Nixon.

So we see that Ashcroft's demeanor—that of a reckless ideologue—often masked a strategic political agenda. Beginning in 2001 Ashcroft kept an eye on his boss's (the president's) next election, a campaign starting in 2003 and lasting until November 2004. Ashcroft himself had taken the point position naturally suited to his polarizing stance: the Republican conservatives' polarizer, taking positions of extreme imbalance on public problems of security and crime vis-à-vis considerations like civil liberties in order to bash the Democrats for not following suit. As the nonpartisan *National Journal* simply described this role in 2003, "Ashcroft has successfully played bad cop to Bush's good cop, thus deflecting criticism away from the president." For example, "mounting arrests of illegal immigrants have angered many Hispanic groups, but their anger is mostly directed toward Ashcroft. Bush still gets high ratings from Hispanics."[64]

Yet, the lighting rod theory explains only the more obvious half of Ashcroft's highly crafted role. In addition, Ashcroft's ultrahard line sets up a polarity: By contrast with his (and the Bush administration's) position "for" security and "against" terrorism and crime, the other side cannot help but be vulnerable to low-style attack for appearing insufficiently "for" security and hence "soft" on terrorism and crime. During 2001–2003 Ashcroft could figure that the other side would mostly be civil liberties groups and the occasional brave congressional Democrat, but in 2004 it would be the Democratic Party's nominee running against President Bush. Ashcroft and surrogates would implicitly, and perhaps even explicitly, accuse that nominee of being AWOL in the war on terror and crime. Meanwhile, the bad cop–good cop split with President Bush permits the latter to avoid sullying his image with these rough, nasty tactics while reaping their benefit and yet portraying himself positively as a compassionate conservative.

The public understands that such role-playing is endemic to politics. Hardball political tactics have a legitimate place in many nondelicate aspects of running the country; Americans like politics rough-and-tumble. However, civil liberties and the Bill of Rights have a special, frail, and vulnerable function in a democracy in time of crisis, for crises often threaten to overwhelm some of the fragile links that sustain liberty and privacy.

Ashcroft's approach amounted to something less forgivable than politics as usual. His approach picked, and sometimes broke, the delicate yet vital constitutional and quasi-constitutional locks by which the nation shackles the dragon it has always dreaded: what its necessarily strong central government could do with excess unchecked power. Now that Ashcroft has picked those locks, we find the dragon loosed amongst us, and sometimes, with reason, we feel fear.

ELECTION-YEAR DEVELOPMENTS

Seeking to score points against his rivals in the 2004 campaign as the leader standing tall against terrorism, President Bush did not want to have to defend Ashcroft's unimpressive and alienating performance or his undermining of the Bill of Rights. In the years since the winter 2001 effort in Afghanistan—the last and basically only gesture at bipartisan centrism it ever made in the effort against terrorism—the Bush administration had choreographed as backup a later election-year legal show by Ashcroft and Rumsfeld. This had long been planned to highlight the detentions in Guantánamo of fighters captured in Afghanistan and the detention of Jose Padilla and to showcase the trials by a sort of military tribunal of some of those detainees.[65] Bush could thereby dwell in his campaign ads and speeches on the detainees' bad acts so as to rally his conservative base— a style alien to presidents in a democracy though familiar to nondemocratic rulers parading foreign war captives.

Besides the images of foreign fighters detained for a sort of military trial, Ashcroft could cite the opinions issued by the Supreme Court in spring 2004 concerning these fighters and Padilla in order to paper over his gross and unnecessary incursions into the civil liberties of citizens. Never mind that the Court's rulings on such matters, as when it upheld the tragic World War II detentions of Japanese Americans, never approved presidential judgments but only fixed responsibility for asserting national security as the justification on the executive and not the courts.[66]

Legal professionals who handle war and terror cases mocked Bush's subversion of legal tradition in such matters.[67] Ashcroft's and Rumsfeld's model for detentions of citizens outside the civil law, as well as for a kind of military tribunal for captured fighters far below the due process standards of American courts martial or prior war crimes tribunals, came down from the political top, not up from those professionals. As to pushing the disdain for citizens' rights to unheard-of extremes, Ashcroft and Rumsfeld had inspired the public's distrust by their other incursions against civil liberties, such as Rumsfeld's tactics during the Iraq war in curbing independent, First Amendment–protected journalism. In years to come, if Ashcroft and Rumsfeld effectively controlled all three branches of government and engaged in more unpopular right-wing/hard-line adventurism in the Third World on a basis like their doctored intelligence about Iraqi WMD stockpiles, they would create much tension: legitimate efforts to bring the truth about these overseas ventures to the American public and to help angry American citizens be heard would clash with Ashcroft's and Rumsfeld's low tolerance for such expression. Certain questionable Bush administration actions—including federal law enforcement moves (later canceled) against anti–Iraq war protesters; the attempted federal prosecution of a famous, if controversial, defense lawyer; unexplained military strikes on journalists in Iraq—gave broad hints at the dangers faced in years to come if Ashcroft and Rumsfeld had the power to treat even American citizens outside the law whose loyalty the two questioned on the thinnest of bases.

As for the election-year treatment of captured foreign fighters, Bush was so determined to produce campaign-usable imagery that he seemed at best oblivious as to how much the disdain his tactics in this regard showed for international law and consensus undermined the United States' vital long-term effort against international terrorism. Recent years had seen such effective examples of real—not victor's—justice as the international war crimes tribunals for the former Yugoslavia that tried Milošević, the Hague tribunal that tried the Libyan defendants in the Lockerbie bombing case, the forward evolution of true American courts martial pursuant to the Uniform Code of Military Justice, and successful civil trials in the United States such as for the 1993 World Trade Center and 1995 Oklahoma City bombings.[68] Building on those successes offered a prize beyond measure in the effort against international terrorism: reinforcing collective effort among the NATO nations and garnering respect in the Third World. Instead, President Bush adopted only those approaches that would promote him domestically in the 2004 election. NATO nations dropped charges against important al-Qaeda defendants several times because the Bush administration deprived foreign courts of what they needed. And Bush forfeited the Islamic world's confidence in the United States to the point that by spring 2004 even Bush's own CIA admitted his Iraq occupation had set America back in dealing with bin Laden's ideology.

Bush did disguise from the American public some aspects of how much was forfeited by his election-oriented approach to detained Taliban and al-Qaeda fighters. In chapter 6 I describe the ill effects of Bush's ideological combat against the International Criminal Court. Chapters 7 and 8 describe the ill effects of Bush's manipulated portrayal of Saudi backing of al-Qaeda in the lead-up to 9/11—including the lengths to which he and his personal lawyer and ambassador to Riyadh, Robert W. Jordan, went in 2001–2003 to relieve the Saudis after 9/11 from American public pressure for their calculated unhelpfulness in controlling their Frankenstein's monster bin Laden. These chapters thus reveal additional dimensions of the Bush administration's harmful subversions of the law as to foreign fighters in order to serve Bush's 2004 campaign purposes.

In the eyes of our NATO allies, the extension of the anti–International Criminal Court crusade, the unilateral preemptive war in Iraq, and the handling of the Afghan captives augmented America's rejection of collective means and measures just when they were most vital to support the effort against terror.[69] Having forfeited so many post–Afghan campaign opportunities to keep our allies in that campaign on board with us, now Bush forfeited one of the last and best. NATO publics and leaders, torn between wanting to join with the United States as they had after 9/11 against terror and feeling alienated by many of the Bush administration's actions, would find his insistence on "victor's justice" for the captives as motivated by his desire to protect his own political interests—chilling their desire to assist. They needed no descriptions of the infamous acts of terrorists—these were quite familiar to them. But Bush would provide no more.

In the eyes of the Islamic world, Bush simply committed further errors by preemptively invading and occupying Iraq. We badly needed a restoration of credibility. Running detentions and military tribunals not even up to the traditional standards of American courts martial and missing opportunities for international tribunal credibility worked no such restoration. And continuing to focus only on the work of the foot soldiers of terror and not on the elite backing, such as the Saudi support, for recruiting and finance reinforced the effect of the refusal to declassify the congressional joint committee report on 9/11. By not using the context of post-Afghan justice for presenting a case that would challenge the earlier backers of *jihadi* terror, but instead addressing only the familiar, albeit horrendous, effects of its foot soldiers, the Bush approach failed to convince either Islamic elites or the general Islamic public that they should not repeat the errors of those earlier backers. In particular, popular discontent in the Islamic world would continue, and elites would be forced to consider various ways of addressing or diverting it. The United States could have demonstrated to elites why they should prevent that discontent from being directed against the West and demonstrated to the Islamic public that America's attention encompassed their concerns as well as its own. Richard A. Clarke, the most relentless of al-Qaeda foes, concluded in 2004 that "far from addressing the popular appeal of the enemy that attacked us, Bush handed that enemy precisely what it wanted and needed, proof that America was at war with Islam, that we were the new Crusaders come to occupy Muslim land."[70] Bush's election-oriented policies regarding justice might well deserve the same criticism: their faults meant they would simply be used by the other side as a basis for attributing to the defendants the status of martyrs.

Again to counter the sense that Ashcroft and the Bush administration generally had undermined the Constitution without sufficiently improving domestic protections, Bush made election-year use of his implementation of the statutorily created Homeland Security Department (DHS). Here too, however, he had undermined the law for conservative causes instead of focusing on effective anti-terrorism. A 2004 report, *America at Risk: Closing the Security Gap,* by the House Homeland Security Committee's minority side, broke through the silence of Bush's partisan loyalists on the committee to paint an elaborate and disheartening picture.[71] For Bush to distinguish his own brand of Homeland Security Department from the original bipartisan brand of Senator Joseph Lieberman, Bush had thrown in extra government agencies better left out while leaving out some of the capacities most needed. Bush's DHS had a threat-warning capacity that was confusing and inadequate and that failed to follow through and force cooperation among intelligence units and watch-list keepers.

Sometimes Bush dropped the ball from underweighting the most serious terrorism risks, as when the administration did so little to follow the recommendations of the bipartisan Baker-Cutler Commission and devote resources to securing nuclear sites and biological materials within the former Soviet Union.[72] Sometimes he dropped the ball because of partisan regional preferences, as in backing formulas and plans for homeland security assistance that slighted the most populous states (California and New York) and coastal ports—obviously places where the nation was exposed to risk but where the aid would not go to his political supporters. Sometimes he dropped the ball from excessive sympathy for industries that were part of his base, as in not pressing the chemical industry to act on the 123 facilities each of which could threaten over one million people in an attack, or in not ensuring stepped-up food inspections of the food industry even after the mad cow threat graphically exposed our vulnerabilities. Bush's bottom line seemed consistent: Ashcroft has supplied me with the required image-making tools, whatever the price; as for the rest, let conservative causes be served.

4 Domestic Affairs Veer Right

In his first year in office, President Bush abused the Budget Act to enact a trillion-dollar regressive tax cut, followed by another, even more regressive cut in 2003. After he rolled back President Clinton's popular legacy initiatives, he mounted from November 2002 through 2004 an anti-environmental campaign, including secrecy aspects discussed in a later chapter. Bush also bent campaign finance to his service, with the anticipated yet still record scale of his 2004 fund-raising providing the engine and the discipline for his whole program.

Most astonishing, President Bush pushed the domestic agenda with little or no popular mandate to do so. Before Bush, presidents needed strong public support for ideological agendas. Ronald Reagan's large victory against President Carter in 1980—including, on Reagan's coattails, the decisive seizure of the Senate for his party for the first time since the 1950s—gave impetus to his conservative domestic programs such as cutting taxes in top brackets, chopping spending for the poor, converting the toxic waste–reducing Superfund into a party slush fund, and despoiling the West's natural resources. President George H. W. Bush in 1988 had, by contrast with his celebrated immediate predecessor, a more modest popular victory and, as to congressional coattails, barely any. His request for a modest capital gains tax cut got the congressional spurning it "richly" deserved. Quite to the contrary, he signed into law a tax increase, the Clean

Air Act of 1990, and even the Civil Rights Act of 1991—each of which made archconservatives apoplectic.

To describe the scale of President George W. Bush's domestic conservatism and to show clearly the legal black magic by which he performed his feats, this chapter starts by looking at how conservatives prepared to take control of the agenda in Washington as of 2001. Only then can the chapter look into the depths of what Bush has done and, even worse, has been preparing to do.

HOW THE RIGHT SEIZED THE DOMESTIC AGENDA

In 2001–2004 the Bush administration sapped the strength, sometimes subtly but in the end unmistakably, of not just the environmental and public interest state the nation had constructed in previous decades but many of the Great Society (1960s) and even some of the New Deal (1930s) programs that most Americans unconsciously assume to be fundamental. Although this development seems quite sudden, almost shocking, the right-wing ascendancy in Washington actually developed over decades. We must start with an appreciation of the tremendous national structure that the right took on—and how it did so.

Just as the Democratic Party as we know it emerged from the New Deal coalition and program of the 1930s, so America accepted in the 1960s the key components of the party's post–New Deal agenda. These included funding a benign social safety net—food stamps, Medicaid—with federal taxes based on ability to pay and levied on a nationally even basis. Meanwhile the country saved itself just in time from environmental disaster by extensive legislation, much of it shepherded through Congress by leaders like Senator Ed Muskie (D-Maine) and, later, Representative Henry Waxman (D-Calif.). For its part, decades ago the Republican Party's most successful (i.e., most moderate) national leaders (President Eisenhower, Senate leaders Everett Dirksen [R-Ill.] and even Howard Baker [R-Tenn.], and as to much of his domestic legislating, even President Nixon) rarely advocated dismantling these programs. Rhetoric aside, successful moderate Republican leaders actually pushed balanced packages of spending and tax cuts and some curbing of regulatory excesses, and the "party of Lincoln" was by no means, at that time, an avowed enemy of civil rights.[1]

However, starting mainly in the mid-1970s, affected business sectors and their wealthy patrons began fighting back, with the far-right-fringe, immensely wealthy Scaife and Olin foundations becoming the hard ideologues' sugar-daddies.[2] Together, conservative businesses and foundations created a potent network of doctrinaire litigation and lobbying groups, from the Business Roundtable to the "libertarian" Cato Institute.[3] This network initiated countless projects for circumventing ordinary democratic channels for action, filling the media and the three branches of government with the din of their credo, and stocking a deep pool of influential conservative activists.[4] A Niagara of conservative campaign fund-raising came out of this 1970s "politicization of the business community,"[5] particularly from wealthy interests in Texas and other conservative states.[6] Big Tobacco's limitless, unaccountable, and morally questionable political funding served the darkest purposes.

President Reagan's historic budget package of 1981 did much to fulfill near-term conservative wishes.[7] His feat, using some provisions of the Budget Act of 1974 and the process it created, started shifting the fiscal direction of government from progressive to regressive.[8] His budget played a large part in how, as Kevin Phillips notes, "between 1979 and 1989, the portion of the nation's wealth held by the top 1 percent nearly doubled, skyrocketing from 22 percent to 39 percent, probably the most rapid escalation in U.S. history."[9] Simultaneously, President Reagan made a series of fox-in-the-chicken-coop appointments to undermine public interest regulation, notably of his infamous anti-environment interior secretary, James Watt, led by a centralized White House regulatory review system.[10] Something of a backlash in the 1982 midterm election defined the legislative limits of what this effort could achieve, and the soaring national debt after the 1981 tax cut preoccupied domestic attention for the following decade.

In 1990 the first President Bush dared to step away from the deficit-ridden policies of Reagan.[11] He and President Clinton each restored some of the taxes on the top brackets and to some degree shored up the nation's environmental and other public interest efforts.[12] President Bush thereby split his party, and the conservative faction took control. In the early Clinton era, the conservative wing of congressional Republicans, who sought control of Congress and eventually the White House, set about enlarging the exchange relationship between their party and conservative donors. Looked at one way, this was a politically farsighted arrangement; looked at another way, it was signing a pact with the Tempter, bearing the usual consequences besides prosperity in the immediate term. Abetted for a time by House Speaker Newt Gingrich's famous subpact, the "Contract with America," the Republican Party began syndicating its institutional prospects to achieve outsized ideological gains.[13] The new relationship was also eagerly embraced by publicly unpopular business sectors, ranging from the insurance lobby—then actively trying to protect itself from reform of the health care finance system—to the increasingly Republican-allied tobacco industry.[14] Capitalizing on early Clinton fumbles that helped turn the faithful out to vote and demoralized some Democratic groups, Gingrich gained control of Congress in 1994, the final stage of a decades-long staggered realignment as the South finally went decisively Republican.

After the election of 1994, the Gingrich Congress attempted a sharp rightward legislative shift. But the public, resentful at Gingrich's dramatic policy lurches and especially put off by House Republicans' shutdown of the government in the winter of 1995–1996, backed Clinton's low-key resistance. The presidential veto, and an effective Senate filibuster,[15] helped defeat legislative action on almost all aspects of the conservative agenda, and Clinton easily won reelection in 1996. He had temporarily staved off his party's cash-poor position by tolerating greater dependence on the new tack of raising "soft money."[16] And with a 1997 fiscal compromise that enacted a capital gains tax cut paid for by some cuts in food stamps and Medicare provider payments and that underfunded welfare reform, Clinton gave the conservative economic base a slice of what it wanted. This reflected the limits on President Clinton's willingness to lead, for what he signed made no progress toward meeting the nation's enormous long-term liabilities for Medicare and Social Security that loom as the baby boom generation nears retirement beginning in 2011. The "comeback kid" was not thinking at his best when he had a chance to lead forward. Still, his 1997 deal remained within the traditional, relatively centrist Budget Act approach of cutting taxes only when also cutting spending for balance in the budget.

In Texas then governor Bush's record from 1994 to 2000[17] foreshadowed how he would advance the domestic causes of his conservative economic base once he became president. Bush mobilized business interests politically (and financially) by undermining environmental and other public interest protections in exchange for support. He did not forget his immensely wealthy far-right backers. Thomas O. Hicks, who threw Bush a personal fortune with the sweetheart Texas Rangers deal, received (according to a series of front-page articles running periodically in the *Houston Chronicle* at least through late 2002) the lucrative placement of a third of the $1.7 billion in so-called private equity investments of the University of Texas trust funds.[18] In a simper move, Bush grandfathered the worst (and most grateful) Texas air polluters by winning passage of a fig leaf of voluntary standards.[19] All this Bush's lawyers concealed from the public as best they could.[20]

For conservative causes, no source of power matters more than this burgeoning exchange of campaign fund-raising for conservative policy action. By the 2000s, meanwhile, the escalating election expense of television advertising put unheard-of levels of fund-raising to use—$529 million and $1.05 billion to fund ads for the 2000 presidential and congressional elections, respectively (up from $331 million and $659 million, respectively, in 1992).[21] Most of the big money came from those who had it. Of the $2.5 billion privately raised for all the 2000 campaign activities, $912 million came from large individual donations (over $200), $498 million from (mostly corporate) soft money, and $267 million from political action committees—with the rest (approximately $823 million) primarily from the candidates' own funds or small donations.[22] As Kevin Phillips summed up in *Wealth and Democracy*, "Some three-quarters of the individual money that fueled turn-of-the-century presidential and congressional races came from donors with incomes over $200,000 a year (in essence, the top 1–1.5%)."[23]

Bush's opponent in 2000, Vice President Al Gore, had made the environment one of his principal concerns both as a senator and as vice president and had a long legislative record in the area of privacy rights as well. Bush had to face the dislike of centrist voters for quite different policies favored by his conservative campaign backers. So on these issues of top public concern he made campaign promises in 2000: he would regulate the principal atmospheric agent implicated in global warming, carbon dioxide emissions from the burning of fossil fuels, and he would protect the privacy of individual medical records from business abuse.[24] While Bush knew his own record to be suspect in both areas, he made implied concessions by campaigning on slogans like "I'm a privacy-rights person" and "The marketplace can function without sacrificing the privacy of individuals."[25]

If the ordinary mechanisms at a president's disposal were the only means Bush had, his extraordinarily narrow victory in 2000 might have cramped him greatly in dealing with domestic affairs. But for his vice president's tie-breaking vote, Bush entered office with no majority in the Senate. Even two years later, the razor-thin 51–49 Republican majority would not have sustained his attempts to pass the controversial ideological legislation sought by his conservative base; it came nowhere near the required sixty votes for cloture on most issues. Moreover, Bush risked a public backlash if he took visible, highly controversial action, just as Reagan found in 1982 and Clinton, for relatively limited attempts, found in 1995–1996. In the end, his ability to deliver for right-wing domestic causes over the long term depended on something special: the political uses of law.

REGRESSIVE TAX CUTS VIA ABUSE OF THE BUDGET ACT

President Bush's made his domestic policy mark with his trillion-dollar tax cut for the higher income brackets in 2001, followed by another regressive cut in 2003.[26] Ordinarily, such controversial fiscal legislation faces the same Senate procedures as other bills, requiring sixty votes for cloture to overcome organized partisan filibuster resistance.[27] However, when Congress enacted the 1974 Budget Act to coordinate taxes and spending in annual budget resolutions, a key provision, section 310, also provided that such resolutions could contain "reconciliation instructions." These would facilitate the enactment of a deficit-reducing reconciliation bill, such as a package of spending cuts and tax increases, by precluding measures that would ordinarily trigger Senate filibusters.[28] Under section 310 a simple Senate majority can overcome resistance to pass even a controversial deficit-reducing package.

The 1974 act and its implementation over two decades remained faithful to the centrist congressional position—taxes could not be cut by reconciliation without raising other taxes or making spending cuts. In 1981 President Reagan used reconciliation only to pass his spending cut bill, not his tax cut bill (albeit the bogus accounting and sweeteners in the reconciliation spending cut bill indirectly helped the atmospherics for the tax cut bill). It was Reagan's political mandate from his decisive 1980 election victory and Senate coattails, and his strategy (i.e., Senate majority leader Baker's and Budget chair Pete Domenici's [R-N.M.]) of moving first a bill that cut spending, that got his tax cut through the Senate with no filibuster.[29]

In 1993 President Clinton, building on his predecessor's 1990 foundation, pushed through a controversial tax rate increase for top tax brackets. As political scientist Keith Krehbiel wrote, "Republicans undoubtedly would have filibustered the Clinton-Democratic reconciliation bill if they had been permitted to do so. But they weren't, so they didn't."[30] They could not filibuster because the 1993 tax increase greatly reduced the deficit and hence could honestly pass the Senate by reconciliation, which precluded filibuster.[31] In contrast, at the same time, President Clinton requested an economic stimulus bill that was not designed to reduce the deficit and that Senate Republicans could and did stall to death for lack of sixty votes for cloture. The same fate—death by Senate Republican filibuster—befell other mildly progressive Clinton agenda items, including campaign finance reform, a restriction of strikebreaking by permanent replacement of strikers, and lobbying disclosure.[32]

From 1995 on, the new, harder-edged congressional conservatives increasingly disdained budget balancing and made cutting upper-bracket taxes per se their cynosure, even if such cuts would go unfunded by accompanying spending cuts.[33] In 1999 and 2000 the Senate passed more large tax cut bills without corresponding savings, although centrist voters actually showed little enthusiasm for these and President Clinton's opposition prevented enactment.[34] Although these efforts failed, Senate conservatives had quietly laid the foundation for their new strategy of abusing the reconciliation provision in order to move unpaid-for tax cuts without having the necessary votes (i.e., without the necessary public support).[35]

Still, as President Bush started his term in January 2001, passing the trillion-dollar tax cut for the rich that he sought presented his party with a daunting task. His controversial passage to power and weak mandate from the 2000 election had shrunk Republican numbers in the Senate by five, from fifty-five two years earlier to a bare fifty.[36] And, as the bursting of the stock market bubble in 2000 increasingly factored into economic models, Bush's 1999 campaign hopes that he'd have large federal surpluses to give away became each day more and more out of touch with rational economic projection. So Senate passage of an outsized cut could not possibly depend on actual public support or actual Senate votes; more than ever, it must depend on the abuse of reconciliation.

The tax legislating process of 2001 began with a general debate in January and February as President Bush's vague oversized campaign promises had to get put before the Senate's unyielding budget processes, the rock on which presidential fantasies so often founder. On February 15 Senator Robert Byrd (D-W.Va.), the Senate's dean of procedure (his multivolume Senate history overflows with his love for and mastery of procedure) delivered a detailed address in which he argued forcefully that "there is no reason whatever to consider the President's tax cut proposal as a reconciliation bill." He explained, "What I believe most Senators fe[el] in their hearts . . . [is that] forcing deficit reduction [through] . . . should be the sole reason for using the highly restricted vehicle called reconciliation."[37] Byrd gave an extraordinary insider's account of why neither of two controversial past initiatives (President Reagan's 1981 [successful] tax cut and President Clinton's [unsuccessful] 1994 health care bill) had received, nor could have received, reconciliation treatment.[38] Anyone who knows the Senate knows that Byrd was unanswerable; after all, he had personally edited the 1974 budget act's reconciliation provision, and its 1982 tune-up is known in the Senate for obvious reasons as the "Byrd Rule." The Senate, especially as to its most august procedure of filibuster and cloture, is not some circus of trained performing seals. This is the most powerful deliberative body in the world and one that had, at that moment in 2001, the most ultraprecarious of 50–50 party splits—a split actually on the verge of flipping to 51–49 against Bush.

Following the president's budget proposal, the House enacted the main proposed cut to top-bracket rates.[39] In the Senate the Budget Committee chair, Senator Pete Domenici (R-N.M.)—a man respected on both sides of the aisle but who, in the crunch, knew to which side he owed his chair— brought his party's version of the budget resolution directly to the Senate floor.[40] Then, however, Senate Republicans discovered to their horror that they had lost their legal excuse to use reconciliation. At the key procedural juncture, the Senate parliamentarian, Robert Dove, declined to sanction the party's first plan for cutting taxes by multiple reconciliation bills.[41]

Senate conservatives, however, were in no mood to accept this. So Chairman Domenici muscled the reconciliation instructions through by a 51–49 vote virtually on party lines, employing a crude method depending only on such partisan power and not on the legitimacy of the parliamentarian giving sanction from the chair.[42] Soon thereafter Senate majority leader Trent Lott (R-Miss.) discharged the Senate parliamentarian—a phenomenon never before seen in the Senate (or for that matter, even in the House).[43] In baseball terms, it was akin to permanently sacking an unquestionably neutral umpire just for making one important honest call against the home team. It had never happened before in these United States.[44] Dove's dismissal was all the more shocking since this particular parliamentarian had provided decades of exemplary service and had a long record of demonstrating ample sensitivity to Senate Republican concerns.[45]

Under the budget resolution's instructions, the tax cut bill soon came to the Senate floor, where several moderate Republicans joined almost all of the Democrats in trying to make the bill less extreme. It was at this point that Bush's supporters used the full procedural clout of reconciliation. They could maximize the bill's benefits for the wealthy and not even bother to seek consensus with the otherwise crucial moderates of their own party. Senator John McCain (R-Ariz.) and several Republican moderates mounted a valiant but doomed effort to amend the bill to mildly reduce tax relief for the wealthiest bracket and benefit some in the middle class. The bill then passed the Senate, heading into conference on May 23.

MAY 25 AND 26, 2001:
THE MISGUIDED CONFERENCE PRODUCT

Since the Senate was divided 50–50, from January to May of 2001, even as strong a partisan as Senate majority leader Trent Lott had respected the rule of equal party memberships on standing committees. But now that rule got broken for President Bush's tax cut bill; Senate Republicans stacked the conference delegation going to meet with House colleagues.[46] The Republican-dominated committee moved at lightning speed, finishing the entire trillion-dollar comprehensive rewrite in two days. It placed its conference report before the House for adoption on May 25 and before the Senate, under the juggernaut of reconciliation procedures limiting debate to ten hours, the next day. Those two days shook the fiscal world by setting several different historic records: (1) for largest number of hundreds of billions of dollars given away, (2) for smallest number of minutes devoted to giving away each of those billions of dollars, (3) for the narrowest focus of a gigantic giveaway on just the wealthiest individuals, and (4) for the greatest concentration of money-policy power in the hands of the fewest (conservative) leaders. To paraphrase Winston Churchill, never before had the power to give so much to those already so well off been exercised by so few—and so fast.

The conference committee had performed unprecedented stunts for President Bush's chief cause. First and most important, it had simply helped him, at the nation's expense, to 10 percent greater tax cuts than either the budget resolution or the Senate bill had approved. The conference tax cut included an extra $130 billion over the first nine years. Nominally it then met its ten-year ceiling of $1.3 trillion by appearing to allow rates to zoom all the way back to prelegislation levels in that tenth year— a crude device, which came to be known as "early sunsetting," that conveyed only the illusion that the tax cuts respected the budget resolution's vital ceiling. Even jaded and cynical contemporary observers upon first meeting this new phenomenon expressed amazement at these "outright frauds."[47]

Second, the conference also phased out, as of 2005, the bill's limited relief for the payers of the ultracomplex alternative minimum tax (AMT). This will receive more discussion later in this chapter, as it influences future prospects. What is relevant here is that the AMT happens to spare taxpayers mainly in states that backed Bush in 2000 while pounding tax-payers in the other states; as *Tax Notes* summed up the matter, not providing AMT relief meant "no tax cuts for the Gore states."[48]

Third, the conference committee had to resolve the tension between the huge scale of President Bush's ongoing desires and the limits, pushed back as they were, of what the Senate had voted. It did so by phasing some cuts in late and phasing out others early. For example, the conference phased in early $138 billion in estate and gift tax relief targeted to the wealthiest taxpayers and $420 billion in income tax rate reductions *solely* for those in the top brackets. Meanwhile, the conference phased out small benefits to middle-income taxpayers, such as the deduction for higher education in 2005. This program had cost only $10 billion. It phased in slowly the married-taxpayer benefits, diluting further that relatively meager relief. Social conservatives helped only one–high earner ("traditional") couples, not two-earner ("working wife") ones.[49] Later studies confirmed the extraordinarily regressive nature of the 2001 tax cut. Whereas four-fifths of all taxpayers would receive nothing more after a single credit the first tax year, by the final year of 2010, of $234 billion in tax cuts, more than half—$121 billion—would go just to the richest 1 percent of the population.[50]

All three feats had been made possible by abuse of the Budget Act's reconciliation provision, which had been passed in good faith by a previous generation of lawmakers. Surely those who created and adjusted the reconciliation provision in an attempt to streamline deficit control processes could never have imagined, much less intended, this kind of abuse. While the 2001 tax cut received enormous publicity, the arcane nature of congressional budget procedure guaranteed—as the White House knew it would—that very little of this public discussion, even by the most sophisticated observers who yet lacked deep background in Congress's inner workings, would recognize how this manipulation could deliver on such a scale to President Bush's wealthiest supporters.[51]

2003

After the giant 2001 giveaway, the federal government's fiscal cupboard seemed pretty bare. Soon after the tax cut, even the spurious prior projections of a budget surplus, inflated to provide the bill's justification, quickly vanished. Enactment of tax cuts then took a year off in 2002.[52] But when President Bush's party regained a 51–49 Senate majority in November 2002, he once again insisted on a large tax cut bill. In 2003, with the Iraq war and occupation (whose cost the Bush administration refused to quantify) about to begin, a large tax cut for the top brackets seemed even less likely to pass muster with the public than it had in 2001. By now, Americans had suffered through two years of economic recession and the subsequent Bush "jobless recovery." The kind of tax cut President Bush had in mind, notwithstanding his rhetoric to the contrary, would do little to create jobs. Economists observed that Bush's proposed tax cut (apart from the camouflaging pittance of a child tax credit) would go to people who were unlikely to spend it immediately. Rather than stimulating the economy, it would simply shift savings: the rich would have more; the rest of the American public, less. And the national debt would rocket past the gargantuan $7 trillion level.[53] The Reagan fiscal package of 1981 had inflicted the economic misery of 1982 by taking from the poor and giving to the rich without useful economic stimulation. The Bush fiscal packages of 2001 and then 2003 played a large part in the economic misery of 2002–2004, for much the same reason.[54]

Once again President Bush was demanding an unfunded and economically unhelpful tax cut, and once again he would drive it through the Senate the same way. He would not seek by consensus or negotiation the necessary sixty votes, which would have required concessions like more assistance that would help the jobless and the states with their desperate budgets and actually stimulate the economy. Rather, he would drive it through by abusing the Budget Act's reconciliation provision. This mattered more than ever. Bush could no longer pretend a massive surplus just lay there in the Treasury to justify a big giveaway. This time the giveaway would be smaller, and he felt he must skew it even more completely to benefit only the very wealthiest taxpayers. He insisted on making it a cut mainly in taxes on corporate dividends. In a country where the middle class holds the bulk of its assets in its home equity and even the upper middle class holds most of its stock in tax-deferred pension plans, hardly anyone besides true millionaires receives substantial streams of taxable corporate dividends from stocks.[55] The guiding rule in understanding politics is always to ask: who benefits? And then: who serves them? And, what do they get in return? On this one a Sherlock Holmes is not needed.

Even with his abuse of the reconciliation provision, however, Bush faced a potential political struggle. He still had to gain fifty Senate votes for a tax cut priced nominally at a ceiling of $350 billion yet aimed solely at the country's wealthiest people.[56] Though the proposed cut would be the third largest in history (after Reagan's in 1981 and Bush's own in 2001),[57] its potential to look like a giveaway to the wealthy made congressional leaders nervous. Once again Bush must use early sunsetting to maintain the illusion that the maxed-out tax cut would fit under a budget ceiling.[58] Congressional leaders used the $124 billion available for the dividend tax cut to slash the tax rate way down in the near term, 2003–2006, to 15 percent, less than half the top income tax bracket. This giant rate cut could fit the $124 billion limit only by sunsetting early, on paper, in 2007. The proposition cleared the Senate only when Vice President Cheney cast his crucial vote, breaking the Senate's 50–50 tie.[59]

The conference used the Senate's ceiling figure but honored the desires of Majority Leader Tom DeLay in shaping the cuts. Ironically, with President Bush's own blessing, the bill's congressional backers discarded his original "double taxation" pretext.[60] In similar fashion, while Bush noisily used the child tax credit (though worth only $32 billion) to tout his budget in public, the small allowance was denied to those working poor who paid Social Security taxes but no other (income) taxes and hence receive tax credits only when refundable; this credit wasn't refundable. If the early sunset device did not actually lead to the tax cuts expiring and President Bush or like-minded lawmakers later kept them in effect, the cost to the government in lost revenue through 2013, estimated under various scenarios at $800 billion to $1.0 trillion.[61] And, putting the misery aside and just looking at the debt burden, it soon became evident the national debt burden from the combined 2001 and 2003 tax cuts fell hardest on middle-income taxpayers, who would bear over $6 of federal debt, with the interest charges, for each single dollar of their own tax savings.[62] No legal ploy could have contradicted—or abused—more glaringly the central original and continuing intent of the bipartisan Budget Act of 1974, to facilitate deficit control bills only. I examine the likely effects of such abuse later in this chapter and again in the book's conclusions.

ROLLBACK OF POPULAR CLINTON INITIATIVES

Bush had used nontraditional means to do what might have seemed unthinkable immediately after the disputed 2000 election: reversing his popular (if controversial) predecessor's prudent fiscal policy and delivering two massive tax cuts for the nation's wealthiest citizens, thus delivering a huge gift to the economic base that had gotten him elected. It is worth noting that Bush accomplished these and other domestic policy feats of legal black magic against a backdrop of Clinton initiatives that had left Bush an unusual political challenge.[63] President Clinton had maintained extraordinary political support, doing better in the second-term off-year congressional elections of 1998 than any predecessor in that spot in a century and a half. Despite his wretched Monica Lewinsky affair and all its fallout, he maintained high ratings with the public—both on issues and performance—to the very end.[64] In contrast to previous White House party changes in 1977, 1981, and 1993, when the new president came in relatively strong, Bush had lost the popular vote, entered office with a substantially negative coattail effect in the Senate, and taken positions that polls showed as lacking in public support. So in his last months in office President Clinton found himself, amazingly, the opposite of a lame duck president. He had ample political support for his last round of highly popular domestic legacy initiatives, such as protecting a million acres of important Western public lands by declaring them national monuments.

Bush had to anticipate the problems in launching direct assaults against those Clinton initiatives; at the very least, such unpopular steps would open him to immediate oversight in Congress, and the precarious 50–50 Senate balance—not that far from becoming 51–49 against him—had to make him wary. But the use and abuse of legal technicalities provided the answer to his conundrum. Some of Clinton's legacy initiatives were easily placed in limbo through a nuanced legal trick, later dubbed the "Card Moratorium."[65] The new president's chief of staff, Andrew Card, issued a memorandum freezing all regulations that had been put forth but had not yet taken effect. Tactically, the memorandum used the president's legal power over administrative activity to seize control of the timing and nature of implementation, without any distinct confirmation that he would overrule the regulations; they just drifted off, without government acknowledgement, into the night and fog. Since Bush thereby obscured whether he would reverse any particular one of the Clinton initiatives, any early negative reaction—either from the public or Democrats—was blunted; opponents could not organize a fight as long as the president might still implement the plans.

And some of the measures—like Clinton's national monument designations—proved so high-profile and popular with the public that Bush did indeed allow them to take effect.[66] But most did not enjoy this fate. Instead, the Bush administration eventually either watered down or stealthily discarded them, following enough delay for the press and the public to begin to forget about them. It was a brilliant if cynical device; by starting with a tentative moratorium rather than a definite rollback, the Bush administration stretched out and shrouded its ultimate actions, minimizing negative fallout. Decisions and announcements would occur piecemeal over the next year or more, making public reaction and congressional oversight harder to mobilize.[67]

The fate of several major late Clinton initiatives, particularly medical privacy, warrants close examination.[68] In 1996 Congress had addressed the rising tide of public concern about a huge loss of privacy in medical record keeping by inserting a key provision in the Kennedy-Kassebaum Act, also known as the Health Insurance Portability and Accountability Act (HIPAA).[69] That provision established federal protection of the privacy of personal medical records. Medical confidences between patients and physicians, even about the most sensitive of subjects, increasingly had fallen under the control of big corporate health services and insurers, and these corporations saw profit in commercial exploitation of those confidences. In HIPAA Congress directed the federal Department of Health and Human Services (HHS) to implement privacy protection through regulation. After four years of consideration, in December 2000 HHS proposed as one of the major late Clinton initiatives a tolerably strong health privacy rule.[70]

President Bush did not try, at first, to undo the privacy rule completely; indeed, he allowed it to move forward.[71] As its centerpiece the new regulation required health care providers to obtain written consent from patients before using their personal health information for various ostensibly care-related or administrative purposes. The regulation also put limits on use and disclosure of patient records for "marketing," which it defined in an inclusive way. Bush waited until March 2002 and then reversed his earlier course, proposing that the consent requirement be dropped.[72] Moreover, his new proposal opened a major loophole in the definition of restricted marketing use.[73] The psychiatric profession in particular rose up in arms about this forfeiture of privacy. Therapists warned such uses would severely impair their efforts to reassure patients, who would have to fear that the most sacred of confidences and diagnoses would be broadcast on corporate money-making loudspeakers. Senator Kennedy's committee held an April 2002 hearing at which senators and experts harshly criticized this reversal, but without political effect.[74]

The privacy rollback signified the success, by March 2002, of President Bush's series of legal tactics. He had positioned himself popularly on the privacy issue while running as a candidate in 2000 and then, in 2001, found the route to temporize through administrative law tactics. By 2002, having achieved heightened popularity as the symbol of an embattled nation, he had the cover he needed to serve his conservative economic base more aggressively. It was then, through delay and subterfuge, that he chose to roll back Clinton's popular reform of leaks in medical privacy regulations. Now President Bush could, and did, assist corporate health care providers' and insurers' increasing their revenues by playing fast and loose with the confidentiality of the public's personal medical information. Not surprisingly, these same entities became big spenders in Republican campaign advertising in 2002 and thereafter in ways strongly benefiting Bush's own political efforts—displaying at its most effective the mutual alliance for conservative causes. The same industries, served in 2003–2004 by camouflaged siphoning of Medicare's resources to them via the drug benefit act, would spend with abandon on Bush's 2004 reelection.

Bush turned to quite a different method to roll back another popular Clinton legacy: an occupational health rule intended to limit exposure to ergonomic injuries for about twenty-seven million workers.[75] The Occupational Safety and Health Administration (OSHA) had spent a decade, starting with the first Bush administration, studying repetitive-motion injuries on the job such as carpal tunnel syndrome. In November 2000 OSHA promulgated its new rule—one with enormous support from workers who feared such injuries but frequently had no standing to bargain with their own employers on the subject. The OSHA rule aroused intense opposition from employer groups, particularly those with the worst workplace conditions—another of the many well-funded and powerful set of semi-outcast industries who were part of George W. Bush's core constituency. After seeing President Bush's weak 2000 election results, congressional Republicans quietly decided not to burden the incoming President Bush with the political responsibility for killing the rule.[76] Instead, in early 2001 the most conservative members of the congressional Republican leadership, working closely with industry lobbyists, mounted a drive themselves, initially keeping it secret. Ordinarily, they might have anticipated an eventual countereffort to stop them, first at the committee level and later, if necessary, by Senate filibuster. But this time conservative Republicans made surprise use—its first—of a statute bequeathed by the 1995–1996 "Contract with America," the Congressional Review Act.[77]

After below-the-radar preparation, conservative senators filed a disapproval petition for the ergonomics rule on March 1, 2001.[78] In a lightning strike, they brought the disapproval resolution to the Senate floor without new committee hearings or meetings, where it achieved victory by a bare 56–44 margin on March 6. The narrow win revealed that without the manipulative expediency the Congressional Review Act afforded, a Senate filibuster would have stalled or defeated the move. The House floor victory vote came the next day. In just one week of swift combat, President Bush's business supporters had won a major victory, killing a public interest regulation with broad potential support, a law embodying a decade of steady, patient, mildly progressive bipartisan effort to spare, at modest cost, tens of millions of working Americans the pain of work-related injury. As further window dressing for this Congressional Review Act subterfuge, Bush eventually proposed, thirteen months later, a set of merely voluntary ergonomics guidelines.

Molly Ivins and Lou Dubose have explored just who in the administration was in charge of the legal scheming and maneuvering to assure that the employers with the worst workplaces got full value from President Bush for supporting him.[79] The Bush Labor Department assigned the issue to Eugene Scalia, a brilliant attorney whose father is Justice Antonin Scalia. Gene came from Ted Olson's firm. Gene's specialty is what he calls "labor law"—that is, what he does for employers of the nature just described.[80]

Even after demonstrating such creativity with the legal weapons at his disposal, President Bush did take a significant hit when his effort to roll back another late Clinton initiative became too public. This was his hugely unpopular attempt to reject a Clinton policy attempting to control arsenic levels in drinking water.[81] Overall, the first four months of 2001 brought a resurgence of broadcast news coverage of environmental policy. This coverage portrayed President Bush's anti-environment positions starkly despite his use of legal tools like the Card Moratorium to obscure the situation.[82]

But not every environmental issue had the sinister ring of arsenic in drinking water. In time the Bush administration found its stride when it came to consistently delivering what its conservative constituents wanted: increased exploitation of public lands and resources and the evasion of pollution controls. Bush had to, and did, find means other than open discussions between the executive branch and Congress to bring his initiatives to fruition, ways to evade Senate confrontation and media scrutiny. Bush achieved great success on two issues concerning energy and the environment—power plant pollution and global warming—by relying on the law rather than open debate. Governor Bush had made an important campaign promise in 2000 of a national program to require old electric plants to reduce emissions.[83] It was a pledge he honored in the breach.

The director of EPA's regulatory enforcement resigned in public protest in March 2002, commenting that forthcoming White House–drafted rules "would turn narrow exemptions into larger loopholes."[84] The new rules, mislabeled as a "Clean Skies" initiative, soon materialized, and they struck the most sweeping blow in a decade at controls on industrial air pollution.[85] As he did in undermining other Clinton legacy initiatives, including environmental rules, Bush used a variety of legal powers that obviated the need for congressional action and obfuscated so as to impede congressional oversight and public objection. In this case, the maneuvers included raising pollution baselines, estimating future pollution levels in a way that lowered the figures, and creating a variety of options and exceptions by which pollution control requirements could be avoided.[86] And once again, timing was everything. Although Bush shaped this program early in 2002, he kept his plan nonfinal until the eve of Thanksgiving 2002, just after the midterm election, when he formally implemented the new rules.[87]

As for global warming President Bush used a combination of strategies, nullifying international law when possible and imposing secrecy as a matter of course, especially when criticism seemed to come from within the administration. As a presidential candidate Governor Bush had had to deflect public attention from his poor environmental record in Texas by endorsing reduction in emissions of the main greenhouse gas, carbon dioxide, which is produced by (among other sources) utilities burning coal and oil.[88] Now, with Bush in the White House, his EPA administrator, former New Jersey governor Christine Todd Whitman, appeared at a February 2001 hearing before a subcommittee of the Senate Environment Committee, the nation's leading oversight forum on the issue, and formally announced the policy of regulating carbon dioxide as a pollutant. Subsequently, Senator John Kerry (D-Mass.) won acceptance in the budget resolution formulation process of an amendment for long-term substantial funding of global warming countermeasures.[89]

However, President Bush forcibly overturned Whitman's position, preferring serving his conservative causes over allowing her to fulfill his campaign pledge. In March 2001 he announced in an open letter to four Republican senators that, using the Kyoto Treaty as a scapegoat, he would not designate carbon dioxide as a pollutant.[90] Only in February 2002 did he finally unveil his long-awaited alternative, a proposal for voluntarily reducing so-called "greenhouse gas intensity," the ratio of greenhouse gas emissions to energy produced. It was a thinly veiled decision to do nothing serious at all.[91] In June 2002 the State Department projected that American emissions of carbon dioxide would rise by 43 percent by 2020, suggesting, according to the best scientific thinking, a serious risk within the lifetime of our children of climatic changes at a level some would consider catastrophic.[92] Yet Bush continued to oppose the meaningful action he had pledged in 2000.[93] Rather, he distorted the government's own statements on global warming, forcing the issue out of EPA reports on air pollution and the environment in September 2002 and June 2003.[94]

INTERIOR SECRETARY NORTON
AND PUBLIC LAND EXPLOITATION

President Bush's interior secretary, Gale A. Norton, personified the overall stealth legal strategy of the administration's anti-environmentalism. Her career connects the prior quarter century's incubation of the conservative approach with the course taken by governor and then president Bush, warranting some study of her background. As a young law school graduate in 1979, Norton found herself recruited by the head of the energy industry–funded Mountain States Legal Foundation (MSLF), James Watt. Watt was just months away from becoming President Reagan's first interior secretary, so Watt was as useful a mentor as the young lawyer could have hoped for. Norton became a dedicated combination of true believer and legal schemer for the anti-environmental position.[95] When President Reagan tapped Watt for interior secretary, Norton took his place in leading MSLF's opposition to required reclamation after strip mining.[96] In 1985–1987 she worked in the Interior Department's legal wing on opening the Arctic National Wildlife Refuge (ANWR) to drilling. In 1991 she ran for and won the office of attorney general of Colorado (later she lost a race for the U.S. Senate). She used her power to slash the office's environmental budget by a third and to attack the Endangered Species Act as unconstitutional.[97]

Subsequently, in private legal practice, Norton lobbied lucratively for the big lead-paint company linked with toxic waste and children's lead poisoning. She cofounded, along with famous Washington right-wing leader Grover Norquist,[98] a group (the Council of Republicans for Environmental Advocacy) that gave unwarranted environmental credentialing to party figures more properly considered anti-environmental, adding a new term to the lexicon, *greenwashing*.[99] During the 2000 campaign, she advised Governor Bush on camouflaging his Texas environmental record.

This was the person Bush chose to be interior secretary, a position historically considered the steward of the nation's natural treasures.[100] The Republican Party, notwithstanding its business base, had a conservationist impulse going back to the celebrated efforts of President Theodore Roosevelt, as well as such officials as President Nixon's interior secretaries, Walter Hickel and Rogers C. B. Morton, both former elected officials who dealt relatively reasonably with the early modern environmental movement. Only in the last two decades, as Richard J. Lazarus has ably documented, have Republican administrations turned hard away from environmentalism in the law.[101]

President Bush's selection of Norton capped his government-wide strategy of appointing industry lawyer-lobbyists for key environmental posts.[102] At the top, this started in the White House with the head of the Council on Environmental Quality, James Connaughton, a lawyer with a lucrative practice representing polluters. To be Norton's deputy secretary Bush appointed J. Steven Griles, a coal and oil lobbyist who later got into ethics mischief in helping his old drilling clients with some particularly harmful projects.[103] The Interior Department posts of top lawyer, top mining official, and top water official, went to lawyer-lobbyists representing, respectively, corporate grazing, mining, and water-exploiting interests.[104]

Tracing the record of just one of Norton's crew, the top Interior lawyer, William G. Myers III, shows their zeal in action. Myers had devoted his career to grazing- and mining-industry lobbying, condemning California wilderness protection as "legislative hubris" and public land protection as "tyrannical."[105] Pressed at a Senate hearing in February 2004 to explain these statements, even he admitted to being "bombastic."[106] In office, Myers met with his cattle lobbyist friends to reverse regulations against public land overgrazing, rules that had passed Supreme Court review with unanimous approval. For such a meeting, Myers was officially investigated for allegedly violating the solemn agreement, which he necessarily signed to enter office, pledging he would not hold such meetings.[107] When Myers reversed a Clinton administration legal opinion so as to approve a huge open-pit gold mine in Imperial County, California, a federal judge in turn reversed Myers because this would, contrary to law, "unduly harm . . . the public lands."[108] Having been concededly bombastic in his anti-environmental statements, legally wrong, and allegedly unethical apparently did not set him back unduly in President Bush's eyes, for Bush nominated him to the high U.S. Court of Appeals for the Ninth Circuit in 2003 and pressed the nomination forward in 2004.

Norton wasted little time in putting her talents and her staff to use. In March 2001 she suspended Clinton regulations that protected public lands subjected to hard-rock mining, rules that had become final just five months before, after years of preparation.[109] She also moved quickly to allow oil exploration and development leases in sensitive areas such as off the coasts and on fragile public lands.[110] In June 2002 she announced this offshore policy for California, the Gore state with a Democratic governor, but not for Florida, where the president's brother faced reelection.[111] A year later, in the summer of 2003, she relented about California, but only if the state cared to buy out the offshore leases itself: an obviously painful burden to the squeezed Sacramento state treasury. Once again, she imposed no such burden on Florida.[112] As President Bush launched his drive to open the Alaska refuge to drilling, Norton joined the White House in using one of its favorite tactics—controlling the timing—to delay release of information about the plans until after the November 2002 election.

Nor was Interior the only cabinet-level department to take action against environmental regulation and serve President Bush's conservative backers. In the Agriculture Department, the administration installed a timber industry lawyer-lobbyist as undersecretary with responsibility for forest management.[113] Under Mark Rey the Forest Service stepped away from defending the Clinton administration's protective rules for roadless areas, prompting both the chief and deputy chief of the Forest Service to resign.[114] After stealthy preparation, in December 2002 the Bush administration moved forward on a massive speeding-up of forest cutting.[115] It was the same at EPA, where former industry lawyer-lobbyists served in top posts—from deputy administrator, to air and radiation administrator, to the official in charge of toxins and pesticides—implementing programs affecting their former clients.[116]

USING JUDICIAL CONSERVATISM

This growing cadre of industry lobbyists-cum–environmental "stewards" couldn't have been nearly as effective as the president desired had they not found sympathetic allies in the courts. Here, as in so many other policy realms, the accumulating conservative appointments on the federal district and especially the appellate benches, and the consolidation of a conservative bloc of five justices on the Supreme Court, created opportunities for serving conservative interests—in this case, industries opposed to environmental regulation. They were further abetted by a valued collaborator, formerly a lawyer with many industry clients, who now managed the Justice Department's environmental litigation.[117]

One important example of cozy relations between the anti-environment cabinet secretaries and the conservative judiciary concerned the "mountaintop removal" mining method, typically proposed as a cheap means to exploit narrow coal seams in the Appalachian region of Kentucky and West Virginia.[118] If permitted, mining companies blast the tops off mountains, burying whole streams under the dumped rubble, which can sometimes result in an environmental disaster. In the first round of courtroom battles early in the Bush administration, a district court ruled in a lawsuit filed against West Virginia state officials that the practice violated federal law. However, the conservative activist Fourth Circuit, employing one of the doctrines pushed by the five-justice conservative bloc on the Supreme Court, held such state officials immune from such a suit.[119]

In a second round, in May 2002 the Bush administration approved the wholesale permission-granting policy for mountaintop removal rejected by its predecessor administration. Environmentalists tried to fight this unprecedented action, and a federal judge promptly ruled for the environmentalists and enjoined the new policy, strongly criticizing the administration. However, in 2003 the Fourth Circuit intervened again to reverse this, dismally demonstrating the Bush administration's ability to play the trump card of the conservative activist judiciary.[120]

SIGNIFICANCE OF ELECTION-YEAR DEVELOPMENTS

A prosecutorial investigation in Texas, as well as a report in the *New York Times*, revealed in 2004 how the right wing had used corrupt campaign financing to overpower majoritarian democracy. Through this funding scheme, DeLay had installed Tom Craddick as the Speaker of the Texas House so he could perform a re-redistricting to purge the U.S. House delegation of Democrats.[121] Bush's Republican National Committee apparently served as a classic Watergate-style money laundry: corporations donated huge sums to the RNC, and the RNC, in turn, wrote checks in the same exact sums, apparently per DeLay's instructions, to particular Craddick supporters. Bush's RNC and DeLay's aide lamely explained they had no record of, and could "not recall," this—a warm-up for the RNC to play similar games of coordination and laundering of conservative funding, covered in similarly amnesiac style, for Bush himself in 2004.[122]

Few of Bush's measures better revealed the conservative agenda in domestic affairs than those subverting both Social Security and Medicare for short-term election advantage. For Social Security Bush aimed to make his reelection both a confirmation of the conservative myth that Social Security inherently faces a contemporary insolvency crisis and a popular mandate to "rescue" the program through privatization.[123] In early 2004 Federal Reserve Chairman Alan Greenspan said what Bush had tried to keep quiet: that the problem loomed only for those who believed top-bracket earners should get off scot-free and that benefit cuts and delays in the retirement age were the only feasible solutions. Bush moved in that direction, not by admitting to the plan to have the nonrich do all the sacrificing, but by helping the rich alone: section 233 of the November 2003 Medicare legislation had shoved billions of tax giveaways for the upper brackets into virtually unregulated "health savings accounts." Now the Treasury Department renewed for 2004 its espousal of similar top-bracket bonanzas called "annual lifetime and retirement savings accounts"; these, together with privatized Social Security accounts, would put wealthy individuals onto their own gilded track and leave the majority of working families carrying the burdens and the cuts.[124]

The immediate payoff for Bush from advocating Social Security privatization came in the huge campaign assistance from Wall Street firms anticipating billions in profits from managing individual accounts. A subtext to the Republicans' decision to hold their September 2004 convention in New York City, where many residents might despise Bush for his hypocritical campaign use of 9/11, may be the feeling of the financiers hosting parties and fund-raisers that they are well taken care of. A subtle aspect of Bush's maneuvers was that he intensified the burdens on Social Security's administrative workforce while holding down its funding with budget caps. In time, Bush would, ostensibly to relieve those burdens, conduct rigged workforce-privatizing competitions, scoring a goal that moderate Republicans had abandoned a half century earlier: shrinking the ranks of the civil service employees who had administered the nation's income security program with impressive efficiency since the New Deal.

As for Medicare, 2004 brought startling revelations of President Bush's subversion of the law and the possibility that a few more years of conservative control would weaken Medicare past the point of saving. The president had pushed through a drug benefit law with enormous costs—not the $400 billion claimed at the time but the $500 billion to $600 billion his administration had kept the system's honest actuary, Foster, from telling. These costs resulted from drug makers reaping 61 percent of Medicare's drug subsidy, or $139 billion over eight years, as windfall profit, as well as large subsidies going to Republican-contributing health insurers.[125] The drug benefit law's other shortcomings included the famous doughnut-shaped coverage that meant half the people with Medicare would not see a gain in net benefits, especially with seniors barred from coupling the drug benefit with a Medigap solution. Among the severe casualties, almost a third of nonfederal retirees would see their health coverage reduced by their former employers, and Medicaid participants would also lose benefits.[126] Bush's supporters knew he would benefit from a flood of double-edged drug company ads in the six months before the election, explicitly touting drug benefit cards (without mentioning the

law's downsides) and implicitly eulogizing Bush for his spurious benefi-
cence in arranging them.

More fundamentally, President Bush had radically undermined Medicare itself by quietly replacing the ill-starred but feeble Medicare+Choice
of Gingrich/DeLay with the much stronger and hence vastly more dangerous Medicare Advantage. Nearly 70 percent of seniors—normally a group
especially alert to such matters—did not even know that Bush had pushed
through a new Medicare law, for he had lulled them in the familiar conservative way of 2003–2004: the administration introduced relatively moderate versions on the House and Senate floor, making overtures to Democrats and offering a veneer of near-term benefits; then a right-slanted secret
rewrite behind closed doors followed, and DeLay's hammerlike campaign
funding threats produced a hasty late-night House adoption of the conference report.

Hitherto, Medicare had stood since 1965 as the greatest progressive
legacy; its legal status as an entitlement seemed to make it an unbreakable
national promise of decent health security for all seniors. As I argued
in 1996, the conservative game plan to overthrow traditional Medicare
depended on splitting it into different segments for different classes. The
ultimate outcome would visit upon the residual seniors in traditional
Medicare "crude reductions in the form of denials of basic health services,
specifically for those with the weakest political representation."[127] Sure
enough, President Bush's November 2003 Medicare rewrite launched so-
called "premium support demonstration projects" affecting at their start
about six million of the forty-one million people in Medicare and expand-
able later.[128] If Bush had his way on the siting of these projects, the harsh
consequences, such as 30 percent hikes in premiums, would hit seniors not
likely to vote Republican.[129]

The better-off and healthier seniors in the areas selected for these projects would leave traditional Medicare for Bush's heavily subsidized and
profit-guaranteed insurers—their departures thus helping conservatives
to accomplish their prime political goal of breaking up Medicare's support.
In the next phase, as these projects expand and insurers continue driving
costs up, Medicare would pass the accounting mark specified in the new
statute as the point when, projecting seven years ahead, the need for a
large infusion of general revenues is manifested. At that mark, the act
obliges the president—whatever his party—to declare Medicare effectively insolvent, and legislation to raise premiums or cut benefits would
get fast-track treatment in the House and in the Senate Finance Committee. This particular fast track would have a rare and nasty twist: it facili-

tates a Medicare-slashing measure even if the Republicans have by then lost control of the House.[130] Even if frightened seniors were to send a Democratic majority to Washington, that leadership could no more bar a conservative coalition from rolling it over on Medicare than the Democrats had been able to bar a similar coalition from using the Budget Act to hammer Medicaid and food stamps in 1981. Conversely, however, the Medicare act precluded a progressive coalition from using that same fast track for reform bills such as curbing drug makers' profits or undoing tax cuts for the rich. In the ultimate battles over such fast-tracked Medicare-slashing measures, conservatives would incentivize the better-off and healthier seniors to play along and to undermine the rights of the less well-off, less healthy seniors. This latter group would find themselves in a variant of Medicaid, losing out in the competition with defense and other necessary annual spending backed by powerful lobbies.

Bush administration defenders might contend that the problem arose apart from what the president did, simply due to medical cost increases or demographics. However, whereas Bush's own Medicare trustees estimated in 2001 that the troubles were twenty-eight years off, in 2004 they said it was only fifteen years away.[131] Bush had found Medicare fairly strong; in four years he had greatly weakened it, and he had put the processes in place to sound in the not too distant future the death knell of that great program in its classic form.[132]

5   The Corruption

Bush's acumen and system in raising money have been truly extraordinary. As governor and then president, Bush took campaign fund-raising to new extremes (to Heaven or to Hades, depending upon one's perspective). He sought not only to fuel his own campaigns but also to advance two portentous conservative causes: strengthening ideological discipline within the Republican ranks and drawing lifeblood funds away from Democrats. His fund-raising efforts continued the cunning strategy started by the Gingrich-DeLay leadership of the House of Representatives in the early 1990s.

Gingrich and DeLay had developed an approach, carefully kept as far from public notice as possible, that handed them the reins—and the whip—to keep Republican members of Congress under their thumb. It worked especially well with the newly elected candidates who arrived in 1994 and the elections afterwards, who arrived in Washington typically without a great deal of prior political capital and, hence, were initially "grateful" for the campaign money help. Later, the more alert among them came to understand just how deeply they had gone into thralldom to the conservative interests from whom Gingrich and DeLay had raised the money they had taken. This was the *real* "Contract with America," by which the new Republicans had signed away their freedom—not the public relations campaign but the real political contract they had signed in blood with the agents of the powerful far-right distributors of campaign lucre. It seemed such a good deal for the Republicans at first; it brought them office and majority power. Only later did they learn the painful lesson about such a deal that would keep wise senior Republicans—even some fairly conservative ones—from yielding to such temptation, a lesson they learned any time they thought of breaking ranks with DeLay and taking the moderate positions that many of their constituents—yes, even some of their own loyal Republican constituents—yearned for: The first rule of congressional politics is he who signs with mammon and takes from mammon must do mammon's bidding.

Because President Bush was so effective with this strategy and so free of any pangs of conscience about using it, he raised funds in unheard-of quantities, with unheard-of ease, from his base among the rich and the semi-outcast industries. The donors knew implicitly he would do what he was paid for, because he liked doing it. When he spread this funding around, the Republicans who eagerly took his money (again, especially the less senior ones, the candidates running for open seats or against incumbents) only later came to understand that they must fulfill the implicit promises made to the rich and the semi-outcast industries. That was the pact with the Tempter: gaining seemingly all the keys to high office, status, and the trappings of power but at a price that must be paid—thralldom.

It took a little longer, until 2003, for the Bush-DeLay alliance to acquire influence in the previously independent and proud Senate. Rove came up with the 2002 campaign strategy, and Bush raised the funds, that got the Senate Republicans back the majority status they craved—even the senior, moderate ones. In the Senate it was Senator Bill Frist (R-Tenn.) who did the campaign fund raising and distributing as chair of the Senate Republican fund-raising committee, a stepping-stone to becoming majority leader and the post in which he came to an understanding with Bush about how the president and his money base must be served. Then it was simply clever politics for Bush nimbly to ease out Senator Trent Lott (R-Miss.) and replace him with the tool better suited to his purposes, Frist. Sure, Lott was conservative, but he was too wily, too senior, too much his own man, and he enjoyed too much making deals across the aisle with the Democratic leader to submit fully to the control of the Bush-DeLay approach. So at the end of 2002, when Lott put his foot in his mouth (while being filmed) with some stupid remarks, Bush (with no fingerprints) let him take the fall and then eased into the leadership post the cat's paw he vastly preferred, Frist. Frist had the perfect characteristics: publicly, he looked like anyone's own warm, caring doctor—a fresh version of Bush as the compassionate conservative.[1] No one understood better than Frist the rarely articulated deal: take the money from the rich and the semi-outcast industries, continue the show for the public of heeding its centrist views, but then at key moments remind the other senators that the one who pays the fiddler calls the tune.

Even worse, the Gingrich-DeLay-Bush-Frist campaign fund-raising strategy had a second, disabling drive across party lines. Strategists worked with artful dexterity to ease business interest groups away from their old bipartisan patterns of giving toward giving much more to Republicans and much less to Democrats. Even nonoutcast industries that used to give in bipartisan patterns learned that they could obtain those ever-so-tempting results from the well-disciplined power-holding Republicans. But then they too were brought to understand that when they yielded to those seemingly irresistible temptations, the goodies were meant for donors who did not give too much to Democrats. DeLay and company tracked carefully who gave what to the wrong side and, woe unto those who still tried in a balanced way to befriend both sides as had been standard.

Now, in 2003–2004, the DeLay-Bush-Frist team could keep control even when poll numbers showed the unpopularity of the party's more extreme conservative policy positions. Bills on key subjects such as the Medicare drug benefit or omnibus government-wide spending were slanted according to donors' bidding in overnight rewrites in conference and then rammed through with tight party discipline. On issues such as the 2003 deficit-financed tax cut on corporate dividends—enacted while the nation's unemployed and the states, even Republican state governors, cried out not just for relief but, at the depths of the recession and the ensuing "jobless recovery," for mercy—Delay, Bush, and Frist could yank hard on the reins and hold their troops in line. The public money would go primarily to the richest who didn't need it and who wouldn't stimulate employment; very little could go to working families. Barely a pittance went for simply easing human suffering (which was felt mostly by groups that not only would probably not vote Republican but might not go to the polls in large proportions, such as poor Hispanics in big cities, and so were beneath Republican political concern).

Bush was following his tried-and-true path in counting on the gratitude of rich donors, not popular steps like stimulating employment, to win elections. Whenever Bush's own campaigns had desperately needed rapid shoring up, he could depend on huge, largely unaccountable, special-occasion funding deployed in legally devious ways. This had occurred at the key stages of his nomination and election and the midterm elections. Money worked hard for Bush in the critical March 2000 South Carolina primary, when ads emerged to smear Senator McCain (but in ways that avoided direct Bush fingerprints).[2] Money worked hard for Bush in the October–November 2000 Florida legal contest, such as when it arranged the infamous "Thanksgiving stuffing" of late absentee ballots of dubious nature.[3] Money worked hard for Bush in the 2002 Senate races, when attack ads linked Democrats to images of Osama bin Laden while politically allied industries purchased pro-Republican "issue ads." And of course, money would work extra hard for Bush's reelection. That is not at all to say that outspending alone won President Bush the nomination and the election, or the Republicans the Senate. But those who underestimated the power of the DeLay-Bush-Frist campaign funds found themselves sidelined, writing their memoirs, sometimes even begging for lobbying jobs that DeLay took a particularly cruel delight in refusing to let them have.

Of central legal interest, though, was the strategy that would protect Bush from one of the greatest challenges of all, campaign finance reform. Bush had to know, of course, that the public—for that matter, even the Republican electorate who had flocked to McCain's banner in the critical New Hampshire primary—had gotten thoroughly fed up with campaign finance abuse. He must control the vulnerability created by his own massive fund-raising efforts and the public's particular repugnance toward some of the sources. Here, for once, Republican efforts at controlling information at first fell short, thanks in part to the tenacity of McCain. McCain first brought much of that will of steel and moral clarity that he had called upon in his years in the Hanoi Hilton to his 1990s war with the seller of the luciferous killer, Big Tobacco. He had also made campaign finance reform his top priority during his presidential campaign. The sleazy ambush in the South Carolina primary by tobacco money had firmed, not weakened, his resolve; so he came back to the Senate brandishing his sword of national centrist support, respected and righteous.

In 2001–2002 Bush risked tearing his party apart—and tearing himself down—if he got publicly in the way of McCain, the reforming knight on this issue. McCain soundly forced the issue right at the start, during the especially critical period just after *Bush v. Gore*, when the country was still adjusting to the bloc of five's having appointed the president, and the organizing of the 50–50 Senate, where only the vice president's vote stood between Republicans and minority status. An intraparty fight with McCain would be the death of Bush's beloved gigantic tax cut for the rich, just as his father had failed to push a capital gains tax cut through the Democratic Senate.[4]

McCain, however, faced a challenge of his own. It lay in his need to assemble the sixty votes that he himself would need to enact campaign finance legislation. Tobacco's chief Senate satraps like senators Jesse Helms (R-N.C., a tobacco state) and Mitch McConnell (R-Ky., another) would not likely roll out the back-alley red carpet routes like reconciliation abuse for a McCain reform bill. McCain would face a powerful filibuster by McConnell—an ally of the president, the party's fund collector, and the staunchest opponent of campaign finance reform (on First Amendment grounds, of course; another abuse of the law)—and must overcome it the old-fashioned way. The price for those sixty votes included critical concessions by the reformers to the moneyed interests, such as opening the back door of a doubled financial ceiling on individual donations of hard money and the Federal Election Commission's enfeebled policing.[5] Bush anticipated mounting an even greater funding onslaught for his "reelection" 2004 campaign (counting 2000 as his having won an election). How he got the McCain-Feingold bill watered down—and hence kept it from seriously impeding his fund-raising in 2004—obliges a brief review of campaign-finance law as the basis for understanding what now took place.

After Watergate the new Federal Election Campaign Act (FECA) limited individual donations to $1,000 per candidate in any given election. It added strict disclosure requirements for donations and further combated corruption by establishing a system of matching public funds for those presidential candidates willing to accept relatively high total spending ceilings. The intent was to diminish candidates' reliance on private funding. But candidates of both parties quickly found loopholes; by 1996 President Clinton was one of the deftest of candidates when it came to using the "soft money" loophole.

Four years later Governor Bush outdistanced even Clinton, running the most extravagant fund-raising machine in all American history—matched, if at all, only in 1896, when Mark Hanna used the money power of the giant trusts for President McKinley's campaign to defeat the populist William Jennings Bryan, who had made the prophetic "Cross of Gold" address. Bush's effort, centered on the "bundling" loophole, also empowered economic conservative voters the most.[6] In bundling, a high-powered fund-raiser—say, the CEO of a corporation in a semi-outcast industry (an employer with poor working conditions or a heavy polluter, for example)—makes himself into a central fund-raising clearinghouse. Bundling works like a feudal system: the CEO assumes the role of feudal lord, pulling in stacks of influence-buying checks from vassals owing loyalty. In return, these vassals receive protection and implicit rewards (but not express reimbursement—that would be illegal). The CEO's subordinate corporate managers (plus outside lawyers, consultants, suppliers, and other retainers) recognize the implicit benefits of being on the CEO's "good boy" list. The CEO, in turn, understands the (implied) quid pro quo his bundling effort will elicit from the recipient. Governor Bush, with his Texas record of protection for unpopular industries such as heavy polluters and facilitators of job exporting to Mexico, had no peer as the candidate to employ bundling in 2000. As an incumbent, he would become infinitely more appealing as a recipient of bundled boodle when he ran for reelection in 2004.

There remained the matter of contending with FECA, and here the maintained and expanded loopholes come into play. Each of these donation checks itself stays under the limit (which was still $1,000 through 2002); but the bundler passes the whole bundle—expressly identified as such, typically by a computer code number put on the checks in the bundle—to the candidate. Governor Bush's premier fund-raisers, the "Pioneers," each pledged to raise a bundle of $100,000, and together they raised $113 million. Thanks to the device of bundling, this gigantic sum consisted entirely of hard money. These funds are more valuable than soft money as they can be used by candidates for any and all purposes. In 2003 it came out that a premium class of Bush donors had pledged to raise $250,000 in the 2000 campaign, and twenty-seven had actually succeeded in raising $200,000 or more before the 2000 primaries even ended. These were sums to make old-timers gasp—sums that could work the black magic.[7] Although bundling at this immoderate level can be legally engineered to stay just this side of the letter of the law, by the time Bush gives each formally deputized Pioneer a personalized computer code to place on the "independently given" checks, it strains the law's spirit and mocks its purpose. The $100,000 (or $250,000) bundler with a special interest agenda might well expect exactly what the $1,000 spending cap sought to forestall.

But that merely sets the stage for the really high-powered manipulation of the law. With governor/candidate (later president/reelection candidate) Bush pulling in funds in such chunks, it followed that avoiding any ceiling on total spending would become preferable to accepting such a ceiling in return for public funds. In one of the most striking primary campaign developments in 2000, Governor Bush legitimated his "opting out" of public financing. That is, he persuaded the public to accept the idea that he was above and beyond the legal system for constraining corruption in presidential candidates, becoming the first major-party candidate since the 1970s to compete successfully without public funding.[8]

By opting out Bush did more than just promote his own campaign. He effectively smashed beyond repair the post-Watergate system for controlling the exchange of big money for presidential favors.[9] In this key respect, Governor Bush had gained a place in the hearts and wallets of wealthy conservative donors not only beyond where his own father or former Senate majority leader Robert Dole—the previous two Republican presidential candidates—had gone but even beyond President Reagan, the gold standard for winning over grateful conservative donors. The damage he inflicted on the campaign spending control system simply could not be repaired, not even by McCain's heroic quest. Even the 2002 McCain-Feingold campaign finance reform statute did not purport to repair the broken presidential spending control system, and so that system had been put effectively out of commission for 2004. Even if Congress considers reform—a long shot at best—it is unlikely that the conservative bloc on the Supreme Court will tolerate any of the best ways to fully repair the system. (Conservative Republicans could hold firm like the Rock of Gibraltar against the "unthinkable" notion, for example, of heavier public financing of presidential campaigns so that a candidate up against one who, like Bush, evades the limits would get extra).

Governor Bush used other techniques to defeat the spirit of the post-Watergate disclosure requirements. To fulfill the FECA's requirements, Bush would disclose the individual donations, but he firmly declined to disclose either the bundles or the bundlers. For his own reference, of course, his campaign meticulously tracked by computer just how much each Pioneer bundled and each industry arranged. These pioneers could later claim their lucrative favors against the public interest. But Bush withheld this identifying information from the public, shrouding the real potential for corruption. To add calculated insult to injury, however, when Bush did report donations, he went to nasty lengths to evade scrutiny. He clogged his reports with vast numbers of tiny donations, such as single-dollar ones that are exempt from reporting, and refused, at least initially, to report electronically rather than on paper—the kind of technique that those who work on the outer edges of the law use so that authorities cannot monitor their flow of funds. As a result, one filing of his contained thirty thousand pages that had to be wheeled to would-be reviewers in boxes, precluding the press from analyzing it meaningfully in timely fashion.[10] Conscientious Texas environmentalists eventually completed this Herculean task. They believed that what their "compassionate" governor had thereby covered up was his sell-out to the polluting interests that they had determined to be increasing asthma among poor children in Houston.

The Texas environmentalists wanted the nation to know what these powerful auguries showed about what lay in its future.

Meanwhile, in order to obtain the sixty votes needed for a Senate cloture, the sponsors of the McCain-Feingold bill found themselves trading away some of the bill's toughest reforms. Not only did the $1,000 ceiling for individual donations double, but corresponding increases occurred in the other aggregate ceilings as well, allowing the money to flow in potent surges.[11] As early as March 2002 the *New York Times* identified Bush as "the one clear winner" of the campaign finance enactment, who in 2004 would opt out entirely from the public finance system. (In 2000 he had opted out only for the primaries; in those relatively "lean" days, that had sufficed to allow him to expend the more "modest" scale of funds he pulled in.)[12]

When the McCain-Feingold bill finally passed the Senate, it went to the House of Representatives, which for this bill was DeLay's lair. The DeLay leadership (meaning all the angry wizards, not just the former gym coach Speaker Hastert) had fought its own party moderates over the bill for years with all its legislative powers as reins and whip to achieve thralldom and subjugation. The House knew the bill as "Shays-Meehan," named for that unstoppable Republican archangel of reform, Representative Chris Shays (R-Conn.). (Later, in 2003, Shays was in line to succeed Burton as chair of the Committee on Government Reform, where Shays's superb qualifications would have done the nation a great service; but as revenge against Shays for the bill, the DeLay leadership blackballed him, giving the committee to their obedient former House campaign contribution collector, Representative Tom Davis [R-Va.].) The Democratic lion on the bill, Representative Nancy Pelosi (D-Calif.), became minority leader in 2003; her caucus could testify to her commitment on this one. By exercise of his powers, DeLay had stalled floor consideration of Shays-Meehan until early 2002, and he looked fully capable of keeping the bill in hopeless strangulation until its clock ran out at session's end in late 2002.

But then Bush and DeLay suffered one of those mysterious turns of fate that can trump even the deuce himself. Their success in holding off floor debate (ironically, by the most cunning of their tricks) meant that it occurred just when the scandal burst that made Enron a nationally despised symbol of deception and corruption—including shady campaign funding. The series of fraudulent corporate accounting disclosures, starting with Enron, caused the public to wonder whether the recession had come from Texas, where Enron is headquartered. Moreover, as the deceptive accounting procedures by which the CEO class (Bush's base) had "managed" its earnings reporting were exposed, not just the voting public's confidence but even investor confidence—that is, even the confidence of those well enough off to own significant securities holdings—would drop to such an extent as to materially retard economic recovery. Now the veil began to drop about how, in one close analyst's words, Kenneth Lay "had helped George W. Bush every step of the way during his journey to the White House," including unsurpassed levels, and laxity in methods, of campaign finance support—for many high Bush administration officials, actual in-the-pocket payments.[13] This was not a pretty picture to a nation muttering about how during depressions CEOs and well-off Republicans never seemed actually to share the unemployed working stiff's pain.[14] (Also at that time the press began reporting Bush's own 1991–1993 SEC investigation for insider trading, with Robert W. Jordan providing his legal representation—also not a very pretty picture right around then.)

At such a time, President Bush simply could not back DeLay in sabotaging McCain's and Shays's bill in the House lest Bush's ties to Kenny Boy get plastered nightly on television, with Bush starring as the poster child for reform's necessity. Shays marched his bill through the valley of the House floor and came out unscathed. Nor could Bush resist openly when McCain and the Senate Democrats took the classic step by which reformers have moved good legislation in the face of overwhelming odds: they simply accepted the House version of the bill verbatim, overcame McConnell's surprisingly feeble last-ditch resistance, and thereby avoided the trap of a conference.

Congress then sent the little bundle of joy right to the White House. No way around it, Bush had to welcome the lovely little baby bill into the world, even if he considered it illegitimate. When McCain-Feingold-Shays-Meehan landed on his desk like a squalling but adorable, seraphic little bastard that everyone in the family is thrilled to welcome even while the Old One is cursing in the corner, Bush could not hide his bitterness; he excluded television cameras from the signing ceremony and wouldn't invite McCain, an astonishing breach of the most elementary legislative etiquette. Grudgingly he signed the new, properly titled Bipartisan Campaign Reform Act (BCRA).

But for all Bush's frustration that any such thing should come into life on his watch, Bush's congressional mischief makers had maneuvered well enough for the bill quite likely to impede Democrats more than those of his own party. Republican threats of a Senate filibuster, House leadership obstruction, and the expected constitutional challenge in the courts had obliged McCain-Feingold supporters to focus most of their reforming effort on soft money—on which Democrats depended far more than President Bush and the Republicans. Though the bill did lightly regulate what it termed "electioneering communications"—the fake issue ads run by the NRA and the semi-outcast industries—it did little more than curb somewhat their being run in unsubtly framed ways on the election's eve. Although BCRA slightly constrained some of the more diabolical ways big far-right backers help Bush in 2004, it did not impair his much more important capacity to opt out of the presidential spending ceiling for the imaginary 2004 Republican primary. Then he could simply purchase his own ads with bundled hard money. That is, Bush could tap his limitless donor base to fund him for the "Republican" primary and dump $100 million in destructive ads on the Democratic candidate, Kerry. Though the reform bill's sponsors had no intention of doing Bush any favors, the strength of the political opposition and the legal *in terrorem* effect of the anticipated Supreme Court challenge, forced the sponsors to focus only on matters that would still leave President Bush's approach relatively unscathed.

And once the bill became law, two mechanisms—one bipartisan, the other strongly backed by Republicans—came into play that limited the significance of the brand-new controls on soft money and fake issue ads. Congress had given some of the rule-making responsibility for BCRA to the Federal Election Commission. In the spring and summer of 2002 the FEC took steps seen by the bill's supporters, including Senator McCain, as grievously undermining the law's intended strength. For example, it allowed various exceptions that suited reform opponents and defined "soliciting" of contributions narrowly enough to permit a great deal of soliciting under other names. President Bush was not publicly identified closely with the FEC's limited implementation of the BCRA, and only three of the four FEC commissioners who pushed through these exceptions were Republicans, so the new rules not be seen as wholly partisan.

The second mechanism, however, fit snugly with the rest of President Bush's political uses of the law. Led by Senator Mitch McConnell (R-Ky.), BCRA opponents began their court challenge, even while expecting the law to minimally crimp their power in 2004. (I learned of the BCRA opponents' expectations in the course of my helping to file an amicus brief on behalf of a bipartisan group of respected House members defending the BCRA.)[15] In this regard, President Bush had chosen to let legal institutions take their course and provide cover for him, thus escaping blame while reform was diluted. He could validly insist that he had signed BCRA into law. This was one case where conservative causes were served without the president's leaving any public fingerprints.

Taken together, the new law's inherent loopholes, its political compromises in anticipation of filibusters and conservative Supreme Court action, its weak implementation by the FEC, and the new Bush campaign tactics such as improved "coordination" in putting otherwise restricted funds to party use turned the would-be reform measure into a green light for large-scale campaign funders, most of whom happened to represent conservative causes. Due to the Enron meltdown, President Bush had not been able to fight the bill vocally, and he signed it only grudgingly; but he could take comfort in the results: a campaign finance reform law that left the power of his conservative economic base unimpaired. BCRA would not get in the way of his record-shattering fund-raising and spending for 2004.

Some may question whether President Bush's attitude and policy toward campaign finance really mattered so much. Presidential fund-raising capacities had not sufficed to reelect such one-termers as President Carter in 1980 or the first President Bush in 1992. President Clinton enlarged the loopholes in the fund-raising law, as already mentioned, when he went after soft money in 1996. Governor Bush beat his wealthy primary opponent, Steve Forbes, despite, rather than because of, Forbes's personal funding of his campaign, and Bush's popularity from late 2001 until 2003 owed more to 9/11 and his display of American military might in Iraq (until the occupation) than to what was done with the ad money.

However, viewed from a historical perspective, the 1990s and early 2000s had set the stage for significant changes in campaign funding. In this President Bush played a key role. The tremendous surge in the concentration of wealth in the United States in the 1980s and 1990s; the politicization and polarization of corporate executives and the wealthy, especially around the issue of reducing their taxes; and the opportunities for advertising and funding under the tottering campaign finance system, all coalesced to produce elections driven, as never before, by the prevalence and might of big money. Kevin Phillips, in *Wealth and Democracy*, likened the period to the Gilded Age of the late 1800s and to the 1920s. As in those periods, big money could once again dominate U.S. politics, buying in exchange a shift in revenue raising toward reliance on soaking those without big wealth.[16] And at the marriage of conservative money and conservative power, it was President Bush's use and sometimes abuse of law that informed the ceremony and made the combination sinister.

REDISTRICTING: CHEATING ON DEMOCRACY

Republican strategy in redistricting amounted, sometimes blatantly, sometimes deviously, to cheating on democracy. After the 2000 census, each state redistricted; that is, it redrew the districts of its House delegation to fit the freshly counted population distribution. Significantly, after previous censuses (in contrast to this one), that process had loosened up the House's party balance, largely because challengers could often beat incumbents running in newly redrawn districts many of whose voters they had not been serving. More contestable seats in the election two or four years after the census meant putting the House's party balance and control up for grabs.[17] So in the early 2000s, redistricting had crucial importance for a closely divided and politically polarized country. Democrats would have their best—if not only—chance for the coming decade to break DeLay's heavy-handed House lockup. All they needed were enough contestable seats that the 50-plus percent of the population voting against the Bush national ticket in 2000 could elect 50-plus percent of the representatives on the side against the DeLay national ticket in 2002 or 2004.

But Republicans found several powerful if abusive strategies for manipulating the drawing of district lines so as to limit contestability. Initially, Republicans who had power over redistricting engaged in intense gerrymandering—drawing districts of distorted shapes for partisan purposes. They used "packing" to concentrate reliable Democratic voters into the smallest number of districts; "cracking," or distributing, their own voters in the largest number of winnable districts; and "kidnapping," or pairing, Democratic incumbents into merged districts, causing half of these popular veterans either to retire or to lose in primaries.[18] By contrast, those Democrats who could get a seat at the table proved less motivated by party money and ideology for a project requiring such a degree of discipline and ruthlessness. The Democrats were more fearful that the maps would end up being drawn by activist Republican federal judges and, frankly, were often just plain beaten by Republican party strength.[19] So they bargained in states where they had any strength to do so principally for the narrow aim of protecting their individual incumbents, not to shoot for the distant goal of winning 51 percent of the House.

For instance, Michigan had gone for Gore in 2000 and would have elected eight Democrats from its fifteen districts on an evenly balanced map. But Republican state legislators drew a packed, cracked, and kidnapped map leaving the Democrats just five seats—a phenomenal 37 percent Democratic disenfranchisement. In Florida, whereas the twelve House seats in the competitive Tampa-Orlando area deserved a 6–6 division, the Republican legislature gerrymandered them as a split of 10–2 Republican.[20] During the Florida contest of 2000 that put Bush in the White House, local Republicans fought hard for the party while local Democrats often took a dive. Insiders knew why: the clear foreknowledge of the redistricting (for local and state as well as federal offices) just two years away was very much on elected officials' minds in Florida. (Florida is perhaps the state in the nation in which the most shifts occur from census to census due to migration, death, and other factors; hence it is the most open to map redrawing.) The insiders knew that the Republicans in command could, and would, administer the coup de grâce to any official of either party elected from a mapped district who dared to arouse their ire. In contrast, the Democrats who had a majority in the California state legislature passed up the opportunity to gerrymander to increase party strength, choosing just to protect incumbents.

Nationally, according to the leading legal study, Republicans pocketed as many as twenty-five Democratic districts—making a fifty-seat difference in the House, enough all by itself to more than lock up the chamber for a decade.[21] Gary C. Jacobson, perhaps the nation's most knowledgeable political scientist on the subject of such House elections, found that the GOP's six-seat gain in the 2002 election was "much more a consequence of redistricting" than of other supposed factors such as a national shift in voter sentiment.[22]

In a particular abuse of law, at a key juncture in 2001–2002 the Commerce Department stalled the release of raw census data that would have allowed states, through a process called adjusting by sampling, to correct House redistricting for the habitual census undercounting of minorities (simply because, among other reasons, poor urban people are harder for census takers to track). California, for example, redistricted on the basis of the literal count rather than one corrected by sampling. Doing so meant adding more Republican districts for the well-counted affluent voters and fewer Democratic ones for undercounted minorities. Democrats sued, but by the time litigation forced the Commerce Department to release the data that patently belonged to the public (let alone to states like California that vitally needed it), it was too late for use in redistricting. The Democrats won the battle but could not win the war.[23]

Most notorious, in 2003–2004 Republicans employed a startling new abuse: an unprecedented second cycle of redistricting. The country watched with amazement as the Texas state legislature, in which Republicans took control after 2002, obeyed Rove and DeLay in 2003–2004 to tear up the redistricting map previously drawn after the 2000 census and to initiate the outrage of a new redistricting. No such "midcycle" redistricting had occurred in a half century,[24] and virtually none in a century, absent a court throwing out a prior map on grounds such as racial prejudice.[25] Texas Republicans, a crew of ideologues that made partisan Republicans elsewhere look thoughtful and humane by comparison, had one purpose: to purge the Texas delegation of more Democrats and send DeLay more myrmidons. Some may say that politics in general isn't beanbag; it's hardball. But this was like one team's supporters opening rifle fire from the bleachers on the other team.

In the special sessions Republicans convened just for this purpose, they went so far as to attempt to fine and to arrest Democratic legislators who fled the state to avoid collaborating with the coup. DeLay's office went so far in May 2003 as to secure the help of thirteen Federal Aviation Administration staff for an all-day tracking of a Democratic state leader, an act on DeLay's own authority that the departmental inspector general denounced in a June 2003 report as being of dubious legality.[26] In the end, the DeLay effort won, big. Out of Texas's thirty-two House seats, the second-round Republican map aimed at keeping their existing fifteen seats and adding as many as five more. This meant, without a single voter actually changing her or his mind, replacing the established House delegation that was 17–15 majority Democratic with one that was 20–12 majority Republican.[27] To put it mildly, "such a seismic shift would significantly strengthen the GOP's hand in the closely divided House."[28]

Republicans in other states followed the same strategy. In only one round after the census, the powerful but hitherto carefully controlled tool of redistricting underwent a nightmarish transformation. Now, a disciplined-enough national ideological party could inflict long-term representative disenfranchisement upon a less well organized centrist majority of voters; the disciplined minority party, run by a central committee of well-funded conservative extremists, would then dictate the rules to the hapless majority. DeLay would say that it is just as much a democracy as ever. Maybe.

Meanwhile the Supreme Court took up the case of *Veith v. Pennsylvania* for a 2004 decision on whether partisan redistricting by the Republican legislature of Pennsylvania had gone so far that the courts should redress it. A neutral group of justices might well have taken the occasion to do something constructive with the case. The Supreme Court justices came to the subject of partisan gerrymandering knowing what was going on. They knew how to remedy it—if they felt like listening to the pleas of the many political scientists who published articles on the subject or took part in filing briefs, urging the Court to do something about the tilted lockup of the House imposed through such redistricting.

Justice O'Connor, the key vote on such a case, had served as Republican majority leader of the Arizona state senate before coming on the Court. Few know better than she the subject of redistricting by state legislatures. And Justice O'Connor had not hesitated to lead the Court's majority into relevant political thickets before. She provided the crucial vote in *Bush v. Gore* to put Bush in the White House.[29] Equally relevant if less well known, she had provided the crucial vote in *Department of Commerce v. House of Representatives*, the 1999 case regarding the ground rules for how, based on the 2000 census, the House got apportioned.[30] She dictated the outcome and wrote the crucial opinion in that case overthrowing the plans of the Census Bureau's professional demographers to use modern statistical sampling techniques for an apportionment that would truly reflect the population.[31] So Justice O'Connor, like the rest of the bloc of five, both understood the issue thoroughly and had shown little restraint or compunction about wielding power to shape it.

However, as the outcomes in both *House of Representatives* and *Bush v. Gore* showed, the bloc of five conservatives made their decisions in such election law cases in ways that seemed conveniently to benefit the conservative wing of their own political party. Whatever political scientists might hope or dream in the way of sensitivity to the needs of a fair democracy, few sober legal analysts really expected O'Connor and the rest of her bloc to desert the Republican cause. On women's abortion rights, even on some minimum gay rights, maybe; not on this. As in *Bush v. Gore*, the issue came down again to whether the Court would approve Republican methods for undemocratically taking over a branch of the government. The outcome, though sad, was predictable.

REGULATORY WEAKENING

President Bush's success in rolling back late Clinton environmental and other regulatory initiatives and setting out on policies of his own showed how much he could achieve for conservative causes. One of the more abstruse approaches his White House established deserves a brief study, not just for what it did early on but also for the opportunities it opened for future abuse. As in other cases, critical efforts to dilute or abolish current regulations or to impose new ones desired by the president's conservative allies could be pursued from an office so obscure (and inserted in measures so seemingly mundane) as to divert any public attention.

This time the White House's own regulatory review system, the Office of Information and Regulatory Affairs (OIRA), led the charge. The Reagan and first Bush administrations had used OIRA, housed in the Office of Management and Budget, as the avenue by which industry could end-run agency action on issues such as clean air and drug safety.[32] In 2001 President Bush appointed the controversial John D. Graham to head OIRA. Graham was a brilliant academic with intellectual credentials a cut above the lawyer-lobbyists of Interior Secretary Norton's crew, but serving the same program nonetheless.[33] Graham's shop had the legal capability to direct environmental, health, safety, public lands, and other regulatory agencies, coordinating their activities closely with industry. When necessary, OIRA manipulated cost-benefit analyses to show that proposed environmental regulations produced high costs and few benefits, even when statutes expressly forbade such an approach.[34]

Under Graham OIRA regularly solicited input from self-interested corporations and other anti-regulation groups about which regulations deserved scrutiny.[35] As early as 2001 he produced what critics dubbed "the hit list" of regulations to which industries wanted "high priority" given. The twenty-three rules slated for probable demolition, including fifteen on the environment, read like a public interest obituary page. They included protections on arsenic in drinking water, medical privacy, roadless-area conservation, animal feedlot pollution, state polluted-water cleanup, and old power plant emissions review. His second annual effort, in May 2002, added a focus on immunizing states and small businesses from public interest requirements.[36] In December 2002, Graham released an expanded survey of rules to undermine, including food poisoning standards for salmonella.[37]

Graham also developed a tool bag for using White House legal power against individual regulations. This included the "return letter," which rejects an agency's proposal to act, and the "prompt letter," which gooses a reluctant agency into acting, usually to water down or terminate environmental or similar regulations.[38] Moreover, OIRA set up "data quality" guidelines, a devious system that effectively browbeats agencies into using counterfeit numbers to justify the desired outcome.[39] Instead of promoting honest effort by industries to demonstrate high costs and minimal benefits in order to thwart a proposed regulation, OIRA was abetting biased efforts to get regulations off the books and forcing affected agencies to comply.

OIRA's changes to another cost-benefit calculation had overtones that were downright grim. Graham had begun pushing agencies to calculate benefits and costs to human lives using a "discount" rate, set at a relatively high 7 percent.[40] Discounting for future lives and for their quality represented a controversial conservative cause. Government could now choose to discount the value it placed on the lives of the elderly, arguing that elderly persons typically earn less money and provide fewer economic benefits to society. When analyzed this way, lives saved in the future get discounted in the present.[41] By the logic of discounting, for example, current anti-smoking efforts might appear less valuable since lung cancer deaths from smoking typically occur years in the future, while cigarette sales benefit the economy—some sectors of it, anyway—right away.[42] Preserving the lives of future elderly people against risks of cancer, heart disease, or environmentally caused disorders—like preserving endangered species, wetlands, or pristine areas—would have a low value after discounting. Conversely, the relaxation of health and safety rules would have a high value. Voters are more likely to base their electoral choices on government policies that affect their lives concretely now than on the obscure connection between the relaxation of an air pollution standard today and their need to carry an oxygen bottle with them in 2020.

At industry's direction OIRA would return or trim proposals for new rules on these subjects and would prompt relevant agencies to make changes that diluted existing rules. And all of this was done through legal channels that were obscure enough to avoid public and congressional oversight. It was the perfect place to deliver otherwise controversial conservative goals.

PROSPECTS WITH SUPREME COURT VACANCIES

Supreme Court vacancies could provide President Bush with his biggest opportunity yet to impose a conservative stamp on his domestic programs. Whether the president chose to fulfill the wishes of his conservative bases through his administrative, legislative, or lawsuit-fighting powers, a more conservative Supreme Court could give the final imprimatur to measures that might otherwise have faced a judicial roadblock.[43]

Though the administration has generally avoided revealing its ultimate goals on environmental and other public interest matters, a push toward relaxed pollution standards and freer industry exploitation of public resources seems a given. With a more conservative Supreme Court, the administration could use the opportunities inherent in federalism as an alibi for letting standards down in many regions, a legal approach known as "downward devolution."

For example, a substantial number of all regulatory standards get enforced in current law by a federal-state division of labor.[44] The federal agency, typically the EPA in the environmental context, sets national goals and standards, while states develop plans and handle detailed implementation and enforcement through such means as issuance of pollution permits. Before the second Bush administration, most states had incentives to maintain discipline when granting permits and enforcing regulations.[45] President Bush could now steer in the opposite direction, allowing individual states to take a more lax approach. An environmental "race to the bottom" would ensue, pushed by two dynamics: First, industry could play off state against state, closing down existing operations and not opening new ones in states that continued to take regulation too seriously. Second, regions of the country that have special reason to fear environmental problems would lose their legal leverage to keep other regions in line. These vulnerable regions include areas downwind of or downstream from pollution, such as the Northeast, and those facing acute problems with air pollution and water shortages, such as California.

A large portion of the natural resources still ostensibly protected by the federal government are in just a few states, including Alaska and the Rocky Mountain states. The Alaska state government, always more Republican and pro-development than the public in the lower forty-eight, presents a particular opportunity for exploitation; so do some of the Western states, whose natural resource policy processes are largely controlled by the "iron triangle" of commodity exploitation interests, captured state agencies, and pliable state legislatures.[46] Devolving control of federal lands and resources in Alaska and these Western states would create entirely new legal channels for special interests to get their way.

With the replacement of one or two justices, the Bush administration would gain considerable leverage to achieve long-term structural anti-environmental goals with the help of judicial rulings. As an example, the Superfund statute obliges localities to pay a share of some toxic waste cleanups, especially when there is simply no other way to get the cleanup going (and when Bush is quietly relieving his friends in the oil and chemical industries of "unfair" tax burdens).[47] With more conservative justices in place, conservative localities might ask the Court to find such "federally imposed" environmental burdens in violation of constitutional principles of federalism. States under the double sway of budget pressures and conservative interests would complain they have higher priorities than cleaning up their environmental problems. The bloc of five conservatives might say that this is not a federal matter. Such a decision with some constitutional language thrown in would not only gut the environmental legislation of the past, with little chance to restore it in the political climate of the 2000s, but might prevent restoration by some environmentally progressive Congress when one comes along in future decades.[48]

After the Supreme Court made such a ruling, Norton and her lawyer-lobbyist colleagues could multiply the effect by developing legal rationales for actions and rule changes, ostensibly to relieve burdens on, and to respect the authority of, conservative anti-environmental state and local governments. In 2003 the Bush administration gave a foretaste of how it could amplify the impact of conservative judicial rulings. Although Bush had made a campaign promise (which he later broke) to take action against greenhouse gases, EPA might still have taken the initiative someday to impose controls. That was until August of 2003, when the agency abruptly disavowed its own long-established legal position, sharply turned course, and announced that it had been granted no such authority by the Clean Air Act.[49] This unusual position bears saying another way: Bush's EPA announced that its charter, despite previous (sound) interpretations of its breadth and strength, actually left it too feeble to do its job. EPA's legal memo acknowledged Congress's "facially broad grants of authority" but cited an opinion by the conservative bloc of five justices, in a completely unrelated context, declining to take a broad regulatory statute at its word.[50]

Putting aside the particular flaws of the Bush EPA's strained legal analogy,[51] the agency's bold reversal of position dramatized the scope for anti-environmental steps that a conservative administration could derive from past conservative Court rulings—and will derive from similar rulings to come. Absent federal standards to maintain a level playing field, industry could be expected to take jobs to the states with laxer standards. Downward devolution would do to the most effective local environmental regulations what it has already done in recent years to poverty support and labor strength. The United States would become a nation with decent environmental standards effective only in a limited number of states (even these feeling the pressure to lower them) and inferior levels in all the others.[52]

Apart from downward devolution, a Bush administration emboldened by a more conservative judiciary might be expected to take action in other constitutional areas. The Takings Clause of the Constitution forbids the government from taking private property for public use unless it provides compensation. Conservative foundations have long argued that much federal regulation, such as the application of the Endangered Species Act's requirements to private lands, falls afoul of the Takings Clause principle. Norton, in Colorado, and Ashcroft, in the Senate, took the same position during the 1990s.[53] In its early years the Bush administration evinced some willingness to cut back on the statutory protection of endangered species on private lands, but, faced with negative reactions in the Senate and public polls, it could not go far on its own in this regard.

The Supreme Court of the early Bush years had a close balance on Takings Clause questions.[54] In a 2002 and a 2003 case it found regulatory impositions not to be constitutional takings.[55] However, those two moderate decisions had strong conservative dissents; with two votes changed, conservative causes would find new leverage to reverse the tide.[56] The Court might start holding that endangered species protection does not justify impositions on uncompensated private landowners. Then the Norton Interior Department could implement property protection principles that would dramatically shift the balance in many contexts, permitting developers to extract benefits from public resources without assuming corresponding burdens. A closely related principle on which the Court also had a tenuous balance in the early 2000s, concerned retroactivity. Conservative rulings would let Norton and her crew establish grandfather protection on a structural basis so that public resource exploiters and polluters might never have to curb their established inroads on the environment.[57] The lay public does not fully understand the implications of these steps, because the Bush administration denies the press what it needs to cover the trend. It means not just no environmental protections of these kinds now, and none in the near future, but possibly none for decades to come; getting back the Congress for environmental laws doesn't count if the Supreme Court has set up constitutional barriers to their enactment.

PAYING FOR TAX CUT EXTENSIONS
OUT OF SOCIAL SECURITY AND MEDICARE

President Bush's tax cuts of 2001 and 2003 had enormous implications for the conservative goals of future fiscal policy. President Clinton had agreed to a capital gains tax cut in 1997, thereby forfeiting—some would say irresponsibly—the first clear opportunity to start saving federal funds for the baby boom generation's impending retirement. In 2001 and 2003 President Bush squandered opportunities more grossly, not only failing to make good use of the surplus he had inherited but replacing it with projected deficits of $400 billion to $500 billion annually. Moreover, he reshaped Budget Act processes to increase the power and wealth of his conservative base at the ultimate expense of those in the middle and lower classes who would depend upon Social Security, Medicare, and poverty aid.

Each year, as some of the sunsetted tax cuts expired, President Bush and other conservatives could demand their extension, condemning opponents as big "tax increasers." The ensuing struggle, assuming one occurred at all, would proceed according to Bush's newly reshaped reconciliation process. Extending the tax cuts would take only fifty Senate votes, with little meaningful Senate debate, limited amendments, and no filibusters permitted. If continuing tax cuts for the wealthy required trimming programs for the middle and lower classes, Bush, with a little more Senate strength, could accomplish this.

Moreover, another potent element subtly established in fiscal law would augment conservative power. The alternative minimum tax (AMT) would soon escalate to impose in effect an income tax surcharge of hundreds of billions of dollars on taxpayers in certain states.[58] The AMT hits taxpayers in states with high state and local taxes, because it denies the deduction for these taxes that is permitted by the regular federal income tax. Thus, the AMT's geographic incidence occurs, not by chance, in politically progressive states like California and New York, which voted against Bush in 2000.

The AMT problem loomed so large in 2003 and 2004 that President Bush appeared to be using it to undermine the income tax completely. He might have had in mind for its replacement conservatives' long-standing preference, a national consumption tax, which would fall most regressively on the lower and middle classes.[59] By arranging for the AMT problem to burgeon, President Bush was preparing to drive a massive wedge into the Democratic Party after 2004. Senators from states where taxpayers would get hit with the AMT would suddenly hear from beleaguered constituents calling for relief. These upper-middle-income voters would become vocal opponents of their less well-off neighbors. The resulting wedge would strain the Democratic Party to the breaking point, making it increasingly impossible for Democrats to maintain unified resistance against Republicans' demands to find savings in benefits programs through what would euphemistically be called "free market" approaches.

Once before, in 1981, reconciliation had briefly empowered conservatives led by President Reagan to take an ax to the major national programs for subsistence support.[60] In the mid-1990s, reconciliation had allowed the Gingrich-DeLay congressional leadership to push large cuts in funding for welfare, food stamps, and Medicare providers through Congress, even though the most extreme of them were blocked by President Clinton's veto.[61] President Bush could use the tool of reconciliation, together with the pressures created by early sunsets of tax cuts for the rich and by the escalating AMT, to promote fiscal projects he did not previously have the tools and the power to force through.

Two of these projects concern the benefit programs that had bound together the middle and lower classes' interests in retirement and health security: Social Security and Medicare. President Bush pushed hard in 2002, but without success, to privatize Social Security.[62] His privatization commission got as far as figuring out how to promote privatization: by confusing the public into believing that it would work. Ultimately, the direction the president sought would change Social Security from the universal retiree safety net into a program that enriches the affluent but sentences the average member of the working poor to abject poverty in retirement.[63] Professor Colleen E. Medill concluded from an in-depth study of the Bush commission's proposals, "Low-income and minority workers will be the group most adversely affected by the Commission's [proposals], which will substantially reduce the future value of scheduled traditional, disability, and survivor benefits."[64] Paul Krugman tells it more bluntly: "The commission's plans include severe cuts in disability benefits, a crucial part of Social Security that privatizers have a habit of overlooking."[65] Gingrich would have put orphans back in orphanages; the Bush concept would have apparently put the disabled back begging on the streets. That's free market efficiency. With more Senate strength and the right concatenation of forces ensuing from reconciliation and the cuts of 2001 and 2003, President Bush or other conservatives could drive through privatization by harnessing two groups in his base that would particularly support it: those in upper-income brackets and the Wall Street securities industry. The latter would get its hands on billions of dollars in Social Security payments— and manage them for its own profit.[66]

Bush proposed similar changes for Medicare.[67] In fact, many of the legal powers Bush needs for these changes were sneaked into the so-called Medicare drug benefit law. His goal, laid out by conservative analysts and recalling the Gingrich-DeLay effort of 1995–1996, was to move toward a system whose federal contribution is defined and capped and that is administered by private for-profit insurers.[68] The limited number of seniors with enough investment income to fall in the upper-income group (benefiting from the Bush tax cuts and not having to worry anymore about such inconveniences as inheritance taxes) could use their own money to buy premium policies, while the much larger numbers of middle- and lower-income seniors would drain their meager bank accounts to pay their share of an inferior level of care.[69] Low-income seniors who currently rely on Medicare to provide a minimal standard of decent care would now face the "Medicaid mill" level of care provided to the poor in the nation's most disadvantaged states. Once again, abuse of the Budget Act would provide the procedural route, and the powerful drive of conservatives to obtain savings to extend tax cuts and fend off some of the AMT escalation would provide the political engine.[70] They would be assisted by upper-bracket voters who stand to gain the most from the proposed changes and by the most profit-oriented, partisan sector of the insurance industry, which would suddenly stand to gain billions of dollars in Medicare funds to manage that are currently managed by less ruthlessly profit-obsessed carriers.[71]

But wait: President Bush's own Senate floor manager, Senator Frist (or as he liked being called, "Doctor" Frist), pushed through a Medicare drug benefit. Sure, he and Frist did that to keep the seniors in line in 2004, but they had to override a bunch of penny-pinching House Republicans who complained about the lack of financing, and the effort was bipartisan, involving Senator Kennedy. Didn't that qualify as compassion?

Two small details did seem still at loose ends. The bill didn't even hint at how to finance the new benefit. Since Medicare currently comes only out of payroll taxes, not income taxes, the new benefit, fiscally, would accelerate the coming crisis-point when the Medicare system starts going deep into the red. "Compassionate" Bush had not offered any money—certainly not out of the huge sums he gave away in eviscerating the estate tax and chopping the tax paid by the richest on their non-pension-plan stock holdings. In effect, Bush brought closer the point at which middle-class Medicare recipients must either get taxes raised—a daunting prospect—or join Bush's war of all against all and take the benefits back from those who have less than they do and who vote less regularly. Another small point: Bush's friends, the drug companies, used to worry about the bill but then stopped worrying. They didn't have to worry about competition from generic or overseas drug makers, about negotiated ceilings on overpricing, or about any questions concerning CEO pay, advertising to push unneeded drugs, and so on. He had taken care of them. They simply would tap the Medicare till themselves until it ran dry. How much neater the Bush plan seemed—no financing, no profit constraints, no regulation—than all that messy Clinton thinking in 1993 about doing something on these points.

Two other Bush fiscal projects might well link up with the conservative drive for funding of reconciliation tax cut extensions. President Clinton's 1993 tax legislation had expanded the earned income tax credit (EITC)—a highly efficient way to put meaningful amounts of support in the hands of low-income earners.[72] The centrist public had generally rallied behind the EITC, for reasons that made conservatives hate it. The EITC used tax funds to allow low-income working families to live above the poverty level, but this meant reducing, even though only by a modest amount, the funds available for Bush to grant tax cuts to the wealthy. The EITC also contradicted the kinds of racist and sexist stereotypes that served conservative political efforts: those that portrayed all government assistance dollars, especially to female-headed and minority households, as being wasted on cheating freeloaders. As it turned out, the EITC actually went predominantly to households of struggling low-wage earners, frequently people working multiple jobs trying their best to keep their families fed and clothed.

President Bush implicitly scorned the EITC, giving it short shrift in his 2001 and 2003 tax cut bills and having the IRS increase the documentation requirements.[73] The new policies demeaned filers and, probably more to the point, depressed participation.[74] His long-term project aimed at both demolishing the EITC and transforming its former recipients into a closer approximation of what the president's supporters had branded them as all along: charity cases. Bush also sought to cut the already reduced federal benefits for the poor in state-run programs like food stamps and Medicaid. This could occur by a version of block granting: cutting federal spending while making the cuts more palatable to conservative states less likely to care through waivers of minimum standards—so-called "superwaivers."[75] Meanwhile, the more generous states (again, typically states like New York and California) would be forced to make up what they could of the difference by raising their own state taxes, while some less progressive states might use their waivers to make even more cuts on their own.[76]

For my purposes here, the details of President Bush's ultimate plans for Social Security, Medicare, EITC, and poverty aid matter less than the general approach. Some reforming approach does warrant implementation, just not his. Demographics makes Medicare in its current form all but unsustainable in decades to come.[77] It is unfortunate that President Bush's predecessor Clinton did not lead the way in 1997–2000 to the painful but necessary compromises that are involved in reform. But action in the legislative context created by President Bush's tax cuts would not likely focus on how to make the programs solvent with the best mix of additional funding sources and necessary impositions on beneficiaries. Rather, it would probably take savings out of the programs, drive wedges among the beneficiary populations, and deliver tax cuts to wealthy, predominantly conservative voters. Clinton didn't make the problem better, but he didn't make the problem worse. If only the same could be said of President Bush.

Prior to the 1980s and again in the early 1990s, the congressional budget system kept entitlement benefits for the elderly and the poor in legal channels that shielded them from easy chopping to suit annual appropriation or tax cut desires. Few expected the Budget Act of 1974 to become the engine for a wholesale assault by the wealthiest Americans against the relatively meager benefits given to the poor. The approach President Bush set in motion in 2001 and 2003 renewed the grim work of President Reagan's 1981 program by squeezing the needy and eventually even the middle class to give to the rich.

If President Bush strengthened his bare Senate majority, he would gain other opportunities to advance conservative domestic policy goals. During two intervals of unified federal government under Democrats, President Carter's in 1977–1980 and President Clinton's in 1993–1994, both presidents ran into conservative Senate filibuster resistance in trying to enact legislative programs.[78] As in those periods, with the ideological pendulum now swung the other way, the one main constraint against President Bush, a Republican Congress, and an increasingly conservative judiciary performing a right-wing rewrite of the laws was again the Senate filibuster.

So President Bush, counting on stronger support from both the Senate and the Supreme Court, sought new legal devices in federalism, just as progressives had in the 1960s—only this time for opposite purposes.[79] He sought, for example, to reduce access to the courts by victims suing either corporate or state defendants, something long desired by the president's conservative business base.[80] In recent decades, as businesses seeking to block such suits increasingly funded conservatives, their opposites representing victims began contributing to the other side, producing a parallel polarization in which the two sides in the courtroom also become the two sides backing the candidates for elective office of different parties. As governor of Texas George W. Bush did what he could to close the courthouse doors to victims' lawsuits, making "tort reform" one of the issues to which he was most personally devoted, a legislative priority.[81] As president he certainly desired to push this same cause from the federal level. However, his initial lack of a mandate and the corporate fraud firestorm after Enron and Worldcom led him to lay off for a time.[82] In 2003 and 2004, with a Republican-majority Senate setting the legislative agenda and much of the Enron scandal in the past, business found increased Bush administration willingness to support a renewed drive on the issue.

The 2003–2004 efforts augured a much more intense drive if President Bush subsequently increased his Senate strength. Several legal models exist for lawsuit-curbing legislation. During consideration of post-9/11 bills, Congress debated putting caps on the recoveries that terrorism victims could obtain in suits for business negligence, a measure President Bush supported. Most important, well-funded industry trade groups pushed so-called "class action" legislation. Ironically, given its policy of downward devolution in other contexts, in this matter the Bush administration championed stripping state courts of their traditional authority.[83] Allowing victims to file class action lawsuits against semi-outcast industries would have been inconsistent with the Bush policy of accommodating those interests.

In the Justice Department, Ashcroft and Olson might even use enactments against victims' lawsuits as part of a grand strategy of bringing together conservative efforts in Congress and the courts. Conservative groups, such as those representing major industries, have been stepping up their efforts to end government funding of public interest lawyers and have relentlessly pressed the Supreme Court to protect them from victims' suits.[84] They have had occasional success, such as a 2003 decision in which the Court struck down a large punitive damages judgment against a bad-faith automobile liability insurer.[85] However, the Court seemed unwilling to go beyond dealing with constitutional provisions or statutes whose meaning had already been largely settled. By contrast, newly enacted measures against lawsuits would offer the Court an opportunity, particularly with Ashcroft's and Olson's encouragement, to give sweeping anti-victim interpretations. For example, any new measure that permitted businesses to move class actions from sympathetic state courts to federal courts would raise a host of legal questions.[86] Ashcroft and Olson could promote the conservative position on all such questions by bringing certain cases before the Supreme Court and by presenting their own arguments as intervenor or amicus. Activist conservative justices would then do the rest.

These examples suggest a new phenomenon. Only rarely in the nation's history have the president, Congress, and the judiciary shifted in the same ideological direction at the same time. They shifted left together during the mid-1960s, when President Johnson, the Great Society legislative program, and the Warren Court together advanced civil rights and liberties, especially in the previously segregated South. The Meese Justice Department and the Rehnquist Court shifted right together during the mid-1980s to cut back on civil rights and liberties. Now the Bush administration and a conservative activist judiciary might well move together to close the courthouse doors to victim suits and entrench new protections and immunities for semi-outcast industries and other conservative causes.

SIGNIFICANCE OF ELECTION-YEAR DEVELOPMENTS

As the 2004 fiscal year wore on, a significant turn was the somber budget deficit forecast.[87] Although the economy continued its "jobless recovery," tax collections continued to fall short of other fiscal factors. And the prescription drug benefit, together with homeland security (that is, the limited kinds of homeland security Bush would support—not aid to beleaguered states and localities), required large expenditures not envisioned only a few years earlier. The tax cuts of 2001 and 2003 took a large toll on revenues since reconciliation had enabled President Bush to get them enacted without regard for budget projections. That perhaps explained the legally a bit weird fact of the enormous shortfalls in tax collections: granted, the jobless weren't paying taxes, but the rich and corporations were doing well, so there had to be some way they apparently had bought their way out of helping with the deficit.

To shore up the Bush reelection campaign in the face of these developments, President Bush had "Rangers" pledge to raise at least $200,000, double the $100,000 raised by the Pioneers for his previous campaign (and perhaps with an inner circle committed to raising bundled contributions that were much higher). From the beginning, observers expected him to raise more than $200 million by summer 2004, doubling his figure of four years earlier—itself a record.[88] Events involving either the president, vice president, first lady, or other surrogates made the fund-raising easy; an invitation list for one reception showed nearly two hundred cochairs, each committed to raising $20,000 for that event alone.[89] President Bush himself sent just one of his fund-raising letters to more than a million supporters.[90]

Meanwhile, public interest studies showed the tilt in contributions from interested industries, especially those benefiting from anti-environmental policies. A study of the sources of campaign contributions found that the timber industry had given 52 percent of its contributions to the Bush-Cheney campaign and the Republican National Committee, 30 percent to other Republican candidates and party committees, and 18 percent to Democrats. The same figures for the mining industry were 50 percent, 34 percent, and 16 percent; for coal-burning utilities, 48 percent, 28 percent, and 24 percent; for the oil and gas industry, 46 percent, 21 percent, and

33 percent; for chemical and miscellaneous manufacturers, 44 percent, 30 percent, and 26 percent.[91] So the basic arrangement seemed firmly established: President Bush would receive record levels of contributions for the 2004 election, he would maintain the loyalty of his party and comparatively defund his opposition, and in return his conservative base would get what it wanted—not through the democratic legislative process as it had long operated under the Constitution but through legal sleight of hand.[92]

The deception might become, over time, even trickier. As downward devolution caught on, the Bush administration might take legal occasions to further erode Congress's authority. The Northeast might be downwind of pollution from the South and West, but it would be left to states in the South and West—not to Congress—to decide whether New York and New Jersey deserved cleaner air. Similarly, the rules that sometimes aided California in addressing its problems—say, by requiring Detroit to build cleaner-emission cars for sale in California—might also go by the wayside. Once the activist justices gave anti-environmental federalism the go-ahead from on high, the increasingly activist lower federal courts could take matters further. The network of legal groups funded by conservative foundations and semi-outcast industries would serve up test cases for conservative district courts and courts of appeals to chop away at the environmental laws. Again, Ashcroft, Olson, and Norton might implicitly or even explicitly support such a campaign.

That kind of change in the Court's composition would also, for the very long term, undermine regulation of the power of wealthy interests exerted through campaign money. President Bush could not afford to take the political responsibility for vetoing the 2002 campaign finance reform law or for not defending its constitutionality.[93] However, as campaign finance issues arise in the future, he can accomplish his conservative goals indirectly. With one more conservative vote on the Court, a wink by Solicitor General Olson (to apply the old saying) would be as good as a nod when it came to campaign finance cases. The ability of well-heeled right-wing and semi-outcast industry interests to buy influence could become entrenched as their sacred First Amendment rights—beyond anyone's ability, even a future reform Congress's, to change.

And Democratic turnout in November 2004 could be countered, as in November 2002, by the uncounted millions of dollars in Republican campaign coffers or in expenditures allied to the party's effort—especially when some of those millions were from donors persuaded to deny all succor to Democratic candidates. Bush knew his campaign managers would find or create the issues for the potent attack ads. They always had.

In the past, the conservative bloc on the Supreme Court has shown a nascent willingness to facilitate, as a matter of interpreting the constitution or the legislation before it, the devolution of regulatory matters to the states. The Court's current drift in favor of states' rights serves the anti-regulatory aims of a conservative president through both strained interpretation of statutes and new constitutional dictates. And as discussed, President Bush stocked his Justice and Interior departments with just the kind of personnel to take advantage of new judicial opportunities. Further activist conservative appointments to the Supreme Court, followed by an accelerated emphasis on devolution by that Court, would finish the job of demolishing public protections.

6 Going It Alone

As of 1992 the United States followed multilateral approaches respecting established international institutions and law and earned grudging respect from the world. By 2004 President Bush had changed that, putting his unilateralist stamp—a conservative partisan stamp—on the conduct of international affairs. This chapter begins with the evolution of conservative causes in the 1990s and describes how the incoming president defined his ideological approach in part by the choices he made for his team, epitomized by Vice President Cheney and two legal lieutenants: Undersecretary of State John R. Bolton and U.S. Trade Representative Robert B. Zoellick. I address the Bush administration's casting the United States as the great nullifier of the international legal regimes that preceding administrations had built, at the cost of increased world suspicion. On another major dimension, by politically twisting the trade fast track and trade law in general, Bush based his international trade stance on partisan terms while bypassing democratic accountability in Congress.

RISE OF THE NEW CONSERVATIVE UNILATERALISM

Post–Cold War Conservatism

When President Bush became the first newly elected Republican president since the end of the Cold War, his conservative base required a replacement for the militant anti-communist crusade—usually presented in moral terms —that had been its central cause. For forty years that base had rallied to various proposals for resort to military solutions untempered by considerations of international consensus and law.[1] However, after 1990 anti-communist crusading lost its appeal as a jingoistic rallying cry.[2]

So conservative leaders sought a replacement ideology to rally their base.[3] As early as the end of World War I, anti-internationalist Republicans teamed with Southern conservatives (at the time, Democrats) to espouse an isolationism which was that era's version of the antipathy to international legal regimes and institutions. Prefiguring the Bush administration's approach, isolationists rejected the legal regimes founded in the Versailles Treaty, the League of Nations, and the International Labor Organization. While they opposed collective security against Nazi and Japanese aggression in the 1930s, they supported active American intervention in the Third World (i.e., Latin America in the 1920s) and "America First" armament as a security means, somewhat anticipating the Bush administration's sentiments as to preemptive war and missile defense.[4]

From World War II through the postwar era, bipartisan moderate efforts made American support the foundation of the new collective, international institutions and legal regimes. These eventually advanced to address collective security via the United Nations charter, the North Atlantic Treaty Organization (NATO), and arms control; ensure human rights with the UN declaration and the human rights law that ensued; tackle Western Hemispheric regional concerns; and make a start on international environmental and labor matters. Eventually, in angry opposition to this internationalist system, particularly with the rise of the Southern Republican party, a vigorous ideological movement called the nation not back to isolationism but forward to unilateralism or American exceptionalism. In an age in which America is the world's superpower, this view casts aside international law, consensus, and reciprocal obligations as parts of a useless structure. Instead it favors chauvinist and moralistic depictions of selected countries as "evil" outlaws. In an earlier era such outlaw states included undifferentiated "Reds," and later they included undifferentiated rogue outlaws of the Middle East. But "outlaws" could never include the oilmen's beloved Saudis, who, if they did not reciprocate with love for everything American, certainly had lots of cash. In this anti-internationalist view the United States, because it held the strategic and moral high ground, should except itself from multilateral legal relations and institutions and be a Lone Ranger of the world with lucrative opportunities for certain businesses.

Senator Jesse Helms (R-N.C.) led the political implementation of the unilateral or American exceptionalist ideology in the Senate from the 1970s until his retirement in January 2003, while House conservatives such as Representative Tom DeLay (R-Tex.) enhanced its status in the 1990s. President Reagan straddled the issues raised by this exceptionalist view, focusing his foreign policy on more traditional anti-communism while dabbling in unilateral intervention elsewhere, such as Lebanon (1983), until the low point of Iran-contra rendered him a lame duck two years before his second term ended.[5] Thereafter, President George H. W. Bush returned to international consensus and multilateralism to ably manage the end of the Cold War and the triumph of the Persian Gulf War. He made significant statements of support for a "new world order" built on strengthened international legal regimes, some of whose aspects might even have been termed progressive, such as his signing in 1992 of the climate change convention that prefaced the Kyoto Treaty. But, ironically, this successful approach of the first President Bush mainly repulsed his party's ideological base in the short run and his own son a few years later. By the 1992 primaries, the ideological base manifested this recoil by rallying to Pat Buchanan's challenge, which was successful in New Hampshire, and H. Ross Perot's independent candidacy, which drew 19 percent of the vote in the general election.[6] Each candidate attracted various extreme ideological elements.[7]

As the son worked in the father's 1992 campaign as liaison to the Christian right,[8] he could see how he himself might ultimately propitiate his party's conservative base on foreign policy as well as other issues. He also saw who could help him: a cadre of elite Republicans who were already in 1991–1992 peeling away from his father's moderate positions to become what would be the nucleus of George W. Bush's later administration. They were epitomized by Dick Cheney (and his deputy, Paul Wolfowitz, already eager to march on to Baghdad), Bolton, and Zoellick.

President Clinton continued and expanded his predecessor's engagement with the legal regimes for collective security and peacekeeping, as well as for human rights and the environment. His military policies—disciplined by tough congressional Republican oversight—helped Europe clean up the Yugoslav messes. He also continued a relatively bipartisan trade agreement approach, at least compared to his successor's, with presidential tools for use when other countries traded unfairly.[9] However, Clinton's approach to international affairs—despite its reliance on continuing the previous, Republican administration's approach—provoked an intensified far-right partisan reaction. From 1995 on, Senator Helms,

Representative DeLay, and their colleagues used majority control of the Congress to promote this new conservative stance. They reveled in extreme positions: dishonoring the United States' UN dues, already in arrears; opposing American participation in NATO's efforts in Bosnia in 1995 and Kosovo in 1999, which even party leaders with moderate internationalist orientations such as Senator Robert Dole supported; and criticizing the Clinton administration's efforts to shape, by participation, the burgeoning legal regimes for arresting global warming and prosecuting war crimes.

In the Senate, these conservative Republicans outright defeated the Comprehensive Test Ban Treaty in 1998, the first treaty handled so roughly by the Senate since the Treaty of Versailles in 1920—an extraordinary U-turn away from multilateral legal efforts against weapons of mass destruction.[10] On security affairs they succored a neoconservative administration-in-exile that espoused unilateralist doctrines like militarization of space by an antimissile defense and occupation (not containment) of Iraq.[11] Congressional Republican leaders also nursed their own vision of how to recast the trade issue once Clinton left office, prying business away from centrist bipartisan trade agreement policy in favor of their own party's agenda.[12]

Bush Enters with His Chosen Team

While congressional Republican leaders thus marked out legal opportunities that would be available to a president of their persuasion, George W. Bush, developing from governor to presidential candidate, had two powerful reasons to say relatively little about specifics on international and security affairs. First, these policy realms bored him. He never lived down the November 1999 pop-quiz press interview in which he failed to name major foreign leaders and flunked the question about America's position in the controversial military coup in Pakistan.[13] Unlike President Clinton, who had been awakened by al-Qaeda's 1998 embassy bombings, as well as other actions, to worry about the Middle East and to strike back at terrorism, candidate Bush found no particular reason to pay attention to the Islamic world, other than its ability to provide oil. Indeed, his inattention to that whole world would continue until 9/11.

Second, avoiding specifics but generally criticizing Clinton suited Bush's campaign needs in 2000.[14] The Bush campaign espoused strong support for anti-missile systems, opposition to the Kyoto Treaty and the Comprehensive Test Ban Treaty, and vague opposition to humanitarian military missions.[15] Otherwise, by muting specifics even from his surrogates and experts, Bush as candidate avoided taking specific, potentially polarizing positions, especially those that would exacerbate the gender gap that had plagued national Republicans generally and Dole in 1996 specifically.[16] He laid a particularly effective smokescreen in restricting his visible foreign affairs personnel picks to Colin Powell and Condoleeza Rice, making it appear as though moderation and diversity would rule. The less he said about how a nondiverse coterie of ideologues would actually predominate, the better.

The one clear warning, for those who understood it, came with Bush's choice of Dick Cheney as his vice presidential candidate. Cheney had all the depth of experience Bush himself lacked.[17] What got less attention were Cheney's extreme views. He glorified the commander in chief's power to act with minimal concern for the positions of congressional Democrats or world leaders of progressive parties, even when they spoke, respectively, for centrist public opinion at home and abroad. While Cheney served as ranking Republican member of the House Iran-Contra Committee, I served on the staff as special deputy chief counsel. It was astounding to see Cheney up close as he brilliantly, but with an extreme orientation, organized the defense, or at least the minimization of political fallout from, the otherwise indefensible illegalities of Oliver North and his extremist cohort.

Upon taking office, President Bush quickly installed a cadre whose writings and later activities defined a particular approach to international affairs. A March 2001 cover article in the *Washington Post* began, "President Bush is quietly building the most conservative administration in modern times, surpassing even Ronald Reagan in the ideological commitment of his appointments, White House officials and prominent conservatives say."[18] The Bush White House had strategically isolated the few relative moderates given prominence such as Secretary of State Powell. In the State Department these key movement conservatives included John R. Bolton, undersecretary of state for arms control and international security; John Negroponte, the United Nations ambassador; and Otto Reich, the assistant secretary for the Western Hemisphere.

The political use of law in selecting this cadre comes out in a closer look at Bolton, who had long established himself as the most vociferous legal spokesman for the Helms wing.[19] Bolton served in a number of posts in the Reagan and first Bush administrations, including assistant attorney general and assistant secretary of state for international operations, the latter post primarily focused on the United Nations.[20] During the Iran-contra scandal, when I had occasion to meet him, Bolton's stonewalling against the bipartisan congressional inquiry was based on such a flawed understanding of the law that it fell out of line even with Attorney General Edwin Meese, his superior.

During the Clinton administration, Bolton worked for a pair of conservative think tanks, prolifically sounding off in op-ed columns, articles, and testimony. He made a career out of taking far-right positions that not only attacked the Clinton administration and fawned over the most conservative elements in Congress but impugned even his former superiors in the first Bush administration. For example, in his legal attacks on the United Nations, he distanced himself even from the senior Bush's prominent role in Boutros Boutros-Ghali's accession as UN secretary-general.[21] Although the first President Bush had sent U.S. troops to Somalia in 1992, where they were never under UN command, Bolton joined those who shrilly blamed the 1993 Mogadishu incident on the alleged sin of UN control—the line of criticism by which the new conservative ideology conveniently, if inaccurately and hypocritically, began overthrowing the multilateral and institutionalist stance championed by their own Bush administration.

During the mid- to late 1990s, congressional Republicans pushed the nation toward the politically popular but legally dicey position of defaulting on UN arrearages. Bolton backed this up with a series of extraordinary positions, arguing, for example, that the formal entry of the United States into the UN treaty was "not legally obligatory" with respect to paying dues and "just not 'law' as we apprehend the term."[22] "Treaties cannot legally bind the United States," he argued, but were merely a dispensable "political obligation." This position served the political posture of his wing of the Republican Party toward its constituents but undermined American credibility abroad. Similarly, in 1998 Bolton penned a series of pieces in the right-wing *Weekly Standard* urging invasion of Iraq, and—when President Clinton did bomb Iraq late that year, an action the rest of the world took as a powerful statement—Bolton criticized the action as inadequate.[23] The senior Bush, who had sized up the downsides of an American occupation of Baghdad in 1991 and found them excessive, might, if he read these articles, have worried about what they signaled for the future if the Bolton wing came into office.

Bolton took payments of $30,000 from a foreign government (Taiwan) in 1994–1996 to write papers supporting its possible declaration of independence, a potential step viewed by every U.S. administration since 1949 as wildly and dangerously provocative. Moreover, he accepted the money while stating his foreign paymasters' case through congressional testimony, something he failed to explain at the time. Senators at his confirmation hearings years later indicated shock at this; they had not known about foreign payments to this seemingly forthright, apparently merely ideologically driven former high official.[24] Bolton had filed, albeit separately and quietly, the legally required disclosure forms for serving foreign interests, so his actions were not prosecutable. Still, by testifying while paid in this way, he recalled the work for Big Tobacco's cause of Rove, Olson, and Dinh, as well as Zoellick's Enron money. Like Bush himself, his lieutenants sustained themselves by an exchange of money for favors with semi-outcast causes.

The second Bush White House installed Bolton in the top State Department post of undersecretary, even though Secretary of State Powell did not want him there. Senator Helms famously commented as chair of the confirmation hearings that "John Bolton is the kind of man with whom I would want to stand in Armageddon, for what the Bible describes as the final battle between good and evil," something less than a nuanced appreciation of shades of gray in international relations.[25]

Bolton's installation occurred at the same time that the White House dashed Powell's hopes about who would serve in the Defense Department, letting Cheney choose Secretary of Defense Donald Rumsfeld and having Cheney's own favored former aide, Wolfowitz, become Rumsfeld's deputy.[26] This way, a tight inner ideological circle would call the shots, with the Helms wing in Congress granting approval. Their controversial commands would flow around the reluctant but outflanked Powell, often going directly to Bolton and the rest of his legal cadre as nuncios. From the outset, observers could see that this opened up the possibility sometime during the Bush presidency of occupying Baghdad, something which, back at the key juncture in 1991, Wolfowitz supported but Powell had successfully opposed.[27] Also at the administration's outset, the White House set up the partisan trade operation, with Zoellick as United States trade representative, discussed later in this chapter.

THE NULLIFYING SUPERPOWER

Starting early, President Bush (often with Bolton as his point man) began the thrust for American unilateralism that pleased his political base but cut back on America's natural and traditional international support. The United States had served not only after World War II but also after the Cold War as the leader of collective and legal efforts toward security based on the UN charter; at times, it had also served as the standard-bearer for progressive international legal regimes, such as for human rights and weapons nonproliferation in the late 1970s. Under the administrations of the first President Bush and then President Clinton, the United States had garnered international support for managing its superpower responsibilities in the Persian Gulf and in the former Yugoslavia, while countering suspicion abroad of hegemonic tendencies. The new Bush administration, by setting forth to nullify international legal regimes, changed this.

Initially, the efforts focused on issues such as global warming and tobacco. After 9/11 the Bush administration moved ahead with its unilateral thrust, turning to security issues like war crimes and arms control. In 2002–2003 the thrust concerned the legal doctrine of preemptive war as a prelude to unilaterally occupying Iraq. We will now examine this progression.

Global Warming

On global warming President Bush combined the unilateral approach discussed in this chapter with his tendency to obscure his anti-environmentalist position (see chapter 4), thus providing legal cover as he served a major conservative cause. Serious international negotiations on the subject of global warming had begun when the first President Bush signed a convention at Rio de Janeiro in 1992, displaying a tolerance for international legal regimes that would stand in marked contrast with his son's hard-line position. In December 1997 the negotiations, after Vice President Gore managed to break several stalemates, produced the Kyoto Protocol, intended to control greenhouse gases and thereby forestall catastrophic climatic change.

Although President Bush criticized the Kyoto Protocol vaguely in the 2000 campaign, it did not present an attractive enough target at the time to warrant a firm position. Meanwhile, the centrist and fairly pro-environmental public heard a drumbeat of increasingly worrisome scientific warnings about global warming. A candidate's carping about the protocol's weaknesses, such as its failure to control pollution by China and India, offered no help with looming problems the public had begun to take seriously. And voters sometimes seemed on the verge of a reaction against Governor Bush's amply demonstrated anti-environmentalism in Texas.[28] So candidate Bush obscured his stance on Kyoto by pledging, if elected, to cap carbon dioxide as a power plant pollutant and by acknowledging in a nationally televised October 2000 presidential debate that "global warming needs to be taken very seriously."[29] Once he was in office, EPA administrator Christine Todd Whitman testified at a February 2001 Senate hearing that the Bush administration would consider imposing limits on such emissions.[30]

At that point, conservative Republican senators, including Helms, struck back in a letter to the president.[31] In a March 2001 open letter, Bush declared formally that he opposed the Kyoto Protocol and, despite his feelings about global warming, wrote, "I do not believe, however, that the government should impose on power plants mandatory emissions reductions for carbon dioxide."[32] This involved some unstated but significant legal subtleties. By staking his position on the global warming problem as a matter of opposition to the Kyoto Treaty, President Bush translated the issue into the realm of international legal regimes rather than domestic anti-environmentalism. This produced a storm of criticism abroad, where his campaign statements about the treaty had not registered.[33] But had he instead fulfilled his campaign pledge about regulating carbon dioxide, congressional conservatives—like Senator Helms and the letter's other signers—could have had their way only by enacting an appropriations rider on the floors of the House and Senate. President Bush's exchange of letters used the law to give conservatives what they wanted while avoiding environmental floor votes, simultaneously easing public reaction to his breaking a domestic policy campaign promise by transforming his move into a statement of American exceptionalism overseas. Whitman and Treasury Secretary Paul O'Neill sized the exchange up as a Cheney-orchestrated trick.[34]

Thereafter, at the key July 2001 global warming conference in Bonn, the European Union, Japan, and other major blocs came together impressively on the significant Bonn Agreement.[35] The Bush administration's continuing legal position of antagonistic nonsupport, at that time and in the following months and years, made the United States almost a disgrace on this issue in the world environmental community. Moreover, Bonn made plain how the Bush administration served only the most obdurate business sectors, not the interests of business as a whole and certainly not the centrist public.[36] Some of the largest business sectors, after all—real estate, agribusiness, property insurance—must begin taking into account the commercial risks of catastrophic climate change. The world business community as a whole had a naturally nonideological impulse to go along with anything political leaders of different nations could work out that would meet a long-term global problem in a way that allowed long-term business planning. The Bush administration's extreme position, designed to wreck long-term collective efforts in controlling real risks, left the major industrial powers of Europe and Japan aghast, as their own business communities, though powerful, had no such taste for global climate anarchy.

Tobacco

In the case of the international tobacco agreement, the Bush administration displayed its unilateralist approach even more starkly than in the Kyoto controversy. The case also revealed Big Tobacco's greed. In dealing with global warming, the energy sectors could at least argue that measures dealing with global warming posed a trade-off with needed economic growth. In contrast, it could hardly be argued that world economic growth required boosting the consumption of a mass addictive carcinogen, the pushing of which made many in the world view the American tobacco industry in public health terms much as America viewed the Medellin Cartel. During the 1990s, the global U.S. tobacco companies, as the extreme example of a pariah interest, had bonded with the conservative wing of the Republican Party.[37] Big Tobacco financed lucrative individual retainers and massive campaign advertising, even including attack ads against Bush's challengers for the nomination claiming they were insufficiently conservative;[38] in return, conservative Republicans, Bush in particular, succored the indefensible industry.[39] The tobacco companies had thereby bought their way through the firestorm of 1990s revelations about their hard-driving, knowing promotion of the addictive killer to the world's children. Tobacco turned up repeatedly as the paymaster of individual Bush administration conservatives: from Karl Rove, who took $175,000 in fees as a Philip Morris consultant in the 1990s, to Viet Dinh, a paid expert for the tobacco companies in litigation.[40] Tobacco's apologia for its largesse came not just from the Cato Institute and from John Ashcroft (who expressed concern as a senator that Janet Reno's brave anti-tobacco lawsuit "could set an unwise precedent") but even from future solicitor general Ted Olson, who listed the anti-tobacco suit as part of President Clinton's "politicizing the Justice Department."[41]

In the 1990s, the World Health Organization (WHO) launched international negotiations on tobacco control.[42] Partially tobacco-related deaths (i.e., from diseases promoted by use of tobacco) accounted for about 20 percent of all U.S. deaths and 17 percent of deaths in developed nations as a whole but only 6 percent of deaths worldwide.[43] Even taking into account the contribution of world poverty to reduced Third World tobacco sales and of other Third World causes to mortality in those regions, these figures still invited the tobacco industry, if uncontrolled, to expand its world markets. Some observers projected that if the industry's plans succeeded, by the year 2020 one in three adult deaths in the world would be partially caused by tobacco. The Clinton administration supported the agreement negotiation effort, particularly pushing the ban on cigarette advertising aimed at minors. Even that position, however, seemed quite lukewarm to observers abroad, reflecting as it did the powerfully constraining effect of the Republican Congress—especially the influential conservative fund-raising masters from tobacco states, senators Helms of North Carolina and McConnell of Kentucky.

Tobacco companies took the need to influence the treaty talks as yet one more reason to contribute overwhelmingly to the Republican Party and to the Bush campaign; they formally contributed $7 million in the 2000 election cycle alone, favoring the Republicans with an extraordinary 83 percent of their total giving. They also secretly purchased professional criticism of international legal regimes. For example, it later came out that Big Tobacco put on a lucrative undisclosed payroll the leading British libertarian commentator Roger Scruton, who wrote a short 2000 book denouncing the "transnational" WHO for this "bureaucratic bullying" effort against cigarette advertising.[44]

When the Bush administration took over the United States' role in the international tobacco talks, ultimately it did move them toward a negotiated treaty in 2003.[45] However, starting from the key spring 2001 Geneva negotiating sessions, the administration's pro-tobacco stance had only a thin camouflage. At the meeting, the long-time chief American negotiator, Thomas E. Novotny, deputy assistant secretary of the Department of Health and Human Services, sharply changed course and took pro-tobacco positions opposed by most other nations. For example, now the U.S. delegation would no longer support an end to tobacco advertising that generally "appeals to" children; to be curbed, ads would have to demonstrate a "special" appeal to children, the precise loophole R. J. Reynolds sought for its Joe Camel cartoon character. Adults, R. J. Reynolds would argue, liked that lovable character, too, so its lethal appeal wasn't "special" to children.

The U.S. delegation objected to warning labels in local consumers' languages, as though only the small multilingual fraction of the world's population fully deserved to know tobacco can kill. And the United States stood against the general—indeed, virtually unanimous—consensus that licensing tobacco retailers would reduce smuggling. The U.S. delegation also changed positions to oppose efforts to reduce tobacco use among adults as well as children. And it now objected to giving the WHO a central role in the agreement. At the time, Novotny, a twenty-three-year federal employee, expressed private frustration over these stances. Afterwards he admitted feeling uncomfortable and distressed; by August, he resigned his post. It was perhaps the most striking case in American diplomatic history of a career negotiator—hitherto a loyal servant of Republican and Democratic administrations alike—disgusted by being forced to take part in a sell-out of the national interest, and it coincided with big campaign help for candidate Bush.[46]

Nonetheless, his departure did nothing to shame the Bush administration, which continued over the following year to oppose the full phased-in bans on cigarette advertising supported by other nations. All this paid off when the watered-down tobacco treaty finally came forth in 2003. The Bush administration had the treaty to show that it had not openly sabotaged world health efforts. But the Bush diplomacy quietly arranged the inclusion of so many loopholes, enfeebling exceptions, and encumbrances against implementation that Big Tobacco could thrive quite well under it.[47]

What President Bush did through the tobacco negotiations involved a sophisticated political use of law. Tobacco could not win an open political and media fight, particularly over the most outrageous issues such as its marketing to children, if its foes had a clear opportunity to attract public attention.[48] More important, Bush wanted to maintain as dignified a distance as he could from Big Tobacco's taint. In particular, as he went into the 2004 election, he would not want both the world and national press to shout about what tobacco cash and paid-for ads had bought in the previous four years. And if there was one thing the tobacco companies had learned over the years, it was when to keep a low profile and just await dividends from their wise investments in political assets.

NULLIFYING THE ABM, BWC, AND ROME TREATIES

September 11, 2001, amounted to the deadliest and most shocking attack by overseas enemies on American civilians in history and the only successful foreign attack on the continental United States since the War of 1812. Televised images of the hijacked planes slamming into New York City's World Trade Center towers and of the towers' collapse, as well as the catastrophic toll in human life, left indelible impressions on the public's consciousness. Afterward, the nation endured an enormous economic toll, including the direct damage, the immediate collateral effects, the national air traffic shutdown, a major drop in the world's securities markets, a disabling injury to several major industries, and the lingering effects of terror-induced insecurity. The revelation of al-Qaeda's global reach and an anthrax scare soon after 9/11 compounded the impact. All this came with no warning from a direction few had even imagined, intensifying the national sense of vulnerability.

I examine in chapter 8 the military actions that followed 9/11. First, however, it is important to continue reviewing how the president had, prior to 9/11, already set in motion an effort toward nullifying international legal regimes, an effort that gained even greater resonance once military action entered the picture. President Bush used his enhanced powers after 9/11 to push on with this nullifying program, a program the rest of the world found counterintuitive, strange, and counterproductive.

President Reagan's famous 1983 speech launching the "Star Wars" initiative had the side-effect of permanently capturing the hearts of ideological conservatives for the dubious notion of a high-tech defensive shield. In the ensuing two decades, a hundred billion dollars was spent on this concept, with little concrete accomplishment. But "Star Wars" enriched government contractors, provoked our erstwhile Cold War rivals, and antagonized our European allies, all of which seemed, to conservatives, notably beneficial; and it purported to help the United States increase its security without the messiness of engaging in the work of the community of nations. For right-wing hawks, the so-called "Strategic Defense Initiative" was a way to get a leg up on both low-level antagonists in the near term and, in the distant future as they imagined it, Russia and China.

President Bush's main thrusts toward anti-missile defense concerned military, diplomatic, and budgetary aspects, but law was to play one very important part: rolling back the ABM Treaty made by President Nixon with the Russians. Conservatives saw this treaty as the worst of the international legal regimes of arms control. President Nixon, despite strong credentials with the conservatives of his time, had created a system of reciprocal international relations to foster peace and stability, rather than relying on American technological and logistical might as the only defense. He had completed the picture by adding an international legal regime reinforcing mutually reliable, reassuring deterrence. Now, according to the present era's conservatives, times had changed, and this needed undoing.

During the 2000 campaign and at the start of the new administration, Bush and Bolton left it vague whether the ABM Treaty would be renegotiated or simply discarded. Either way, missile defense gave Bush, both as a candidate and as president, something specific and major to push that appeared suitably nationalistic. Bush's imprecise position with respect to the ABM Treaty allowed conservatives to coast on their confidence that he would do the right thing and ditch it while lulling the press into inaction. Once in office, taking legal action to undo the ABM Treaty had special advantages. It did not require him to muster the strength in the Senate to enact new measures, nor did it have a specific price tag in the budget, nor did it require demonstration that antimissile technology actually had surmounted its huge problems.[49] So for President Bush to focus on his legal strategy assured a concrete accomplishment that he could tout—the actual elimination of something he could describe as a problem or obstacle —even without corresponding progress on the truly difficult problems or obstacles such as the huge expense, destabilizing effects, and uneven results in testing.[50]

A key moment in 2001 illuminates how President Bush, through Bolton, served his conservative supporters by arranging behind the scenes a major abuse of law to rip up the ABM Treaty. Russian premier Vladimir Putin had signaled willingness to stretch the treaty greatly in America's favor, something to which Secretary of State Colin Powell also aspired. Putin had long understood President Bush's rapture with anti-missile defense. He knew saving the treaty at all was hard but worthwhile, and he would risk his own prestige by serving personally as Russia's legal representative in talks on the treaty. Had the White House let Powell negotiate, he could readily have obtained a reinterpretation or modification allowing missile defense development on terms extremely advantageous to the United States. That this was not what actually happened was an insulting rebuff to Putin's overtures.

Rather than let Powell negotiate, the White House had Bolton go to Moscow on behalf of the State Department, along with Secretary of Defense Rumsfeld, known as a rigid hawk on the issue. Rumsfeld presented a militant American stance, to which Putin objected, saying, "You are asking to effectively gut the treaty."[51] Bolton, far from countering Putin with a clarifying proposal as Powell would have done, quickly took this comment as a basis for declaring the meeting pointless. Bolton said the United States was "asking for the ability to test" in a manner that was completely "unrestrained by the treaty."

When Putin, himself trained as a lawyer, demurred that the American demand seemed too broad, Rumsfeld took the opening to confirm that the United States would withdraw from the treaty. Putin then had no choice but to decline to stand down his own strategic force. But the loser in this deliberately derailed negotiation was the centrist American public. It lost, by this secret lawyer's maneuver, the benefits to be had from a deal on favorable terms—preservation of vital mutual confidence between the two sides, as well as world confidence in American designs. The maneuver thereby undermined nuclear deterrent stability, drove Russia and China into shared distrust of the United States, revived the destabilizing possibilities of nuclear weaponry placed at the ready or built up in arms races, and in many ways renewed the barely controlled risks of unthinkable wars.

Similarly, the Bush administration deliberately discarded the world's receptivity to a strengthened biological weapons pact, just at the time that escalating risks posed by weapons of mass destruction made that a doubly regrettable ideological choice. Following the model of the Nuclear Non-Proliferation Treaty of 1970, a vast membership of nations in 1972 launched the Biological Weapons Convention (BWC), barring development and transfer of biological weapons. Like its nuclear model, the BWC beneficially encouraged superpowers and Third World countries to avoid a wide-open weapons race. In the 1990s, negotiations began toward what became the chemical weapons convention of 1995 and a BWC-strengthening protocol, but American conservatives opposed both. The ideological conservatives complained about unwelcome incursions on American sovereignty and military interests, while certain businesses disdained even the most necessary and appropriate incursions on their proprietary facilities and information.

When Bush came to office, the previous administration's progress on these fronts stopped. In July 2001 President Bush rejected the BWC protocol draft resulting from the 1990s talks and opposed any further negotiations. After the 9/11 attack and the anthrax-bearing letter scare that followed, the president acted briefly as though he had gotten the message; in November 2001 he announced support for a stronger BWC. But just a month later, through Bolton, the administration went hard right again by an unsettling legal ploy. Bolton left the promising December 2001 conference on a BWC protocol in disarray by alone urging, on the meeting's last day, that the negotiating group terminate its own mandate and start over. Without support from other countries, the United States single-handedly ditched the national and international consensus on controlling biological weapons. Instead, as the British magazine the *Economist* commented, "alongside Mr. Bush's refusal to ratify the Comprehensive Test-Ban Treaty, and his moves to scrap the ABM treaty, this was more than an undiplomatic blunder. It seems to represent a dangerously ideological aversion to any sort of binding arms control." This came from a business-oriented publication that often supported the president's direction.[52]

Bolton then turned to making a special ideological abuse. The BWC system had served in the past, like the parallel Nuclear Non-Proliferation Treaty, as a consensus mechanism by which advanced military powers like the United States and Russia built confidence with the dozens of countries capable of sustaining some form of advanced weapons development. With this consensus, it was hoped, all would slow the spread of those dreadful technologies. However, Bolton manipulated the regime in the direction preferred by movement conservatives, turning the BWC system into just another theater for trading charges between the United States and "evil" enemies. He started playing this suit in November 2001 by publicly attacking Iraq and North Korea and, in a lesser vein, Iran, Libya and Syria.

In May 2002 the Bush administration needed a propaganda tactic to counter worldwide approval of former president Jimmy Carter's dialogue-promoting visit to Cuba. Bolton issued a sudden, dramatic denunciation of Castro for asserted past breaches of the 1972 Biological Weapons Convention. No one could approve of what Bolton denounced, but the right wing's forty years of predictably playing the Castro card had long worn out the centrist public's patience. Still, nothing could prevent the Bush administration, through Bolton, from using its legal approach of dissipating the interest the United States shared with the rest of the globe, especially after 9/11 and the anthrax scare, in real progress on an international weapons-control regime.

A final security-related treaty was the Rome Treaty, which created the newest of international legal institutions, the International Criminal Court (ICC). Since the Nuremberg Trials, international justice had moved toward the punishment and deterrence of genocide and war crimes in countries lacking their own domestic justice system. The Clinton administration took part in the international effort, formally begun in 1993, to charter a standing worldwide tribunal for such crimes.[53]

Movement conservatives in Congress, fed by testimony and writings from Bolton, seized on this as an issue. From the start, the conservative critique had little objective legal merit, and it lost even that as the Clinton administration negotiated layer after layer of safeguards for American interests, both in the launching of the Rome Treaty in 1998 and over the following two-year countdown. The ICC existed only for those whose own countries had no effective tribunals, while the United States has one of the world's strongest systems of military justice.[54] Ultimately, at the December 31, 2000, deadline, President Clinton signed the Rome Treaty rather than abandon influence over the system's later development. Of course, this did not ratify the treaty; only the Senate could do that, and there was no prospect of that happening for a very long time.

The Bush administration took a virtually legal action on this treaty. Hitherto, treaties signed by Democratic presidents that lacked support from their Republican successors might not get ratified for many years, but they did eventually reach the Senate calendar and stand the test of a Senate vote. President Truman signed the Genocide Convention in 1948, and the Senate ratified only in 1986; President Johnson signed the Convention against Racial Discrimination in 1965 and the International Covenant on Civil and Political Rights in 1966, ratified, respectively, only in 1994 and 1992; President Carter signed the Convention to Eliminate All Forms of Discrimination against Women (CEDAW) in 1980, which remained unratified in the second President Bush's tenure. Many of these agreements, like CEDAW, had not even a prayer of advancement under the Reagan administration. Even so, that conservative president had avoided steps that might bring his own signature on international proposals into contempt after he left office. Keeping the signed but unratified agreements quiescent and in limbo satisfied Reagan.

However, the Bush administration, led on this issue by Bolton, wanted to make a noisy, provocative legal statement. Echoing conservatives' virulent hostility to the Rome Treaty from the moment it took office, the Bush administration planned to attack the treaty in the fall of 2001 but was forced to postpone action when it became clear that the post-9/11 anti-Taliban coalition was exactly the sort of quest for justice that the treaty had envisioned. Denouncing it then would have been particularly unseemly (especially to the other coalition partners); but by May 6, 2002, the White House was ready to unleash Bolton. On that day, he gave the United Nations a one-paragraph notice declaring that "the United States does not intend to become a party to the treaty" and "the United States has no legal obligations from its signature." The press dubbed this the "unsigning" of the Rome Treaty—the only term available for this strange tactic. Ratified treaties that interfered with contemporary policy had been renounced before this, but since the Rome Treaty had not been ratified and the signature had not entered into effect as to the United States, what was renounced was, mainly, the electorate's right to put someone differently minded in after Bush who would go forward on the issue. Neither the United States nor any other world power in a closely comparable situation had ever before taken the legally peculiar action of disavowing its own signature on a UN treaty.[55]

With Bolton continuing in the lead, the Bush administration did not stop there but looked for even noisier symbolic gestures. It undertook an active campaign, by diverse tactics, to demand immunity for the United States to violate the Rome Treaty, and to continue vocalizing its contempt for the treaty and its supporters. The administration tried to get a UN Security Council resolution to confer immunity. It pressured vulnerable nations to agree to special deals releasing the United States. Its threats to undo international peacekeeping arrangements if it did not have its way became unsettling annual rituals. None of this seemed in proportion to the insignificant actual chance that, despite the Rome Treaty's many safeguards and the "unsigning" as well, the ICC would take on the American military.

There had been nothing comparable to this campaign in the history of the UN system. Only to American ideologues of the extreme right did angering the rest of the world, abandoning the American claim in war to the high ground of jural legitimacy, and weakening the fabric of international law seem perfectly wonderful. Conservatives did want not merely to influence the direction of the international legal system but to act out their disdain and to make their contempt the official expression of the United States. It recalled the reaction of isolationists in the 1920s and early 1930s to the attempted post–World War I legal system. Unlike those earlier efforts, however, these were aimed not primarily at withdrawing America from world affairs but rather at dressing active and powerful worldwide American military intervention in the garb of some ultimate version of legalized symbolic irresponsibility.

The struggle over the International Criminal Court highlighted several aspects of the Bush administration's political use and abuse of law. Here too the administration catered to the far right without concern for any mandate from the centrist public: "unsigning" a treaty and squabbling with allies required no voting in Congress at all. Also, by striking these legal themes in the course of posturing to "protect" the American military, the administration could position itself the better to resort to these themes when promoting special commercial interests that world consensus sought to regulate. For example, as to tobacco, that industry's legal defender at the right-wing Cato Institute, Robert A. Levy, could complain, in terms meant to echo the administration's general sovereignty posturing, that under World Health Organization agreements, "a perfectly legal product [tobacco] would be controlled by an arm of the United Nations" that would "undermine the sovereignty of its member states and impact U.S. domestic priorities."[56]

PARTISAN FAST-TRACK TRADE DEALS

I now turn to an entirely separate part of U.S. relations abroad: trade agreements and their legal mechanisms. Economically and diplomatically, as world trade and economic integration increased after World War II, trade agreements became of the highest importance to the United States, increasing in both scale and in the sensitivity of the issues.[57] However, the political and legal stakes also increased. To persuade trading partners to participate, the United States must sometimes take steps that increasingly risked other countries' taking away large numbers of jobs in specific sectors paying decent wages to American workers. The United States must try to avoid tolerating and even exacerbating the bad labor and environmental records of trade partners.[58] And to bring trading partners into legal mechanisms in which the United States could challenge some of their domestic practices as protectionist, it must reciprocally open to those partners and to multinational companies avenues to challenge as protectionist a host of American federal and state domestic laws, including safety and health standards.[59]

Political scientists call trade deals a "two-level" presidential game: on the domestic level, Congress authorizes negotiations and ratifies and implements legal agreements; on the other, international level, the president horse-trades and enforces and defends disputed legal issues with other nations. Changes in legal mechanisms on one level affect the politics on the other level.[60] Starting with the Trade Act of 1974, Congress created a powerful new legal mechanism, the "fast track," that periodically expires and requires renewal and that can be altered toward either bipartisan or partisan orientations.[61] The fast-track mechanism authorizes presidents to negotiate trade deals that Congress then may approve by passing implementing bills. Such approval by implementing bill makes the often major changes in both federal and state domestic law necessary to meet the requirements negotiated in the implemented trade agreement or enunciated by the organs it empowers, such as the World Trade Organization and its dispute resolution machinery.

Under the fast track's powerful but controversial central procedure, the president can write these implementation bills in his own chosen way and then receive swift up-or-down House and Senate votes, without delays or amendments. On the international level, this mechanism promotes deals because foreign negotiating partners can swap concessions with the president's negotiators and have confidence when they achieve closure. However, at the domestic level, when Congress enacts a fast-track agreement, it thereby entrusts presidents with unique and enormous future domestic legislating power.[62] When the president proposes an implementation bill, Congress may only approve or disapprove it, even if, under other legislative circumstances, the Senate or House would have regarded the bill as unacceptably ideological, partisan, and unpopular and accordingly filibustered, defeated, or amended it. Trade talks increasingly raise issues of whether to repeal or weaken environmental and labor measures (e.g., safety standards for imported genetically engineered food) or job-saving measures (e.g., anti-dumping safeguards against predatory pricing of imports or "Buy American" provisions). So the fast track potentially allows the president to repeal or weaken, relatively easily, a great array of sensitive domestic laws that he could hardly hope to change through the ordinary democratic processes of House and Senate action.[63] The laws that the president gets repealed or weakened may be highly popular with the American public but not with global businesses.

In 1994 the trade fast track provided President Clinton with the means for securing approval and implementation of two key agreements: NAFTA with Mexico and Canada and the Uruguay Round that launched the WTO. After that, the Republican Congress let fast-track authority lapse, and when President Clinton sought its renewal, a bipartisan effort brought him just short of success in November 1997.[64] In the 1990s, NAFTA's implementation produced environmental and labor controversies. Ensuing pollution in the maquiladora zone along the Mexican border, for example, produced tragically heightened levels of birth defects. As to labor, the loss of good jobs as manufacturing shifted to Mexico, China, and elsewhere fell disproportionately and often intensely on less educated, less well-off workers. Meanwhile, NAFTA's benefits went disproportionately to global corporate coffers and, to some extent, more to those with well-paid, secure positions than to those with jobs most vulnerable to offshore competition. At a time of increasing economic inequality in North America and elsewhere and environmental controversy, the political struggles in Congress about trade tended increasingly to focus on these environmental, labor, and job-saving controversies, in addition to the economic issues traditionally related to trade such as farm subsidies and tariffs. The controversies became the points that brought out the different ways that fast-track trade deal mechanisms could be handled: bipartisan ways with sensitivity to the constituencies of both parties, or partisan ways that pushed just a conservative Republican agenda.

The participants in the WTO held a new round of negotiations launched at Doha, Qatar, in November 2001 and known as the "Doha Round."[65] Also, Western Hemisphere nations held rounds of talks set on a specific schedule at a Quebec summit enthusiastically attended by President Bush in April 2001. These talks aimed for a hemispheric trade bloc called the Free Trade Agreement of the Americas (FTAA), somewhat like expanding NAFTA to integrate the whole of South and North America.[66]

The stakes of the Doha Round and the FTAA explain the political concerns that caused fast-track authority to lapse from 1995 through 2002 and to become one of the thorniest issues for President Bush. President Clinton had achieved considerable, if not unlimited, success—on centrist bipartisan terms and with reservation of safeguard mechanisms that meliorated somewhat the environmental, labor, and job-saving issues—in winning congressional approval of NAFTA and the Uruguay Round and China's entry into the WTO in 1999–2000. Ironically, most global business could accept to some degree his bipartisan centrist approach. Congressional conservatives, however, did not wish President Clinton to continue further on such centrist terms, for that meant trade-oriented business would divide its political support between the two parties and have no reason to support only the conservative side. Conversely, President Bush took office notably eager for trade deals not on bipartisan compromise terms but on a partisan basis that would consolidate conservative business interests as his base. This approach entailed completely defeating environmental and labor defenders on trade matters and inflicting a disproportionate share of the economic pain on Democratic constituencies. That was his legacy as governor of Texas and that was the position he inherited from the conservative party leadership in the House of Representatives. Most Democrats, knowing this, would not readily trust President Bush with unchecked authority to dictate enactment of the likely ideological contents of his implementation bills of world and hemispheric trade deals. With this implicit but potent tension in whether trade deal mechanisms would have a bipartisan or partisan orientation, the new president as he took office chose as his czar on this subject the legal impresario of partisan trade dealing, Zoellick.

Zoellick

The partisan background of Robert B. Zoellick, President Bush's choice for the cabinet-level post of United States trade representative, indicated how the president would use and abuse this part of the law. A graduate of Harvard Law School and Harvard's public policy school, Zoellick had risen rapidly in the Reagan and Bush administrations as a protégé of James A. Baker III, the first President Bush's campaign manager and secretary of state. Besides holding a series of Treasury, State, and White House posts,

Zoellick held important campaign responsibilities in both presidential campaigns of Bush senior. In 1988 he was the Bush campaign's issues director; in 1992 he not only managed the White House while Baker was campaign manager but churned out issue positions for Bush's addresses.[67] For a 1990 profile in the *New York Times*, he commented, "I'd be quite pleased if there was a period of Republican hegemony for the next 40 years"; the younger Bush later offered him his chance to work for this goal.

When in 1991 Zoellick went to Japan in advance of a presidential visit to discuss opening the Japanese market, he proposed lowering Japanese auto safety and environmental standards, the sign of an intensely partisan operative.[68] Some Republican conservatives had joined the Pat Buchanan campaign in 1992 to signal their opposition to trade deals like NAFTA, but the young Bush and Zoellick both took a strong line in favor of trade deals. From 1993 on, Zoellick prospered serving business interests and issued opinion pieces and media comments criticizing the Clinton administration's foreign policy. Recalling his loyalty in 1992, Governor Bush made Zoellick a foreign policy adviser to his presidential campaign.[69] The appointment's potential was not lost on Enron chairman Kenneth Lay, who paid Zoellick $50,000 in 2000 just to lend his name to Enron's advisory board. This was a transparent way for Lay to put cash directly in the pocket of a Bush adviser.[70]

Most of what Zoellick said in the media at the time hewed to the safe line of shrill partisan criticism of the incumbent without specifics.[71] In November 2000, when the Florida election contest began, Governor Bush sent Baker to manage his effort. Baker kept Zoellick at his side for five weeks, plotting strategy, doling out assignments, and drafting public statements.[72] In other words, Zoellick served the younger Bush in handling top-level, legally oriented campaign responsibilities, doing so, as he had served the elder Bush, in the most intensely partisan way.

FAST-TRACK RENEWAL AFTER 9/11

Zoellick had dismissed the bipartisan Clinton approach on trade even before assuming his new office. Once installed, Zoellick would act under the cover of free market slogans, abusing the opportunities of his office to pursue a partisan strategy of outflanking the normal, democratic operations of Congress. By summer 2001 President Bush's strategy to renew fast-track authority went forward in the form of a bill filed by House Republicans that was stripped of the meaningful efforts on labor and envi-

ronmental issues that had characterized President Clinton's bipartisan successes.[73] The president's approach, pursued by Zoellick, instead aimed for a
fast-track mechanism that would dismiss environmental, labor, and job-
saving concerns; thrill the extreme side of conservative business and consolidate the whole of trade-oriented business with that side; and thereby
lock up business campaign funding as a conservative base while relatively
defunding the other party.

For its first months in 2001 the bill made only limited progress. However, the 9/11 attack afforded President Bush the opportunity he needed to
push it on. For this issue, he would skip the bipartisan unifying approach
that gained him near-universal domestic support for the Afghan military
campaign and instead advance a pure partisan agenda. It soon became clear
that President Bush viewed implementation of the fast track on his own
terms as absolutely key, and passing the bill became his earliest and biggest
post-9/11 partisan thrust. On September 20, nine days after the attacks,
Zoellick launched a salvo designed to tar opponents of the bill as undermining the anti-terrorism war. The administration, he made clear, would
slur them as unpatriotic.[74] While Zoellick demonized even free trade Democrats as failing to rally around the American flag, he himself wrapped that
flag around a bill intended in no small measure to consolidate party-line
fund-raising support from business.

Zoellick's low tactics of polarization succeeded as intended. By December 7, when the House vote came, the outcome differed totally from those
of the previous eight years. Time and again President Clinton had assembled a bipartisan free trade coalition—for NAFTA and WTO (1994),
attempted fast-track renewal (1997), and China's WTO entry (2000)—
with House Democratic support ranging from 100 to 167 votes.[75] Zoellick's tactics brought unity in his own party but support from barely 20
Democrats. The effects of his approach were memorialized in a floor speech
by Representative Robert T. Matsui (D.-Calif.), long renowned as the
Democrats' leading enthusiast and expert on bipartisan free trade. Matsui
noted that for the preceding twenty-three years he had loyally supported
every trade initiative offered by any president, Republican or Democrat—
until this one.[76]

Zoellick's approach to approval required not only holding the support of
the House Republicans with even slight free trade sympathies but also
buying the support of Republicans from districts where fears of job loss
produced intense suspicion about trade dealing. This required making
strongly protectionist promises to those Republicans that cost much more
than what it would have taken to obtain the votes of centrist Democratic

free trade supporters like Matsui. Zoellick thereby brought on one of the most nakedly revealed episodes of vote buying seen in modern times on the House floor.

Normally, House rules require a vote to end in fifteen minutes, and watching the floor process itself reveals little about what motivates members. Occasionally, the vote will stay open a bit longer, and observers see whether reluctant members who held back their votes at first bargain their way to a choice in the end.[77] In this instance, the House Republican leadership held the vote open and, in front of the television cameras, kept bargaining with protectionist Republicans for what seemed then a phenomenal thirty-eight minutes in a bid to win over the most recalcitrant holdouts.[78] The most protectionist Republicans came from the Carolinas, because over a hundred thousand textile employees in those states felt their jobs to be threatened by cheaper Third World imports and their representatives had united in the single-minded Textile Caucus.[79] The House Republican leadership signed a letter promising protection from Caribbean and Latin textile imports to Jim DeMint (R-S.C.), who switched his vote from no to yes. They made more deals with an almost-in-tears Representative Robin Hayes (R-N.C.) to achieve a 215–214 victory.[80]

Centrist business commentators, far from applauding Zoellick's partisan tactics, recognized their extremist and costly nature. The *Wall Street Journal* reporters covering the House vote noted that "by forcing through a bill tailored narrowly to Republicans, the Bush administration may have alienated pro-trade Democrats who will be needed the next time a trade deal comes up for approval."[81] The *Financial Times* of London, the international business voice of free trade, entitled its critical editorial "The High Price of Fast Track" and described "the many concessions made to producer interests to drum up votes" as making "the fast track bill that squeaked through the House of Representatives [look] like a protectionists' charter."[82] After the December 2001 House vote, the rest of the enactment process occurred in the Senate in 2002, without cliff-hangers. Senators exchanged their support for trade deals as usual, without the friction seen in the House action.

As the business press mournfully observed, Zoellick's pushing through of a partisan fast-track legal mechanism launched an escalation of administration concessions to intraparty protectionist sentiment. Ensuing Bush administration protectionist efforts included

- creating a barrier against steel imports that predictably enraged Brazil, Russia, and South Korea;

- pushing through the 2002 farm bill laden with expensive subsidies amounting over six years to as much as $180 billion, angering developing nations and making Zoellick's own later proposals to Europe about mutually reduced agriculture subsidies seem hypocritical;[83]

- passing a bill in the House to impose the protectionist barriers that were Representative DeMint's price for partisan fasttrack support against the poorest Caribbean nations;[84] and

- reneging, for partisan political reasons, on textile concessions promised to Pakistan, thereby undermining the Musharraf regime, which the United States desperately needed to shore up for the anti-terrorism effort. This move, in particular, showed the cynicism in Zoellick's slur that abjuring his own partisan course was in effect unpatriotic.[85]

If Zoellick cared more for maximizing free fair trade or minimizing the price in domestic American dislocation, he would have made common cause with trade-oriented House Democrats in passing a bipartisan fast track legal mechanism. Instead, by choosing the partisan path to getting a fast-track mechanism, he obliged the United States to make further controversial protectionist concessions to the American textile, steel, and agriculture industries.

In late 2002, following the midterm election when the administration sought ways to serve its conservative economic base, President Bush demonstrated just how hard-line he was on the domestic use of trade-related power. At one point, Congress had taken seriously concerns about the safety of inadequately inspected Mexican trucks displacing the American trucking industry, not merely on the border but deep in the American heartland. The president waited until after the November 2002 election and then implemented wide-open Mexican trucking on American highways.[86] Evidently he was willing to put highway safety in jeopardy primarily in order to attack the Teamsters Union, which had been doing its bipartisan best to engage with him in an issues dialogue.

During 2003–2004 at times the Bush administration's approach appeared to have reached a dead end. Internationally, the WTO meeting in September 2003 in Cancun collapsed. And discussions at a late 2003 FTAA ministerial meeting went almost equally downhill. Zoellick had no success in either arena in coaxing the rest of the world past a series of stumbling blocks. A major one, epitomizing all of them, one that President Bush could not let him budge much, was the newly increased U.S. farm subsidies.[87] These combined with the already excessive subsidies in Europe to create a situation in which, for internal political reasons, the rich countries poured their wealth into domestic subsidies that acted to keep the poor countries poor.

So progress at group meetings like Cancun or the FTAA ministerial meeting wasn't possible. The ever busy Zoellick hardly found himself at a loss. He simply moved forward with bilateral talks between the United States and whatever countries in the world liked doing his kind of deals—partisan ones—the most. Actually, a pre-presidential-election hiatus in trade talks made good sense. The issue of massive job loss to other countries, cheered by White House economists, became important in the 2004 campaign. It was best to bend with the wind until it passed. For a Republican president presiding over an endless "jobless recovery," the prospect of more jobs lost to countries abroad was very unwelcome. (It conjured up Ross Perot's "giant sucking sound" of jobs going down to Mexico, an image that had haunted Bush senior in the 1992 election.) Better to look sheepish and say, "Nothing much happening on the trade front."

Still, it would be a mistake to describe these years as all suffering and sadness for the cause of business making money off sweet trade deals. Take the story of trade with China. The public began noticing in 2003–2004 that the "jobless recovery" seemed to put wealth in the hands of the already wealthy but not good jobs in the hands of the unemployed and, further, that this seemed to correlate with the ballooning of the trade deficit with China. Factory jobs seemed to flee the United States, perhaps first stopping in Mexico but ending up in China. China did not reform its low wages, pollution, absence of labor rights, or other internal practices. In macroeconomic terms, the Bush administration took a lot of heat for its inability to persuade the Chinese to do anything any time soon about the absurdly undervalued Chinese currency that accelerated the effects of the unfair trade competition.

Surely someone profited from these Chinese trade deals. It wasn't George W. Bush's personal style; his background was in oil deals. But there was another Bush—his younger brother Neil, who seemed to have his hand in the Chinese fortune-cookie jar. At the end of 2003 legal documents became public in Neil's divorce from his wife, Sharon Bush. It seemed that a Chinese semiconductor company contracted to pay him $2 million in stock over five years. As Reuters reported, "The corporation is backed by Jiang Mianheng, son of former President Jiang Zemin of China."[88] It might simply seem fitting for the sons of former presidents of the two countries to profit together. Then again, in the 1990s, conservative congressional Republicans had demonized President Clinton for the mere possibility that campaign contributions to him had come through indirect channels from that direction. Even as late as early 1999, when Jiang Zemin visited the United States, Republicans unleashed their vilifiers to keep Clinton from getting the credit and leave him only with aspects that involved blame by stalling the closing of the China trade deal until long after the state visit, whereas Clinton could have showcased the foreign policy aspects of the deal.[89]

Under questioning, Neil Bush admitted that he had "absolutely no educational background in semiconductors." He explained that he knew a lot about business. He had joined the board of that company, he explained, at the request of a major Chinese figure who had also invested in Neil's latest venture, Ignite, an educational software firm in Austin, Texas. Of course, every presidential family has some members with the potential to embarrass the president; that is not a problem peculiar to conservatives and does not in itself say anything about the president. In this case, though, it did focus attention on just how much profit there was in trade deals for the well-off, while the factory workers lost their good jobs. Clinton's policies had favored steps to help those who suffered from the dislocating effects of trade return to contributing to the economy and kept some safeguards in the deals that could be triggered when other countries traded unfairly. Bush's policies had more of a "free market" approach, letting those whose families suffered from such dislocations wait for help from an invisible hand.

FTAA AND DOHA ROUND: ENGINES OF GLOBAL ECONOMIC CONSERVATISM

The most dynamic international legal element in a second term might well be the Bush administration's approach to the FTAA and the Doha Round. These held the prospect of becoming global mechanisms for lowering labor and environmental standards and even for weakening or repealing progressive domestic laws, all by circumventing the normal democratic process in Congress.

Lowering Labor and Environment Standards

Among the strong indications that the Bush-Zoellick approach could transform trade deals into global engines of conservatism was Bush and Zoellick's pressuring the WTO to turn away from dialogue with the

International Labor Organization. For President Bush, the political benefits of trade deals that fostered a hemispheric and worldwide tide against
organized labor were exceedingly attractive. This prospect loomed as
China continued its volcanic outpouring of exports into the United States
and the world, with WTO talks serving as the world's principal forum for
trade talks with China. In the past, American law governing exports to the
United States had operated as an ultimate limit on Chinese violations of
world labor standards, which included its use of a vast prison labor manufacturing system to produce cheap goods. At the very least, such export
laws reduced American complicity in these violations by limiting imports
of the products of exploitation. President Bush's hard-right views about
keeping labor standards out of the Doha Round legal mechanism signaled
China that it might concern itself less with curing such abuses and gave a
green light to all countries seeking to relax labor standards.

Similarly, on some of the key environmental concerns, the Bush-
Zoellick approach also held the prospect of blocking some of the best
opportunities for environmentally sustainable world development. FTAA
talks with Brazil, like the Doha Round talks with China, allowed the United
States and other advanced countries to discuss environmental concerns as
they reviewed potential paths for development. Unless guided otherwise,
Brazil and China could be expected to take paths that alarmingly worsened
global warming, Brazil by cutting down its rain forests and China by
increasing the burning of coal. Among the few available ways to engage
those countries in joining world efforts to head off global warming, the
FTAA and Doha Round trade talks could have put trade issues of interest
to them—their bristling at American protectionism, for instance—on the
table.

Using the FTAA and Doha Round to Repeal Progressive Laws

The Bush administration threatened even to pursue, through the FTAA and
Doha Round talks, possibilities for actively using the fast track to establish
a legal system by which conservative business interests could repeal or
jeopardize America's domestic anti-dumping, labor, and environmental
standards. Implementing bills for the FTAA and Doha Round agreements
could get through Congress on the fast track without the ordinary democratic machinery of House floor amendments or Senate filibuster.

During consideration of the fast-track bill, the Senate did pass a bipartisan compromise, known by its sponsors' names as Dayton-Craig, that
would have preserved American anti-dumping remedies from easy repeal

in trade deals by requiring a separate congressional vote. Zoellick responded by making a rare presidential veto threat, forcing the conference committee to remove the amendment.[90] This episode provides a unique insight into the uses contemplated for the fast track. In the 1980s and 1990s, congressional Democrats had sharpened American legal trade sanctions for anti-dumping and countervailing duty remedies, as well as section 301 penalties, in order to force foreign countries to alter predatory or protectionist trade practices. If a country subsidized its steel industry to dump product in America or if semiprivatized economies like China used government-arranged assistance to help producers compete unfairly, these laws kicked in.[91] Zoellick could not have gotten repeals of the anti-dumping laws through the House and Senate on their own. If he tried, he must answer arguments from the worst examples of multinational business destroying American enterprises and jobs using predatory tactics for ignoble reasons. But instead, by insuring a repeal of anti-dumping laws would occur as part of a fast-track trade agreement, he could achieve it without the full democratic process.

The more complex questions concerned how far the Zoellick-Bush fast track would go to empower global businesses—either directly or indirectly, working through foreign nations—to attack domestic state or local green laws. The prospect that global business could knock out U.S. environmental laws seems so far-fetched as to warrant analysis of how particular legal vehicles could serve this right-wing purpose. The Uruguay Round agreements already included conventions allowing one country to challenge, within the WTO panel system, another country's import-restricting environmental laws as lacking sufficient scientific support. President Bush might well push, through trade deals, sharpened legal tools permitting other nations to challenge American domestic standards. He might allow global business to contest state and local laws in federal court as inconsistent with international trade conventions and obtain court orders enjoining American localities from pursuing certain green goals. For example, such decisions might order American localities to set stringent restrictions on pesticide residues in items sold within their borders only based on completed scientific proof of the need, not on suspicion-based early warnings.

Under existing international trade conventions, while other countries might contend that restrictions without such proof operated as protectionist barriers, President Clinton, in alliance with state attorneys general, had largely kept those conventions from authorizing domestic federal court cases.[92] In contrast, the Bush administration's approach, arranged as part of a trade deal, might allow foreign countries and companies to do just that, much as federal courts can strike down local laws deemed barriers to interstate commerce under what is known as the doctrine of the "dormant" Commerce Clause.

Also instructive is NAFTA's chapter 11, originally rationalized mainly as protecting foreign investors from Mexican governmental expropriation measures. However, this "investor protection" provision also serves as a model for the conservative engine multinational businesses could seek in the FTAA or Doha Round agreement.[93] Down the road, conservative interests could challenge American procedures or rules, not just at the federal level but even at the state and local level, as reducing their market or increasing their risk. Business could use foreign investors as fronts for such challenges, just as interior secretaries James Watt and Gail Norton, in representing conservative legal foundations, used small-property and small-business owners as fronts for legal challenges to environmental rules when the real interests at stake were those of large companies. Issues about an investor protection provision go not to a court but to arbitration, a forum peculiarly insensitive to public policy and democratic governance concerns. Using those provisions, by the early 2000s, a Canadian steel beam company had challenged the federal buy-American construction provisions, and a U.S. waste management company had forced a Mexican municipality to approve a hazardous-waste landfill.[94]

Conservative interests never gave up trying to defeat the centuries-old, constitutionally protected power of citizen juries to give punitive damages against businesses engaged in outrageous conduct, such as toxic dumping or selling consumer products with unsafe pesticide residues. Now the Bush administration could railroad investor protection provisions through Congress as part of trade deals on the fast track, giving a new, potentially potent tool for multinational corporations to argue for immunity from jury verdicts.[95]

More broadly, the Bush administration had other ways via the partisan-tilted fast track to create powerful, self-perpetuating global engines of economic conservatism.[96] The previous bipartisan centrist mode of free trade agreement dealings had put limits on how many lost jobs a trade deal could impose on any large segment of the American population. Groups intensely injured by a trade deal could revolt within each of the two political parties.

By contrast, the partisan fast-track legal mechanism allowed a conservative administration to impose serious pain on particular areas and groups so long as the pain fell largely on Democratic, not Republican, states and districts. Concessions extracted from other countries might open them to global companies eager to take over public services such as water supply—sources of corporate profit but not jobs for American workers.[97] The deals might even continue protectionist shelters for those areas and groups that elect or support Republicans. In 2003 Zoellick muscled Chile in the final hours of a seminal fast-track accord, contrary to prior policy, to drop its tariff on tobacco, always an administration-favored industry. This held alarming potential as a springboard to doing the same using FTAA, thereby increasing the likelihood of youthful cigarette tobacco addiction throughout the Western Hemisphere.[98] The Republican Carolinas make textiles, while Democratic areas like Los Angeles and New York City make apparel. Zoellick's partisan approach suggested he might retain and even strengthen protectionism for textiles to win Republican House support while freely negotiating away American apparel jobs.[99]

SIGNIFICANCE OF ELECTION-YEAR DEVELOPMENTS

The mushrooming figures on American job exports in 2004 blew the lid off the Bush-Zoellick trade policy. American manufacturing and the loss of jobs to China epitomized the problem, though it increasingly affected the service sector and involved job losses to other countries, including Latin America and India, as well. From January 2001 to early 2004 American manufacturing lost 2.89 million jobs, about half of that loss occurring after the "jobless recovery" began. Meanwhile, the United States' annual trade deficit with China zoomed to $124 billion in 2003. Many imagined that the problem might in time solve itself through economic stimulation or sectoral adjustment, particularly if China eventually—although even in 2004 it had postponed dealing with this indefinitely—relaxed its artificially undervalued currency. Belatedly, in 2004 Bush began making his first minimal public relations gestures on the trade issue for campaign effect.

At that time, however, the nightmare effects of Bush's prior undermining of trade law were just starting. The potential was foreshadowed in the late 1990s. After a 1997 trip to China, where I conferred with trade scholars, it was clear to me that Beijing's system augured "problems [that were] likely to persist regarding China's compliance with WTO and accession agreement rules."[100] These problems required vigilance and a willingness to use "particularly potent tools available to the United States, such as antidumping remedies, countervailing duties, import surge safeguards, retaliations for failure to achieve accession agreement 'benchmarking,' and encouraged negotiation of bilateral trade restraint agreements with China."[101] Although Bush, in his 2000 campaign and thereafter, embraced effectively dropping the vulnerable American market's fair trade protections as to China, China's exploding Communist-controlled export engine engaged in numerous export-subsidizing and import-reducing policies, ranging from subsidy-like state bank loans to local protectionism, that flouted WTO and accession agreement undertakings—and increasingly devastated American industry.

Mark Barenberg of Columbia Law School argues that China's wide-scale violation of its workers' rights contributed heavily to its ability to unfairly undermine American manufacturing and broke the rules of international and domestic trade law, justifying American resort to tough trade remedies.[102] China's authoritarian exploitation of its workers created a cost advantage on the order of 47 percent, thereby taking an estimated three-quarters of a million American jobs. Most chillingly, China's ongoing capital investment, bank loans, and foreign direct investment set new records in 2003, warning of a blind drive toward overcapacity that would produce a major supply shock to global trade over the following five years. The American economy had continued its job hemorrhage to China even during the (jobless) economic recovery of 2003–2004, so in those coming years, when problems from enormous federal deficits and long-term interest hikes did hurt the United States, its job-losing sectors would already be on their knees.

Bush understood as much of what was going on as he wanted to—his window-dressing gestures on China trade in the election year showed as much—but while a Gore or McCain administration might have used the potent tools enumerated above earlier and forcefully, Bush would not. Bush allowed the transition review mechanism and the trade remedies planned for monitoring and policing China's accession to the WTO to stall out, and he threw away the methodologies developed in the Clinton administration for holding China to account for dumping as the country racked up violations.[103] Given that Bush evinced no dissatisfaction with Zoellick, who symbolized the kowtow-to-Beijing policy, it would seem that more years of Bush in charge would see no policy change on the requisite grand scale. A calamitous exporting of American jobs would continue to China and, as Zoellick made new deals shorn of meaningful labor rights and fair trade protections, to other countries as well.

7 Veering from Riyadh to Baghdad

President Bush wielded power far beyond that of his two centrist predecessors to lead the country by means of the sense of urgency he created, secrecy, and his legal redefinition of America's enemies and foreign commitments. After 9/11 he used his legal doctrine of preemptive war, which seemed a nice fit with his party's goals in 2002 and 2004 but a poor one with international law and world consensus. And the results mattered; his early approach shaped the international and local terms of the occupation of Iraq, and these in turn shaped ensuing international relations and the situation in Iraq.

Although fifteen of the nineteen hijackers and Osama bin Laden himself came from Saudi Arabia, President Bush first paused and then systematically excused the Saudis from their responsibility and instead took us into Iraq. Why? His approach to occupation alienated the world community and shut out even supportive elements of his own government, such as State Department and military service planners. The timing, in particular, of many steps seemed far more attuned to the calendars of the 2002 and 2004 elections than to the national interest. Why?

This chapter follows a particular line of reasoning, mostly legal: I describe the legal arrangement set up by a president whose background lay in the oil industry and in Texas and a vice president whose background lay in strategic thinking about the Middle East as an oil source—both of whom thought of the national strategic interest as interwoven with their party's interests. Cheney approached oil-related matters with little thought of personal payoff, notwithstanding his stint at Halliburton, for he had spent his working life in national politics. Bush, in contrast, had a pattern of thought going back to his personal situation in the international oil industry. Both understand that the United States' success in the world economy revolves considerably around the future of international oil and gas supplies and that these will come largely from the trifecta of Saudi Arabia, the current heart of OPEC; Iraq, holder the second largest reserves in the world; and the Caspian Sea region.

How would Bush and Cheney see their ideal, finely adjusted legal relationships with such valuable and strategically vital oil suppliers? Until the 1970s, the United States had the ideal arrangement: Saudi Arabia, possessing the world's largest oil reserves, was a very loose, informal protectorate that guaranteed both world oil supplies and enormous profits, starting with the oil find in the 1930s and continuing when Nasser's Egypt scared the Saudis in the 1960s. Since the 1970s, the Saudis have remained just as strategically vital, but they have served us less while we have increasingly been made to serve them. So with world oil needs still enormous and the United States the lone superpower, the ideal, or at least the necessary, legal arrangement became working out a modus vivendi with the increasingly powerful, albeit internally shaky, state of Saudi Arabia. As to Iraq, the arrangement called for ending the dog-in-the-manger regime in Baghdad withholding that country's second largest reserves and instead setting up a productive regime under another informal American protectorate. Perhaps the same could occur in Central Asia, particularly in the Caspian Sea region.

There happens to be a lawyer on Bush's team who serves as a marker of the working out of such a vision. That lawyer is much closer to Bush than, say, John Ashcroft, a rival through 1998 for the 2000 nomination, or Robert Zoellick or Gail Norton, who were useful but whom he barely knew. It's young George's own personal lawyer, the Texas white-collar-defense hired gun who helped him in 1991–1993 when he was caught by the SEC on two counts of insider trading. This lawyer is from the Bush family law firm, the supergiant Texas firm of Baker Botts, mentioned in chapter 1, a friend occupying a trusted role both in defending Bush and cutting a deal for him in 1993 and in seconding James Baker as head of the Florida contest in 2000: Robert W. Jordan. When Bush posted his trusted personal lawyer to Riyadh in 2001–2003, he signaled his actual interests much more clearly than he did in any of his speeches made for public consumption.

An angry nation after 9/11 might have expected that Bush would bring to terms the nation most involved in providing the men and money for 9/11—Saudi Arabia—and maybe even do something about the corrupt theocracy that causes some young Saudi men to become Osama's warriors. But instead, Bush and Jordan played out an approach requiring acceptance of the ruling Saudis' indifference and contempt toward us, their noncooperation in the financial probe into the roots of 9/11, and the United States' withdrawal from Saudi Arabia, something Osama and the Saudi rulers had long wanted to achieve. Let us follow the trail along which American attention after 9/11 got diverted from Riyadh, a source of the terror, to Baghdad, long targeted by the Republican right as a country to occupy. And let us examine how the occupation came about in a way that did not serve the national interest so much as the administration's partisan interest. In chapter 8 I discuss how the Bush administration pursued its goals using secrecy and deception.

PREEMPTIVE WAR AND THE OCCUPATION OF IRAQ: BACKGROUND

Briefly, the late-2001 Afghan campaign showed America could still be the world's hero even though acting as the lone superpower. Even the Bush administration could earn tremendous national and international support when it subordinated its devotion to conservative causes to the centrist vision of national security. The Bush administration's preemptive invasion of Iraq in 2003, without any fresh cause for war, and its occupation of that country, continuing through 2004, involved a painful return to the administration's basic subversion of law, at odds with both centrist and international consensus. One of these methodologies depended on secrecy and served as part of Rove's successful strategy of redirecting public attention for the 2002 and 2004 elections—a subject for chapter 8. Another method, discussed here, consists of a cluster of stretched or counterfeited doctrines, particularly that of preemptive war, that would justify the administration's unilateral action in Iraq.

From 1991 on, both the first Bush and Clinton administrations had treated Iraq as a dangerous enemy. Both painstakingly gathered and maintained international support for keeping Iraq weak. Both Bush and Clinton voiced the same unvarnished criticisms of Saddam Hussein as would be heard in 2002 and 2003—that he was dictatorial, vicious, a plague on his people, a potential threat to his region, addicted to chemical weapons, and maybe even committed to programs for building up others. Both presidents treated Iraq more harshly than Europe or Middle Eastern nations liked, what with the cruelty the blockade worked in practice and the provocative no-fly zones, but did so without requiring the United States to go alone in the world. All such actions were carried out under UN resolutions that strained U.S. relations with other nations, perhaps, but were acceptable to the world as a way of dealing with a tough situation.

The Bush administration's change of course in 2002–2003 had its legal roots in a neoconservative viewpoint that split from the mainstream in 1991, one that downgraded the importance of international law and consensus on the use of force in general and on Iraq in particular. Only after 9/11 did this neoconservative view take control, as exhibited in President Bush's unprecedented embrace of the legal doctrine of unilateral preemptive war against sovereign, nonterrorist nations.

In this chapter I work from international law, though it may seem abstract, to the concrete; I start with doctrine and end with Mr. Jordan the lawyer. To start with the background for the administration's legal self-aggrandizement, the first Bush administration and then the Clinton administration treated Saddam Hussein as a dangerous enemy while following a course consistent with the basic international legal regime governing the use of force.[1] From the American perspective, this collective security regime, in place since World War II (and reformulated but maintained by the first Bush administration in the Persian Gulf War), involved just a few basic building blocks. The United Nations charter imposes a general prohibition on waging war except in self-defense, granting the Security Council a large role in collectively authorizing use of force in response to aggression. The NATO alliance provided the great legal institution connecting European allies with the United States. And, although the United States took diverse stances against nonstate threats (e.g., Communist insurgencies or terrorist groups), it generally relied upon deterrence, containment, and responsive action to ward off or repel invasion by sovereign states—not unilaterally and preemptively initiated attack.

Iraq's possession of chemical weapons, its quest for other weapons, and the other negative, even dangerous aspects of Saddam Hussein's government did not create an exception to this international legal regime. I wrote at length in 1994 about the first Bush administration's courtship of Saddam Hussein right up to the eve of his invading Kuwait—while he was making just as much use of chemical weapons, pursuing other unconventional weapons, ruling with the utmost brutality, and acting aggressively toward his neighbors.[2] Bush senior courted him anyway. To a large extent we *created* Saddam. Without us he could never have pulled out of his disastrous, bloody, costly eight-year invasion of Iran and then swiveled around to the west and confidently marched into Kuwait. He misread the signals from Bush senior, but those signals emboldened him in 1989–1990. We built him up, led him on.

It was not some mistaken belief in Saddam's positive qualities or weakness on its own part that led the first Bush administration to initially court him and then, when he overplayed his hand and took over Kuwait, to defeat and then contain and weaken Iraq rather than occupying Baghdad. Partly, of course, the first President Bush sized up the instability in the region and the burdens on the United States and decided an occupation was unwise. However, he also took into account how occupation would alienate America's allies. His administration thus interpreted and applied international law to the specific case of Iraq. By choosing not to occupy Iraq unilaterally, the first Bush administration ensured that the United States—even when it employed a large measure of its superpower status—would be seen by its allies and cooperating countries as acting within the loose confines of international law and staying far away from the appearance of hegemonic arrogance.

In 1991 a conservative splinter group dominated by Paul Wolfowitz, then undersecretary of defense for policy, disagreed with the administration's decision not to occupy Baghdad and broke away from the more centrist view. The split widened during the 1990s as various foreign policy voices emerged in the Republican right. Most relevant, a group of neoconservatives boldly embraced the concept, articulated in a key 1996 article by William Kristol and Robert Kagan, of "benevolent global hegemony."[3] This new doctrine included "actively pursuing policies in Iran, Cuba, or China, for instance—ultimately intended to bring about a change of regime."[4] In other words, neoconservatives believed that the United States should—alone, if necessary—project its military might abroad, especially toward foreign governments it refused to tolerate. They favored inciting public anger, if necessary, to legitimate the doctrine as a security concept and build normative consensus as to those regimes' evil nature.

In this way the neoconservatives added a radical foreign policy construct to the mix of other doctrines, programs, and policies espoused by the Republican right, particularly after Clinton's reelection in 1996. Some, like Cheney and Rumsfeld, joined only in the most essential shared points: disdain for Clinton and desire for a more aggressive foreign policy.[5] The Southern Republican congressional leadership under Helms and DeLay emphasized, in opposition to Clinton, the element of American exceptionalism. And the ideological base harbored an unvarnished chauvinistic support, dormant as long as the hated Clinton was commander in chief, for use of more force in pursuit of moralistic objectives. These conservatives' hatred of Clinton mounted because he failed to fit their ideal of a warrior leader, creating a problem for governor and then president Bush to offset his Texas Air National Guard history, which is touched on in the chapter on secrecy.

While these various elements on the right thereby created the opportunity for an incoming president later to make political use of law, other factors led governor and candidate Bush to avoid, once again, awakening a centrist backlash by expressly joining the chorus. For one thing, to publicly embrace measures far beyond those of the Clinton administration would have required recklessness. After all, contemporary Iraq policy issued from Secretary of State Madeleine Albright and Secretary of Defense William Cohen. Albright took a hawkish line and explicitly wanted Saddam ousted; Cohen had been a lifelong Republican. Both acted in close consultation with congressional Republicans. The strong exponents of a belief in Saddam Hussein as an American nemesis had just as many ties to President Clinton as to Republicans; Iraq simply had not been an issue for the Democratic Party.[6] Moreover, in 1998 President Clinton himself took hard-line actions, including missile strikes, both as to Iraq and, after al-Qaeda's embassy bombings, as to Afghanistan and Sudan. He justified preemption against nations harboring terrorists, and he further said the United States "simply cannot allow" Saddam Hussein to acquire advanced arsenals.[7] So if candidate Bush embraced views so extreme as to sharply break with the first President Bush or President Clinton, he risked a centrist backlash.[8] In 2000 there was little popular support for sending the nation's young men and women to Baghdad. Bomb Iraq, sure, but don't send our troops.

The incoming Bush administration in 2001 continued to project force against Iraq at the same level as its predecessor through military maintenance of a no-fly zone. CIA director George Tenet, a Clinton appointee, continued under Bush, and the basic intelligence analysis of Iraq remained the same: Saddam Hussein was bad but containable. The president did allow Cheney to install the hard-liners who would set to work nullifying international legal regimes. These included Wolfowitz and Bolton, who espoused a military campaign in Iraq.[9] Secretary of the Treasury Paul O'Neill's memoirs have opened an important window, allowing us to see that Bush himself, from his earliest days in office, hungered to force a regime change in Iraq. However, policy did not move that way at first. Quite the opposite: at first, in 2001 Secretary Powell proceeded to line up international support for so-called "smart sanctions," a way of maintaining the embargo of Iraq in the face of declining international support for the human pain it inflicted. The containment system of the two prior administrations continued in effect and continued more or less to succeed.

AFTER 9/11: THE RISE OF PREEMPTIVE WAR

After 9/11 President Bush turned the nation's indignation, logically directed at Saudi Arabia, the source of fifteen of the nineteen hijackers and Osama, into not merely hatred of Iraq, uninvolved in 9/11, but into a casus belli, a justification for invasion and occupation. The president made this move in stages. In his immediate campaign against al-Qaeda and the Taliban in Afghanistan, he stayed within the classic legal framework of his two predecessors' approaches in the Persian Gulf War and in the conflict with Slobodan Milošević's Serbia. For the Afghan campaign, Secretary Powell lined up the United Nations and NATO, and President Bush dealt with Congress through meaningful bipartisan negotiations for the war authorization vehicle—one that satisfied wary Senate Democrats. Following military success, the Bush administration arranged for peacekeeping, not occupation, of Afghanistan along multilateral lines, just as his predecessors had arranged in other countries, such as the former Yugoslavia after its 1990s conflicts. Hence, in the relatively respectful attention given to international law, the Afghan campaign contrasted with controversial aspects of the neoconservative proposal to march on Baghdad.

The next chapter discusses how planning and preparations for action against Iraq began, immediately but clandestinely, pursuant to a secret directive issued September 17, 2001. I focus in this chapter on what ensued in 2002, not by use of secrecy to control the timing for political benefit, but by overt means to implement hard-liner ideology. Step-by-step the Bush administration embraced the legal doctrine of preemptive unilateral war and occupation, not against terrorist groups in disorganized locales but against sovereign nations demonstrating no terrorist tendencies toward the United States.

September 11 created a political premium for this legal doctrine by changing American public attitudes on both the right and the center about America's exceptionalist right to make war preemptively. On the right, 9/11 ended a period during which militant chauvinism had been muted, lasting from Buchanan's and Perot's campaigns in 1992 through the Clinton administration. The conservative base, now able to rally behind a president it trusted ideologically, eagerly demanded that the military be unleashed to make "regime changes," in the muscle-flexing terms most blatantly provocative to the rest of the world.

And the shock of 9/11 diminished the possibility of a centrist backlash (indeed, the president won new, if temporary, support from the center), offering President Bush an opportunity to move in the direction his ideological base desired. Before 9/11 proposals to legally sanction an American-initiated invasion risked just such a centrist backlash. Before 9/11 an expanded defense budget would bring charges of spending down the Social Security surplus and leaving domestic needs unmet. Before 9/11 centrists typically saw unilateral preemptive American military invasion and occupation of a sovereign nation—of, say, Nicaragua in the 1980s or Iraq in the 1990s—as going too far. To say that the American public in general paid direct attention to international attitudes, even in the halcyon pre-9/11 days, would be reading a lot, perhaps too much, into that centrist attitude of restraint. Still, until 9/11 the public would take its cues from respected Republican moderates like Secretary Powell or, in Congress, Senator Richard Lugar (R-Ind.), in line to chair the Foreign Relations Committee in 2003. And these internationally attuned moderate leaders did caution against taking on the consequences of transgressing international law and consensus by unilateral preemptive war making.

After 9/11, however, there naturally arose a strong yearning even among centrists to restore America's shattered sense of security. Another president would have satisfied this with a major shift in policy—an international effort against terrorism—but nothing particularly to do with Iraq. Moreover, another president would have let the natural anger at Saudi Arabia run its course. All points of the political spectrum from left to right were receptive to understanding the Saudi role (on this receptivity chapter 8, on secrecy, goes into more detail). Few alert observers could overlook the basic facts: not only did the hijackers come from Saudi Arabia, but the financing for 9/11 seemed to come from the protection-paying machine of the Saudi ruling class, a bountiful wallet for Middle Eastern terrorism generally.[10] Conservatives were not particularly unreceptive to these facts: they could read a main selection of the Conservative Book Club, Dore Gold's *Hatred's Kingdom: How Saudi Arabia Supports the New Global Terrorism*, published by a conservative press and praised by conservative reviewers.[11] As Gold noted, "Six of the fifteen Saudis involved in the hijackings went through a process of religious recruitment while they were in Saudi Arabia," whereas, he continued, "there is serious doubt whether any of the fifteen Saudi hijackers ever set foot in Afghanistan, except for one or two cases."[12] Not just centrists but even social conservatives as well could realize how the intense Wahhabi sect of Saudi Arabia had nurtured fierce *jihadi* fanatical elements, for such conservatives readily understood that this sect had been driving Saudi Arabia to become very anti-Christian. The expanded Saudi religious police operation in the 1980s, as one observer noticed, meant that "hit broadest by the [religiously zealous] movement are (1) Christian church gatherings; (2) women; (3) westernized Muslims."[13]

But if President Bush could turn public attention away from the Saudis, first toward Afghanistan and then especially toward Iraq, he had a remarkable opportunity for a political use of law. September 11 rendered budgetary concerns out of order in the security context and suppressed sensitivity to what Middle Eastern states (or, indeed, to what most other states) might argue. In international security affairs the president has vast legal powers to heighten a sense of urgency, redefine external threats, and initiate far-reaching projects in response to those redefined threats. So Bush had to transmute and redirect the public feeling of insecurity into what his conservative base wanted him to address, ideally by military means: "bad" nations like Iran, Libya, North Korea, Cuba, and the one those conservatives placed in a class by itself, Iraq.

In this matter, one particular bit of public confusion greatly helped the president: the public's unfounded willingness to believe in an alleged direct connection between Saddam Hussein and 9/11. Once the Afghan campaign succeeded but Osama bin Laden escaped, President Bush took every opportunity to manipulate the imagery of public discussion so as to shift blame onto the Iraqi dictator.

Whenever it could, the administration associated the terms "terrorism" and "weapons of mass destruction" and the images those terms evoked not with the actual terrorists and weapons (the hijacked planes) but with Saddam Hussein's name. As sheer Pavlovian associational conditioning, this accomplished a great deal. By January 2003 President Bush's efforts convinced half of those polled that one or more of the 9/11 hijackers were Iraqi citizens (none was).[14] Such manipulation of public opinion would give Republican candidates an important advantage in November 2002 and, in the administration's hopes, even in 2004.[15] What made this such an impressive propaganda exercise was how casually, almost nonchalantly, in late 2003 Bush eventually said he'd seen no evidence for an Iraqi role in 9/11. Thus Bush skillfully avoided taking the heat for mobilizing support with this exercise.

Bush's successful groundwork for this bogus mass belief in Iraqi culpability for 9/11, however, revealed a basic dilemma of unilateral action: it might serve the president's domestic political interests, but internationally it made the United States seem arrogant and threatening. Top administration conspiracy theorists might privately try tracing, and leaking to the domestic press, tenuous threads from Baghdad to 9/11, drawing on the signs of a vengeful Saddam Hussein behind early 1990s terrorism.[16] However, running these threads all the way to 2001 so lacked objective credibility that when the United States put its case to foreign audiences, they were consistently unconvinced. Domestic public opinion might allow President Bush to blur the line between 9/11 and Saddam Hussein, but for other nations, even American allies, the line existed unblurred in objective reality.[17] After 9/11 they saw good legal and moral reason to support the United States when it struck back at fanatical Islamic terrorism—even beyond Afghanistan in actions including rooting out terrorist cells in Europe and the Near East, carrying out military strikes in states such as Yemen or Somalia that might harbor terrorist bases, giving combat advice to counterterrorism forces in the Philippines, and pressuring states like Indonesia to do more against indigenous Islamic terrorism. But they saw no persuasive reason to lump an invasion and occupation of Iraq in with any of this. Without a credible basis, such a tack alienated even NATO allies and regional supporters, let alone those not so sympathetic.

President Bush's "axis of evil" State of the Union address in January 2002 signaled his direction in this regard. Commentators were confused by the list; historically the term *axis* had been used primarily to characterize concrete relations among foreign nations. This axis could better be understood as what Bush wanted to run against, an artificial unification of nations that scored low with the American public. By labeling Iraq, Iran, and North Korea an "axis of evil," President Bush lined up domestic support for aggressive action against his choice of targets among these sovereign nations—and by then no one doubted his first choice was Iraq.

The "axis of evil" speech accentuated the alienation of international support. The rest of the world observed the absence of any alliance whatever between Iraq and Iran, which had committed six-figure slaughter upon each other in 1980–1988, let alone between either of them and distant, isolated North Korea.[18] It also saw each country in its own situation, with world relations only worsened by misbranding them alike as scorned kin.[19] The phrase "axis of evil" suggested that America was supplanting the universalistic norms of international law with purely self-referential ones.

Then, in spring 2002, came President Bush's key step of spelling out the new position legally: his strained doctrine of preemptive war making.[20] Historically, international law approved by the United States had always confined preemptive attacks of any kind by one nation upon another to an extremely narrow role. In the historic *Caroline* incident, U.S. Secretary of State Daniel Webster established the requirements to justify a preemptive strike even against mere raiders based in the territory of another nation: there must be a "necessity of self-defense, instant, overwhelming, leaving no choice of means, and no moment for deliberation."[21] At the beginning of World War II, Germany's and Japan's abuse of preemptive excuses for war—the justifications they cited for surprise attacks on neutral nations' forces like Pearl Harbor—stamped the doctrine in the world's eyes as the script of powerful lawless aggressors. The Nuremberg Trials and the UN charter enshrined a legal heritage that made it greatly difficult to introduce a broader version of the doctrine to international law.

Over the past half century, while the United States had very occasionally resorted to the terminology of preemption, it responded to specific attacks: for example, the bombing of Libya for its own attack in 1986 and President Clinton's strikes in Afghanistan and Sudan in response to al-Qaeda's embassy bombings in 1998. As to the issue of security problems posed by other nations' capabilities and intentions before they supported or took some concrete hostile act, the United States had adhered to international law and consensus by eschewing not only preemptive land invasion and occupation but even preemptive air strikes.[22] To begin expanding the preemption doctrine, therefore, the United States had to struggle to find ways the world could accept. It also had to avoid justifying the preemptive leanings of nations like India and Pakistan, each of which believed the other to be a source of terrorist attacks and a wielder of "weapons of mass destruction." To expand the preemption doctrine without breaking down world order, the United States might have placed the doctrine in some self-limiting framework, as the Clinton administration did when it used support from multilateral institutions (like NATO) to justify its initiation of a bombing campaign to stop Serbian "ethnic cleansing" in Kosovo.[23] But it would have been inconsistent for President Bush, having nullified a number of international legal regimes, to confine his preemption doctrine visibly to what multilateral institutions would support.

In announcing this new doctrine at West Point in June 2002, Bush said, "Containment is not possible when unbalanced dictators with weapons of mass destruction can deliver those weapons on missiles or secretly provide them to terrorist allies.... [Since] the only path to safety is the path of action...our security will require all Americans...to be ready for preemptive action."[24] Note the centrality of what became the explanation in 2002–2003 for invading Iraq: the country would soon (if it did not already) have superpotent weapons of mass destruction (WMD) and would "secretly provide them to terrorist allies." Actually, that paranoid Saddam would undertake such action was no more likely than Stalin's using the Red Army against the United States had been—paranoids are the least likely to undermine their own preciously defended security by bringing down enormous retribution on themselves. Only in 2004, when the search for WMD in occupied Iraq proved so embarrassing, did President Bush conveniently and casually slide away from that justification for the occupation.

However, three months after that first speech in 2002, Bush used the issuance of his first formal National Security Strategy to flesh out his position.[25] The strategy's thirty-one pages covered much ground, with its central point reemphasizing preemption: the right to "anticipatory action to defend ourselves, even if uncertainty remains as to the time and place of the enemy's attack."[26] Preemption's justification rested on the claim that deterrence alone, the classic method of preventing hostile attack, failed for nations like Iraq and North Korea because "deterrence based upon the threat of retaliation is less likely to work against leaders of rogue states more willing to take risks." Yet the American response to the North Korean crisis—reliance on deterrence, containment, and multilateral diplomacy—belied a sincere belief in this logic. In this strategy President Bush also disavowed reliance on international legal institutions of security, in this case formal alliances.[27]

In September 2002 President Bush did speak to the United Nations in tones seeming to invite international support for a limited, diplomatically achievable goal of disarming Iraq.[28] Then he pressed Congress for a novel form of authority to use force, which he received. It authorized war, but on a basis allowing him complete discretion as to whether and when to employ it. By obtaining this authority, Bush wrested responsibility for the ultimate decision on war or peace away from Congress, an extraordinary preemption of another kind since it ran counter to the Framers' intent.[29]

The timing of this request for novel authority represented another dubious use of law. The president elicited congressional votes on October 20 and 21. This made no special sense in foreign affairs—late October held no significance for his self-initiated invasion of Iraq. But the dates made only too much sense for turning public attention to the issues he wanted accentuated for campaign use in the November 2002 midterm congressional election.[30]

As a matter of the law of war powers, Bush's timing, coupled with the discretionary format, allowed him to obtain the vote in Congress without having to discuss concrete aspects of the occupation he preferred not to clarify, if at all, until much later. That is, by obtaining a vote in October, months before he actually initiated the invasion, he did not have to discuss such unpleasant practicalities as the cost of both the war and the occupation, the contingency planning in case alienated allies did not join, and the real reasons for the occupation if UN weapons inspectors found no WMD in Iraq. Rather, the October vote got the country's mind off of that annoying "jobless recovery," the kind that had hurt Republicans badly at the polls in 1982 and 1992.

After President Bush achieved his objective in 2002 of regaining control of the Senate, he could proceed with a freer hand. According to close observers of Prime Minister Tony Blair's arrangements with Bush, the president had apparently agreed on an invasion in spring 2003, after further expected-to-fail international overtures in late 2002.[31] In November Secretary Powell did obtain an initial, unanimous resolution from the Security Council.[32] Resolution 1441 showed that the administration could still turn away from unilateralism, if it chose, by using an approach acceptable to international law and multilateral institutions.

Instead, however, the administration went forward with its plans for war. It made strenuous efforts to obtain a second resolution from the Security Council authorizing hostilities. Faced with a triple pledge of vetoes from not just France and Russia but even China—a real marker that the United States had grossly exceeded international consensus (the Chinese try very hard to avoid sparring with Washington over issues outside their own region)—the administration made a visible effort to obtain the vote of nine members of the Council, lobbying the six uncommitted members.

Even that failed.[33] American observers often ignore the nuances of international law and politics in the protocol followed at the Security Council. With the Bush administration completely bereft of the classic reason for preemption—a definite and imminent expectation of attack—or indeed any classic casus belli (cause of war), it had to push the boundaries of international law on use of force quite far. Absent a current Security Council resolution expressly authorizing force, special arguments may still help make the use of force palatable to other nations or at least less obnoxious to their view of international law. In 1999, for example, the special arguments in favor of the Kosovo bombing were NATO's support and humanitarian goals.[34] In this case the special arguments were the history of Saddam Hussein's transgressions, among them his unreliable adherence to UN resolutions concerning weapons inspections. When the United

States has such special arguments but no Security Council resolution, it matters whether Washington can cite a partial or arguable quantum of institutional support, albeit not a formally complete one.[35] As to Kosovo in 1999, while the United States could not obtain a Security Council resolution because of the potential Russian veto, the institutional support of NATO quieted some of the world's objections.

Had President Bush succeeded in obtaining even the nine votes he sought in the Security Council, or perhaps just eight votes (a majority of the Security Council),[36] even the subsequent veto of the resolution would have recalled the 1999 situation: the United States would have had the potential votes but no prospect of securing a resolution. The formal requirement of a Security Council resolution would have gone unmet, but worldwide public opinion and collective legal arrangements would have seemed less sternly arrayed against what the United States did.

While a host of reasons combined to deny the United States the support of eight or nine nations,[37] Bush's startling and sad inability to come anywhere near that number damaged any chance of gaining world sympathy for his unilateral approach. The president's unilateralism on human rights and environmental matters hardened opposition in Europe; unilateralism on space warfare and anti-missile defense had the same effect in Russia and China; unilateralism on immigration issues and trade relations stiffened objections from Latin America. Governments and public opinion around the world, in unison, withheld support from the United States. Never prior to President Bush had the United States been so friendless in the United Nations, so diplomatically isolated, even in the community of nations prior to the UN—this, despite the genuine wave of world sympathy a year earlier, after 9/11.

Only when the diplomatic efforts proved a failure did Secretary Powell fall back on the claim that previous resolutions dating as far back as 1991, after the Kuwait invasion, authorized hostilities.[38] Far from convincing the world, Powell's grasping for justifications reflected only his willingness to wear the fig leaf after having lost out to the Cheney-Rumsfeld squeeze.[39] Powell evidently figured he had fought the idea of going on to Baghdad for a dozen years, the deal was going down, and his remaining in office would make it easier for his beloved military and country as they veered into the (wrong) desert.

Among the key nations of the Middle East, perhaps the most singular manifestation of the American unilateral position's isolation was the Turkish Parliament's unwillingness to approve a deal, very much desired by U.S. armed forces, by which the army would pass through Turkey en route to opening a northern front in Iraq. No one could accuse Turkey of sympathy for Saddam Hussein.[40] Against this diplomatic background, the success of the American armed forces' action in overcoming the organized resistance of the weak Iraqi forces, while welcome and a great relief, failed to vindicate President Bush's overall international and domestic legal approach— not in the way success in 1991 had vindicated the first President Bush, or success in protecting Kosovo and bringing down Milošević in 1999 had vindicated President Clinton, or even success in Afghanistan in 2001 had vindicated President Bush himself. In 1991, 1999, and 2001, the presidents— including even Bush—arranged multilateral institutional support for military as well as postwar action. In none of these actions did the United States go it alone (or, as now, proceed with a "coalition" mocked by the foreign press as a transparent veiling of what British leaders meeting with Cheney at the time called the Bush administration's "visceral unilateralism"). While America's isolation in the 2003 conflict had little effect on the U.S. military's ability to enter Iraq, the U.S. decision to unilaterally inflict punishment on a Third World country caused the world to react in a way not seen since the condemnation of the millions of civilian casualties in the Vietnam conflict. American unilateral isolation prompted other nations to say, as they might not have said before about U.S. ventures, that in international law as in other legal realms, might alone does not make right.

EERIE ECHOES OF VIETNAM AND LEBANON

Suddenly the United States found itself occupying Iraq. There was one brief moment of triumph, marked by one of the most astounding visual images of the whole four years: Bush in a U.S. Air Force uniform pretending to help land a jet on an aircraft carrier right off the California coast and then circulating among real Air Force flyers. That image provides a special window into what President Bush was doing immediately before and after, because it was a strange gamble on his part that he lost. We might call that the image of the "Heroic Pilot." As an icon it mattered because President Bush always carried with him the image of young George in the rich sons' unit of the Texas Air National Guard. This was an image that he certainly wanted buried in time for the 2004 election but that also may have weighed upon him psychologically—his father having been a genuine World War II pilot, shown in navy wartime footage being picked up after the Japanese shot down his plan in fierce combat, and the son perhaps feeling he had not measured up in his youth to the father. We will shelve the issue of that specially managed image until chapter 8.

Shortly after the "Heroic Pilot" touched down on the carrier fifty miles from the U.S. coast, Iraq began turning out totally different than the Bush administration's propaganda had promised. By evoking memories of World War II or the 1991 conflict that got the Iraqi invaders out of Kuwait, the administration had fostered the expectation that the American military would be welcomed as liberators. Instead, within weeks guerrilla warfare sprang up, and American casualties mounted daily. American reserves were called up and stretched to a dangerous point, facing an ice-cold attitude from the world community and flat-out hostility—at best—throughout the Arab world. What a contrast between Bush junior in 2003 and Bush senior in 1991. The latter—up against the same country, except much stronger then—had won allies in the Middle East—not just the relatively easy ones like Turkey but even the tough nut Syria (a country that now baited Rumsfeld and got away with it)—making it infinitely harder for local eyes to look at the conflict as just the Americans pursuing their own narrow agenda.

And now a whole series of factors stemming from the way Bush and Cheney had arranged the invasion combined to make the occupation bloody and treacherous for the U.S. military and to render the profound U.S. interest in regional stability precarious. The two had stymied the efforts of the State Department to make useful plans for the postwar situation, so the occupation started without these.[41] Militarily, by overruling American commander Tommy Franks's call for more time and forces, they had virtually insured that the Iraqi conventional weapons arsenals would fall into the hands of guerrilla forces. And internationally, by alienating potential allies, they made it easy for those who wanted a fight in Iraq—both the foreign *jihadi* fighters entering Iraq and, more important, the native antipathetic forces—to maintain one, because to the eyes of Iraqis there was no disguise, no veiling, no ambiguity. They saw only U.S. troops, armed with fearsome weaponry but not speaking any Arabic, not practicing Islam, giving no sign that they were there for any interest but the narrow national interest of the United States, presumably (to Iraqi eyes) to get their oil.

And inside Iraq an enormous range of unheralded problems suddenly fell on the miserable Americans there, images of which—despite administration maneuvers to sanitize them—horrified Americans at home who watched on television. The chasm between, on one hand, President Bush's propaganda myth going in about our being treated by the Iraqis as beloved liberators and, on the other, the sudden awful reality hit Americans like a punch in the solar plexus. When the "defeated" enemy blasted the heavily protected UN headquarters in the heart of Baghdad, killing the leading diplomat the world had lent us there, the insurgents trumpeted the message that Allah (or for non-Islamic viewers, Fate) would treat cruelly and mercilessly anyone giving the United States succor in this hostile, foreboding desert.

As months and seasons went by, the situation at first got worse. The changing Bush administration line could not keep up with the increasingly awful reality. That line started with the ostensibly confident search for nuclear and other weapons, Cheney's main public justification for this venture into the desert. That one got old fast, though we did find some bits and pieces buried before 1990 and not unearthed since. The neoconservatives' moment came: they told us the United States would leisurely build a shining Western-style, true democracy in Baghdad. The Iraqis would embrace it and the whole Middle East would follow. In a flash the neoconservative moment was over, and the responsible high Bush officials got shuffled into hiding not to remind us of that line anymore.[42]

And as the Baghdad nightmare wore on into late 2003 and then 2004, the eerie echoes of past legal matters such as Lebanon (1983) and Vietnam (1964–1965) began forcing themselves on the attention of that unhappy centrist public. Suddenly, the October 2002 congressional vote hardly seemed, in retrospect, a real national decision to send our boys and girls into this desert. Legally, stage-managed congressional votes for such ventures seem to come easy to Texan presidents of either party. In 1964 President Lyndon Johnson got a nearly unanimous congressional vote for the Gulf of Tonkin Resolution. Only later, over the ensuing decade, as American boys died in Vietnam, did the public discover the scale of the Vietnam debacle that its elected representatives had technically authorized. Congress then repealed the resolution, but Nixon said the repeal didn't matter, and so the killing went on. From 2003 on, an easy initial attack, but on terms of deception about the in-country reality, meant an occupation increasingly bedeviled with problems. A hoodwinked congressional vote going in (compared to, say, the real votes in 1917 for World War I or in 1991 for the Gulf War) meant no real national commitment and resolve and, when the going got tough, not so much "shock and awe" for the Iraqis as shock and horror back home for Americans.

So the real congressional oversight hadn't come with the initial, stage-managed vote in October 2002, which the president handled—as Johnson had the 1964 vote—as though it were merely a successful preelection stunt. No, the real oversight would come after American sons and now daughters started to die and when, each year, Congress must vote the money for the president's war and decide whether the people want to impose some conditions on turning their tax money over to the commander in chief, such as how long he can keep troops where the people don't like them to be. A constitutional point: the Framers had placed the purse strings for war in the hands of the Congress because of their painful experience with the disastrous wars waged by the previous regime's chief executive, King George III.

Actually, to compress two hundred years of constitutional history into a sentence, the public scarcely realizes how many times Congress has used its purse-string and related powers, often in subtle and indirect ways, to help avoid or shorten disastrous military adventures. The bipartisan congressional leadership in 1954 scotched the proposal of Eisenhower's version of Cheney, John Foster Dulles, to throw U.S. forces into the pit of Vietnam right after the disaster of our anti-communist allies the French at Dien Bien Phu. And in the 1980s, congressional spending restrictions known as the Boland Amendments, after Tip O'Neill's no-nonsense friend Representative Eddie Boland (D-Mass.), made it illegal for President Reagan to commit American personnel or treasure to a war against Nicaragua, which Reagan therefore couldn't do—legally.[43] (But as the Iran-contra scandal revealed, the Reagan White House subverted the law anyway.)

Of what significance were the backdoor maneuvers of late 2003 regarding the spending in Iraq? Real congressional oversight using the purse strings was unlikely to occur any later, in the election year of 2004. President Bush would finance the occupation through the election on a temporary basis, presenting the real tab afterwards for payment in a supplemental appropriation. Not only would Bush do his best that year to calm Iraq down for the election, but calm or not, the congressional conservative leadership would never, in the last analysis, allow a "no confidence" vote on its standard-bearer (the incumbent seeking reelection) to occur in the election year. It might tolerate a little debate and a few votes, but the endless flows of campaign spending orchestrated by those hard-working wizards would keep the conservative leadership in control.[44] Since Bush would attempt to calm Iraq in 2004 and since the president's party leadership that year would protect Bush from preelection rebuke, any purse-string oversight, to occur at all, must occur when the reality hit hardest, in 2003. That was precisely why Bush, with an eye on the election calendar, administered the shock, ice cold, right then.

And when the shock hit, many in Congress in both parties did try hard to have representative democracy in this country about Iraq. To bite the bullet—and to handle things the Bush way—the president must ask the congressional holders of the purse strings for $20 billion to pay contractors (lumped in with money for the military, this was part of the $87 billion total that Bush requested). How should we understand that $20 billion? The Senate Republican leader from 1959 to 1969, Everett Dirksen (R-Ill.), had a favorite saying.[45] While holding forth, in his honey-tongued oratory, about spending, particularly spending for big foreign construction projects like those undertaken by Halliburton and Bechtel in Iraq, he would say that "a billion here, a billion there, and pretty soon you're talking about real money." With today's inflation that might become "five or ten billion here, five or ten billion there, and pretty soon . . ." Even without Dirksen's reminders, when Bush wisely timed his demand to the public for $20 billion to come prior to the election year, the country went into something the wags called "sticker shock." If the reaction of the general television watcher not committed to Bush could have been translated into words, it might have been "Huh? What? Did that nice president who said some things about Iraq that I was trying to follow but just basically went along with, did he just take out of my own wallet (which is none too thick these days though there's some rich supporters of his probably doing better than me), did he just remove $20 billion for a bunch of contractors he's picking?"

When the television-watching public has that kind of shocked reaction, members of Congress on both sides of the aisle hear it and factor it into their exercise of purse-string power—in particular, appropriations and the conditions upon them. Bush wanted Congress to vote an unconditional $20 billion for his picked contractors in Iraq. He camouflaged the diversion of the public's funding to his loyal and largely unaccountable machine, but the rest of the world recognized the game of awarding contracts for loyalty, and so did the press and Congress. In a long segment on the *Lehrer NewsHour* in 2003, Gwen Ifill questioned me about reconstruction contracting in Iraq; the polled reactions to that segment and to the wave of press coverage of which it was part showed the public had the situation pretty well scoped out.[46] Legally, President Bush achieved his ideological goals by putting as much of the occupation as possible in the hands of politically loyal and well-rewarded contractors. While this precluded real international support and created new impervious layers between the contractors and American public oversight, it foreshadowed the new conservative approach to projecting American power worldwide: operating not through public instruments responsible to oversight and to some extent dedicated to the public interest, but rather through privatized instruments. These private entities would do the bidding of the corporate interests ultimately responsive to the administration's partisan will and also, in this region, to the long-term financial incentives to make occupational machinery self-supporting.

By October 2003 a bipartisan coalition in Congress—truly bipartisan, with impeccable credentials—had come together to pass on to President Bush the centrist public's sticker-shock message. The coalition didn't ask for much—just a condition upon the taxpayer funds (which would never be seen again) going to the emerging government, or "Bush's Baghdad," we'll call it. (Bush's own name, "Coalition Provisional Authority," which yields the same acronym as "certified public accountant," seems inapropos. The CPA was set up as a mix of personnel from Rumsfeld's Defense Department and Powell's State Department; an observer in Baghdad noted a lot of "Bush/Cheney 2004" T-shirts worn by the partisan ideological crew.[47] In theory the CPA would give way to an Iraqi government acceptable to Bush. In any event, Bush created the circumstances for the whole process, and Bush decided what it could do and when, so why not call it Bush's Baghdad?) The proposal: Bush's Baghdad should be requested to pay back—some day, in return for the $20 billion we were investing up front—$10 billion. That is, give it $2 now and ask back, someday when the oil flowed like honey, only $1?

Certainly in the long run, a suitably occupied Iraq would be good for a loan. That was the interesting thing about Bush's decision to pick Iraq as the country to occupy—the interesting thing that remained after eliminating the phony association of Iraq with 9/11, and the manufactured intelligence about the imminent threat of WMD, and the mythology that a generous Bush sought oppressed Islamic peoples who would gratefully receive his Christian liberation. And that was the interesting difference with Afghanistan, where there at least had been a real Osama who had launched 9/11 (even if his source of men and money was not Afghanistan but Saudi Arabia). Afghanistan needed help, it had covetous neighbors, but the country didn't interest Bush or Cheney. Afghanistan wasn't good for a loan, because there wasn't oil in Afghanistan.

But there was oil in Iraq—a whole lot. More than you might think given Bush and Cheney's coyness about it—an odd reticence on their part, considering how much they talked about the rationales that evaporated. Even the old data from before the Gulf War measured proven oil reserves in the area under Bush's Baghdad at 112 billion barrels, with oil in place at 250 billion barrels.[48] As Dirksen might say, a billion barrels here, a billion there . . . And that's just for openers. Iraq is one of the least explored among the rich oil countries, yet it possesses the most enormous and easy-to-tap fields outside the territory of our great friend Saudi Arabia. I hope I don't violate the USA PATRIOT Act in voicing the thought that Bush of Harken Oil and Cheney of Halliburton might have realized the potential of the oil fields of Iraq when they decided that this country, unlike the others in Asia that might have cruel dictators, warranted special attention. Certainly the Iraqis themselves had that view: when polled, they distinctly attributed Bush's motivation in occupying their country to oil.

If Bush's Baghdad never pays back that $20 billion unconditional appropriation, then the whole sum comes from American middle-class taxpayers and their children. It gets added to the national debt that must be serviced over their lifetimes. That debt service would not be paid by the rich, who had farsightedly backed Bush, as previously discussed, and it couldn't come from the poor, from whom not much more could be squeezed. The world community showed little willingness to contribute much toward the $20 billion for Bush's contractors. Even the Japanese—who have the world's second largest economy and whom the American military defends for free against North Korea, China, and Russia—were slow getting up their little $1.5 billion.

What does it mean when the Bush administration, either directly or through Bush's Baghdad, picks the contractors?[49] For major American companies, given the opportunities afforded by constrained competition on White House orders, government contracting law usually means cleverly boosted profits. Such contractors, staying within the law by using their PACs, often make generous campaign contributions for the conservative cause. They need not give to Bush—they may give to "good" congressional Republicans. For those contracting or subcontracting firms run by Iraqis who have administration connections, government contracting law means something very different, for full-scale congressional oversight of the spending that goes through them is unlikely. Iraqis connected to the administration's hard-liners who handle taxpayer money from rich America and hope to survive (and prosper) in this nearly lawless environment will handle the money "wisely"—that is, a fair amount in the end may well flow after a few steps into Swiss bank accounts or the like.

Fortune magazine, in an October 2003 article entitled "The Iraq Fixers Are Circling: No, Not the Rebuilders, the Washington Lobbyists," revealed who gets hired to help with the pesky little details of government contracting law.[50] The top such contractor is Joe Allbaugh, who ran Bush's campaign for governor in 1994 and managed his presidential campaign in

2000. Allbaugh chairs "New Bridge Strategies," which he runs with two former aides of Bush's father. The company's Web site touts how it is "particularly well suited to working with" what it cheerfully calls "the American rebuilding apparatus." Allbaugh says his lobbying clients include "telecommunications, food services, transportation, construction, [and] oil and gas."[51] If anyone were to ask me who to hire in connection with government contracting of this kind—me (coauthor of *Government Contract Law*) or Allbaugh—I would say, don't be a fool. Hire Allbaugh.

So as Bush's ice-cold shock message about the $87 billion, including the unconditional $20 billion for the contractors in Bush's Baghdad, worked its way through the public, Congress also noticed lobbyists like Allbaugh in action. One strong bipartisan purse-string proposal became the central and essential vehicle for moving the public's message through Congress to Bush. As *Congressional Quarterly* reported, "The most prominent proposal to emerge in the Senate came from Kay Bailey Hutchison, R-Texas, and Susan Collins, R-Maine, and would have made half of the $20.3 billion reconstruction package into a loan administered through the World Bank. . . . The final version of the amendment would have provided . . . . [that the] $10 billion [to] be structured as a loan would be converted to a grant if 90 percent of Iraq's prewar sovereign foreign debt . . . was forgiven by other countries."[52] One senator was not fooled into voting for the bill on the expectation that the amendment would survive to enactment: Senator Kerry flatly declared, "The best way to support our troops and take the target off their backs is with a real strategy to win the peace in Iraq—not by throwing $87 billion at George Bush's failed policies."[53] For this position Bush vilified Kerry during the 2004 campaign as falling short of his own seemingly strong support for the troops. The bill had the inestimable advantage that its passage would not deny one cent to the troops. It would not deny one cent even to the contractors. The bill would not even solicit any foreigners like the Japanese or, perish the thought, ask the Saudis to ante up one cent. It may be indelicate here to recall that in 1990 Congress "suggested" to the first President Bush, and he impressively arranged, to make foreigners, principally the Saudis and the other gulf states, pay virtually the entire $50 billion bill for the Gulf War. The money all went through careful appropriation accounting and basically got spent in the traditional way—no special funny business.

Bush's ice-cold shock hit very hard—as he intended. This takes some explaining. For example, Orange County congressman Dana Rohrabacher (R-Cal.), who normally beams with pride when told his politics is to the right of Attila the Hun, roared about how the public thought: "We're going to borrow this money so that we can give it to Iraq, which will be rich with oil in 10 years? That's obscene." It was safe to say that in the House: DeLay, "the Hammer," had the tools, which he used, not to let "the People's House" even vote on the issue. Ah, democracy.

But Senate procedure does not preclude a vote—in the first round. So despite intense presidential lobbying, the Senate voted 51–47 to impose the requirement of repaying $1 for each $2 to the contractors in order to send this message on October 16, with front-page headlines blaring, "Senate Defies Bush on Iraq Assistance."[54] Eight Senate Republicans abandoned Bush, including the seemingly ungrateful Saxby Chambliss (R-Ga.). (Readers will recall that Chambliss, who did not serve in Vietnam, got helped into his Senate chair by Rove and by Bush, who did not serve in Vietnam, by running ads condemning incumbent Max Cleland—who lost three of his four limbs in a grenade accident while honorably serving in Vietnam—as a pal of Osama and Saddam.) It would appear that Rohrabacher and Chambliss really took their responsibilities seriously and stood up to Bush—right? But that Senate vote only sends the spending bill, the appropriation of the $87 billion, to the conference committee. As *Congressional Quarterly* drily explained, "Bush's lobbying [in that conference] focused most intently on two Republicans—Sam Brownback of Kansas and Ben Nighthorse Campbell of Colorado."[55] Even Bush's success in turning around those two conservatives was no foregone conclusion. Kansas used to elect Democratic representatives from Wichita and Topeka, where the populist slogan "Raise less wheat and more hell" used to reverberate. Senator Nancy Kassebaum politely stood fast many a time against the congressional Republican right wing, and many Kansans now watched this Iraq venture on television and didn't want to send their money, one way, to the contractors of Bush's Baghdad. Senators Brownback and Campbell had voted on the Senate floor before their colleagues, their country, and their constituents (I won't mention their consciences) to send Bush their public's message.

But perhaps someone hadn't quite understood President Bush's full purpose in delivering that ice-cold shock in late 2003, to get it out of the way before the election year. So the vote in conference came on October 29. On that day "Brownback and Campbell were conspicuously absent—though they cast votes by proxy that reversed their earlier support."[56] That is, they flipped around to pull back on the message to Bush, just used the indirect method (the proxy) to hide their faces. Even so, the administration's lobbying of them had to be fierce, because they had already gone on record, a real embarrassment to them. At such moments, when presidential arm-twisting bears down on a senator who knows that reversing him- or herself means appearing before the political world as supinely pusillanimous, senators like to say you can hear the shoulder joint snap. Brownback and Campbell should be pitied, not criticized. It must have hurt like the dickens.

Then came the last act for the power of the purse in 2003. Bush's $87 billion for his mistake must come back from conference unencumbered by any message from the public or Congress, not even the symbolic one about the reconstruction money getting paid back from future Iraqi oil revenues. The Senate must pass it—no way around it—on November 3, 2003. Each senator must say whether he or she supports it without that message attached to it, right? No. For the eight Republicans who voted for the October 16 version, that would hurt too much. (It also might hurt for some of the Democrats, particularly those running for president. So the Democrats would lie down and go along, but forgoing a final Senate vote was traceable to control over the wavering [Republican] Senate conferees, and that control lay in the hands of the sole person who could twist those Republican senatorial right-of-moderate arms hard enough: President Bush himself.) Now, from a commonsense view, the main reason the public puts up with senatorial high jinks is that it hopes senators will use their independence, their conscience, and their constituents' reactions and go on record on the hard decisions as voting "yea" or "nay." Isn't that what we mean by representative democracy? But as noted, the country's conservative leadership decided that this bill on Iraq would be decided by a voice vote. No record. No formal listing to reflect that the eight Republican senators had reneged on their prior vote, that they changed their mind and said to Bush, "The people simply won't get to send a message through me for you on Iraq."

Senator McCain knew sadly what this meant. He had endured years of privation and much pain but attained great honor as a prisoner of war in Vietnam. He had traveled the road to the White House and, perhaps better than anyone, could imagine how different things would be if he were the Republican president. Some very similar maneuverings, equally irresponsible, had taken place in the Senate in the years leading up to his stay in what his buddies called the "Hanoi Hilton," and he did not like seeing them repeated. Perhaps had McCain become president and the same mistakes as to Iraq had occurred (indulging this supremely counterfactual hypothetical), McCain would not have prevented the Senate from going on record on the subject of sons and daughters serving their country by going to a foreign land and, in some instances, not coming back. McCain said at the time in a serious public talk, "It's not wise to have the vote go unrecorded. . . . I do not understand why we did it by voice vote."[57] It took a long time for Congress to exercise the power of the purse on Vietnam. It finally did so in 1975 under President Ford, when it shut down combat operations in and over Indochina—the year Ford's secretary of defense, Rumsfeld, and White House chief of staff, Cheney, presumably shook their heads at how wrong Congress had been to thus interfere.

Vietnam is too strong a legal and practical analogy for Iraq. President Bush could calm Iraq in the short term. Unlike the regime in Vietnam— the enemy that had outlasted the Japanese, the French, and then us—Saddam Hussein's regime had merely crushed its own people and sparred bloodily but ineffectually with Iran. This showed the deep disease that afflicts really any regime in Baghdad: Iraq has several quite distinct nationalities that do not easily coexist together and that have trouble living in that rough neighborhood of Shiite Iran, Sunni Saudi Arabia, and Kurd-fearing Turkey.

Hence, self-interested yet cool observers drew analogies not to Vietnam but instead to Lebanon, the one-time "Switzerland of the Middle East" that fell to pieces in a violent civil war starting in the late 1970s. In Lebanon, as in Iraq, the ostensible regime before the American troops entered (in 1983) lacked legitimacy on the ground. So in Iraq in 2003–2004, as an astute columnist paraphrased his interview of the Turkish ambassador to the United States, "there is a 'very good possibility' that Iraq could end up as another Lebanon—a nation of warring factions with each supported by a meddling neighbor."[58] When President Reagan insisted on sending Marines on a murky mission into Lebanon in 1983, wise senior senators of both parties held hearings, gave speeches, and otherwise tried to warn him. They got a preliminary legal message to Reagan by enacting an authorization for his military intervention in Lebanon that signaled, albeit subtly, their reservations.

Calamity occurred in Lebanon: by use of suicide bombing the enemy killed over three hundred Marine officers. Horrible as this was, the congressional hearings and debates had created a framework in which the Reagan administration now understood what it must do: get out of Lebanon right away. The stunned President Reagan, who had not apprehended the dangers of sending American troops into that part of the world, now got the message and pulled out fast. Some would call that defeat, but no one criticized Reagan for pulling out—quite the contrary, the pullout saved the Reagan presidency, and today many conservatives call him a foreign affairs genius. Perhaps President Bush received the message on the same frequency broadcast by the Turkish ambassador, who when asked "to give his opinion on the Bush administration's odds for successfully remaking the country [Iraq], thought for a moment and replied, '60-40.'"[59]

To the legal and legislative eye, it told a great deal that Bush could and did extraordinarily crush congressional ability to send him the message elicited by his own $87 billion shock. Bush had so subverted the normal oversight process that he could time his biggest preelection problem for his political convenience; could absorb the courage of even his own conservative Republican senators, such as Chambliss, as they faithfully tried to pass on to him the people's message; and could run things his own way in the end, regardless. By breaking the resistance of his own conservatives Brownback and Campbell, he displayed how firmly he held the whip and the reins over a previously sovereign and democratic centrist public.

So Bush had the power. That left the question of what he wanted to make of Iraq. Here is an analysis. What is in Bush's mind cannot be documented in footnotes. What evidence there is I present in the following section. But first let me state the analysis.

Bush wanted what he had known of paradise in this context. Most other Americans after 9/11 had not forgiven the Saudis for their role and didn't think of Saudi Arabia as paradise. Only Bush (and a few like-minded rich Texas oil executives) still thought of creating another country like Saudi Arabia, or more precisely, like Saudi Arabia prior to 1974. Before 1974 Saudi Arabia had been an informal American "protectorate" with its own native satraps who kept things quiet—kept the women and the poor down and so forth—while Aramco—the consortium of the Texas Oil Company ("Texaco") plus three of John D. Rockefeller's Standard Oil companies (now known as Exxon, Mobil, and Socal)—reaped the oil profits. The Texas leaders in Washington kept the oil business exempt from pesky taxes, while the American taxpayer paid for military protection of the vulnerable Saudi riches via the American navy cruising offshore (ready to "fight communism," as anyone who wanted a different deal was of course labeled). Just so Bush's Baghdad, if it worked out: an oil-producing state, with native satraps, making money for the international oil company executives; low taxes of course, with everyone at the top who is in on the deal keeping a huge cut; big but discrete payoffs to the Republican conservative machine via the contractors; and the middle-class American taxpayer paying all of the bill.

How can we find out just what Bush thinks about Saudi Arabia—not how Cheney or Rove thinks, but how Bush himself thinks and how he himself uses the law to implement his approach? We could ask him, but there's a better way. To follow the trail of the Bush administration's subversion of the Constitution and laws in the Middle East, we must travel to the ultimate source. We must study the previously unanalyzed record concerning who Bush sent to Saudi Arabia to represent him. We must study just how little Bush cared about having competent foreign affairs officers watching out for American vulnerability to terrorism by Saudi hijackers at the most fearsome base of that terrorist threat. We must study Bush's own personal hired-gun defense lawyer and why Bush sent him to be our man in Riyadh.

BACKGROUND: SAUDIS AND HARD-LINE REPUBLICANS

Briefly, the ruling class of Saudi Arabia, the House of Sa'ud (hereafter, "the Saudis," unless the context includes the nonruling classes) consists of about a thousand very wealthy relatives. They share two forms of quasi-absolute international power that, like any such power (and unlike power in a truly accountable democracy), can corrupt absolutely. Within the Islamic world, the Saudis control the holy sites at Mecca and Medina, which all Islam prays toward five times a day and desires to visit in the Hajj. For the rest of the world, the Saudis control through OPEC the easiest world oil spigot to turn on or off and thereby manage the world price of oil almost to the same extent that Alan Greenspan manages short-term interest rates in the United States.

As power and money over the decades have increasingly corrupted the House of Sa'ud, as its lack of accountability and vices have taken their toll, the Saudis nonetheless have refused to reform. They keep much of their country's own population powerless, angry, and relatively poor. They hold the population down by a mixture of religious (Wahhabi) police and highly paid, mostly American, private "corporate warrior" services that "train" the force that guards the Saudi royal class.[60] They treat women as chattels, thereby squandering half the precious talent available to make a strong nation—in contrast to, say, the Egyptians, a nearby Islamic and Arab people who, at least until recently, viewed their daughters as real people.[61] This is based on sources spanning the ideological spectrum from books and articles written by centrists to Dore Gold's popular 2003 book, *Hatred's Kingdom: How Saudi Arabia Supports the New Global Terrorism*, which became a main selection of the Conservative Book Club.

Until 1974 the Saudis were, as noted above, ideal partners for the American-centered international oil business. But since the quadrupling of oil prices by OPEC in 1974 and 1978, the Saudis have been a difficult "ally."

When we give them a chance, in fact, we don't manage them. They manage the American government, particularly under conservative Republicans from Texas like Armey, DeLay, and Bush, in ways a country proud of its sovereignty should find unacceptable. To manage our government, the Saudis primarily use the high road of their world economic and regional political power. Also they use the low road of directing the flow of benefits to those in America who help them obtain "understanding" and "deference" from American policy makers—that's the better way to put it, for the crude term, *corruption*, again may overstate the matter and also fails to do justice to the Saudi skill in manipulating the supposed superpower capital of the free world. *Corruption* doesn't acknowledge Saudi artistry in flattering the receivers of their baksheesh while, behind their backs, holding them and their whole country in contempt as foolish infidel dogs deserving whatever awful fate Allah has in store for them when they enter or leave the desert. And it fails to reflect the Saudis' feeling that it was they rather than he who had gone to Paradise when Bush came into office under them.

As to the high road, from Nixon to Cheney the Saudis offered Republicans a basic deal. The Saudis and the Republican presidents allied to project power into Central Asia to oppose communism during the Cold War and, after that, to fill in the new regional vacuum before others, such as Iran or China, did so.[62] In Reagan's two terms, according to public sources, when we backed the Afghan Islamic-extremist elements, we did so alongside the Saudis, who trained and sent their own son Osama to join the local warlord with the strongest Saudi backing and declare himself the Saudis' "representative in Afghanistan."[63] Afterwards, in the 1990s, the Saudis and the proxy service built up by the Reagan CIA, the ISI (Pakistani intelligence), sustained the takeover of Afghanistan by the Taliban.[64] So Reagan, his proxies, and the Saudis stirred up devils that would later torment us: Osama plus his Taliban base.

Off the high road, the Saudis played the Republicans other ways. (They could hold their own in Democratic administrations also, but as we'll see, that wasn't quite as good for them.) They are said to have given Nixon, through Adnan Khashoggi, a cool million in a suitcase of cash as lagniappe (during Nixon's pre-Watergate cash orgies); Prince Bandar bin Sultan gave Reagan thirty million to fund his private illegal war against Nicaragua; and when Bush senior left office, the Saudis proved very generous through the plush payroll of the Carlyle Group.[65] From some point after 1992 until late 2001, the Bakr bin Laden family—the billionaire family close to the ruling class, with its scion Osama—had millions invested with partnerships of the Carlyle Group.[66] CIA veteran Robert Baer writes, "With embarrassment spreading on both sides, Carlyle and the bin Ladens parted company in October 2001, some five weeks after the World Trade Center and Pentagon attacks."[67]

Let's connect up the Saudis to the post-1992 rise of Republican hard-liners in general and George W. in particular. Baer interestingly describes 1992–2000 for the Saudis as "the dark interregnum of the Clinton years." Democrats had not always been that way. Back before the OPEC years, Lyndon Johnson got on just fine with oil interests at home and with the informal protectorate of the Saudis. Indeed, he ran the Senate as majority leader (and Sam Rayburn, the House, as Speaker) and, later, acted as president to ensure that the foreign tax credit would continue shifting count-less billions from the American taxpayer to domestic and foreign oil inter-ests alike. (That tax code provision gives oil companies a 100 percent credit for Saudi royalties, rather than a mere deduction for it as a business expense, as royalties to the landowner usually are treated. In this way the American taxpayer foots the whole bill for the high cost to the Saudi rul-ing class of vice, "protection," and bribery.)

But with OPEC's rise through the quadrupling of oil prices in 1974 and 1978, and with the corresponding American economic stagflation that made the 1970s a decade of pain and destroyed first President Ford and then President Carter, the American public took an interest in discourag-ing one of its two parties from taking the crudest Saudi bait. (True, Amer-ican Jews, most of whom supported Democrats, feared that Saudi wealth and the Saudi ability to get top-of-the-line high-tech weaponry from Washington would produce peril for Israel. But Lyndon Johnson managed to get plenty of American Jewish support notwithstanding his discrete Texan love affair with the oil companies and the Saudis; what changed in the 1970s and pushed the Saudis more into the Republican than the Democratic camp was the painful effect on the broad American public of OPEC, not the factor of one ethnic group's loyalties.)

Apart from the Saudis' fondness for what Bush senior had done in the Gulf War and Clinton's political coolness toward them, other elements in the 1990s brought them into synch with the rising conservative Republi-cans, particularly those of the wealthy Southwestern base.[68] For a post-2001 example, American gasoline prices spiked an average of twelve cents a gallon during a one-week period in August 2003, making television headlines and annoying the public. Thirty-two Senators signed a protest led by Senator Chuck Schumer (D-N.Y.) and Democratic leader Tom Daschle, noting the reason for the price spike: the Saudis curtailed sales of crude from 2 million barrels per day to 1.5 million in the middle of the American summer driving season. Who knew why? It didn't interest the Bush administration to fuss about it. Saudi ambassador Prince Bandar did not deny the facts, just airily dismissing the conclusion as "nonsense" and "a trend to blame anything and everything on the Saudis."[69]

The 2001 inauguration of young George brought the Saudis to their greatest influence, their greatest degree of American deference, ever. At least Bush senior, in his early years, had wildcatted his own domestic oil company, Zapata Petroleum. He had some of the independent entrepreneur in him, even if his Carlyle Group later sought Saudi payoffs. His son built no oil company, and as he "made" his "own" fortune, young George presumably told himself that he was doing international oil deals at Harken Oil based on his brains and his Harvard MBA: who tells the sons of the rich and powerful who don't serve in a war that there are no honest gains without pains? And who would tell Bush junior that he was just part of a system for suborning his father, legally? What a convenient setup for the Persian Gulf paymasters, who invested in an early "business relationship" with Bush senior for that reason and then discovered that, just like at home, the sons of the ruling class became the new ruling class.

Actually, for the Saudis, having Governor Bush care nothing about international affairs worked fine. Bush picked Cheney of Halliburton, a tight Saudi friend fresh from a company just about buried in lucrative contracts, as his foreign minister, the best of all possible worlds. The less he talked about foreign affairs in 2000 and the less he complicated the Saudi task in bribing and steering his administration, the better. Baer comments, "With the Bush II administration, [Ambassador] Bandar retook the White House as spectacularly as when the British burned it in 1814, turning himself into a permanently visiting head of state."[70]

BUSH'S LAWYER ROBERT W. JORDAN, THE SAUDIS, AND 9/11

With the foregoing background, let's now focus on Bush's own uses and abuses of law—this book's subject. For the Saudis, international relations does not consist of paper treaties or United Nations actions. They make their legal deals as in the desert—orally, senior negotiator to senior negotiator. So the choice of ambassadors matters more to them than it does to any other country in the world; it decides who is master at the negotiating table and who is, with many flattering words, basically taking orders and getting bought off.

The Saudis have made themselves the master by ensuring that their ambassador to Washington is a virtual Talleyrand, a diplomatic master, and Washington's ambassador to Riyadh is something quite different, basically someone close to the president whom they can flatter and fawn over but pay and direct as one would any top-quality servant on loan from a rich friend. For their potent Talleyrand, the Saudis have what Baer describes as the legendary and matchless access, funding, and power in Washington of Prince Bandar, who has served as Saudi ambassador since 1983. He whistles and the White House quickly comes; CIA directors barely match his access and never dare to challenge him; he end-runs any diplomatic or military objections without breaking a sweat; he pals with his leadership allies in Congress and brushes off the rest.[71]

As a small example, in mid-2002 it surfaced that the Defense Policy Board had endorsed an assessment that "the Saudis are active at every level of the terror chain, from planners to financiers, from cadre to foot-soldier, from ideologist to cheerleader."[72] This wasn't some Democratic analysis; this was from the board headed by Richard Perle, in any other context considered a guru of Bush administration policy. Not on this. Bandar broke Perle instantly. Bandar didn't stop with Secretary Powell's immediate abject disavowals. Bush invited Bandar to the Crawford ranch for personal reassurance.[73] It happened only once; it wouldn't happen again.

In Riyadh the shoe is on the other foot. Once, just once, in late 1987, right after the Iran-contra sobering-up kicked the misguided little junta of Ollie North and company out of the Reagan White House and put Howard Baker and Brent Scowcroft (neither one a fool) in to clean up, Washington tried to put someone in Riyadh, Hume Horan, capable of doing the vitally needed real work. In April 1988 the Saudis made Reagan take Horan back after only six months, a real slap in the face to the former actor who had been so nice to them but whom they now viewed as just a very lame duck. Thomas L. Friedman wrote in the *New York Times* the month after 9/11, "What the Saudis didn't like about [Horan], though, was that he was the best Arabic speaker in the State Department, and had used his language skills to engage all kinds of Saudis, including the kingdom's conservative religious leaders who were critical of the ruling family."[74]

Ambassador Horan seemed likely to start finding out how things really stood, such as the fact that Saudi sons like Osama were learning in the Afghan guerrilla war how to destroy even the most formidable of world powers. Horan seemed likely to find out that the basic Saudi plan was just to keep paying protection to whoever it would propitiate, including terrorist movements. All the Saudis wanted was to persuade Islamic jihadists like

Osama not to punish them for permitting themselves to be corrupted by the West but instead to attack some other target. Soviets were fine. Israel was fine. He could help the Islamic Pakistanis against the Hindus in Kashmir for all they cared. And if he attacked the United States—well, wasn't that better ultimately than having him turn those skills and weapons on the Saudis?

Wouldn't this Saudi way of thinking, indicating the direction things might take, be something the United States would want a Horan in Riyadh to start trying to find out? But that isn't the role the Saudis dictate for the American ambassador in Riyadh. Friedman continues: "The Saudis didn't want someone so adroit at penetrating their society, so—of course—we withdrew Mr. Horan. Ever since then we've been sending non-Arabic-speaking ambassadors to Riyadh—mostly presidential cronies." The reporter politely went on to other points without discussing the details of how Bush's own ambassador, Robert W. Jordan, fit this latter category.

We met Jordan in an earlier chapter. Recall that he came from Baker Botts, the supergiant firm headquartered in Houston that has long served the Bush family and been run by the James Baker family, reflecting an interfamilial multigenerational lawyer-protecting-client network. Recall also Jordan's own background: he's a trial lawyer, basically a hired-gun defense lawyer for special Texas interests under legal challenge. Bush senior's law firm picked Jordan as the defense attorney for young George when he stumbled into two different kinds of alleged insider trading and the SEC had no choice but to notice his hand in the cookie jar. As young George's personal defender, Jordan did just fine in 1991–1993. He beat the case by making a bogus privilege claim to withhold the offense's key proof, persuading the SEC to refrain from questioning the president's son about his multiple self-contradicting explanations and to drop the whole matter. This was an SEC top-heavy with "sensitive" colleagues from Jordan's own firm (some recused, of course), put there directly or indirectly by his client's father, the president.

There was an irony in Jordan's representing Bush on Harken. As Kevin Phillips has pointed out, during this period "Harken would turn out to have links to Saudi money, . . . the emir of Bahrain, and the shadowy Bank of Credit and Commerce International [BCCI]. . . . Harken was described in the *Texas Observer* as having 'direct links to institutions involved in drug-smuggling [and] foreign currency manipulation. . . . Bush received over $500,000 from the deal [i.e., the acquisition of his prior company, Spectrum 7, by Harken], annual consulting fees, and, presumably, the unmistakable message that his financing rested on his name and connections."[75]

BCCI was the target of serious investigation by a Senate subcommittee chaired by John Kerry, who used his findings to develop legislative proposals to prevent money laundering by foreign criminal groups (such as al-Qaeda). Later, President Bush stuffed those proposals into one of the more respectable titles of the USA PATRIOT statute. In effect, Bush took credit for enacting what Kerry drafted to deal with dicey connections like Bush's own. Next round, Jordan will advise Saudi businesses how to circumvent the Kerry-drafted statute so as to continue buying influence in America, as they did around 1990 with young George of Harken, and "protection" from terrorists, as they did at the same time from young Osama bin Laden. Meanwhile Bush attacks Kerry for failing to be like Bush portrays himself—tough on money-laundering terrorist connections.

Of course Jordan and Bush bonded during the latter's SEC troubles; in a situation like that, the son who is aware of his guilt but doesn't want a bad mark on his record thinks Jordan is a swell guy for using these methods to get him off scot-free. In 2000, when former secretary of state James Baker himself took over management of the strategic and legal side of the Florida contest, he put Jordan to work—bonding him still more closely to Bush.

In January, at Bush's inaugural, Baker Botts threw a private party for, among others, Bandar. Bush senior had gone to Riyadh shortly before the 2000 election; Baker himself often went to Riyadh for the Carlyle Group to get a generous squeeze of the "gratitude" for the Gulf War; and now, Baker Botts opened a Riyadh office.[76] Riyadh was not exactly rolling out the welcome mat to every American law firm seeking to come there.

Meanwhile, President Bush gave every other plum ambassadorship to someone who had contributed heavily (in money) to his campaign. Only Jordan did not have to give some big amount. It's not that he couldn't or was unwilling. The "free" ambassadorship tells us much. Bush may or may not have known the other ambassadors—Rove and others handle most donors—but he knew this one, directly, personally. When Bush posted Jordan, the Saudis must have smiled with absolute delight. Better even than the usual types they got (apart from Horan), this one was much better than just a presidential crony. Al Smith (of Tammany Hall in its corrupt prime) once said of a young lawyer that he was "learning to take a bribe and call it a fee"; in American experience, only the viewpoint of Tammany Hall approaches that of the Saudis. They would see in Jordan, as a partner of Baker's supergiant firm, one who knew perfectly how to build the firm, build his own financial blessings, and serve his clients. And the Saudis' record sent the message for them that for services rendered to them, they could be expected to pay afterwards even better than during or before. The Carlyle Group received fabulous sums. Jordan and Baker Botts were perfect for them.

Officials in the State Department know exactly who will pick the ambassador to the Saudis after a party change in the White House. At the U.S. embassy in Riyadh, officials must listen through the grapevine for who it will be and plan smoothly so the policies the new bosses want get into place quickly. In 2001 these officials didn't feel (and they were probably right) they could let little things like the bombing of the U.S.S. *Cole* next door in Yemen cause them to worry about al-Qaeda; that was the FBI's problem, not theirs. As we have discussed, Ashcroft regarded terrorism as a Reno issue, not one of his; Bush never raised the issue except to promote missile defense. At the Riyadh embassy, they would read these tea leaves and put aside worrying about possible connections to the 1993 World Trade Center bombing or the 1996 Khobar Towers bombing in Dharhan, Saudi Arabia.

No, in June 2001 American embassy officials in Saudi Arabia, reading the open book of the new administration's desires, adopted an extraordinary delegated approach to allowing noncitizens from one country into the United States without even the minimum of legal precautions. They called this by the typically cheerful Bush administration name "Visa Express." Visa Express relied on Saudi travel agents to process non-U.S.-citizen Saudis, including young men, often sparing them even the briefest visit to the embassy to pick up the ticket to enter that gigantic wide-open target range, the United States. Apparently hoping to avoid putting young Saudi men through the nervous experience of walking into a place where a CIA or FBI agent might even lay eyes on them, embassy officials made a visa application process that previously hadn't been that difficult even easier.

All fifteen of the Saudis among the nineteen 9/11 hijackers were in the United States on visas from our embassy in Riyadh. Three had not even been interviewed by a consular official. (This is not to withhold blame from the Clinton administration; the laxness preceded Bush.)

Jordan's confirmation hearing before the Senate Foreign Relations Committee occurred on September 21, 2001. It was the period of time right after 9/11 when senators didn't ask any questions; it was time to rally around President Bush and pray he'd use the limitless power invested in him to fight back wisely. His advisers had been debating whether to go after both the Taliban and, for some reason, Iraq or to attack only the former, and the public word was, it would be just the former. The White House assiduously redirected the country's attention away from the count that soon emerged: fifteen of the nineteen hijackers were Saudi.

As for Jordan's hearing, his statement was a model of reassurance to the Saudis, reminding the senators that the Saudis were "our real friends." Aside from "coalition building"—his only term for relations with the Saudis concerning terrorism—the statement included no such unpleasantries as the name *bin Laden,* which resonates throughout Saudi Arabia, or any complaint about how the Saudis had frustrated inquiries into the attacks on American targets from the first World Trade Center attempt, to the Khobar Towers, to the U.S.S. *Cole.* Indeed, Jordan spoke of how "relations with Saudi Arabia encompass a number of other areas, including energy, political-military cooperation, commerce, education, and health"—leaving out reform, rights, and democracy. As to why he had gotten this all-important nomination at this all-important moment, Jordan explained that his father had been a foreign service reserve officer. He himself had lived as a child in Peru and Hong Kong and had "traveled extensively." He also credited his personal qualities, especially his "listening" ability.[77] There may not have been a single notable press report covering the hearing, apart from Jordan's fan press back in Texas.

Jordan kept an incredibly low profile after that. The American press and public periodically went through fits of anger as the evidence about the Saudi role in 9/11 continued to mount. During the summer of 2001, the press seems not to have connected Jordan, the president's defense lawyer, that much with the Saudis and 9/11. Of course, the press did lambaste the Saudis, who must have wondered whether Jordan was working as hard as he should.

Powell angrily canceled Visa Express and sacked his assistant secretary of state over the policy—an extraordinary act, rare at State. Why Powell got enraged—Powell, former military, familiar with the Saudis but not a recipient of their largesse nor really part of the Republican conservative wing—hardly needs spelling out. Yet when the *Washington Post* reported about Visa Express after 9/11, both Jordan and administration spokespersons were as bland as ever. Jordan said he was "deeply troubled about the prevailing perception in the media and within Congress and possibly among the American public at large" that the Riyadh embassy's red carpet for the Saudi hijackers "represent[s] a shameful and inadequate effort on our part." Powell couldn't touch Jordan, nor could Congress or the public. And he knew it.

Only one corner of the press seems not to have felt the way the rest did. In Jordan's hometown the *Dallas Morning News* kept running editorials preaching tolerance of the Saudis, the same line as in Jordan's Senate confirmation testimony. These editorials mentioned Ambassador Jordan by name, even though he himself was not in the news. One might think he kept in good contact with those writing the editorials and kept saying something like, "Can you give me some clippings, with my name in them, to show the Saudis that I'm on the job for them about all this awkward 9/11 stuff?" It would have to be editorials; news simply isn't managed quite so backstage. Sure enough, on June 25, 2002, Jordan himself penned a "Viewpoints" op-ed run by the *Dallas Morning News* entitled "Saudis Reliable Allies." The ambassador wrote that "in the months since September ... [g]roups from the FBI, the Treasury Department and the like have been to Saudi Arabia [i.e., to his embassy] to gather and share information." That month, *U.S. News & World Report*, the leading (conservative) business weekly, ran a tough, smart column observing that "al Qaeda was supported by large contributions from Saudis, including members of the Saudi royal family. The Saudis' cooperation with our efforts to track down the financing of al Qaeda appears to be somewhere between minimal and zero."[78] This matched detailed Bush administration leaks to the *New York Times* that "the Treasury Department was increasingly frustrated by the reluctance of the Saudi government to provide information about at least five Islamic charities ... suspected of having financed terrorist groups"— that is, the pipeline from top Saudis right into Osama's Swiss financing shell.[79]

On the subject of how precisely the Saudis treated the Treasury Department investigators in Riyadh, under Jordan's roof, a large gulf separated what, on one hand, the Treasury Department itself was unhappily confessing to *U.S. News & World Report* and the *New York Times* and what, on the other, Jordan wrote in the *Dallas Morning News*. Jordan told the American public, "The Saudis have assisted us every step of the way. . . . The Bush administration is pleased with that cooperation." *Every* step of the way? Did the presumably crestfallen and humiliated Treasury investigators stationed in Jordan's embassy who indirectly let *U.S. News* know they received actual cooperation "between minimal and zero" believe Jordan had secured them cooperation "*every* step of the way"?

And Saudi officials reading Jordan's clippings from the *Dallas Morning News* would know (both directly from Jordan's self-promotion and from their own excellent intelligence in Texas) how closely Jordan spoke for Bush himself. Saudis analyzing the Bush White House would know how tightly it controlled its own releases, so that Jordan's speaking in this way in Texas counted as a finely calculated signal on behalf of Bush himself—in front of the safest segment for Bush of the American public—confirming the message of Bush's that Jordan would deliver ever so much more deferentially to the Saudis in person. In person Jordan could bluntly state Bush's needs in handling American public opinion. The Saudis would factor this into their vital decision not to reveal what the royalty knew, not just about how they had fueled Osama before 9/11, but about how they were continuing to do so even then, in late 2001 and early 2002. Prince Turki left his top post in Saudi intelligence, but hardly in disgrace; he could soon be found as the Saudi ambassador in London, a splendid post, really a reward for a job well done to one who now required a discrete relocation. There Turki could specifically play his accustomed role in the background as Tony Blair joined with Bush against Iraq.[80]

The Bush administration would defend Jordan's touting Saudi reliability by saying that Jordan was engaging in quiet diplomacy, was pressing the Saudis for cooperation all the more effectively in private by praising them in public. That this was a self-serving explanation was the smallest of its flaws. The first Bush administration provides us an especially helpful and relevant example of what actually occurs, behind the scenes, in these situations. In July 1990, on the eve of Saddam Hussein's invasion of Kuwait, the Bush administration ostensibly engaged in such quiet diplomacy through its ambassador. It, too, tried hard to keep the lid on its actual ambassador-to-Arab-leader exchanges. But it failed. After the war, the Iraqis released a transcript, and Senate Democrats got the classified ambassadorial records. Almost without fully appreciating what he was saying, President Bush had sent, via his ambassador, the signal to Saddam Hussein that he took as the green light to invade Kuwait.[81]

Saudis reporting to Abdulla, from reading Jordan's op-ed and talking to him privately, would interpret Bush's apparent message to the Saudi royal family as meaning "If you stonewall Treasury investigators, the president will see that you get defended as reliable allies. So don't feel pressured to detail your 9/11 financing and terrorist support links to Treasury investigators; ignore the American public's demands to find out what happened; keep in mind how that would embarrass the president's extensive efforts, which you see every week in the media, to get the American public's attention about terror to veer from Riyadh to Baghdad." What more effective way to impede the 9/11 financial investigation than to send a message the Saudis would read this way?

By the way, in discussing our "reliable allies" and preaching tolerance, Jordan didn't mention one little item. According to one poll conducted in October 2001, 95 percent of educated Saudi males between the ages of twenty-five and forty-one supported Osama.[82] That's better even than Bush's support in Houston. If Jordan had really been providing useful information to us from Riyadh about 9/11, not producing clippings for his Saudis, he'd have explained why Osama had no trouble recruiting those fifteen of the nineteen. He'd have explained that the group from which they came, the 95 percent, wants to replace the current regime with an Islamic government, as the Iranians did in 1979 (just Sunni, not Shiite). He'd have explained that this 95 percent of Saudi adult men—not the Iraqis—hate America the way the Iranians did in 1979, enough to support terrorist violence against us.

And Jordan would have added that, as with the quadrupling of prices in the 1970s, if the lid blows in Saudi Arabia, prices will blow sky-high, too, sending the international and then the American economy into a tailspin. But Jordan didn't tell us that, nor did Bush. Why not? Jordan can't have missed that poll. Presumably he just bet that the Saudi ruling class would remain in power long enough at least for good things to happen for his family and the families he cares about.

It wasn't Saudi or 9/11 items that brought Jordan's name into the limelight as summer became fall in 2002. Rather, after Enron and WorldCom the press finally took something of a look at the SEC's insider-trading investigation of Bush in 1991–1993. It told the story of Jordan's role previously recounted. But the SEC file containing the key documents never came out, even after Bush again flubbed the explanation for not filing the insider-trading notification. As noted earlier, Bush had Harvey Pitt sitting on the SEC, and the premier former defense lawyer for the accounting industry does not release the file on the former defense lawyer for the president's son who is now president.

Releasing that file might kindle public interest in, among other technicalities, just why the SEC in letting him off had not even made young George himself answer questions on the record. Of course, a defense lawyer would note that one ought to respect young George's privacy and due process rights. Then again, a cynic might cite what the Bush administration itself indicates about respecting privacy rights (when, say, the public's medical records fall into corporate hands) or about respecting the due process rights of those accused without, in the end, being formally charged with the offense that was the point of the inquiry (as illustrated, say, in Ashcroft's haughty dismissal of the huge review underlying the Justice Department inspector general's 2003 report about Ashcroft's noncitizen detainees). Here's a fresh reason for White House reporters to ask for the government file that has never yet come out on the president's alleged insider trading. Let the White House press secretary feign a yawn and assert there's no fresh reason; then ask whether anyone who previously asked for the file mentioned 9/11, Jordan in Riyadh, and the rest.

Anyone who understands the trade of the hired-gun defender in the post in Riyadh may now see the dilemma—the potential trap—Bush and Jordan found themselves in once Jordan's name came into the Bush insider-trading matter. If Jordan spoke, no matter what he said, and drew attention to where he now was, the press would connect his name and his role as young George's lawyer with the way Visa Express overlapped with Jordan's early tenure as ambassador. And the president had his hands full without that kind of press coverage. Until October 2002 he had to carefully time the congressional vote on Iraq. Then, after winning back the Senate in November 2002, the heat was off—no Senate inquiries would occur, whatever the press. But still, he had to lead the nation to the invasion of Iraq despite the lack of world support and the thinness, to put it mildly, of the case that Iraq really had the kinds of weapons Cheney kept alluding to. Cheney didn't talk about Saudi hijackers, who had been terribly real, but rather about Iraqi weapons of mass destruction, which turned out to be hard to find after the invasion.

In short, Bush must make it appear that his agenda regarding Iraq had nothing to do with oil and must distract the public from focus too much on the Saudi role in 9/11. All this would get a bit mussed up if public attention was focused on the president's lawyer being in Riyadh, especially in 2003 as public evidence of the Saudi role in 9/11 kept mounting. During 2003 the struggle was on for the release, which Bush fought tooth and nail, of the portion of the 9/11 congressional joint inquiry report that detailed the Saudi role.

Moreover, the Saudis performed one of their less subtle maneuvers with American lawyers. Naturally the families of 9/11 victims went to the courts for redress of their grievances. These families have a lot of potential support in the American public, to put it mildly. The Saudis were made defendants: a very interesting lawsuit if it ever reached the facts. Not that the Saudis would confess, but the 9/11 victim families might put together a fair amount of circumstantial evidence—fifteen of the nineteen hijackers, plus Osama, being Saudi and so forth—inconvenient both to the Saudis and to Bush.

The Saudis are what is known in legal parlance as a "deep pocket," and deep pockets pay their defense lawyers very well; the more sympathetic the plaintiffs, the better for the defense lawyers. It's a plum. To whom did the plum go in these 9/11-related suits? After all, the country has quite a lot of firms that can do legal defense work. Why, Baker Botts, of course—the firm of James Baker and (before his ambassadorship) of Robert Jordan—was among, let me make clear, a number of firms hired for the work. This connection the press, legal and otherwise, didn't miss;[83] it just didn't walk the trail back to our ambassador to Riyadh. Technically, with the same law firm defending both the Saudis and the Bush family on all kinds of matters, the Saudis and Bush seemed to get closer to the relationship between fellow clients of the same lawyer on related matters—one of them, 9/11—that is delicately referred to as a "community of interest."

That was particularly tricky for Jordan, with his having preached in the press of tolerance for the Saudis about 9/11. "In a statement on behalf of [Saudi] Prince Sultan," *American Lawyer* noted, "Baker Botts called the [9/11 victims'] claims that the prince and other Saudi royal family members assisted in terrorist attacks 'utterly false.'"[84] Increasingly, Jordan's firm and Jordan himself in his Riyadh role defended the Saudis on 9/11 as the evidence mounted while people could have recalled at any time that he had been the President's personal defense lawyer—two things not so pleasant to contemplate simultaneously. So he must find some way to get out of Riyadh, preferably a way allowing him to "go public" without the press connecting up his roles.

And he did—the one and only time anyone ever saw him, in effect, jumping up and down in Riyadh to get in front of television cameras. Maybe he just had the knack to adapt himself to circumstances quickly and luckily. Or maybe, the occasion involved prepared steps by Saudi authorities, who were helping him with his problem because it was also their problem. But that belongs in the chapter on secrecy and deception. So we will put a finale for now on Ambassador Jordan, the Saudis, 9/11, and Iraq.

PROSPECTS FOR SECURITY UNDER NULLIFIED LEGAL REGIMES

President Bush made a two-part change in how international legal regimes shape America's security, casting a shadow over the future. He both stepped down the level by which these international regimes maintain security and stepped up his own power to involve the country in unilateral preemptive war. Without trying to predict the unpredictable, some scenarios grounded in reality illustrate how, in a second term, these shifts could mean lowered legal barriers to dubious American military interventions overseas.

President Bush's actions put other countries on notice to place less reliance for their own security on international legal regimes. To see the effects, the starting place is Russia and China, both with delicate internal balances between nationalists nursing memories of the Cold War and those who hoped for reassurance that they could devote their nations' resources to economic growth. Part of the internal debate within each country centers on whether the United States will behave in a way respecting those legal regimes. For example, in the two countries' internal debates about America's strategic nuclear capability, experts could take some comfort in the ABM Treaty, since it kept the United States years away from any effort that would call their own deterrent strategic capabilities into question.

As the United States releases itself from the ABM Treaty's legal constraints, however, certain factions in those countries—such as nationalists whom the United States may consider either overly hawkish or actually paranoid—will predict dangerous consequences. They can seize on the United States' displayed willingness to unleash its military in the face of unified opposition in the Security Council. To engender fears of the United States, these factions do not have to make a convincing case that the United States plans a first strike on their country. They need only raise public concern that the diminished trust in the strategic balance and in American restraint gives substance to hypothetical scenarios involving confrontation. Russia can imagine confrontations over NATO's stationing nuclear arms in the Baltic states or undermining the country's vulnerable flank with Islamic Central Asia. Hawks in China can always raise the specter of confrontations about Taiwan declaring independence or over oil drilling in the South China Sea. China particularly must worry because of the prospect of American "local" or "theater" anti-missile defenses stationed in Japan, South Korea, and possibly Taiwan. The relatively small Chinese force of intercontinental missiles, which China considers a potential deterrent to U.S. action, becomes a question mark in its own military's mind if such antimissile defenses ring it.[85]

As a growing economic and technological superpower, China may decide at some point to redirect its strength toward a strategic military buildup. Russia, still possessing an enormous if decreasingly controlled nuclear arsenal, may push its own strategic weapons to a higher state of readiness, returning the world partially to the Cold War's shadow of fear that miscalculation or mistake would trigger a nuclear exchange.[86] The Bush administration has made both of these developments more likely by nullifying reciprocal international legal constraints and brandishing its present and future weaponry. In 2003 the administration issued a directive that its anti-missile policy aimed at "undermining the confidence of our adversaries" in their ability to threaten a missile strike on the United States.[87] In 2004 the administration sold anti-missile radar to Taiwan with a range of three thousand kilometers—Rumsfeld's way of providing off-budget funding for, and setting up, a system provocatively covering not just China's short-range missiles across the Taiwan straits but virtually the whole country.[88] Some factions in China and Russia might experience undermined confidence in their own present deterrent capacities, redounding to render the United States less secure.

If these two nations reacted with alarm, one may hope that the Bush administration would respond by negotiating away the tensions, perhaps through a substitute anti-missile defense agreement that could legally reassure the other countries of their ability to deter an American first strike. But President Bush would not necessarily, or even likely, react by seriously looking for reassuring mutual legal restraint. Rather, the Bush administration would more likely respond by pointing to any such Russian or Chinese moves as a reason to step up its own military capabilities and readiness—for its domestic political base's consumption as much as for the world's.

A parallel range of increased tensions might characterize U.S. relations with potentially antagonistic Third World regional powers, such as India, Pakistan, and Iran. In each the parties of militantly religious zeal, backed by national followings, might step up their commitment to weapons of mass destruction as needed both to fight their local enemies and in some cases to deter the United States. Each country responds much more to its internal dynamics than to what the Bush administration does in terms of nullifying treaties or occupying Iraq. Still, because of the global electronic media, these countries do react when America, now apparently unhindered by traditional legal restraints or by what the Security Council resolves, flexes its military might, particularly in their immediate vicinity.

Yet another type of increased tension characterizes the large tier of nations that at present lack a potent deterrent capability of their own and whose concerned factions (often their military) could without extreme paranoia regard themselves as potential targets for action like what happened to Iraq. Prime examples include unstable but strategically important countries whose future regimes might anger or alarm Washington enough to trigger some form of intervention. Because of economic and social instability, Indonesia, Egypt, or another important country from the Near East to the Far East could undergo an internal political swing toward sympathy with violent Islamic fundamentalism. If such a regime set out, like Iran, to acquire weapons of mass destruction, Washington would inevitably take notice.

Other examples include countries that the Bush administration has already labeled as supporting or plagued with terrorism and that it has already shown it does not regard as immune from special attention: Cuba, Colombia, and Sudan.[89] Cuba illustrates how countries in this group can regard their situation. Until the Bush administration, the centrist American public looked to a gradual policy of engagement, including a successful 2000 law allowing cash sales of American farm products to Cuba.[90] However, the Bush administration sharply changed the tone of U.S.-Cuba relations, appointing Otto Reich, with his Iran-contra past, to the position of assistant secretary of state for Latin American affairs, in effect ceding control to shrill anti-Castro elements in the Cuban-American exile community. Rove does not forget the preoccupation with Elian Gonzalez in 2000 or Cuban Americans' role in the Florida electoral contest in 2000 and in Governor Jeb Bush's reelection two years later. Conservatives never cease ideological barrages about Cuba.[91] An example from 2002, as noted already, is John Bolton's sudden creation of a legal stir about biowarfare simply to divert attention from former president Carter's successful peace-promoting visit to Cuba. Any number of scenarios would make the Bush administration think more about unilateral action as to Cuba, whether or not such action was consistent with traditional international law.

SIGNIFICANCE OF ELECTION-YEAR DEVELOPMENTS

Having found himself mired in an Iraq occupation much costlier than he had ever led the American public to imagine—meeting few of the stated objectives—Bush sought, as he headed for the November 2004 election, to minimize the downsides and, without allowing Americans to see where his hard-liners would lead the country, to secure what they would deem a mandate. Having gotten through the sticker shock of the Iraq war the year before, he would minimize the shocks in 2004, trying to portray himself as a commander in chief protecting the public against terrorists.

In particular, Bush would manipulate legal symbols mightily to dress up appearances about Iraq for the 2004 election. He would proclaim, by moves toward a purported transfer of sovereignty to an interim Iraqi group, that the United States could soon get out of Iraq, satisfied both with having ended the old regime and having installed an independently viable replacement regime. Never mind that the U.S. military and Bush's Treasury-paid contractors were still the actual "changed regime" and that, since Bush refused to ask Congress to fund the continuing cost until after the election, the U.S.-funded regime actually in control was meanwhile free of democratic accountability to the American public. Similarly, Bush would proclaim, by shows of diplomatic legitimation, that his flexing of American military muscle would avoid the price and pain of world public disfavor and, in the Middle East, outright broad-based antagonism. Never mind that with the United States' continuing refusal to come to terms with the other members of the Security Council, and with the fall of the conservative government in Spain early in 2004 due to its support for Bush's Iraq policy, prospects for durably harmonizing the invasion and occupation with international law and consensus looked dubious.

Overall, Bush would create what symbolism he could as a backdrop to his election in order to show that he had been standing tall against terrorism, asking of Americans only a reasonable sacrifice in blood, treasure, and international standing. Never mind that, in the words of Richard A. Clarke, former White House counterterrorism czar, "nothing America could have done would have provided al Qaeda and its new generation of cloned groups a better recruitment device than our unprovoked invasion of an oil-rich Arab country."[92] Bush's preelection performance recalled three other presidents who, in war situations, put on comparable preelection shows in 1964, 1972, and 1984 on pretenses that, although transparent in retrospect, actually had had more of a basis for credibility at the time than Bush's in 2004.[93] After each of those elections the elaborately staged fronts fell, bringing American intervention in an overseas conflict quickly to a satisfactory end, as Bush's front would fall after 2004. President Bush had barged into Iraq as his predecessors had barged into Vietnam and Nicaragua. After the election, Bush would, like his predecessors, refuse to allow the locals to work out their own destiny even if they accepted the condition that they not threaten key American interests.[94] In short, what Bush actually prepared to do after the election regrettably matched the prospects after the similar preelection posturing of 1964, 1972, and 1984.

As Richard Clarke's disclosures in spring 2004 made only too clear, Bush had, in his intense desire to occupy Iraq, cared little before or after 9/11 about Osama bin Laden's terrorism.[95] And as chapter 8 explains more fully, Bush's post-9/11 position had nothing to do with aligning the United States, as he claimed, against *jihadi* terrorism. He not only alienated the

Arab street and potential Arab allies such as Egypt but chose to join tightly from 9/11 on with the Saudi royalty, whose charitable contributions had actually bankrolled al-Qaeda's buildup starting in 1991. His campaign contentions in 2004 about having stood tall against terrorism signified, not that he had done so, but rather that after the election, he would claim a mandate to go forward with his original reasons for occupying Iraq, reasons that did not match the centrist public's yearning to put the problem of Iraq in the hands of the Iraqis and the international community, on their terms rather than ours.

On the contrary, with Powell likely to leave and, hence, the Cheney-Rumsfeld-Wolfowitz school of thinking likely to be more dominant than ever, the postelection period would see Bush pursuing his own international vision harder than ever. The legal shows of legitimation Bush set up within and outside Iraq were empty; Cheney and Rumsfeld would not actually allow the Shiite majority in Iraq to move very far toward a degree of Islamic self-governance—even if nonjihadist—that the Shiites would accept, and the Shiites would not put up indefinitely with Cheney and Rumsfeld effectively calling the shots. Worse, the same tension would occur elsewhere in the Islamic world. A Bush administration that believed in preemption and that continued to see global security in sync with makers of advanced weapons and international oil suppliers would continue to align itself with policies and regimes that were insufficiently acceptable to America's key NATO allies and that antagonized Middle Eastern locals in a way that would drive many into Islamic militancy. As the tensions increased, the Cheney-Rumsfeld-Wolfowitz school's recourse to a greater use of force than the UN Security Council would countenance would keep the United States mired in unilateralism. Prospects for reducing the American commitment to force abroad would dim.

Why did Bush strive so hard to push his real agenda, verging on subverting the Constitution, to defeat this primal drive of the American centrist public? His agenda wasn't of the international strategic type his father had pursued. Even before 2001 Bush junior, like Cheney, saw the huge untapped potential of Iraqi oil reserves and resources, for the only oil industry he knew (unlike his father, who had wildcatted in West Texas and had built a real company, Zapata Petroleum) was that of sweet international deals. Iraq's oil potential would remain untapped so long as Saddam played out his low-production, smuggle-through-Syria approach inside the American-policed UN sanctions blockade, and Bush understood that the Saudi impatience about getting American bases out forced him to act soon or never.[96] In 2001–2003 he, like Cheney, could rationalize the expected political cost after the 2004 election of maintaining an unpopular occupation as the price of gaining the expected politically valuable stroke of a popular war and of replacing the skunk-porcupine Saddam atop the huge oil reserves with an American protectorate.

Regular, congressionally overseen troop strength would not suffice. The Bush administration had already begun abusing its legal powers to circumvent congressionally set troop strengths by what it did with the military reserve system. In 2004 it slated National Guard and Army Reserve units to reach 40 percent of the U.S. military personnel in Iraq, an unprecedented use of reservists. It issued thousands of stop-loss orders to force reservists to extend their tour of duty, which under these circumstances amounted to Rumsfeld reviving a kind of conscription to compel them to serve Bush's military aims beyond the terms they had voluntarily accepted.[97] To the affected thousands of reservists' families and their communities, this policy forced those who had signed the reservist's contract with their nation—to defend it in special occasions of need—to submit instead to a cruelly imposed levy for Bush's aims.[98]

But beyond that, the strategic visionaries serving the hard-line partisan machine saw a new age in which privatized soldiers, both Americans and foreigners, would constitute the new imperial forces. As the $20 billion rolled out for Bush's contractors through Rumsfeld's contracting officers starting in spring 2004, journalistic investigators worked with me to figure out why a key award initially went to the company connected to Ahmed Chalabi. Chalabi had always been Rumsfeld's chosen exile-returned-as-satrap for occupied Iraq despite—or, more likely, because—he had helped build the bogus case about extensive, ready nuclear and similar WMD stockpiles. As I explained on the March 3, 2004, broadcast of *NBC Nightly News*, the award to Chalabi's friend of a government contract to arm the new Iraq army could not possibly be justified on the merits: the company had been formed less than a year earlier, in May 2003, from personnel with construction, not army-equipping, experience.[99] Rather, the Chalabi-sponsored firm put in a low bid in order to get the positioning contract as controller, for Cheney and Rumsfeld, of the American money backing the new army—a traditional leverage point for corrupt rule.

A leading scholarly study published in 2003, *Corporate Warriors: The Rise of the Privatized Military Industry*, by P. W. Singer, explains how American-linked multinationals can both recruit, and arm with superior power, private forces set up through corporate structures as "private military firms," or PMFs.[100] Singer naturally uses "oil industry facilities and pipelines" as a prime example of a "focal point of fighting" where multinational corporations stand ready to make "huge outflows of money" to PMFs.[101] In the Bush-Cheney-Rumsfeld vision, as Iraqi oil eventually came on stream, it could pay for this new privatized way to exercise force in Iraq—free of congressional oversight. Iraqi nationalists and the international community would have trouble stomaching a foreign military rule paid for from Iraq's own oil (while Iraqi civilian needs and past debts were ignored), but Bush and hard-liners after him would simply make political use of PMF casualties by labeling all critics of the evolving occupation as soft on terrorism.

President Bush had displayed respect for Congress's constitutional role in voting to authorize war. In September 2001 he asked for and received congressional authorization for the Afghan campaign, although after 9/11 that was a foregone conclusion; in October 2002 he asked for and received congressional authorization for the Iraq campaign, although he did so to create a useful campaign issue. Each time, though, the Bush White House signaled that it might not seek such authorization in the future. As discussed in the next chapter, the administration took several steps in September 2001 that reflected a belief in presidential, not congressional, war powers. More pointedly, in August 2002 the White House counsel expressly announced that the president could authorize an Iraq invasion on his own, without a congressional vote.[102] The counsel's finding apparently represented a deep well of conservative hard-line legal opinion eager for President Bush to decide on his own, without Congress, on invasions and occupations.[103]

Similarly, Rumsfeld's assertions of power in 2004 to make heavily funded, no-holds-barred, and virtually oversight-free deployments of Special Forces reinforced the Bush White House capacity to decide on its own—without Congress, without diplomacy, and without support from the locals—whether and where to invade and occupy. This recalled similar warning signs before such fiascos as the Bay of Pigs invasion of Cuba in 1961.[104]

If we look beyond Iraq and Central Asia, Bush had altered the overall legal environment that would come into play during debates about intervening in countries such as Indonesia, Iran, Cuba, Sudan, or Colombia. He had changed the international legal climate to the extent that the need to resort to unilateral force was increased; and he had demonstrated a willingness to act without international, and possibly without domestic, legal authority and shown how doing so could have political advantages. With respect to military intervention in the Third World, he had swung the pendulum back from the 1980s to the 1960s, the period before the War Powers

Resolution of 1974. He had returned the country to the period of the failed American assassinations, interventions, and regime changes that ultimately led to a hardened Castro regime in Cuba (after the Bay of Pigs fiasco); the militant rule of the ayatollahs in Iran (after our installation of the shah ultimately failed); Pol Pot's genocidal regime in Cambodia (after Nixon's destabilizing invasions); and many other sour legacies of an earlier era's Rumsfeld-style overreaching.

8 Blindfolding the Public

President Bush needed to blindfold the public, and he succeeded. He ran the most secretive presidency since Watergate, thirty years ago: secretive as to both foreign and domestic affairs, secretive about matters that lie outside the scripted presidential "message" prescribed for Congress and the public, and particularly secretive about plans for achieving conservative political and ideological goals.[1] Along with formal uses and manipulations of law—such as secrecy policies, concealment measures, invocations of privilege, and strategies for fending off lawsuits for information and stalling or disabling congressional probes—also comes brilliant stage-managing. The formal and what we might term "informal" uses of law work in combination and have a common purpose: to deter, divert, or otherwise diminish efforts that might otherwise circumvent Bush's structure of information confinement, the key to his conservative triumphs.

We may thus distinguish between the administration's formal and less formal uses of the law for political purposes, but the two efforts reinforce each other. The administration maintains and employs secrecy formally when it blocks probes or lawsuits and informally when it assigns a high priority to confining information from public view through nonlegal means. For example, it chooses subordinates who can be trusted not to reveal the conservative ideological drift of policy efforts; directs subordinates to maintain such secrecy; takes measures to make sure any information released to the public conforms to the approved "message"; minimizes the ordinary governmental response to queries; leads the press corps to stay within the favored spin, even when there are revelations to the contrary; and of course, simply implements its own plans with care, especially as to timing, so as to reduce public scrutiny. Among more exotic tactics, the administration has sabotaged congressional overseers by accusing them of unpatriotically violating intelligence rules and by creating tame dummy bodies like the intelligence review commission; rearranged the timing and structure of environmental decision making to minimize public disclosure of exploitative quid-pro-quo policies; and conducted the most important coordination of its Middle Eastern policy through the back channel of the president's strategically posted personal lawyer so as to box in the wisely reluctant moderates and take away the role of the State Department, CIA, and military service bureaucracies.

To analyze the uses of law for secrecy thus calls for more than a narrow review of privilege claims for withholding information. It takes a broader analysis of how legal maneuvers render President Bush's far-ranging management of congressional and public relations more controlling. The Bush administration's use of secrecy explains, as none of its other mechanisms can, how this president accomplishes so much for conservative causes.

Two early examples reveal Bush and Cheney unfurling their domestic secrecy policy: the first formal executive privilege claim and the vice president's effort to shield lobbying by Enron and other energy industry companies. After considering those initiatives, I'll turn to the greatest secrecy maneuver of them all, President Bush's use of his personal lawyer in Riyadh as a back channel around his administration's moderates in order to coordinate his Saudi dealings with the hard-line Cheney-Rumsfeld Iraq occupation approach and to cynically and even ruthlessly accomplish his partisan and personal goals. To implement and then cover up the back-channel deal from 9/11 on, President Bush impeded oversight of Saudi involvement in 9/11; hid his strategy from 9/11 to the occupation of Iraq; and with accelerating intensity as the Iraq occupation soured and the election approached, concealed the reasons he had made many, seemingly accidental mistakes all the way through that painful occupation. Thus he not only obscured the relation of the invasion and occupation to his dealings with the Saudis but also faked a warrior image for display in 2004 vis-à-vis Kerry.

After that, I devote a section to addressing how secrecy in domestic affairs helped key domestic initiatives, from anti-environmentalism to the filling of key judgeships with ideologues. A final section anticipates the future prospects, both in international and domestic affairs, for President Bush to advance conservative and hard-line causes through secrecy.

Several other matters warrant brief preliminary comment. First, in this section I draw more heavily than in most other parts of the book on my own involvement in the issues considered here, as a former solicitor of the House of Representatives and a continuing participant in executive privilege debates. I have spent my career not just analyzing bogus secrecy claims, from President Jimmy Carter's about Billy Carter in 1980 to the present, but also calculating what lies under the secrecy claim. It is not so hard; there are really only a few familiar reasons for claims of privilege, and each has its telltales. Observers who analyzed President Johnson's public deception about the Tonkin Gulf "attack" in 1964 to justify tragically escalating the Vietnam War encountered challenges similar to those the House Iran-Contra Committee, on which I served, had in analyzing the Reagan administration's deceptive statements justifying its covert war in Nicaragua in 1984–1986. Presumably, historians years from now will have more direct evidence in hand about President Bush's dealings as to Saudi Arabia and Iraq. For now, judicious marshalling of the facts that are available about what President Bush did and sensible conclusions from surrounding circumstances, such as the known Saudi positions on crucial issues at key moments, must suffice.

A BRIEF HISTORY OF RECENT PRESIDENTIAL SECRECY

President Bush's predecessors generated plenty of controversy over real and alleged abuses of law relating to secrecy. Indeed, of all the subjects treated in this book, it's in the matter of secrecy that Bush's immediate predecessor, Clinton, creates an interesting record to compare and contrast with Bush's as to abusing the law. Clinton endured a House impeachment and a Senate trial mainly on charges that he lied under oath about his affair with Monica Lewinsky. This capped years of allegations that Clinton had resisted investigations on subjects such as Whitewater, Travelgate, and the financing of his 1996 campaign.

There is no question that President Clinton engaged in deception in the Lewinsky matter, stemming from the lies he told about Lewinsky at his deposition in the Paula Jones case. Such presidential lying under oath cannot be excused or condoned, regardless of all that can be offered in explanation: the origin of the charges as a trap set by right-wing organizations; Kenneth Starr's biased prosecution; the Gingrich-DeLay House leadership's view that a sexual dalliance was a fair basis for overturning the 1996 election through impeachment; or in general, that leadership's preference for focusing on questions about Clinton's personal character flaws as opposed to his administration's governmental policies and practices.[2] After all the excuses, presidential lying under oath is simply wrong, and the resulting domination of national political life by the proceedings amounts to a national penalty for the former president's flaws. Thus, any analysis of secrecy in the Bush administration must recognize that Bush is not alone.

Further back in time, the Cold War greatly enlarged the dimensions of presidential secrecy, partly for national security reasons, partly as a rationalization for executive self-aggrandizement. President Johnson's deceptions in escalating the war in Vietnam in the 1960s and President Nixon's in covering up Watergate in the 1970s launched an extended period of severe public suspicion of White House credibility, reflected in newly energized press and congressional scrutiny. Efforts at public scrutiny on one hand and the withholding of information by presidents on the other came into particularly intense conflict from 1987 to 2000, during the successive administrations of presidents Reagan, Bush, and Clinton. From Iran-contra through Monicagate, the phenomenon of the "specially investigated president" took center stage in national affairs.[3] Statutorily appointed independent counsels, especially Lawrence Walsh and Kenneth W. Starr, and special congressional investigating committees combined to produce unusually high levels of legally intense scrutiny of all three presidents, and each executive fought back by wielding various tools of diversion, obfuscation, delay, and resistance.

Although there were obvious differences among the controversies involving these presidents, all three fought more complex and continuous battles over secrecy and scrutiny than any recent president prior to Watergate.[4] What matters most when we consider secrecy in the George W. Bush administration, however, is that by 2000 the public had become tired of the Clinton impeachment proceedings and tired of the special prosecutors. This public burnout, ironically, cleared the way after 2000 for the incoming president to engage in greater secrecy about policy than had been possible for any president in the preceding thirty years.[5] Quite simply, the public, and therefore the press and Congress, lacked the will in the immediate post-Clinton era to support the high level of suspicious, combative scrutiny of presidents characteristic of preceding decades.

Into this new situation Governor Bush brought a personal drive of his own to diminish and to control oversight through use, and sometimes abuse, of secrecy, an ambition derived from several sources. Well before he became president, Bush had demonstrated his control of information flow. His adviser, Karl Rove, taught him to keep his Texas gubernatorial campaigns strictly "on message" and to stay away from frank answers to the press or openness about controversy. As Molly Ivins and Lou Dubose put it, "The Texas press was supine."[6] "In Bush's management style" when he was governor, Dubose and his colleagues found, "what mattered was keeping all disagreement inside the tent."[7] Hence, Governor Bush arranged a minimum of public revelation when his budget process redistributed wealth from poor to rich, when he virtually deregulated the state's worst air polluters, and in general, when he steadily delivered for right-wing causes in Texas.

Once Governor Bush ran for president, even jaded Texas Republicans described his record-shattering campaign fund-raising methods as "very stealthy."[8] Most extraordinary, he raised huge sums without addressing large groups of donors; instead, key donors and fund-raisers came to Bush, meeting with him individually or in very small, discreet groups.[9] Texas law prohibits such fund-raising by candidates for state offices while the state legislature is in session, as it was from January to June 1999—precisely when Bush so effectively used these methods.[10] Even the relatively wide-open campaign finance code of Texas anticipates that during the state legislative session, governors may obtain funds from the raw selling of gubernatorially arranged favors. But Bush managed to exploit a loophole in Texas law to raise his millions during the session anyway,[11] and he used bundling techniques to avoid the kind of public scrutiny that the federal post-Watergate campaign finance law had intended.

Later, in November–December 2000, many aspects of his campaign's successful legal effort to forestall a full and accurate count of the Florida undervotes depended upon secrecy. These included the discarding of thousands of minority votes; the tight secret coordination between the Republican campaign and the biased state election official who made the key rulings, Katherine Harris; and the "Thanksgiving stuffing" of quantities of highly dubious, "late-discovered" absentee ballots.[12]

Hence, even before his presidency began, Bush had mastered the use of secrecy both in governing and in electoral strategy. When he finally arrived in Washington, where he might have expected a more intense brand of scrutiny, he found the times had changed. In the new atmosphere of public exhaustion with investigations and special prosecutors, Bush benefited from the expiration without renewal of the independent counsel statute and the lack of public pressure on Congress after 2000 to mount high-powered oversight investigations.[13] Unlike former governors Carter, Reagan, and Clinton, who arrived in Washington to find a vastly more intense glare of press and congressional oversight than they had experienced at the state level, Bush found conditions in the nation's capital not so dramatically different than they had been for him in Austin.[14]

Moreover, as president, Bush would now deal with foreign, military, and intelligence affairs, policy areas where a degree of secrecy was from the start a legitimate given. He had picked Cheney as his running mate specifically to make him his chief minister in these areas. Throughout his career Cheney had firmly maintained Republican presidents' rights to resist public and especially congressional oversight of the foreign, military, and intelligence affairs.[15] This Cheney displayed most visibly as ranking Republican on the House Iran-Contra Committee in 1987. As the committee's special deputy chief counsel, I observed Cheney up close as he insisted unceasingly that the congressional hearings be controlled and constrained, ostensibly lest there be leaks, rather than open them to sanitize the Reagan administration.[16]

As Bush senior's secretary of defense, Cheney held backroom talks with the Saudi royal family in August 1990 that played a key part in arranging the military buildup for the Persian Gulf War. In 1990, as he would again in 2002–2003, Cheney exaggerated intelligence on an alleged imminent Iraqi military peril (to suggest in 1990 that Iraqi tanks were poised to conquer Saudi Arabia), while insisting that American and Saudi political interests were identical—all to foment war against Iraq. (The 2002–2003 assertion about identical Saudi and American interests proved particularly troubling in light of the Saudis' pre-9/11 support for the Taliban and Osama bin Laden's Saudi recruiting and financing service to al-Qaeda.)[17] In 1990–1991 Cheney also advocated, albeit unsuccessfully, launching the war with Iraq without having any vote in Congress.[18] Once President Bush and Vice President Cheney took office in 2001, their administration prepared quietly to strain the law in avoiding oversight.[19] A potential difficulty in this effort was posed by their politically unavoidable appointment of the very popular Colin Powell as secretary of state. Powell did not share the White House's aversion to congressional and press scrutiny, nor did he represent the same right-wing constituency; instead, he saw a need for at least minimal responsiveness to the public, as well as a credible dialogue with the international community and its institutions. So Bush and Cheney must choose a national security team capable of neutralizing Powell, including key figures such as Cheney's long-standing conservative mentor Rumsfeld.[20] They particularly imposed on Powell a key subordinate, John Bolton, who shared their views both about serving the conservative base in general and about fending off scrutiny in particular.[21]

On the domestic stage, Bush's appointment of Ted Olson as his solicitor general sent a strong, if subtle, message of zealotry on executive privilege. Olson espoused the most fully elaborated, conservative executive privilege doctrines of any major public legal figure in two decades.[22] Thus Mr. Executive Privilege was chosen for the administration's most honored legal post.

As if to provide an early signal of its formal line on secrecy, the administration immediately waged two cover-up fights, the first of which Cheney personally picked and then won. In 2001 congressional Democrats asked Congress's auditing arm, the General Accounting Office (GAO), to examine the massive lobbying of the Cheney Energy Task Force by such big energy companies as the then revered, later reviled Enron. Of course the energy bills the task force proposed involved enormous taxpayer and consumer giveaways to Big Oil.[23] This task force was an extremely valid choice as subject of an inquiry: the public rightly distrusted the lobbying spectacle Cheney had invited so soon after coming to office.[24]

However, Cheney (with Bush's support) resisted the audit, shrewdly seizing the opportunity to demand a decision on executive secrecy from the increasingly conservative judiciary. When the GAO sued Cheney, Olson eagerly descended from the solicitor general's office, which almost never handles such cases at the trial-court level, and personally led the administration's side in *GAO v. Cheney*.[25] Thereby President Bush sent the strongest possible legal signal of the supremely high value he placed on shrouding corporate lobbying in secrecy. Cheney drew, as district judge on the case, a Bush appointee formerly in the Justice Department who predictably followed his benefactor's line and ruled that the GAO did not have the right to sue to overcome secrecy.[26] In deciding not to appeal, the GAO was perceived as yielding to intense pressure from the Republican congressional leadership.[27]

The second fight was President Bush's own and, without having to be as successful as Cheney's, did reinforce the new administration's commitment to executive privilege. Bush cleverly seized a safe opportunity. A House committee chaired by Representative Dan Burton (R-Ind.) investigated allegations that the Boston FBI over several decades had protected and nearly partnered with violent informants, only to find in December 2001 that President Bush signed a formal executive privilege claim covering the relevant Justice Department memoranda.[28] Initially the administration attempted to argue that historically, Congress had not reviewed similar materials. However, at key House hearings in March 2002, I had the honor of testifying in detail, and without effective contradiction, that this privilege claim subverted the law, for Congress had repeatedly obtained just such materials in the past.[29] To his credit, Chairman Burton stood rock-steady on the principle of congressional access to oversight materials, notwithstanding intense White House pressure to back down.

But the press gave the battle minimal attention, still thinking that executive privilege must concern personal presidential vice to matter. Eventually, Bush yielded so that Burton could review the documents, but with minimal personal damage to Bush's image.[30]

In picking these particular fights, the Bush White House restored barriers to congressional oversight of the White House—barriers hitherto lowered from the high levels of the Nixon stonewall in 1969–1974. Picking and directing these particular fights signaled within the administration, from top to bottom, a strong determination to resist any kind of information release—formally or informally, to the press, to Congress, to the public—other than releases that would abet the administration's own political agenda. Tactically, the Bush White House demonstrated skill in picking both the GAO and the Boston FBI battlegrounds to organize its layered defenses.[31]

Apart from these particular battles, the administration undertook several broader legal courses early on to promote secrecy. The Presidential Records Act of 1978 legally obliged the release in 2001 of most presidential records from the Reagan administration, after a twelve-year delay meant to desensitize the material.[32] However, many former Reagan administration figures—from the president's father, George H. W. Bush (Reagan's vice president) to Powell to OMB director Mitchell Daniels—would not welcome the prospect of reporters poring over Reagan-era records. Nor would former officials of the first Bush administration likely want such disclosures to be made a few years later. So, President Bush issued Executive Order 13233, hamstringing the Presidential Records Act.[33] When hearings ensued in which neutral scholars and even congressional Republicans decried the obstruction, Bush brushed them aside.[34]

Now it was Ashcroft's turn, and in October 2001 he issued a hostile memorandum about the Freedom of Information Act (FOIA).[35] It intimated that federal records officers should withhold records in any "discretionary" case and the Justice Department would back them up—effectively reversing the bedrock presumption of openness underlying the FOIA.[36] The memo would have far-reaching effects since a large number of cases could be construed as "discretionary." Such a memo would later constrain the Environmental Protection Agency and the Interior Department, for example, when environmentalists demanded greater disclosure of the administration's anti-environment policies. In March 2002 White House Chief of Staff Andrew Card followed this memorandum up with another, accompanied by guidance to all federal departments and agencies, suggesting they reduce information disclosure regardless of whether the disclosure fell under the FOIA's stated exemptions. Now, the memo advised, information could be withheld if it were merely judged "sensitive."[37] When Card said "sensitive," the bureaucrat who wanted to survive had better understand that to mean anything "politically sensitive" must be withheld.

It took two years for the administration to put up these high legal barriers to scrutiny. In the meantime, the legal shield of new court findings and internal directives had firmed up the surrounding informal policies of secrecy. By the end of the 107th Congress, in late 2002, senators and representatives of both parties facing the Bush administration's refusal to cooperate with even the most routine and basic congressional oversight expressed outrage.[38] White House reporters said they could not remember a White House that was more grudging or less forthcoming in informing the press.[39] Of course, after the election of November 2002 returned Senate control to President Bush's party, the loss of the only formal federal opposition forum for oversight meant President Bush could set the secrecy levels that much higher. It reminded one of Nixon before Watergate overwhelmed his layers of secrecy.[40]

A more particular analysis of the administration's secrecy divides into two parts: first, as to 9/11 and the Iraq occupation and, second, as to domestic policy.

SECRECY ABOUT 9/11 AND THE IRAQ OCCUPATION

Immediately after 9/11, Bush faced a basic challenge that he could overcome only with secret maneuvers on several levels. We know from the Saudi lobbying (about to be discussed) and from Paul O'Neill that Bush had, from the start, an interest in actions that would pull off a certain grand play: invade Iraq, give up the bases in Saudi Arabia as asked, and for 2004, offer the Iraqi oil reserves to his economic base and offer a warrior image of himself to his social base. But reflecting his electoral weakness, he had within his administration the hobbling presence of wise moderates like Powell and Tenet, who can be termed "tentatives" about taking down Iraq without a casus belli and hence without the approval of international consensus and law. Correspondingly, in the Senate Bush faced the externally hobbling combination of Democrats (in the majority from June 2001 through the end of the Congress and potentially, until late 2002, thereafter) and moderates in his own party such as Senator Richard Lugar (R-Ind.). If he pushed Powell and Tenet over the edge, the Senate would revolt. If he lost control of the increasingly damaging secrets accumulated in the back channel and created by the fictitious rationalizations for his moves, such as the "uranium from Niger" fable, the Senate would investigate and expose. Secrecy beget the need for further secrecy not only to achieve the fruits of the previous strategic moves but also to cover for the vulnerabilities to exposure those moves created.

Let me start by making clear I do not blame President Bush for 9/11 more than President Clinton deserves blame. A whole generation of American leadership failed to gauge the gathering *jihadi* storm against us, especially because of the lulling effect that the Saudi backers' cover-up had. The 2002 hearings of the congressional joint inquiry extracted specific regrettable details about the security bureaucracy's failings. These included the FBI and the CIA failing to talk to each other, ignoring pleas to investigate the al-Qaeda plot from the FBI agents in Phoenix and Minneapolis who glimpsed it, and ignoring warnings to both agencies' headquarters of aspects to the plot.[41] These specific bureaucratic problems stand for a much larger problem. All of us in Washington, from top to bottom, from right to left, shared the limits of vision. The evil was so powerful, so new, that it succeeded on a terrible scale; the lessons must be learned not just by some but by all. America's unreadiness for the 9/11 attacks was a systemic shortcoming, and both the Bush and Clinton administrations had demonstrated inadequate leadership.

To understand the significance of what President Bush concealed requires working further into perhaps the ultimate puzzle of this book: how did his dealings with the Saudis, particularly after 9/11, frame the occupation of Iraq in the unfortunate form it took?

Bush Sets Up His Back Channel (Jordan)

We explore this ultimate puzzle of the book by analyzing how Bush placed his loyal personal lawyer from the days of the 1991–1993 SEC insider trading charges, Robert W. Jordan, as his back channel to the Saudi ruling elite at the critical time when the Saudi role in 9/11 had to be finessed—including impeding the law enforcement investigation of 9/11—so that Bush could handle the Iraq occupation in his chosen way.

Here's how Bush's more secret ruses enabled him to set up his Iraq agenda as he wanted it for November 2004. Understanding the Saudi dealings starts with identifying the linchpin from the Saudi perspective. This was removal of America's military strongpoint in the Saudi-Iraqi neighborhood—the U.S. military buildup in Saudi Arabia and especially the huge, ultrasophisticated Prince Sultan Air Base fifty miles southeast of Riyadh. Carrier fleets, the island of Diego Garcia in the Indian Ocean, Turkish bases, and other forces and installations in the region served important functions. But when Saddam Hussein invaded Kuwait in 1990, the Saudis originally invited the United States to build up this base, right next to that sensitive Saudi/Iraqi border. For over a decade thereafter, this gigantic complex supported 286,000 completed flight missions enforcing the southern no-flight zone that kept Baghdad bottled up.[42]

But a gigantic military base fifty miles from the Saudi capital is not quite the same as a base in some remote corner of a nation whose history and national attitude puts it on easy terms with the largely Christian and wholly Western U.S. superpower. The Saudis are intensely Islamic and intensely Arabic, and they became a world powerhouse in their own right—as to oil and money—only after 1970. With the Saudi royalty keeping so much of its population down and managing it by feeding not only the *jihadi* sentiments held by many religious leaders and a substantial fraction of the men but also a kind of anti-Western nationalism, a powder keg is created of anti-American sentiment. From 1991 on, the Saudis increasingly doubted the American military presence was for their own good. They certainly never bought into the myths peddled later by Bush and Blair that Saddam posed an imminent nuclear threat. They knew how little he threatened them after the Gulf War inflicted $200 billion in damage on Iraq from the air, crushed his military, and blockaded his economy into feebleness.

Rather, the Saudis disliked that heavy-handed American military presence, producing tensions reminiscent of Iran under the shah (up to 1979). Those tensions lent credence to the "outs'" depiction of the "ins" as a kind of neocolonial stooge that let armed Christian infidels "occupy" the Islamic holy land of Mecca and Medina. The "outs" felt like revolting over it; the "ins" feared that revolt. Imagine how Americans would have felt during the Cold War if a corrupt U.S. regime had invited Stalin to build a giant military powerhouse for godless communist atheism about fifty miles south of Washington, supposedly to protect the United States from attack from the Bahamas but actually with the main effect of making all Western nations of faith look down on America. More broadly, the popular Saudi feelings about the U.S. military commitment and the base crystallized the deeper Saudi ambivalence about exploitation in the recent past, rapid modernization, and an uncertain positioning vis-à-vis the rest of the Arabic and Islamic world.

With the Saudi population and factions of the Saudi ruling class itself holding these sentiments to various degrees, the Saudi nation applied pressure on two tracks—one terrorist, one diplomatic—from 1991 to 2003 to persuade the United States to pull out its military. On each track, they decreasingly saw any point in supporting the American feud with Saddam. After all, skunk though he was, he had invaded Kuwait in 1990, not Saudi Arabia. His weak but intact Iraq served as a way that a Sunni ruling class held down a potentially dangerous Shiite population; the whole country was a useful buffer against the hostile Iraqi Shiite power of Iran. And by keeping his oil reserves undeveloped, he made it that much easier for the Saudis to manage oil prices through OPEC. As a precedent for what the Saudis now did, for years before the Gulf War, the Saudis had paid off what could alternately be described as "protection" or "support" to Middle Eastern terrorist groups with the awareness that they would attack infidel, not Saudi, targets.

As the conservatives' own inquirer into the Saudi backing of terror, Dore Gold, explains, "Osama bin Laden and Prince Turki al-Faisal, a son of King Faisal, knew each other during bin Laden's university days. Turki would make use of his relationship with bin Laden after the prince became the Saudi intelligence chief in September 1977. After the Soviet invasion of Afghanistan, he put bin Laden in charge of moving Arab volunteers who wanted to fight the Soviets from Saudi Arabia to Peshawar, Pakistan."[43] When the Soviets pulled out and their puppet fell and then after the Gulf War ended, Turki faced an angry Osama, whose offer to come home to fight the Baathist (secular) Saddam with the strength of faith had been spurned by Saudi rulers embracing infidel America instead. Turki and Osama talked as like-minded anti-Western Saudi patriots, the way a CIA director might talk to a talented but fanatical field chief following something that the director had to admit looked like a sellout. Since Turki coordinated Saudi royal support (or protection, depending on how you look at it) to *jihadi* terrorists, Turki made an offer Osama couldn't refuse: "an explicit deal with the Saudi royals to desist from violence in the kingdom in exchange for Saudi financing" for terrorism elsewhere.[44]

Prince Turki admits a half-dozen meetings with Osama while of course denying that he made such a deal.[45] But a few years later, Turki's arranging of Saudi backing played a pivotal part in the Taliban taking over Afghanistan, and the Saudis then pushed Osama to go there for his countdown to 9/11.[46] Gold, the conservative analyst, explains that when Sudan expelled Osama to the Saudi-backed Taliban's Afghanistan in 1996, "high-level U.S. intelligence officials became convinced that Saudi Arabia had struck a deal with bin Laden. . . . U.S. and British officials had actually identified the two Saudi princes who funded bin Laden. . . . Before bin Laden left Sudan for Afghanistan, at least three Saudi delegations . . . explained [to him], 'Your fight is with the United States, not with us.'"[47]

To go forward in time and look at the other end of the Saudi support pipeline—within the United States—the ultimate example of Saudi intelligence support for Osama was money from Ambassador Bandar's wife, Princess Haifa—so warm a friend of the Bushes that Laura Bush personally showed her around the Crawford ranch. That money ended up, via regular transfers, supporting Khalid Almidhar and Nawaf Alhamzi, two of the nineteen hijackers—the ones who on 9/11 ploughed the plane into the Pentagon.[48] It is naive to think of this as some individual whim of Princess Haifa's. The Saudi embassy, like any other, would (I infer, solely from public sources of information) have placed Turki's intelligence operatives under diplomatic cover, and the latter would write checks from the ambassador's wife's account, ostensibly for charity, and dispatch them through the usual disintermediation processes as financial cover. Looking at the two ends—(1) the Saudis setting up Mullah Omar in Afghanistan and moving Osama to his side and (2) the Saudi embassy's financing serving as support for Osama's hijackers as they arrive in America—one may begin to understand just what Bush steered the American government and public away from after 9/11, so that, instead of going down the trail to the real Saudi culprits, he could instead make his deal with the Saudis, control his internal and external "tentatives," and occupy Iraq as he wished.

On the diplomatic track, the rising Crown Prince Abdullah (King Fahd having suffered an incapacitating stroke in 1995) bluntly told the Clinton administration in 1996, as Turki sent Osama to Afghanistan, that he wouldn't tolerate indefinitely those U.S. bases to remain.[49] But the diplomacy failed with the Clinton administration. Nor did Osama's early attacks, such as the Khobar Towers bombing, persuade the United States to pull out. By late 2000 Abdullah issued strong anti-American warnings at an Arab summit in Cairo.[50]

Quite naturally, the Saudis turned to the Bush family, particularly since former president Bush officially joined the Carlyle Group, lined up on the Saudi payroll, and then turned out to be a twofer—a powerful former president and a back channel to his son, the new chief executive. In 2000, near Riyadh, Bush senior met with Abdullah on behalf of Carlyle. Carlyle was pursuing one of its numerous ultralucrative partnerships, this time with the Texas-based SBC Communications to buy a 25 percent stake in the Saudi national phone system. This would mean a nice piece of change for already very rich Texans, typical of the wonderful Saudi-Texas deals that danced like sugar-plum visions for both Bush senior and junior.[51] Shortly after the November 2000 election, the former president flew to Spain with Ambassador Bandar for a hunting trip.

So with Bush senior presumably giving junior lessons in the rewards and challenges for a Republican president in keeping the Saudis happy, Bush junior presumably got the message that he needed a coordination back channel in Riyadh. For Bush junior would need to coordinate his actions with the Saudis if he intended to reckon with Saddam Hussein. It would be most inconvenient to do so while pulling U.S. forces out of Saudi Arabia, not only because of the practical loss of the great base but also because of the confusion likely to arise when Americans saw proof that Iraq's neighbor scoffed at the claim that it needed protection from Saddam. The incoming secretary of state, Powell, had for a decade remained opposed, on military and diplomatic grounds, to occupying Baghdad.

Powell and Bush senior thought much alike—indeed, Bush senior probably still counted largely as a "tentative," since he had good reason to want to see Saddam go but only with international and domestic support if it involved a big military move. Bush junior probably could not frankly tell his father that the embarrassment of his own reserve service meant he could benefit from the enhancement of a warrior image that just such a military move would give him for 2004, and that he would go with less support than the "tentatives" required. Bush junior needed an emissary to the Saudis whom he could trust beyond anyone else to keep secrets not just from the public but from oversight or even the inquiries of others in his own administration. His trusted personal defense lawyer, Jordan, from the 1991–1993 SEC inquiry (and the Florida contest) already knew his weaknesses; had proven untroubled by excessive scruples (e.g., about the bogus privilege claim in 1993 and Bush's subsequent fables as to the SEC "losing" the required disclosure filings); and having been raised up from junior status by Bush, would treasure and respect him. In short, Jordan could become the back channel to the Saudi elite so that it understood that coordinating a military pullout from Saudi Arabia, as the Saudis demanded, with Saddam Hussein's removal, as Bush wanted, was not just Cheney's project; Bush himself would set the order of priorities; and for once, Cheney and Rumsfeld would just be useful tools, their agendas folded into his own larger and secret one.

Jordan was, of course, a diplomatic tyro with no knowledge of Arabic, and from Powell and Tenet's perspective, he would find out nothing to guide American policy makers through the mysteries of Saudi internal royal power struggles or royal relations with the *jihadi* Islamic clergy and the disaffected population; he would just be Abdullah's window to look right into Bush's mind. Too bad for Powell and Tenet; on this score they were not all that far from playing the role Paul O'Neill revealed had been created for himself and Christine Whitman—making the administration look more moderate while it actually pursued right-wing or hard-line plans. Powell and Tenet could assure the public and the Senate that Bush would not move too fast against Iraq, while Jordan could assure Abdullah privately that Bush would move against Iraq soon enough and then get the bases out, if Abdullah would just be a little patient.

Then came 9/11. As Bush recovered from the shock and as he listened to the code language in the debates before him between Powell and Rumsfeld and then in the back room with Cheney, he personally understood that 9/11 created both political problems and opportunities as to the Saudis and Iraq. These could not get talked about in public or with the "tentatives," and only to a limited extent even with Cheney and Rove. The tentatives would accept Bush's desire to preserve the Saudi royal alliance by deflecting some of the American public's anger at Saudi Arabia for its apparent connections to 9/11. But the tentatives would not fully know what Bush would say to Abdullah only via Bush senior, Bandar, and Jordan to persuade the crown prince to play ball, if grudgingly, with a politically timed invasion of Iraq. Abdullah would give polite denials that there had been a Saudi support apparatus for Osama and would remove its most visible signs: he'd let his far-out Taliban allies get whacked, reduce Prince Turki's visibility, and give low-level cooperation even to the despised, disrespectful FBI—so long as it stayed on the relatively insignificant details of the backgrounds of the violent fighters and didn't dig into connections between either the financial backing or the religious indoctrination and the Saudi elite. But Bush must get specific about removing those bases. And he must accept many actions and statements by top Saudis catering to internal *jihadi* sentiments and just hope that the awakened American defenses would, without much Saudi help, keep the huge funds and other support still going into Osama's pipeline from producing another 9/11.

That exchange would make sense to Abdullah only if he was convinced that Bush, for Bush's own reasons, would invade and occupy Iraq, unilaterally if need be, and would push the project through at whatever political price its half-baked, internationally isolated nature required. Only Bush's own personal lawyer in Riyadh could convey Bush's determination by explanations that the tentatives could never approve of: (1) the political usefulness to Bush in 2002 and 2004 of scoring what he considered a politically and militarily easy victory—the U.S. occupation of Baghdad (a message conveyed perhaps by allusions to the Democratic Party's containing more of the anti-Saudi elements); and (2) the value Bush placed on the long-term maintenance of Saudi friendship (conveyed as gratitude for his father's Carlyle Group payola, a message the Saudis would hear as carrying the implicit message that Bush himself wanted to be on what Baer calls the generous Saudi retirement plan). This kind of talk could be channeled only through Robert W. Jordan. Among the problems created by such a powerful back channel, though, was that in the long term, it cut the State, intelligence, and even military service bureaucracies so much out of the play that their attempts to shape the occupation in order to reduce its terrible costs—first in world opinion and later in American blood and treasure—would achieve only limited success.

Bush's "Suspect's Express" Service

Immediately after 9/11 the Bush White House had to deal, going on pure instant reflex, with a decisive turn of events. The FBI and Treasury investigators would awaken from their slumber. Bush's and Condoleeza Rice's pre-9/11 understanding of the Saudis may have been lightweight, but Bush should have understood at least that Osama was a sort of wayward Saudi son with a good deal of Saudi support. Rice probably understood a good deal more: that the Saudi global intelligence service and charitable network backed up terrorism elsewhere; that these had been tolerated to function in the United States from the misguided expectation that they would stay relatively benign; and that an operation like the 9/11 attacks would put a harsh spotlight on these. Inquiries would press forward in the United States and in Saudi Arabia on the trail from the fifteen Saudi hijackers, Osama, and Osama's Saudi-linked hierarchy back to the charitable supporters in Saudi Arabia. America just might boil over with rage at the Saudi regime.

Meanwhile, Wolfowitz in open meetings talked up the reasons now to go ahead with the Iraq invasion project, and Cheney in the back talked up the reasons to do it a little later—both being ignorant of Bush's own back channel. And Cheney would explain how tough Abdullah would find it, in allowing the Iraq invasion, to keep certain Saudi popular factions from vocalizing their opinion that Osama was the greatest warrior against the infidels since the medieval struggles. The Bush White House would hobble its foreign policy if it sided overly with the FBI and Treasury investigators who were building a case against the all-too-exposed Saudis.

So immediately after 9/11 the Bush White House almost reflexively gave its real signal that it would protect against FBI probing into the global Saudi covert intelligence and charitable support for Osama. This had to occur right then, as the FBI began awakening from its slumber under Louis Freeh and the terrorism-downgrading Ashcroft. In particular, the awakening FBI might use the chance to question the bin Ladens and other higher-level Saudis who had been in the United States—caught there by the fact that Osama's Saudi backers had not wanted to know, and had not known, enough of the details of what he was doing with their support to get them out earlier. All those exposed Saudi sources might enable the FBI to break through the "lone gunman" cover story of the Saudi royalty—that Osama was some kind of isolated nut and his hijackers were a bunch of psychopaths wandering around without any traceable connection to the large-scale charitable support for *jihadi* violence provided from the Saudi top. The FBI needed just a few talking top Saudis to give them all they needed to present the picture that the press and the terrorism experts soon had anyway: that the Saudi hierarchy back home had made its peace with a well-funded global al-Qaeda run by a leadership who used to work with them hand in glove. But if the angry, awakening FBI got it, then there would be consequences, and Bush would lose control of the effort to turn American anger away from the Saudis and instead, when he could in a few months, toward Iraq.

So in the two days after 9/11, the Saudi government worked with the bin Laden family to jet more than one hundred family members and other prominent Saudis out of a number of United States airports and then to Saudi Arabia. As a mirror image of "Visa Express" to get young Saudi males (fitting the hijacker profile) in before 9/11, let's call this operation of the Bush administration's that conveniently got bin Ladens out of the country after 9/11 "Suspects' Express." Here again, the Bush administration's skill at secrecy and deception really helped.

No one in the Bush White House wanted to say out loud just why it would not do to have television cameras filming the takeoff of the bin Laden jet while the actual smashing of the 9/11 suicide planes into the twin towers of the World Trade Center was still being shown over and over and after all passenger airline flights had been grounded. The public would be enraged from even a few visuals of bin Ladens leaving and a few lame quotes obtained by reporters from departing bin Ladens and Saudi royals. Those relatively unhardened, untrained figures simply would not know what to say to avoid either a obvious lie or clues revealing what those at the top in Saudi Arabia and in the bin Laden family knew about Osama and his murderous warriors and how much support he had back home.

Craig Unger explains in his study of the flights that "before 9/11, coincidentally, President Bush had invited Bandar to come to the White House on September 13, 2001, to discuss the Middle East peace process. The meeting went ahead as scheduled, but in the wake of the terrorist attacks, the political landscape had changed dramatically."[52] Bandar had spent the previous two days frantically organizing the flights. The top CIA and FBI figures could find out easily that Bandar would still meet with the president almost as soon as he got back to Washington, which powerfully indicated to them how deeply Bandar was in favor at the Bush White House. Indeed, at that meeting Bandar would even tell Bush that the Saudis would gladly take over the questioning of al-Qaeda operatives captured in America. For the Saudis actually to take away from America any al-Qaeda operatives the FBI managed to capture would have set the Bureau back so far in both the perception and the reality of its discharging of its responsibilities that the FBI probably heaved a sigh of relief at merely letting Bandar walk (or rather, fly) away with the bin Ladens and the Saudi elite. After all, at the time, the FBI had little in the way of counterterrorism files on the vast majority of these elite figures and no reason to link even the few it did have files on with these hijackings.[53]

The White House approval was managed, as it must be, from the very top: the spokesman on this matter at later hearings (and the writer of an account of it in his memoirs) was Richard Clarke, who ran the post-9/11 White House crisis team. Presumably Condoleeza Rice quickly figured out where this new development fit in Bush's well-known desire to stay as supportive of the Saudis as possible and not handle their terrorism role in a way that would upset the planned September 13 meeting. She would translate Bandar's urgent suggestions into what Clarke would say to the outside agencies, particularly the FBI. And now we begin to see how important it had been for Bush to lay down, during the campaign and from day one in the White House, broad secrecy principles, so that even on so utterly important a matter as this, Rice would know there would never be any real oversight. Neither Bush nor Rice need fear ever having to answer such hard questions as: given that Osama's demand was to get the American base out of Saudi Arabia, when had he or she received that request from any Saudi, and through whom? Bandar? Bush senior? Jordan? And how had Bush previously responded?

For the Bush White House, the challenging part, as always in such potentially scandalous matters, lay in giving the FBI just enough of the low-level insignificant symbols of respect that it needed to keep it from blowing the whistle but not enough for it to function too effectively. (This was no idle concern. Recall that when, not long afterward, Ashcroft and Dinh too-bluntly blocked the FBI from getting terrorist suspects' gun purchase logs, the FBI leaked to the press, and eventually the Senate Democrats extracted the lame tooth-fairy explanation of Ashcroft's respect for newly fabricated "firearms privacy rights." The real explanation in that case (Ashcroft's deal with the NRA) was relatively benign, but an explanation that involved Saudi payola and desires to manipulate American public opinion would be explosive by comparison, and the FBI leaks that would expose this story must simply not occur.)

So Bandar via Rice via Clarke—among other routes blessed implicitly by Bandar's 9/13 meeting with Bush—gave the still-groggy FBI its marching orders. The FBI should just to do a quickie, "Hey, you don't know anything, do you?" kind of airport interview with the departing Saudis. The FBI counterterrorism chief later sheepishly admitted that the bin Ladens "were not subject to serious interviews or interrogations."[54] He hadn't pressed the point on September 13. After that it was too late.

And now let us get concrete about what the FBI could have asked the bin Ladens and the Saudi royalty if not for their swift removal, implicitly blessed by Bush, aboard the "Suspects' Express." For this purpose let's examine the press reports of the classified annex to the 9/11 joint congressional inquiry report (drafted in late 2002 but its declassified sections not released until summer 2003), which "represented a searing indictment of how Saudi Arabia's ruling elite have, under the guise of support for Islamic charities, distributed millions of dollars to terrorists through an informal network of Saudi nationals, including some in the United States."[55] Robert Baer speculates that federal authorities might well have wanted to charge a number of Saudis whom they suspected of playing roles in the al-Qaeda financing network.[56] Some searching questioning of the bin Ladens and other rich Saudis, using the evidence the FBI and Treasury rapidly developed but did not have in hand at the airport on 9/13, would have led to one of two things. Either some of those Saudis would have provided a lot of information about the background of Saudi charitable financing and support in the United States to people who fit the hijacker profile, or if too many of them told lame lies, a couple would have stumbled into making false statements to the FBI that would have put them on public trial. There simply was not time for all those Saudis to coordinate their stories about the details of the charity work in the United States and to describe how they themselves respected what might be called "guidance" from Saudis at the embassies (and indirectly from Turki). One way or the other, the FBI questioning would permanently wreck the image of our "reliable allies" the Saudis.

For example, Omar al-Bayoumi, whom both the *Los Angeles Times* and the (media leaks about the) 9/11 joint inquiry pegged as a Saudi intelligence agent working with the Saudi consulate in Los Angeles, supported the aforementioned pair of Saudis, Khalid Almidhar and Nawaf Alhamzi, who flew the plane into the Pentagon on 9/11.[57] After 9/11 Bayoumi went to London, beat the FBI's effort to extradite him to the United States, and later resided in Riyadh. Questioning of those rushed aboard the "Suspect's Express" could presumably have led both to figures such as Bayoumi who had previously been in the United States and were later spirited to Saudi Arabia and to the couple of bin Laden's own brothers known to be on his side and fully capable of passing him directly a helpful portion of the bin Laden billions.

With this material in the FBI's hands, the legal problem would become the Saudis' refusal to yield up high-level figures fingered by the FBI, either for interrogation or for indictment. FBI demands for folks like Bayoumi and the Osama-sympathetic bin Laden brothers would be a world-class embarrassment for Bush. We had, after all, invaded Afghanistan and engaged in hands-on regime change because the Taliban had "harbored" some of those involved in the 9/11 planning—and now Saudi Arabia too would be seen as "harboring" plotters. That fits precisely what the September 14 congressional authorization of war said: legally, it didn't cover Iraq (not a harborer), but rather Afghanistan (a harborer), and it would then cover Saudi Arabia (a harborer). A tricky problem, that one, in the real practical law of authorizing war, especially with a Democratic Senate able to publicly debate the matter without overmuch sympathy for Bush's personal and political plans.

Conversely, Jordan, a sophisticated defense lawyer observing the White House run a "Suspects' Express," took his cues for the following stage. He would now know that his job as ambassador would not include excessively and embarrassingly pressuring the Saudis to help with 9/11 investigations over there. As Jordan managed the reins in Riyadh, he must take great care not to undermine Bush's patient efforts to persuade Americans to forget the Saudi role in 9/11 and instead, after Afghanistan, come to believe that the world terror problem somehow connected, not to the Saudi regional financial powerhouse, but to the bottled-up, kept-down, effectively enfeebled, and quite frightened Iraq.

So, Bush's "Suspects' Express" flew off like the plane at the end of the movie *Casablanca* did, carrying those who knew just where the gun had come from that shot Major Strasser. Just as the movie plane left the Vichy police behind with the task of "rounding up the usual suspects" (dangerous-looking characters without an actual role in the high-level plot), so this plane left Ashcroft behind to round up his usual suspects, also dangerous-looking characters who fit the politically convenient "lone gunman" theory of the terrorist attack but were far too poor and far too non-

Saudi to have any real clues about how the half billion dollars in Saudi financing for Osama had flowed down to 9/11. Ashcroft would demonstrate to the blindfolded American public how "serious" the Bush administration was about protecting this country against terror by posturing on television, making far-fetched proposals for convening military tribunals to try American civilians, threatening leak probes to unmask those who would talk about the administration's cover-ups, and so forth. How scornful the Saudi intelligence service must be of Ashcroft, with his partisan quickness to accuse senators of aiding the enemy when their inquiries were the only actual hope of keeping the administration honest.

The Bush White House's complicity in immediately throwing a cover over the lead-up to 9/11 had a long-term and deep significance. Because in recent American history the public has been denied a sense of closure on and final accounting for some of the major tragedies in national affairs, it has been haunted by theories, a few possibly true, many unthinkably far-fetched. As for 9/11, two successive major national investigations—the 9/11 joint congressional inquiry in 2002 and the Kean-Hamilton Commission in 2004, would attempt to provide a final accounting of the causes and the responsibility. But these inquiries and their conclusions might well suffer in the long run the fate that overtook the Warren Commission and its study of the assassination of President Kennedy in November 1963. Once official complicity in cover-ups immediately after that tragic event, such as the FBI's destruction of its file on Lee Harvey Oswald, became known, the public could have little confidence that the inquiries on its behalf had uncovered the whole story. In the large gap opened by such complicity, questions, doubts, and theories of varying plausibility would inevitably arise.

Down the road from 9/11, observers would inevitably ask, given their understanding of the Saudi role in providing charitable financing and recruits, what had gotten covered up by the White House's immediate (and subsequent) protection of the Saudis. All the hijackers themselves lay dead, much as Oswald, the asserted "lone gunman" of November 1963, lay dead shortly after the tragedy. Public inquiries like the Warren Commission's might try to place all the active blame on the obvious culprits. But when the official reaction immediately afterward fit the profile of a White House attempting to obstruct the trail leading beyond those culprits and that official reaction was suspect, in the end, the public might find its questions no more finally and certainly answered than it had with the Warren Commission report. Perhaps the administration acted out of simple reflex, steering (as its conservative economic base would want) to align itself with whatever the Saudis wanted and nothing more. Even if this was so, it might turn out that in steering that course, the Bush White House, by making it that much more difficult to lay to rest the ghosts haunting the lead-up to 9/11, had cost the American people something they vitally needed: the hope that eventually, in absorbing and dealing with the most foul and awful of blows against the country, they would at least know how the blow had come about.

The Secret 9/17 Directive and the Start of Iraq War Planning

President Bush wasted no time starting the war-planning machinery. He began with two legal instruments. The first, dealing with Afghanistan and al-Qaeda, emerged on September 14 from the legitimate democratic process of working with Congress. The second instrument, issued by the White House three days later, evolved in a very different, nondemocratic process, was never released officially, and became known only when it was leaked later on. It was this document that named Iraq as a target.

Immediately after the terrible Tuesday of 9/11, congressional leaders and the White House held three days of meetings and exchanges to prepare the functional equivalent of a declaration of war. Although these exchanges occurred out of the public eye rather than in hearing rooms, what they resolved—or at least what Congress could legitimately believe they resolved—becomes clear from a comparison of two important legal texts: that of the White House's first proposed resolution, issued Wednesday, the 12th,[58] and that of the resolution Congress actually adopted, with President Bush's blessing, on Friday, the 14th.[59]

The "Resolved" clause of the White House's 9/12 proposal would have authorized force both to punish those involved in the 9/11 attacks and—significantly—also "to deter and pre-empt any future acts of terrorism or aggression against the United States." This would have been an incredibly sweeping attack authorization—presumably covering, at a minimum, Iraq. As discussed in chapter 7, the legal doctrine of initiating war unilaterally against nations not themselves now or recently supporting terrorism in order simply to "deter and pre-empt" disfavored nations constituted a quantum leap in asserted war-making authority. President Bush's core supporters might applaud giving him a free hand to wage war against anyone he chose to "deter," but centrists wanted some of the traditional steps taken before presidents attacked other nations.[60]

For a time it appeared the centrists had prevailed. The final Force Authorization Resolution enacted September 14 contained no such legal authorization for preemptive war against other nations in the effective or

"Resolved" clause. It simply did not authorize deterrent or pre-emptive use of force.[61] Congress voted for, and the American public and the world saw as the legally enacted product of the democratic legislature, the 9/14 open resolution against those harboring the 9/11 terrorists—that is, an authorization for force against Afghanistan, but not Iraq. This fit with the public's and the world's sensible perception: after the Taliban, the next suspect wasn't Iraq—it was the Saudis.

In contrast, no one outside the circle of executive secrecy could examine the secret directive that followed on Monday, the 17th, and whose stance toward Iraq was quite different. To discuss this kind of secret directive calls for some legal background.[62] Presidents have a powerful means of directing national security that is parallel to enacting laws but very different in operation. Presidents can issue "national security directives," such as that of September 17, that function somewhat like executive orders but are not openly issued. Instead, these directives are meant to communicate policy commands on military and international matters through special channels. Although presidents may legitimately use secret directives in order to avoid international awareness and repercussions, they may also use this clandestine mechanism to accomplish their own politically controversial objectives.

In a previous book, *The Semi-Sovereign Presidency*, I detailed the classic abuse of the power to issue such directives: how the first President Bush in June 1989 issued National Security Directive 26 (NSD-26), which secretly implemented a policy of courting Saddam Hussein as a valued friend and ally in the critical year when this courtship played a part in Saddam coming to believe that the United States would not punish him much for invading Kuwait.[63] In that instance, the directive later proved so misguided that the same administration employed strenuous legal efforts to keep as much of it as possible classified for years thereafter—long after the Gulf War and long after the end of all legitimate reasons to do so. Keeping the directive secret helped impede postwar congressional inquiries that sought to uncover the reasons for America's earlier courtship of Saddam Hussein.[64] Days after the September 2001 attacks, the George W. Bush administration apparently had a similar mixture of motives for applying secrecy to its own Iraq policy, but this time for much larger stakes.[65] President Bush's top secret 9/17 national security directive focused primarily on the war in Afghanistan as part of the anti-terrorism effort.

However, the president also decisively stamped his imprimatur on Pentagon planning of an invasion of Iraq.[66] This forever altered the Cabinet's pre-9/11 consensus on Iraq. Before 9/11, Bush had let Powell have the play to pursue his ingenious if difficult course of maintaining and fine-tuning the Clinton policy of an economic blockade stranglehold. Bush had said that Rumsfeld "should examine our military options," according to O'Neill's recollection, but not given orders in writing.[67] The secret directive meant an immediate but unheralded change of course. Bush desired neither an immediate war nor immediate, bipartisan consultations with congressional leaders about a possible war. Instead, he wanted to shift decisions on Iraq into Cheney's picked national security network—especially Secretary Rumsfeld, Undersecretary Wolfowitz, and Undersecretary Bolton—all of whom had long nursed a vision of war with Iraq, even if it had to be conducted unilaterally. Meanwhile Bush would make the ultimate calls based on his own private circle, with Rove at home and Jordan in the field.

Acting under the secret 9/17 directive's authority, by early November the White House deputy national security adviser for counterterrorism, retired army general Wayne Downing, began secretly working up plans for the invasion of Iraq.[68] Downing had been identified since the late 1990s with devising a military strategy for attacking Iraq. This he worked on with Dewey Clarridge, perhaps the wildest and most anti-democratic CIA figure in the Iran-contra scandal, who was spared from an indictment for multiple felony counts for lying—not just lying before the scandal broke but even lying to the Iran-contra committee itself—only by Bush senior's presidential pardon in December 1992. Bush junior's use of Iran-contra culprits reached a new high, or low, in putting the infamous Dewey Clarridge's plans into play via a secret directive. (We're lucky Clarridge's plans didn't include, too, the great idea of financing this unpopular occupation by selling missiles to the ayatollahs in Iran and lying to Congress about it.) Although Downing's plan was not to mount the full-scale invasion ultimately undertaken, it did include the enduring feature of heavy reliance on the exile figure Ahmed Chalabi. Chalabi continued to be the Cheney-Rumsfeld darling, and his lack of actual in-country support foreshadowed one of the reasons that the eventual occupation faced the resistance of a suspicious and potentially hostile population.[69]

Rumsfeld had his top legal aide Undersecretary Douglas Feith create a secret Pentagon intelligence system, the Office of Special Plans, to distort the government's official analysis on the inconvenient facts about Iraq, such as its not being involved in the 9/11 terrorist attacks.[70] These steps began to box in Powell and Tenet by generating a new stream of exaggerated or doctored intelligence claims designed ultimately to leave no choice but to occupy Iraq. One had to reach back to President Johnson's deceptions about Vietnam for a similar instance of a president using legal tools to supply doctored intelligence that promotes such a war. And as with Vietnam, using doctored intelligence meant basing the military commitment on war aims—in this instance, eliminating the asserted stockpiles of nuclear and other weaponry ready for use against America—that were doomed to evaporate, leaving the occupation much more insecure—internationally and domestically, within the military and in relation to the occupied population—than if the commitment had been based on truth.

Bush's engine for pushing the Iraq war came from the terrorist attacks, which gave a large short-term boost to his popular support and allowed Ashcroft to conduct a complete image makeover so that he became a fighter against shadowy enemies. With the passage of time, however, the public pressed its representatives in Congress to learn by way of a major joint House-Senate inquiry in 2002 just how its government had failed to prevent the devastating attacks.

But the Bush administration stood to lose much of its newly heightened popularity if the public obtained too vivid a picture of a sitting president and attorney general whose pre-9/11 reality clashed so much with their carefully cultivated post-9/11 image makeover. Whatever its inadequacies, during the prior administration, Attorney General Reno had personally pushed counterterrorism efforts.[71] President Clinton had personally supervised, according to press reports, multiple CIA efforts that came close to eliminating Osama bin Laden.[72] At least the record showed they had cared and had tried to act.[73] In contrast, a portrait of Ashcroft and Bush before 9/11 might have revealed that they simply had not responded to the imminence of the threat and sometimes demonstrated how little they cared about the issues.

In the 1990s, Ashcroft, like other conservative Republican senators, had treated Reno's urgent requests for additional counterterrorism authority coolly.[74] Ironically, Ashcroft later drafted his post-9/11 statute (described in chapter 3) using her proposals—as well as proposals for controlling money laundering from the senator who, in contrast, had warned loudly and clearly about transnational flows of financing for evil purposes, John Kerry (D-Mass.). Moreover, the Senate had a number of former prosecutors, Kerry being only one of them, fully capable of laying out the difference between the semblance of counterterrorism staged by Ashcroft and the reality of following the money trail.

In the months before 9/11, as we saw in chapter 3, Ashcroft had actually downgraded counterterrorism as a Justice Department priority.[75] As for President Bush, it required strenuous White House spin-control efforts to deal with the public reaction to even partial revelations. The public took hard his continuing to be more passive about Osama bin Laden than about his own, far-less-vital pet security projects despite his having been briefed—on August 6, 2001—about an impending al-Qaeda threat.[76] When there was still time, Bush held neither the Taliban nor al-Qaeda to account for either the October 2000 attack on the U.S.S. *Cole* or the discovered plans for attacks on the United States on January 1, 2001.[77] Quite the contrary, he revoked the Clinton administration's deployment of cruise missiles and gunships on alert near Afghanistan, let the Afghan Northern Alliance almost collapse, and permitted Rumsfeld to redirect spending on counterterrorism toward Bush's own pet project, missile defense. President Bush said virtually nothing publicly about the dangers of terrorism between his inauguration and 9/11, except when he used the words to move missile defense along and to justify on three occasions discarding the ABM Treaty. Bush missed the opportunity as president to awaken public concern about the looming al-Qaeda threat.

If the Bush White House had not invoked executive privilege, he would have allowed the actual text of the August 6 briefing about al-Qaeda (with its heading, "Bin Laden Determined to Strike in the U.S.") to become public.[78] Televised hearings about this would have brought his post-9/11 image closer to reality. President Clinton's use of privilege failed to keep embarrassing details having a minor impact on the public interest secret; President Bush's, as to big matters, succeeded.

President Bush now had a strong interest in splicing a revised version of his pre-9/11 agenda onto the new national counterterrorism mandate. However, to promote hard-line causes that had little to do with the 9/11 attack (such as invading Iraq), Bush had to find ways to obscure the artificiality of that connection, not just sell his agenda to the public and Congress. Otherwise, the press and public would have reason to wonder why Iraq, which had not sponsored 9/11, was suddenly replacing bin Laden as the nation's principal nemesis. The administration also perceived that further evidence of Saudi financing and involvement with 9/11, obtained by the congressional joint inquiry and not really warranting the classification stamp the administration wanted to keep on it in 2002 and early 2003, would further stir public doubt and anger.

As war planning unfolded covertly, the president gradually began moving the public toward anti-Iraq fervor, beginning with his "axis of evil" comments in January 2002. But even conflating Iraq with Iran and North Korea did not constitute a formal and public espousal of war.[79] Starting in April 2002, the president apparently initiated serious interdepartmental meetings about war planning. Army general Tommy R. Franks, later the combat commander, traveled to the White House every three or four weeks to brief the president privately about military planning.[80] By June it had been leaked that the Pentagon's secret war-planning options did not just encompass the small strike force of the Downing-Clarridge plan but extended to use of 250,000 troops in 2003. The White House did not want to admit it, but the notion that the Iraqi population would fight for liberation as so much of Afghanistan had was a myth, and the desires of the White House required a large and lengthy American military occupation. This meant a whole fresh layer of secrets that needed to be kept, for the American public must not know about the nature of and reasons for that occupation.

Still, the covert nature of presidential war preparations continued to have several inestimable advantages for the administration. It gave the war hawks time to control the "tentatives." Cheney did this by taking the bogus intelligence manufactured by Feith for Rumsfeld and pressuring Tenet's subordinates until they began to accept it.[81] Cheney especially wanted the CIA to bolster his favorite claim, that Iraq could soon have the ability to attack the United States with nuclear explosives.[82]

Most famously, Cheney prepped Bush to insist that Iraq had tried to buy uranium from Niger. In the first half of 2002, the CIA and the State Department declared the documents assertedly supporting this claim to be forgeries. But the Bush administration bottled this awareness up. The American public did not realize the roundabout method by which it was lied to, but the administration allowed Blair to use it in his key September 2002 intelligence-based war debate (the British press later nicknamed the intelligence file the "dodgy dossier"), which spawned war-pushing headlines that "Saddam 'could have nuclear bomb in year.'"[83] Then, in America Bush himself served up in his infamous January 2003 State of the Union address—long after the reminders of the forgery had saturated the government, the latest version of the Thousand and One Tales of the Arabian Nights (fewer flying carpets but ample WMD).[84] By letting Blair's bunkum go uncorrected and then recycling it, the Bush administration produced the supreme example of the technique called intelligence "blowback," in which intelligence-generated false propaganda circulates overseas and then comes back to America to undermine our own democracy.

The blowback from the official espousal of the Niger forgeries mattered so much that the exposure by the CIA's investigating emissary, former ambassador Joseph Wilson, triggered Bush White House backlash. The infamous leak about Wilson's wife being with the CIA led to a criminal investigation, which followed a trail of notes by Cheney's staff, to determine whether to indict Rove himself on this. This had double significance. It showed how much of the Iraq war planning and selling did not go through even Rumsfeld, but rather came out of Bush's private circle of Rove and Jordan. And, the fact that Ashcroft had his Criminal Division look hard at this suggested both the strength of the case against Rove and the cracks between the different conservative bases within the party. A substantial wing of the party (including Pat Buchanan) recognized the Saudi role in 9/11, would not put up with Bush hard-liners suppressing criticism of that Saudi role, and somewhat disdained the prolongation of the occupation of Iraq. The hard-liners' leak tactics against Wilson's wife epitomized what this wing disdained.

This brings us to the Bush White House's tactical use of the leak investigation—not, as with the Rove-Wilson matter, to trace real, harmful shenanigans but rather, under Cheney's expert handling, to suppress criticism of the administration. For the background of the Bush-Cheney use of this special legal weapon, we start with the fact that the information later indignantly dealt with as a dangerous leak lay already plastered in the public record. On September 22, 2001, the *Washington Times*, the pro-administration organ published by followers of South Korea's far-right Reverend Sun Myung Moon, published a first lead story on the failure of American intelligence, "Intercepts Foretold of 'Big Attack.'" Based on comments from a "senior administration official," the article said that American intelligence agencies had intercepts of "discussions between Osama bin-Laden's lieutenants of an impending 'big attack.'"[85] Naturally, this leak, from a pro-administration newspaper, aroused no sign of indignation from the White House. After all, it took some pressure off the Bush White House and put blame on the security bureaucracy. Then, on September 30, Attorney General Ashcroft went on CBS and CNN, proclaiming heatedly that bin Laden's terrorists currently at large in the United States "have plans . . . to do things."[86] These disclosures again drew no criticism from the White House, which approved of the purpose behind them of scaring Congress into passing Ashcroft's USA PATRIOT bill.[87]

However, when others not anointed by President Bush later made such statements, he whipped out the criticism-stifling tactic of the leak inquiry. The press reported the following week that members of Congress—apparently those on the intelligence committees—had repeated what Ashcroft had said on television: that bin Laden terrorists seemed likely to try another attack. But what Ashcroft could shout at top volume to White House applause no one else must be allowed to say. In response, the president issued on October 5 one of the most extraordinary secrecy orders in American history. Entitled "Disclosures to the Congress,"[88] it permitted administration officials to respond to only eight leading members of Congress—not the other 527—when faced with a query, even if the query dealt with nonclassified information deemed merely "sensitive" (which meant just about anything and everything). Four of the eight were congressional leaders, and the other four, senior intelligence committee members; half were of the president's own party. This extraordinary directive basically would have put Congress out of the business of oversight of the administration's spending or legislative proposals, since the administration would no longer have to answer any congressional questions on anything called "sensitive" unless the questioners were among the four tolerated House and Senate Democrats. The president basically threatened to administer the country on a secret basis. Bush seems to have acted toward Congress without much consideration of the reaction to his approach; he later let the directive slide, and the Congress, far from showing any indignation, just sighed with relief at his relenting about putting it out of business.[89]

And Ashcroft, who now had to answer for his own reduction of counterterrorism efforts prior to 9/11, got even more than a free pass from scrutiny. To describe his own resistance to scrutiny of his abuses after 9/11 is a large undertaking, one that a number of scholars have ably tackled. His withholding from the press the discrediting details of his department's bumbling sweeps of hundreds of alien immigration detainees who bore no trace of terrorist tendencies; his advocating the inflammatory anti-constitutional concept of seizing American citizens, stripping them of elementary rights, and trying them before secret military tribunals; his withholding from objective scrutiny his staff's dicey legal opinions; his stonewalling Judiciary Committee queries about civil liberties; and many other, parallel steps amounted to placing himself above criticism and beyond the law.[90] In this, Ashcroft once again demonstrated his ability to place self-image above responsibility. His predecessor, Janet Reno, was certainly not perfect, but she did accept scrutiny and criticism as part of the powerful job, even tolerating frequent leaks to Republicans in Congress from the staff of her politically freelancing FBI director, Louis Freeh.

Ashcroft's tactics worked. Avoiding references to the coolness he'd shown to Reno's anti-terrorism efforts in the 1990s, Ashcroft now paraded himself constantly in front of the media as a zealous fighter for national security. This extraordinary cosmetic makeover campaign continued for two months, until Ashcroft finally appeared for a Senate hearing in December 2001 to answer questions about whether he had misused his legal powers after the emergency. By then, the press had reported Ashcroft and Dinh's blocking of the post-9/11 FBI terrorism investigation, which had sought firearms records Ashcroft wished to keep secret (see chapter 3). It was in his dramatic opening statement that Ashcroft famously implied that Democratic senators, by daring to ask him oversight questions, were "aiding" the terrorist enemy. To be precise, he chillingly told the senators whose opening statements that day had dared question the erosion of civil liberty by the post-9/11 actions, "To those who scare peace-loving people with phantoms of lost liberty, my message is this: Your tactics only aid terrorists."[91] The archconservative who had been an administration-baiting senator just a year before thus smeared his Senate colleagues, some of whom had done a lot more to promote anti-terrorism legislation than he ever had, by portraying them as traitors. Few single sentences have so polarized and poisoned American governance.

Nor did the spin-control effort stop with Ashcroft. As the joint congressional 9/11 inquiry moved beyond the specific details of missed CIA and FBI opportunities to crack the terrorists' conspiracy, attention now turned to what President Bush had heard about the looming al-Qaeda menace in the August 6, 2001, intelligence briefing at his Crawford ranch. By July 2002 Bush faced mounting questions in the press—potentially the worst press firestorm of his term and one of the last before the November 2002 election could free him from oversight by a Democratic Senate.

Then CNN broadcast information about a closed congressional hearing focused on National Security Agency intercepts from the eve of 9/11 that had indicated a coming attack—effectively the same information the *Washington Times* had printed the preceding September 21.[92] Bush did not care that this CNN report revealed little beyond what his own administration itself previously leaked to the *Times* the preceding September. He directed Cheney to pounce, and Cheney forced the intelligence committees to allow a full FBI leak probe on Capitol Hill.[93] Because I had experience with Capitol Hill leak probes, the *Washington Post* and MSNBC invited my comments, and reporters shared their own insights with me on this issue.[94] The press itself knew the point of President Bush's tactic—to frighten their already intimidated sources into silence and to divert attention from what the joint inquiry might uncover about the president's alleged negligence. Despite the press's awareness of Bush's intent, the tactic nevertheless worked like a charm. President Bush cooled the firestorm, buying himself all the room to maneuver that he needed.

SECRECY AND THE NOVEMBER 2002 ELECTION

As midterm elections approached in the summer of 2002, the possibility of Republican gains looked doubtful absent some especially effective strategy. Bush's support had retreated from its peaks during his bipartisan phase after 9/11 and during the Afghan campaign. Record-breaking campaign fund-raising in the spring had filled GOP coffers but given Bush a distinctly partisan appearance. The 9/11 joint inquiry had put some heat on Bush, whose professed unconcern with his failure to capture or kill Osama began to seem forced. The continuing recession and the third year of the stock market plunge debunked his repeated line that the Bush tax cut of 2001 had significantly relieved the bad employment situation. To the contrary, the 2002 corporate accounting scandals shone a harsh new light on the nation's economic situation. Now it began to seem that part of the fault for the stock market bubble and the depth of the recession following its burst resulted from corporate accounting misdeeds by a class of chief executives and managers, such as Enron's, who were, now and always, uncomfortably close to President Bush. Republican candidates facing the upcoming election may well have wondered whether the campaign contributions they had accumulated with President Bush's help could suffice to distract the centrist public from blaming the president's party for the continuing economic pain.

Manipulation of jingoistic public sentiment offered President Bush one possible way out; he could time several intense national debates about security for the eve of the election. This latest effort at window-dressing would contain two main elements: authorizing war against Iraq and casting blame for delay in creating a "homeland security" department on the opposition.

Bush finally unveiled some of his previously concealed war aims just a couple of months before the election, when he indicated his desire for a congressional war resolution. By then, nearly a year had passed since actual war preparations had begun with the secret directive of 9/17. The directive itself had never been released, and its partial leaking had gone largely unanalyzed, so there was no need to account for the year's worth of preparations undertaken *before* he asked for any congressional action. The administration suppressed as secrets many other inconvenient elements of the ensuing war debate,[95] including the encouragement of the illusion of Iraq's connection with 9/11; Bush's proof allegedly showing Iraq on the verge of having nuclear weapons; failure to face the negative international impact from unilaterally proceeding with occupation;[96] the absence of an exit strategy; inability to explain how Powell's earlier cautious antiwar stance had changed; and many other flaws.[97] Indeed, the White House held the CIA back from reporting to the Senate about Iraq, provoking bitter reproaches.[98] Bush also avoided openness as to the administration's own previous internal divisions about the wisdom of unilateral war and occupation, which would have impaired the image Rove wanted to project. Above all, Bush concealed from Congress the core calculations on post-9/11 reshaping of relations with the Saudis and the concerns about oil that actually drove him.

The technical form of the Iraq invasion authorization has an interesting aspect that, though less important than the secret planning and the control of timing, contains much for reasonable scholars to debate. After all, President Bush did ask Congress for approval; he did not bypass Congress. He obtained a binding public law as authorization from the House and Senate, as his father had in 1991 prior to the first Persian Gulf War, and in contrast with President Clinton's bombing of Serbia in 1999, which was carried out without such a formal congressional authorization.

But it looked much like the Tonkin Gulf Resolution of 1964. The authorization Bush sought and obtained did predate the actual land conflict by months, amounting to a blank check. Some would reasonably defend this chain of events as constitutional, since all declarations or authorizations of war leave the president some discretion on whether and when to initiate combat. But Bush defeated the spirit, if not the letter, of the war authorization system established in the Constitution and the War Powers Resolution. That system seeks to have Congress, on behalf of the people themselves, take responsibility for war, even if its authorization leaves some discretion to the president.[99] Bush's methods diffused and undermined congressional responsibility since actual combat would not start for an indeterminate period, after unknown intermediate steps including an as-yet-unclear United Nations role. The vote was not a responsible congressional decision on war based on the president's frank assessment of imminent costs and problems but instead an election-eve referendum on who the public liked better—their own president or the beast of Baghdad. President Bush had, by his uses of secrecy and his related control of timing, set it up that way.

Part two of Rove's strategy for the 2002 midterm election concerned manipulating the issue of creating a Department of Homeland Security. Up until this time President Bush had cloaked with executive privilege the planning efforts of his homeland security director, Tom Ridge.[100] Throughout the first six months of 2002, congressional Democrats had, with bipartisan support, demanded answers and accountability from Ridge. Senate Appropriations chairman Robert C. Byrd (D-W.Va.) sought to plan the appropriations for homeland security; by May Senate Governmental Affairs Committee chairman Joseph I. Lieberman (D-Conn.) had elaborately prepared and now sought to introduce a bipartisan bill to organize a Department of Homeland Security.

But Bush asserted that Ridge, occupying a post created by executive order, stood beyond oversight, just like the national security adviser. Senators, even those addressing Ridge's $38 billion homeland security budget, were going to have to settle for briefings, not the televised hearings the public would want. President Bush's executive privilege claim stonewalled Congress in its efforts to organize the new homeland security department and decide what it would do. It was an abuse of executive privilege, as invalid as the Boston FBI claim.

The resulting silence from Ridge paid off handsomely for Rove's midterm election strategy. By thus avoiding months of congressional hearings on funding and organizing the new effort, Bush could wait until the timing was ideal—in June 2002—to unveil his own Homeland Security Department plan.[101] The long secrecy made possible by executive privilege gave the administration enough control to transform the issue from its natural status as the perfect place for bipartisanship into Rove's partisan trap. Now the White House pasted partisan poison pills into the bill, creating a Homeland Security Department with its own, previously prepared "Freedom to Manage" initiative, a conservative-inspired plan for turning the federal civil service into a politically run patronage and cronyism machine. Inserting this politically charged addition into what might have been a bipartisan bill constituted a poison pill. Democrats would be certain to vote against this version, since it no longer focused on the consensus goal of a consolidated Homeland Security Department but veered off toward serving the administration's partisan interest. Clearly Rove did not want a law; he wanted a campaign issue. Senate Democrats tried to move the bipartisan version of the homeland security bill they had developed earlier. However, following the White House script, after Congress returned from its August recess, Senate Republicans filibustered for seven key weeks, refusing reasonable compromise until Congress adjourned in mid-October without enacting a law.[102]

This sprang Rove's trap, as the president could now campaign in his most shrill, negative way against Democrats for what he called their "special interest" opposition to homeland security; he implied that Democrats were soft on terrorism—in contrast with the only patriotic candidates, the Republicans. His distortions abused important national security issues as election hostages and trashed bipartisan cooperation. But as politics the strategy worked brilliantly. Republicans could attack Democratic Senate and House candidates who had voted against their version—or attempted to move homeland security past the Republican filibuster in the Senate—without restraint.

The famous victim was Senator Max Cleland (D-Ga.).[103] Cleland had lost both legs and an arm fighting in Vietnam, received the Silver Star, and served as secretary of veterans' affairs. This ordinarily would have ended any room for President Bush to attack him as unpatriotic (Bush, the "veteran" of the Texas Air National Guard who always had on his conscience that period of his service when he moved to Alabama, for which there didn't seem to be any human or other convincing corroboration that he had shown up for duty). In effect, Cleland represented in 2002 the challenge Bush would face even more directly in 2004: which legal tactics could help him survive the natural comparison between him, the leader of a preemptively attacking nation who had that less-than-stellar reservist's record, and those—McCain, Kerry, Cleland—who had actually traded bullets with America's enemies and knew firsthand the pain and price of war? Moreover, Cleland had voted for Bush's trillion-dollar tax cut, burnishing his credentials not just with centrists but with conservatives.

But Rove had Cleland trapped because the senator had dared vote to end the Senate Republican filibuster waged against the bipartisan Lieberman version of the homeland security bill. Now Republicans blanketed the airways with a negative ad that flashed pictures of Osama bin Laden and then blasted Cleland for votes "against" President Bush's domestic security bill. Similar attack ads used this issue to put Saddam Hussein's picture with Cleland's, effectively deceiving the electorate about where he stood on the Iraq issue, since he had in fact voted for the authorization of war against Iraq. Cleland lost. So did Senator Jean Carnahan, a Missouri Democrat. President Bush's party took the two seats needed to regain Senate control by a combination of secrecy and manipulative timing.

Having made such election use of the Iraq issue, it remained to force through, against world resistance, an occupation with no new rationale. Here also, secrecy was to continue to play a role. The administration refused to discuss the war's possible price tag until the annual fiscal year 2003 budget had largely gone through, making a mockery out of Congress's power of the purse and promoting Bush's 2003 tax cut without acknowledging the huge looming deficits, which would be exacerbated by the occupation.[104] The administration whipped up domestic feeling against Iraq by inflated claims about nuclear explosives and other weapons of mass destruction, though such efforts were scarred by knowledgeable foreign publics and leaders.

And once again putting secrecy to use, the Bush administration from January to March 2003 started arranging the contracting for Iraq's postwar reconstruction to go only to its picked friends. The press, once again learning the facts only bit by bit after the deals had largely been done, eventually came to note in particular the favoritism shown companies like Halliburton, which had previously been headed by Cheney, and Bechtel, whose leaders were almost as well connected to the Bush administration. This time the anger was both domestic and international, since the administration had prevented companies from allied countries like Tony Blair's Britain from taking part.

Many reporters also pointed out that the Bush administration had found yet a new method of covering up. Normally the letting of large contracts for postwar reconstruction would occur by open solicitation of proposals and then a relatively open process of competition, especially for contracts like those for public health facilities and schools that had no military significance. Normally the State Department's Agency for International Development (AID), which gave the juicy contracts out, would gladly allow British companies to bid in order to help keep prices down (through competition) and procedures honest (through openness). Instead, on White House orders, AID solicited bids in secret, restricting the circle of competitors just to those the administration liked enough to invite. Invitees knew to tell the press nothing and, if they got awards, knew who they owed campaign contributions to—amounting to, in this instance, a legally though thinly veiled variant of kickback.

Though the administration's main reasons for secrecy may never be fully revealed, they ranged beyond seeking to cover up simple corruption. Rather, Cheney had found himself, as he steered the Bush administration to war, wanting to minimize the role of the State Department in the planning and, later, the handling of the occupation, and seeking to deny the public a window into either the planning or the occupation. In January 2003 the vice president followed so rigidly unilateral a path, he could not even spare much concern for Britain's sensibilities. So he wanted a privatized and unilateral way of controlling the money that Bush would make Congress put into the occupation. That meant contracts kept as much under his thumb as possible and awarded to companies grateful and obedient enough to suit his total top-down control and secretive planning, even though that meant subverting the contracting laws otherwise written to ensure openness and accountability.[105] Cheney didn't care much about the insult to America's fighting allies, whose soldiers shed their blood in Basra as bravely as ours shed theirs in Baghdad. So the opportunity to bid was denied not only to American firms, except for select invitees, and to nonallied countries' firms but even to British firms—with valuable experience (Iraq being at one time run by the British).

Meanwhile, President Bush had succeeded on many levels in avoiding the hard questions about his and Ashcroft's pre-9/11 roles: his White House had invoked executive privilege (and other privileges); his administration's disputes about declassification had stalled the 9/11 joint inquiry report's final release until long after the Iraq invasion; the war provided cover when the nearly nine-hundred-page report eventually came out in August 2003; and above all, the Saudis' role still didn't get probed. The report did include a revealing account of the privilege claims used against the 9/11 inquiry. In May 2002 the administration had informed the inquiry in a general way about Bush's written "President's Daily Briefing" for August 6, 2001, with its in-depth analysis of Osama's terrorist plans. Simultaneously, National Security Adviser Condoleeza Rice had mentioned to the press in as low-key a way as she could that briefing. Nothing could keep the story from gaining enormous attention in the broadcast and print media. But Rice succeeded in spinning the briefing as vague—"a generalized warning."[106] "I don't think anybody could have predicted that these people would take an airplane and slam it into the World Trade Center, take another one and slam it into the Pentagon," Rice told reporters.[107] Cutely phrased, but the warning President Bush ignored wasn't so zilch as Rice portrayed it.

Only when the administration finally declassified (most of) the report in August 2003, belatedly allowing it to be published, was it revealed that the White House had refused to provide the congressional inquiry with an actual copy of the president's August 6 briefing. Without it, the report could hardly lift the veil on President Bush's state of knowledge even a little.[108] Only a very few media reports caught on that the president had withheld dramatic evidence that he had been told to expect a "spectacular" attack and that he had remained passive. He had used his power to invoke executive privilege to cover up the flaws in his so-carefully built-up image.[109] An unusually penetrating report came from John W. Dean, the famous White House counsel who advised President Nixon about executive privilege during Watergate and surely, in his own way, the star analyst on Republican presidents who use executive privilege for cover-ups. Dean did not mince words: in refusing to release this record, "After pulling together the information in the 9/11 Report, it is understandable why Bush is stonewalling."[110] Stonewalling, Dean said.

Also, veteran intelligence agency personnel, fed up with Bush's Iraq intelligence distortions, came out similarly, emphasizing the headline of the withheld August 2001 briefing, "Bin Laden Determined to Strike in the U.S.," and its allusions to plane hijackings. Dean amplified this, drawing on clues in the joint inquiry report: apparently the president's briefing included 1998 intelligence that "Bin Laden's next operation might involve flying an explosive-laden aircraft into a U.S. airport and detonating it" and that revealed a "Bin Laden plot involving aircraft in the New York and Washington, D.C., areas," as well as 2000 intelligence of his intended targets—"skyscrapers, ports, airports, and nuclear power plants."[111] The joint inquiry report also cited Justice Department sources confirming that Ashcroft had actually downgraded counterterrorism as a priority on the eve of Osama's attack. But the administration invoked privilege on the actual budget documents detailing this. The joint inquiry calmly noted that the withholding "limited the Inquiry's ability to determine where in the budget process requests for additional counterterrorism resources were changed."[112]

As the election came closer in 2004, some might have thought President Bush had hoisted himself on his own secrecy petard as to 9/11. For example, President Bush's fending off of the joint congressional inquiry on 9/11, including resisting its release in declassified form from December 2003 to May 2003 (and beyond), and his further stalling of the follow-up, Kean-Hamilton 9/11 commission, meant that some discrediting aspects of 9/11 would come out within months of the 2004 election. However, this view underappreciates the significance of what President Bush had concealed. Whatever limited revelations occurred in 2004 would be largely dismissed as they came out, well after the events, amidst the general high volume of rancorous exchanges close to the election, and the broader aspects might not come out at all, even then. It appeared that by abusing the law to maintain secrecy, President Bush had won.

COORDINATING THE U.S. PULLOUT FROM SAUDI ARABIA

To return to the role of the Saudi dealings in shaping the Iraq occupation, from September 2001 through spring 2003, Robert Jordan's public line (as previously noted, he especially favored the *Dallas Morning News* editorial page) must be the cock-and-bull story that the Saudi ruling elite were splendid reliable allies of America and anything to the contrary must merely be foolish calumnies and slurs. Meanwhile, in 2001–2002, through Jordan's embassy went a stream of very unhappy Treasury agents whom the Saudis virtually stonewalled about the 9/11 trail and whom Jordan himself would know better than to help in any real way, as I reveal shortly.

Jordan had a huge coordination job, much bigger than mere public relations about how reliable Saudi allies were in the war on terror. As Bush's plans for a unilateral invasion of Iraq moved forward despite the near-universal opposition of the world community, Bush ran into an additional problem: the Saudi view of the United States, which had plunged after 9/11, now plunged even further. By the time of the April 2002 Bush-Abdullah summit, the *New York Times* quoted a source familiar with Abdullah's thinking as saying the crown prince was talking "of using the 'oil weapon' against the United States and demanding that the United States leave strategic military bases in the region."[113] We can only dimly understand the internal struggles within the Saudi royal family, but Dore Gold explains that with a struggle for Saudi succession approaching, "Abdullah was expected to become king, and he would be expected to name [Prince] Sultan as his crown prince. Sultan was already [in 2002] voicing some of the most hard-line positions with respect to the United States."[114] By 2003 Bush's doctrine of preemptive war (i.e., in Arab eyes, occupation whenever Bush felt like it) made America so unpopular in Saudi Arabia that, as the *New York Times* reported, "barbs against the Americans [are now] laced through newspaper editorials, Internet chat rooms and even text messages on cellphones."[115]

So early in 2003 Abdullah had to ban American air strikes against Iraq from the Prince Sultan Air Base. For a contrast recall that in 1990–1991, Bush senior had persuaded the Saudis and other gulf states to bankroll, to the tune of $50 billion, the Gulf War against Iraq. So it's not as though the Saudis were inherently unwilling to accept the word of a President Bush about the need for a fight with a genuinely threatening Iraq. They just weren't blindfolded like the American public; they had a much better sense than we did about just what Bush was doing and why, and they intended to extract the price demanded by Osama, namely, an end to U.S. military bases on their soil. Bush would want to promise them that price, but doing so constrained his interaction with Iraq. No matter that Iraq complied with demands about weapons, no matter that UN inspectors reported correctly the absence of a need to invade, no matter that the United States would occupy in a way that permitted arsenals to fall into hostile hands and insured an occupation fraught with risks and horrors—Bush must convince Abdullah to wait until spring 2003, box in his "tentatives" and Blair by then, and go ahead with the premature occupation.

To be persuaded to wait, Abdullah must have confidence that Bush would adhere to that rigid occupation plan—confidence he might gain by seeing in Jordan the living proof that the contemporary President Bush was still the young George W. of Harken Oil—a fellow who had taken Bahrainian baksheesh and then afterwards pulled off the pretense it was all a coincidence. In other words, to Saudi eyes that see American politicians and their lawyers (especially conservative Republican ones) as readily purchased commodities, Bush as represented by Jordan would seem what Tammany Hall used to call an "honest" politician—that is (again, to Saudi royal eyes), one who, once bought, can be trusted to stay bought. With the Senate in Republican hands after November 2002, Bush could reassure the Saudis that his complete control of the government meant he would fulfill his invasion and occupation pledge. Until then, the Saudi rulers had carefully avoided any action so strong that it would force a break with Osama. A reporter visiting the Saudi area where five of the 9/11 hijackers were recruited found a year after 9/11 "the same radical religious leader who was suspected to have recruited them, Sheikh Ahmad al-Hawashi, was still in charge of the local mosque."[116] After the invasion itself—with the Saudi rulers sourly refusing to allow combat missions out of Prince Sultan Air Base—Rumsfeld announced on April 30, 2003, the day before President Bush announced (prematurely, triumphantly) the successful conclusion of combat operations in Iraq, the pullout of the American military from Saudi Arabia. This meant particularly abandoning Prince Sultan Air Base for a new Kuwaiti one, which formally occurred later, in August and September 2003.[117]

So Bush timed and concealed well what was, in effect, the virtual expulsion by Osama's country of the U.S. military, whose presence had by this time, because of Bush himself, become bitterly resented. High officials on both sides and American military leaders must realize—and must know to keep their mouths shut—that in a terribly sad way, Arabic observers would conclude that through his evil act on 9/11, Osama had won the duel between him and Bush. Bush was now hastening to haul down the American flag over the former military protectorate of Saudi Arabia, as Osama demanded, having kept it there just long enough to get the American public's attention to veer from the Saudi origins of the attack to the target much more useful for him politically in the elections of 2002 and 2004, Iraq. In Arabic eyes, Bush had effectively surrendered, with Jordan as the messenger, to the demands of America's most vicious and awful enemy in history. It took a good deal of very skillful Bush propaganda to keep that surrender obscured enough so that it did not cramp the upcoming cavorting fifty miles off the U.S. coast by the "Heroic Warrior" president. He pretended to help land the plane; then, wearing the air force uniform, mingled with those who had fought and, for TV purposes, took the victory for himself.

And that brings up the most delicate point of all about the need to blindfold the American public. The conservative base had spent eight years reviling Clinton for not fitting their ideal of a commander in chief. That base had given Bush a pass in 2000 because America was at peace with the world. But after 9/11 America was no longer secure and at peace with the world. Bush had to make himself fit that warrior ideal. His time in the unit of the Texas Air National Guard for the sons of the well-connected rich was a new problem after 9/11; it would get in the way of his 2004 reelection pitch. In fact, it became a double problem when his records became the focus in early 2004, because no documents seemed to disprove the charge that Bush had failed to show up for duty from May of 1972, with two years to go on his six-year commitment to wear the uniform of his country, to April of 1973.[118] Bush's apparently being AWOL in wartime (the winter of 1972–1973 was a period of very heavy air combat over Indochina) would not harmonize perfectly with his bellicose and jingoistic rhetoric in 2001–2004. To many in the military, it was a nice question: who is worse—Clinton, who simply didn't serve (but didn't use any kind of special privilege to get out, either) or someone who gets into a special unit by way of his father's connections and then, in wartime, apparently does not show up for duty. Later, in 2003–2004, when Bush shirked his presidential duty to attend the funerals of those who died in Iraq obeying his orders, he would particularly need some cover.

WHITEWASH

Anyway, two weeks after the announcement of the U.S. military pullout from Saudi Arabia, came the final act for Jordan, the most peculiar of all, allowing him to exit and be replaced with a different Bush pal. This act was the highly publicized Saudi crackdown after the May 12 bombings by three trucks inside Saudi Arabia itself.[119] The bombings were the work of al-Qaeda, an outfit that could kill three thousand Americans, almost destroy the American airline industry, and wipe out hundreds of billions of dollars in the American economy. But in Osama's own country, the source of recruiting and financing, it seemed they couldn't do even a tiny fraction of that kind of damage. It makes one wonder whether 9/11 would have come off if the Saudi authorities Bush and Jordan kept praising to the skies as our "reliable allies" had merely cared a little more not to see all those Americans die. They cared about their own people, but did they care about us? Or with reference to the planning and financing needed to train young Saudi males at American flight schools for one-way flights, we'd want to ask of the Saudis in key intelligence and police positions, as Howard Baker used to ask: what did they know, and when did they know it?

As for May 2003, one must focus, not on the ineffective truck bomb-ings, but on Jordan's adept political uses of the Saudi official crackdown. As Robert Baer notes, the Saudi police authorities, politically motivated and corrupt as they are, use such crackdowns with a lot of savvy. After a 1995 bombing that killed five Americans, the Saudis executed four "suspects." Some thought the Saudi police were "taking advantage of the bombing to get rid of political opponents," especially because the Saudis wouldn't let the FBI talk to even a single one of the four before the execution.[120] That was Saudi-style "cooperation" with the Louis Freeh FBI, before 9/11, and it didn't change all that much after 9/11 with the Treasury agents operat-ing out of Jordan's Riyadh embassy.

Those same Saudi police handled their "crackdown" to serve marvelously Jordan's previously desperate public relations needs. A skeptic might even imagine that the Saudi authorities, relieved that the American bases were now gone, were in effect giving Jordan a nice going-away party, carefully informing him about the crackdown's times, places, and so forth. He was a trial attorney who knows how to work with cooperative authorities, especially such politically savvy ones. Looking at it from a media perspec-tive, which is what counts, their help meant he could play to the hilt the role in which he was cast—the "Two-Fisted Ambassador," helping fight terror in Saudi Arabia.

For, as the crackdown began, Jordan didn't stop just with maximum-publicity press conferences.[121] (Press conferences had been the sort of thing he couldn't make time for back when Powell went ballistic about the Riyadh embassy's "Visa Express," or the press blew a gasket about "Sus-pect's Express," or the pack of reporters clamored in 2002 for the withheld SEC file of how Jordan neatly resolved Bush's insider trading case.) Only now did Jordan go on to use whatever information the apparently helpful Saudi police/intelligence authorities gave him to get a series of just-him-on-camera interviews on American television networks. After all, Saudi police don't encourage TV cameramen ordinarily to roam free in Riyadh; if they want good footage quick and easy of a breaking crackdown story, the right way to get it is to take Jordan up on his generous offer to stand out on a Riyadh street in an open short-sleeved shirt and give the camera a spirited (trial lawyer's) spiel. For the "Two-Fisted Ambassador," that's like open mike day on American television. I just happened to turn on the TV after the May crackdown out of curiosity and saw Jordan—repeatedly—on the TV screen. Remarkable. One must admire his trial lawyer skills, creating instantly so perfect an image for himself in the mind of the otherwise blindfolded American public.

To consider the political uses of law, let's just speculate why the Saudi police would be so nice to Jordan. Sure, it was the will from the Saudis on high. But also, it may just be that these were Saudi police authorities Jordan had cultivated while they were virtually stonewalling the FBI agents stationed in his embassy who were trying to follow the key post-9/11 trails. Such are the uses of law. Jordan would serve the personal and political interests of his client Bush a whole lot better by getting in position to obtain that coat of American TV whitewash from the Saudi police than by the alternative.

Suppose instead in 2001–2002 Jordan had made a lot of trouble, had thrown his weight around as the president's personal guy, and had helped the FBI pry out of the suspects and out of key document collections—all in plain sight—some details of just which Saudis' backing of Osama's fundraising and recruiting really underlay 9/11. That would have taken the focus off of Iraq and put it back on Saudi Arabia. That would have bollixed up Bush's grand strategy of redirecting American anger about 9/11 off the involved Saudis, who weren't going to be occupied (quite the opposite; the troops would be kicked out) and onto the uninvolved Iraqis, who would instead be occupied. Partners in Baker & Botts don't get their six- and seven-figure draws by disrupting their conservative clients' elaborately conducted maneuvers like that.

So now, with a nice fresh coat of televised whitewash, Jordan could get away from the post-9/11 hot seat in Riyadh and return to his Texas roots. And come home he did, replaced as back channel to the Saudi elite by Bush's next choice, Jim Oberwetter, oil lobbyist extraordinaire. Oberwetter started out as a young press secretary to Bush senior in the late 1960s, when the latter was just a Texas congressman and Bush junior was a youngster. Oberwetter was Texas campaign chair for Bush senior in 1992, played an important role in the oil lobby in Washington (the American Petroleum Institute), and served on George W. Bush's transition team in

2000. He has worked since about 1975 for the family oil business of the famous H. L. Hunt (an early rich Texas backer of the rising conservatism) who first discovered oil in Yemen in 1984.[122]

Oberwetter's "great friend," famous Bush counselor Karen Hughes, considers him someone who knows how to keep political secrets. A combination of such personal loyalty to the Bush family with such insider experience with the big-money payoff system by which the oil industry fuels the right-wing machine is not easy to find. Those in Texas who know say "Jim is one of the president's best friends."[123] Thank goodness Abdullah will have a new back channel to cut out Colin Powell and George Tenet (to say nothing of the congressional Democrats, who could never hope to get the time of day out of him) when the oil deals get down to the lick-log, as they say in Houston—and Riyadh.[124]

Saudi Arabia had ceased to be an American oil protectorate, all expenses paid for by the U.S. taxpayer, with big American military bases flying the United States flag—the Texas conservative paradise. But Bush, Jordan, and now Oberwetter could, despite that temporary unpleasantness over 9/11, still keep the Saudi ruling elite relatively content paying off the American oil executives and (usually indirectly) the American conservative politicos. And now, Iraq was on the way to becoming a replacement American oil protectorate—the new frontier for the conservative money machine, so to speak. It had taken a very smooth job of blindfolding the public. What else would induce the centrist public to accept the price to be paid—in the blood of its children, in the blood of the 9/11 victims never avenged, and in taxpayers' treasure for decades to come—for all those oil millionaires to thrive and to gratefully finance the Texas-based conservative machine that had seized power in Washington?

DOMESTIC POLICY SECRECY

Secrecy on international and security matters in large part resulted from the administration's desire to make the most of the post-9/11 hand; secrecy on domestic matters, by contrast, was designed mainly to protect a more basic transaction: favors for special business interests in return for campaign finance. Secrecy fit the style already manifested by Governor Bush in Texas and the style of the appointees he picked, such as the lawyer-lobbyists who filled so many posts in EPA and Interior. Secrecy surrounding this particular cash-for-policy transaction had more to do with carefully managing information and the timing of its release than with completely squelching public knowledge.

Three examples reflect the Bush administration's use of secrecy on domestic issues. The most important has to do with promoting anti-environmental policies. Fulfilling the wish of President Bush's conservative economic base to contain or curtail environmental regulations—while the majority of the public favors such regulations—requires a concerted effort to restrict public knowledge of new policies. A second use of information control comes into play in the administration's all-important effort to stack the judiciary with conservative activists. Finally, a stealth effort, hard to quantify, is aimed at obscuring ideological changes in the law itself— that is, the administration's shadowy promotion of a "secret law" policy.

The Stealth Anti-Environmental Policy

President Bush brought from Texas and from his presidential campaign a determination to serve industries seeking to exploit public resources, as well as heavy industrial polluters. These constituencies consistently funded Republican political campaigns while cutting off funding for opposing candidates and could be expected to do so as long as Bush found ways to deliver for them. As I have shown, President Bush immediately filled most top posts at the Department of the Interior, the Environmental Protection Agency, and other environmental agencies with industry lawyer-lobbyists, such as Interior Secretary Gail Norton, or with people who could be expected to take a laissez-faire attitude. Notwithstanding his appointees' skills and direction in proceeding quietly, their numerous and dramatic early moves gave the public too clear a picture of the anti-environmental direction. EPA's approval of relaxed arsenic levels in drinking water crystallized this trend.[125] So did President Bush's breaking his campaign promise to regulate the greenhouse gas causing global warming, carbon dioxide; his freeze on Clinton administration pro-environmental regulations; his approval of controversial offshore drilling (except in Florida, where his brother was governor); and the Cheney Energy Task Force's pursuit of drilling in the Arctic National Wildlife Refuge.[126] All of these moves provoked a public that registered strongly pro-environmental views in polls,[127] and they failed to prevent a level of press coverage unusually strong and blunt for the Bush administration.

The high negative response elicited from the press and public mattered even more when Vermont senator Jim Jeffords departed from the Republican Party and handed control of the Senate to the Democrats for the rest of 2001–2002, himself taking the chair of the Senate's environment committee. Following 9/11, the president sought to temporarily mute some of the most jarringly divisive aspects of his legislative approach, which further weakened his ability to move a distinctly anti-environment agenda. All told, the experiences of 2001 led the administration to look for stealthier ways to reach its goals affecting the environment.

Enhanced public recognition of legitimate security needs provided a much better cover for intensified secrecy than the administration had enjoyed previously. Just as the Nixon and Reagan administrations had tried to invoke Cold War security concerns to justify those presidents' politically motivated deceptions involving the CIA, the Bush administration now invoked concerns about terrorism to advance positions that had little or nothing to do with such security.[128] For example, observers noted that the Bush administration obtained a new statute in collaboration with industry lobbyists, ostensibly to protect homeland security secrecy, but actually more calculated for the cover-up of environmental problems.[129] Companies with huge, fearfully dangerous facilities, such as those filled with toxic chemicals that could, by accident or attack, inflict giant casualties, didn't want to solve the problem. They wanted the public not to know. So Bush helped them to close the shades.

The most important of the new stealth approaches called for planning controversial steps secretly and making potentially unpopular moves only at the safest moment—after the November 2002 election.[130] By then, congressional forums of debate were closed until the new Congress started up in 2003. Moreover, when the Republicans regained 51–49 control of the Senate, President Bush claimed to have received a policy mandate. Environmentalists might have countered that mandates come from running on, not running away from, an issue and Republican candidates had largely (though not exclusively)[131] attempted to avoid the administration's environmental record.

Mandate or not, the change in Senate control meant that Democrats lost control of the country's main forum for raising the administration's controversial environmental actions. Moreover, Bush could now drop his charade of having New Jersey's Christie Todd Whitman as EPA head. He had never let her have any real say anyway. Now he brought in a Utah governor more attuned than her to the developer's perspective. Not that so much would happen before the November 2004 election. But as in 2002, the plans would be quietly readied to move on the anti-environmental agenda in the postelection "dark" period.

For after November 2002 the administration didn't wait for the new Senate to take its seats. President Bush showed "renewed vigor," as one commentator put it, in moving his anti-environment agenda forward in November and December.[132] In late November 2002 the EPA implemented the president's main pollution idea: letting owners of the oldest and most air-polluting facilities out of the legal requirement to update their anti-pollution equipment when upgrading and expanding their production facilities.[133] Also right after the November 2002 election, the White House approved guidelines for developers by which more private wetlands could be turned over to them so long as they made plans to restore the wetland functions later, a largely ineffective stipulation.[134] And the administration commenced in January 2003 a review of federal public lands classified as wetlands to open many for development, a plan that might ultimately shrink federal wetlands as much as 20 percent.[135] All of these initiatives moved quickly and relatively quietly while Congress was out of session.

Another part of the postelection anti-environmental wave concerned public forests and logging. Shortly before Thanksgiving 2002 the Forest Service issued a proposal that would greatly undermine forest planning by eliminating wildlife protections and reducing the public role. In December the administration slipped out its new policy of encouraging commercial logging precisely in the areas of concern to environmentalists.[136] Its claim that this had to do with wildfire suppression, though tentatively accepted by some observers, looked more dubious when it turned out that most of the areas slated for logging happened to be among the most commercially desirable—stands of old-growth trees. It also happened that such trees tended to be the farthest from the populated areas most threatened by wildfires.

Getting all these actions out of the way in the postelection window did not, of course, mean that the rest of 2003 would prove safe for trees and wetlands. However, it raised the prospect that Norton and her colleagues would offer a repeat performance in the run-up to the 2004 elections, preparing plans that could be unveiled as soon as the elections were over. Meanwhile, President Bush could count on record-shattering fund-raising as payback from loggers, developers, and the owners of aged industrial plants.

The Bush administration also made moves, as quietly as possible, to replace precious accountability mechanisms related to environmental decisions with a new business model that would avoid such mechanisms. One effort involved shuttering the main window for public environmental oversight, the National Environmental Policy Act (NEPA).[137] NEPA requires preparation of a public environmental impact statement (EIS) for major actions and entails much public openness and disclosure. When the government refuses to prepare an EIS or prepares an inadequate one, environmental groups often sue. Where possible, Norton and her fellow administrators sought to avoid such oversight by failing to fulfill the NEPA statute altogether; but when they got sued, the Justice Department weighed in with a program to resist firmly, including appeals if necessary. A scholarly study of 219 NEPA cases during 2001–2002 found that the Bush administration had doubled the Clinton administration's rate of challenging such lawsuits yet won only 55 percent of the time (the Clinton administration had prevailed in 74 percent of cases).[138] Judges rejected Bush administration legal arguments about NEPA as tending to "eviscerate NEPA"[139] or as constituting an "extralegal effort to circumvent the law" and "mystical legal prestidigitation."[140]

Besides fighting individual actions, the Bush administration used several large-scale approaches. It attempted to segment highway construction into separate federal and state divisions, evading NEPA for the state projects—an approach the court that rejected it called "deliberate evasion ... [that] cannot and should not be tolerated."[141] In September 2002 President Bush issued an executive order giving the Transportation Department authority to expedite NEPA reviews for highways and airports. In November and December 2002 the administration cut back on NEPA compliance with respect to forest use, and the Interior Department similarly indicated, generally, that it would cut back on NEPA.[142] Beyond the overall reduction of NEPA's role, the public planning process for forests was specifically targeted for rollbacks, closing a key window in the struggle over public land exploitation.[143]

Stealth Appointments of Right-Wing Judges

As one of its first acts, the Bush White House ended the long-standing practice of vetting judicial nominations with the American Bar Association (ABA) before nomination, a major reduction in openness.[144] In earlier decades Republican administrations had supported that system, as had Democrats, as an impartial way to screen out political choices that might lack basic judicial qualifications. The ABA rating system reflected the values of the establishment bar. Both parties could subscribe, however warily, to a consistent system of checks designed to weed out nominees without experience, credentials, or other basic qualifications. ABA prescreening had played a part in limiting President Clinton's options, just as they might have limited President Bush's. If Clinton wanted judicial nominees who could survive the gauntlet of Senate opposition, he had to first choose nominees who could survive ABA screening.[145]

But social conservative organizations focusing on the politics of ideological patronage had come to see the ABA system as an obstacle.[146] They asserted, from old grievances, that the ABA was slanted against them.[147] More seriously, they apparently worried that screening would inhibit the choice of far-right judges, and they cared little that the same screening process might ease the way for the administration's more mainstream candidates. So Rove, Ashcroft, and their lieutenants deliberately had the White House counsel, Alberto Gonzales, shut off this previously accepted mode of outside, objective scrutiny.

To push through many of his nominations, President Bush counted on concealment, an effort greatly eased by discarding the ABA vetting process. Typically, the administration spoke with apparent frankness but in general about nominees' conservatism while looking for ways to conceal their more specific, controversial positions, especially in opposing women's rights or civil rights. With the obscuring of many facts about nominees' records and ideologies, confirmation struggles now often shifted largely to arguments about the administration's refusal to provide specifics.

The privileges claimed during the abortive confirmation effort in 2002–2003 for Miguel Estrada to an appellate judgeship dramatized the issue. Estrada was a relatively young Honduran immigrant who had held top-level nonjudicial positions and who seemed to have a hard-right ideology; but his lack of a public judicial record made him something of a mystery. Bush and Rove apparently intended to cast him in the Clarence Thomas role—the minority conservative for whom the absence of a public record stymies confirmation critics. Had Estrada gotten confirmation, he might later have become the first Latino on the Supreme Court—a political coup Rove hoped to set up years in advance.[148] The social conservative base cared little about diversity but showed support for this young, former Honduran right-wing activist and not for the less young, less radical Texas Latino Alberto Gonzales.

Democrats gave Estrada a Judiciary Committee hearing in September 2002 and found him dodging concrete answers to questions about just how much of an activist he would be. They had no choice but to demand the only available record of Estrada's legal views, memos he had written while serving in the solicitor general's office between 1992 and 1997. Here they were thwarted by the White House, whose counsel—Gonzales—sent a letter withholding the memos as privileged to "maintain the integrity of the Executive Branch's decisionmaking process."[149] The administration tried to bolster this claim by producing a bipartisan letter from seven former solicitors general, covering a truly wide ideological spectrum from Clinton's Walter Dellinger to Nixon's Robert Bork, supporting in the abstract the idea of a privilege claim as vital to the office of the solicitor general.[150] However, the deputy solicitor general who actually supervised and worked closely with Estrada, Paul Bender, warned concretely and strenuously against allowing him to be confirmed, as he was "ideologically driven" by "extreme conservative views" with "an agenda similar to Clarence Thomas'."[151]

Many times in the past, as I noted in my own 2002 House testimony on executive privilege, the Senate had made access to records—including Justice Department memoranda—the price of moving nominations.[152] Ultimately, a *Los Angeles Times* editorial expressed it well: "Estrada, a corporate lawyer who helped make Bush's case in the Florida recount battle, has virtually no public writings and no judicial experience. The committee needs to see the memos he wrote at the U.S. solicitor general's office, which Atty. Gen. John Ashcroft has refused to release."[153] The two sides fought the issue to a standoff. In September 2003, as Senate Democrats held together, insisting they would not let Estrada be confirmed when he had not produced his memos nor answered their questions, Estrada withdrew his nomination.[154] Bush lost the nomination but could still claim the attempt to place an ideological conservative on the federal bench as a way of showing his pro-Latino values. He could also assail Senate Democrats as obstructionist, dodging the real obstruction: his administration's refusal to own up to the ideological basis of the appointment.

Stealth Law

As the anti-environmental and anti-judicial disclosure schemes went into operation, the Bush administration was setting out to impose secrecy in a third area, attempting thereby to change the very nature of federal law. This was a broad quest for government-made law to become "secret law" by which even most of the government's legal pronouncements would become secret.

Traditionally, the vast majority of important federal government legal opinions—those that do not pertain to intrinsically secret matters such as classified intelligence—have not been deemed secret themselves.[155] The large general counsel offices of the many Cabinet departments and agencies opine constantly about new and old federal statutes, regulations, guidelines, and other authorities. Difficult though this task may be, they keep law as the public's visible servant rather than its covert master.

For example, as the Interior Department continuously coordinates new and old authorities about the use of public lands and resources, its opinions eventually come to the attention of both industries and environmentalists, so that neither side comes to feel itself oppressed by unaccountable governance. The lay public barely realizes how much these kinds of government legal pronouncements and opinions really matter.[156] Many legal issues come before government lawyers far more frequently than they arise in court, and some may not arise in court very often or at all. To take examples from issues discussed in this book, President Bush's various executive orders raise countless legal issues on subjects from "faith-based" funding of discriminatory religious institutions to reducing environmental safeguards. Most of the opinions on issues arising from these executive orders or exemptions will come from the government, not the courts.

The administration of President Bush's father made an effort in one controversial matter to switch to a policy of secret opinions. After House hearings, congressional overseers led by House Judiciary chairman Jack Brooks (D-Tex.) fought and defeated that early attempt at a secret opinions policy.[157] At the end of that Bush administration, its Office of Legal Counsel dropped the secrecy and published the volumes of opinions it had withheld.[158] During the Clinton administration, no secret opinions policy existed.[159]

However, George W. Bush's administration appears to have revived the "secret law" project on a widespread but (unsurprisingly) unacknowledged basis. For example, in August 2002 the White House press office cited an administration legal opinion that the president could invade Iraq without asking Congress—this in the months prior to President Bush's actual decision to ask and receive congressional authorization. Yet the White House never released the actual legal opinion as a whole and only cited bits of it. Similarly, Attorney General Ashcroft often indicated that legal opinions backed his controversial views, from replacing courts with military tribunals to a constitutional right to individual use of firearms, but did not release the actual opinions as wholes.[160] The public cannot nail down how far President Bush moved toward a policy of secret law. However, unmistakably, the shades were being pulled down on this vital window into the powers asserted and exercised by the Bush White House and Ashcroft.

THE RETURN TO AN "IMPERIAL PRESIDENCY"

The events of 9/11 and the Iraq occupation inaugurated a greater reliance by the administration on the political use of secrecy in manipulating the tools of law, especially (though not exclusively) in the security realm. Like the struggle against world communism before 1990, the current struggle to defeat Islamic terrorism and unpopular figures like Saddam Hussein provides a president who chooses to invoke it the ability to conjure a virtually omnipresent, shadowy threat as well as specific unpopular enemies. By focusing openly on these enemies and secretly handling the timing of action and of less popular aspects of U.S. policy, the president can take a very large share of power away from Congress and away from the kind of public scrutiny that the Constitution intended Congress to provide.

Two very different types of geopolitical projects illustrate the president's new secrecy powers in international and security affairs. These projects matter less for their foreign affairs specifics than for their use in concretely illustrating how the means of secrecy, deployed in the Bush administration's initial years, may have uses in a second term. One consists of perhaps the single largest economic resource prize in the world: the underdeveloped natural resources of Central Asia, specifically the huge oil and gas resources of the Caspian Sea region.[161] Nothing could appeal more to President Bush and an administration top-heavy with fellow former oilmen than a region containing the largest undeveloped oil resources outside the Middle East. Where the Soviet Union once stood in the way, Putin's Russia now seeks to overcome regional instability by developing its own oil lifeline.[162]

The geopolitical challenge lies both in developing the fields in countries such as Kazakhstan—or in the Caspian Sea itself, which involves conflicting claims from surrounding countries, including Iran—and in transporting the oil across an area unstable in every direction. Problems range from the unsavory and potentially unstable nature of several of the region's authoritarian regimes to the difficulty of reaching accommodation with the hostile Caspian Sea power of Iran. More generally, the problem comes in building a base in a region where popular discontent may further destabilize national governments. When the United States rooted out the Taliban in Afghanistan, it dealt with the only Central Asian country (putting the special problem of Iran aside) where the regime itself directed militant Islamic fundamentalism into violent action against America. What the United States does elsewhere in the region determines whether the inevitable popular discontents and uprisings, including those rooted in militant Islam, are directed only against often corrupt local rulers or also against the United States.

Through 2000 Central Asia seemed far from the centers of traditional American geopolitical attention. Hence, prior to 9/11 and the Iraq occupation, limited development prospects in the near term hinged upon a crude multilateral "rule of law" model for achieving stability. Efforts by Western and other nations to reform corrupt authoritarian regimes, international cooperation through open negotiation, and establishing fair terms for trade and development seemed the only way.[163] Before the 2000s, the United States' own quite limited security stake in Central Asia would not have supported unilateral American military involvement in the region, anyway. Observers hoped that the United States would use its leverage for needed reforms, so that popular discontent would find outlets other than through potentially jihad-minded groups like the Islamic Movement of Uzbekistan.[164]

In the first nine months of the Bush administration, despite its interest in the oil industry and evident preference for unilateral action, American activity in the region seemed likely to stay limited. Heavy-handed attempts to pursue Central Asian oil and gas resources would arouse too much suspicion. After 9/11 and the Iraq occupation, however, the administration foresaw exercising expanded legal authority and tools for projecting American power into Central Asia, deflecting the inevitable domestic and international criticism, once again, through a program of secrecy. In the aftermath of 9/11, President Bush could insist that the region's potential as a base for future terrorism justified whatever the administration did there and, further, justified the administration's policy of making its decisions in utmost secrecy.

President Bush's secrecy in the preparation and implementation of the moves regarding Iraq, from the 9/17 secret directive to closed-door reconstruction contracting, became exhibit A for demonstrating how secrecy would work in the new projection of power in adjoining Central Asia. Clearly, the days of the Marshall Plan and the Alliance for Progress— when many controversial aspects of America's foreign policy were handled openly—are behind us.[165] Indeed, by 2004 Rumsfeld's aggressive, unaccountable covert operations prompted a rebuke from Congress. Even Trent Lott (R.-Miss.), no lefty pinko, expressed alarm.[166]

In contrast, done unilaterally and in deep secrecy, American commitments of credibility, money, and military might in Central Asia would raise the suspicion that they owe too little to actual public security imperatives and too much to private economic interests. It would serve American security interests better, as open congressional debate would reflect, to press reforms on the local authoritarian regimes and to let popular discontent find outlets other than Islamic militancy. We lost Iran in 1979; we must lose Saudi Arabia. Why not lighten up on the greed and do something to make the populations feel they have a stake in their nation's government and economy? Decisions made without open debate will reflect more the preference of global businesses and their state backers, who may decide that development needs complete support from the existing regimes, even though they resist reforms and eagerly label all opposition as terrorist. Authoritarian regimes of Central Asia, lacking popular support, have every incentive to work with multinational businesses and to line up the Bush administration to suppress all "terrorist" opposition. In this way, secret processes may take the United States down the path of inevitable armed confrontation between the regimes it backs and popular uprisings forced for lack of any other alternative into *jihadi* channels.[167]

By going this way in secrecy, the Bush administration could repeat some of the most regrettable episodes of the Cold War: the overthrow of progressive regimes from Guatemala in the 1950s to Chile in 1973; adherence to regimes such as that of the shah of Iran, until it fell in 1979; and ever deepening commitments to unstable regimes such as that of South Vietnam and the apartheid system in South Africa. Unfortunately, the Bush administration's trajectory, shaped by secrecy, sometimes seems headed in precisely that tragic direction.

An entirely separate and different geopolitical project consists of what other target countries or regimes that the Bush administration's conservative electoral base dislikes could receive the preemptive "regime change" treatment meted out to Iraq. In one variant, this might involve a regime in the course of changing on its own, like Haiti in the 1990s, but one in which President Bush wields the tools of secrecy and unilateral action to achieve the goals of his conservative backers.

Any number of regimes around the world might fall under this heading, but an obvious example—on which the American right wing has remained fixated for more than forty years—is Cuba as Fidel Castro's time comes to an inevitable end. Until the Bush administration, the centrist American public looked to a gradual policy of engagement to replace the failed policies of decades of confrontation.[168] Bush took a different tack, dedicating a substantial part of his Latin American policy to serving the desires of the right-wing Cuban American exile community in Florida. Karl Rove had not forgotten that community's preoccupation with Elian Gonzalez in 2000 or the key role of Bush's Cuban American supporters during the Florida electoral controversy later that year or during Governor Jeb Bush's reelection campaign in 2002. He couldn't: conservatives never cease ideological criticism of Cuba.[169] Even former president Carter's innocuous visit to Cuba in 2002 occasioned an international legal incident in the hands of John Bolton, as reported in chapter 7. As Castro relinquishes control, the Bush administration can be expected to impose secrecy and exert maximum pressure on behalf of the reactionary Cuban American exile community, especially as to its assertion of old property claims.[170]

DOMESTIC POLICY STEALTH

The administration's progress in executing an anti-environment policy shift under the cloak of secrecy gives some sense of how far it might ultimately go in other domestic policy areas. Obviously, in a general sense much can be accomplished by placing more conservative appointees on the federal bench. It is more challenging to analyze the administration's prospects for expanding its network of secret, unaccountable legal practices throughout the government. The network itself, rather than any particular use of secret law, is what worries those who want full oversight of government. Once such a network takes root, its political convenience encourages its growth, and the dependence of political officials on unaccountable legal practices leads to a permanent shift from a government of public laws to one of privately interested persons.

Privacy law may furnish an example of such a shift in action. As discussed in the chapters on domestic affairs and on Ashcroft, the Bush administration swept aside individual privacy in several contexts. It discarded the fragile privacy of medical patients so as to enhance the ability of health care providers to use their medical data for marketing purposes; and under the surveillance provisions of Ashcroft's post-9/11 statute, it allowed unchecked inroads into the privacy of phone and Internet communications.

Whether individuals have "rights" to maintain the confidentiality of their medical data or to communicate in private depends on the legal opinions by which government lawyers give guidance either to respect or to disrespect such rights. Bush administration lawyers who expect shielding from oversight or outside review might grant greater access to "private" records to both companies and government bodies and might dilute, if not destroy, the rights of privacy in those areas. For example, since most individuals now obtain most of their medical care pursuant to insurance arrangements that waive confidentiality for insurability-verification purposes, commercial enterprises have potential access to a great deal of confidential personal medical data. If agencies can pyramid one secret opinion diminishing the privacy protection for such data atop another, eventually it becomes all but impossible to argue seriously that the data must receive firm privacy protections when new issues arise.

Similarly, vast amounts of individual communications about the most intimate of matters go out unencrypted daily as phone or Internet conversations. Of course the federal government can intercept these with court-issued search warrants, but in the post-9/11 security world, that government has enhanced powers that are limited by no meaningful judicial consideration. The Bush administration at various times discussed collecting and "mining" private data, supposedly only as a means of combating terrorism, with the administration's conservative supporters hastening to defend the concept legally.[171] Once again, federal agencies set the parameters for how "public" such "private" records may become. In this way the blindfolded come to have no idea of just how little privacy they have left, how they get scrutinized and overheard in purely nonterrorism contexts by eyes and ears that mock.

SIGNIFICANCE OF ELECTION-YEAR DEVELOPMENTS

Former Nixon White House counsel John W. Dean, in *Worse than Watergate: The Secret Presidency of George W. Bush*, lists the potential secrecy-related scandals that the Bush administration had accumulated by early 2004. Paraphrased (with some omissions), the list includes:

1. Bush's character issues and prepresidential business conduct;

2. Cheney's lack of candor about his pre–vice presidential business conduct and his health problems;

3. Bush's squelching of dissent and secrecy about presidential records;

4. Concealment of business, environmental, health, and safety information so as to benefit campaign contributors;

5. Bush and Cheney's efforts to block inquiries into 9/11;

6. Bush and Cheney's motives and negligence in not addressing terrorism;

7. Bush's misleading statements to Congress about war with Iraq; and

8. The allegedly criminal leak of Valerie Plame Wilson's covert CIA identity.[172]

Although Dean and I both address the most significant matters in this list, such as misleading Congress about war with Iraq, at least half of Dean's list does not get addressed in this book. On the other hand, many topics I address here fall outside Dean's list, such as unilateralism in international affairs, Medicare, and trade law abuses.[173] Even when we treat the same broad topics, we address the tactics of deception and concealment from quite different angles. This chapter focuses on how Bush frustrated the 9/11 inquiries by protecting the Saudis; chapter 7, on the war with Iraq, focuses on Bush's implementing of the secret 9/17 directive. Dean focuses on these broad topics from entirely different, yet equally discomfiting, perspectives. In trying to describe Bush administration secrecy and the potential for scandal in 2004, we are like the parable of the several blind-folded people who try to describe the elephant by poking at its different parts. But in this version our blindfolding, and everyone else's, has been arranged by the critter itself, taking advantage of special historical oppor-tunities and trends, described in the first chapter, that have been in the making for over thirty years.

In many ways, the most striking development of 2004 reflected how many more legal abuses to advance conservative causes still lay undis-closed or would bear their main fruit only in years to come. What little the public came to know about the administration in 2004 emerged from a remaining channel likely soon to be closed off: Bush had tolerated in his service, and in positions to learn some of his outer secrets and even a few of his inner ones, a few officials willing to blow the whistle. These included, of the original senior moderates in the Cabinet, Treasury Sec-retary O'Neill; of the very few carried-over senior national security fig-ures, Richard Clarke and a lesser figure who became the victim of outra-geous tactics, Ambassador Wilson; of the senior domestic civil servants, the Medicare actuary Richard S. Foster; and some high EPA officials. Even Christine Whitman would not go public, albeit enough of her cards turned over to allow reporters to see the gross slacking on enforcement of key pollution standards urged by the White House for the benefit of big contributors.[174]

Thus only a handful of whistle-blowers revealed incredible potential scandals, showing the Bush White House to be, like a building with ter-mites, infested with a problem whose outward manifestations indicate much more, soon to be found within. The Bush administration's reaction to O'Neill's revelations was to attack the source; yet a few months after-ward, Richard Clarke confirmed a central allegation—that President Bush's Iraq war fever dated to his arrival in office. The Bush White House breezily dismissed the worsening trade figures and accompanying job losses all through 2002 and 2003; yet in 2004, when trade deficit figures reached astronomical levels, it implicitly admitted, by futile gestures about the overvalued but immovable Chinese yuan, that it had dropped the ball.

More important, the press and the public still barely apprehended that these revelations occurred in the absence of the functioning revelatory machinery—the hard-driving regular House oversight subcommittees, special congressional investigations armed with subpoena power, and special prosecutors—that had operated for three decades, since Vietnam, Watergate, and other scandals in the 1970s revealed the dangers of leaving the executive branch unwatched. President Bush's powerful concealment strategies had matured. After the 2002 election, congressional Republicans virtually shut down regular oversight. And Republican secret game playing during conferences on House and Senate–passed bills, disciplined by contribution-controlling congressional leaderships, effectively neutered what administration opponents had done with specific issues on the floor, often by majority vote.

The powerful simultaneous congressional and prosecutorial inquiries of the past had worked effectively, not just because they overcame executive privilege but also because they then made the spinning of fables by White House officials a limited and dangerous tactic. But when Condoleeza Rice testified about Richard A. Clarke's eyewitness account of Bush's interest in Iraq rather than al-Qaeda as the engine of national security affairs in 2001–2003, she remained free to repeat her message without admitting the truth.[175] The Bush White House had no fear of special prosecutors and was not besieged by waves of questioners like virtually all its predecessors for thirty years, and so it did not open its document drawers and e-mail systems. What few documents it did provide and what information did come out was controlled by abuse of classification; even Clarke lost some of the best material for his book this way. Inquiries without teeth provided only platforms for spin. Bush himself held so few press conferences and disciplined his staff so tightly about talking on background that the press had no way to get at the White House truth. The master strategist of secrecy and deception, Cheney, had run, and still would run, the show. Significantly, Cheney, and the rest of these secrecy mechanisms (other than classification), operated as much on the domestic as on the foreign side.

Moreover, the Bush White House had not reacted to any of the whistle-blower revelations by cleaning house, but by doing the opposite. The doctored intelligence about Iraq's supposed nearness to nuclear capability and similar overblown claims about other weapons of mass destruction had pointed overwhelmingly to a particular pipeline. Rumsfeld supplied raw distorted intelligence from ambitious Iraqi exiles whom he favored to help run the country, and Cheney pressured the CIA and organized high-level use of the distortions. Bush did not fire Rumsfeld, punish the dissembling exiles, or remove the vice president from the parts of the loop in which he had done the mischief. After the election, Powell or Tenet or both would be gone, and in other ways State and the CIA would lose their counterweight ability. Cheney and Rumsfeld, opponents of giving democracy a place in foreign affairs, would have a much larger role, with less accountability, than ever.

Fiscal year (FY) 2005, for example, would bring a bonanza for Rumsfeld's imperial aspirations, as his Special Operations command, which had gotten a 47 percent increase from FY 2003 to FY 2004, was enlarged by another 47 percent in Bush's FY 2005 request.[176] Bush and Cheney also now arranged, under Rumsfeld, an undersecretary of intelligence overseeing a sprawling bureaucracy. This relegated the CIA—which had strict requirements for reporting to Congress and which cared about its long-term reputation—to junior partner in the intelligence business. Bush concluded after the Iraq WMD fiasco that he should shift around the power, money, and control involved in wielding of force so that after the election, no one could blow the whistle.[177]

Nor did the White House do any housecleaning on the domestic side as 2004 brought the exposure of its suppression of Foster's true estimates that the administration's drug maker and insurer subsidies had added over $100 billion to the Medicare bill's costs. It did no housecleaning as the massive hemorrhage of jobs overseas was revealed as considered quite acceptable by its economic team as well as by Zoellick. Quite the contrary, Bush had replaced O'Neill and other moderates at Treasury with those more willing to follow the conservative line. For his unyielding positions on questions and criticisms regarding social conservatives and threats to civil liberties, Ashcroft was rewarded with approval and expansions of power. And a Republican-controlled Congress shut down most of the regular oversight by which these figures would have been forced to respond to angry centrist questions about their stances.

For the secrecy and deception wrapped around conservative causes did not constitute some isolated abuse separate from those right-wing stances. Bush's machine, operating in a way that had been evolving in both domestic and foreign affairs for decades, worked so powerfully by dint of its camouflaged cross-deals for different conservative constituencies. Each conservative base could get its own kind of patronage or payoff without unduly disturbing the support of the other base nor fully alarming the centrist public. Bush's middle-class social conservative shock troops never fully understood that he was destroying their Medicare future or that his tax cuts simply exploded deficits that they would have to pay for. His upper-class economic conservative backers never fully had to face the reign that Ashcroft's agenda would impose, in the long run, of reduced civil liberties and government-sponsored intolerance on everyone, not just out-groups. And the centrist public was not told, as it had not been told in 2000, that a Bush victory would mean a hard-right turn after the election. Secrecy and deception were not occasional and dispensable vices extraneous to the way the administration centrally worked; they were integral to parts of the machine delivering for conservative causes.

So the squeezing out or voluntary departure in 2001–2004 of moderates or senior civil servants across the government, from Clarke's post to EPA to the Medicare agency, marked not the ceiling of the deception problem but rather its floor. Bush's bidding farewell to those few whistle-blowers meant to him the end of what amounted effectively to the last real means of scrutiny. A Republican Congress would not oversee him. The press, unaided, could not. The public remained, more than ever, blindfolded. The accomplishment of conservative causes by abuses and subversions of law, wrapped in secrecy and deception, would continue, not merely unabated but intensified.

9 If This Goes On

What does President Bush's approach to governance in his 2001–2004 term tell us about the future? We can measure those prospects against the standard of his apparent goal: consolidating a national power structure under the dominance—for the foreseeable future—of his party's most conservative wing despite the public's opposition or indifference to its policies. In many ways, the unprecedented speed and intensity with which Bush implemented his agenda from 2001 to 2004 can be expected, barring major upsets, to lock in many aspects of that agenda for at least the next two presidential terms (through 2012). But the political, economic, judicial, and even constitutional sea change that Bush and his administration set in motion may cause ripple effects even further into the future, especially when a successor president attempts to duplicate his tactical successes. That alone is an unprecedented milestone in American governance and one, I would argue, that augurs ill for the nation's future in a number of ways.

Because most Americans hold views far less radical than those of Bush's right-wing bases, for a conservative power structure centered in the executive branch to dominate it must subvert rather than accept the balancing powers in the Constitution. As Bush's presidency showed almost from the beginning, constitutional checks and balances can be circumvented and weakened through the political abuse and subversion of the law. With new extralegal mechanisms in place, we would be right to ask: What kinds of projects already under way would be advanced even further during the terms of future conservative leaders? What larger, grander projects would emerge? Conversely, what kinds of negative repercussions, even scandals, may result from a political structure built on secrecy and the abuse of law to serve special interests? How might the mainly centrist American public—kept in the dark but uncomfortably aware after the fact of the damage to its constitutional structures—belatedly fight back?

TOWARD A DOMINATING NATIONAL CONSERVATIVE POWER STRUCTURE

As is often the case, it is useful to turn to history, which here reveals the emerging conservative power grab as built on an extraordinary power-accumulating trend now several decades in the making. President Bush's projects ride a wavelike, three- to four-decade reaction against the preceding wave of national reform policy.[1] That reform era began in the desegregation and Great Society steps of the late 1950s to mid-1960s and in legislative initiatives that continued into the 1970s. We may call that period the establishment of a national centrist governance system, and we may call the subsequent countertrend a thirty-year conservative reaction against that system. That national centrist system raised ample funds efficiently through federal ability-to-pay taxation, which progressively funded a relatively decent level of government benefits and services. The system increasingly dismayed wealthy economic conservatives, who had to pay what they considered an unfair share. Drawing on the interaction of all three branches of government (and fed especially by Warren and Burger Court precedents), that system sustained a national minimum level of equality, liberty, and tolerance but contributed to the growing fears and outright anger of social conservatives and the power structure they supported in more conservative states.[2] Many of those states, of course, were in the South, where reforms like the Voting Rights Act and the dislocations of the civil rights era signaled the end of the pro–states' rights, pro-segregation status quo. It is worth noting that in those days, many of the most powerful "movement conservatives" were Southern Democrats.

Indeed, the centrist governance system tended to constrain conservatives' power, because both parties spanned broad political spectrums, inclusive of Republican liberals and Democratic conservatives. Moreover, even when Republicans got into the White House or onto the Supreme Court, they sometimes proved disappointingly centrist or even liberal to their most conservative supporters. Chief Justice Burger was one of these; so, after the Reagan presidency, were George H. W. Bush when it came to fiscal policy and the Republican-appointed Supreme Court justices John Paul Stevens and David Souter on civil rights and liberties. Conservatives thus faced the daunting potential opposition of national broad-based coalitions that sustained the fiscal system underlying Social Security, Medicare, and poverty benefits and the regulatory system underlying environmental, privacy, and other public-interest regulation.

During the half-century reaction, especially beginning in the mid-1970s and accelerating in the 1990s, aroused conservative elements—both economic and social conservatives—organized and fought their way toward supplanting the centrist system with an alternative capable not only of taking power but of keeping it. To do this, they would first need a president willing to govern almost totally from the top down, without seeking the kind of consensus enshrined in the Constitution and the nation's political traditions. Meanwhile, they prepared the way by coordinating extragovernmental institutions like far-right foundations, business alliances, and organizations of social conservatives; forming deep pools of ideological spokesmen and propaganda themes; and developing approaches for overcoming opposition when it came time to take control of the Republican Party and finally the government itself. The Reagan program of 1981 provided a key interim rallying point, as did the Gingrich-DeLay program of the mid-1990s. As wealth inequality and the political role of money increased in the 1980s and 1990s, conservatives found their overwhelming economic might could now provide the engine to redress their discontents.[3] The staggered realignment that created the Southern Republican bastion and gave it control of the congressional Republican party, and the consolidation of a conservative bloc on the Supreme Court, set the stage in the late 1990s for assumption of national control. Now, President Bush's successes suggested the route to further consolidation of conservative power in the mid-to-late 2000s.

THE MONEY JUGGERNAUT

Each election of the 2000s enlarged the volcanic outpouring of campaign contributions from the economic conservative base. No longer did contributions by businesses buy merely a limited protection of their interests from a two-party, relatively moderate national government. The mechanisms developed in the 1990s by congressional Republicans and given peak power by President Bush harness enormous resources from semipariah special interests and from wealthy social and economic conservatives offered in exchange for a vast array of favors. With unprecedented central

control the Republican Party reshapes government to serve those interests. The longer this vast exchange of favors continues, the bolder and
grander becomes the collective project marrying conservative money and
conservative power. Each year, this growing conservative exchange relationship ramps up the pressure on the potential moderate donors whose
financial contributions used to provide balance. To maintain some stake for
their own interests, these moderates, both individuals and businesses, find
themselves forced to contribute their resources to conservative candidates,
effectively defunding candidates of the moderate center, not to mention
the anti-conservative opposition. This siphoning off of funds fuels the
entrenchment of conservative incumbents and the marginalization of
minority-party (Democratic) challengers.[4] Elections, swayed increasingly by the effects of massive right-wing campaign funding, thus decreasingly reflect the centrist public's preferences. Money-powered manipulation defuses the public's reactions against conservative policies like anti-
environmentalism, hostility toward the poor and minorities, and religiously
moralizing intolerance. Increasingly, centrist voters lack contestable districts and states in which to mount credible challenges to conservative control of the Senate and House. Republican conservative incumbents emerge
from each election with their preexisting advantages often strengthened
and with new ones.

President Bush promotes this exchange relationship, which provides
the engine for his ideological project in multiple ways. His own leadership
in conservative fund-raising knit his machine together in 2000, 2002,
and 2004. He freed himself and similar future candidates from the shackles
of the post-Watergate presidential fund-raising regulatory system. By
arranging rewards on a never-before-imagined scale for his moneyed supporters, he inspired them to continue the work for many years to come of
supplanting the old political order.

Moreover, the legal sinews of this conservative fund-raising machine
now safeguard its system against public criticism or calls for reform—to
the extent the public is aware, let alone recognizes the impact, of the unin-
hibited buying of influence for highly suspect purposes. Thanks to Bush,
conservatives need not fear the constraints of statutory funding controls
(now meaningless for well-financed conservatives) nor investigations of
fund-raising abuses along the lines of those held in 1997 and 1998, nor
even scrutiny and regulation from the Federal Election Commission and
the courts.[5]

With these sources of strength, the conservative movement would
readily claim a mandate and exercise concomitant power over national

policy, even with the thinnest of victories at the polls. Forget the moderation shown by presidents who came in by squeakers, such as Truman in 1948 (whose election was sufficiently in doubt to produce the famous next-morning headlines that Dewey had won and who conducted the Cold War on down-the-middle bipartisan lines) or Kennedy in 1960 (whose election by less than 50 percent precluded his confronting pro-segregation congressional committee chairs in 1961–1962). Bush had shown after losing the popular vote in 2000 and after "winning" the Senate with a 51–49 majority in 2002 how to claim a "mandate" and make the claim stick. Thus, having run on the implicit platform that his opponent had nothing on him in special interest favoring, he could claim a mandate to put supportive businesses on an even richer diet. The semi-outcast contributors who had patiently restrained their appetites during the campaign could now batten on the outsourcing of the former civil service's work, rollbacks of pesky privacy and pollution rules, lucrative international opportunities created by America's new world influence in the "fight against terrorism," and double helpings from the cupboard of public lands and resources. Having run on the implicit platform that the world understood nothing from America but displays of might, he could claim a mandate to let go most of the last few administration moderates—the "reluctants," the Powells and Tenets, those in the military who had questioned the straining of resources to stay in Iraq. Cheney and Rumsfeld, who had gone somewhat undercover during the campaign, could now come out swinging against followers of the Iraqi Ayatollah Sistani or "Old Europe" social democrats, groups that had equally failed to appreciate that, whether they formed majorities in their own land, those not with us must necessarily be with the terrorists.

THE CONSERVATIVE FISCAL PROGRAM

President Bush's fiscal moves of the early 2000s suggest ways in which conservatives will bend the government's whole taxation and spending structures. The trillion-dollar, unpaid-for tax cut of 2001 and the smaller but still potently regressive deficit-financed tax cut of 2003 cast a much longer shadow than just the immediate specific near-term giveaways, important though these were. By front-loading trillions of dollars in upper-bracket tax cuts with various sunsetted components on an expiring schedule over the following decade, President Bush moved not just toward a new budget system but to a new class system as well. While he manipulated the system of the Congressional Budget Act, he produced something radically different from its previous legal form. It is as if Congress had enacted a new constitutional provision, or a potent new Budget Act. His new system almost guarantees periodic fiscal struggles, but on a playing field now tilted toward victory for the interests of the rich. Their taxes will continually shrink, at the cost initially of mushrooming national debt on the backs of the middle class and eventually of cuts in basic benefits vital to low-income seniors and working families.

Under the fiscal system established by President Bush in 2001 and 2003 and custom-built for conservative augmentation later in the decade and beyond, every biennial Congress will witness the combination of expiring sunsetted tax cuts, large overhanging deficits, and the renewed availability of the juggernaut of budget reconciliation favoring the buttered upper crust. Each time, conservatives will further damage the political prospects of their opponents by claiming—falsely but woundingly— that the Democrats and anyone standing in the juggernaut's way seek to "increase" taxes.[6]

As taxes either end (as with estate taxes) or fall for the wealthiest Americans, benefits for the poorest Americans will correspondingly shrink and expire. Thanks to the Bush administration's distortion of the Budget Act, the rich need only fifty-one Senate votes to win their tax cut renewals and expansions, while the others need sixty Senate votes to repair holes torn in the social safety spending net.[7] Even the briefly unified Democratic government of 1993–1994, which just barely managed to pass the progressive fiscal package that supported the ensuing impressive years of economic gains, could not pass any direct spending for the poor—because that would have required sixty Senate votes, a virtual impossibility.[8]

The larger conservative project for the future, however, assumes that Bush's Ponzi scheme of deficit financing by itself won't always provide for extending sunsetted tax cuts for the wealthy. Sooner or later, Bush's heirs and their colleagues in Congress must start "reforming" benefit programs for the nonaffluent.[9] Provisions in such reconciliation bills might incrementally start privatizing Social Security; capping Medicare for some groups as a defined-contribution program; altering if not clipping the earned-income tax credit; and paring already reduced subsistence benefits for those in poverty such as food stamps and Medicaid. What warrants focus is not so much the details or relative probabilities of each of these in the short term as the grim overall, longer-term vista.

Simply by setting the terms of national fiscal debates for the rest of the decade, the Bush administration has gone far beyond the dreams of the Gingrich-DeLay drive after the 1994 election.[10] Of course, both Social Security and the core of the Medicare program will constitute a political "third rail," to be touched by the wealthy only with caution. But the coming demographic shifts as the baby boom generation begins retiring, the limited ability of payroll taxes to finance boomer benefits, and the rising cost of boomer medical care have already undermined the ability of Social Security and Medicare to continue in their past fiscal forms indefinitely. Bush's Medicare prescription drug benefit, a transparent "compassionate" campaign ploy, had absolutely no financing. He just broke the economic back of the middle class that he saddled with all his other burdens that much sooner.

President Bush's colossal deficit-financed tax cuts simply set the inevitable day of reckoning that much sooner. The Social Security and Medicare systems will not be overthrown in a day, a year, or even substantially in a few years. But, the demographic problems that Social Security and Medicare (the latter exacerbated by rising health care costs) must soon face will last for the next half century at least, until the ultimate demise of all the baby boomers, well into the twenty-first century, finally relieves the overburdened workers of Generation X of the cost of boomer income and health security. Social Security and Medicare as we know them (let alone the EITC and Medicaid) will shrivel under the Bush plan much sooner. In much the same way that welfare as we knew it shrank in the 1990s and 2000, these programs will be fiscally drained for other purposes, their burdens shifted by various devices onto the recipients or onto local taxpayers in the progressive states, and otherwise repeatedly "reformed," each time on stingier terms. Bush's heirs will smooth over the political difficulties of implementing these changes with the irresistible force of conservative campaign fund-raising, which will strain and eventually loosen the ties that today bind middle- and low-income Americans together in supporting uniform Social Security and Medicare benefits for all. Conservatives will craft versions of these programs, such as a privatized version of Social Security (or a defined-benefit Medicare supplemented by tax deduction or tax-deferred subsidies), so as to convince better-off groups of middle-class families that these changes, while not wholly welcome, will mainly affect those below them in income, not themselves.[11]

Each time, the conservative terms of debate over conservative proposals will split the inherently fragile coalition of the somewhat vocal middle class and the largely unorganized poor and pit groups in different states against each other. Bush's confreres thereby have the opportunity to use their superior ideological discipline and internal unifying mechanisms to gain a political victory. And the legal subversion of the budget process provides conservatives with power sufficient to time the issues, as they did in 2001 and 2003, to unite their forces while constraining the mobilization of diffuse and divided groups in opposition.

A similar wedge will gradually help conservatives overcome some of the difficulties of moving toward abolishing the progressive income tax and replacing it with either a flat income tax or, even more regressively, a national consumption tax. In actual implementation the switch has some enormous practical problems, including the dislocation it will cause home owners, pension funds, and charitable organizations when the tax deductions they rely on disappear—not to mention the sheer difficulty of raising enough revenue through such regressive taxes to keep the government from quick insolvency. But President Bush does not need to enact such a sweeping change of the tax system to use the issue to rally his faithful. In this case, the workings of the alternative minimum tax (AMT) alone will operate as a powerful wedge to break the ability of elected leaders from Democratic-leaning states to maintain a unified defense of Social Security and Medicare in the national debates to come. Their upper-middle-class constituents in higher-tax states will demand a deal that provides some degree of the AMT relief Bush withheld, even if it means going along as conservatives "reform" the AMT (that is, shift more of the tax burden to lower income brackets).

Once again, Bush's grasp of the terms of the debate will fragment and overpower the inherently fragile coalition of beneficiaries, enhancing conservative dominance of the fiscal debate. The results would be different if the federal government could still make its decisions fully democratically. But as we have seen, the tide has been inexorably in the opposite direction. In ways too cleverly obscured for the general public to follow, truly even-handed democratic institutions and processes play a shrinking role in the exercise of fiscal control by the richest 1 percent—Bush's core base.

USING A CONSERVATIVE JUDICIARY

President Bush inherited five conservative Supreme Court justices and accumulated more chances to fill life-tenured lower-court judicial posts. The long-term muscle of his conservative activist appointments was increased not only by his selection criteria but by the relative youth of the appointees. He not only would adhere to the social conservative rallying cry of "no more Souters" but would appoint few jurists of mature years whose tenure was likely to last just a decade or two. His lifetime picks of activists in their forties embeds a hard ideological tilt more permanently than any other federal legal process short of an ideologues' constitutional convention. Coupled with Ashcroft's activities, the revamped Bush judiciary provided the most enduring available payoff to the religious right, as its intellectual leaders themselves unabashedly proclaim.[12]

Of course, in the late 1990s and early 2000s, the potential "swing" justices among the conservative bloc of five, O'Connor and Kennedy, had stood against outright overruling of *Roe v. Wade*. Even during President Bush's own tenure, the courts still had flashes of their previous beneficent spirit. In 2003 the Supreme Court struck down the criminalization of private gay conduct in *Lawrence v. Texas* and upheld affirmative action for classroom diversity.[13] And some of the Court's rulings of the late 1990s and early 2000s, such as those against Internet censorship, acted more to reinforce than to undermine the structure of the national minimum of tolerance and civil liberty built up during the Warren and Burger courts.

Understanding the potential for what conservatives can do with their judges thus requires subtlety. I have argued many times in somewhat politically sensitive cases before relatively mature Republican-appointed judges, and even those with established conservative stances regularly took their responsibility to be independent and neutral with great seriousness, including ruling without hesitation against "their" side when they saw the law made doing so appropriate. *Bush v. Gore*, of course, showed conservative activist justices at their worst, in a decision more important than whole years of the Court's regular docket put together. But *Bush v. Gore* was exceptional, and conservative victories of the future cannot and will not depend upon mere excesses of judicial crassness.

It is worth allowing, then, that even Bush's handpicked conservative-activist judicial appointees merely enhance the *potential* disposition to provide the results Bush wants. And if future Supreme Court justices prove as unpredictable as some of their predecessors, then the right wing cannot guarantee full triumph even if a couple of moderates resign and Bush replaces them with justices like Scalia and Thomas.[14] Moreover, conservative tacticians know that Supreme Court decisions that are too extreme can sometimes cause an effective public backlash.[15]

But a subtle combination of political and judicial maneuvering can pave the way toward conservative victories at a time when appointed judges are increasingly conservative. The Ashcroft agenda for undermining *Roe v. Wade* provides the model for understanding the complex and intricate maneuvers by which social conservatives work toward their goals through simultaneous political and judicial processes. The game plan involves nothing as stark as a constitutional amendment or an undisguised attempt to overrule wholesale all recent Supreme Court precedents on social issues. Social conservatives have shown a canny ability to avoid objectives that are beyond their political strength or judicial support. Instead, they have tended to take incremental, tactically wise steps, achieving at least symbolic victories while avoiding an excessive public backlash. With Ashcroft's and Olson's help, they can be expected to continue shaping judicial test cases that bring them favorable rulings without stirring up judicial resistance—that is, without asking the courts to look too nakedly pliant and political.

Chapter 2 describes the next steps of this kind in the anti–abortion rights campaign: legislation limiting the D&X and other methods, state laws creating impediments to (not outright prohibitions of) abortion, federal interstate-movement legislation, and the corresponding judicial tests of these federal and state actions. Perhaps the next major front concerns the upcoming years of struggle in the wake of the Supreme Court's 2003 decision decriminalizing private gay conduct.[16] This may be the second main legal issue around which social conservatives will seek pronouncements from Washington legitimating them and delegitimating the targets of their moralizing.

Politically, apart from the constitutional amendment drive, social conservatives might choose to focus on battles in particular communities where their own views predominate and that can be expected to fight against having to accept gay marriages or other gay rights sanctioned in more tolerant jurisdictions.[17] What may seem to start as a fight for local self-determination (and hence for local and states' rights) may in reality be a carefully chosen set of skirmishes in a larger war fought ultimately in Washington. Politically, the campaign to institutionalize social conservative objectives begins with President Bush's important careful signals of understanding to his coreligious constituency, accompanied by less restrained but still carefully coordinated signals of sympathy from Ashcroft, social conservative organizations, and conservatives in Congress. It will play out further in tailored legislative action in which symbolism matters at least as much as results—for example, action that maintains the "defense of marriage" theme rather than attempting to limit civil liberties outright. Unduly arousing the anger of centrists (including many Republicans) about intolerance toward those within the core American political family (that today includes homosexuals, of course) would not advance Bush's social conservative goals.[18]

Once some local and federal laws produce test cases in the judiciary, however, Ashcroft's Justice Department can swing into action, using the same tactics it used to pump up the personal right to possess lethal weapons; that is, it will support what it would term congressionally supported "local choice" on the matter of "defending marriage." These tactics include public statements mostly for the benefit of social conservatives, briefs written with their political impact in mind, and the careful choice of test cases that can further promote the anti-gay agenda. Inevitably, one or two seminal cases will reach the high court, where Olson will ask the justices (again with an eye toward social conservative voters) to view the matter not as politically inspired religious moralizing but as an important chance to consider the American tradition of federalism—and other seemingly lofty, neutral values.

Only much further down the road, after years of success in using symbolic stances to rally the social conservative troops—and perhaps after a few Supreme Court replacements—would Bush's or a succeeding conservative administration offer more concrete anti-gay political and legal action for the right-wing cause. This might involve implementing laws, then getting them approved in favorably disposed courts, that would enshrine the exclusion of gays from certain kinds of anti-discrimination regulations—perhaps through the backdoor device of federal funding of social services increasingly provided by religious institutions.[19] During the 1950s McCarthy era, the right wing taught gay people to fear the FBI and the rest of the restrictive conservative establishment. It could happen again.

In another vein, the Rehnquist Court of the 1990s and early 2000s made important though limited forays into building up principles of constitutional and statutory interpretation to strike down or hobble the great progressive milestone legislation of the past. With support from the Bush administration, the judiciary could continue along these lines. Considering how difficult even a conservative president and Congress find it to repeal popular progressive legislation like anti-pollution laws, activist judges could do the right a favor at a cheap political price. Victories in coordinated judicial and legislative campaigns will keep social conservatives energized and wealthy contributors ready with their checkbooks while filling the media with the desired message and maintaining congressional ideological discipline. Above all, such campaigns help conservatives from widely different backgrounds—from wealthy Orange County Episcopalians to low-income Bible Belt born-agains—recognize that they're all part of one controlling structure.

Judge Robert Bork once wrote that "the New Deal is not going to be undone, certainly not by the stroke of a judicial pen." But he also described in constitutional terms how courts might (and, in his view, should) stop

Congress from regulating intrastate waters for "noncommercial" reasons—that is, how to keep local waters free of pollution controls. Bork's argument centered on limiting Congress to what he deemed the original intent of the Commerce Clause, drafted over two centuries ago.[20] Using this deceptively simple line of attack to smash one relatively simple environmental law, however, shows how each such campaign has a host of repercussions. It would place in permanent constitutional jeopardy federal protections of surface waters such as lakes and of underground waters such as local aquifers, toxic waste disposal laws, and even safe drinking water laws.[21] It would prevent Congress from applying the Superfund law to locally operated landfills or the Endangered Species Act to private landowners. Likewise, Congress could not promote transportation safety standards, since these apply to state as well as interstate highways.[22]

Judge Bork's Commerce Clause campaign shows just one route among many by which New Deal reforms and a full range of other laws that are anathema to social and economic conservatives could be undone. As Mark Tushnet put it, if President Bush could pack the Court, "the U.S. political system could be *transformed* into one committed in principle to a sharply reduced role for government in supporting economic growth and achieving economic and social justice."[23] As President Bush and his Congress implemented new laws and rules to suit this program, in Tushnet's chilling phrase, the activist conservative "Supreme Court then could assist the new unified government by cleansing the statute books of legislation left over from the prior system."[24] Each of the Court's holdings, starting with the one Judge Bork proposed in his illustration, would add to the "cleansing" "transformative" effect. Each could demolish not only the regulation under challenge but perhaps also an entire system of regulations. And each such ruling calls into doubt another host of parallel ones. The Warren Court used to make whole lines of judicial dominoes progress to the left, at least when overcoming the previously entrenched system of segregation and denial of fundamental equality and civil liberties, especially in the South. An Ashcroft campaign along lines like Bork's, using more activist conservatives on the courts, would send the dominoes crashing in the other, potentially repressive direction.

FEDERALISM: FROM NATIONAL CENTRIST
FLOOR TO NATIONAL CONSERVATIVE CEILING

Farther down the road, President Bush and his heirs might implicitly undermine the very notion of national minimums in key civil rights and liberties and in certain kinds of regulation such as pollution rules. In the new civil order, no longer would conservative states like South Carolina, Texas, or Utah have to respect federally protected minimum requirements to tolerate social or racial differences or to obey EPA regulations completely. Now, Ashcroft and his administration colleagues, working with a conservative judiciary on certain subjects and disciplined congressional conservatives on others, could increasingly devolve social and regulatory direction in conservative states to the local established power structure.

Several of the individual policy thrusts explored in this book—for example, industry's quest for weakened environmental regulations—depend on this mechanism of devolving social and regulatory policy to states and localities. Whether affected groups mount resistance at the national level or not, this program can come to fruition through processes that quiet opposition. For example, federalism by its very nature currently allows groups in more progressive states to guarantee accustomed levels of tolerance and regulation, but only within the borders of those states. So conservatives might be able to enact bills in Congress curtailing restored guarantees of civil liberty and equality and, by merely providing for such flexibility, satisfy the Supreme Court's conservative bloc that the Constitution has been honored. Although this may develop piecemeal, certain overall thrusts might advance it—breakthrough rulings from the Supreme Court or the use of "block grants," vouchers, privatization, and other vehicles to permit more state and local administration of federally funded benefits programs (for as long as they survive).

But with principles of uniformity among the states weakened, conservative governors would be free to do what Bush did as governor of Texas when he diverted available funding from poor areas (such as the "colonias" near the Texas-Mexico border) to rich ones, leaving the areas of the poor as sinks of neglect and deprivation.[25] It is not inaccurate to describe the logical end of this project as the de facto release of conservative states from a half century of equality principles built up by the Warren Court and the Great Society programs of the 1960s. This would be the modern equivalent of the end of Reconstruction in the Southern states in 1877, when federal troops went back North and the local power structure in the former slaveholding states got to restore the system of inequality it liked.[26] Let us not forget that the Klan-based power structure in the conservative states did not just repress racial minorities but religious and social ones too. And Washington turned a deaf ear to the cries of the oppressed.

Yet reliance on federalism to undo national civil rights and regulatory standards also will allow the Bush administration and its progeny to impose a ceiling on the civil liberties now cherished by those living in more progressive regions of the country. Ashcroft has already tried—and will continue to try—to impose social conservative views on progressive states on such issues as assisted suicide, the death penalty, and firearms possession and, pursuant to the PATRIOT Act, on such issues as domestic surveillance and the denial of civil liberties to immigrants and suspects. Ashcroft could seek to build on the Rehnquist opinion that kept New Jersey from holding the Boy Scouts' national organization accountable for its violation of the state law against anti-gay discrimination.[27] Many progressive states have stronger anti-discrimination or pro-labor regimes than the Constitution and federal statutes necessarily require for the nation as a whole.[28] A long-term Ashcroft agenda would find ways to impose a national ceiling on just how far progressive states and localities can go in providing specific rights and liberties.[29]

INTERNATIONAL AFFAIRS

Three simple aspects of the Bush administration's approach govern the future in the context of international affairs and the related use of secrecy. President Bush always favored unilateralism—or in blunter terms, "going it alone." National security problems, such as those posed by 9/11, traditionally provide Republican presidents with the political opportunities to prove themselves "stronger" than the opposition. And the Iraq occupation committed the Bush administration to a forward projection of force without support in international law and consensus.

Between 2000 and 2004 conservatives achieved many of their initial goals for unilateralism. Now future conservative administrations may consider themselves free to erect a U.S.-centered alternative to the remaining structures of international law, consensus, and governance. That collective framework—embodied in the United Nations Security Council, international peacekeeping arrangements, regional organizations such as NATO, and multilateral treaties against weapons proliferation—enables all nations —large or small, strong or weak, rich or poor—to participate in the collective quest for security. It also allows them the chance to join social progress on environmental, labor, and other issues through agreements and organizations. The administrations of George H. W. Bush and Bill Clinton generally made use of these structures, even if they sometimes took different approaches. But George W. Bush envisions a radically different structure for international governance, one built around unilateral American decisions, ad hoc coalitions, bilateral negotiations, and economic interaction concerned mainly with trade relations. He will continue to undermine the Security Council, steer around NATO, avoid meaningful multilateral treaties, and reduce the role of international institutions. Environmental agreements and similar collective legal efforts, other than those affecting trade and investment, will get short shrift, as they did from 2001 to 2004.

The rest of the world can be expected to attempt to continue upholding collective structures, hobbled though they may be by America's rejection of them. In regions not considered of strategic interest to America, such as much of Africa, the UN and regional organizations might continue to carry out peacekeeping missions; the rest of the world might also maintain or develop weakened legal structures, as with the Bonn Protocol that followed up the Kyoto Treaty on global warming. However, any suggestion that such international legal arrangements represent a collective conscience, as was claimed for the Rome Treaty on genocide and war crimes, might well trigger strenuous antagonism from the Bush administration—efforts not just to steer clear of international conventions but to assault them. It would suit conservatives fine if the world just abandoned some aspects of its collective progress altogether, as when John Bolton broke up the international conference working toward a stronger bioweapons protocol. In these and other ways the chill from the United States would reduce the level of the world's collective legal and institutional effort. It already has.

Although it is not often stated in epistemological terms, one question with respect to international legal conventions is: what is truth? The Bush administration conducted a huge worldwide campaign in 2002–2003 to promote its view of the imminent threat posed by Iraqi weapons of mass destruction, notably Iraq's supposed nearness to nuclear weaponry. This marketing blitz triggered a rhetorical competition between unilateral pronouncements from the administration and multilateral ones from institutional and collective forums. In that instance the statements of UN arms inspectors turned out considerably closer to the truth than the administration's. In the world's eyes, the U.S. failure to substantiate its charges—during an ongoing U.S. occupation—called the veracity of all future unilateral pronouncements into question. As far as other countries, even America's allies, are concerned, the Bush administration engages in convenient propaganda, not truth telling.

This approach to truth in international and security matters exposes the Bush administration to special risks. These start in general with conservatives' misplaced sense that America's interests will necessarily thrive on unilateralism and in particular with the hubris underlying the unilateral occupation of Iraq. To the Bush White House, only good can come from unshackling America's lone-wolf superpower capacities by tearing up the ABM treaty so anti-missile defense can go forward; pulling out of world social agreements; and undermining collective efforts such as those against global warming. From 2001 to 2004 President Bush and his supporters promoted the image, and to some extent believed, that the United States could broaden its initial battles against terrorists in Afghanistan into a prolonged war in Iraq (also ostensibly against terrorism), even without international support. In conservatives' eyes President Bush's unilateralism was appropriate in the face of the rest of the world's caution; better to go it alone (or nearly so) than knuckle under to international law and consensus.

No administration since Lyndon Johnson's has exhibited such an overconfident belief in its own ability to project power into remote and hostile quarters without international support. No American administration has stretched the international law to a greater degree in launching a preemptive war on another country. Even the Clinton administration, whose decision to bomb Serbia without Security Council authorization in 1999 raised serious questions, made itself part of a NATO effort, whatever excessive price must be paid to propitiate the French. Nor has any administration other than presidents Johnson and Nixon, who engaged in the Vietnam deceptions, stretched the bounds of truth more fully in its pronouncements to Congress and the public than did the Bush administration in its express assertions about Iraqi weaponry, its wrongful silence about the start of planning and the potential cost, its cultivation of the public misimpression linking Iraq with 9/11, its dispensing of contract patronage to loyal retainers like Ahmed Chalabi and Halliburton, and its misleading statements to Congress about whether the invasion and occupation would go ahead in the near absence of foreign support. As a result, the extended, bloody Iraq occupation, with all the difficulties that ensued from the absence of international support, came about as the product of hubris and of a fundamental decision to control rather than level with the American people.

The Bush administration got itself ready, as a matter of doctrine and public pronouncement, to send troops preemptively wherever it saw fit, without either a valid basis in accepted international law or all that much in the way of solid public support. President Bush spread a cloak of stealth, and even played fast and loose with the truth, in his international actions—as in the secret planning for the Iraq invasion and the shrill claims about Iraqi weaponry. The Bush administration's approach may indeed spell a return to the pattern of imperial presidential prerogative seen in the Johnson and Nixon years and to the accompanying pattern of scandal and national intelligence failures that are all but guaranteed in the end when congressional and public oversight are thwarted.

And there are other risks to conducting international policy so recklessly and under such a heavy cloak of secrecy. Unilateralism and stealth may seem magically to release President Bush in the short run from what would otherwise seem to him like a short leash to the bipartisan center of the country and the Congress.[30] But by junking international law and institutions and escaping the need to credibly justify action, an administration forgoes some of the few options it has—other than unilateral force—when it faces confrontations with dangerous or unstable countries. It sacrifices the availability of the Security Council, of regional agreements and structures such as NATO, and of nonproliferation treaties and institutions such as the International Atomic Energy Agency and loses the support of potential allies that would help much more within a collective framework, as the international community helped Bush's father with the 1991 Persian Gulf War. As President Bush goes forward with his approach, he may find the United States' options, and his own, tragically limited.

For example, we have already noted the temptation the Bush administration may experience to prop up Central Asian countries, ostensibly for post-9/11 security but actually, at least in part, to promote the commercial ambitions of Bush's favored oil industry. The world must of course continue to develop its energy resources, but the basic elements of a political quagmire threaten to develop if right-wing administrations overplay their hand. Unilateral commitments can turn out like Indochina in the 1960s, Lebanon in 1983, and Somalia in 1992–1993, with American forces in the wrong place at the wrong time, bereft of allies, not really knowing how they got there and lacking a real decision back home to support a long-term commitment. Then the American public, no longer in the dark when flag-draped caskets begin returning to Dover Air Force Base, will rightly ask how and for whom American blood and resources came to be so tragically squandered, without international support or a genuine national interest at stake. They will begin to wonder whether all this was not done on behalf of some global commercial interest, like Big Oil, one with access to skillful lobbyists and the financial resources of so many Rangers and

Pioneers. In the wake of the ensuing public backlash, the Bush administration's seeming cleverness in displacing existing global legal structure so that the White House could make decisions to its political benefit in splendid isolation will appear a vice rather than a virtue.

Meanwhile, conservative administrations could make their international economic polestar the push for enhanced legal arrangements on trade. The United States might either keep up the drive toward an Free Trade Agreement of the Americas or a Doha Round agreement or settle for assembling a network of bilateral agreements with other countries. The new trade agreements would operate as powerful global engines for conservative economic causes. In return for a role in the global economy, countries in regions such as Latin America could well find themselves either having to accept trade on Robert Zoellick's partisan terms or doing without. Other countries' lower environmental, labor, and safety standards would become the basis for bringing down American standards as well.[31] The ensuing deals might sacrifice the American productive sectors that President Bush views unsympathetically, like unionized manufacturing or services found in Democratic-leaning regions and capable of being performed in other countries. But that would just teach Democratic-leaning areas the price of betting against those holding the reins, and that expecting the leaders in a moderate and democratic republic to try their best to represent the interests of the country as a whole in the international arena is an illusion.

President Bush will use continued access to the U.S. import market to bribe or extort compliance with his party's international gambits. For example, the time may come when conservatives' obsession with anti-missile systems leads them to desire locating some near Russia and China. Presumably this would occur with a cover story—some imagined threat from a regional power or terrorists. Yet Eastern European and Asian countries can be expected to express queasiness about participating in a needless, strategically destabilizing effort. American economic strength would then be employed to teach such countries that engaging in trade with conservative presidents obliges them to go along with anti-missile systems. While this approach to international and trade law may have a questionable effect on real U.S. security, President Bush presumably sees it as enhancing his political prospects.

Presidents have always used their national security initiatives to build up their authority and popularity at home. Congress tends not to assert itself in the face of perceived security threats but to abdicate its own authority.[32] So the new security situation might again furnish an array of tools for President Bush, as well as other conservative presidents, to undertake (initially) popular jingoistic moves in international affairs. This is not to say that conservatives are unpatriotic or that they undertake international efforts only when these serve a domestic political objective. Vice President Cheney espouses a principled ideology about national security affairs that takes into account his patriotism, wisdom, and expertise. But his way, the conservative way, often happens neatly to serve both what he and fellow conservatives see as the national interest and also the interest of their president in getting, holding, and enhancing his political power—and theirs.

Most of President Bush's efforts during 2001–2004 aimed primarily at securing his own reelection, with conservative causes, particularly social conservative ones, advancing principally, as far as he cared, more as a means to his personal ends than as an end in themselves. But the movement to which he attached himself had a momentum that would continue despite interim hindrances, even on the scale of his losing the reelection, so long as he and that movement could view such a defeat as an "honorable" one and the movement could regroup for the next campaign. Many in the conservative movement had viewed the succession in 1989 of Bush senior (as compared to, say, the Christian-right candidate, Pat Robertson), the election of Clinton in 1992, and the end of Newt Gingrich's Speakership after the midterm election of 1998 as precisely such interim hindrances— and the triumphs of the early 2000s had proven them, measured by their set of political values, as quite right about what mattered in the long term.

Such right-wingers could coolly predict that their movement would survive and even do quite nicely regardless of how the election of 2004 came out. The small number of contestable districts and states made it virtually certain that the House and Senate would remain under Republican control. Republican congressional leadership would not revert to the centrism characteristic of Howard Baker, Robert Dole, and Robert Michel in the 1980s and early 1990s. No Republican Senate would allow Supreme Court vacancies to fall into progressive hands; the trend to the right on the Court might slow but not reverse. Thus, conservatives knew that they would keep control of two branches and that their core platform of keeping taxes low for the rich and arousing the base against women's and gay rights would maintain that control despite any setback, even on the scale of a White House loss.

Although this book focuses on the personal strategy and tactics of George W. Bush, it has also shown how the 1990s program and personnel of the Gingrich-DeLay House leadership, its Senate allies of the Helms wing, and their supporters in the spheres of lobbying and sectarian politics became—with an extra infusion from Texas—the program and personnel of the Bush administration. It would not crush or fracture the movement to pull back temporarily into its secure bastions for any single four-year hiatus during the 2000s or early 2010s.

A Democratic president any time during that period would find it too dangerous to radically reorient American foreign policy from Bush's— that would be called going "soft" on "the enemy" (and even those supporting international consensus on environmental, labor, or human rights would be viewed as suspicious in their insufficiently pugnacious versions of American exceptionalism). That president would find it virtually impossible, given Senate Republican dominance, to challenge the Bush-imposed economic structure. And, the president's every step toward tolerance, inclusion, and respect for privacy in national values would invigorate with fresh hostility the social conservative base. Even if the national vehicle were pulled back momentarily from its veer right, it would not get very far left, and the powerful and effective yanking of the steering wheel hard toward the right would not relent. It was a real question in early 2004 whether anything on the horizon could be worse than merely a temporary check on the conservative movement's forward sweep. Not even an honorable (i.e., limited) loss in November 2004 would do it.

SECOND-TERM ELECTORAL SWINGS

Before we wholly accept the idea Bush found for guaranteeing conservatism's development into a political colossus of ever increasing scope, some offsetting and counterbalancing patterns deserve consideration, as well. Two entirely distinct kinds of mechanisms—one electoral, the other having to do with scandals or failures—have often operated in recent second presidential terms. Both puncture simplistic expectations that whatever helped President Bush and his movement in the early 2000s must necessarily work for him later. Each of these deserves detailed analysis by those trying to peer into the crystal ball.

In most of the second terms of the last half century, the midterm congressional election evinced a strong swing away from the presidential party. This occurred in 1958, 1966, 1974, and 1986.[33] In that last episode, President Reagan, who had won a forty-eight-state reelection sweep in 1984, saw the Senate swing dramatically against him two years later. After that, notwithstanding his personal popularity, he faced a confident Democratic majority in both chambers of Congress that enacted a progressive miniprogram in 1987–1988—on issues from trade to health care benefits very much the mirror image of Reagan's own successful conservative program in 1981–1982.

Political scientists have elaborate, somewhat quantitative analyses for the second midterm congressional election swing against the president's party. The so-called "negative surge" analysis takes into account that in presidential reelection years (e.g., 1956, 1964,[34] 1972, 1984), coattails produce a surge for the president's party in Congress. This owes both to enhanced levels of voting by groups favorable to the president's party and to the actual degree of straight-ticket voting following the president at the top of the ticket.[35] The surge means that a certain number of marginal states and districts just barely produce a majority for the president's party, including a certain number of House races with weak candidates of that party whom the voters barely approve. Two years later, in the midterm election, the president's supporters are less likely to vote and less likely to vote a straight ticket when they do go to the polls. The surge for the president's party of two years earlier evaporates, leaving, by contrast, a "negative surge" in which the president's party loses the races in the close states and districts, or the ones with the barely viable candidates, that it had marginally won two years earlier.

For various reasons, in second-term midterm elections, the average loss for the president's party actually doubles.[36] Occasionally, though, even a first-term midterm election exhibits a different phenomenon: a reaction against the sitting president, producing substantial losses for his party. This phenomenon came into play in 1982, damaging Republicans in Congress, and again in 1994, when a negative reaction to President Clinton absolutely pounded congressional Democrats. And the traditional pattern may not hold in the immediate future. It broke in 1998, when President Clinton bucked the curse of the second-term midterm.[37] That year, the preparations by Ken Starr and Newt Gingrich to impeach the popular president for Monicagate so antagonized Clinton's supporters that he seemed to gain rare midterm coattails; Democrats made no gains, but neither did the Republicans.[38] The pattern broke again in 2002, presumably for special reasons arising from 9/11 and the presidential strategy for using it, and President Bush enjoyed a special kind of midterm coattails.[39]

Although 1998 and 2002 have their explanations, the appearance of an exception to a political rule, twice in a row, always inspires doubt about the continued predictive validity of a past political pattern. Perhaps the factors underlying the past pattern of midterm swings, like the contribution of straight-ticket voting to the "negative surge," have declined over time.[40]

Despite all the recurring patterns, intriguing theories, and statistical data available for these phenomena, however, no one can hope to predict election results long in advance, any more than they can predict the stock market or the weather long beforehand. Still, just noting the patterns and their limits cautions against making any overly simplistic projection of the long-term enduring effect of President Bush's approach.

For a historical analogy, the pro-business, WASP-based Republican Party stayed largely dominant in national politics from the 1860s to the 1920s (with interludes for presidents Grover Cleveland and Woodrow Wilson). However, this owed more to major societal trends after the post-1860 realignment—the industrialization of the North and Midwest and the politically potent concentration of capital there—than to the particular stratagems of Republican Party leaders. Democratic control of Congress from the 1930s to the 1990s (interludes such as Eisenhower's aside) similarly owed a great deal to major societal trends after the New Deal realignment, favoring a decentralized party that could field left (Northern) and right (Southern) wings appealing to urban labor and rural interests, respectively. It owed much less to the political stratagems of party leaders. The success of President Bush's approach may turn out to have been the result of emerging societal trends that will become clear only with hindsight; or it may indeed rank as nothing more than a well-calculated temporarily effective use of political strategy. Without the backing of the kind of major societal trends that create long-term realignments, the regular cycles of the past that have interrupted the political successes of even the most popular administrations may recur.

SCANDALS AND FIASCOES

Before further assessing the question of the endurance of President Bush's approach, a quite separate pattern also deserves notice: the second-term scandal. Modern presidents simply tend to get into deeper trouble in their second than in their first term. Not only did President Johnson stumble in Vietnam in his second term, but President Nixon did in Watergate, President Reagan in Iran-contra, and President Clinton in impeachment for Monicagate. Nothing on that scale occurred to any of them in their first term.

If there is any common thread to these second-term scandals, it's that each had a legal component. Second-term troubles often involve a president's exposure after he lied about or at least wrongfully covered up a legal stretch. The political system or the legal system, or both, then sets about

punishing the president for his dissembling. And—also a common thread
—each president's usual approach to governing and communicating, previously a source of great strength, suddenly turns into a great liability. The
more he conducts business as usual, the worse matters become. It may
not be a complete overgeneralization to say that modern two-term presidents demonstrate relatively firm discipline at first, ruthlessly avoiding
scandal and, if they get into real trouble, covering up problems in order
to gain reelection.[41] After the election, in the second term, more troubles
arise: the discipline relaxes, the self-indulgence grows, the willingness
to coldly troubleshoot problems falters, and the dissembling snowballs.
Clinton did not fall into adultery and the related lying until his second
term. President Reagan let Oliver North and others make full-scale war
in Nicaragua and shocking deals with Iran only after his big reelection
victory.

The unifying thread through these scandals is presidential secrecy. Perhaps that will prove, in the end, to be Bush's undoing. Sunlight is the best
disinfectant; shutting it out produces corruption, which usually comes to
light in the second term. President Bush runs the most secretive administration in thirty years (but that may turn out to be less a benefit for him
than a curse). His supporters like to contrast his fidelity in marriage and
his story of religious redemption from early sins with his predecessor's
marital infidelities and his failure to talk like Bush about religious faith.
They would undoubtedly scoff at the notion that merely keeping policy
secrets, as opposed to engaging in marital infidelity, could lead to scandal.

But the history of presidential scandals includes more Hardings and
Nixons than Clintons. A White House giving out favors to contributors
runs a risk of a corruption scandal. A White House manipulating information about security in order to justify the way it prefers to handle international affairs—sometimes, as in October 2002, timed for evident electoral
impact—runs a risk of an intelligence or defense scandal. Presidents Nixon
and Reagan thought that the legal protection given national security
secrets would limit their exposure to scandal if the Watergate and Iran-
contra affairs ever became public. Both were wrong.

OTHER RISKS AND SCENARIOS

President Bush's seeming success in legitimating Ashcroft-style social
conservatism may constitute a long-term route to power, but it also creates
an ever present possibility of centrist backlash. To deliver for the long
term, the effort depends upon keeping faith with movement conservatives

and, in particular, delivering an activist conservative judiciary. Bush's approaches worked for a while, and this success has a historical precedent. While neither conservatives nor progressives would particularly relish the comparison, the Bush approach to tilting the judiciary bears a sort of distorted mirror-image resemblance to the Kennedy-Johnson judicial appointments that moved the early Warren Court to its last more liberal stage. The Warren Court of the mid-1960s, with justices like Goldberg and Fortas, energetically brought previously marginalized groups into the mainstream.

As President Bush's judicial legacy takes hold, contemporary social conservatives may feel enormous entitlements themselves. President Bush and his political advisers, such as Karl Rove, can hope these newly empowered social conservatives exhibit the same kind of loyalty to Republicans that their minority counterparts gave to Democrats for a generation. The Warren Court analogy, however, carries a double-edged moral. The late Warren Court and early Burger Court engendered a political backlash; conservatives came to power running on issues such as reducing protections for "criminals' rights." President Bush's judiciary could trigger a similar response from the opposite side of the ideological spectrum.

Every radical judicial step cutting back on *Roe v. Wade*, curbing minority and women's rights, and using government power for sectarian moralizing risks stirring up minorities, feminists, and centrists generally. And these potential opposition groups are not like the freedmen in the states of the former Confederacy in 1877: the deprivation of judicial support may hurt disfavored groups, eroding their equal rights and letting social conservatives feel high and mighty, but it will not crush them into disenfranchisement. Stirring them up will confront conservatives with their basic nightmare: the transformation of standard poll numbers showing the overall public disagrees with them on particular issues into majorities of votes against them at the next election.

Some astute observers calculate that the demographic trends of the long-term future—including projected increases in the numbers of minorities; single, working, and highly educated women; professionals; and other key voting groups—favor growth in Democratic and centrist-progressive strength.[42] The outrages of a right-wing Court may wake these particular groups out of dogmatic slumber, as Gingrich's outrageous stances brought them to the polls in significant numbers in 1996 and 1998. Many lawyers assume the judiciary automatically reigns supreme in these confrontations, particularly considering that a potent conservative movement would back a far-right Court. But in the long term, when democratic institutions that enjoy centrist public support find themselves in conflict with non-elected judges favoring fringe positions, smart observers bet on democratic institutions to win.[43] So even the conservatives' most permanent monument, a judiciary stacked with young Scalias, cannot stand against a fully aroused public.

RESPONSIBILITY AND POSSIBILITIES

The Bush administration has been, by its own reckoning, a tremendous success. It has demonstrated a vast capacity to promote conservative causes. It has engendered what may turn out to be a long-term alteration of the power structure bringing with it a boundless flow of campaign funding and a right-wing judiciary. It has perceived and exploited potent opportunities to manipulate the budget process, to devolve power to conservative states (and disempower more progressive ones), and to use real needs for national security to justify even great augmentation of the president's legal and political authority. The Bush administration may continue a fruitful exchange relationship with conservative bases that acquire, in return, the sweet rewards of a powerful grip on national power.

Yet the conservative swing may ultimately fall prey to the same political and legal undermining that hobbled the second-term Nixon and Reagan presidencies. The 2004 and 2006 elections may not surely and definitively mark the final outcome. It may take many years for the real results of President Bush's attempt at revolution to become known. The study of how the Bush administration has veered right through the subversion of law, while disturbing, does not, finally, show the centrist public to be facing the ineluctable and dismal prospect of ceding governance to those with plutocratic or theocratic dreams. We may hope for a better result. I do. Each individual in the American polity who believes in democracy's infinite possibilities bears a personal responsibility to work honestly and morally for the triumph of his or her ideals.

Notes

1. GETTING READY TO VEER RIGHT

1. William C. Berman, *America's Right Turn: From Nixon to Clinton* (2d ed. 1998).

2. See generally Jon. R. Bond & Richard Fleisher, eds., *Polarized Politics: Congress and the President in a Partisan Era* (2000).

3. For a conservative's favorable review of the Reagan administration's handling of legal affairs, see Terry Eastland, *Energy in the Executive* (1992).

4. Theodore J. Lowi, *The End of the Republican Era* (1995); Dan Balz & Ronald Brownstein, *Storming the Gates: Protest Politic and the Republican Revival* (1996); Douglas L. Koopman, *Hostile Takeover: The House Republican Party, 1980–1995* (1996).

5. David W. Rohde, *Parties and Leaders in the Postreform House* (1991).

6. Ronald Radosh, *Divided They Fell: The Demise of the Democratic Party, 1964–1996* (1996).

7. Nicol C. Rae, *The Decline and Fall of the Liberal Republicans from 1952 to the Present* (1989).

8. For a full treatment of this subject, see Charles Tiefer, *Congressional Practice and Procedure* (1989).

9. This theory has been most fully developed in a series of works by Aldrich and Rohde. A good overview is John H. Aldrich & David W. Rohde, *The Logic of Conditional Party Government: Revisiting the Electoral Connection*, in Lawrence C. Dodd & Bruce I. Oppenheimer, eds., *Congress Reconsidered* 269 (7th ed. 2001).

10. Charles Tiefer, *Budgetized Health Entitlements and the Fiscal Constitution in Congress's 1995–1996 Budget Battle*, 33 Harv. J. on Legis. 411 (1996).

11. The Republican Party fared worse in the 1998 elections than any out-of-White-House party had done in a second-term midterm election in the previous century and a half. See Paul R. Abramson et al., *Change and Continuity in the 1996 and 1998 Elections* 252 (1999).

12. In studying realignment over the past century, political scientists have analyzed the two separate activist groups within the party. See Gary Miller & Normal Schofield, *Activists and Partisan Realignment in the United States*, 97 Am. Poli. Sci. Rev. 245, 247–48 (2003).

13. Some of the disapproved lifestyle varieties had to do with family or sexuality issues framed in moral terms, such as sex education in school or homosexuality. Some of the disapproved diversity issues had to do with racial or other group-identity attitudes framed in code words, such as putting a "pro-crime" or "pro-welfare" label on minority candidates or minority judicial nominees.

14. Edward N. Wolf, *Top Heavy: A Study of the Increasing Inequality of Wealth in America* (1998).

15. Kevin Phillips, *Wealth and Democracy* 321–29 (2002).

16. Jeffrey M. Stonecash, *Class and Party in American Politics* 32–33 (2002).

17. Sheldon D. Pollack, *Refinancing America: The Republican Antitax Agenda* (2003).

18. See generally Paul Begala, *It's Still the Economy, Stupid: George W. Bush, the GOP's CEO* 3–15 (2002) (favorably recounting Clinton economics).

19. See Balz & Brownstein, *supra*, at 334.

20. See Thomas B. Edsall, *Big Business's Funding Shift Boosts GOP: Trend May Put Squeeze on Democrats' Finances*, Wash. Post (Nov. 27, 2002), at A1.

21. See generally Richard Briffault, *The Political Parties and Campaign Finance Reform*, 100 Colum. L. Rev. 620 (2000).

22. The strength of the defunding effect depends on the particular situation. In mild situations, secure Democratic incumbents might experience nothing more than some limits on access to a few of the sources of additional contributions. In severe situations, Democratic challengers facing difficult races against massively funded incumbents might find themselves cut off from the levels of funding they need to run effectively, and might find their party unable within its constrained budget to fill the gap.

23. This bias is underlined, although without strong acknowledgement of the partisan aspects, in Twentieth Century Fund Working Group on Campaign Finance Litigation, *Buckley Stops Here: Loosening the Judicial Stranglehold on Campaign Finance Reform* (1998).

24. Melissa Levitt & Katherine C. Naff, *Gender as a Political Constant: The More Things Change, the More They Stay the Same*, in Stephen J. Wayne & Clyde Wilcox, eds., *The Election of the Century* 67, 70 (2002).

25. James M. Lindsay, *From Containment to Apathy*, 79 Foreign Affairs (Sept.–Oct. 2000), at 2.

26. The leading study of rates of passage of major bills is David R. Mayhew, *Divided We Govern: Party Control, Lawmaking, and Investigations, 1946–1990* (1991).

27. The best study of the filibuster is Sarah A. Binder & Steven S. Smith, *Politics or Principle? Filibustering in the United States Senate* (1997).

28. Id. at 135.

29. See, e.g., John H. Kessel, *Presidents, the Presidency, and the Political Environment* (2001); Shirley Anne Warshaw, *The Domestic Presidency: Policy Making in the White House* (1996); Mark A. Peterson, *Legislating Together: The White House and Capitol Hill from Eisenhower to Reagan* (1990).

30. Arthur M. Schlesinger Jr. *The Imperial Presidency* (rev. ed. 1989).

31. Cecil V. Crabb Jr. & Pat M. Holt, *Invitation to Struggle: Congress, the President, and Foreign Policy* (4th ed. 1992).

32. Andrew Bennett & Troy White, *Foreign Policy in the Presidential Campaign*, in Wayne & Wilcox, *supra*, at 19, 35–36.

33. See Paul R. Abramson et al., *Change and Continuity in the 1996 and 1998 Elections* 266 (1999).

34. Martin Garbus, *Courting Disaster: The Supreme Court and the Unmaking of American Law* (2002).

35. Joseph A. Pika et al., *The Politics of the Presidency* 260 (5th ed. 2002).

36. Nancy Scherer, *Are Clinton's Judges "Old" Democrats or "New" Democrats?* Judicature (Nov.–Dec. 2000), at 151.

37. Charles Tiefer, *How to Steal a Trillion: The Uses and Abuses of Laws about Lawmaking in 2001*, 17 J.L. & Pol. 409, 432 & n.108 (2001).

38. Id. at 433–34, 450.

39. Roger Pilon, ed., *The Rule of Law in the Wake of Clinton* (2000).

40. A full treatment is given in chapter 2. A snappy background profile is in David Corn, *The Fundamental John Ashcroft*, Mother Jones (March–April 2002).

41. Charles Tiefer, *Adjusting Sovereignty: Contemporary Congressional-Executive Controversies about International Organizations*, 35 Tex. Int'l L.J. 239, 257–59 (2000).

42. John R. Bolton, *Saddam Wins*, Wkly. Standard (Aug. 24, 1998); John R. Bolton, *Our Pitiful Iraq Policy*, Wkly. Standard (Dec. 21, 1998).

43. I participated in many of these special investigative matters, from serving as the House Iran-Contra Committee's special deputy chief counsel (1987) to representing the Clinton White House chief of staff, John Podesta, at House inquiries on Travelgate (1990s) and the matter of presidential pardons (2001). During this period, the special investigations cycle ran its course from an aroused democracy's reassertion its oversight of public powers in the 1980s down to a mere witch hunt for crass objectives. For a general legal treatment of this era, see Charles Tiefer, *The Specially Investigated President*, 5 U. Chi. Roundtable 143 (1998).

44. Charles Tiefer, *The Controversial Transition Process from Investigating the President to Impeaching Him*, 14 St. John's J. Legal Comment. 111 (1999).

45. Charles Tiefer, *The Senate Impeachment Trial for President Clinton*, 28 Hofstra L. Rev. 407 (1999).

46. Samuel Kernell, *Going Public: New Strategies of Presidential Leadership* (3d ed. 1997).

47. Kevin Phillips, *American Dynasty: Aristocracy, Fortune, and the Politics of Deceit in the House of Bush* (2004).

48. Molly Ivins & Lou Dubose, *Shrub* 28–31 (2000 ed.).

49. Id. at 28–29.

50. Richard W. Stevenson, *Old Business in New Light*, N.Y. Times (July 9, 2002), at A1; Begala, *supra*, at 126.

51. The firm's cofounder's grandson was friends of Prescott Bush. His son, James Baker, served Prescott's son, the first President Bush, as campaign manager and secretary of state.

52. Nicholas M. Horrock, *White House Watch: Credibility Problem*, U.P.I. (June 17, 2002).

53. George W.'s first paying job had been in the Baker & Botts mailroom. Phyllis D. Brandon, *Arkansans Tip Their Hats for Texans as Nation Embraces a New President*, Ark. Dem.-Gaz. (Jan. 28, 2001), at D1.

54. And James Baker joined Baker & Botts, then went to the Carlyle Group and served as an Enron consultant. The SEC's general counsel went on to handle the sale of the Texas Rangers to Bush and his partners and to head the Baker & Botts Washington office. *Inadmissible*, Texas Lawyer (Jan. 1, 2001), at 3; Horrock, *supra*.

55. Martin Peretz, *Audit This*, New Republic (July 22, 2002), at 46.

56. Elisabeth Bumiller & Richard A. Oppel Jr., *Bush Defends Sale of Stock and Vows to Enhance S.E.C.*, N.Y. Times (July 9, 2002), at A1.

57. Pika et al., *supra*, ch. 3 ("Public Politics," including going public), ch. 6 ("Executive Politics," including executive privilege).

58. Lou Dubose, Jan Reid, & Carl M. Cannon, *Boy Genius: Karl Rove, the Brains behind the Remarkable Political Triumph of George W. Bush* (2003); James Moore & Wayne Slater, *Bush's Brain: How Karl Rove Made George W. Bush Presidential* (2003).

59. Ivins & Dubose, *supra*, at xvi.

60. Ivins & Dubose, *supra*; Dubose, Reid, & Cannon, *supra*.

61. Ivins & Dubose, *supra*, at 94–96.

62. Rick Abraham, *The Dirty Truth: George W. Bush's Oil and Chemical Dependency: How He Sold Out Texans and the Environment to Big Business Polluters* 39–76 (2000).

63. Robert Bryce, *Pipe Dreams: Greed, Ego, and the Death of Enron* 88–92 (2002).

64. Abraham, *supra*, at 13, 56.

65. Lee Walczak, Rich Miller, Howard Gleckman, & Richard S. Dunham, *A Politically Correct Tax Plan*, Bus. Week (Dec. 13, 1999), at 44.

66. Jeremy D. Mayer, *The Incorrigibly White Republican Party: Racial Politics in the Presidential Race*, in Wayne & Wilcox, *supra*, at 45, 46–48; Clyde Wilcox, *Wither the Christian Right? The Elections and Beyond*, in Wayne & Wilcox, *supra*, at 107, 111; Dubose, Reid, & Cannon, *supra*, at 139–42.

67. See Richard E. Cohen & James Kitfield, *Cheney: Pros and Cons*, 32 Nat'l J. (July 29, 2000), at 2456.

68. Most relevant, as Ford's chief of staff, Cheney shifted national security power from Secretary of State Henry Kissinger to the further-right, harderline Secretary of Defense Donald Rumsfeld. Jason Vest, *Darth Rumsfeld*, Am. Prospect (Feb. 26, 2001), at 20. Rumsfeld had been Cheney's mentor, starting him in the White House under President Nixon.

69. Charles Tiefer, *The Semi-Sovereign Presidency* 127–130 (1994).

70. James F. Simon, *The Center Holds: The Power Struggle inside the Rehnquist Court* (1995).

71. Tinsley E. Yarbrough, *The Rehnquist Court and the Constitution* (2001).

72. *United States v. Morrison*, 529 U.S. 598 (2000).

73. *Adarand Constructors, Inc. v. Pena*, 515 U.S. 200 (1995).

74. *Board of Trustees of the University of Alabama v. Garrett*, 531 U.S. 356 (2001).

75. *Food and Drug Admin. v. Brown & Williamson Tobacco Co.*, 529 U.S. 120 (2000).

76. *Dept. of Commerce v. U.S. House of Representatives*, 525 U.S. 316 (1999).

77. *Printz v. United States*, 518 U.S. 1003 (1996); *United States v. Lopez*, 514 U.S. 549 (1995).

78. My brief for the House Democratic Leadership can be found in the Westlaw Supreme Court brief database, 2000 WL 126192.

79. *Dickerson v. United States* 530 U.S. 428 (2000). A good analysis of Rehnquist's hidden agenda in the opinion is in Garbus, *supra*, at 71–72.

80. Charles Tiefer, *A True Ballot: Florida Law Makes Clear That Confusing Design Must Never Distort the Voice of the Voters*, Legal Times (Nov. 13, 2000), at 58.

81. *Bush's Legal Team*, Orlando Sentinel (Nov. 29, 2000), at A10.

82. It bought fake threatening demonstrations to cow local election boards; it bought legal challenges to valid votes, particularly minority votes, throughout the state; and it bought a special phenomenon called "Thanksgiving Stuffing" in which after-the-election absentee ballots of the most dubious nature got stuffed into the ballot boxes. Fresh information on the absentee ballot issue as a whole, and particularly the Thanksgiving Stuffing issue, is developed in Jeffrey Toobin, *Too Close to Call: The Thirty-Six-Day Battle to Decide the 2000 Election* 170–76, 197–210 (2001), which is based in part on David Barstow & Don Van Natta Jr., *How Bush Took Florida: Mining the Overseas Absentee Vote*, N.Y. Times (July 15, 2001), at 1.

83. The details of Jeb Bush's string pulling are laid out in Toobin, *supra*.

84. 531 U.S. 70 (2000).

85. Howard Gillman, *The Votes That Counted: How the Court Decided the 2000 Presidential Election* (2001), at 86 (initial Scalia deployment of issue), 146 (later revelation by Souter that the Court had earlier been split despite its surface unanimity).

86. 121 U.S. 512 (2000).

87. Charles Tiefer, *Skirting a Constitutional Crisis*, Legal Times (Dec. 4, 2000). The other two were Charles Tiefer, *Heads Up! Ready or Not, the Election Might Be Congress' to Decide*, Legal Times (Nov. 20, 2000), at 59, and Tiefer, *A True Ballot, supra*.

88. 531 U.S. 1026 (2000).

89. Tiefer, *Skirting a Constitutional Crisis, supra*.

2. "ASHY": THE SOCIAL CONSERVATIVE AGENDA

1. 410 U.S. 113 (1973).

2. A bit more obscurely, in the late 1970s the Internal Revenue Service adopted a clear-cut policy against tax exemptions for segregated private schools. Many of the affected schools were sectarian, and politically active evangelicals now had a legal cause to organize behind the new, harder-edged Southern right wing of the Republican party led by Sen. Jesse Helms (R-N.C.). By the time the Supreme Court, led by Chief Justice Burger, roundly rejected the Reagan Justice Department's championing of that cause in the case of *Bob Jones University v. United States*, 461 U.S. 574 (1983), a wave of Republican organizers, such as Richard Viguerie and Paul Weyrich, and religious leaders, such as Jerry Falwell and Pat Robertson, had used it to jump-start a social conservative movement with a particular foandness for legal causes outside the mainstream. For the rise of conservatives within the Republican Party and their success through it, see Lowi, *supra*; Balz & Brownstein, *supra*; Koopman, *supra*.

3. Berman, *supra*, at 79 (Reagan); 133, 139 (Bush).

4. Mastery of the political uses of law, it became clear, meant not only keeping social conservatives loyal and active but also somehow doing this without galvanizing centrists into a high-turnout opposition. The previous Republican generation had known a good deal about pushing conservatism by legal means but before 1992 had not resolved the knotty dilemma posed by social conservative legal causes far outside the mainstream.

5. For conservative antagonism toward Reno, see Theodore B. Olson, *The Most Political Justice Department Ever*, Am. Spectator (Sept. 2000); Pilon, *supra*; David Limbaugh, *Absolute Power: The Legacy of Corruption in the Clinton-Reno Justice Department* (2001).

6. The Christian Coalition was founded by Pat Robertson, then ingeniously made over by Ralph Reed. Both men used it consistently to support the Republican Party, with which both had long associations. For a full treatment, see the excellent work by former *Los Angeles Times* reporter Nina J. Easton, *Gang of Five: Leaders at the Center of the Conservative Ascendancy* 208–21 (2000). Reed subsequently became chair of the Georgia Republican Party. As the *New York Times* said respectfully about Reed, "He brings formidable political skills to the [Republican] chairman's job. He is telegenic, verbally nimble, has a record as a first-class fund-raiser, and under his leadership the Christian Coalition rose to its highest peak of national political influence." B. Drum-

mond Ayres Jr., *Ralph Reed Wins Election to Lead Georgia Republicans*, N.Y. Times (May 6, 2001), at 1.

7. Figures for the 1994 election are from Balz & Brownstein, *supra*, at 56, 198.

8. For Ashcroft's rise, see Nancy Gibbs & Michael Duffy, *His Opponents Call John Ashcroft an Extremist, So Why Did George W. Bush Think He Was Picking an Attorney General Who'd Be a Cinch to Confirm?* Time (Jan. 22, 2001); Brian Doherty, *John Ashcroft's Power Grab: The Saga of a Troubled— and Troubling—Attorney General*, Reason (June 1, 2002); Dana Slavin, *Faith in Justice: Attorney General John D. Ashcroft*, Fed. Lawyer (Oct. 2001); Peter Schrag, *Ashcroft's Hypocrisy*, Am. Prospect (Jan. 1, 2002).

The dictionary defines *religiosity* as "1. The quality of being religious; piety; devoutness. 2. Affected or excessive devotion to religion" (*American College Dictionary* 1024 [1965 ed.]). To be clear, I am not questioning the sincerity of Ashcroft's faith; it is the faith of his father and his youth, and he has demonstrated his sincere adherence to it on countless nonpolitical occasions. But during eleven years in my post in the House of Representatives I observed effective political leaders of faith to deal with care, rather than naive spontaneity, whenever they bore witness to their faith. In campaigning for office, Ashcroft at times manifested his religion prominently, such as in his appeals to the Christian Coalition and in his May 1999 speech at Bob Jones University (Neil A. Lewis, *Much-Sought Speech by Ashcroft Is Found*, N.Y. Times [Jan. 12, 2001], at A18) while at other times, such as before centrist audiences, he did not deny his faith, of course, but manifested it more subtly.

Ashcroft's political use of his religiosity contrasted with such prior-generation conservative leaders as Senator Barry Goldwater (R-Ariz.) and President Nixon, who effectively inaugurated the Republican appeal to Southern conservative voters without any such emphasis on a shared religion.

9. Important research went into Walter V. Robinson, *In Ashcroft's Past, a Vietnam Deferment*, Boston Globe (Jan. 16, 2001), at A1. Robinson explains: "Ashcroft's teaching position was arranged by an SMSU [Southern Missouri State University] business professor [Vencil Bixler] who was an active member of the Assemblies of God church where Ashcroft's father was pastor and an influential figure in the community.... Bixler, asked what he knew of Ashcroft's draft status, said, 'I do know he realized he would not get a deferment in all probability if he didn't teach.'...Ashcroft, he said, 'may have raised the deferment issue with the [business] department head. What they worked out I don't know.' In late 1968, while he still held the occupational deferment, Ashcroft also established a private law practice in Springfield with his wife, Janet."

10. He had built his statewide reputation and prestige fighting the main racial issue of his time, school desegregation. He fought it in the Kansas City and St. Louis metropolitan areas, opposing it not only when it was court ordered but even when arranged voluntarily.

11. The speech can be found at *Road to Victory Watch* for Sept. 19, 1998, at http://www.pfaw.org. The quote above about how Ashcroft personally argued *Webster* is from that speech.

12. Thomas W. Ross, *The Faith-Based Initiative: Anti-Poverty or Anti-Poor?* 9 Geo. J. on Poverty L. & Pol'y 167 (2002).

13. *Roe v. Wade: Has It Stood the Test of Time?* Hearing before the Sub-comm. on the Constitution, Federalism and Property Rights of the Senate Comm. on the Judiciary (Jan. 21, 1998) (prepared remarks of Chairman John Ashcroft).

14. *Privacy in the Digital Age: Encryption and Mandatory Access,* Hearing before the Subcomm. on the Constitution, Federalism and Property Rights of the Senate Comm. on the Judiciary (March 17, 1998).

15. *Gun Control,* Hearing before the Subcomm. on the Constitution, Federalism and Property Rights of the Senate Comm. on the Judiciary (Sept. 23, 1998) (prepared remarks of Chairman John Ashcroft).

16. *Road to Victory Watch, supra.*

17. Clinton was still practicing a variant of old-style judicial appointments, nominating women and minorities of largely centrist principles, less for ideological reasons than to seek gender and ethnic balance. Appointment of centrist women and minority judges of tolerant dispositions appalled social conservatives. A diverse judiciary would send a message contrary to what political manipulators of the intolerance theme sought, in this case, through reduced diversity and increased repression with sectarian overtones.

18. Doherty, *supra.*

19. Ashcroft brought White down but hurt himself and some in his party in the process. Republican moderates recall a G.O.P. lunch just before the White vote, when Ashcroft and fellow Missouri Senator Christopher ("Kit") Bond stood up to galvanize the caucus to vote en bloc against White. Senators usually defer to the home-state lawmaker on nominations and rarely investigate a nominee's background. But neither Ashcroft nor Bond ever mentioned during the meeting that White is African American. . . . [F]or the moderates, voting against a black judge was always politically dangerous, and many might not have done so if they had known White was black. Some even felt that Ashcroft had deliberately deceived them. Nancy Gibbs & Michael Duffy, et al., *The Fight for Justice,* Time (Jan. 22, 2001), at 20.

20. Jean Carnahan, like a figure out of a Greek tragedy, was named to fill the Senate vacancy her deceased husband would have occupied. Observers were impressed with the grace Ashcroft displayed in such circumstances; he did not resist or challenge, was the opposite of petty or bitter, was simply at his best. Putting aside the strange immediate circumstances, however, Ashcroft's defeat was no isolated phenomenon but fit the broader pattern of Senate Republican losses in 2000. Their ranks were thinned from fifty-six two years earlier to a mere fifty, with minimal actual recovery to fifty-one in 2002. President Bush's own shortfall among the electorate mattered doubly because of his party's Senate losses. It meant that ordinary politics, absent the political uses of law,

would be pumping a dry well in the Senate and would leave social conservatives as unprovided-for as ever.

21. The relationship Bush constructed with social conservatives is detailed in Ivins and DeBose, *supra*; Fred Barnes, *The Impresario: Karl Rove, Orchestrator of the Bush White House*, Wkly. Standard (Aug. 20, 2001).

22. John C. Green, Mark J. Rozell, & Clyde Wilcox, *The Christian Right in American Politics* 67–73 (2003).

23. Id. at 23.

24. DuBose, Reid, & Cannon, *supra*.

25. It began with the development and promotion of a case against him by Princeton professor Robert P. George, conducted as far as possible from the eyes of the press by the internal communications of the social conservative movement. By 2000 it was no longer taken as remarkable that one of the nation's leading Catholic intellectuals taking part in the political world would help unseat a nonsectarian candidate for attorney general so an ardent Pentecostal could get the post. George's role itself represented the culmination of a decades-long development: an ecumenical approach that came, not from the left (ordinarily considered more the sponsors of interfaith tolerance dialogue), but from the right within each faith. Its developers were spurred on by a shared low tolerance for cultural freedoms—in short, an ecumenical intolerance.

George spoke with authority as a leading philosopher on the relation of law to Thomistic philosophy in general and social conservative legal issues in particular. A fine account of the campaign that unseated Racicot for Ashcroft is in Mike Allen, *Montana Gov. Didn't Have Right Stuff*, Wash. Post (Jan. 2, 2001). Also see James Carney, *How Bush Chose Ashcroft*, Time (Jan. 22, 2001).

26. The president wanted someone at the RNC who would not unduly surrender the party's organizational apparatus to social conservatives, as the Texas Republican Party had been surrendered. Social conservatives gained a form of ideological patronage, while the regular patronage of party organization was reserved for those with personal loyalty.

27. *Justice: Lightning Rod Defends "Aggressive" Tactics*, Nat'l J. (Jan. 25, 2003) (interview with Ashcroft).

28. Ashcroft's confirmation may well have been in some early doubt. With *Bush v. Gore* barely a month old, minorities remained highly incensed about disenfranchisement in Florida. Moderate Northern Senate Republicans worried seriously about identification with Ashcroft, who symbolized both the intolerant strain in Southern Republicans and, by losing his own border state to a dead opponent, the large extent of Republican Senate losses. The collapse of Linda Chavez's nomination for secretary of labor showed what could happen.

29. Asked about the constitutionality of firearms restrictions, he repeated his Second Amendment views, with the seeming concession that "I don't believe the Second Amendment to be one that forbids any regulation of guns" (apparently meaning only that his view would not preclude all regulation of

every type of gun; maybe children should not bring machine guns to school, for example).

30. Coming from Racicot, this pledge could have been taken at face value. Coming from Ashcroft, it merely meant undermining *Roe* in a different fashion when the time came—by chipping away rather than by frontal assault. Asked about legislation he had opposed that protected access to abortion clinics, Ashcroft now promised to enforce it, a promise he honorably fulfilled. Neil A. Lewis & David Johnston, *In Hearing's Second Day, Ashcroft Says He Would Not Challenge* Roe *Ruling*, N.Y. Times (Jan. 18, 2001); David Johnston & Neil A. Lewis, *In Testimony, Ashcroft Vows to Enforce Laws He Dislikes*, N.Y. Times (Jan. 17, 2001).

31. Regarding the nominating and confirmation of Olson, two opposing views can be found in Alexander Wohl, *Bush's Tenth Justice*, Am. Prospect (May 21, 2001); Kate O'Beirne, *The Olson Project: Democrats against a Bush Nominee*, Nat'l Rev. (June 11, 2001).

32. In an interesting essay for the far-right (but self-described "libertarian") Cato Institute entitled "Politicizing the Justice Department," Olson threw into the stew dozens of conservative complaints, including that Clinton was too hard on tobacco companies, under the label that "the rule of law has suffered under the reign of Janet Reno." Theodore B. Olson, *Politicizing the Justice Department*, in Pilon, *supra*, at 156.

33. When it emerged that Olson had indeed worked very closely with the key figures in the Arkansas Project, who paid him for marshaling legal support for their positions, he justified his sweeping sworn denial by claiming that he did not understand his involvement to be formal. Olson thereby repeated the kind of problematic statement under oath that had nearly led to his indictment for false testimony in the 1980s in a Reagan-era environmental matter; but this simply enhanced his right-wing credentials.

Olson suffered terrible personal tragedy later under special circumstances, when his wife was killed aboard one of the highjacked planes on 9/11.

34. Jim Oliphant, *Profile of Viet Dinh*, Legal Times (Dec. 17, 2001).

35. Intellectually Dinh, like Olson, supported the isolated legal positions held only by justices Scalia and Thomas or social conservatives. In time, Dinh received an especially outsized opportunity, because occupants of two posts that would normally overshadow his, the White House counsel and the head of the department's Office of Legal Counsel, gladly ceded him the role of point man.

36. Peter Nicholas & Matea Gold, *Schwarzenegger Team Focuses on 2 Key Posts*, L.A. Times (Oct. 11, 2003), at 1.

37. Siobhan Gorman, *Ashcroft's Invisible Hand*, Nat'l J. (May 25, 2002).

38. Vanessa Blum, *John Ashcroft's Inner Circle*, Legal Times (Oct. 13, 2003). Ms. Blum has developed over the 2000s some of the best Justice Department sources in Washington; the story had about as much information as any reporter could get out of so closed a political operation.

39. Id. Having done oversight of the Justice Department during the entire Reagan–first Bush years, I would have to say that even Ed Meese, though as close an adviser to Reagan as anyone and intensely political in what he did, had a less political style—that is, was more open to, and relied more on, senior officials with official responsibility and accountability—in his running of the department. For background on previous attorneys general up to and including Meese, see Nancy V. Baker, *Conflicting Loyalties: Law and Politics in the Attorney General's Office, 1789–1990* (1992); Cornell W. Clayton, *The Politics of Justice: The Attorney General and the Making of Legal Policy* (1992).

40. Dan Eggen, *Minorities Less Visible at Justice after Departures*, Wash. Post (Oct. 12, 2003), at A9.

41. The administration's legal strategy on abortion rights and particularly on the D&X procedure is discussed in Heather A. Smith, Comment, *A New Prescription for Abortion*, 73 U. Colo. L. Rev. 1069 (2002). For background on the relation of politics and law on the abortion rights issue, see Neal Devins: *Shaping Constitutional Values: Elected Government, the Supreme Court, and the Abortion Debate* (1996).

42. Sarah Wildman, *Bullies in the Pulpit: Will a Political Catholic Church Help or Hinder the GOP?* Am. Prospect (Oct. 2003), at 19–20.

43. Michael Barone with Richard E. Cohen, *The Almanac of American Politics, 2002*, at 621.

44. The stem cell discussion is based on David L. Corn, *The Lies of George W. Bush* 117–25 (2003).

45. The term "Mexico City Policy" derives from the Reagan administration's announcing conservative's new direction on this issue at the second International Population Conference in Mexico City in 1984. The actual implementing executive order was issued in March 2001. For a discussion of the policy, see Elizabeth Rohrbaugh, *On Our Way to Ten Billion Human Beings: A Comment on Sustainability and Population*, 5 Colo. J. Int'l Envt'l. L. & Pol'y 235 (1994).

46. Ann H. Ehrlich & James Salzman, *The Importance of Population Growth to Sustainability*, 32 Envt'l L. Rep. 10559 (2002).

47. Smith, Comment, *supra*, at 1070.

48. Julia Duin, *Abortion Words Block U.N. Draft*, Wash. Times (Aug. 31, 2001), at A14.

49. James Dao, *At U.N. Family-Planning Talks, U.S. Raises Abortion Issue*, N.Y. Times (Dec. 15, 2002).

50. Sharon Lerner, *Saviors of the Children*, Village Voice (May 14, 2002), at 45.

51. Rachel Farkas, *The Bush Administration's Decision to Defund the United Nations Population Fund and its Implications for Women in Developing Nations*, 18 Berkeley Women's L.J. 237 (2003).

52. Mike Allen, *Powell Calls Resignation Report "Gossip,"* Wash. Post (Aug. 5, 2003), at A2. Some speculated that the slot, if open, could go to

Condoleeza Rice. She didn't bring the difficulties of Powell, who had a national constituency among moderates. That rankled the conservative vote manipulators. Rice had no constituency of her own—surely the black community did not consider her one of their own fighters for social justice. She did what she was told and let Cheney and Bush call the shots.

53. Juliet Eilperin & Dana Milbank, *Bush May Cut U.N. Program's Funding: No Final Decision, But State Department Told to Plan Withholding Family Planning Aid*, Wash. Post (June 29, 2002), at A4.

54. Farkas, *supra*, at 251–52.

55. D&X is not the only method used late in pregnancy, so even this term reflects the way anti-abortion activists have shaped the issue.

56. "[Led by their] commander, House Speaker Newt Gingrich . . . the [congressional] Republicans . . . barred federal employees health insurance from covering abortions. They outlawed the use of American military hospitals for abortions on U.S. servicewomen and dependents of soldiers stationed abroad. They banned federal funding of abortions for federal prisoners. And they eliminated 35 percent of U.S. aid to international family planning programs." William Saletan, *Bearing Right: How Conservatives Won the Abortion War* 229 (2003).

57. Id. at 234.

58. 530 U.S. 914 (June 28, 2000).

59. Id.

60. The story of Bush's 1978 position is best told in Corn, *Lies of George W. Bush, supra*, at 21–22.

61. Green, Rozell, & Wilcox, *supra*, at 71. This is from the illuminating chapter about Texas, cowritten by Professor James W. Lamare, author of *Texas Politics: Economics, Power and Policy* (7th ed. 2000).

62. Saletan, *supra*, at 251.

63. *Transcript of Debate between Vice President Gore and Governor Bush*, N.Y. Times (Oct. 4, 2000), at A30.

64. *Women's Medical Profession Corp. v. Taft*, 162 F. Supp. 2d 929 (S.D. Ohio 2001).

65. Clinton beat Bush in 1992—another "technicality," but he was elected by the people of the United States, not by five conservative Justices.

66. Partial-Birth Abortion Ban Act of 2002, H. Rept. no. 107-604, 107th Cong., 2d Sess. 152–53 (2002) (dissenting views).

67. Jennifer A. Dlouhy, *Court Challenge a Sure Thing for "Partial Birth" Abortion Ban*, Cong. Q. Wkly. Rep. (June 7, 2003), at 1385, 1387.

68. Id.

69. Melissa C. Holsinger, *The Partial-Birth Abortion Ban Act of 2003: The Congressional Reaction to Stenberg v. Carhart*, 6 N.Y.U. J. Legis. & Pub. Pol'y 603, 609–10 (2003).

70. "Repeatedly through the [2003] process . . . critics faulted the legislation for its lack of a health exception. . . . [O]pponents offered such language, but

each time, the proposals were defeated, mostly along party lines." Jennifer A. Dlouhy, *Cleared "Partial Birth" Ban on Fast Track to Court*, Cong. Q. Wkly. Rep. (Oct. 25, 2003), at 2635.

71. For perspective on the Family Research Council and its tight connection to the Republican right wing, see Laurie Goodstein, *Religious Right, Frustrated, Trying New Tactic on G.O.P.*, N.Y. Times (March 23, 1998), at A1.

72. Jim Whittle, *War of the Worldviews: Family Research Council, Washington Allies Fight for Religious Right Agenda in Nation's Capital*, Church & State (May 1, 2003).

73. Richard M. Doerflinger, *Challenges for a Somewhat Pro-life Congress*, America (June 9, 2003).

74. Gail Glidewell, Note, *"Partial Birth" Abortion and the Health Exception: Protecting Maternal Health or Risking Abortion on Demand?* 28 Fordham Urb. L.J. 1089 (2001).

75. Ramesh Ponnuru, *Abortion Now: Thirty Years after Roe, a Daunting Landscape*, Nat'l Review (Jan. 27, 2003).

76. The current status of state legislation imposing such requirements can be found on Web sites such as http://www.reproductiverights.org.

77. As noted above, in Ohio the test case on late-term abortion legislation concerned a particular clinic, Women's Medical Professional Corporation. For other legal attacks on that clinic, see, e.g., *Women's Medical Professional Corp. v. Baird*, 2003 Lexis 15623 (S.D. Ohio Aug. 15, 2003).

78. Keith Perine, *Abortion Rights Advocates Spurn Fetus Protection Bill*, Cong. Q. Wkly. Rep. (July 19, 2003), at 1825, 1826.

79. Jennifer A. Dlouhy, *Abortion Foes' Busy Agenda*, Cong. Q. Wkly. Rep. (July 19, 2003), at 1827.

80. Smith, Comment, *supra.*

81. The so-called legal "conscience clause" in federal law protects Catholic doctors who have personal objections to abortion from having to perform any. Such a provision, in itself, was widely accepted.

82. This could occur even if the institution was essential to the procedure's availability, was not intrinsically objectionable, and basically was being held hostage by that movement's pressure.

83. Dlouhy, *Cleared "Partial Birth" Ban on Fast Track to Court, supra*, at 2634.

84 In this situation Ashcroft's judges might protect the doctors from harassment. Maybe.

85. This could occur without either the newly appointed justice having to expressly champion overruling *Roe* right away or the previously sitting justices having to renounce already stated positions.

86. Fine treatments of the support for the classic interpretation of the Second Amendment, and the debunking of the NRA theory of the personal right to firearms, occur in Carl T. Bogus, *The History and Politics of Second Amendment Scholarship: A Primer*, 76 Chi.-Kent L. Rev. 3 (2000); Robert J. Spitzer,

Lost and Found: Researching the Second Amendment, 76 Chi.-Kent L. Rev. 349 (2000); Michael C. Dorf, *What Does the Second Amendment Mean Today?* 76 Chi.-Kent L. Rev. 291 (2000).

87. Repeatedly, the Supreme Court addressed the Second Amendment—in 1876, 1886, 1894, and definitively again in 1939. Each time, the Court held that it precludes only infringement of the people's collective right to bear arms within the militia and establishes no individual right to firearms for personal use. Around twenty lower courts held the same. After the 1939 Supreme Court case, the issue of firearms rights was not meaningfully posed again until the Gun Control Act of 1968. By the early 1990s the individual right theory did enjoy a slight degree of acceptance from academics most of whom did not espouse conservative views, especially Sanford Levinson, Lawrence Tribe, and Akhil Amar.

88. In 1993–1994 the Clinton administration helped enact two firearms regulation measures—the Brady Bill, for background checks before sale of guns, and a general ban on sales of assault weapons.

89. Ivins & Dubose, *supra,* at 44.

90. To counter that impression, the NRA in 1995 orchestrated congressional hearings on the 1993 standoff between a heavily armed apocalyptic cult in Waco, Texas, and federal authorities. I represented Joyce Sparks, a Waco social worker called as a witness in those hearings. Sparks played a message left on her telephone answering machine by the NRA, revealing the organization's extensive role in the ostensibly government-run hearings.

91. A thorough study is Violence Policy Center, *John Ashcroft: Year One* (Jan. 2002).

92. This stance went back to the 1939 Supreme Court case, where the Justice Department successfully opposed the notion of an individual right to firearms. To show the venerable nature of the position, a 1973 Nixon administration letter from the Office of Legal Counsel to this effect was quoted in a 2000 letter from the solicitor general (and the department had issued nothing to the contrary between 1973 and 2000 or indeed since it first took a position at all in 1939):

> The language of the Second Amendment . . . makes it quite clear that it was the right of the States to maintain a militia that was being preserved, not the rights of an individual to own a gun. . . . [I]t must be considered as settled that there is no personal constitutional right, under the Second Amendment, to own or to use a gun.
>
>> Letter by Solicitor General Seth P. Waxman, Aug. 22, 2000 (quoting letter by Mary C. Lawton, deputy assistant attorney general, Office of Legal Counsel, July 19, 1973), reprinted as appendix B to Violence Policy Center, *Shot Full of Holes: Deconstructing John Ashcroft's Second Amendment* (July 2001). This report cites the pertinent congressional testimony and Justice Department briefs.

93. The quotes are from David S. Cloud, *Justice Department Is Shifting Stance on Gun Rights,* Wall St. J. (July 11, 2001), at A3.

94. 270 F.3d 203 (5th Cir. 2001).

95. The decision in *Emerson* upheld a 1993 provision barring firearms purchases by persons under court order not to threaten their spouses or children. It was not a hard or close case, and it most certainly did not call for reaching and deciding the ultimate issues of Second Amendment jurisprudence.

96. *United States v. Emerson, supra,* at 273–74 (Justice Parker specially concurring).

97. The November 2001 memo is discussed in Violence Policy Center, *John Ashcroft: Year One, supra,* at 7.

98. That request was virtually frivolous, and was even filed in forma pauperis (meaning by a poor person under exceptions to the normal rules)—a form of petition that ranks extremely low in the Court's priorities. Or he might have filed a brief confined to a simple explanation to the Court why the case should be considered unworthy of its attention.

99. 536 U.S. 639 (2002).

100. "Although Racicot was often described as 'pro-life' during his previous campaigns and had been endorsed by the Montana chapter of the National Right to Life Committee, his new conservative critics said they felt he had not expended political capital to promote additional restrictions on abortion. His critics had the same feeling about his views *on school choice:* his stated views were fine, but *he had not done as much* as [others] to show leadership on the issue, they said." Allen, *Montana Gov. Didn't Have Right Stuff, supra,* at A1 (italics added). "School choice" is conservatives' phrase for the voucher issue. That "he had not done as much . . . to show leadership on the issue" means he had just not displayed the intensity required by social conservatives. Mike Allen's article was the *Washington Post's* front-page contemporaneous exploration of how social conservatives shot down Ashcroft's rival and made him attorney general; it was good journalism.

101. On Election Day 2000, ballot initiatives to create voucherlike statewide tax-refund programs lost in California and Michigan, despite multimillion-dollar campaigns. In December 2000 a federal appeals court affirmed in a 2–1 decision a district court decision invalidating the Cleveland program. Goldstein, *supra.*

102. Lizette Alvarez, *Senate Rejects Tuition Aid, a Key to Bush Education Plan,* Wash. Post (June 13, 2001).

103. Greenhouse, *supra.*

104. Usually, absent a request from the Court for an expression of views, the solicitor general does not file a brief on whether it should hear a case in which the United States is not a party and has no direct institutional stake.

105. Olson echoed the Bush campaign's rhetoric about "expanding education opportunity for children enrolled in failing public schools."

106. *Bush Administration Urges High Court to Uphold Religious School Vouchers, supra.*

107. When the district court initially invalidated the Cleveland program, the Supreme Court had temporarily blocked the order. This suggested that the conservative justices who wanted to take up the issue of vouchers had their eyes on the case.

108. That specific constitutional issue consisted of whether vouchers, as an indirect method by which taxpayer funding went to religious institutions, constituted an "establishment of religion," and, hence completely against the First Amendment's Establishment Clause. Precedent gave a large role on this question to examining factually whether such indirect aid flowed evenly to sectarian and nonsectarian alternatives.

109. *Equal Protection of the Law for Faith-Based and Community Organizations*, Executive Order 13279, 67 Fed. Reg. 77141 (Dec. 12, 2002).

110. Bill Swindell, *Renewed Push for "Faith Based" Law Faces Hostile Democrats, Tight Calendar*, 61 Cong. Q. Wkly. Rep. 511 (March 1, 2003).

111. For descriptions of the sequence on this issue, see Brad Knickerbocker, *Assisted-Suicide Movement Gets a Boost*, Christian Sci. Mon. April 19, 2002; Adam Liptak, *Judge Blocks U.S. Bid to Ban Suicide Law*, N.Y. Times, April, 18, 2002. For fuller legal analysis, see Christina E. Manuel, *Physician-Assisted Suicide Permits Dignity in Dying: Oregon Takes on Attorney General Ashcroft*, 23 J. Legal Med. 563 (2002); Lindsay F. Wiley, *Assisted Suicide: Court Strikes Down Ashcroft Directive*, 30 J. L. Med. & Ethics 459 (2002).

112. Senate Judiciary Hearing, April 25, 2000; House Judiciary Hearing, June 24, 1999.

113. He would tolerate states' autonomy—such as when lax states wanted to ease up on industrial water polluters—or bring the federal boot down on states—such as when a state implemented the public's tolerance for individual choice on physician-assisted suicide—as it served his political convenience. Because the administration shrouded its policy deliberations in secrecy, it was never revealed whether the initial impetus to do what the social conservatives wanted came, as rumor had it, through their pipeline on such issues to Rove at the White House or the White House simply unleashed Ashcroft to implement his Senate stance. Jim Barnett, *Bush Policy on Suicide Is Shielded in Secrecy*, Oregonian (Nov. 11, 2001).

114. *State of Oregon v. Ashcroft*, 192 F. Supp. 2d 1077 (D. Ore. 2002).

115. Joe Klein, *How the Supremes Redeemed Bush*, Time (July 7, 2003), at 27.

116. For the spectrum of Catholic comments on Santorum's remarks, see Gill Donovan, *Santorum's Remarks Draw Both Affirmation, Criticism from Catholics*, Nat'l Catholic Rep. (May 9, 2003), at 12. On the Bush strategy, see Eleanor Clift, *Standing by Their Man*, Newsweek Web Exclusive (April 25, 2003) in Lexis-Nexis database for news sources.

117. Who knows, maybe he'd actually get some mileage, compassion image–wise, out of ultraright criticism of Cheney for standing by his openly lesbian daughter. After all, wasn't it compassionate to stand by Cheney on this

matter, Bush refraining himself from putting a fingerprint down anywhere except to say that he thought men and women got married? Even in his beloved Saudi Arabia, that proposition was true (only they allowed the man a few extras and the woman's legal status was more like that of a camel than a person).

118. *The War over Gay Marriage*, Newsweek (July 7, 2003), at 38.

119. Two fine overviews of the issue can be found in Michael J. Gerhardt, *Norm Theory and the Future of the Federal Appointments Process*, 50 Duke L.J. 1687 (2001); Tracey E. George, *Court Fixing*, 43 Ariz. L. Rev. 9 (2001); and sources cited in each.

120. For example, President Eisenhower put Earl Warren and William Brennan on the Court for political reasons relating, respectively, to California and to Catholics and obviously not to their ideology, which he did not share. Even conservatives of Nixon's era were satisfied with some general reinforcement of the judicial center and cared more about the historic Republican regard for judicial temperament and objective qualifications than about archconservative ideology. Apart from the choice of Justice Rehnquist, President Nixon had, after all, appointed moderates like justices Blackmun and Powell. Even his appointment of Chief Justice Burger, though he was somewhat conservative by that era's standards, hardly qualified according to the standards of the 2000s—considering that he joined in *Roe v. Wade*—as a social conservative choice.

121. For a conservative defense of the Reagan administration's appointments, see Eastland, *supra*, at 235–77.

122. His Supreme Court picks, justices Breyer and Ginsburg, each had some definitely centrist attitudes (he being market-oriented on regulation, she prosecutorial on rights of the accused). Most of his lower court choices brought much-needed gender and race diversity but took their doctrinal lead from the Rehnquist Court without balking. In 1995–96 and 1999–2000, President Clinton faced a Republican Senate that tried to hold back his judicial choices for the lower courts in order to keep vacancies open for a hoped-for Republican President, generating controversy over delay tactics.

123. *Halting the Juggernaut: Can the Dems on the Senate Judiciary Committee Block the Takeover of the Courts?* Am. Prospect (July 2, 2001).

124. Distinguished witnesses, from Lawrence Tribe on the left to Ronald Rotunda on the right, discoursed on the Senate confirmation process for judges. The hearings made clear how unique was the contemporary confrontational process. For example, witnesses explained that until 1955, it was virtually unheard of for Supreme Court nominees to appear at a Senate hearing for any questioning at all. The political patronage of the past had focused upon geographic and ethnic balance, for which a grilling of the nominee about ideology was irrelevant as well as unseemly. Ideological judicial patronage was a comparatively recent development.

125. People for the American Way, *John Ashcroft's First Year as Attorney General: Judicial Nominations* (2002), http://www.pfaw.org.

126. My brief is noted in Erwin Chemerinsky, *The Court Should Have Remained Silent: Why the Court Erred in Deciding Dickerson v. United States,* 149 U. Pa. L. Rev. 287, 308 (2000).

127. *Dickerson v. United States,* 530 U.S. 428 (2000).

128. Brown made the speech before the Chicago chapter of the Federalist Society in 2000. Jonathan Groner, *Rough Hearing Bodes Ill for Nominee,* Legal Times (Oct. 27, 2003), at 10.

129. Jonathan Groner, *Survival Guide: The Politics of Judicial Nominations Is More Complicated Than Ever: Why Some Controversial Picks Are Making It Through, While Others Are Getting Stopped Cold,* Legal Times (May 5, 2003), at 1. Groner had the unique combination of his own excellent journalistic and legal skills and his long-term cultivation, from the special listening post of the *Legal Times,* of the city's most useful sources.

130. Groner, *Rough Hearing Bodes Ill for Nominee, supra.*

131. *President's State of the Union Message to Congress and the Nation,* N.Y. Times (Jan. 21, 2004), at A15.

132. In discussing what moved Pryor into the position of poster child on this issue, the *National Catholic Reporter* noted that Judiciary Committee Democrats had questioned Pryor "for supporting the recently overturned Texas anti-sodomy statute" and about "a canceled family excursion to Disney World; it was 'gay day' at the park and Pryor didn't want his children exposed to it." Feuerherd, *supra.*

133. Bush's lawyer in charge of protections against wrongful retribution against federal employees, Scott L. Bloch, removed references to sexual orientation from the list of what could not be used as a justification for dismissal. Stephen Barr, *Gay Rights Information Taken off Site,* Wash. Post (Feb. 18, 2004), at A17. Bloch was previously counsel to the Task Force for Faith-Based and Community Initiatives at Ashcroft's Justice Department. He noted "that sexual orientation is not mentioned as a basis for discrimination in existing civil rights laws or in the statute under which [his office] operates," as Washington's conservative newspaper gleefully trumpeted. Jerry Seper, *Counsel Questions "Protected-Class" Status of Gays: Suspends Enforcement of Harassment Claims During Analysis,* Wash. Times (March 22, 2004), at A3. The White House later announced that it would continue to view the law as prohibiting discrimination on the basis of sexual orientation. However, Bloch remained in place, and the view he had expressed probably signaled where the administration would eventually end up, if not precisely how it would get there.

134. David Orgon Coolidge & William C. Duncan, *Reaffirming Marriage: A Presidential Priority,* 24 Harv. J.L. & Pub. Pol'y 623, 649–50 (2001).

135. Patricia A. Cain, *Federal Tax Consequences of Civil Unions,* 30 Cap. U. L. Rev. 387 (2002).

136. Alimony in marriages is said, in the vernacular, to be tax "deductible" by the support-paying partner (more precisely, it is excludible from adjusted gross income). Child support obligations of one partner affect tax treatment of various items. Some believe DOMA already resolves all these issues, but the

future of the law in this context, especially given the possible constitutional considerations, is hardly crystal clear.

137. See, generally, Tony Mauro, *Rocky Path for Gay Rights Cases despite Lawrence*, Legal Times (Feb. 9, 2004), at 1.

3. FLOUTING CIVIL LIBERTIES: LIBRARIES OR WEAPONS?

1. For a look back at how reactions involving heightened security have historically been coupled with repression, see David Cole, *The New McCarthyism: Repeating History in the War on Terrorism*, 38 Harv. C.R.-C.L. L. Rev. 1 (2003).

2. Jim McGee & Brian Duffy, *Someone to Watch over Us*, Wash. Post (June 23, 1996), at W9.

3. Id. The article by McGee and Duffy is based on extracts from their book *Main Justice*.

4. *Cong. Q. Almanac* (1995), at 6-18–6-21; *Cong. Q. Almanac* (1996), at 5-18–5-26.

5. The shrill critique of Reno as too strongly opposed to far-right causes spanned her whole tenure, from her confrontation in 1993 with the armed cult group in Waco to her removal in 2000 of the refugee boy Elian Gonzalez from the Cuban American group making propaganda use of him. A conservative treatment of these subjects is in Pilon, ed., *supra*.

6. Dan Eggen & Guy Gugliotta, *FBI Secretly Trying to Re-create Anthrax from Mail Attacks*, Wash. Post (Nov. 2, 2002), at A9.

7. A conservative account of the 2000 rejection is James Bovard, *Rise of the Surveillance State*, American Spectator (May 2000).

8. For background on the 1996 legislation that coupled only some of what Clinton sought as counterterrorism provisions with promotion of the conservative Republican agenda on the death penalty, see James S. Liebman, *An "Effective Death Penalty"? AEDPA and Error Detection in Capital Cases*, 67 Brook. L. Rev. 411 (2001).

9. Congress's responsibility started with Republicans rewarding FBI director Louis Freeh for lending political help against Reno and Clinton, which meant the bureaucratic flaws of FBI counterterrorism escaped what turned out to be urgently needed scrutiny. Daniel Franklin, *Freeh's Reign: At Louis Freeh's FBI, with Carte Blanche from Congressional Republicans, Real Cops Didn't Do Intelligence and Counterterrorism*, American Prospect (Jan. 1, 2002), at 20.

10. Adam Clymer, *How Sept. 11 Changed Goals of Justice Dept.: Fighting Terror Didn't Lead Ashcroft's List*, N.Y. Times (Feb. 28, 2002), at 1.

11. *Justice: From the Ashes of 9/11: Big Bad John*, Nat'l J. (Jan. 25, 2003).

12. These included undermining efforts to pass federal hate crimes legislation and overturning career prosecutors to push for increased use of the death penalty in what turned out to be a racially disproportionate fashion. Staff Report, *The Death Penalty Becomes a High-Profile Issue*, Fed. Lawyer (Sept. 2002), at 34, 39–40.

13. See Cole, *supra,* at 24. That sweep, in its nonpolitical components, inevitably reflected law enforcement's desperation. The FBI must know that, of the thousands of noncitizens they rapidly went about detaining, relatively few actually deserved detention of serious duration. However, in the short run, the FBI lacked any other sufficient response in the wake of 9/11.

14. Law enforcement had no way effectively to sort out the hundreds of thousands of noncitizens with some degree of Islamic or Arabic identification present in the country. The detention discouraged further arrivals and encouraged rapid departures in suspicious categories, and hurriedly if crudely remedied to some degree the suddenly intolerable extent of law enforcement ignorance about that population.

15. To quote the Vichy police chief who orders a postcrime sweep in the movie *Casablanca.*

16. On the Judiciary hearing, see Eric Lichtblau, *Ashcroft Seeks More Power to Pursue Terror Suspects,* N.Y. Times (June 6, 2003), at A1. The Justice Department's line to the press is in Eric Lichtblau, *U.S. Report Faults the Roundup of Illegal Immigrants after 9/11,* N.Y. Times (June 3, 2003), at 1.

17. Adam Liptak, Neil A. Lewis, & Benjamin Weiser, *After Sept. 11, a Legal Battle on the Limits of Civil Liberty,* N.Y. Times (Aug. 4, 2002), at 1; David Cole, *Enemy Aliens,* 54 Stan. L. Rev. 953 (2002).

18. Ashcroft and Dinh justified the proposed order on their interpretation of the Supreme Court's precedent on this subject, the case of the World War II Nazi saboteurs. See Louis Fisher, *Nazi Saboteurs on Trial: A Military Tribunal and American Law* (2003).

19. Neil A. Lewis, *Ashcroft's Terrorism Policies Dismay Some Conservatives,* N.Y. Times (July 24, 2002), at 1.

20. The conservative side of the issue is laid out in David Kopel, *Terrorism and Guns,* Nat'l Rev. (Dec. 17, 2001), and in Byron York, *Gunning for Ashcroft,* Nat'l Rev. (Dec. 6, 2001).

21. The NRA sued to challenge the retention period, but a federal appeals court dismissed the suit in July 2000. That court's thoughtful opinion noted that the NRA-supported attempts to insert the word *immediately* in the provision had failed both during passage of the original Brady Law and in the 1998 effort. Social conservatives who wanted rapid destruction of the NICS records trail simply lacked the support to win through ordinary political processes. *National Rifle Association v. Reno,* 216 F.2d 122 (D.C. Cir. 2000).

22. Meanwhile, Republicans dropped efforts to pass an immediate-destruction provision in Congress. Quite likely, social conservatives calculated they had a better chance at achieving their goal via the administration than through the regular appropriation processes in Congress. A losing effort made through democratic processes on Capitol Hill would only highlight the public's continued condemnation of such unpopular and extreme gambits.

23. Fox Butterfield, *Justice Dept. Bars Use of Gun Checks in Terror Inquiry,* N.Y. Times (Dec. 6, 2001), at A1.

24. Id. As a former Clinton administration attorney involved in writing such rules, Mathew Nosanchuk, explained, "A fair interpretation is that if there is a terrorist act, and that if you have a basis to think a person was in a prohibited category, it would be O.K. for law enforcement to check the records to see if a person purchased a gun."

25. Fox Butterfield, *Ashcroft's Words Clash with Staff on Checks*, N.Y. Times (July 24, 2002), at A14.

26. Id. (emphasis added).

27. Peter Slevin, *Ashcroft Blocks FBI Access to Gun Records: Critics Call Attorney General's Decision Contradictory in Light of Terror Probe Tactics*, Wash. Post (Dec. 7, 2001).

28. Gene Collier, *Bill Takes Aim at Checks on Gun Buyers*, Pittsburgh Post-Gazette (Feb. 1, 2004).

29. Debra Rosenberg, *Gun Control; "Gored"? Note in '04*, Newsweek (Jan. 19, 2004), at 8 (noting the "major pieces of gun legislation on deck in Congress—including the assault weapons ban and a proposal to grant gun makers and dealers immunity from lawsuits").

30. H. L. Mencken's comment that "patriotism is the last refuge of the scoundrel" raises a question about a leader who would give his proposed statute such a title.

31. Nat Hentoff, *The War on the Bill of Rights and the Gathering Resistance* (2003).

32. Sign quoted in Nikki Swartz, *Information at a Price: Liberty vs. Security*, Info. Mgmt. J. (May 1, 2003).

33. June Kronholz, *Patriot Act Riles an Unlikely Group: Nation's Librarians*, Wall St. J. (Oct. 28, 2003), at A1, A6.

34. Audrey Hudson, *Librarians Dispute Justice's Claim on Use of Patriot Act*, Wash. Times (Sept. 19, 2003), at A10.

35. One of the nation's premier legal news reporters explained the paperwork in a related context: "The reason the FISA court grants so many of the wiretap requests, the official added, is that by the time they reach the court they have been exhaustively reviewed.... When the FBI wants to wiretap someone, it sends over a two- or three-page document known as a letterhead memorandum, signed by the assistant FBI director for national security. A special office at the Justice Department . . . decides whether to recommend to [the attorney general] that [he or she] seek the wiretap." Naftali Bendavid, *China Spy Probe Puts Spotlight on Hush-Hugh Court*, Chicago Trib. (May 27, 1999), at 1.

36. It is also possible that if a librarian said, "Come back with your court order," the FBI agents, having mentioned their PATRIOT Act authority, simply shrugged and walked away. Many of their inquiries may not have mattered that much to them; for example, snoopy library patrons may call the FBI with a "tip" that the agents barely think worth even a visit, not worth going up the chain of command to get the court order. In other words, sometimes FBI agents may bluff, and librarians may call their bluff.

37. A subsequent book by two *Wall Street Journal* reporters, Jane Mayer and Jill Abramson, found the following (from a *Newsweek* review): "During the hearings, Thomas claimed he had no interest in pornography. But Abramson and Mayer interviewed a video-store owner who said Thomas was a regular in the X-rated section, and found a prominent Washington lawyer who said he saw Thomas leaving the store with a film called 'The Adventures of Big Mama Jama.'" Lincoln Caplan, *Who Lied?* Newsweek (Nov. 14, 1994) (reviewing Jane Mayer & Jill Abramson, *Strange Justice* [1994]).

38. Clarence Thomas's opening statement on October 11, 1991, included the following:

> I will not allow this committee or anyone else to probe into my private life. This is not what America is all about. To ask me to do that would be to ask me to go beyond fundamental fairness. . . . No job is worth what I've been through—no job. . . . I never asked to be nominated. . . . I enjoy and appreciate my current position, and I am comfortable with the prospect of returning to my work as a judge on the U.S. Court of Appeals for the D.C. Circuit. . . .
>
> I will not provide the rope for my own lynching, or for further humiliation. I am not going to engage in discussions, nor will I submit to roving questions of what goes on in the most intimate parts of my private life, or the sanctity of my bedroom. These are the most intimate parts of my privacy, and they will remain just that: private.
>
> > Thomas, *This Is Worse Than Any Obstacle . . . That I Have Ever Faced,* Wash. Post (Oct. 12, 1991), at A8 (quoting Thomas's statement).

39. David Streitfeld, *Lewinsky to Turn Over Book Purchase Information: Agreement Resolves 1st Amendment Dispute between Starr and Bookstore Owners,* Wash. Post (June 23, 1998), at A4.

40. It is technically redundant to say "FISC Court" since the C in *FISC* stands for "Court," but it might be clearer to the layperson who already may be aware of and confused by such terminological problems as that *fisc* is a word meaning "treasury" and *FICA* means (to every worker who sees a portion of his or her wages evaporate this way) the Social Security payroll tax.

41. Kathryn Martin, Note, *The USA PATRIOT Act's Application to Library Patron Records,* 29 J. Legis. 283, 299–300 (2003). The quoted material draws upon another article, by one of the nation's top experts on this subject, James X. Dempsey, *Civil Liberties in a Time of Crisis,* 29 Hum. Rts. Q. 8 (2002).

42. Roy Tennant, *Patriotism As If Our Constitution Matters,* Libr. J. (July 15, 2003), at 32.

43. Audrey Hudson, *"Patriot II" Bid Garners Little Favor on Hill,* Wash. Times (Sept. 12, 2003), at A1. When the hard-right *Washington Times* supportively quotes Senator Lieberman to lambaste Bush, the reader may well suspect that the president has gone too far.

44. On FBI abuses not revealed in FISC court proceedings, see McGee & Duffy, *supra*.

45. I emphasize that what follows is based wholly on reports in the *Washington Post* and the *Chicago Tribune* and that I myself do not confirm or deny anything said in those reports.

46. There is no finer treatment of the background before 9/11 than William C. Banks & M. E. Bowman, *Executive Authority for National Security Surveillance*, 50 Am. U. L. Rev. 1 (2000).

47. Gerald H. Robinson, Article, *We're Listening! Electronic Eavesdropping, FISA, and the Secret Court*, 36 Willamette L. Rev. 50, 70–71 (2000).

48. See David Hardin, Note, *The Fuss over Two Small Words: The Unconstitutionality of the USA PATRIOT Act Amendments to FISA under the Fourth Amendment*, 71 Geo. Wash. L. Rev. 291 (2003).

49. To take a simplified example, routine shoplifters, joyriders, forgers, smugglers, or anyone else of a criminal nature used to get investigated by the Fourth Amendment method—after all, the Bill of Rights says so. But now, if the FBI got the notion that even one connection or customer of such types might possibly hypothetically somehow get mixed in with the type of target FISA exists for—and the "underworld" is not like a department store, it's never clear where some teenager's quest for an ID to buy beer underage ends and some FISA suspect's quest for an ID for their own purposes begins—end of story for civil liberties.

50. Why bother with the labors required by the Fourth Amendment to get regular warrants for the shoplifter, joyrider, forger, smuggler, or anyone else, intended to protect the privacy of all of us who can easily, despite the best of personal records, find ourselves in an investigation's path, when, by waving the magic PATRIOT Act wand, everything became so much easier.

51. Stephen J. Schulhofer, *No Checks, No Balances: Discarding Bedrock Constitutional Principles*, in Richard C. Leone & Greg Anrig Jr., eds., *The War on Our Freedoms* 74, at 81 (2003).

52. Id. at 85.

53. At the request of bipartisan senators upset even at that early date by the PATRIOT Act, it gave the application of the Fourth Amendment in such circumstances a straightforward reading.

54. *In re: All Matters Submitted to the Foreign Intelligence Surveillance Court*, 18 F. Supp. 2d 611 (Foreign Intel. Surv. Ct. 2002).

55. The court did allow briefs to be filed by civil liberties groups.

56. *In re: Sealed Case*, 310 F.3d 7817, 746 (Foreign Intel. Surv. Ct. Rev. 2002).

57. Nat Hentoff, *No "Sneak and Peek": The House Rejects Funds for the Patriot Provision*, Wash. Times (Aug. 4, 2003), at A17. Hentoff has led the way in awakening the public to how the PATRIOT Act works.

58. Eric Lichtblau (Sept. 28, 2003), at 1; the spokesperson quote is on page 21.

59. Their bill updated surveillance laws to allow secret searches, tracking of Internet communications, nationwide court orders, information sharing by

grand juries with intelligence agencies, "roving wiretaps" covering different phones, and more curbs on money laundering.

60. The story is told in Robert Dreyfus, *John Ashcroft's Midnight Raid*, Rolling Stone (Nov. 22, 2001), at 47. My research assistant, Philip J. Sweitzer, did impressive research subsequently to document extensively the hard-to-track details.

61. The comment is quoted in Eric Lichtblau with Adam Liptak, *On Terror, Spying and Guns, Ashcroft Expands Reach*, N.Y. Times (March 15, 2003), at 1. Armey and the USA PATRIOT Act are discussed in Jeffrey Rosen, *Civil Right*, New Republic (Oct. 21, 2002).

62. A typical account reflecting how he built up his public image is Edward Klein, *We're Not Destroying Rights, We're Protecting Them*, Parade Magazine (May 19, 2002).

63. Lisa Finnegan Abdolian & Harold Takooshian, *The USA PATRIOT Act: Civil Liberties, the Media, and Public Opinion*, 30 Fordham Urb. L.J. 1429, 1445 (2003).

64. *Justice: From the Ashes of 9/11, supra.*

65. Padilla was the ineffective but nevertheless frightening American citizen who was caught coming into the United States allegedly to scout a terrible attack. His case went to the Supreme Court on the question of whether he could be treated, notwithstanding his citizenship, the way that, by legal tradition, only noncitizens are.

66. These cases would concern the government's ability to try citizens before military tribunals and the obstacles for the Guantánamo detainees in obtaining a review in federal courts. For a discussion of the issues in the cases, see Michael I. Greenberger, *Three Strikes and You're outside the Constitution*, Md. Bar J. (March–April 2004), at 14.

67. For a forum of the professionals, see http://www.crimesofwar.org. The Web site includes an exposition of the traditional due process safeguards in a tribunal under the heading "Prosecuting Al Qaeda: September 11 and Its Aftermath," posted by Jeffrey Walker on Dec. 14, 2001.

68. The historical background is treated in the sources cited in chapter 6 regarding the International Criminal Court. For application of this history to the detainees, see K. Elizabeth Dahlstrom, *The Executive Policy toward Detention and Trial of Foreign Citizens at Guantanamo Bay*, 21 Berkeley J. Int'l L. 662 (2003).

69. Josef Braml, *Rule of Law or Dictates by Fear: A German Perspective on American Civil Liberties in the War against Terrorism*, 27 Fletcher F. World Aff. (summer–fall 2003), at 115.

70. Richard A. Clarke, *Against All Enemies: Inside America's War on Terror* 246 (2004).

71. The report is available at the committee Web site, http://www.house.gov/hsc/democrats.

72. For sources on the following paragraph, see *America at Risk, supra*, at 12 (subchapter on preventing attacks by securing nuclear material), 35 (sub-

chapter on port security), 82 (subchapter on protecting chemical plants and the food supply), and 114 (chapter on preparing communities to deal with attacks).

4. DOMESTIC AFFAIRS VEER RIGHT

1. In earlier periods, the Republican Party's central purposes had been, to oversimplify, dealing with the Civil War and Reconstruction after 1860, keeping the tariff high from the late 1800s on, and serving business in other ways in the 1920s. It may seem ironic today that in the days when tariffs largely financed the federal government, the Republican Party, its conservative economic base craving protectionism, had loved high tax rates.

2. Richard Mellon Scaife, an eccentric, public-hating reactionary heir of the enormous Mellon fortune, ploughed vast sums into ginning up a far-right movement.

3. The best study is John B. Judis, *The Paradox of American Democracy: Elites, Special Interests, and the Betrayal of the Public Trust* (2001). See also Jean Stefancic & Richard Delgado, *No Mercy: How Conservative Think Tanks and Foundations Changed America's Social Agenda* (1997).

4. For an account from the viewpoint of key individual activists and their cohort, see Nina J. Easton, *Gang of Five: Leaders at the Center of the Conservative Ascendancy* (2002 ed.).

5. Thomas Byrne Edsall, *The New Politics of Inequality* (1984).

6. These interests decided to pour funds through the new channel of corporate and far-right ideological political action committees (PACs). Their money helped mobilize a turning of the tide so that the elections of 1978 and 1980 furnished a Republican Senate majority and a House majority of conservatives (Republicans plus cooperative conservative Southern Democrats) for President Reagan.

7. Pollack, *supra*, at 57–63.

8. The various components of the shift are summarized in Stonecash, *supra*, at 32–33.

9. Kevin Phillips, *Wealth and Democracy* 92 (2003 paperback ed.).

10. Watt vigorously opened previously safeguarded parks, wildlife refuges, and other public lands to overuse, clashing hard with environmentalists in Congress. For a fuller description of these steps by the Reagan administration, see Tiefer, *The Semi-Sovereign Presidency, supra*, at 27–28 (1994).

11. He joined the Congress in a bipartisan package of tax increases, spending cuts, and the Budget Enforcement Act, a set of tough budget enforcement procedures.

12. The first President Bush signed a genuinely reasonable revision of the Clean Air Act, with meaningful regulatory authority, in 1991 and a civil rights restoration act the same year, and in other respects took a breather from his predecessor's swing right in domestic affairs. However, even the first Bush White House had a powerful office, known as the "Quayle Council" (for Vice President Quayle), to curb environmental and other public-protecting

regulation in order to obtain special interest campaign support. For more on the Quayle Council, see Tiefer, *The Semi-Sovereign Presidency, supra,* at 61–88.

13. Specifically, the strategy involved quests for funds by senior party or committee leaders, used not for their individual purposes but for distribution through "leadership PACs" to promising challengers for seats held by Democrats. Hitherto, donors gave funds to party leaders or committee leaders for their own use, and by giving to those whose position gave them the most to sell in terms of moderate goals, this system maintained favorable aspects of the legislative status quo. Under the new funding scheme, senior party figures, some of them personally holding moderate views, now had to raise more money for use by others and do so by taking the positions pleasing to the hard-line donors. These party figures had to increasingly forgo moderate appeals, such as for the fiscally responsible course of limited tax cuts paid for with savings. For more on this strategy, see Balz & Brownstein, *supra,* at 48–49.

14. The insurance lobby's spending, and the larger polarization of conservative business elements against the Clinton health plan, is discussed in Judis, *supra,* at 213–16. For more on tobacco companies' involvement, see Darrell M. West, *Checkbook Democracy: How Money Corrupts Political Campaigns,* chapter 7 (2000).

15. Charles Tiefer, *Congressional Oversight of the Clinton Administration and Congressional Procedure,* 50 Admin. L. Rev. 199, 204 (1998).

16. This was money given, technically, for expenditure in nonfederal races and therefore treated by federal regulations differently than federal election "hard money." Used with skill, soft money could indirectly help federal candidates as a partial substitute for hard money. See Briffault, *supra,* at 628–31. For tables of soft money giving by year and party, see Ray La Raja, *Sources and Uses of Soft Money: What Do We Know?* in Gerald C. Lubenow, ed., *A User's Guide to Campaign Finance Reform,* 83, 93 (2001).

17. Abraham, *supra.*

18. The best explanation of Hicks's role is in Paul Krugman, *The Great Unraveling* (2003) at 291–92. For the 2002 stories about the university trust funds, see R. G. Ratcliffe, *UTIMCO Records Show Favors, Failures, Fortune,* Houston Chron. (Oct. 5, 2002), at A1; R. G. Ratcliffe, *The UTIMCO Connection,* Houston Chron. (Sept. 16, 2002), at A7. Earlier stories were published in 1999.

19. Abraham, *supra.*

20. R. G. Ratcliffe, *Return to Secrecy: Overseer of UT's Trust Fund Conceals Details on Investment Performances,* Houston Chron. (Sept. 16, 2002), at A1.

21. Phillips (2003 ed.), *supra,* at 324.

22. Id. The $2.5 billion figure for private funding comes from adding, to the hard money totals, soft money, but not public funding.

23. Phillips (2003 ed.), *supra,* at 326.

24. Each of these promises is discussed later in this chapter in connection with what he actually did in office.

25. Amy Borrus, *Surprise! Bush Is Emerging as a Fighter for Privacy on the Net,* Bus. Wk. (June 5, 2000), at 63.

26. This section draws on Tiefer, *How to Steal a Trillion, supra,* in which the technical issues are discussed in detail with extensive documentation.

27. The requirement of sixty Senate votes to pass controversial partisan bills became rock solid in the past quarter century when the array of subjects for the filibuster came to include more than civil rights contests, the previous era's focus. For a fine exploration of filibuster and cloture, see Catherine Fisk & Erwin Chemerinsky, *The Filibuster,* 49 Stan. L. Rev. 181 (1997). In 1989–1990 President Bush could not move his capital gains proposal because Senate Democrats would not clear it as free from a sixty-vote requirement. In 1993, as noted below, President Clinton could not move his economic stimulus bill for want of sixty votes in the face of a Republican filibuster threat.

28. For studies of reconciliation, see Anita S. Krushnakumar, *Reconciliation and the Fiscal Constitution: The Anatomy of the 1995–96 Budget "Train Wreck,"* 35 Harv. J. on Legis. 589 (1998); Elizabeth Garrett, *Rethinking the Structures of Decisionmaking in the Federal Budget Process,* 35 Harv. J. on Legis. 387 (2001). The description in the text is simplified on technical points; e.g., the 1974 act initially provided for a pair of resolutions annually—only later was the second resolution obviated.

29. During the rest of the Reagan and the first Bush terms, Congress passed reconciliation bills, but all dealt with reducing the deficit; there were no unpaid-for tax cuts that way, and in 1990 there was a centrist tax increase.

30. Keith Krehbiel, *Pivotal Politics,* 204 n.25 (1998). Barbara Sinclair makes the same point: "The president's program [in 1993] would never have passed were it not for the special procedures.... Most important, of course, was the budget process.... Budget rules gave the budget resolution and the reconciliation bill protection against a filibuster and amendments in the Senate that is enormously advantageous." Barbara Sinclair, *Unorthodox Lawmaking: New Legislative Processes in the U.S. Congress* (2d ed. 2000), at 182–83.

31. Sinclair, *supra,* at 182–83.

32. Tiefer, *How to Steal a Trillion, supra,* at 432 & n.107.

33. During 1995–1996 the new congressional Republican majority made a sustained effort to enact large tax cuts, along with anti-regulatory measures. I discuss this in Tiefer, *Budgetized Health Entitlements, supra.*

34. Pollack, *supra,* at 98–104.

35. They asserted the right to use the Budget Act, particularly the reconciliation provision, to cut taxes on a grand and unpaid-for scale with a mere simple majority. By this method they did not need to achieve cloture to overcome the anticipated filibuster resistance by the otherwise unbreakable combination of most of the Democratic Party plus traditional Republican moderates. For two accounts of this period, see Tiefer, *How to Steal a Trillion, supra,* at

433–34, 450; Michael W. Evans, *The Budget Process and the "Sunset" Provision of the 2001 Tax Law*, 9 Tax Notes 405, 407–8, 410–12.

36. Even if Senate Democrats suffered a few defections, with their new strength they could not fail to demand, against a controversial party-defining measure such as a grossly overlarge tax cut, what Senate Republicans had insisted on in 1993 to defeat the various Clinton measures, including a stimulus bill: sixty votes for cloture to pass.

37. 147 Cong. Rec. S1532 (daily ed. Feb. 15, 2001).

38. Senator Byrd recollected that in 1994 "President Clinton also pressed me to allow his massive health care bill to be insulated by reconciliation's protections. . . . I said to the President, . . . 'I cannot in good conscience allow the rule to be abused.' . . . [M]y view prevailed. . . . It is time for this abuse of the reconciliation process to cease." 147 Cong. Rec. at S1535.

39. On March 28 the House adopted a budget resolution providing for $1.6 trillion in tax cuts over ten years, the sum President Bush had proposed.

40. When the key substantive amendment was offered, four Republican moderates, including Senator Jim Jeffords (R-Vt.), provided the winning votes to reduce the size of the tax cut target by $448 billion, down to $1.187 trillion. Tiefer, *How to Steal a Trillion, supra*, at 427–28.

41. Warren Rojas, *Bush Budget Rolls through House; Senate Budget Bar Keeps Rising*, 91 Tax Notes 15, 19 (April 2, 2001). "'It appears [the Parliamentarian] reflected very carefully on what Sen. Byrd has said and came to a conclusion,'" [Senator] Nickles' chief of staff, Eric Ueland, said of Dove. 'The legislative history as interpreted by Bob [Dove] is that you can only give reconciliation protection to a bill or bills that increase taxes, decrease mandatory spending or make changes in the public debt.'" Andrew Taylor, *Law Designed for Curbing Deficits Becomes GOP Tool for Cutting Taxes*, 59 Cong. Q. Wkly. Rep. 770, 771 (April 7, 2001).

42. "Fearing that Senate Parliamentarian Bob Dove would rule against [the method], Domenici said his budget does not include reconciliation instructions for the president's tax bill, although he expects to introduce an amendment addressing reconciliation during the budget debate." *Senate Kicks Off Budget Debate*, 2001 Tax Notes Today 64-1 (April 3, 2001), in Lexis, Fedtax Library, TNT file. "Domenici was forced to pursue this auxiliary course on reconciliation after the Senate parliamentarian took notice of a Democratic challenge to the use of limited protections for Bush's $1.6 trillion tax cut and threatened to rule against Republicans." 2001 Tax Notes Today 67-1 (April 6, 2001), in Lexis, Fedtax Library, TNT file. As the press noted after interviewing the principals, "By declining to force a futile party-line vote, Byrd spared his party from squarely establishing a precedent about reconciliation in favor of Republican tax cutters." Taylor, *supra*, at 771. The highlight of the debate on the Domenici amendment for reconciliation instructions consisted of the speeches by Chairman Domenici (142 Cong. Rec. S3499–S3501 [daily ed. April 5, 2001]) and Senator Byrd (id. at S2502–S2504. The Senate adopted the budget resolution

the next day (147 Cong. Rec. S3696 [daily ed. April 6, 2001]) (adopting H. Cong. Res. 83, 107th Cong., 1st Sess.).

43. For an expert and moderate account of the 2001 debate, including the Domenici amendment and the sacking of the parliamentarian, see Evans, *supra,* at 412–14. Evans was chief counsel and deputy staff director of the Senate Finance Committee in 2001–2002; there is no better-informed expert on the parliamentary procedure and issues of that momentous time.

44. I assert this as the author of a thousand-page treatise, with two thousand footnotes, on congressional procedure. Tiefer, *Congressional Practice and Procedure, supra.*

45. The discharge is discussed in Charles Tiefer, *Out of Order: The Abrupt Dismissal of the Parliamentarian Threatens Senate Procedure,* Legal Times (May 14, 2001). When Byrd edited the reconciliation provision in 1974, Dove was his parliamentary scribe, and when the senator wrote the Byrd Rule in 1982, Dove was parliamentarian; so Dove, too, knew exactly why what Bush wanted could not, rightly, be done.

46. Although the power-sharing 50–50 Senate had equal representation on standing committees, "looking ahead to conference, [Majority Leader] Lott said Republicans would enjoy a one-seat majority in the House-Senate budget conference. [Minority Leader] Daschle said that because of budget rules favoring the majority, the conference split would be four Republicans to three Democrats." *Senate OKs $1.2 Trillion Tax Cut, Sets Up Budget Standoff,* 2001 Tax Notes Today 68-1 (April 9, 2001), in Lexis, Fedtax Library, TNT file. That is, ordinarily, the fifty senators in the minority could enforce their rights to equal representation on all committees by filibustering the floor motions relating to bills, and this would be true of the motions for going to and from conference. However, reconciliation treatment meant such motions as to a reconciliation conference did not face this threat.

47. A long-time Washington commentator who is a self-declared sympathizer for deep tax cutting commented, "A whole series of outright frauds have been employed to massage the figures. . . . When I first read the arithmetic had been done this way, I assumed I had missed something. Whatever the conference had done, it could not have done *that.* . . . Presto: The cost of 10 or fewer years' worth of tax cuts is spread over 11 years, at a savings (entirely imaginary) of hundreds of billions of dollars. The imaginary savings is then spent on extra cuts. Amazing." Clive Cook, *How to Take a Flawed Tax Bill and Turn It into a Joke,* 23 Nat'l J. 1707, 1708 (June 9, 2001).

48. Lee A. Sheppard, *News Analysis: No Tax Cuts for the Gore States,* 91 Tax Notes 1480 (May 28, 2001).

49. "Because it is being phased in so slowly, the alleviation of the 'marriage penalty' [which helps more middle-income taxpayers] will cost just $63.3 billion in the next decade, 5 percent of the total." Daniel J. Parks with Bill Swindell, *Tax Debate Assured a Long Life As Bush, GOP Press for New Cuts,* 59 Cong. Q. Wkly. Rep. 1304, 1309 (June 2, 2001). The bill provided some relief

to married couples with a single very high earner not experiencing an actual tax rate penalty by getting married, and correspondingly provided even less to couples with two moderate-earners who were experiencing such an actual penalty. For background on the distributional effect of these marriage benefits as compared with alternatives that would have helped low- and middle-income two-earner families more, *see, e.g.,* Lawrence Zelenak, *Doing Something about Marriage Penalties: A Guide for the Perplexed,* 54 Tax L. Rev. 1, 55–58 (2000); Robert S. McIntyre & Michael J. McIntyre, *Fixing the "Marriage Penalty" Problem,* 33 Val. U. L. Rev. 907 (1999).

50. Citizens for Tax Justice, *Year-by-Year Analysis of the Bush Tax Cuts Shows Growing Title to the Very Rich* (2002). Further extensive studies of regressiveness and other flaws are at http://www.ctj.org.

51. Paul Krugman's superb economic treatment of the 2001 act is an education to read. Krugman, *supra,* at 176–209. But he has not preempted the discussion here of reconciliation procedure.

52. Members of the Senate Democratic majority produced by Senator Jeffords's departure from the Republican Party knew the budget would not support new cuts.

53. Even the Republican Congress's own Congressional Budget Office—releasing a study conducted under a director just recently a Bush adviser and handpicked by the conservative leadership—could not gainsay what Federal Reserve Board chair Alan Greenspan, too, had implied in this regard. Martin A. Sullivan, *Mandated JCT Report Says House Bill May Hurt Economy,* 99 Tax Notes 948 (May 19, 2003).

54. Krugman, *supra.*

55. Even those affluent enough not only to have home ownership, the main asset of the middle class, but also to own fairly substantial stock holdings would nevertheless own stocks mostly in pension plans (like 401[k]s) that defer income taxes.

56. Patricia Mohr & Warren Rojas, *Senate GOP Bets That $500 Billion Tax Deal Can Break Budget Logjam,* 99 Tax Notes 167 (April 14, 2003).

57. Alan K. Ota, *Tax Cut Package Clears Amid Bicameral Rancor,* 61 Cong. Q. Wkly. Rep. 1245 (May 24, 2003).

58. For a treatment of why reconciliation required sunsetting to satisfy the Byrd Rule, see Evans, *supra.*

59. Jill Barshay, *White House Bonds with Moderates for Victory on Dividend Cuts,* 61 Cong. Q. Wkly. Rep. 1173 (May 17, 2003).

60. As enacted, the measure dropped any relation to whether the dividend-paying corporation had itself paid taxes. The slogan of ending "double taxation" on corporate dividends (once as corporate income, a second time as shareholder income) had served President Bush's purpose, and now he could unceremoniously discard it as legal double-talk that presumably had never really mattered. For example, it applied to dividend-issuing foreign companies paying no American corporate income taxes, even to the despised "expatriate" companies like Stanley Works that unpatriotically reincorporated in Bermuda

to evade taxes, and to the broad array of companies that by any of the many other legal dodges paid little or no taxes. Jill Barshay, *Who Benefits from New Rates for Dividends, Capital Gains,* 61 Cong. Q. Wkly. Rep. 1246, 1247 (May 24, 2003).

61. Robert Greenstein, Richard Kogan, and Joel Friedman, *New Tax Cut Law Uses Gimmick to Mask Costs* (Center on Budget and Public Policy, June 1, 2003).

62. David Cay Johnston, *Studies Say Tax Cuts Now Will Bring Bigger Bill Later,* N.Y. Times (Sept. 23, 2003), at C2.

63. In the preceding quarter century, the three presidents who departed with party changes in the White House—Ford (1977), Carter (1981), and Bush (1993)—adopted virtually nothing in the way of late major domestic initiatives. When their successors defeated them at the polls, they simply, as defeated lame ducks, served out their time as caretakers.

64. He had cleverly husbanded that mandate, avoiding fights with Congress in 2000 while the spotlight deservedly stayed on the campaign contest of Gore and Bush and then on the delicate Florida election contest.

65. The subject is discussed in William M. Jack, *Taking Care That Presidential Oversight of the Regulatory Process Is Faithfully Executed: A Review of Rule Withdrawals and Rule Suspensions under the Bush Administration's Card Memorandum,* 54 Admin. L. Rev. 12479 (2002).

66. The subject is discussed in Christine A. Klein, *Preserving Monumental Landscapes under the Antiquities Act,* 87 Cornell L. Rev. 1333 (2002).

67. Bush appointees could modify Clinton initiatives in complicated ways, so that even as they scuttled the important aspects of the initiative, they could emphasize that they retained some other aspects and hence twist their position as having modified, rather than abandoned, the whole initiative. Different Clinton initiatives could ultimately get undermined in different ways that obscured the overall picture: some by amending regulations; some by consolidating them with other plans; and some by changes in administrative, permitting, or enforcement policies. Moreover, if any particular reversals of Clinton initiatives proved too individually controversial, it could be returned to limbo without clarifying its own obscure fate, keeping in perpetual fog the status of the overall Clinton initiatives.

68. For an introduction to the legal issues, see Lawrence O. Gostin, *Health Information Privacy,* 80 Cornell L. Rev. 451 (1995).

69. Pub. L. No. 104-191, 110 Stat. 1936 (1996).

70. Standards for Privacy of Individually Identifiable Health Information, 65 Fed. Reg. 82462 (Dec. 28, 2000).

71. Lawrence O. Gostin, James G. Hodge Jr., & Mira S. Burghardt, *Balancing Communal Goods and Personal Privacy under a National Health Informational Privacy Rule,* 46 St. Louis U. L.J. 5 (2002).

72. See Robert Pear, *Democrats Say Bush Revisions Ruin Medical Privacy Rules,* N.Y. Times (April 17, 2002); Robert Gellman, *Bush Team Stumbles on Health Privacy,* Gov't Compensation News (April 29, 2002).

73. Namely, marketing would not include literature that pushed an individual to purchase health care tailored to their own conditions. In other words, a patient with a condition about which she felt acutely sensitive and vulnerable to embarrassment could nevertheless receive a barrage of targeted exploitative sales tactics, revealing that her data had been circulated—and this would be considered no violation of her privacy.

74. See Pear, *supra*.

75. See Julie A. Parks, Comment, *Lessons in Politics: Initial Use of the Congressional Review Act*, 55 Admin. L. Rev. 187 (2003).

76. The issue mattered so much, both to the public and to business, that it constituted one of the main reasons Congress planned, when it adjourned before the November 2000 election, to reconvene for a lame-duck session. Congressional Republicans had thereby retained until after the election the option to resolve the issue by striking a last-minute postelection deal with President Clinton in the form of an appropriation rider on a bill he would sign.

77. Gingrich's team had created a legally unique channel for disapproving a regulatory rule, bypassing the committees that hold hearings and meetings on such measures and precluding Senate filibuster. So it could hustle a House anti-regulatory attack to a decisive Senate partisan vote well before the forces of potential broad-based opposition could mobilize to arouse the general public's slowly awakened alarm and give it voice in the Senate. Morton Rosenberg, *Whatever Happened to Congressional Review of Agency Rulemaking? A Brief Overview, Assessment, and Proposal for Reform*, 51 Admin. L. Rev. 1051 (1999).

78. Deirdre Davidson & Tatiana Boncompagni, *The Swift Demise of OSHA Rules*, Legal Times (March 12, 2001).

79. Molly Ivins & Lou Dubose, *Bushwhacked: Life in George W. Bush's America* 50–71 (2003). Ivins and Dubose go into this in much greater detail, all of it fascinating, than there is room for here. The account here derives from my earlier legal analysis in Tiefer, *How to Steal a Trillion, supra,* at 471–77 & nn.262–300.

80. An employer who makes millions from unsafe workplace conditions should definitely hire the firm of Ted Olson and Gene Scalia to obtain, at any price, even a small amount of their proven and excellent services. But such employers may not find it easy to get much of Olson's or Scalia's personal attention, because so many will be ahead of them, begging for the privilege of paying their firm huge legal fees—at least, that has been the experience at Ken Starr's firm, where tobacco companies bid for his excellent services.

81. Robin Kundis Craig, *The Bush Administration and the Environment: An Overview and Introduction*, 25 W. New Eng. L. Rev. 1, 5–7 (2003).

82. The level of environmental stories on the three major-network nightly newscasts, a nice quantitative measure, shot up to 264 minutes in that time, from 174 minutes in 1996 and 195 in 1998—and that high level preceded the high-profile announcements in May of President Bush's major new controversial energy proposals. Jane Hall, *How the Environmental Beat Got Its Groove Back*, Colum. Journalism Rev. (July 2001), at 10.

83. Richard Stavros, *The Candidate: An Interview with Texas Gov. George W. Bush*, Pub. Utilities Fortnightly (Feb. 1, 2000).

84. Katharine Q. Seelye, *Top E.P.A. Official Quits, Criticizing Bush's Policies*, N.Y. Times (March 1, 2002), at A19.

85. Katharine Q. Seelye, *White House Seeks a Change in Rules on Air Pollution*, N.Y. Times June 14, 2002.

86. See John Boyd, Note, *The New New Source Review: Teaching Old Sources New Tricks?* 11 Southeastern Envtl. L.J. 401 (2003).

87. On the program's development, see Natural Resources Defense Council, *Gutting the New Source Review: Letting the Polluters Avoid Cleanup for 10 Years and Beyond with a New Right to Pollute*, NRDC Backgrounder (March 20, 2002) (http://www.nrdc.org). On the timing of its implementation, see Matthew L. Wald, *E.P.A. Says It Will Change Rules Governing Industrial Pollution*, N.Y. Times (Nov. 23, 2002), at A1.

88. On Sept. 29, 2000, in a speech in Saginaw, Michigan, Bush outlined a comprehensive energy policy, saying, "We will require all power plants to meet clean air standards in order to reduce emissions of sulfur dioxide, nitrogen oxide, mercury and carbon dioxide." Begala, *supra*, at 62.

89. 147 Cong. Rec. S3644 (daily ed. April 6, 2001).

90. Thomas O. McGarity, *Jogging in Place: The Bush Administration's Freshman Year Environmental Record*, 32 Envtl. L. Rep. 10709 (2002).

91. This ratio does improve with progress in energy efficiency, but not enough to offset the rising levels of energy consumption and greenhouse gas buildup and, hence, irreversibly worsening climate conditions.

92. See David A. Wirth, *The Sixth Session (Part Two) and Seventh Session of the Conference of the Parties to the Framework Convention on Climate Change*, 96 Am. J. Int'l L. 648 (2002).

93. Greg Kahn, *The Fate of the Kyoto Protocol under the Bush Administration*, 21 Berkeley J. Int'l L. 548 (2003).

94. Andrew C. Revkin, *With White House Approval, E.P.A. Pollution Report Omits Global Warming Section*, N.Y. Times (Sept. 15, 2002), at 30.

95. Natural Resources Defense Council, *Gale Ann Norton: An Environmental Profile* (Jan. 2001) (e.g., abolishing the Bureau of Land Management).

96. Norton filed MSLF's brief in an unsuccessful in 1982 effort to persuade the Supreme Court to strike down the entire body of federal surface mining reclamation regulations as an unconstitutional interference with property rights.

97. Jim Motavalli, *Scorched Earth Policy: Environmental Policy of the George W. Bush Administration*, E Magazine (May 1, 2001).

98. For background on Norquist's potent right-wing organizational efforts, see Easton (2000), *supra*, at 360–65.

99. Motavalli, *supra*.

100. Presidents Nixon and Ford chose Rogers C. B. Morton; President Carter, Stewart Udall; President Reagan (after the disaster with Watt), his close friend William Clark; and President Clinton, Bruce Babbitt.

101. Richard J. Lazarus, *A Different Kind of "Republican Moment" in Environmental Law*, 87 Minn. L. Rev. 999 (2003).

102. The organization Earthjustice maintains a full Web site of profiles of the anti-environmental lawyers and lobbyists with environmental posts at http://www.earthjustice.org/policy/profiles/index.html.

103. Both Connaughton and Griles have Earthjustice profiles (see id.). Connaughton lawyered and lobbied for a range of polluting companies and their trade associations. Griles served Watt during the Reagan administration as assistant secretary of the notoriously slashed and curtailed Office of Surface Mining. On Griles's ethics problems, see Michael Grunwald, *Interior Official's Memo Raises Conflict Issue*, Wash. Post (May 23, 2002), at A2.

104. Earthjustice profiles for William Geary Myers III, interior solicitor; Rebecca W. Watson, assistant secretary for land and minerals management; and Bennet W. Raley, assistant secretary for water and science may be found at http://www.earthjustice.org/policy/profiles/index.html.

105. Earthjustice, *The Nomination of William G. Myers III to a Lifetime Federal Judgeship Threatens Environmental Protection* (Oct. 2003), http://www.earthjustice.org.

106. Henry Weinstein, *Democrats Hammer at Court Choice*, L.A. Times (Feb. 6, 2004), at B7.

107. *Agency's Top Lawyer under Investigation for Ethics Violations*, Greenwire (Aug. 20, 2003).

108. Henry Weinstein, *Groups Fight Nominee for 9th Circuit*, L.A. Times (Feb. 5, 2004), at B1.

109. McGarity, *supra*, at nn.29–31.

110. Craig, *supra*, at 7–9.

111. Kenneth R. Weiss, *U.S. Refuses to Buy Back Oil Leases*, L.A. Times (June 8, 2002), at 1.

112. Kenneth R. Weiss, *White House Pulls Back on Offshore Oil Drilling*, L.A. Times (April 1, 2003), at 1.

113. Mark Rey, undersecretary for natural resources and environment, has an Earthjustice profile (see http://www.earthjustice.org/policy/profiles/index.html).

114. Lazarus, *supra*, at 1017.

115. Katharine Q. Seelye, *Bush Proposes Change to Allow More Thinning of Forests*, N.Y. Times (Dec. 12, 2002), at A32.

116. See the Earthjustice profiles (http://www.earthjustice.org/policy/profiles/index.html) for Linda Fisher, deputy administrator; Jeffrey Holmstead, assistant administrator for air and radiation (who was an adjunct scholar for Citizens for the Environment, formed in 1990 as a project of Citizens for a Sound Economy, funded by the Scaife and Olin foundations, among others); Jean-Marie Peltier, counselor to the administrator on agriculture policy; and Adam J. Sharp, associate assistant administrator of the Office of Prevention,

Pesticides, and Toxics (who dealt with pesticides and other issues at the American Farm Bureau Federation from 1995 to 2001).

117. Thomas Sansonetti, the Justice Department's assistant attorney general for environment and natural resources, has an Earthjustice profile (see id.). His practice in (anti-)environmental law included lobbying for corporate mining interests.

118. See the report at http://www.nrdc.org/bushrecord/wildlife_mining.asp.

119. *Bragg v. West Virginia Coal Association*, 248 F.3d 275 (4th Cir. 2001); Robert V. Percival, *Environmental Implications of the Rehnquist Court's New Federalism*, 17 Natural Res. & Env. (summer 2002), at 3.

120. Paul A. Duffy, *How Filled Was My Valley: Continuing the Debate on Disposal Impacts*, 17 Natural Res. & Env. (winter 2003), at 143.

121. The prosecutors uncovered a stream of hundreds of thousands of DeLay's dollars flowing to Craddick's supporters' ads, not by the permissible route of donations, limited in amount and properly disclosed, to regulated PACs, but directly out of corporate treasuries, in violation of regulatory and disclosure requirements. Richard A. Oppel Jr., *Inquiry Focuses on Group DeLay Created*, N.Y. Times (Feb. 16, 2004), at A14.

122. Id.

123. Dean Baker and Mark Weisbrot, *Social Security: The Phony Crisis* (1999).

124. The health savings accounts are in section 1201 of the Medicare Prescription Drug, Improvement, and Modernization Act of 2003 (MPDIMA), Pub. L. No. 108-173. As to the other Treasury plans, see Jonathan Weisman, *Treasury Renews Campaign for Tax-Free Savings Accounts*, Wash. Post (Dec. 6, 2003), at E1.

125. The debate between, on one side, academic experts Alan Sager and Deborah Socolar of the Boston University School of Public Health and Robert E. Moffit of the Heritage Foundation and, on the other side, consultants hired by the industry-supported Pacific Research Institute is laid out in Alan Sager and Deborah Socolar, *How Much Would Drug Makers' Profits Rise under a Medicare Prescription Drug Benefit?* (March 19, 2004), http://www.healthreformprogram.org.

126. Theda Skocpol, *A Bad Senior Moment*, Am. Prospect (Jan. 2004), at 26.

127. Charles Tiefer, *"Budgetized" Health Entitlements and the Fiscal Constitution in Congress's 1995–1996 Budget Battle*, 33 Harv. J. on Legis. 412, 414 (1996).

128. For nontechnical accounts, see http://www.kaisernetwork.org and http://www.medicarerights.org.

129. For a study of the harm to minorities from MPDIMA, see Maya Rockeymoore and Laura Hawkinson, *Structured Inefficiency: The Impact of Medicare Reform on African Americans*, Center for Policy Analysis and Research (Jan. 2004), http://www.cbc.org.

130. Section 803 of MPDIMA, Pub. L. No. 108-173.

131. Edmund L. Andrews and Robert Pear, *Entitlement Costs Are Expected to Soar: Medicare and Social Security May Need Twice as Much as Thought,* N.Y. Times (March 19, 2004), at A13.

132. Amy Goldstein, *A Dire Report on Medicare Finances: Under New Law, Hospital Fund May Run Out by 2019,* Wash. Post (March 24, 2004), at A1.

5. THE CORRUPTION

1. Actually, his family ran Columbia HCA, one of the more notorious of the giant health care companies, perhaps better termed "anti-health" care companies for how they pocketed the money and even ripped off the government.

2. For scholarly analysis, see Mayer, *supra,* at 45, 46–48; Wilcox, *supra,* at 107, 111. For journalists' detailed accounts, see the descriptions of the smears and the evidence connecting them to Rove in Dubose, Reid, & Cannon, *supra,* at 139–42. The role of money is evident in the description of the smears' propagation: "These canards were repeated on handbills, in phone calls, in push polls, on the radio, in conversation." Id. at 143. Push polls and radio promotion, in particular, make use of funds being handled in legally untraceable ways, like the expenditures by highly loyal pariah interests, such as tobacco companies, able to operate with impunity in South Carolina.

3. Toobin, *supra,* at 170–76, 197–210 (2001), based in part on Barstow & Van Natta, *supra.* Although the Bush side in the contest greatly outspent the Gore side, and although this gave it many advantages, this is not a contention that it was simply outspending that won the Florida contest. That would be overweighting one cause of victory among many.

4. The first Bush had at least won his own 1988 election without needing Scalia's intervention, and he could count on at least some support from Southern Democrats, whom he treated as fellow leaders.

5. For the striking of the compromise, see Philip Shenon, *A Top G.O.P. Senator Hints at Soft Money Compromise,* N.Y. Times (March 23, 2001), at A1; Alison Mitchell, *Campaign Finance Bill Passes in Senate, 59–41,* N.Y. Times (April 3, 2001), at A1.

6. This is well analyzed in Victoria A. Farrar-Meyers, *In the Wake of 1996: Clinton's Legacy for Presidential Campaign Finance,* in David Gray Adler & Michel A. Genovese, eds., *The Presidency and the Law: The Clinton Legacy,* at 135, 147–48 (2002).

7. Mike Allen, *"Pioneers" Paved Bush's Way with Big Dollars,* Wash. Post (May 6, 2003), at A7.

8. Richard Briffault, *The Future of Reform: Campaign Finance after the Bipartisan Campaign Reform Act of 2002,* 34 Ariz. L.J. 1180, 1215 (2002).

9. For the striking nature of the decreased significance of public financing in presidential election politics in 2000, see David B. Magleby, ed., *Financing the 2000 Election* (2002).

10. Abraham, *supra*, at 13.

11. Richard L. Berke, *The $2,000 Answer*, N.Y. Times (March 21, 2002), at A1.

12. Alison Mitchell, *The Calculus of Campaign Finance*, N.Y. Times (March 17, 2002).

13. Bryce, *supra*, at 272.

14. Sure, Bill Clinton cheated on his wife and lied about it, but Hillary Clinton could probably handle it. This was about how the greed of a few inflicted pain on the many; and the unemployed mothers and fathers and their children were likely less able to handle it.

15. The brief was filed on behalf of an amicus group including Michael Castle (R-Del.) and David Price (D-N.C.) and twenty-three other representatives. Two disclaimers are in order. The counsel of record and the principal author of the brief deserving the lion's share of credit for it was Richard Briffault of Columbia University School of Law, who has written extensively about campaign finance law. And the amici representatives, major backers of the BCRA, came together solely to back the BCRA in the way expressed in that brief; none thereby associated themselves with any of the views expressed in this book or my other writings (many of which ideas, quite to the contrary, many of them would of course vigorously dispute). I admire the willingness of those amici and Professor Briffault, with their distinguished records of contribution to the cause of campaign finance reform, to tolerate my much more modest contribution to that cause being pooled with theirs.

16. Phillips, *supra* (2003 ed.), at 323.

17. After the redistricting of 1981–1982, House Democrats did well in 1982, the loosening-up effect of the redistricting enabling them to benefit from the public's dislike at that time of the Republican budget action of 1981 and the ensuing 1982 recession. The redistricting of 1991–1992 prefigured the Republican takeover of the House in 1994 because the opening of many contestable seats, especially in the South, made room for the election of a new generation of Republicans with the help of the Gingrich-DeLay strategies and much public dissatisfaction with the Clinton administration's first two years.

18. The premier study is Sam Hirsch, *The United States House of Unrepresentatives: What Went Wrong in the Latest Round of Congressional Redistricting*, 2 Election L.J. 179 (2003), discussing packing and cracking at 194.

19. The best discussion of Democratic weakness in this process is Cohen, *supra*.

20. Id.

21. Hirsch, *supra*.

22. Gary C. Jacobson, *Terror, Terrain, and Turnout: Explaining the 2002 Midterm Elections*, 118 Pol. Sci. Q. 1 (2003).

23. The background of the case is recounted and analyzed in Louis Fisher, *The Politics of Executive Privilege* (2004). I filed the brief on behalf of the House Democratic leadership in one of the key cases seeking to overcome the Commerce Department's illegal withholding of the census data.

24. According to a report by the Congressional Research Service cited in Leif Strickland, *Texas Showdown*, Newsweek (Aug. 21, 2003).

25. Charles Cook, *Round and Round the Acrimony Goes . . .*, Nat'l J. (May 17, 2003).

26. Strickland, *supra*.

27. *Texas Redistricting to Go to Conference*, N.Y. Times (Sept. 25, 2003), at A25.

28. Louis Jacobson, *Back to the Redrawing Board?* Nat'l J. (April 12, 2003), at A22.

29. 121 S. Ct. 525 (2000).

30. 525 U.S. 316 (1998).

31. For the author's analysis of her opinion, see Charles Tiefer, *The Reconceptualization of Legislative History in the Supreme Court*, 2000 Wisc. L. Rev. 205, 240–41.

32. Tiefer, *The Semi-Sovereign Presidency, supra*, at 64, 77.

33. For background and critique of Graham and his approach, see Frank Ackerman & Lisa Heinzerling, *Pricing the Priceless: Cost-Benefit Analysis of Environmental Protection*, 150 U. Pa. L. Rev. 1553 (2002), and the prior writings of Heinzerling and Ackerman referenced therein.

34. Rena I. Steinzor, Book Review, *Pragmatic Regulation in Dangerous Times*, 20 Yale J. on Reg. 407, 416–17 (2003).

35. Rena I. Steinzor, *Toward Better Bubbles and Future Lives: A Progressive Response to the Conservative Agenda for Reforming Environmental Law*, 32 Envtl. L. Rep. 11421, n.76 (2002).

36. OIRA again proved a magnet for wish lists, including such items as curbing impending controls on toxic lead pollution.

37. Cindy Skrzycki, *267 Rules Up for Review; Referendum Names Environmental, Auto Standards*, Wash. Post. (Dec. 19, 2002), at E1.

38. Steinzor, *Toward Better Bubbles and Future Lives, supra*, at 11421, n.75.

39. *New Guidelines Open U.S. Data to Challenge*, Wash. Post (Oct. 1, 2002), at E1.

40. Discounting at 7 percent meant that ten lives saved in thirty-five years was barely worth one life saved now, while the social value of the elderly's health could be accounted particularly low because of their lower earnings.

41. Ackerman & Heinzerling, *supra*.

42. Deaths from lung cancer typically occur decades later among those in or near retirement, while current tobacco sales pump up the current (not discounted) gross national product. For a discussion of the infamous Arthur D. Little study commissioned by Philip Morris that found that smoking was a financial boon to the government, see Ackerman & Heinzerling, *supra*.

43. For a leading constitutional scholar's more theoretical treatment of the potential for President Bush to work a conservative transformation in alliance with a conservative Supreme Court, see Mark Tushnet, *Alarmism versus*

Moderation in Responding to the Rehnquist Court, 78 Ind. L.J. 47, 67–70 (2003).

44. Philip J. Weiser, *Towards a Constitutional Architecture for Cooperative Federalism,* 79 N.C. L. Rev. 663 (2001).

45. Through such discipline they keep the authority at the state level, can harmonize their federally supervised work with other state-level activity, and lose nothing in terms of competition with other states because all must satisfy the same firm federal requirements.

46. See generally Thomas M. Koontz, *Federalism in the Forest: National versus State Natural Resource Policy* (2002).

47. The Superfund statute for cleaning up toxic waste sites obliges municipalities (that contributed waste to landfill sites), as it obliges businesses, to contribute to the cleanup. Moreover, because of the statute's cleanup imperatives, it has no strict principles for sharing burdens, so in some situations a lawsuit could stick a large share of the cleanup cost on a municipality when some now-insolvent business ought to have that burden.

48. For example, the Bush administration could argue that issues of the pace of cleanup of isolated polluted surface or underground water reservoirs, particularly those that do not directly affect some downstream state, ought be resolved by the state containing the problematic body of water, as a matter of its traditional power over its own land and water use. For background on the controversy over the federally supervised program for states to clean up local water supplies, see Linda A. Malone, *The Myths and Truths That Threaten the TMDL Program,* 32 Envtl. L. Rep. 11133 (2002).

49. EPA general counsel Robert E. Fabricant, *EPA's Authority to Impose Mandatory Controls to Address Global Climate Change under the Clean Air Act* (Aug. 28, 2003), http://www.epa.gov/oar. Previously, in 1998, DeLay had attacked EPA administrator Carol Browner on the theory that her agency could not regulate these emissions; she had taken the formal legal position that her agency's sweeping Clean Air Act authority encompassed doing so. This is discussed in an April 10, 1998, memorandum by EPA general counsel Jonathan Z. Cannon, *EPA's Authority to Regulate Pollutants Emitted by Electric Power Generation Sources* (1998).

50. The memo said that "the Supreme Court has ruled that facially broad grants of authority must be interpreted in the context of the statute's purpose, structure and history and other relevant congressional actions." It cited the decision (by the bloc of five conservatives) against the Clinton administration FDA's regulation of cigarettes, saying that "in light of the Supreme Court's decision in *Food and Drug Administration v. Brown & Williamson Tobacco Corp.,* 120 S. Ct. 1291 (2000), . . . it is clear that an administrative agency properly awaits congressional direction on a fundamental policy issue such as global climate change." Fabricant, memo, *supra,* at 4.

51. Whatever one thinks of the Court's decision against the FDA in the tobacco case, it did at least cite a history of congressional enactments considering

just how far to go in regulating cigarettes during decades in which the health problems they pose had become increasingly apparent. The EPA's August 2003 memo could only argue, in contrast, that the Clean Air Act had been comprehensively amended in 1990, years before the increasing clarity and urgency of the global warming problem had reached the point that even Governor Bush, surely the least likely enthusiast on this subject, had in his 2000 campaign promised action.

52. Critics noticed that the Bush administration had put this into informal practice early, in 2001, by approving the Houston-Galveston area prospective smog plan, which fell far short of necessary efforts even though that area already has the nation's highest smog readings. McGarity, *supra* at 10709 n.108. Maybe under this regime the environment would stay clean and nice in the few choice spots where CEOs live or vacation, like the opulent River Oaks area of Houston where many of Bush's supporters are and the oil refineries aren't.

53. On Norton, see Motavalli, *supra*. On Senator Ashcroft, see *Vindication of Property Rights*, Hearing before the Subcomm. on Constitution, Federalism and Property Rights of the Senate Comm. on the Judiciary (Oct. 7, 1997).

54. Charles Tiefer, *Did* Eastern Enterprises *Send Enterprise Liability South?* 51 Ala. L. Rev. 1305 (2000).

55. *Tahoe-Sierra Preservation Council, Inc. v. Tahoe Regional Planning Agency,* 535 U.S. 301 (2002); *Brown v. Legal Foundation of Washington,* 123 S. Ct. 1406 (2003).

56. See generally Charles Tiefer, *Helping Those Who Can Help Themselves: The Rehnquist Court's Direct and Indirect Conservative Activism,* 1 Geo. J. L. & Pub. Pol'y 103 (2002).

57. Tiefer, *Did* Eastern Enterprises *Send Enterprise Liability South? supra.*

58. The AMT's role escalates for two reasons. Unlike the regular income tax, the AMT is not indexed for inflation, and it kicks in when the taxpayer owes more under the AMT than under the regular income tax. So each year, inflation results in earners at certain levels of income paying lower (indexed) regular income tax than the (unindexed) AMT, and the AMT's impact begins at those levels. Second, as the tax cuts of 2001 and 2004 phase in, without a corresponding AMT cut, other groups find themselves paying lower (cut) regular income tax than the (uncut) AMT, and the AMT's impact begins for those groups.

59. Leonard E. Burman, William G. Gale, & Jeffrey Rohaly, *The AMT: Projections and Problems,* 100 Tax Notes 105 (July 7, 2003); William Rojas, *Pick Your Battles: Weighting Bush's Dividend Cut against AMT Reform,* 100 Tax Notes 458 (April 28, 2003).

60. In his 1981 spending-side reconciliation bill, President Reagan rammed through Congress his staggering conservative domestic agenda of cuts in programs like food stamps, Medicaid, and housing aid. Only reconciliation gave him the procedural power to steamroll over what, without reconciliation, would have been spirited and effective congressional resistance. Tiefer, *Congressional Practice and Procedure, supra,* at 885–86, 896.

61. This occurred through the rewrite-with-cutbacks of welfare law; taking away food stamps from legal immigrants including hungry children; and the capital gains tax cut paid for by siphoning off hundreds of billions from the Medicare system. See Charles Tiefer, *Treatment for Medicare's Budget: Quick Operation or Long-Term Care?* 16 St. Louis U. Pub. L. Rev. 27 (1996).

62. For a description of conservatives' enthusiasm for this effort, see, e.g., Ramesh Ponnuru, *How's the Granny Card Playing? The Evolving Politics of Social Security,* Nat'l Rev. (Nov. 11, 2002).

63. See generally Colleen E. Medill, *Challenging the Four "Truths" of Personal Social Security Accounts: Evidence from the World of 401(K) Plans,* 81 N.C. L. Rev. 901, 953–62 (2003).

64. Id. at 975.

65. Krugman, *supra,* at 211.

66. A parallel scenario is how Bush's pal Dallas billionaire Tom Hicks, the one who made him really rich by buying the Texas Rangers, got to manage (without accountability) his part of the University of Texas trust funds.

67. For background, see Jennifer Rak, Note, *An RX for Reform: A Medicare Prescription Drug Benefit,* 12 Health Matrix 449 (2002).

68. Walter Francis, *The FEHBP as a Model for Medicare Reform: Separating Fact from Fiction* (Heritage Foundation Reports, Aug. 7, 2003). Conservatives used the model of the Federal Employees Health Benefits Program (FEHBP). In Medicare the government pays the cost of the health services (apart from manageable deductibles and copayments). In FEHBP the insured must pay 25 percent of the cost of the health insurance—that's what it means to say that the government defines and caps its contribution.

69. When the vast number of lower-income seniors (and even a substantial number of middle-income seniors) can afford to pay only a relatively low amount for their 25 percent, then they get, in terms of health services, only what they can afford—with corresponding savings for the government. Id.

70. For the lack of fit of tax action with Medicare's needs, see generally Maureen B. Cavanaugh, *On the Road to Incoherence: Congress, Economics, and Taxes,* 49 U.C.L.A. L. Rev. 685 (2002).

71. "The Golden Rule Insurance Company . . . the leading underwriter of high-deductible medical insurance policies . . . is a big donor to the Republican Party and Republican politicians." David E. Rosenbaum, *Bush Seeks Tax Cuts He Had Scorned,* N.Y. Times (Feb. 9, 2003), at 28.

72. Leslie Book, *The IRS's EITC Compliance Regime: Taxpayers Caught in the Net,* 81 Ore. L. Rev. 351 (2002).

73. Jonathan Alter, *Between the Lines, Online: Whacking the Waitresses,* Newsweek Web Exclusive, May 30, 2003; Joe Klein, *Blessed Are the Poor—They Don't Get Tax Cuts,* Time (June 9, 2003), at 29.

74. See Senator Max Baucus et al., *Baucus, Colleagues Urge End to "Burdensome" EITC Precertification,* Tax Notes Today, Doc. 2003-17055 (July 18, 2003).

75. For conservative enthusiasm about waivers, see John Hood, *Take Your Medicine! If the GOP Neglects Health Care, It Is in Deep Trouble—Period,* Nat'l Rev. (June 30, 2003).

76. The superwaiver is "a very one-way kind of flexibility: the flexibility to cut." Drake Bennett, *Freedom to Fail: The False Flexibility of the President's Welfare Plan,* Am. Prospect (April 2003), at 18, 20 (quoting Deborah Weinstein of the Children's Defense Fund). Conservative states might aim to let employers dump their existing employee health insurance programs on state programs, purloining some funding for this from Medicaid sources previously required to be spent on decent care for the poor.

77. Tiefer, *Treatment for Medicare's Budget, supra.*

78. For example, conservative Senate filibusters derailed efforts to strengthen legislation affecting labor organizing in both periods. The law as it stood effectively guarded the federalism barriers permitting conservative-controlled states—"right to work" states—continue to make labor organizing difficult. In 1978 Senate Republicans filibustered legislation to strengthen the antiquated remedies of the National Labor Relations Act for unfair labor practices. In 1994 Senate Republicans filibustered a bill to limit corporation's practice of permanently replacing strikers, the most feared tool for breaking strikes.

79. Progressive successes in benefit programs starting in the 1960s owed much to legal innovations in cooperative federalism—federal programs administered partly through the states. These extended national standards, both for program goals in a narrow sense and for other national progressive goals such as civil rights, into conservatively controlled regions. For example, federal aid to education not only raised school standards in the South but also carried with it civil rights requirements that played a part in ending state-backed school segregation. Warren Court legal doctrines relating to federalism on many levels also helped. These subjected states to federal constitutional requirements and opened the federal courthouse doors to newly created or expansively interpreted remedies.

80. These included workers with occupational harms, consumers hurt by defective products or price-fixing, smokers following up on the revelations about Big Tobacco, investors harmed by securities fraud and insider trading like Enron's (and not unlike George W. Bush's own in the early 1990s), patients harmed by medical malpractice, victims of pollution, and so forth.

81. "Dubya, who ran on the issue in '94, declared tort reform a 'legislative emergency.' ... It was good electoral politics, encouraging business funders to give generously.... And it cut into the income of plaintiffs' lawyers, a major source of campaign contributions for Democrats." Ivins & Dubose, *Shrub, supra,* at 88–89.

82. Moreover, in 2002, the public firestorm regarding bad corporate financial practices, starting with Enron, put conservative ideologues in business greatly on the defensive. The public, hurting from burst stock market bubble

and the recession, took umbrage at business abuses. Temporarily, President Bush had to lay off defending legal protections for business misconduct.

83. This legislation aimed at allowing businesses to remove cases from the state courts that in some states still stayed open to victims' suits. The removed cases would go to federal courts, with their accumulating conservative judicial appointments and correspondingly decreasing openness to such suits. See Shawn Zeller, *Tort Reform's Massive War Chest*, Nat'l J. (March 29, 2003), at 1008.

84. David Luban, *Taking Out the Adversary: The Assault on Progressive Public-Interest Lawyers*, 91 Cal. L. Rev. 209 (2003).

85. *State Farm Mut. Auto. Ins. Co. v. Campbell*, 2003 WL 1791206 (2003).

86. These would range from how comprehensively such legislation acted to preclude any cases, however shaped, from remaining in state court to how much state substantive law and procedure would follow a case initiated in state court when removed to federal court.

87. Andrew Taylor, *Grim Budget Deficit Forecasts Still Too Rosy, Say Critics*, 61 Cong. Q. Wkly. Rep. 2088 (Aug. 30, 2003).

88. *Billionaires for Bush*, The Nation, July 21, 2003.

89. Michael Isikoff & Tamara Lipper, *Bush Campaign: We're in the Money*, Newsweek (June 16, 2003), at 8.

90. Edwin Chen, *Bush Cites War in Letter Seeking Campaign Funds*, L.A. Times, May 25, 2003, at 25.

91. Earthjustice and Public Campaign, *Paybacks: Policies, Patrons and Personnel—How the Bush Administration Is Giving Away Our Environment to Its Corporate Contributors* (Sept. 2002). The figures were for 2000 through July 2002.

92. Id.

93. In 2002–2003, immediately during and after the Enron scandal, taking such responsibility would have subjected him to intense criticism from reformers, particularly McCain, who would have the media on his side.

6. GOING IT ALONE

1. John Spanier & Steven W. Hook, *American Foreign Policy since World War II* (15th ed. 2000).

2. Governor Bush, like most Republican leaders, far from disputing the Clinton arrangements for China to enter the World Trade Organization (WTO), endorsed them, as his conservative business base wished. Ultimately, President Bush so valued Beijing's necessary cooperation on his agenda that he bottled up the anti-communist rhetoric—e.g., during the early 2001 American intelligence plane detention on Hainan Island—reaping the benefits during the post-9/11 Afghan campaign and the 2003 dealings with North Korea. See generally Charles Tiefer, *Sino 301: How Congress Can Effectively Review Relations with China after WTO Accession*, 34 Cornell Int'l L.J. 56 (2000).

3. It has been well argued by Michael Lind that this vein of thought drew on the Southern regional ideology that had long favored projecting unrestrained military power in the Third World and evincing unconcern, if not hostility, toward European or other social views and multilateral institutions. Michael Lind, *Made in Texas: George W. Bush and the Southern Takeover of American Politics* (2002).

4. A recent critical treatment of this viewpoint is in Johan D. van der Vyver, *American Exceptionalism: Human Rights, International Criminal Justice, and National Self-Righteousness,* 50 Emory L.J. 775 (2001).

5. Theodore Draper, *A Very Thin Line: The Iran-Contra Affairs* (1991).

6. For Buchanan's positions, see the very critical Franklin Foer, *Home Bound: Buchanan's Surefire Flop,* New Republic (July 22, 2002), at 12; and a more complex analysis from a neoconservative perspective, William Kristol & Robert Kagan, *Toward a Neo-Reaganite Foreign Policy,* Foreign Aff. (July–Aug. 1996), at 18.

7. The positions of Buchanan and Perot variously included intense antagonism toward the United Nations (despite its valuable support in the Persian Gulf War), xenophobic attitudes toward immigrants, retreat from bipartisan reciprocal agreements on trade, and distrust of traditional U.S. alliances and collective efforts.

8. Ivins & Dubose, *Shrub, supra,* at xvi.

9. He secured bipartisan congressional approval of the NAFTA deal by adding side agreements on the environment and labor and won similar bipartisan approval of the WTO in 1994 and of China's membership in 2000. Charles Tiefer, *Alongside the Fast Track: Environmental and Labor Issues in FTAA,* 7 Minn. J. Global Trade 329 (1998).

10. Terry L. Deibel, *The Death of a Treaty,* Foreign Aff. (Sept.–Oct. 2002), at 142.

11. Zalmay M. Khalilzad & Paul Wolfowitz, *Overthrow Him,* Wkly. Standard (Dec. 1, 1997), at 14.

12. Tiefer, *Alongside the Fast Track, supra.*

13. The polls after the pop quiz are in Bennett & White, *supra,* at 19, 35.

14. See James Kitfield, *Bush and Gore's Positions on Foreign Policy,* 32 Nat'l J. (April 1, 2000), at 1034. The party ideological base so hated Clinton that they needed no specifics. For example, it sufficed that Bush's surrogates criticized the Clinton commitment to Bosnia, as congressional Republicans had. See Charles Tiefer, *War Decisions in the Late 1990s by Partial Congressional Declaration,* 36 San Diego L. Rev. 1 (1999). Bush himself never specifically promised to change that commitment and never tried to.

15. Sydney J. Freedberg Jr., *Bush and Gore's Positions on Defense,* 32 Nat'l J. 1026 (April 1, 2000).

16. Levitt & Naff, *supra,* at 67, 70.

17. Experience from serving as President Ford's chief of staff, as the number two House Republican leader, and as President Bush's secretary of defense during the Gulf War, all before spending the 1990s as CEO of Halliburton.

Washington knew Cheney as a brilliant strategist in both national security and partisan politics, superb at leading both the defense establishment and the Republican Party. A good treatment of Cheney, although one less unsympathetic toward his ideology than I, is Nicholas Lemann, *The Quiet Man: Dick Cheney's Discreet Rise to Unprecedented Power,* New Yorker (May 7, 2001).

18. Dana Milbank & Ellen Nakashima, *Bush Team Has "Right" Credentials: Conservative Picks Seen Eclipsing Even Reagan's,* Wash. Post (March 25, 2001).

19. A range of his positions is collected in John R. Bolton, *Should We Take Global Governance Seriously?* 1 Chi. J. Int'l L. 205 (2000).

20. Bolton's profile is in Foreign Policy in Focus, at http://www.fpif.org.

21. *Selecting the Next United Nations Secretary General,* Hearing before the Subcomm. on International Organizations and Human Rights of the House Comm. on International Relations (Sept. 24, 1996).

22. *U.S. Peacekeeping Endeavors,* Hearings before the House Comm. on International Relations (April 9, 1997).

23. Bolton, *Saddam Wins, supra;* Bolton, *Our Pitiful Iraq Policy, supra.*

24. His Senate Foreign Relations Committee confirmation hearing occurred on March 29, 2001.

25. *Bolton Nomination,* Hearing before the Senate Comm. on Foreign Relations (March 29, 2001).

26. Lawrence F. Kaplan, *Containment,* New Republic (Feb. 5, 2001), at 17.

27. Id.

28. Abraham, *supra.*

29. Patrice Hill, *Bush Takes Centrist Stance on Utility Emission Limits,* Wash. Times (Oct. 17, 2003), at A3; *Second Presidential Debate between Gov. Bush and Vice President Gore,* N.Y. Times (Oct. 12, 2000).

30. Eric Pianin, *EPA Mulls Limits for Power Plant Emissions: Environmentalists Laud White House Effort on Pollutant,* Wash. Post (Feb. 28, 2001), at A13.

31. The senators' letter is at http://www.lavoisier.com.

32. Letter from the president to senators Hagel, Helms, Craig, and Roberts, March 13, 2001, at http://www.whitehouse.gov.

33. "Seldom in history has the United States suffered the kind of international criticism that its decision to withdraw from Kyoto elicited." Miranda A. Schreurs, *Competing Agendas and the Climate Change Negotiations: The United States, the European Union, and Japan,* 36 Envtl. L. Rep. 11218 (2001).

34. Ron Suskind, *The Price of Loyalty: George W. Bush, the White House, and the Education of Paul O'Neill* 120 (2003).

35. Wirth, *supra.*

36. The Bonn Agreement embraced a wide variety of flexible mechanisms for meeting greenhouse gas reduction goals, just as the Clinton administration had anticipated in making the key stalemate-breaking proposals in 1997. Schreurs, *supra.*

37. Useful later accounts by leading tobacco industry critics about what this meant for candidate Bush are Dan Zegart, *Bush, Marlboro's Man: George W. Bush's Policy towards Tobacco Industry,* The Nation (Nov. 6, 2000), at 8; Michael Pertschuk, *When It Comes to Tobacco Legislation, Who Wins in November May Matter a Lot,* The Nation (April 17, 2000), at 15.

38. The industry-funded National Smokers Alliance ran attack ads against McCain assaulting his honesty—and the purity of his conservative credentials—in the critical South Carolina primary, because McCain, in Senate legislating, had not followed the pro-tobacco line of party conservatives loyal to the industry. Troy K. Schneider, *At the Races: A Weekly Review of Campaign 2000,* 7 Nat'l J. 496 (Feb. 12, 2000); Eric Pooley et al., *Read My Knuckles: To Win Big in South Carolina, Bush Found His Anger, Battered McCain—and Moved Sharply to the Right,* Time (Feb. 28, 2000), at 28.

39. David A. Breaux, *Checkbook Democracy: How Money Corrupts Political Campaigns* (2000).

40. On Rove, see Dubose, Reid, & Cannon, *supra.* I was on the anti-tobacco side in a lawsuit in which the court received a copy of Dinh's expert written testimony, originally from another matter. The tobacco companies paid Dinh to argue that although documents revealing the industry's misdeeds had been obtained and published by Congress, they could not be used in court against the tobacco industry.

41. Olson, *Politicizing the Justice Department, supra,* at 151, 157.

42. Background on the legal issues is in David J. Malcolm, *Tobacco, Global Public Health, and Non-governmental Organizations: An Eminent Pandemic or Just Another Legal Product?* 28 Denv. J. Int'l L. & Pol'y 1 (1999).

43. The figures are from Stephen D. Sugarman, *International Aspects of Tobacco Control and the Proposed WHO Treaty,* in Robert L. Rabin & Stephen D. Sugarman, eds., *Regulating Tobacco* (2001).

44. Alexander Stille, *Advocating Tobacco, on the Payroll of Tobacco,* N.Y. Times (March 23, 2002) (quoting Scruton's publication).

45. Alison Langley, *World Health Meeting Approves Treaty to Discourage Smoking,* N.Y. Times (May 22, 2003), at A11.

46. A summary of the sequence of events involving Novotny is in Marc Kaufman, *Negotiator in Global Tobacco Talks Quits,* Wash. Post (Aug. 2, 2001). Further details were in documents released by Representative Henry Waxman (D-Cal.), a leading anti-tobacco voice in Congress.

47. For example, the administration had been quite vague about what kind of legislative implementation of the advertising ban it would support within the United States. The seemingly bland condition it had inserted, that the ban must be implemented "consistent" with the Constitution, left plenty of room for the tobacco industry tie up the progress of domestic implementing legislation until the administration honored the industry's extremely expansive views of its First Amendment rights to push its product. The administration had carefully avoided encouraging critics' skepticism that a killer addictive drug had a full complement of constitutionally guaranteed rights of commer-

cial promotion. And overseas, some observers predicted that if the treaty squeezed any tobacco sellers, it would be the little companies, not the big ones. *Puffed Up or Stubbed Out?* Economist (May 24, 2003) (noting prospects of "gradual and uneven implementation").

48. For example, if the press made a firestorm about Novotny's having put forth pro-tobacco stances, members of Congress could propose appropriation limitation riders against spending for those purposes. Under some circumstances, this could force Republican members from affluent centrist-leaning districts where the tobacco industry's selling to children had always been unpopular to have to vote in ways putting on painfully explicit display whose cash they, through their party, took.

49. These problems are described in Steven Weinberg, *Can Missile Defense Work?*, N.Y. Rev. of Books (Feb. 14, 2002), at 41.

50. Walter C. Uhler, *Missile Shield or Holy Grail? How to Kill: The New Battle over Shielding America from Missile Attack*, The Nation (Jan. 28, 2002), at 25.

51. This paragraph is based on David E. Sanger & Patrick E. Tyler, *Officials Recount Road to Deadlock over Missile Talks*, N.Y. Times (Dec. 13, 2001), at A1.

52. *Bush's Hang-Ups*, Economist (Dec. 15, 2001).

53. The international effort to create war crimes tribunals drew on idealistic appeals to the European and American publics and, through the 1990s, on the so-called "CNN factor"—public sympathy for populations facing dramatic mistreatment, such as the innocent victims of Serbian brutality.

54. The Clinton administration heeded its Defense Department's legitimate concerns about protecting the U.S. military, while recognizing its State Department's sensitivity to the benefits the United States stood to gain from a legal regime that delegitimated the war criminals it would proceed against in places like Rwanda and Serbia.

55. For debates about the "unsigning" tactic, including background on the distinguishable predecessor gambits, see Harold Hongju Koh, *On American Exceptionalism*, 55 Stan. L. Rev. 1479 (2003) (decrying the "unsigning"); Edward T. Swaine, *Unsigning*, 55 Stan. L. Rev. 2061 (2003) (producing a framework that legitimates the "unsigning" as "forthright").

56. Robert A. Levy, *Federal Tobacco Policy: Return to Reason?* (June 4, 2001), http://www.cato.org.

57. For general background, see I. M. Destler, *American Trade Politics* (3d ed. 1995).

58. Tiefer, *Alongside the Fast Track*, supra.

59. Some of these points are covered in Charles Tiefer, *Free Trade Agreements and the New Federalism*, 7 Minn. J. Global Trade 45 (1998).

60. Robert Putnam, *Diplomacy and Domestic Politics: The Logic of Two-Level Games*, 42 Int'l Org. 427 (1988).

61. See Tiefer, *Alongside the Fast Track*, supra.

62. This point is further developed and documented in Tiefer, *How to Steal a Trillion, supra*, at 456–71 (and sources cited).

63. For an introduction to the legal literature on the "democracy deficit" issue in trade policy, of which this analysis is part, see Patti Goldman, *The Democratization of the Development of United States Trade Policy*, 27 Cornell Int'l L.J. 631 (1994).

64. Tiefer, *Adjusting Sovereignty, supra.*

65. See, e.g., Inaamul Haque, *Doha Development Agenda: Recapturing the Momentum of Multilateralism and Developing Countries*, 17 Am. U. Int'l L. Rev. 1097 (2002).

66. Christopher M. Bruner, *Hemispheric Integration and the Politics of Regionalism: The Free Trade Area of the Americas (FTAA)*, 33 U. Miami Inter-Am. L. Rev. 1 (2002).

67. Bill Javetski, *He's Selling the Free Market to the World*, Bus. Week (June 3, 1991), at 110.

68. Such an operative would have steered the serious Japanese American trade talks toward an attack on environmental rules. Japanese officials had unhappily noted that low American auto sales had more to do with Detroit's marketing of left-hand-drive cars in their right-hand-drive country than with their allegedly excessive environmentalism.

69. James A. Barnes, *Inside Bush's Campaign Shop*, Nat'l J. (Aug. 7, 1999).

70. *Some in Bush Administration with Financial Ties to Enron*, USA Today (Jan. 21, 2002), at 8A.

71. Robert B. Zoellick, *A Republican Foreign Policy*, Foreign Aff. (Jan. 2000).

72. Steven Pearlstein, *Bush Selection Zoellick Is a Free-Trader on a Mission*, Wash. Post. (Jan. 13, 2001), at A2.

73. Bruce Stokes, *Talk about Unintended Consequences*, Nat'l J. (May 26, 2001).

74. Robert B. Zoellick, *Countering Terror with Trade*, Wash. Post (Sept. 25, 2001).

75. The precise figures of House Democratic support were 102 for NAFTA (1994) and 167 for the Uruguay Round bill that launched the WTO (1994). In 1997 President Clinton and Speaker Gingrich decided to pull the fast-track renewal bill before a floor vote for lack of support, but the estimated House Democratic support was perhaps 140.

76. Helene Cooper et al., *House Votes Wide Trade Powers for Bush*, Wall St. J. (Dec. 7, 2001).

77. Tiefer, *Congressional Practice and Procedure, supra*, at 354–55.

78. The House Republican leadership held the 2003 vote on final passage of the Medicare drug benefit for three hours, dwarfing this prior phenomenon.

79. Franklin Foer, *Fabric Softener: The Textile Lobby v. the War on Terrorism*, New Republic (March 5, 2002).

80. Jeff Faux, *A Deal Built on Sand*, American Prospect (winter 2002), at A22.

81. Cooper et al., *supra.*

82. *The High Price of Fast Track*, Fin. Times (Dec. 17, 2001).

83. On the farm bill, see Daniel Altman, *Global Trade Looking Glass: Can U.S. Have It Both Ways?* N.Y. Times (Nov. 9, 2002), at B1. Zoellick discusses his proposed deal with the Europeans in *Bringing Down the Barriers: Robert Zoellick Says the US Is Prepared to Tackle Its Own Trade-Distorting Policies on Agriculture If Others Agree to Do the Same*, Fin. Times (July 26, 2002), at 21.

84. *Notebook: DeMint Condition*, New Republic (May 27, 2002), at 8.

85. Faux, *supra*, at A22; *DeMint Condition, supra*; Foer, *supra*.

86. Steven Greenhouse, *Mexican Trucks Gain Approval to Haul Cargo throughout U.S.*, N.Y. Times (Nov. 28, 2002).

87. These were not Bush's sole fault; he and the Democrats had gotten into a bidding war in 2002 for farm-state Senate seats. It was a fact of the American federal system (although the Republican party under Bush did have to forget its temporary belief in the deregulated free market during the 1990s): House Republicans had to learn that while welfare was something certainly to be pulled away from poor women and children, especially minorities, one could not take a cavalier attitude toward pulling back welfarelike subsidies from well-connected agribusiness.

88. *Deposition Lists Lucrative Deals for Bush Brother*, N.Y. Times (Nov. 27, 2003), at A23.

89. The conservative movement seemed to care not so much about the China issue in itself as about its utility for embarrassing a Democratic president. Apparently the issue could be shrugged off when Bush junior was in office and his brother was accepting Chinese millions and putting them, not indirectly through a chain of obscuring intermediaries into campaign fund pools, but directly into his own wallet.

90. On Zoellick's threat, see Guy De JonQuieres & Frances Williams, *Stalled in Geneva: After Doha, a Further Trade Liberalization Round Seemed Imminent, but Wavering US Commitment to the Cause Has Robbed It of Its Impetus*, Fin. Times (June 19, 2002), at 22. The withdrawal of the amendment is reported in Rob Hotakainen, *Senate Passes Trade Bill, Giving Bush a Victory*, Minn. Star Trib. (Aug. 2, 2002), at 1A.

91. Tiefer, *Sino 301, supra*, at 76–79 (2000).

92. These allowed only the U.S. government, not companies or foreign governments, to obtain court orders invalidating certain kinds of state laws on trade grounds.

93. A scholarly treatment of this prospect is Vicki Been & Joel C. Beauvais, *The Global Fifth Amendment? NAFTA's Investment Protections and the Misguided Quest for an International "Regulatory Takings" Doctrine*, 78 N.Y.U. L. Rev. 30 (2003).

94. See Bruce Stokes, *Talk about Unintended Consequences*, Nat'l J. (May 26, 2001).

95. See Harold Meyerson, *Senatorial Heresy: The Democrats Rethink Free Trade*, Am. Prospect (June 17, 2002), at 12.

96. See Marjorie Cohn, *The World Trade Organization: Elevating Property Interests above Human Rights*, 29 Ga. J. Int'l & Comp. L. 427 (2001).

97. Maude Barlow & Tony Clarke, *Who Owns Water?* The Nation (Sept. 2, 2002).

98. *Notebook: Puff Peace*, New Republic (Jan. 20, 2003), at 10.

99. Foer, *Fabric Softener, supra*.

100. Charles Tiefer, *Sino 301: How Congress Can Effectively Review Relations with China after WTO Accession*, 34 Cornell Int'l L.J. 56, 59 (2001).

101. Id.

102. Barenberg's discussion is in a section 301 petition filed on behalf of the AFL-CIO in March 2004 with the Office of the U.S. Trade Representative and is available at http://www.aflcio.org.

103. China's export surplus to the United States had indeed grown during the Clinton years, and the Clinton administration had negotiated the China WTO accession agreement. However, that administration had also shown itself willing to fight: it had fought hard and well regarding Chinese export of pirated information technology. Of China's $70 billion of exports to the United States prior to 1999, $10 billion fell under U.S. antidumping orders. Tiefer, *Sino 301, supra*, at 78. Sandy Berger cited the continuing availability of those remedies as a major basis for the accession agreement. Id. Bush and Zoellick had the tools; it was their choice not to use them.

7. VEERING FROM RIYADH TO BAGHDAD

1. I have discussed this in Charles Tiefer, Book Review, 96 Am. J. Int'l L. 489 (2002) (reviewing Michael J. Glennon, *Limits of Law, Prerogatives of Power: Interventionism after Kosovo* [2001]).

2. Tiefer, *The Semi-Sovereign Presidency, supra*, 89–118.

3. Kristol & Kagan, *supra*.

4. Id.

5. In 1997 they joined in founding a group called the Project for a New American Century, a step on the long road to the preemption doctrine. Steven R. Weisman, *Pre-emption: Idea with a Lineage Whose Time Has Come*, N.Y. Times (March 23, 2003), at B1.

6. The bible of those tracing terrorism to Saddam Hussein was Laurie Mylroie, *Study of Revenge: Saddam Hussein's Unfinished War against America* (2000). Mylroie was a fellow of the American Enterprise Institute, a conservative bastion, and AEI published her book. Yet she had been a consultant to the Clinton campaign in 1992. Another major voice about such issues, James R. Woolsey, had been the first CIA director in the Clinton administration. While working on two different congressional investigations, in 1987 and 1995, I met Woolsey and each time found him quite credible and, while not especially pro-Democratic, not strongly partisan the other way either. In other

words, Mylroie and Woolsey's line of analysis, though in the end more useful to hard-line Republicans than anyone else, originally crossed party and ideological lines. To put it another way, the inherently difficult issues of how dangerous to consider Saddam Hussein and how to handle him were not intrinsically partisan or ideological, just as the issues of how to handle North Korea were not partisan or ideological. The issue became so only in 2002–2003 because of the political uses to which President Bush put it.

7. *In Clinton's Words: Containing the "Predators of the 21st Century,"* N.Y. Times (Feb. 17, 1998).

8. In one obscure but memorable May 2000 comment, though, Robert Zoellick, the foreign policy adviser who later became U.S. trade representative, said, as reported by the London *Independent,* that the United States should dismember Iraq, "taking away pieces of [its] territory" and thereby splitting it into several different states. Sensible observers regarded Zoellick's as the single proposal demonstrably worse for the region than Saddam Hussein, offering the ayatollahs of Iran a Shiite satellite and threatening Turkey with an independent Kurdish enemy. Andrew Marshall, *Take Iraq Apart, Says Bush Adviser,* The Independent (May 21, 2000).

9. Stephen Fidler & Gerard Baker, *America's Democratic Imperialists: How the Neo-Conservatives Rose from Humility to Empire in Two Years,* Fin. Times (March 6, 2003), at 11.

10. The immediate support marshaled to deflect criticism away from our "ally" Saudi Arabia was contemporaneously discussed in Ken Silverstein, *Saudis and Americans: Friends in Need,* The Nation (Dec. 3, 2001), at 35.

11. Dore Gold, *Hatred's Kingdom: How Saudi Arabia Supports the New Global Terrorism* (Regnery, 2003).

12. Id., at 183.

13. Id., at 122 (quoting a Western observer in Dhahran).

14. Martin Merzer, *Unilateral Iraq Attack Losing Support,* Milwaukee J. Sentinel (Jan. 12, 2003), at 3A.

15. Karl Rove noted the potential advantage for his party in a January 18, 2002, speech at the Republican National Committee's winter meeting: "We can go to the country on this issue because they trust the Republican Party to do a better job of protecting and strengthening America's military might and thereby protecting America." Dubose, Reid, & Cannon, *supra,* 216. The remark became well known.

16. James Kitfield, *Next Stop—Baghdad,* Nat'l. J. (Oct. 13, 2001).

17. Not only in the United States but also abroad, objective observers traced the participants in the airplane hijackings, the attacks' planning and financing, and the motivation for them to a tight-knit fanatical conspiracy of a *jihadi* nature—i.e., a distorted version of Islam bent on zealots' combat. These characteristics and indications utterly failed to fit Baghdad. The rest of the world understood as well as or better than American observers what underlay Osama bin Laden's attitudes as expressed in his 2003 tape scorning Saddam

Hussein as a "socialist" and hence an "infidel": bin Laden's internationally widespread self-sacrificing religious zealots abhorred Saddam Hussein's personal and Iraqi nationalist interests.

18. Mansour Farhang, *A Triangle of Realpolitik: Iran, Iraq and the United States*, The Nation (March 17, 2003), at 18.

19. Howard W. French, *North Korea Has an Axis All Its Own*, N.Y. Times (Feb. 10, 2002), sec. 4, at 4; Abbas Amanat, *A Risky Message to Iran*, N.Y. Times (Feb. 10, 2003), sec. 4, at 15.

20. The sequence leading there is traced in Mike Allen & Barton Gellman, *Preemptive Strikes Part of U.S. Strategic Doctrine* (Wash. Post), Dec. 11, 2002.

21. Bruce Ackerman, *But What's the Legal Case for Preemption?* Wash. Post (Aug. 18, 2002), at B2.

22. The United States went overtly beyond deterrence and containment only in its limited response to very grave provocation: During the crisis in 1962 when Cuba installed Soviet nuclear missiles, the United States imposed a quarantine by a mere interdictive step outside Cuba's territory—not a preemptive air strike, which senior American officials at the time disapprovingly likened to Pearl Harbor.

23. Tiefer, (book review) *supra*.

24. Remarks by the President at 2002 Graduation Exercises of the United States Military Academy. West Point, New York (June 1, 2002).

25. Stephen Murdoch, *Preemptive War: Is It Legal?* Wash. Lawyer (Jan. 2003), at 24.

26. *The National Security Strategy of the United States of America* (September 2002).

27. Ivo H. Daalder, James M. Lindsay, & James B. Steinberg, *The Bush National Security Strategy: An Evaluation*, http://www.brookings.edu.

28. David E. Sanger & Elisabeth Bumiller, *Bush Presses U.N. to Act Quickly on Disarming Iraq*, N.Y. Times (Sept. 13, 2002), at A1.

29. The best comment on the constitutional implications of Congress's authorization came from Senator Robert C. Byrd, *Congress Must Resist the Rush to War*, N.Y. Times (Oct. 10, 2002), at A39.

30. Gebe Martinez, *Concerns Linger for Lawmakers following Difficult Vote for War*, 60 Cong. Q. Wkly. Rep. 2671 (Oct. 12, 2002).

31. Dilip Hiro, *Secrets and Lies: Operation "Iraqi Freedom" and Thereafter* 61 (2004) (drawing on what was said by Clare Short, the British cabinet minister who resigned in May 2003 in protest of Blair's Iraq policy).

32. Julia Preston, *Security Council Votes, 15–0, for Tough Iraq Resolution*, N.Y. Times (Nov. 9, 2002), at A1.

33. David E. Sanger, *Canvassing the Votes to Gain Legitimacy*, N.Y. Times (March 13, 2003), at A12.

34. Tiefer, (book review) *supra*.

35. I have made a similar argument about partial or arguable justifications in congressional votes when a full authorization has not occurred. Tiefer, *War Decisions in the Late 1990s by Partial Congressional Declaration, supra*.

36. "'With eight votes,' one friend of Mr. Bush's said today, 'he could go on television the night of the U.N. vote and say, "We are backed by a majority of the Security Council." And that would help a lot.'" David E. Sanger, *Canvassing the Votes to Gain Legitimacy*, N.Y. Times (March 13, 2003), at A12.

37. Steven R. Weisman, *A Long, Winding Road to a Diplomatic Dead End*, N.Y. Times (March 17, 2003), at A1.

38. A good review of the sequence is in id.

39. The British foreign minister resigned when the war began, showing just what a perceptive secretary of state might do. Secretary Vance had resigned over the ill-fated "rescue mission" for the Iran hostages in 1980; President Wilson's secretary, William Jennings Bryan, resigned rather than take part in his chief's nonpacific policy; it happens sometimes. See "Who's Who: William Jennings Bryan," www.firstworldwar.com.

40. Turkey had stood by the United States against Iraq through the dozen years of allowing U.S. fighter jets patrolling the no-fly zone to use Turkish air bases. The Turkish military, having fought an internal war for years against the Kurds, desperately desired to move into northern Iraq and prevent its nemesis from rising to autonomous state stature. But the proud and increasingly Islamic-nationalist Turkish public found Bush's position intolerably alienating, along with the fact that neither he nor his top lieutenants traveled around, met and listened, or paid even the minimal attention to the views of "inferior nations" shown by every other superpower in history.

41. James Fallows, *Blind into Baghdad*, Atlantic Monthly (Jan.–Feb. 2004), at 53.

42. Julie Kosterlitz, *Neoconservatives in Eclipse?* Nat'l J. (Oct. 25, 2003), at 3284.

43. These stories are told in Tiefer, *War Decisions in the Late 1990s, supra*, at 20 & n.90; 25 & n.109.

44. Whether the game would change once Congress reconvened after the November 2004 election was of course another story. (Recall that DeLay reconvened Congress after the November 2000 election to finalize spending, including putting the final touches on how he and Senator Nickles would kill the ten-year initiative to reduce the employer-caused workplace injuries threatening twenty-seven million Americans ["ergonomics"].)

45. First, the Republican leader would remind listeners of something you don't hear much today, that he and all his party colleagues called themselves "the party of Lincoln." While Republican leaders today may talk about wartime leadership in their fund-raising talks back in Texas and other Southern states, presumably Lincoln and his Emancipation Proclamation are not overemphasized.

46. Adam Nagourney, *White House Tries to Dismiss Iraq Claim as Campaign Issue*, N.Y. Times (July 15, 2003), at A11.

47. Private communication to me from a journalist.

48. Issam al-Chalabi, *Iraqi Oil Policy: Present and Future Perspectives*, Cambridge Energy Research Associates (March 24, 2003), at 42.

49. A fuller explanation can be found in Charles Tiefer and William A. Shook, *Government Contract Law* (2d ed. 2004).

50. Jeffrey H. Birnbaum, *The Iraq Fixers Are Circling,* Fortune (Oct. 2003), at 56. Birnbaum has proven himself one of the best reporters in Washington about lobbying, both in his work for the *Wall Street Journal* and for his coauthorship of the classic *Showdown at Gucci Gulf.*

51. Birnbaum, *Iraq Fixers, supra.*

52. Joseph J. Schatz, *Senate Rejects White House Plea, Adopts Iraqi Loan Amendment,* Cong. Q. Wkly. Rep. (Oct. 18, 2003), 2573, at 2574–75.

53. Id. at 2577 (quoting Kerry).

54. Jonathan Weisman, *Senate Defies Bush on Iraq Assistance,* Wash. Post (Oct. 17, 2003), at A1.

55. Carolyn Skorneck, *Bush Wins Supplemental Battle, May Face Loss in War on Terror,* Cong. Q. Wkly. Rep. (Nov. 1, 2003), at 2715.

56. Id.

57. Carolyn Skorneck, *Supplemental sans Roll Call Provides Cover All Around,* Cong. Q. Wkly. Rep. (Nov. 8, 2003), 2783, at 2784.

58. George C. Wilson, *Iraq Could Be Another Lebanon,* Nat'l J. (Nov. 8, 2003), at 3436.

59. Id.

60. P. W. Singer, *Corporate Warriors: The Rise of the Privatized Military Industry* (2003).

61. For the full Saudi story, look to the best-seller *Sleeping with the Devil* (2003), by Robert Baer, a knowledgeable thirty-year CIA veteran fed up with the Saudis; and, for the relation to current events of the Saudi ruling class's flaws, to the coverage in *Time* and *Newsweek,* especially articles in the latter by Michael Isikoff and Mark Hosenball. This is not an ideological analysis. The foregoing centrist writers basically agree about Saudi Arabia with Dore Gold's popular 2003 book, *Hatred's Kingdom: How Saudi Arabia Supports the New Global Terrorism,* which became a main selection of the Conservative Book Club.

62. It was a variation on the Great Game, played by Britain and Russia in Central Asia in the 1800s and early 1900s, that appealed to Republican presidents; plus now, the Americans understood the economic importance of the oil.

63. Gold, *supra,* at 130.

64. The best description is in Ahmed Rashid, *Taliban: Militant Islam, Oil, and Fundamentalism in Central Asia* (Penguin, 2003) (written by the best foreign correspondent in the region and originally published by Yale University Press).

65. Baer, *supra,* at 43, 64.

66. Id., at 52.

67. Id.

68. Actually, the Christian conservatives had their own problem with the Saudis, epitomized by Bush repeatedly calling his ventures into South Asia a

"crusade"—a phrase he used for his religious Christian base but one that made the Wahhabi Saudis wince at his ignorance of history. Bush's "crusading," like Robertson and Falwell making nasty remarks about the religion of Islam, reminded the Middle East that it viewed the Christian occupation of the Holy Land from roughly 1000 to 1200 (what we call the Crusades) as an act of Western barbarians—especially because the contemporary people of the Middle East associate this period much more with the heroism of Saladin and the Arab "liberation" of the area from the Latin Kingdoms temporarily set up in the name of the Church than we do.

The new ideological heart of the conservative Republican party lay in Texas, with Dick Armey of Houston, Tom DeLay of Dallas, and the state's 1994–2000 governor, young George. The simple economics of energy prices always bound Texas with the limited number of American energy-profiting states on one side and the mainly energy-consuming, hence energy "money-losing," states such as California and the New York, on the other. Houston became the American center of the world oil industry, partly because Arabs found it infinitely more simpatico (focusing now not on the religions of faith but the religion of making oil money) than New York (where the United Nations lived, which bored them) or Washington (which usually didn't devote all its thinking to oil money; that, is until after 2001).

So as the conservative takeover of the South, of Texas in particular, and then of Washington unrolled, the remunerative ways of the Saudi-Republican alliance became much simpler. Conveniently, in 1993 Clinton made the fatal error of proposing an energy tax. This would shift some of the quasi-monopoly profits of OPEC into the U.S. Treasury. The Saudis didn't like that, and the Republicans portrayed it as a tax increase to milk the rich party donors and the angry anti-tax activists alike, an argument that material helped the 1994 Republican takeover of Congress. The anti-communist cause might be kaput, but the Saudis and conservative congressional Republicans now discovered common interests such as a successful partnership dividing up fat rewards. Congressional Republicans hated as much as the Saudis how California and New York Democrats kept talking, at home and even (in a muffled way) toward Riyadh, about investing in the education of potential workers rather than just in big construction projects; how the centrist public yammered about renewable energy resources and energy conservation (as practiced in Europe and Japan) instead of just oil, oil, oil; how the uppity women's movement at home and abroad kept demanding that more women be allowed into higher education and into the seats of power in business and government instead being kept below the glass ceiling (or in the harem).

69. Maureen Lorenzetti, *DOE to Investigate Last Month's Gasoline Price Spike*, Oil & Gas J. (Sept. 15, 2003), at 32.

70. Baer, *supra*, at 66.

71. Id., at 60–68.

72. Id., at 67.

73. Id.

74. Thomas L. Friedman, *Drilling for Tolerance,* N.Y. Times (Oct. 30, 2001), at A17.

75. Phillips, *American Dynasty, supra,* at 47, 130 (quoting Robert Sherrill, *What Fertilized the Bushes,* Texas Observer [July 12, 1991]).

76. Martin Peretz, *Audit This,* New Republic (July 22, 2002).

77. Testimony by Robert W. Jordan before the Senate Foreign Relations Committee, Sept. 21, 2001 (in FDCH Lexis database).

78. Michael Barone, *Our Enemies the Saudis,* U.S. News & World Rep. (June 3, 2002). Barone may have touched a raw nerve in Jordan when he concluded a powerful brief analysis by saying, "It may not be prudent yet to speak the truth out loud, that the Saudis are our enemies. But they should know that it is increasingly apparent to the American people that they are effectively waging war against us." *U.S. News & World Report* got a lot of attention for showing that American anger extended even to those speaking for our (conservative) business elite. Jordan's op-ed reads like a response to Barone very heavy on currying favor with the Saudis—a lucrative endeavor in the long run—but not exactly heavy on the truth about the level of Saudi cooperation on terrorism financing.

79. Judith Miller, *U.S. Examines Donations of 2 Saudis to Determine If They Aided Terrorism,* N.Y. Times (March 25, 2002).

80. Turki himself did not join in the Bush administration's line about linking Osama with Saddam Hussein. He commented, "Iraq does not come very high in the estimations of bin Laden. He thinks of Saddam Hussein as an apostate, an infidel or someone who is not worthy of being a fellow Muslim." Hiro, *supra,* at 28 (quoting Turki in the *International Herald Tribune* on Nov. 22, 2001).

81. Tiefer, *The Semi-Sovereign Presidency, supra,* at 112–13 ("The April Glaspie Myth") (citing the *New York Times* and *Congressional Quarterly Almanac*).

82. Baer, *supra,* at 202.

83. Michael Steinberger, *Bush's Saudi Connections: And Why This Is a Crucial Issue in 2004,* Am. Prospect (Oct. 2003), 15, at 16.

84. Bartalk Column, *And There Should Be No Shortage of Firms Willing to Pitch In,* Am. Lawyer (Feb. 2003).

85. Weisberg, *supra,* at 41, 45.

86. Helen Caldicott, *The New Nuclear Danger: George W. Bush's Military-Industrial Complex* 172–74 (2002).

87. David E. Sanger, *Bush Issues Directive Describing Policy on Antimissile Defenses,* N.Y. Times (May 21, 2003), at A16.

88. Lilian Wu, *Taiwan Legislators Question Radar Purchase from U.S.,* BBC Worldwide Monitoring (April 1, 2004), available on Lexis-Nexis.

89. See Mark Zepezauer, *Boomerang!* 30–38 (2003) (Sudan); Phillis Bennis, *Before & After: US Foreign Policy and the September 11th Crisis* 174–77 (2003) (Cuba, Colombia).

90. Jerry Hagstrom, *Cows Chip Away at the Cuban Trade Embargo*, 34 Nat'l J. 1650 (Oct. 5, 2002).

91. Fred Barnes, *The Bush Doctrine Comes to Cuba*, Wkly. Standard (July 15, 2002), at 9.

92. Richard A. Clarke, *Against All Enemies: Inside America's War on Terror* 246 (2004).

93. Johnson's Tonkin Gulf Resolution, making it look as though American ground troops need not go to Vietnam, helped him get the landslide of 1964 (after which the troops went in). Nixon's seminormalization of U.S. relations with China, invasions of Laos and Cambodia, and "Vietnamization" policy (which seemingly neutralized the North Vietnamese while extracting American ground troops) helped him get the landslide of 1972 (though by 1975 his house of cards in Indochina had collapsed). And Reagan's signing of the Boland Amendments and making of accords with the Senate Intelligence Committee to stay out of Nicaraguan fighting helped him get the landslide of 1984 (after which Oliver North unleashed the American proxy war underlying the Iran-contra scandal).

94. Bush was not the kind of president it had taken—Eisenhower in Korea in the 1950s, Bush senior after the Gulf War in 1992, Clinton in Bosnia in 1995—to let the locals and the international community set up their own stable, if imperfect, government and get the United States out of any deeper faraway involvement than Americans wanted to authorize through the full democratic process. Tiefer, *War Decisions in the Late 1990s, supra,* at 9–15 (describing Bosnia).

95. Clarke, *supra.*

96. Saddam's paranoid-vicious style, though unspeakably cruel to his own people, was keeping him in power. Without the wells pumping much, it would take a decade or more to make up for Saddam and for the oil profit to come on really strong, and no one around seemed able to make that kind of investment.

97. Joseph C. Anselmo, *Pentagon Plans for Bigger, Better Army with "Spike,"* Cong. Q. Wkly. Rep. (Jan. 31, 2004), 170, at 272.

98. Id.

99. Knut Royce, *Start-up Company with Connections: U.S. Gives $400M in Work to Contractor with Ties to Pentagon Favorite on Iraqi Governing Council,* Newsday (Feb. 15, 2004); Sue Pleming, *U.S. Halts Deal for Iraqi Army after Protests,* Reuters (Feb. 27, 2004).

100. Cornell University Press.

101. As a prime example, Singer notes that "Halliburton received over $200 million to develop oil well services in the rebellion-ridden Angolan Cabinda enclave. Without the protection guarantees against rebel attacks provided by the PMF Airscan and its local joint ventures, this contract would be worthless." P. W. Singer, *Corporate Warriors* 81 (2003).

102. Mike Allen & Juliet Eilperin, *Bush Aides Say Iraq War Needs No Hill Vote,* Wash. Post, Aug. 26, 2002, at A1.

103. Michelle Goldberg, *Above the Law*, Salon.com, Aug. 28, 2002 (tracing the White House counsel's opinion back to the administration's many ties to the Federalist Society and to a Federalist Society white paper on President Bush's war-initiating power).

104. Helen Fessenden, *Hill's Oversight Role at Risk: Lawmakers Question Accountability as Military Expands Clandestine Operations*, Cong. Q. Wkly. Rep. (March 27, 2004), at 734.

8. BLINDFOLDING THE PUBLIC

1. Patrice McDermott, *Withhold and Control: Information in the Bush Administration*, 12 Kan. J.L. & Pub. Pol'y 671, 671 (2003).

2. Tiefer, *The Controversial Transition Process from Investigating the President to Impeaching Him*, supra.

3. I have given a universal legal treatment to this era in Tiefer, *The Specially Investigated President*, supra.

4. Of course there had been a long history of major and minor legal scrutiny of presidents, from President Washington's earliest discussions of executive privilege, to President Andrew Johnson's impeachment, to the Teapot Dome investigations of the 1920s, through the red-hunting investigations of the 1940s and 1950s. New studies continue to shed light on this history. See Louis Fisher, *The Politics of Executive Privilege* (2004). Discussing the post-1987 specially investigated presidents does not deny the past, but just telescopes it to focus on the immediate background to the Bush administration.

5. Tiefer, *The Senate Impeachment Trial for President Clinton*, supra.

6. Ivins & Dubose, *Shrub*, supra, at 54 (2000 ed.).

7. Dubose, Reid, & Cannon, *Boy Genius*, supra, at 129.

8. Id. at 164.

9. Id.

10. Dubose, Reid, & Cannon, supra, at 118.

11. He was not violating the letter of the law, because he was running for the federal office of president, not a state office, but that must seem a distinction without a difference when the governor is raising funds.

12. Toobin, supra.

13. See Mark J. Rozell, *Executive Privilege: Presidential Power, Secrecy, and Accountability* (2d ed. 2002), at 83–92 (Carter administration), 93–105 (Reagan administration), 123–46 (Clinton administration).

14. Tiefer, *The Specially Investigated President*, supra.

15. Cheney's baptism in office came as a Rumsfeld protégé and as President Ford's young chief of staff, when Ford repeatedly claimed executive privilege on national security affairs. Ford came to office, after Watergate, determined to run a relatively "open" presidency with less executive privilege in most areas than the disgraced President Nixon. As an appointed vice president who became president without ever running in a national election, Ford faced an aroused and reinforced "Watergate" (pro-oversight) Congress elected in

November 1994. Although Ford must ration the exercises of executive privilege, he claimed it as to national security matters. Rozell, *supra*, at 79–82.

16. For example, the Iran-Contra Committee hearings had to discuss President Reagan's infamous "tin cup" diplomacy by which contributions from other governments were solicited for the contras. Because of an insistence on maintaining the technically undisclosed status of the contributing governments' identities, the hearings used the euphemism that contributions came from "Country 1," "Country 2," and so forth. Meanwhile, the press gave its contemporaneous translation, for the millions of television viewers and more millions of next-day newspaper readers, of which specific countries this meant. (In saying this, I myself neither confirm nor deny anything about those press translations, merely noting that they occurred.) Cheney led the committee in insisting on not publicly using country names. He treated this as a matter of respect for the system of classifying such things. The effect of this and related matters was to reduce the overall extent to which the hearings could clearly and forcefully convey to the public the extent of Iran-contra abuses; for example, it served as a helpful backdrop for Oliver North's insistence that his own elaborate and wrongful efforts (and those of others in the White House) to keep the Iran-contra abuses from contemporaneous congressional knowledge in 1984–1986 had justifications in national security akin to those still used to keep matters classified at the time of the 1987 hearings.

On Cheney's behalf, it is appropriate to note that his defense of executive secrecy was a consistent long-term principle, not something opportunistically or cynically devised just at the moment of the 1987 hearings. On the other hand, if Cheney ever made a public point of raising his principle at a point where it would come to the defense of Democratic presidents, the author has not been able to find it. In this regard, he is like the separate fount of executive privilege in the Bush administration, Olson, who also had a consistent long-term principle on the subject but who also never came to the defense of a Democratic president on it. The political uses of secrecy can occur without necessitating that the expositors be crassly cynical, just selective.

17. For accounts of the critical period of the first week of August 1990, see Jean Edward Smith, *George Bush's War* 80–95 (1992); Bob Woodward, *The Commanders* 228–56 (1991). It is said that, following the Iraqi invasion of Kuwait on August 2, 1990, the Saudis were not particularly motivated to liberate Kuwait, which was not a close friend. Secretary Cheney transformed their reluctance to allow a large U.S. military buildup on Saudi territory by showing them, according to public reports, satellite photographs of Iraqi tank forces lined up facing toward Saudi Arabia; the photos helped convince the Saudis they were the next target. Objective interpreters of such photographs would not necessarily have drawn that conclusion, absent some other indications to be expected had the Iraqis had any such imminent invasion plan.

This is not necessarily to criticize what Cheney did in 1990, when Iraq had, of course, actually engaged in the inexcusable aggression of invading and occupying Kuwait. Rather, it is to identify a consistent Cheney approach to national security by which he may have helped bring on both American wars against Iraq, in 1991 and in 2003: describing intelligence in slanted ways that portrayed Iraq as prone to press on with further aggressive use of weapons. Both times, Cheney used to the hilt the advantages that the legal secrecy surrounding intelligence provides to those with his kinds of preexisting objectives.

18. Tiefer, *The Semi-Sovereign Presidency, supra,* at 128–30.

19. Rozell, *supra;* Vanessa Blum, *Why Bush Won't Let Go: To the White House, the Paper Fight with Congress Is Part of a Bigger Plan to Restore Presidential Power,* Legal Times (Feb. 4, 2002).

20. Vest, *supra.*

21. Bolton's background—such as his testifying to Congress in favor of Taiwan's independence without mentioning that he was on the Taiwanese payroll, and his close association with Senator Jesse Helms—is discussed in chapter 5.

22. He had published lengthy jurisprudential justifications of executive privilege during the most bitter formal executive privilege battle of the entire Reagan-Bush years—Olson's unsuccessful fight to use executive privilege to cover up environmental abuses in 1981–1982. This Olson fought for on such extreme terms that he himself became the target of a lengthy criminal investigation for obstruction and false statements, something that became his badge of honor in conservative circles. For a survey of the sources on executive privilege, several of which recount the Superfund matter, see Tiefer, *The Specially Investigated President, supra,* at 144 & n.7. As to the independent counsel's investigation of Olson, see *Morrison v. Olson,* 487 U.S. 654 (1988).

23. The final GAO report drily noted: "In developing the National Energy Policy report, the NEPDG [National Energy Policy Development Group] Principals, Support Group, and participating agency officials and staff met with, solicited input from, or received information and advice from nonfederal energy stakeholders, principally petroleum, coal, nuclear, natural gas, and electricity industry representatives and lobbyists." General Accounting Office, *Process Used to Develop the National Energy Policy* 1 (Aug. 25, 2003).

24. For background on the case, see Mark J. Rozell, *Executive Privilege Revived? Secrecy and Conflict during the Bush Presidency,* 52 Duke L.J. 403, 411–13 (2002).

25. Charles Lane, *Olson's Role in War on Terror Matches His Uncommon Clout,* Wash. Post (July 3, 2002), at A21.

26. *Walker v. Cheney,* 230 F. Supp. 2d 51 (D.D.C. 2002).

27. GAO Press Statement on *Walker v. Cheney* (Feb. 7, 2003).

28. For background on the case, see Rozell, *Executive Privilege Revived? supra,* at 413–19.

29. Charles Tiefer, *Overcoming Executive Privilege at the Justice Department,* in *The History of Congressional Access to Deliberative Justice Department Documents,* Hearings before the House Committee on Government Reform, 107th Cong., 2d sess. (Feb. 6, 2002).

30. Charles Tiefer, *President Bush's First Executive Privilege Claim*, 33 Presidential Studies Q. 201 (2003).

31. When Cheney beat the GAO so badly that it dropped its appeal, the pro-oversight forces in Congress were embarrassed. The Boston FBI fight allowed the White House to associate its secrecy drive with seemingly lofty principles (i.e., presidential independence from scrutiny by prosecutors from predecessor administrations) rather than its usual, self-serving political reasons for secrecy. The fight served as a practice run for the administration's enthusiastic privilege-asserting legal staff, conducted on a safe topic and at a safe time—the months right after 9/11, when the public and press would not find fault in the administration even for an unsustained privilege claim.

32. The issue is treated in Marcy Lynn Karin, Note, *Out of Sight, But Not Out of Mind: How Executive Order 13233 Expands Executive Privilege While Simultaneously Preventing Access to Presidential Records*, 55 Stan. L. Rev. 529 (2002).

33. See Martha Joynt Kumar, *Executive Order 13233: Further Implementation of the Presidential Records Act*, 32 Presidential Studies Q. 194 (2002).

34. McDermott, *supra*, at 680–83.

35. Mark S. Zaid, *Too Many Secrets*, Nat'l Law J. (March 25, 2002).

36. See McDermott, *supra*.

37. Id.; John D. Podesta, *Shadow Creep: Government Secrecy since 9/11*, 2002 J. Tech. L. & Pol'y 361 (2002).

38. Alexander Bolton, *Members Hit White House over Secrecy*, The Hill (Aug. 7, 2002).

39. Jim Rutenberg, *White House Keeps a Grip on its News*, N.Y. Times (Oct. 14, 2002).

40. Kristen Elizabeth Uhl, *The Freedom of Information Act Post-9/11: Balancing the Public's Right to Know, Critical Infrastructure Protection, and Homeland Security*, 53 Am. U. L. Rev. 261, 304 & n.255 (2003) (noting the similarity between "the recent erosion of FOIA" and "FOIA's strengthening after the Watergate scandal").

41. See House Permanent Select Comm. on Intelligence & Senate Select Comm. on Intelligence, *Report of the Joint Inquiry into the Terrorist Attacks of September 11, 2001* (drafted Dec. 2002; declassified and released 2003).

42. Don Van Natta, *Last American Combat Troops Quit Saudi Arabia*, N.Y. Times (Sept. 22, 2003), at A8.

43. Gold, *supra*, at 130.

44. The quote is from Lisa Beyer et al., *After 9/11: The Saudis: Friend or Foe?* Time (Sept. 15, 2003), at 38. It paraphrases the fuller exploration of this deal in Gerald Posner, *Why America Slept* (2003). Posner drew on the interrogation of Abu Zubaydah, who attended the meetings between bin Laden and the Saudi intelligence chief, Prince Turki. Interestingly, the meetings predated the Taliban takeover of Afghanistan, which Turki strongly backed and which gave bin Laden his nation-sized base there. For those who wondered why Mul-

lah Omar let his regime be attacked and overturned rather than yield up bin Laden, just look at who installed him in the first place, and why.

45. Beyer et al., *supra.*

46. Gold, *supra,* at 132 & n.40 (citing Nawaf E. Obaid, *Improving U.S. Intelligence Analysis of the Saudi Arabian Decision-Making Process* [master's thesis, John F. Kennedy School of Government, Harvard University, 1998], at 33).

47. Gold, *supra,* at 181–82 (citing a wide array of sources, from the *Wall Street Journal* to terrorism expert Peter L. Bergen's *Holy War, Inc.: Inside the Secret World of Osama bin Laden* [2001]).

48. Linda Robinson et al., *A Question of Complicity,* U.S. News & World Report (June 30, 2003), at 20.

49. Baer, *supra,* at 183.

50. Gold, *supra,* at 205 (the topic was the second Palestinian intifada, which began in September 2000).

51. Beyer, *supra* (chronology following text of article; entry for 2000).

52. Craig Unger, *Saving the Saudis,* Vanity Fair (Oct. 2003), at 162.

53. For a description of just which Saudis on the flight had open FBI investigations or files, see id.

54. Eric Lichtblau, *White House Approved Departure of Saudis after Sept. 11, Ex-Aide Says,* N.Y. Times (Sept. 4, 2003), at A19.

55. David Johnston, *Classified Section of Sept. 11 Report Faults Saudi Rulers,* N.Y. Times (July 26, 2003), at A6.

56. Christopher Dickey, *Saudi Arabia: The Kingdom & the Power,* Newsweek (Aug. 11, 2003), at 14.

57. Joseph Meyer, *Report Is Wary of Saudi Actions,* L.A. Times (July 25, 2003), at 1.

58. Senator Byrd had the text printed in the *Congressional Record* a few weeks later. 147 Cong. Rec. S9950–S9951 (daily ed. Oct. 1, 2001).

59. Introduced as S.J. Res. 23, it was enacted as Pub. L. No. 107-40 on Sept. 18, 2001.

60. The press at the time noted the political resistance to the wording of the 9/12 proposal, as did later legal commentators. Michael J. Glennon, *Presidential Power to Wage War against Iraq,* 6 Green Bag 183 (winter 2003), citing Helen Dewar & Juliet Eilperin, *Emergency Funding Deal Reached: Hill Leaders Agree to Work Out Language on Use of Force,* Wash. Post (Sept. 14, 2001), at A30.

61. In its list of five "Whereas" clauses, it did say, "Whereas, the President has authority under the Constitution to take action to deter and prevent acts of international terrorism against the United States." President Bush might later point to that, but as a merely precatory clause it lacked effect, particularly as to Iraq. Glennon, *Presidential Power to Wage War against Iraq, supra,* at 188: "Material set out in a whereas clause is purely precatory. Such material may be relevant for the purpose of clarifying ambiguities in a statute's legally operative terms, but in and of itself such a provision can confer no legal right or obligation." Such material was part of a long tradition of merely hortatory

congressional references to presidential pretensions, poles apart from Congress's legally binding authorization of war in the "Resolved" clause.

62. For an overall treatment, see Philip J. Cooper, *By Order of the President: The Use and Abuse of Executive Direct Action* (2002).

63. Tiefer, *The Semi-Sovereign Presidency, supra*, ch. 5, "National Security Directives and the Cover-up of the Courtship of Saddam Hussein."

64. For example, by keeping NSD-26 classified long after the Gulf War, President Bush prevented open Senate hearings for the public to see how the president's mistaken guidance led the U.S. ambassador to Iraq, April Glaspie, to send a very wrong signal to Saddam Hussein of American unconcern about Kuwait on the eve of his invasion, a signal Saddam could only too readily mistake as the green light for his invasion.

65. The Clinton administration did have secret directives, as had all administrations going back decades. However, for all President Clinton's other sins— including, above all, Monicagate—he had not used secrecy as the way of getting to war. President Clinton's steps in sending troops to Bosnia in 1995, striking Iraq from the air in 1998, and bombing Kosovo in 1999 had drawn not merely criticism from congressional Republican, but vitriolic criticism. Yet even his critics could hardly accuse President Clinton of effectuating these steps by secret directives. He provided congressional Republicans every opportunity, which they indulged to the limit, to probe and debate, in the open, his long, difficult, ultimately successful prewar preparations and then the war with Milošević itself, as well as his long and difficult duel with Saddam Hussein.

66. Glenn Kessler, *U.S. Decision on Iraq Has Puzzling Past: Opponents of War Wonder When, How Policy Was Set*, Wash. Post (Jan. 12, 2003), at A1.

67. Suskind, *supra*, at 75.

68. Kessler, *supra*, at A1.

69. Hiro, *supra*, at 20, 34.

70. "The C.I.A. also had scant new evidence about links between Iraq and al-Qaeda, but specialists began working on the issue under the direction of Douglas J. Feith, the under secretary of defense for policy. Those analyses did not develop any new intelligence data, but looked at existing reports for possible links between Iraq and terrorists that they felt might have been overlooked or undervalued." James Risen et al., *After the War: Weapons Intelligence: In Sketchy Data, Trying to Gauge Iraq Threat*, N.Y. Times (July 20, 2003), at 1. See also Eli J. Lake, *The Pentagon v. the CIA on Iraq*, New Republic (Sept. 23, 2002).

71. *1995 Cong. Q. Almanac* at 6-18–6-21; *1996 Cong. Q. Almanac* at 5-18–5-26.

72. Barton Gellman, *Broad Effort Launched after '98 Attacks*, Wash. Post (Dec. 19, 2001), at A1.

73. The Clinton administration had received the loud wake-up calls of the 1993 World Trade Center bombing, the 1995 bombing in Oklahoma City, and the 1998 bombings by al-Qaeda of the American embassies in Kenya and Tanzania.

74. A conservative account of this cool treatment that Reno's requests got is Bovard, *supra*. See also *Privacy in the Digital Age, supra*.

75. Clymer, *supra*.

76. See Dan Eggen & Dana Priest, *Bush Aides Seek to Contain Furor: Sept. 11 Not Envisioned, Rice Says*, Wash. Post (May 17, 2002), at A1.

77. This paragraph is based mostly on a comprehensive study in Barton Gellman, *A Strategy's Cautious Evolution: Before Sept. 11, the Bush Anti-Terror Effort Was Mostly Ambition*, Wash. Post (Jan. 20, 2002), at A1.

78. See Mark Follman, *Spooked by the White House*, Salon.com (July 18, 2003), an interview with Ray McGovern of Veteran Intelligence Professionals for Sanity, a group of retired intelligence personnel. McGovern, who has no partisan affiliation, commented: "I don't subscribe to the more sinister theories; I take the more charitable interpretation: gross incompetence on the part of the president and the CIA director."

79. Rather, President Bush signed a covert intelligence order directing the CIA to undertake a comprehensive program to oust Saddam Hussein. This apparently allowed him to strongly signal, out of the public eye, the internal victory of the Cheney-Rumsfeld approach and put Powell and Tenet under increasing pressure to muffle their previously decisive diplomatic and intelligence doubts about the necessity for unilateral invasion of Iraq. Bob Woodward, *President Broadens Anti-Hussein Order: CIA Gets More Tools to Oust Iraqi Leader*, Wash. Post (June 16, 2002), at A1.

80. Kessler, *supra*.

81. Id.; Follman, *supra*.

82. "The specter of a nuclearized Saddam Hussein was the primary fear of Bush, Cheney, and administration policy makers; it was invoked repeatedly by them." Carl M. Cannon, *What Bush Said*, Nat'l J. (July 26, 2003), 2412, at 2418.

83. Hiro, *supra*, at 71.

84. James Risen, *C.I.A. Aides Feel Pressure in Preparing Iraqi Reports*, N.Y. Times (March 23, 2003).

85. Rowan Scarborough, *Intercepts Foretold of "Big Attack,"* Wash. Times (Sept. 22, 2001), at A1.

86. Eric Lichtblau, *Attorney General Stresses the Risk of More Attacks*, L.A. Times (Oct. 1, 2001), at A4; James Dao, *Defense Secretary Warns of Unconventional Attacks*, N.Y. Times (Oct. 1, 2001), at B5.

87. Ashcroft's purpose, besides to change his image from Christian right champion to personal fighter against terrorism, was to overcome the resistance from even conservative Republicans against the extreme legislative provisions on domestic surveillance he was pushing.

88. President George Bush, *Disclosures to the Congress* (Oct. 5, 2001).

89. President Bush's anger is described in Bob Woodward, *Bush at War* 198–99 (2003). Despite the universal unconditional support for President Bush at that moment, this bizarre order elicited, even from members of his own party, complete disbelief until the order was quietly withdrawn. Members

observed that President Bush must have been planning to put out of business the congressional Foreign Relations, Armed Services, Judiciary, and Appropriations committees, since the administration would not tell anyone on those committees anything of importance.

90. For an entry into the debates on these issues, see Anthony Lewis, *Civil Liberties in a Time of Terror*, 2003 Wis. L. Rev. 257; Stephen R. McAllister et al., *Life after 9/11: Issues Affecting the Courts and the Nation*, 51 U. Kan. L. Rev. 219 (2003).

91. *Anti-Terrorism Policy Review*, Hearings before the Senate Comm. on the Judiciary (Dec. 6, 2001) (prepared testimony of Attorney General John Ashcroft). The media immediately took the phrase's meaning and, no more willing or able now to deal with such tactics than they had been to deal with similar ones from Senator Joseph McCarthy (R-Wis.) in the early 1950s, let his attack overawe the rest of the hearing. As he presumably intended it, his attack cowed the senators into limiting their inquiries and expressing safe sentiments. The administration thus effectively flaunted its immunity from oversight by deterring would-be questioners from even trying. Ashcroft's statement was reminiscent of his own tactics in calling the judicial nominee Judge Ronnie White "pro-criminal" to the extent that it publicly mislabeled as favoring evil those upon whom the fragile constitutional system depends to check the abuses of those who possess great power.

92. Todd S. Purdum & Alison Mitchell, *Bush, Angered by Leaks, Duels with Congress*, N.Y. Times (Oct. 10, 2001), at A1.

93. The probe meant that members of the intelligence committees must now submit to FBI questioning and have FBI dossiers assembled on which innuendos could be based that might later be used as blackmail material—matters infinitely more of concern to those who must face surprise attack advertisements every election. Not surprisingly, for a while these members visibly lost some of their bravery for publicly commenting on the FBI's negligence—or the president's.

94. Dana Priest, *FBI Leak Probe Irks Lawmakers*, Wash. Post (Aug. 2, 2002); Dan Eggen, *Ashcroft Assailed on Policy Review*, Wash. Post (Aug. 21, 2002).

95. It was hard enough on Rove that many Democrats were hawks, some of them vociferous, and that the Republican chairman of the Senate Foreign Affairs Committee, Richard Lugar (R-Ind.), worked publicly with Democrats for a compromise bipartisan position on the issue.

96. The administration kept up a front that its private exchanges with foreign countries, such as Iraq's neighbors, reflected more willingness to support an invasion than their public expressions of opposition indicated. This administration story line matured later into the propaganda about America leading a "coalition of the willing." In reality, judging from how relatively friendless the United States actually was at the time of the invasion, any frank private exchanges with foreign leaders may well have expressed even more *un*willingness to join the war than what they said publicly at the time.

97. See generally Louis Fisher, *Deciding on War against Iraq: Institutional Failures,* Pol. Sci. Q. (Sept. 2003).

98. James Risen, *C.I.A. Rejects Call for Iraq Report,* N.Y. Times (Oct. 3, 2002), at A1.

99. See John Hart Ely, *War and Responsibility: Constitutional Lessons of Vietnam and Its Aftermath* (1993).

100. Louis Fisher, *Congressional Access to Information: Using Legislative Will and Leverage,* 52 Duke L.J. 323, 398–400 (2002).

101. As to that unveiling, see Jill Barshay & Gebe Martinez, *Democrats Embrace Homeland Security While Working on Separate Political Persona,* 60 Cong. Q. Wkly. Rep. 1586 (June 15, 2002).

102. Adriel Bettelheim, *Senate's Failure to Resolve Personnel Management Issue Stalls Homeland Security Bill,* 60 Cong. Q. Wkly. Rep. 2741 (Oct. 19, 2002).

103. Jeffrey Gettleman, *Senator Cleland Loses in an Upset to Republican Emphasizing Defense,* N.Y. Times (Nov. 6, 2002).

104. Stevenson, *Delaying Talk about the Cost of War, supra.*

105. I have received press inquiries about these reconstruction contracts because one of my substantive areas of expertise is government contracting law. I am the coauthor, with William A. Shook, of the casebook for law students, *Government Contracting Law: Cases and Materials* (2d ed. 2004).

106. Eggen & Priest, *supra.*

107. John W. Dean, *The September 11 Report Raises More Questions about the White House,* CNN.com (July 29, 2003) (text on Lexis-Nexis).

108. Apparently, the briefing told the president that "bin Laden had wanted to conduct attacks in the United States since 1997" and FBI information "acquired in May 2001 indicated a group of bin Laden supporters was planning attacks in the United States with explosives." Walter Shapiro, *What We Know Is Bad: Secrecy Just Makes It Worse,* USA Today (July 25, 2003), at 4A.

109. *Stonewalling: Press Bush on 9/11 Report,* Minneapolis Star Trib. (Aug. 5, 2003), at 10A.

110. Dean, *supra.*

111. Id. (citing material in the 9/11 joint inquiry report).

112. Ashcroft would doubtless have spoken of someone else who got in the way of counterterrorism efforts—and whom he didn't like politically—in overtones suggesting treason. Perhaps his familiarity with Scripture did not extend to the suggestion that only the one without sin himself should cast the first stone.

113. Patrick E. Tyler, *Mideast Turmoil: Arab Politics; Saudis to Warn Bush of Rupture over Israel Policy,* N.Y. Times (April 25, 2002).

114. Gold, *supra,* at 209.

115. Sarah Kershaw, *U.S.-Saudi Ties Frayed over Mideast Tensions,* N.Y. Times (April 30, 2003), at A14.

116. Gold, *supra,* at 210.

117. Van Natta, *supra.*

118. Corn, *The Lies of George W. Bush, supra,* at 23–27.

119. Beyer, *supra.*

120. Baer, *supra,* at 160.

121. Neil MacFarquhar, *Saudis Arrest 8 in Deadly Riyadh Bombing,* N.Y. Times (May 29, 2003), at A13.

122. *Oil Man for Ambassador,* N.Y. Times (Nov. 18, 2003).

123. A quote from Oberwetter's ex-college roommate and Texas Republican politico Steve Bartlett. Jim Landers & Todd J. Gillman, *Nominee as Saudi Envoy Naturally Diplomatic, Friends Say,* Dallas Morning News (Nov. 20, 2003).

124. As Senator Kay Bailey Hutchison (R-Tex.) said quite accurately, the Saudi ruling elite prefers an ambassador "who has the president's ear and is a personal friend, and Jim Oberwetter fits that description." Jim Landers, *Schumer Contests Bush Ambassador Nominee,* Dallas Morning News (Nov. 22, 2003).

125. Craig, *supra,* at 5–7.

126. Id. at 4–9.

127. Steinzor, *Toward Better Bubbles and Future Lives, supra,* at n.5.

128. As an immediate illustration, the GAO's quest for lobbying records of the Cheney Energy Task Force and Congress's oversight of the Boston FBI were instantly sidetracked, stalled, and undermined politically by long post-9/11 stays of action, though of course neither of these pre-9/11 matters had the remotest connection to terrorism.

129. Rena Steinzor, *Democracies Die behind Closed Doors: The Homeland Security Act and Corporate Accountability,* 12 Kan. J. L. & Pub. Pol'y 641 (2003); Podesta, *supra.*

130. More concretely, secrecy until just after the election avoided an environmental backlash at the polls in such key elections as the Senate race in Colorado, narrowly won by conservative Republican senator Wayne Allard, a vulnerable incumbent with a dismal environmental record that would have put him on the spot if the administration had not held off preelection controversies. "As the November 2002 elections approached, however, the Bush Administration scaled down its environmental work. Cynics might suggest that the Administration was simply trying to keep the environment—traditionally a Democratic issue—off the election agenda." Craig, *supra,* at 19.

131. There were a few environmental issues the administration addressed during the 2002 campaigning: it tried, for example, to lump its relaxation of air pollution standards for utilities with its other efforts to help the energy industry and claim credit for the whole package to boost its support in the Appalachian coal region.

132. Craig, *supra,* at 20.

133. Wald, *supra.*

134. Natural Resources Defense Council, *Rewriting the Rules, Year-End Report 2002: The Bush Administration's Assault on the Environment* 13–14 (2003).

135. Douglas Jehl, *On Environmental Rules, Bush Sees a Balance, Critics a Threat,* N.Y. Times (Feb. 23, 2003).

136. Seelye, *Bush Proposes Change to Allow More Thinning of Forests,* supra.

137. 42 U.S.C. 4332. I have been writing about NEPA since not that long after its enactment in 1970. Charles Tiefer, *NEPA and Energy Supply: A Case Study,* 22 BNA Envtl. L. Monograph (1976).

138. William Snape III and John M. Carter II, *Weakening NEPA: How the Bush Administration Uses the Judicial System to Weaken Environmental Protections,* 33 Envtl. L. Rep. 10682 (2003).

139. *Wyoming Outdoor Council v. U.S. Forest Service,* 157 IBLA 259, 269 (2002).

140. *Wilderness Society v. Rey,* 180 F. Supp. 2d 1141, at 1148 (D. Mont. 2002).

141. *Old Town Neighborhood Ass'n v. Kauffman,* 2002 WL 31741477 (S.D. Ind. Nov. 15, 2002), at 22.

142. Katherine Pfleger, *Bush Proposes Changes to Way Forests Are Zoned,* Seattle Times (Nov. 27, 2002), at A6.

143. For background, see John C. Dernbach, *Learning from the President's Council on Sustainable Development: The Need for a Real National Strategy,* 32 Envtl. L. Rep. 10648 (2002); Dave Owen, *Prescriptive Laws, Uncertain Science, and Political Stories: Forest Management in the Sierra Nevada,* 29 Ecology L.Q. 747 (2002).

144. Laura E. Little, *The ABA's Role in Prescreening Federal Judicial Candidates: Are We Ready to Give Up on the Lawyers?* Wm. & Mary Bill Rts. J. 37 (2001).

145. Ironically, not so long before, Republicans had been the ones most loudly preaching the gospel of ABA prescreening, back when that party depended upon this procedure to constrain Democratic presidents like Clinton as they nominated more women and minorities. The discriminatory aspects of the profession until relatively recently limited the pool of women and minorities who had acquired the kinds of credentials, such as certain kinds of experience and activities often hard to acquire without seniority, that the ABA measures.

146. Thomas L. Jipping, *From Least Dangerous Branch to Most Profound Legacy: The High Stakes in Judicial Selection,* 4 Tex. Rev. L. & Pol. 365 (2000).

147. For the large role of the confirmation defeat of Supreme Court nominee Robert Bork, see Easton, *supra* (Touchstone ed. 2002), at 191–93.

148. Rove put heavy emphasis on a quest for Hispanic votes. Dubose, Reid, & Cannon, *supra,* at 168–69.

149. Jonathan Groner, *Privilege Fight Looms over Estrada: Leahy's Request for Memos May Spark a Showdown,* Legal Times (June 3, 2002). The Gonzales memo is quoted in Michael Crowley, *Private Opinion,* New Republic (April 7, 2003), at 17.

150. The letter is in 148 Cong. Rec. SS10033 (daily ed. Oct. 7, 2002).

151. Jack Newfield, *The Right's Judicial Juggernaut: Nomination of Miguel Estrada,* The Nation (Oct. 7, 2002).

152. In a classic 1986 example, as the price for confirming Justice Department official Stephen Trott as appellate judge, senators successfully insisted on reading memoranda about an independent counsel probe of Reagan family friend Faith Ryan Whittlesey. Memoranda from Frank Easterbrook's time in the solicitor general's office came out during his appellate judgeship nomination. Tiefer, *Overcoming Executive Privilege at the Justice Department, supra.*

153. L.A. Times, Oct. 3, 2002.

154. Nina Totenberg, *Miguel Estrada Withdraws His Name from Consideration as a Bush Nominee,* National Public Radio: All Things Considered (Sept. 4, 2003) (transcript in Lexis-Nexis database).

155. Obviously, the government does deem certain matters intrinsically secret because they address secret matters (e.g., opinions on classified intelligence activities) or because their particular situations require maintaining secrecy for their uses (e.g., opinions in preparation for litigation or similar action). But such categorizations apply only in a limited number of situations. In contrast, matters of large and small importance in governance become the subjects of opinions not necessitating tight secrecy.

156. The vast bulk of appropriation act provisions, for example, receive interpretation by the government yet rarely arise in court. Similarly, the vast majority of statutes, regulations, guidelines, and so forth governing the Department of Defense receive interpretation by its legions of lawyers yet rarely arise in court.

157. I testified at that hearing. See Charles Tiefer, *The Attorney General's Withholding of Documents from the Judiciary Committee in Department of Justice Authorization for Appropriations, Fiscal Year 1992,* Hearings before the House Comm. on the Judiciary, 102nd Cong., 1st sess. (July 11, 1991), at 76–125.

158. This is recounted in Louis Fisher, *The Politics of Executive Privilege* (2004).

159. For example, the head of the Office of Legal Counsel in the early Clinton administration, Walter Dellinger, explained what he did about the legal issue of sending troops to Haiti, in *After the Cold War: Presidential Power and the Use of Military Force,* 50 Miami L. Rev. 107, 108 (1995):

> The President asked the Department of Justice ("Department") to determine whether he would have the legal authority to order the deployment of American troops into Haiti without the consent of the military regime.... The Department concluded that the President had that authority. Later, in response to a letter to the President from Senators Bob Dole, Strom Thurmond, Alan Simpson, and William Cohen, I responded with an opinion letter setting out the basis of our conclusion.

Releasing that opinion letter meant the Clinton administration endured scrutiny and criticism of its position; it did not make secret law.

160. Allen & Eilperin, *supra.* This is discussed in chapter 3 in the section on firearms rights. In 2001–2002 the Ashcroft Justice Department alluded to its opinion on the Second Amendment, but only put out bits and pieces in its letter to the NRA and its solicitor general's filing in the Supreme Court in opposition to a pro se cert petition.

161. Owen Matthews, *The Next Move Is Check,* Newsweek (April 8, 2002), at 44.

162. *Security in Insecure Times,* Petroleum Economist (Feb. 10, 2003), at 21.

163. Shawn E. Cantley, Book Review, *Black Gold or the Devil's Excrement? Hydrocarbons, Geopolitics and the Law in the Caspian Basin,* 3 Eur.-Asia Studies 477 (2002).

164. A fine study of the region pleading for recognition by the United States of its own interest in pressing regimes to reform rather than suppressing popular discontent is Ahmed Rashid, *Jihad: The Rise of Militant Islam in Central Asia* (Penguin ed. 2003).

165. In the late 1940s, Congress debated openly, and the president arranged multilaterally, the comparatively revolutionary step, as to foreign aid, of the Marshall Plan to aid Europe rebuilding after World War II. The Korean War, although entered by President Truman on his own authority, nevertheless occurred under United Nations auspices, and the Senate managed, with considerable difficulty, the all-important public debate of the subsequent escalation proposals by General Douglas MacArthur. By the 1970s, Congress debated openly the end to American military involvement in Indochina; in the 1980s, it debated openly the limits on aid to the Nicaraguan contras. In the 1990s, it openly debated the Persian Gulf War, conducted under United Nations auspices, and the military involvements in the former Yugoslavia, conducted under NATO auspices.

166. Cong. Q.

167. A complex example consists of the United States' increasing support for the government of Uzbekistan as it brutally represses potential internal opposition. See Nick Paton Walsh, *US Looks Away As New Ally Tortures Islamists: Uzbekistan's President Steps Up Repression of Opponents,* The Guardian (May 26, 2003), at 13; Muhammad Salih, *America's Shy Ally against Terror,* N.Y. Times (March 11, 2002), at A21 (op-ed by party in exile).

168. A 2000 law allowing cash sales of American farm products to Cuba was enacted with the Republican Senate's strong support, reflecting the large body of quite conservative Republican senators who represent farm states. The law's enactment vividly demonstrated the promising centrist approach of support for gradual engagement. Hagstrom, *supra.*

169. Barnes, *The Bush Doctrine Comes to Cuba, supra.*

170. The administration would not let events in Cuba follow the course that unfolded in the new Eastern European regimes at the Cold War's end, which made progress for their countries and for alliance with the West, but accorded only limited concrete rewards to exiles. Exiles can have just claims that, however, may retard organic regime transitions only if pushed by external powers for political ends.

171. Rosenzweig & Scardaville, *supra;* Heather MacDonald, *Total Misrepresentation,* Wkly. Standard (Jan. 27, 2003).

172. John W. Dean, *Worse Than Watergate* 189–191 (2004).

173. I do not address, in the way Dean treats them, Bush's character issues, Cheney's own lack of candor, Bush's squelching of dissent, or the Wilson leak. This list of eight is compressed from Dean's list of eleven. By his count, there is more that he addresses that I do not.

174. Christopher Drew & Richard A. Oppel, Jr., *How Power Lobby Won Battle of Pollution Control at E.P.A.,* N.Y. Times, (March 6, 2004), at A1.

175. Adam Liptak, *Prosecutions for Perjury in Legislative Settings Are Unusual,* N.Y. Times (March 31, 2004), at A15. As the article quotes me, I believed Rice did face some potential perils because her testimony was shadowed by her earlier statements to the media. There are national security advisers whose rigid sense of honor makes it extremely hard for them to depart from telling the truth: Bud MacFarlane, Reagan's adviser, was one. He felt such dishonor after the Iran-contra scandal broke that it led him to a suicide attempt. Rice did not have that rigid sense of honor. Bush had picked her carefully—and not for her having much interest in or concern about terrorism. Her accounts to the press, nimbly adapted over the years to Bush's needs at the time, contradicted facts that came out later. Even so, Rice was not facing the kind of perjury risk that makes a witness break out in cold sweats. The questioning she would receive was not of that kind. She was not in the position of a witness obliged to turn over an extensive paper trail and uncomfortably explain it, because the Bush White House simply didn't turn over the records that could be put to that use. And congressional Republicans had suffered acute amnesia about how to obtain records since the days of the Clinton administration, when they set historic records with such infinite-loop methods as asking for records of the handling of previous inquiries and then records for the handling of the inquiry about the handling of the previous inquiries.

176. Helen Fessenden, *Hill's Oversight Role at Risk: Lawmakers Question Accountability as Military Expands Clandestine Operations,* Cong. Q. Wkly. Rep. (March 27, 2004), at 734, 735.

177. In that regard, Bush's course in 2004 about his biggest secrecy-abusing debacle resembled Reagan's in 1984 in having the CIA mine the Nicaraguan harbors: both White Houses temporarily feigned, before the election, having learned from their mistakes, but both actually yearned to forge on after reelection without accountability.

9. IF THIS GOES ON

1. A useful legal treatment of this historical period as a whole is Harry N. Scheiber, *Redesigning the Architecture of Federalism—An American Tradition: Modern Devolution Policies in Perspective,* 14 Yale L. & Pol'y Rev. 227 (1996).

2. For background (albeit by an author who argues that "cooperative federalism is a rotten idea"), see Michael S. Greve, *Against Cooperative Federalism,* 70 Miss. L. J. 557 (2000).

3. Phillips (2002), *supra,* at 326.

4. Thomas E. Mann, *Linking Knowledge and Action: Political Science and Campaign Finance Reform,* Perspectives on Politics (March 2003), 69, at 76.

5. If either McCain or Gore had won the presidency in 2000, the 2002 Bipartisan Campaign Reform Act might just have taken a form that opened the door to further serious reform. Once experience developed with loopholes and ambiguities after 2004, as after 1996, the press and public might have stimulated further action. As for the relation of campaign finance legal issues to other conservative causes, see Tiefer, *Helping Those Who Can Help Themselves, supra.*

6. What most swamped the prior political system in place from the 1960s was the tidal wave of conservative contributions, mobilization, organization, and turnout in the 1994 election, crucially backed by the well-financed reaction against congressional Democrats' 1993 tax increase to pay down the deficit. Now, conservatives have created a legal mechanism so that they can repeat constantly the rallying cry that worked so well for them in 1994.

7. In those periods when either the House or the White House might come ultimately into Democratic hands, this abuse of the Budget Act creates a playing field on which the rich need not despair. Even then, the Democratic branch must and still will bargain with conservative Republicans for a bipartisan package, as President Clinton gave in to the capital gains tax cut in 1997, for no such package could pass as long as the Republicans have strength anywhere. But, conversely, the Bush system creates a very high hurdle for those seeking to restore any sizable funding specifically for low-income groups.

8. The one exception in 1993 proves the rule. The 1993 Clinton budget did strengthen the earned-income tax credit, which helps the working poor. However, the Democrats could do that in 1993 because the EITC is a tax credit, not a spending program, so it only required fifty-one votes, not sixty, to include it in a package that raised ample offsetting taxes. However, not all programs for the poor and the middle class can be tax cuts, and not all those other programs that involve spending can pass the way the EITC did.

9. This would resemble the pattern of reconciliation bills for the decade after the Reagan tax cuts of 1981.

10. Tiefer, *Budgetized Health Entitlements, supra.*

11. As long as two-earner families can avoid a personal setback—such as a costly illness, a heavily dependent elderly family member, or a prolonged

period of unemployment—that drops them out of the middle class through the major gaps being torn in the social safety net, the proposed changes may not seem to put them in jeopardy.

12. As a leading archconservative Thomistic academic proclaimed, "All right, my Republican Friends. We had a great victory on Tuesday. But let's clear our minds of cant. This is not the time for magnanimity." As for judicial appointments, "now it is our turn to play to win." Robert P. George, *No Time for Magnanimity*, Nat'l Rev. (Nov. 8, 2002).

13. *Lawrence v. Texas*, 123 S. Ct. 2472 (2003); *Grutter v. Bollinger*, 123 S. Ct. 2325 (2003).

14. A well-researched and written report is People for the American Way, *Courting Disaster: How a Scalia-Thomas Supreme Court Would Endanger Our Rights and Freedoms* (June 2000). I use different standard of comparison. While the shift analyzed in that report could happen, it would take more resignations over more time and an overcoming of Senate resistance for such a steady stream of extreme ideological appointments to vacancies.

15. The Supreme Court's anti–civil rights statutory interpretation decisions of the 1980s actually set the conservative cause back by awakening such an angry public reaction as to fuel enactment of the civil rights restoration statute of 1991, embarrassing the Court's conservatives into backing off. For a discussion of the enactment of that law, particularly President Bush's 1991 signature, see Tiefer, *The Semi-Sovereign Presidency, supra*, at 54–59.

16. *Lawrence v. Texas*, 123 S. Ct. 2472 (2003).

17. For a legally advanced treatment of the issue, see *Developments in the Law—The Law of Marriage and Family: Constitutional Constraints on Interstate Same-Sex Marriage Recognition*, 116 Harv. L. Rev. 2028 (2003).

18. To understand the administration's caution until the 2004 campaign, simply check the Web site monitoring gay rights issues, http://www.hrc.org /issues/index.asp.

19. See Karen Lim, Note, *Freedom to Seclude after* Boy Scouts of America v. Dale: *Do Private Schools Have a Right to Discriminate against Homosexual Teachers?* 71 Fordham L. Rev. 2599 (2003). Similarly, gays might be deemed "unfit" for employment in religious and other institutions that provided federally funded services.

20. See, e.g., Robert H. Bork & Daniel E. Troy, *Locating the Boundaries: The Scope of Congress's Power to Regulate Commerce*, 25 Harv. J. L. & Pub. Pol'y 849 (2002).

21. Bork contended that the courts should stop Congress from using its commerce power to federalize inappropriately the punishment of crimes, adding that "most crime has nothing to do with 'commerce.'" Id.

22. For example, Bork argued, "If speed limits do not burden interstate commerce, Congress should not be able to set maximum speeds just because . . . [this] would promote the safety of the people." Id.

23. Tushnet, *supra*, at 69 (italics added).

24. Id.

25. Ivins & Dubose (2000 paperback ed.), *supra,* at 169–79 (describing Governor Bush's treatment of the "colonias" near the Mexican border).

26. The school voucher proposal championed by President Bush illustrates how this would work. Conservative states can use these vouchers to help finance good private schools in affluent white areas. Meanwhile, they can undercut the already inadequate budgets of the only schools—public schools —that many poor children, particularly the minority poor in large families, can realistically afford to attend. With a new legal structure that omits directness and statewide uniformity requirements, conservative states would find ways to use each of the various pots of federal funds to reinforce patterns of separate and unequal treatment.

27. *Boy Scouts of America v. Dale,* 530 U.S. 640 (2000).

28. Although, the Ninth Circuit did rule that federal antidiscrimination laws had some teeth in this regard. Andrew Brownstein, *Title VII Protects Gay Workers from Sexual Harassment, Ninth Circuit Finds,* Trial (Jan. 2003), at 76.

29. See Michael A. Woods, Comment, *The Propriety of Local Government Protections of Gays and Lesbians from Discriminatory Employment Practices,* 52 Emory L.J. 515 (2003).

30. The classic study of how the taste for imperial prerogatives grew in the. White House is Schlesinger, *supra.*

31. For this the model may be the way the policy allowing Mexican trucking to use U.S. highways, slipped through after the 2002 election by way of NAFTA, undercuts highway safety.

32. See generally Louis Fisher, *Congressional Abdication in War and Spending* (2000); Barbara Hinckley, *Less Than Meets the Eye: Foreign Policy Making and the Myth of the Assertive Congress* (1994).

33. President Eisenhower won reelection handily in 1956 and then faced a Democratic swing in Congress in 1958. President Johnson received a landslide in 1964 that powered his civil rights and Great Society programs of 1965–1966, but then his party lost significant ground in the House in 1966. President Nixon's decisive reelection victory of 1972, when he swept forty-nine of fifty states, completely reversed upon his resignation and President Ford's accession.

Then, 1974 produced the so-called "veto-proof" post-Watergate Democratic Congress, a high tide of liberal strength. The "Watergate Congress" overthrew the prior two-thirds Senate cloture requirement and also cracked that other bastion of conservative power, the congressional seniority system for appointing committee chairs.

34. Technically, Lyndon Johnson was elected vice president in 1960, became president in 1963, and so was elected rather than reelected president in 1964.

35. James E. Campbell, *The Presidential Pulse of Congressional Elections* (2d ed. 1997).

36. One of the reasons for this larger "negative surge," historically, may be that each president received more support in his reelection than in his first

election. (This is somewhat the result of the selection method; presidents who receive much less support in their reelection effort than in their first election—such as presidents Hoover, Carter, and Bush senior—got defeated for reelection, and so, of course, there is no second-term midterm election, nor anything else about a second term, to study for them.) Perhaps it owes to asymmetric turnout. By late in a president's term, this theory goes, discontent with the party in power compounds, so the lower-turnout supporters get swamped by motivated discontented opposition voters. See Paul R. Abramson, John H. Aldrich, & David W. Rohde, *Change and Continuity in the 1996 and 1998 Elections* 252 (1999).

37. Id. at 258–60.

38. Gingrich paid for this immediately by surrendering the Speakership.

39. James E. Campbell, *The 2002 Midterm Election: A Typical or an Atypical Midterm?* PS (April 2003), at 203, 205–06.

40. Straight-ticket voting in presidential years, which partly explains the presidential election year surge so as to account for the midterm negative surge two years later, has greatly declined. The absence since 1994 of any large swings at all in Congress suggest no further big realignments have hit, and this, coupled with incumbent-friendly redistricting and other incumbent entrenchment, dampens expectations of any other big swings, all else being equal.

41. Johnson solved his Vietnam problem before November 1964, and Nixon covered up the Watergate burglary before November 1972—in ways that came back to haunt them.

42. John B. Judis & Ruy Teixeira, *The Emerging Democratic Majority* (2002).

43. Ultimately, the ensuing confrontation would resemble one of those eras, such as the mid-1930s, when congressional liberals ran against and fought a right-wing Court (or the late 1950s, when congressional conservatives ran against and fought a left-wing [compared to them] Court). Charles Tiefer, *The Flag-Burning Controversy of 1989–90: Congress' Valid Role in Constitutional Dialogue*, 29 Harv. J. on Legis. 357–98 (1992).

Bibliography

Abraham, Rick. *The Dirty Truth: George W. Bush's Oil and Chemical Dependency: How He Sold Out Texans and the Environment to Big Business Polluters* (2000).

Abramson, Paul R., John H. Aldrich, & David W. Rohde. *Change and Continuity in the 1996 and 1998 Elections* (1999).

Ackerman, Bruce. *But What's the Legal Case for Preemption?* Wash. Post (Aug. 18, 2002).

Ackerman, Frank, & Lisa Heinzerling. *Pricing the Priceless: Cost-Benefit Analysis of Environmental Protection*, 150 U. Pa. L. Rev. 1553 (2002).

Adams, Rebecca. *Senate's Energy Policy Rift Grows as Democrats Unfurl Their Bill and GOP Loses ANWR Vote*, Cong. Q. Wkly. Rep. (Dec. 8, 2001).

Adler, David Gray, & Michel A. Genovese, eds. *The Presidency and the Law: The Clinton Legacy* (2002).

Aldrich, John H., & David W. Rohde. *The Logic of Conditional Party Government: Revisiting the Electoral Connection.* In Lawrence C. Dodd & Bruce I. Oppenheimer, eds. *Congress Reconsidered* (7th ed. 2001).

Allen, Mike. *Montana Gov. Didn't Have Right Stuff: GOP Conservatives Derailed Racicot for Attorney General*, Wash. Post (Jan. 2, 2001).

———. *Powell Calls Resignation Report "Gossip,"* Wash. Post (Aug. 5, 2003).

———. *"Pioneers" Paved Bush's Way with Big Dollars*, Wash. Post (May 6, 2003).

Allen, Mike, & Barton Gellman. *Preemptive Strikes Part of U.S. Strategic Doctrine*, Wash. Post (Dec. 11, 2002).

Allen, Mike, & Juliet Eilperin. *Bush Aides Say Iraq War Needs No Hill Vote*, Wash. Post (Aug. 26, 2002).

Alt, Robert. *Democratic Racism*, Nat'l Rev. (Sept. 5, 2003).

Alter, Jonathan. *Between the Lines, Online: Whacking the Waitresses*, Newsweek Web Exclusive (May 30, 2003). Lexis-Nexis database.

Altman, Daniel. *Global Trade Looking Glass: Can U.S. Have It Both Ways?* N.Y. Times (Nov. 9, 2002).

Alvarez, Lizette. *Senate Rejects Tuition Aid, a Key to Bush Education Plan,* Wash. Post (June 13, 2001).

Amanat, Abbas. *A Risky Message to Iran,* N.Y. Times (Feb. 10, 2003).

Anselmo, Joseph C. *MTBE Trips Filibuster Target,* Cong. Q. Wkly. Rep. (Nov. 22, 2003).

———. *Pentagon Plans for Bigger, Better Army with "Spike,"* Cong. Q. Wkly. Rep. (Jan. 31, 2004).

Anselmo, Joseph C., & Allison Stevens. *Regional Issues Leave Energy Bill a Hair Too Unwieldy for Senate,* Cong. Q. Wkly. Rep. (Nov. 22, 2003).

Ashcroft's Invisible Hand, Nat'l J. (May 25, 2002).

Ayres, B. Drummond, Jr. *Ralph Reed Wins Election to Lead Georgia Republicans,* N.Y. Times (May 6, 2001).

Baer, Robert. *Sleeping with the Devil* (2003).

Baker, Nancy V. *Conflicting Loyalties: Law and Politics in the Attorney General's Office, 1789–1990* (1992).

Balz, Dan, & Ronald Brownstein. *Storming the Gates: Protest Politics and the Republican Revival* (1996).

Banks, William C., & M. E. Bowman, *Executive Authority for National Security Surveillance,* 50 Am. U. L. Rev. 1 (2000).

Barlow, Maude, & Tony Clarke. *Who Owns Water?* The Nation (Sept. 2, 2002).

Barnes, Fred. *The Bush Doctrine Comes to Cuba,* Wkly. Standard (July 15, 2002).

———. *The Impresario: Karl Rove, Orchestrator of the Bush White House,* Wkly. Standard (Aug. 20, 2001).

Barnes, James A. *Inside Bush's Campaign Shop,* Nat'l J. (Aug. 7, 1999).

Barnett, Jim. *Bush Policy on Suicide Is Shielded in Secrecy,* Oregonian (Nov. 11, 2001).

Barone, Michael, with Richard E. Cohen, *The Almanac of American Politics 2002*

Barshay, Jill. *White House Bonds with Moderates for Victory on Dividend Cuts,* 61 Cong. Q. Wkly. Rep. (May 17, 2003).

———. *Who Benefits from New Rates for Dividends, Capital Gains,* 61 Cong. Q. Wkly. Rep. (May 24, 2003)

Barshay, Jill, & Gebe Martinez. *Democrats Embrace Homeland Security While Working on Separate Political Persona,* 60 Cong. Q. Wkly. Rep. (June 15, 2002).

Barstow, David, & Don Van Natta Jr. *How Bush Took Florida: Mining the Overseas Absentee Vote,* N.Y. Times (July 15, 2001).

Bartalk Column, *And There Should Be No Shortage of Firms Willing to Pitch In,* Am. Lawyer (Feb. 2003)

Baucus, Senator Max, et al. *Colleagues Urge End to "Burdensome" EITC Pre-certification,* Tax Notes Today, Doc 2003-17055 (July 18, 2003).

Been, Vicki, & Joel C. Beauvais. *The Global Fifth Amendment? NAFTA's Investment Protections and the Misguided Quest for an International "Regulatory Takings" Doctrine,* 78 N.Y.U. L. Rev. 30 (2003).

Begala, Paul. *It's Still the Economy, Stupid: George W. Bush, the GOP's CEO* (2002).

Bendavid, Naftali. *China Spy Probe Puts Spotlight on Hush-Hush Court*, Chicago Trib. (May 27, 1999).

Bennett, Andrew, & Troy White. *Foreign Policy in the Presidential Campaign*. In Stephen J. Wayne & Clyde Wilcox, eds. *The Election of the Century* (2002).

Bennett, Drake. *Freedom to Fail: The False Flexibility of the President's Welfare Plan*, Am. Prospect. (April 2003).

Bennis, Phillis. *Before & After: US Foreign Policy and the September 11th Crisis* (2003).

Berke, Richard L. *The $2,000 Answer*, N.Y. Times (March 21, 2002).

Berman, William C. *America's Right Turn: From Nixon to Clinton* (2d ed. 1998).

Bettelheim, Adriel. *Senate's Failure to Resolve Personnel Management Issue Stalls Homeland Security Bill*, 60 Cong. Q. Wkly. Rep. (Oct. 19, 2002).

———. *Wilderness Drilling Defeat Results in Cropped Energy Bill*, Cong. Q. Wkly. Rep. (April 20, 2002).

Beyer, Lisa, et al. *After 9/11: The Saudis: Friend or Foe?* Time (Sept. 15, 2003).

Billionaires for Bush, The Nation (July 21, 2003).

Binder, Sarah A., & Steven S. Smith. *Politics or Principle? Filibustering in the United States Senate* (1997).

Birnbaum, Jeffrey H. *The Iraq Fixers Are Circling; No, Not the Rebuilders, the Washington Lobbyists*, Fortune (October 2003).

———. *Showdown at Gucci Gulf* (1988).

Blum, Vanessa. *Why Bush Won't Let Go: To the White House, the Paper Fight with Congress Is Part of a Bigger Plan to Restore Presidential Power*, Legal Times (Feb. 4, 2002).

Bogus, Carl T. *The History and Politics of Second Amendment Scholarship: A Primer*, 76 Chi.-Kent L. Rev. 3 (2000).

Bolton, Alexander. *Members Hit White House over Secrecy*, The Hill (Aug. 7, 2002).

Bolton, John R. *Our Pitiful Iraq Policy*, Wkly. Standard (Dec. 21, 1998).

———. *Saddam Wins*, Wkly. Standard (Aug. 24, 1998).

———. *Should We Take Global Governance Seriously?* 1 Chi. J. Int'l L. 205 (2000).

Bond, Jon. R., & Richard Fleisher, eds. *Polarized Politics: Congress and the President in a Partisan Era* (2000).

Book, Leslie. *The IRS's EITC Compliance Regime: Taxpayers Caught in the Net*, 81 Ore. L. Rev. 351 (2002).

Bork, Robert H., & Daniel E. Troy. *Locating the Boundaries: The Scope of Congress's Power to Regulate Commerce*, 25 Harv. J. L. & Pub. Pol'y 849 (2002).

Borrus, Amy. *Surprise! Bush Is Emerging as a Fighter for Privacy on the Net*, Bus. Week (June 5, 2000).

Boyd, John. Note, *The New New Source Review: Teaching Old Sources New Tricks?* 11 Southeastern Envtl. L.J. 401 (2003).

Brandon, Phyllis D. *Arkansans Tip Their Hats for Texans As Nation Embraces a New President,* Ark. Dem-Gaz. (Jan. 28, 2001).

Breaux, David A. *Checkbook Democracy: How Money Corrupts Political Campaigns* (2000).

Briffault, Richard. *The Future of Reform: Campaign Finance after the Bipartisan Campaign Reform Act of 2002,* 34 Ariz. L. J. 1180 (2002).

————. *The Political Parties and Campaign Finance Reform,* 100 Colum. L. Rev. 620 (2000).

Brownstein, Andrew. *Title VII Protects Gay Workers from Sexual Harassment, Ninth Circuit Finds,* Trial (Jan. 2003).

Bruner, Christopher M. *Hemispheric Integration and the Politics of Regionalism: The Free Trade Area of the Americas (FTAA),* 33 U. Miami Inter-Am. L. Rev. 1 (2002).

Bryce, Robert. *Pipe Dreams: Greed, Ego, and the Death of Enron* (2002).

Bumiller, Elisabeth, & Richard A. Oppel Jr. *Bush Defends Sale of Stock and Vows to Enhance S.E.C.,* N.Y. Times (July 9, 2002).

Burman, Leonard E., William G. Gale, & Jeffrey Rohaly. *The AMT: Projections and Problems,* 100 Tax Notes 105 (July 7, 2003).

Bush's Hang-ups, The Economist (Dec. 15, 2001).

Bush's Legal Team, Orlando Sentinel (Nov. 29, 2000).

Butterfield, Fox. *Ashcroft's Words Clash with Staff on Checks,* N.Y. Times (July 24, 2002).

————. *Justice Dept. Bars Use of Gun Checks in Terror Inquiry,* N.Y. Times (Dec. 6, 2001).

Byrd, Senator Robert C. *Congress Must Resist the Rush to War,* N.Y. Times (Oct. 10, 2002).

Caldicott, Helen. *The New Nuclear Danger: George W. Bush's Military-Industrial Complex* (2002).

Campbell, James E. *The 2002 Midterm Election: A Typical or an Atypical Midterm?* PS (April 2003).

————. *The Presidential Pulse of Congressional Elections* (2d ed. 1997).

Cannon, Carl M. *What Bush Said,* Nat'l J. (July 26, 2003).

Cantley, Shawn E. Book Review, *Black Gold or the Devil's Excrement? Hydrocarbons, Geopolitics and the Law in the Caspian Basin,* 3 Eur.-Asia Studies 477 (2002).

Caplan, Lincoln. *Who Lied?* Newsweek (Nov. 14, 1994) (reviewing Jane Mayer & Jill Abramson, *Strange Justice* [1994]).

Carney, James. *How Bush Chose Ashcroft,* Time (Jan. 22, 2001).

Cavanaugh, Maureen B. *On the Road to Incoherence: Congress, Economics, and Taxes,* 49 U.C.L.A. L. Rev. 685 (2002).

Chalabi, Issam al-. *Iraqi Oil Policy: Present and Future Perspectives,* Cambridge Energy Research Associates (March 24, 2003).

Chemerinsky, Erwin. *The Court Should Have Remained Silent: Why the Court Erred in Deciding* Dickerson v. United States, 149 U. Pa. L. Rev. 287 (2000).

Chen, Edwin. *Bush Cites War in Letter Seeking Campaign Funds,* L.A. Times (May 25, 2003).

Citizens for Tax Justice. *Year-by-Year Analysis of the Bush Tax Cuts Shows Growing Tilt to the Very Rich* (2002).

Clayton, Cornell W. *The Politics of Justice: The Attorney General and the Making of Legal Policy* (1992).

Clift, Eleanor. *Standing by Their Man,* Newsweek Web Exclusive (April 25, 2003) (Lexis-Nexis database).

Cloud, David S. *Justice Department Is Shifting Stance on Gun Rights,* Wall St. J. (July 11, 2001).

Clymer, Adam. *How Sept. 11 Changed Goals of Justice Dept.: Fighting Terror Didn't Lead Ashcroft's List,* N.Y. Times (Feb. 28, 2002).

Cohen, Richard E. *Broken Barometer,* Nat'l J. (July 12, 2003).

Cohen, Richard E., & James Kitfield. *Cheney: Pros and Cons,* 32 Nat'l. J. 2456 (July 29, 2000).

Cohn, Marjorie. *The World Trade Organization: Elevating Property Interests above Human Rights,* 29 Ga. J. Int'l & Comp. L. 427 (2001)

Cole, David. *Enemy Aliens,* 54 Stan. L. Rev. 953 (2002).

———. *The New McCarthyism: Repeating History in the War on Terrorism,* 38 Harv. C.R.-C.L. L. Rev. 1 (2003).

Cook, Charles. *Round and Round the Acrimony Goes . . . ,* Nat'l J. (May 17, 2003).

Cook, Clive. *How to Take a Flawed Tax Bill and Turn It into a Joke,* 23 Nat'l J. (June 9, 2001).

Cooper, Helene, et al. *House Votes Wide Trade Powers for Bush,* Wall St. J. (Dec. 7, 2001).

Cooper, Philip J. *By Order of the President: The Use and Abuse of Executive Direct Action* (2002).

Cong. Q. Almanac (1995, 1996).

Corn, David, *The Lies of George W. Bush* (2003).

Crabb, Cecil V., Jr., & Pat M. Holt. *Invitation to Struggle: Congress, the President, and Foreign Policy* (4th ed. 1992).

Craig, Robin Kundis. *The Bush Administration and the Environment: An Overview and Introduction,* 25 W. New Eng. L. Rev. 1 (2003).

Crowley, Michael. *Private Opinion,* New Republic (April 7, 2003).

Daalder, Ivo H., James M. Lindsay, & James B. Steinberg. *The Bush National Security Strategy: An Evaluation* (2002), at www.brookings.edu.

Dao, James. *At U.N. Family-Planning Talks, U.S. Raises Abortion Issue,* N.Y. Times (Dec. 15, 2002).

———. *Defense Secretary Warns of Unconventional Attacks,* N.Y. Times (Oct. 1, 2001).

Davidson, Deirdre, & Tatiana Boncompagni. *The Swift Demise of OSHA Rules,* Legal Times (March 12, 2001).

Dean, John W. *The September 11 Report Raises More Questions about the White House,* CNN.com (July 29, 2003) (text in Lexis-Nexis database).

Deibel, Terry L. *The Death of a Treaty,* Foreign Affairs (Sept.–Oct. 2002).

Dellinger, Walter. *After the Cold War: Presidential Power and the Use of Military Force,* 50 Miami L. Rev. 107 (1995).

Dempsey, James X. *Civil Liberties in a Time of Crisis,* 29 Hum. Rts. 8 (2002).

Deposition Lists Lucrative Deals for Bush Brother, N.Y. Times (Nov. 27, 2003).

Dernbach, John C. *Learning from the President's Council on Sustainable Development: The Need for a Real National Strategy,* 32 Envtl. L. Rep. 10648 (2002).

Destler, I. M. *American Trade Politics* (3d ed. 1995).

Developments in the Law—The Law of Marriage and Family: Constitutional Constraints on Interstate Same-Sex Marriage Recognition, 116 Harv. L. Rev. 2028 (2003).

Devins, Neal. *Shaping Constitutional Values: Elected Government, the Supreme Court, and the Abortion Debate* (1996).

Dewar, Helen, & Juliet Eilperin. *Emergency Funding Deal Reached: Hill Leaders Agree to Work Out Language on Use of Force,* Wash. Post (Sept. 14, 2001).

Dickey, Christopher. *Saudi Arabia: The Kingdom & the Power,* Newsweek (Aug. 11, 2003).

Dlouhy, Jennifer A. *Abortion Foes' Busy Agenda,* Cong. Q. Wkly. Rep. (July 19, 2003).

———. *Cleared "Partial Birth" Ban on Fast Track to Court,* Cong. Q. Wkly. Rep. (Oct. 25, 2003).

———. *Court Challenge a Sure Thing for "Partial Birth" Abortion Ban,* Cong. Q. Wkly. Rep. (June 7, 2003).

———. *Estrada Battle Just Part of the War over Who Controls U.S. Judiciary,* 61 Cong. Q. Wkly. Rep. (Feb. 15, 2003).

Doerflinger, Richard M. *Challenges for a Somewhat Pro-life Congress,* America (June 9, 2003).

Donovan, Gill. *Santorum's Remarks Draw Both Affirmation, Criticism from Catholics,* Nat'l Catholic Rep. (May 9, 2003).

Dorf, Michael C. *What Does the Second Amendment Mean Today?* 76 Chi.-Kent L. Rev. 291 (2000).

Draper, Theodore. *A Very Thin Line: The Iran-Contra Affairs* (1991).

Dubose, Lou, Jan Reid, & Carl M. Cannon. *Boy Genius: Karl Rove, the Brains behind the Remarkable Political Triumph of George W. Bush* (2003).

Duffy, Paul A. *How Filled Was My Valley: Continuing the Debate on Disposal Impacts,* 17 Nat. Resources & Env. (Winter 2003).

Duin, Julia. *Abortion Words Block U.N. Draft,* Wash. Times (Aug. 31, 2001).

Earthjustice and Public Campaign. *Paybacks: Policies, Patrons and Personnel—How the Bush Administration Is Giving Away Our Environment to Its Corporate Contributors* (Sept. 2002).

Eastland, Terry. *Energy in the Executive: The Case for the Strong Presidency* (1992).

Easton, Nina J. *Gang of Five: Leaders at the Center of the Conservative Ascendancy* (2000).

Edsall, Thomas B. *Big Business's Funding Shift Boosts GOP: Trend May Put Squeeze on Democrats' Finances,* Wash. Post (Nov. 27, 2002).

———. *The New Politics of Inequality* (1984).

Eggen, Dan. *Ashcroft Assailed on Policy Review,* Wash. Post (Aug. 21, 2002).

———. *Minorities Less Visible at Justice After Departures,* Wash. Post (Oct. 12, 2003).

Eggen, Dan, & Dana Priest. *Bush Aides Seek to Contain Furor: Sept 11 Not Envisioned, Rice Says,* Wash. Post (May 17, 2002).

Eggen, Dan, & Guy Gugliotta. *FBI Secretly Trying to Re-create Anthrax from Mail Attacks,* Wash. Post (Nov. 2, 2002).

Ehrlich, Ann H., & James Salzman. *The Importance of Population Growth to Sustainability,* 32 Envtl. L. Rep. 10559 (2002).

Eilperin, Juliet, & Dana Milbank. *Bush May Cut U.N. Program's Funding: No Final Decision, but State Department Told to Plan Withholding Family Planning Aid,* Wash. Post (June 29, 2002).

Ely, John Hart. *War and Responsibility: Constitutional Lessons of Vietnam and Its Aftermath* (1993).

Evans, Michael W. *The Budget Process and the "Sunset" Provision of the 2001 Tax Law.* 9 Tax Notes 405 (2003).

Fallows, James. *Blind into Baghdad,* Atlantic Monthly (Jan.–Feb. 2004).

Farhang, Mansour. *A Triangle of Realpolitik: Iran, Iraq and the United States.* The Nation (March 17, 2003).

Farkas, Rachel. *The Bush Administration's Decision to Defund the United Nations Population Fund and Its Implications for Women in Developing Nations,* 18 Berkeley Women's L.J. 237 (2003).

Farrar-Meyers, Victoria A. *In the Wake of 1996: Clinton's Legacy for Presidential Campaign Finance.* In David Gray Adler & Michel A. Genovese, eds. *The Presidency and the Law: The Clinton Legacy* (2002).

Faux, Jeff. *A Deal Built on Sand,* Am. Prospect (winter 2002).

Feuerherd, Joe. *Too Extreme or . . . Too Catholic? Pryor Nomination Puts Religion to the Test,* Nat'l Catholic Rep. (Aug. 29, 2003).

Fidler, Stephen, & Gerard Baker. *America's Democratic Imperialists: How the Neo-conservatives Rose from Humility to Empire in Two Years,* Fin. Times (March 6, 2003).

Finnegan Abdolian, Lisa, & Harold Takooshian. *The USA PATRIOT Act: Civil Liberties, The Media, and Public Opinion,* 30 Fordham Urb. L.J. 1429 (2003).

Fisher, Louis. *Congressional Abdication in War and Spending* (2000).

———. *Congressional Access to Information: Using Legislative Will and Leverage,* 52 Duke L. J. 323 (2002).

———. *Deciding on War against Iraq: Institutional Failures,* Pol. Sci. Q. (Sept. 2003).

———. *Nazi Saboteurs on Trial: A Military Tribunal and American Law* (2003).

———. *The Politics of Executive Privilege* (2004).

Fisk, Catherine, & Erwin Chemerinsky. *The Filibuster*, 49 Stan. L. Rev. 181 (1997).

Foer, Franklin. *Fabric Softener: The Textile Lobby v. the War on Terrorism*, New Republic (March 5, 2002).

———. *Home Bound: Buchanan's Surefire Flop*, New Republic (July 22, 2002).

Follman, Mark. *Spooked by the White House*, Salon.com (July 18, 2003).

Francis, Walter. *The FEHBP as a Model for Medicare Reform: Separating Fact from Fiction*, Heritage Foundation Reports (Aug. 7, 2003).

Franklin, Daniel. *Freeh's Reign: At Louis Freeh's FBI, with Carte Blanche from Congressional Republicans, Real Cops Didn't Do Intelligence and Counterterrorism*, Am. Prospect (Jan. 1, 2002).

Freedberg, Sydney J., Jr. *Bush and Gore's Positions on Defense*, 32 Nat'l J. 1026 (April 1, 2000).

French, Howard W. *North Korea Has an Axis All Its Own*, N.Y. Times (Feb. 10, 2002).

Friedman, Thomas L. *Drilling for Tolerance*, N.Y. Times (Oct. 30, 2001).

Garbus, Martin. *Courting Disaster: The Supreme Court and the Unmaking of American Law* (2002).

Garrett, Elizabeth. *Rethinking the Structures of Decisionmaking in the Federal Budget Process*, 35 Harv. J. on Legis. 387 (2001).

Gellman, Barton. *A Strategy's Cautious Evolution: Before Sept. 11, the Bush Anti-Terror Effort Was Mostly Ambition*, Wash. Post (Jan. 20, 2002).

———. *Broad Effort Launched After '98 Attacks*, Wash. Post (Dec. 19, 2001).

Gellman, Robert. *Bush Team Stumbles on Health Privacy*, Gov't Compensation News (April 29, 2002).

George, Robert P. *No Time for Magnanimity*, Nat'l Rev. (Nov. 8, 2002).

George, Tracey E. *Court Fixing*, 43 Ariz. L. Rev. 9 (2001).

Gerhardt, Michael J. *Norm Theory and the Future of the Federal Appointments Process*, 50 Duke L.J. 1687 (2001).

Gettleman, Jeffrey. *Senator Cleland Loses in an Upset to Republican Emphasizing Defense*, N.Y. Times (Nov. 6, 2002).

Gibbs, Nancy, & Michael Duffy, et al., *The Fight for Justice*, Time (Jan. 22, 2001).

Gillman, Howard. *The Votes That Counted: How the Court Decided the 2000 Presidential Election* (2001).

Glennon, Michael J. *Presidential Power to Wage War against Iraq*, 6 Green Bag 183 (winter 2003).

———. *Limits of Law, Prerogatives of Power: Interventionism after Kosovo* (2001).

Glidewell, Gail. Note, *"Partial Birth" Abortion and the Health Exception: Protecting Maternal Health or Risking Abortion on Demand?* 28 Fordham Urb. L.J. 1089 (2001).

Gold, Dore. *Hatred's Kingdom: How Saudi Arabia Supports the New Global Terrorism* (2003).

Goldberg, Michelle. *Above the Law,* Salon.com (Aug. 28, 2002).

Goldman, Patti. *The Democratization of the Development of United States Trade Policy,* 27 Cornell Int'l L. J. 631 (1994).

Goodstein, Laurie. *Religious Right, Frustrated, Trying New Tactic on G.O.P.,* N.Y. Times (March 23, 1998).

Gostin, Lawrence O. *Health Information Privacy,* 80 Cornell L. Rev. 451 (1995).

Gostin, Lawrence O., James G. Hodge Jr., & Mira S. Burghardt. *Balancing Communal Goods and Personal Privacy under a National Health Informational Privacy Rule,* 46 St. Louis U. L. J. 5 (2002).

Green, John C., Mark J. Rozell, & Clyde Wilcox. *The Christian Right in American Politics* (2003).

Greenhouse, Linda. *White House Asks Court for Voucher Ruling,* N.Y. Times (July 8, 2001).

Greenhouse, Steven. *Mexican Trucks Gain Approval to Haul Cargo throughout U.S.,* N.Y. Times (Nov. 28, 2002).

Greve, Michael S. *Against Cooperative Federalism,* 70 Miss. L. J. 557 (2000).

Groner, Jonathan. *Privilege Fight Looms over Estrada: Leahy's Request for Memos May Spark a Showdown,* Legal Times (June 3, 2002).

———. *Rough Hearing Bodes Ill for Nominee,* Legal Times (Oct. 27, 2003).

———. *Survival Guide: the Politics of Judicial Nominations Is More Complicated Than Ever. Why Some Controversial Picks Are Making It Through, While Others Are Getting Stopped Cold,* Legal Times (May 5, 2003).

Hagstrom, Jerry. *Cows Chip Away at the Cuban Trade Embargo,* 34 Nat'l J. 1650 (Oct. 5, 2002).

Hall, Jane. *How the Environmental Beat Got Its Groove Back,* Columbia Journalism Rev. (July 2001).

Halting the Juggernaut: Can the Dems on the Senate Judiciary Committee Block the Takeover of the Courts? Am. Prospect (July 2, 2001).

Haque, Inaamul. *Dohu Development Agenda: Recapturing the Momentum of Multilateralism and Developing Countries,* 17 Am. U. Int'l L. Rev. 1097 (2002).

Hardin, David. Note, *The Fuss over Two Small Words: The Unconstitutionality of the USA PATRIOT Act Amendments to FISA under the Fourth Amendment,* 71 Geo. Wash. L. Rev. 291 (2003).

Hentoff, Nat. *No "Sneak and Peek": The House Rejects Funds for the Patriot Provision,* Wash. Times (Aug. 4, 2003).

———. *The War on the Bill of Rights and the Gathering Resistance* (2003).

The High Price of Fast Track. Financial Times. Dec. 17, 2001.

Hill, Patrice. *Bush Takes Centrist Stance on Utility Emission Limits,* Wash. Times (Oct. 17, 2003).

Hinckley, Barbara. *Less Than Meets the Eye: Foreign Policy Making and the Myth of the Assertive Congress* (1994).

Hiro, Dilip. *Secrets and Lies: Operation "Iraqi Freedom" and Thereafter* (2004).

Hirsch, Sam. *The United States House of Unrepresentatives: What Went Wrong in the Latest Round of Congressional Redistricting,* 2 Election L.J. 179 (2003).

Holsinger, Melissa C. *The Partial-Birth Abortion Ban Act of 2003: The Congressional Reaction to* Stenberg v. Carhart, 6 N.Y.U.J. Legis. & Pub. Pol'y 603 (2003).

Hood, John. *Take Your Medicine! If the GOP Neglects Health Care, It Is in Deep Trouble—Period,* Nat'l Rev. (June 30, 2003).

Horrock, Nicholas M. *White House Watch: Credibility Problem,* U.P.I. (June 17, 2002).

Hotakainen, Rob. *Senate Passes Trade Bill, Giving Bush a Victory,* Minneapolis Star Trib. (Aug. 2, 2002).

Hudson, Audrey. *"Patriot II" Bid Garners Little Favor on Hill,* Wash. Times (Sept. 12, 2003).

———. *Librarians Dispute Justice's Claim on Use of Patriot Act,* Wash. Times (Sept. 19, 2003).

In Clinton's Words: Containing the "Predators of the 21st Century," N.Y. Times (Feb. 17, 1998).

Inadmissible, Texas Lawyer (Jan. 1, 2001).

Isikoff, Michael, & Tamara Lipper. *Bush Campaign: We're in the Money,* Newsweek (June 16, 2003).

Ivins, Molly, & Lou Dubose. *Bushwhacked: Life in George W. Bush's America* (2003).

———. *Shrub: The Short But Happy Political Life of George W. Bush* (2000 ed.).

Jack, William M. *Taking Care That Presidential Oversight of the Regulatory Process Is Faithfully Executed: A Review of Rule Withdrawals and Rule Suspensions under the Bush Administration's Card Memorandum,* 54 Admin. L. Rev. 12479 (2002).

Jacobson, Gary C. *Terror, Terrain, and Turnout: Explaining the 2002 Midterm Elections,* 118 Political Science Quarterly 1 (2003).

Jacobson, Louis. *Back to the Redrawing Board?* Nat'l J. (April 12, 2003).

Javetski, Bill. *He's Selling the Free Market to the World,* Bus. Week (June 3, 1991).

Jehl, Douglas. *On Environmental Rules, Bush Sees a Balance, Critics a Threat,* N.Y. Times (Feb. 23, 2003).

Jipping, Thomas L. *From Least Dangerous Branch to Most Profound Legacy: The High Stakes in Judicial Selection,* 4 Tex. Rev. L. & Pol. 365 (2000).

Johnston, David. *Classified Section of Sept. 11 Report Faults Saudi Rulers,* N.Y. Times (July 26, 2003).

Johnston, David, & Neil A. Lewis. *In Testimony, Ashcroft Vows to Enforce Laws He Dislikes,* N.Y. Times (Jan. 17, 2001).

Johnston, David Cay. *Studies Say Tax Cuts Now Will Bring Bigger Bill Later,* N.Y. Times (Sept. 23, 2003).

JonQuieres, Guy De, & Frances Williams. *Stalled in Geneva: After Doha, a Further Trade Liberalization Round Seemed Imminent. But Wavering US Commitment to the Cause Has Robbed It of Its Impetus*, Fin. Times (June 19, 2002).

Judis, John B. *The Paradox of American Democracy: Elites, Special Interests, and the Betrayal of the Public Trust* (2001).

Judis, John B., & Ruy Teixeira. *The Emerging Democratic Majority* (2002).

Justice: From the Ashes of 9/11: Big Bad John, Nat'l J. (Jan. 25, 2003)

Justice: Lightning Rod Defends "Aggressive" Tactics, Nat'l J. (Jan. 25, 2003).

Kahn, Greg. *The Fate of the Kyoto Protocol under the Bush Administration*, 21 Berkeley J. Int'l L. 548 (2003).

Kaplan, Lawrence F. *Containment*, New Republic (Feb. 5, 2001).

Karin, Marcy Lynn. Note, *Out of Sight, but Not Out of Mind: How Executive Order 13233 Expands Executive Privilege While Simultaneously Preventing Access to Presidential Records*, 55 Stan. L. Rev. 529 (2002).

Kaufman, Marc. *Negotiator in Global Tobacco Talks Quits*, Wash. Post (Aug. 2, 2001).

Kernell, Samuel. *Going Public: New Strategies of Presidential Leadership* (3d ed. 1997).

Kershaw, Sarah. *U.S.-Saudi Ties Frayed over Mideast Tensions*, N.Y. Times (April 30, 2003).

Kessel, John H. *Presidents, the Presidency, and the Political Environment* (2001).

Kessler, Glenn. *U.S. Decision on Iraq Has Puzzling Past: Opponents of War Wonder When, How Policy Was Set*, Wash. Post (Jan. 12, 2003).

Khalilzad, Zalmay M., & Paul Wolfowitz. *Overthrow Him*, Wkly. Standard (Dec. 1, 1997).

Kitfield, James. *Bush and Gore's Positions on Foreign Policy*, 32 Nat'l J. 1034 (April 1, 2000).

———. *Next Stop—Baghdad*, Nat'l. J. (Oct. 13, 2001).

Klein, Christine A. *Preserving Monumental Landscapes under the Antiquities Act*, 87 Cornell L. Rev. 1333 (2002).

Klein, Edward. *We're Not Destroying Rights, We're Protecting Them*, Parade Mag. (May 19, 2002).

Klein, Joe. *Blessed Are the Poor—They Don't Get Tax Cuts*, Time (June 9, 2003).

———. *How the Supremes Redeemed Bush*, Time (July 7, 2003).

Knickerbocker, Brad. *Assisted-Suicide Movement Gets a Boost*, Christian Sci. Monitor, (April 19, 2002).

Koontz, Thomas M. *Federalism in the Forest: National versus State Natural Resource Policy* (2002).

Koopman, Douglas L. *Hostile Takeover: The House Republican Party, 1980–1995* (1996).

Kopel, David. *Terrorism and Guns*, Nat'l Rev. (Dec. 17, 2001).

Krehbiel, Keith. *Pivotal Politics* (1998).

Kristol, William, & Robert Kagan. *Toward a Neo-Reaganite Foreign Policy*, Foreign Aff. (July–Aug. 1996).

Kronholz, June. *Patriot Act Riles an Unlikely Group: Nation's Librarians,* Wall St. J. (Oct. 28, 2003).

Krugman, Paul. *The Great Unraveling* (2003).

Krushnakumar, Anita S. *Reconciliation and the Fiscal Constitution: The Anatomy of the 1995–96 Budget "Train Wreck,"* 35 Harv. J. on Legis. 589 (1998).

Kumar, Martha Joynt. *Executive Order 13233: Further Implementation of the Presidential Records Act,* 32 Pres. Studies Q. 194 (2002).

La Raja, Ray. *Sources and Uses of Soft Money: What Do We Know?* In Gerald C. Lubenow, ed. *A User's Guide to Campaign Finance Reform* (2001).

Lake, Eli J. *The Pentagon v. The CIA on Iraq,* New Republic (Sept. 23, 2002).

Lamare, James W. *Texas Politics: Economics, Power and Policy* (7th ed. 2000).

Landers, Jim. *Schumer Contests Bush Ambassador Nominee,* Dallas Morning News (Nov. 22, 2003).

Landers, Jim, & Todd J. Gillman. *Nominee as Saudi Envoy Naturally Diplomatic, Friends Say,* Dallas Morning News (Nov. 20, 2003).

Lane, Charles. *Olson's Role in War on Terror Matches His Uncommon Clout,* Wash. Post (July 3, 2002).

Langley, Alison. *World Health Meeting Approves Treaty to Discourage Smoking,* N.Y. Times (May 22, 2003).

Lazarus, Richard J. *A Different Kind of "Republican Moment" in Environmental Law,* 87 Minn. L. Rev. 999 (2003).

Lemann, Nicholas. *The Quiet Man: Dick Cheney's Discreet Rise to Unprecedented Power,* New Yorker (May 7, 2001).

Leone, Richard C., & Greg Anrig Jr., eds. *The War on Our Freedoms* (2003).

Lerner, Sharon. *Saviors of the Children,* Village Voice (May 14, 2002).

Levitt, Melissa, & Katherine C. Naff, *Gender as a Political Constant: The More Things Change, the More They Stay the Same.* In Stephen J. Wayne & Clyde Wilcox eds., *The Election of the Century* (2002).

Levy, Robert A. *Federal Tobacco Policy: Return to Reason?* (Cato Institute, June 4, 2001), www.cato.org.

Lewis, Anthony. *Civil Liberties in a Time of Terror,* 2003 Wis. L. Rev. 257 (2003).

Lewis, Neil A. *Much-Sought Speech by Ashcroft Is Found,* N.Y. Times (Jan. 12, 2001).

———. *Ashcroft's Terrorism Policies Dismay Some Conservatives,* N.Y. Times (July 24, 2002).

Lewis, Neil A., & David Johnston. *In Hearing's Second Day, Ashcroft Says He Would Not Challenge Roe Ruling,* N.Y. Times (Jan. 18, 2001).

Lichtblau, Eric. *Ashcroft Seeks More Power to Pursue Terror Suspects,* N.Y. Times (June 6, 2003).

———. *Attorney General Stresses the Risk of More Attacks,* L.A. Times (Oct. 1, 2001).

———. *U.S. Report Faults the Roundup of Illegal Immigrants after 9/11,* N.Y. Times (June 3, 2003).

————. *U.S. Uses Terror Law to Pursue Crimes from Drugs to Swindling: Broad Steps Anger Critics of Expanded Powers.* N.Y. Times (Sept. 28, 2003).

————. *White House Approved Departure of Saudis after Sept. 11, Ex-Aide Says,* N.Y. Times (Sept. 4, 2003).

Lichtblau, Eric, with Adam Liptak. *On Terror, Spying and Guns, Ashcroft Expands Reach,* N.Y. Times (March 15, 2003).

Liebman, James S. *An "Effective Death Penalty"? AEDPA and Error Detection in Capital Cases,* 67 Brook. L. Rev. 411 (2001).

Lim, Karen. Note, *Freedom to Seclude after* Boy Scouts of America v. Dale: *Do Private Schools Have a Right to Discriminate against Homosexual Teachers?* 71 Fordham L. Rev. 2599 (2003).

Limbaugh, David. *Absolute Power: The Legacy of Corruption in the Clinton-Reno Justice Department* (2001).

Lind, Michael. *Made in Texas: George W. Bush and the Southern Takeover of American Politics* (2002).

Lindsay, James M. *From Containment to Apathy,* Foreign Affairs (Sept.–Oct. 2000).

Liptak, Adam. *Judge Blocks U.S. Bid to Ban Suicide Law,* N.Y. Times (April 18, 2002).

Liptak, Adam, Neil A. Lewis, & Benjamin Weiser, *After Sept. 11, a Legal Battle on the Limits of Civil Liberty,* N.Y. Times (Aug. 4, 2002).

Little, Laura E. *The ABA's Role in Prescreening Federal Judicial Candidates: Are We Ready to Give Up on the Lawyers?* 10 Wm. & Mary Bill Rts. J. 37 (2001).

Lorenzetti, Maureen. *DOE to Investigate Last Month's Gasoline Price Spike,* Oil & Gas J. (Sept. 15, 2003).

Lowi, Theodore J. *The End of the Republican Era* (1995).

Luban, David. *Taking Out the Adversary: The Assault on Progressive Public-Interest Lawyers,* 91 Cal. L. Rev. 209 (2003).

Lubenow, Gerald C., ed. *A User's Guide to Campaign Finance Reform* (2001).

MacDonald, Heather. *Total Misrepresentation,* Wkly. Standard (Jan. 27, 2003).

MacFarquhar, Neil. *Saudis Arrest 8 in Deadly Riyadh Bombing,* N.Y. Times (May 29, 2003).

Magleby, David B., ed. *Financing the 2000 Election* (2002).

Malcolm, David J. *Tobacco, Global Public Health, and Non-governmental Organizations: An Imminent Pandemic or Just Another Legal Product?* 28 Denv. J. Int'l L. & Pol'y 1 (1999).

Mann, Thomas E. *Linking Knowledge and Action: Political Science and Campaign Finance Reform,* Perspectives on Politics (March 2003).

Manuel, Christina E. *Physician-Assisted Suicide Permits Dignity in Dying: Oregon Takes on Attorney General Ashcroft,* 23 J. Legal Med. 563 (2002).

Marshall, Andrew. *Take Iraq Apart, Says Bush Adviser,* The Independent (May 21, 2000).

Martin, Kathryn. Note, *The USA Patriot Act's Application to Library Patron Records,* 29 J. Legis. 283 (2003).

Martinez, Gebe. *Concerns Linger for Lawmakers following Difficult Vote for War*, 60 Cong. Q. Wkly. Rep. (Oct. 12, 2002).

Matthews, Owen. *The Next Move Is Check*, Newsweek (April 8, 2002).

Mayer, Jeremy D. *The Incorrigibly White Republican Party: Racial Politics in the Presidential Race*. In Stephen J. Wayne & Clyde Wilcox, eds. *The Election of the Century* (2002).

Mayhew, David R. *Divided We Govern: Party Control, Lawmaking, and Investigations* (1991).

McAllister, Stephen R., et al. *Life after 9/11: Issues Affecting the Courts and the Nation*, 51 U. Kan. L. Rev. 219 (2003).

McDermott, Patrice. *Withhold and Control: Information in the Bush Administration*, 12 Kan. J.L. & Pub. Pol'y 671 (2003).

McGarity, Thomas O. *Jogging in Place: The Bush Administration's Freshman Year Environmental Record*, 32 Envtl. L. Rep. 10709 (2002).

McGee, Jim, & Brian Duffy. *Main Justice* (1997).

———. *Someone to Watch over Us*, Wash. Post (June 23, 1996).

McIntyre Robert S., & Michael J. McIntyre. *Fixing the "Marriage Penalty" Problem*, 33 Val. U. L. Rev. 907 (1999).

Medill, Colleen E. *Challenging the Four "Truths" of Personal Social Security Accounts: Evidence from the World of 401(K) Plans*, 81 N.C. L. Rev. 901 (2003).

Merzer, Martin. *Unilateral Iraq Attack Losing Support*, Milwaukee J.-Sentinel (Jan. 12, 2003).

Meyer, Joseph. *Report Is Wary of Saudi Actions*, L.A. Times (July 25, 2003).

Meyerson, Harold. *Senatorial Heresy: The Democrats Rethink Free Trade*, Am. Prospect (June 17, 2002).

Milbank, Dana, & Ellen Nakashima. *Bush Team Has "Right" Credentials: Conservative Picks Seen Eclipsing Even Reagan's*, Wash. Post (March 25, 2001).

Miller, Gary, & Norman Schofield. *Activists and Partisan Realignment in the United States*, 97 Am. Poli. Sci. Rev. 245 (2003).

Mitchell, Alison. *Campaign Finance Bill Passes in Senate, 59–41*, N.Y. Times (April 3, 2001).

Mohr, Patricia, & Warren Rojas. *Senate GOP Bets That $500 Billion Tax Deal Can Break Budget Logjam*, 99 Tax Notes 167 (April 14, 2003).

Moore, James, & Wayne Slater. *Bush's Brain: How Karl Rove Made George W. Bush Presidential* (2003).

Motavalli, Jim. *Scorched Earth Policy: Environmental Policy of the George W. Bush Administration*, E Magazine, (May 1, 2001).

Murdoch, Stephen. *Preemptive War: Is It Legal?* Wash. Lawyer (Jan. 2003).

Mylroie, Laurie. *Study of Revenge: Saddam Hussein's Unfinished War against America* (2000).

Natural Resources Defense Council, *Gale Ann Norton: An Environmental Profile* (Jan. 2001).

————. *Gutting the New Source Review: Letting the Polluters Avoid Cleanup for 10 Years and Beyond with a New Right to Pollute*, NRDC Backgrounder (March 20, 2002) www.nrdc.org.

————. *Rewriting the Rules, Year-End Report 2002: The Bush Administration's Assault on the Environment* (2003).

New Guidelines Open U.S. Data to Challenge, Wash. Post (Oct. 1, 2002).

Newfield, Jack. *The Right's Judicial Juggernaut: Nomination of Miguel Estrada*, The Nation (Oct. 7, 2002).

Nicholas, Peter, & Matea Gold. *Schwarzenegger Team Focuses on 2 Key Posts*, L.A. Times (Oct. 2003).

Notebook: DeMint Condition, New Republic (May 27, 2002).

Notebook: Puff Peace, New Republic (Jan. 20, 2003).

O'Beirne, Kate. *The Olson Project: Democrats against a Bush Nominee*, Nat'l Rev. (June 11, 2001)

Olson, Theodore B. *The Most Political Justice Department Ever*, Am. Spectator (Sept. 2000).

Oil Man for Ambassador, N.Y. Times (Nov. 18, 2003).

Olson, Theodore B. *Politicizing the Justice Department.* In Roger Pilon, ed. *The Rule of Law in the Wake of Clinton* (2000).

Ota, Alan K. *Tax Cut Package Clears Amid Bicameral Rancor*, 61 Cong. Q. Wkly. Rep. (May 24, 2003).

Owen, Dave. *Prescriptive Laws, Uncertain Science, and Political Stories: Forest Management in the Sierra Nevada*, 29 Eco. L. Q. 747 (2002).

Parks, Daniel J., with Bill Swindell. *Tax Debate Assured a Long Life as Bush, GOP Press for New Cuts*, 59 Cong. Q. Wkly. Rep. (June 2, 2001).

Parks, Julie A. Comment, *Lessons in Politics: Initial Use of the Congressional Review Act*, 55 Admin. L. Rev. 187 (2003).

Pear, Robert. *Democrats Say Bush Revisions Ruin Medical Privacy Rules*, N.Y. Times (April 17, 2002).

Pearlstein, Steven. *Bush Selection Zoellick Is a Free-Trader on a Mission*, Wash. Post. (Jan. 13, 2001).

People for the American Way. *Courting Disaster: How a Scalia-Thomas Supreme Court Would Endanger Our Rights and Freedoms* (June 2000).

————. *John Ashcroft's First Year as Attorney General: Judicial Nominations* (2002), www.pfaw.org.

Percival, Robert V. *Environmental Implications of the Rehnquist Court's New Federalism*, 17 Natural Res. & Env. (summer 2002).

Peretz, Martin. *Audit This*, New Republic (July 22, 2002).

Perine, Keith. *Abortion Rights Advocates Spurn Fetus Protection Bill*, Cong. Q. Wkly. Rep. (July 19, 2003).

Pertschuk, Michael. *When It Comes to Tobacco Legislation, Who Wins in November May Matter a Lot*, The Nation (April 17, 2000).

Peterson, Mark A. *Legislating Together: The White House and Capitol Hill from Eisenhower to Reagan* (1990).

Pfleger, Katherine. *Bush Proposes Changes to Way Forests Are Zoned*, Seattle Times (Nov. 27, 2002).

Phillips, Kevin. *Wealth and Democracy* (2002; paperback ed. 2003).

Pianin, Eric. *EPA Mulls Limits for Power Plant Emissions: Environmentalists Laud White House Effort on Pollutant*, Wash. Post (Feb. 28, 2001).

Pika, Joseph A., et al. *The Politics of the Presidency* (5th ed. 2002).

Pilon, Roger, ed. *The Rule of Law in the Wake of Clinton* (2000).

Podesta, John D. *Shadow Creep: Government Secrecy since 9/11*, 2002 J. L. Tech & Pol'y 361 (2002).

Pollack, Sheldon D. *Refinancing America: The Republican Antitax Agenda* (2003).

Ponnuru, Ramesh. *Abortion Now: Thirty Years after Roe, A Daunting Landscape*, Nat'l Rev. (Jan. 27, 2003).

———. *How's the Granny Card Playing? The Evolving Politics of Social Security*, Nat'l Rev. (Nov. 11, 2002).

Pooley, Eric, et al. *Read My Knuckles: To Win Big in South Carolina, Bush Found His Anger, Battered McCain—and Moved Sharply to the Right*, Time (Feb. 28, 2000).

Posner, Gerald. *Why America Slept* (2003).

Preston, Julia. *Security Council Votes, 15–0, for Tough Iraq Resolution*, N.Y. Times (Nov. 9, 2002).

Priest, Dana. *FBI Leak Probe Irks Lawmakers*, Wash. Post (Aug. 2, 2002).

Puffed Up or Stubbed out? Economist (May 24, 2003).

Purdum, Todd S., & Alison Mitchell. *Bush, Angered by Leaks, Duels with Congress*, N.Y. Times (Oct. 10, 2001).

Putnam, Robert. *Diplomacy and Domestic Politics: The Logic of Two-Level Games*, 42 Int'l Org. 427 (1988).

Rabin, Robert L., & Stephen D. Sugarman, eds. *Regulating Tobacco* (2001).

Radosh, Ronald. *Divided They Fell: The Demise of the Democratic Party, 1964–1996* (1996).

Rae, Nicol C. *The Decline and Fall of the Liberal Republicans from 1952 to the Present* (1989).

Rak, Jennifer. Note, *An RX for Reform: A Medicare Prescription Drug Benefit*, 12 Health Matrix 449 (2002).

Rashid, Ahmed. *Jihad: The Rise of Militant Islam in Central Asia* (2000; Penguin ed. 2003).

Ratcliffe, R. G. *Return to Secrecy; Overseer of UT's Trust Fund Conceals Details on Investment Performances*, Houston Chron. (Sept. 16, 2002).

———. *UTIMCO Records Show Favors, Failures, Fortune*, Houston Chron. (Oct. 5, 2002).

Revkin, Andrew C. *With White House Approval, E.P.A. Pollution Report Omits Global Warming Section*, N.Y. Times (Sept. 15, 2002).

Risen, James. *C.I.A. Aides Feel Pressure in Preparing Iraqi Reports*, N.Y. Times (March 23, 2003).

————. *C.I.A. Rejects Call for Iraq Report*, N.Y. Times (Oct. 3, 2002).

Risen, James, et al. *After the War: Weapons Intelligence: In Sketchy Data, Trying to Gauge Iraq Threat*, N.Y. Times (July 20, 2003).

Robinson, Gerald H. Article, *We're Listening! Electronic Eavesdropping, FISA, and the Secret Court*, 36 Willamette L. Rev. 50 (2000).

Robinson, Linda, et al. *A Question of Complicity*, U.S. News & World Rep. (June 30, 2003).

Robinson, Walter V. *In Ashcroft's Past, a Vietnam Deferment*, Boston Globe (Jan. 16, 2001).

Rohde, David W. *Parties and Leaders in the Postreform House* (1991).

Rohrbaugh, Elizabeth. *On Our Way to Ten Billion Human Beings: A Comment on Sustainability and Population*, 5 Colo. J. Int'l Envt'l. L. & Pol'y 235 (1994).

Rojas, William. *Pick Your Battles: Weighting Bush's Dividend Cut against AMT Reform*, 100 Tax Notes 458 (April 28, 2003).

Rosen, Jeffrey. *Civil Right*, New Republic (Oct. 21, 2002).

Rosenbaum, David E. *Bush Seeks Tax Cuts He Had Scorned*, N.Y. Times (Feb. 9, 2003).

Rosenberg, Morton. *Whatever Happened to Congressional Review of Agency Rulemaking? A Brief Overview, Assessment, and Proposal for Reform*, 51 Admin. L. Rev. 1051 (1999).

Rosenzweig, Paul, & Michael Scardaville. *The Need to Protect Civil Liberties While Combating Terrorism: Legal Principles and the Total Information Awareness Program*, Heritage Foundation Rep. (Feb. 5, 2003).

Ross, Thomas W. *The Faith-Based Initiative: Anti-Poverty or Anti-Poor?* 9 Geo. J. on Poverty L. & Pol'y 167 (2002).

Rozell, Mark J. *Executive Privilege: Presidential Power, Secrecy, and Accountability* (2d ed. 2002).

Rozell, Mark J. *Executive Privilege Revived? Secrecy and Conflict during the Bush Presidency*, 52 Duke L.J. 403 (2002).

Rutenberg, Jim. *White House Keeps a Grip on Its News*, N.Y. Times (Oct. 14, 2002).

Saletan, William. *Bearing Right: How Conservatives Won the Abortion War* (2003).

Salih, Muhammad. *America's Shy Ally against Terror*, N.Y. Times (March 11, 2002).

Sanger, David E. *Bush Issues Directive Describing Policy on Antimissile Defenses*, N.Y. Times (May 21, 2003).

————. *Canvassing the Votes to Gain Legitimacy*, N.Y. Times (March 13, 2003).

Sanger, David E., & Patrick E. Tyler. *Officials Recount Road to Deadlock over Missile Talks*, N.Y. Times (Dec. 13, 2001).

Sanger, David E., & Elisabeth Bumiller. *Bush Presses U.N. to Act Quickly on Disarming Iraq*, N.Y. Times (Sept. 13, 2002).

Scarborough, Rowan. *Intercepts Foretold of "Big Attack,"* Wash. Times (Sept. 22, 2001).

Scheiber, Harry N. *Redesigning the Architecture of Federalism—An American Tradition: Modern Devolution Policies in Perspective,* 14 Yale L. & Pol'y Rev. 227 (1996).

Scherer, Nancy. *Are Clinton's Judges "Old" Democrats or "New" Democrats?* Judicature (Nov.–Dec. 2000).

Schlesinger, Arthur M. *The Imperial Presidency* (rev. ed. 1989).

Schneider, Troy K. *At the Races: A Weekly Review of Campaign 2000,* 7 Nat'l J. 496 (Feb. 12, 2000).

Schrag, Peter. *Ashcroft's Hypocrisy,* Am. Prospect (Jan. 1, 2002).

Schreurs, Miranda A. *Competing Agendas and the Climate Change Negotiations: The United States, the European Union, and Japan,* 36 Envtl. L. Rep. 11218 (2001).

Schulhofer, Stephen J. *No Checks, No Balances: Discarding Bedrock Constitutional Principles.* In Richard C. Leone & Greg Anrig., Jr., eds. *The War on Our Freedoms* (2003).

Second Presidential Debate between Gov. Bush and Vice President Gore, N.Y. Times (Oct. 12, 2000).

Security in Insecure Times, Petroleum Economist (Feb. 10, 2003).

Seelye, Katharine Q. *White House Seeks a Change in Rules on Air Pollution,* N.Y. Times (June 14, 2002).

———. *Bush Proposes Change to Allow More Thinning of Forests,* N.Y. Times (Dec. 12, 2002).

———. *Top E.P.A. Official Quits, Criticizing Bush's Policies,* N.Y. Times (March 1, 2002).

Senate Kicks Off Budget Debate, 2001 Tax Notes Today 64-1 (April 3, 2001), in Lexis, Fedtax Library, TNT file.

Senate OKs $1.2 Trillion Tax Cut, Sets Up Budget Standoff, 2001 Tax Notes Today 68-1 (April 9, 2001), in Lexis, Fedtax Library, TNT file.

Shapiro, Walter. *What We Know Is Bad; Secrecy Just Makes It Worse,* USA Today (July 25, 2003).

Shenon, Philip. *A Top G.O.P. Senator Hints at Soft Money Compromise,* N.Y. Times (March 23, 2001).

Sheppard, Lee A. *News Analysis: No Tax Cuts for the Gore States,* 91 Tax Notes 1480 (May 28, 2001).

Silverstein, Ken. *Saudis and Americans: Friends in Need,* The Nation (Dec. 3, 2001).

Simon, James F. *The Center Holds: The Power Struggle inside the Rehnquist Court* (1995).

Sinclair, Barbara. *Unorthodox Lawmaking: New Legislative Processes in the U.S. Congress* (2d ed. 2000).

Singer, P. W. *Corporate Warriors: The Rise of the Privatized Military Industry* (2003).

Skorneck, Carolyn. *Bush Wins Supplemental Battle, May Face Loss in War on Terror,* Cong. Q. Wkly. Rep. (Nov. 1, 2003).

———. *Supplemental Sans Roll Call Provides Cover All Around,* Cong. Q. Wkly. Rep. (Nov. 8, 2003).

Skrzycki, Cindy. *267 Rules Up for Review: Referendum Names Environmental, Auto Standards,* Wash. Post. (Dec. 19, 2002).

Slavin, Dana. *Faith in Justice: Attorney General John D. Ashcroft,* Fed. Lawyer (Oct. 2001).

Slevin, Peter. *Ashcroft Blocks FBI Access to Gun Records: Critics Call Attorney General's Decision Contradictory in Light of Terror Probe Tactics,* Wash. Post (Dec. 7, 2001).

Smith, Jean Edward. *George Bush's War* (1992).

Smith, Heather A. *A New Prescription for Abortion,* 73 U. Colo. L. Rev. 1069 (2002).

Snape, William, III, and John M. Carter II. *Weakening NEPA: How the Bush Administration Uses the Judicial System to Weaken Environmental Protections,* 33 Envtl. L. Rep. 10682 (2003).

Spanier, John, & Steven W. Hook. *American Foreign Policy since World War II* (15th ed. 2000).

Spitzer, Robert J. *Lost and Found: Researching the Second Amendment,* 76 Chi.-Kent L. Rev. 349 (2000).

Staff Report. *The Death Penalty Becomes a High-Profile Issue,* Fed. Lawyer (Sept. 2002).

Stavros, Richard. *The Candidate: An Interview with Texas Gov. George W. Bush,* Public Utilities Fortnightly (Feb. 1, 2000).

Stefancic, Jean, & Richard Delgado. *No Mercy: How Conservative Think Tanks and Foundations Changed America's Social Agenda* (1997).

Steinberger, Michael. *Bush's Saudi Connections: And Why This Is a Crucial Issue in 2004,* Am. Prospect (Oct. 2003).

Steinzor, Rena I. *Toward Better Bubbles and Future Lives: A Progressive Response to the Conservative Agenda for Reforming Environmental Law,* 32 Envtl. L. Rep. 11421 (2002).

———. Book Review, *Pragmatic Regulation in Dangerous Times,* 20 Yale J. on Reg. 407 (2003).

———. *Democracies Die behind Closed Doors: The Homeland Security Act and Corporate Accountability,* 12 Kan. J.L. & Pub. Pol'y 641 (2003).

Stevenson, Richard W. *Delaying Talk about the Cost of War,* N.Y. Times (March 23, 2003).

———. *Old Business in New Light,* N.Y. Times (July 9, 2002).

Stille, Alexander. *Advocating Tobacco, on the Payroll of Tobacco,* N.Y. Times (March 23, 2002)

Stokes, Bruce. *Talk about Unintended Consequences,* Nat'l J. (May 26, 2001).

Stonecash, Jeffrey M. *Class and Party in American Politics* (2002).

Stonewalling, Press Bush on 9/11 Report, Minneapolis Star Trib. (Aug. 5, 2003).

Streitfeld, David. *Lewinsky to Turn Over Book Purchase Information: Agreement Resolves 1st Amendment Dispute between Starr and Bookstore Owners,* Wash. Post (June 23, 1998).

Strickland, Leif. *Texas Showdown,* Newsweek (Aug. 21, 2003).

Sugarman, Stephen D. *International Aspects of Tobacco Control and the Proposed WHO Treaty* In Robert L. Rabin & Stephen D. Sugarman, eds. *Regulating Tobacco* (2001).

Sullivan, Martin A. *Mandated JCT Report Says House Bill May Hurt Economy,* 99 Tax Notes 948 (May 19, 2003).

Swartz, Nikki. *Information at a Price: Liberty vs. Security,* Info. Mgmt. J. (May 1, 2003).

Swindell, Bill. *Renewed Push for "Faith Based" Law Faces Hostile Democrats, Tight Calendar,* 61 Cong. Q. Wkly. Rep. (March 1, 2003).

Taylor, Andrew. *Grim Budget Deficit Forecasts Still Too Rosy, Say Critics,* 61 Cong. Q. Wkly. Rep. (Aug. 30, 2003).

———. *Law Designed for Curbing Deficits Becomes GOP Tool for Cutting Taxes,* 59 Cong. Q. Wkly. Rep. (April 7, 2001).

Tennant, Roy. *Patriotism As If Our Constitution Matters,* Libr. J. (July 15, 2003).

Texas Redistricting to Go to Conference, N.Y. Times (Sept. 25, 2003).

Thomas, Clarence. *This Is Worse Than Any Obstacle . . . That I Have Ever Faced,* Wash. Post (Oct. 12, 1991).

Tiefer, Charles. *Adjusting Sovereignty: Contemporary Congressional-Executive Controversies about International Organizations,* 35 Tex. Int'l L. J. 239 (2000).

———. *Alongside the Fast Track: Environmental and Labor Issues in FTAA,* 7 Minn. J. Glob. Trade 329 (1998).

———. (Book review) 96 Am. J. Int'l L. 489 (2002).

———. *Budgetized Health Entitlements and the Fiscal Constitution in Congress's 1995–1996 Budget Battle,* 33 Harv. J. on Legis. 411 (1996).

———. *Congressional Practice and Procedure* (1989).

———. *The Controversial Transition Process from Investigating the President to Impeaching Him,* 14 St. John's J. Legal Comment. 111 (1999).

———. *Congressional Oversight of the Clinton Administration and Congressional Procedure,* 50 Admin. L. Rev. 199 (1998).

———. *Did Eastern Enterprises Send Enterprise Liability South?* 51 Ala. L. Rev. 1305 (2000).

———. *The Flag-Burning Controversy of 1989–90: Congress' Valid Role in Constitutional Dialogue,* 29 Harv. J. on Legis. 357 (1992).

———. *Free Trade Agreements and the New Federalism,* 7 Minn. J. Global Trade 45 (1998).

———. *Heads Up! Ready or Not, the Election Might Be Congress' to Decide,* Legal Times (Nov. 20, 2000).

———. *Helping Those Who Can Help Themselves: The Rehnquist Court's Direct and Indirect Conservative Activism,* 1 Geo. J. L. & Pub. Pol'y 103 (2002).

———. *How to Steal a Trillion: The Uses and Abuses of Laws about Lawmaking in 2001*, 17 J. Law & Politics 409 (2001).

———. *NEPA and Energy Supply: A Case Study*, 22 BNA Envtl. L. Monograph (1976).

———. *OMB's New A-76: Tilting the Contracting-out Process*, Federal Bar Association Government Contracts Section Newsletter (spring 2003).

———. *Out of Order: The Abrupt Dismissal of the Parliamentarian Threatens Senate Procedure*, Legal Times (May 14, 2001).

———. *President Bush's First Executive Privilege Claim*, 33 Pres. Studies Q. 201 (2003).

———. *The Reconceptualization of Legislative History in the Supreme Court*, 2000 Wisc. L. Rev. 205 (2000).

———. *The Semi-Sovereign Presidency* (1994).

———. *The Senate Impeachment Trial for President Clinton*, 28 Hofstra L. Rev. 407 (1999).

———. *The Specially Investigated President*, 5 U. Chi. Roundtable 143 (1998).

———. *Sino 301: How Congress Can Effectively Review Relations with China after WTO Accession*, 34 Cornell Int'l L. J. 56 (2000).

———. *Skirting a Constitutional Crisis*, Legal Times (Dec. 4, 2000).

———. *Treatment for Medicare's Budget: Quick Operation or Long-Term Care?* 16 St. Louis U. Pub. L. Rev. 27 (1996).

———. *A True Ballot: Florida Law Makes Clear That Confusing Design Must Never Distort the Voice of the Voters*, Legal Times (Nov. 13, 2000).

———. *War Decisions in the Late 1990s by Partial Congressional Declaration*, 36 San Diego L. Rev. 1 (1999).

Toobin, Jeffrey. *Too Close to Call: The Thirty-Six-Day Battle to Decide the 2000 Election* (2001).

Totenberg, Nina. *Miguel Estrada Withdraws His Name from Consideration as a Bush Nominee*, National Public Radio: All Things Considered (Sept. 4, 2003) (transcript in Lexis-Nexis database).

Transcript of Debate between Vice President Gore and Governor Bush, N.Y. Times (Oct. 4, 2000).

Tushnet, Mark. *Alarmism versus Moderation in Responding to the Rehnquist Court*, 78 Ind. L.J. 47 (2003).

Twentieth Century Fund Working Group on Campaign Finance Litigation. *Buckley Stops Here: Loosening the Judicial Stranglehold on Campaign Finance Reform* (1998).

Tyler, Patrick E. *Mideast Turmoil: Arab Politics; Saudis to Warn Bush of Rupture over Israel Policy*, N.Y. Times (April 25, 2002).

Uhler, Walter C. *Missile Shield or Holy Grail? How to Kill: The New Battle over Shielding America from Missile Attack*, The Nation (Jan. 28, 2002).

Van Natta, Don. *Last American Combat Troops Quit Saudi Arabia*, N.Y. Times (Sept. 22, 2003).

van der Vyver, Johan D. *American Exceptionalism: Human Rights, International Criminal Justice, and National Self-Righteousness,* 50 Emory L.J. 775 (2001).

Vest, Jason. *Darth Rumsfeld,* Am. Prospect (Feb. 26, 2001).

Violence Policy Center. Appendix B to *Shot Full of Holes: Deconstructing John Ashcroft's Second Amendment* (July 2001).

———. *John Ashcroft: Year One* (January 2002).

Walczak, Lee, Rich Miller, Howard Gleckman, & Richard S. Dunham. *A Politically Correct Tax Plan,* Bus. Week (Dec. 13, 1999).

Wald, Matthew L. *E.P.A. Says It Will Change Rules Governing Industrial Pollution,* N.Y. Times (Nov. 23, 2002).

Walsh, Nick Paton. *US Looks Away As New Ally Tortures Islamists: Uzbekistan's President Steps Up Repression of Opponents,* The Guardian (May 26, 2003).

The War over Gay Marriage, Newsweek (July 7, 2003).

Warshaw, Shirley Anne. *The Domestic Presidency: Policy Making in the White House* (1996).

Wayne, Stephen J., & Clyde Wilcox, eds. *The Election of the Century* (2002).

Weinberg, Steven. *Can Missile Defense Work?* N.Y. Rev. of Books (Feb. 14, 2002).

Weiser, Philip J. *Towards a Constitutional Architecture for Cooperative Federalism,* 79 N. Caro. L. Rev. 663 (2001).

Weisman, Steven R. *A Long, Winding Road to a Diplomatic Dead End,* N.Y. Times (March 17, 2003).

———. *Pre-emption: Idea with a Lineage Whose Time Has Come.* N.Y. Times (March 23, 2003).

Weiss, Kenneth R. *U.S. Refuses to Buy Back Oil Leases,* L.A. Times (June 8, 2002).

———. *White House Pulls Back on Offshore Oil Drilling,* L.A. Times (April 1, 2003).

West, Darrell M. *Checkbook Democracy: How Money Corrupts Political Campaigns* (2000).

Wilcox, Clyde. *Wither the Christian Right? The Elections and Beyond.* In Stephen J. Wayne & Clyde Wilcox, eds. *The Election of the Century* (2002).

Wildman, Sarah. *Bullies in the Pulpit: Will a Political Catholic Church Help or Hinder the GOP?* Am. Prospect (Oct. 2003).

Wiley, Lindsay F. *Assisted Suicide: Court Strikes Down Ashcroft Directive,* 30 J. L. Med. & Ethics (2002).

Wilson, George C. *Iraq Could Be Another Lebanon,* Nat'l J. (Nov. 8, 2003).

Wirth, David A. *The Sixth Session (Part Two) and Seventh Session of the Conference on the Parties to the Framework Convention on Climate Change,* 96 Am J. Int'l. L. 648 (2002).

Wohl, Alexander. *Bush's Tenth Justice,* Am. Prospect (May 21, 2001).

Wolf, Edward N. *Top Heavy: A Study of the Increasing Inequality of Wealth in America* (1998).

Woods, Michael A. Comment, *The Propriety of Local Government Protections of Gays and Lesbians from Discriminatory Employment Practices,* 52 Emory L.J. 515 (2003).

Woodward, Bob. *The Commanders* (1991).

———. *Bush at War* (2003).

———. *President Broadens Anti-Hussein Order: CIA Gets More Tools to Oust Iraqi Leader,* Wash. Post (June 16, 2002).

Yarbrough, Tinsley E. *The Rehnquist Court and the Constitution* (2001).

York, Byron. *Gunning for Ashcroft,* Nat'l Rev. (Dec. 6, 2001).

Zaid, Mark S. *Too Many Secrets,* Nat'l Law J. (March 25, 2002).

Zegart, Dan. *Bush: Marlboro's Man: George W. Bush's Policy towards Tobacco Industry,* The Nation (Nov. 6, 2000).

Zelenak, Lawrence. *Doing Something about Marriage Penalties: A Guide for the Perplexed,* 54 Tax L. Rev. 1 (2000).

Zeller, Shawn. *Tort Reform's Massive War Chest,* Nat'l J. (March 29, 2003).

Zepezauer, Mark. *Boomerang!* (2003).

Zoellick, Robert B. *A Republican Foreign Policy,* Foreign Affairs (Jan. 2000).

———. *Countering Terror with Trade,* Wash. Post (Sept. 25, 2001).

———. *Bringing Down the Barriers: Robert Zoellick Says the US Is Prepared to Tackle Its Own Trade-Distorting Policies on Agriculture If Others Agree to Do the Same,* Fin'l Times (July 26, 2002).

PUBLIC DOCUMENTS

Anti-Terrorism Policy Review. Hearings before the Senate Comm. on the Judiciary (Dec. 6, 2001).

Bolton Nomination. Hearing before the Senate Comm. on Foreign Relations (March 29, 2001).

Bush, President George, *Disclosures to the Congress* (Oct. 5, 2001).

EPA's Authority to Impose Mandatory Controls to Address Global Climate Change under the Clean Air Act (Aug. 28, 2003). www.epa.gov/oar.

Equal Protection of the Law for Faith-Based and Community Organizations. Executive Order 13279, 67 Fed. Reg. 77141 (Dec. 12, 2002).

General Accounting Office. *Process Used to Develop the National Energy Policy* 1 (Aug. 25, 2003).

Gun Control. Hearing before the Subcomm. on Constitution, Federalism and Property Rights of the Senate Comm. on the Judiciary (Sept. 23, 1998) (prepared remarks of Chairman John Ashcroft).

House Permanent Select Comm. on Intelligence & Senate Select Comm. on Intelligence, *Report of the Joint Inquiry into the Terrorist Attacks of September 11, 2001* (drafted Dec. 2002; declassified and released 2003).

Partial-Birth Abortion Ban Act of 2002. H. Rept. No. 107-604. 107th Cong., 2d Sess. (2002).

Privacy in the Digital Age: Encryption and Mandatory Access. Hearing before the Subcomm. on Constitution, Federalism and Property Rights of the Senate Comm. on the Judiciary (March 17, 1998).

Roe v. Wade: *Has It Stood the Test of Time?* Hearing before the Subcomm. on Constitution, Federalism and Property Rights of the Senate Comm. on the Judiciary (Jan. 21, 1998) (prepared remarks of Chairman John Ashcroft).

Selecting the Next United Nations Secretary General. Hearing before the Subcomm. on International Organizations and Human Rights of the House Comm. on International Relations (Sept. 24, 1996).

Standards for Privacy of Individually Identifiable Health Information, 65 Fed. Reg. 82462 (Dec. 28, 2000).

Tiefer, Charles. *Overcoming Executive Privilege at the Justice Department.* In *The History of Congressional Access to Deliberative Justice Department Documents.* Hearings before the House Committee on Government Reform, 107th Cong., 2d Sess. (Feb. 6, 2002).

Tiefer, Charles. *The Attorney General's Withholding of Documents from the Judiciary Committee in Department of Justice Authorization for Appropriations, Fiscal Year 1992.* Hearings before the House Comm. on the Judiciary. 102nd Cong., 1st Sess. (July 11, 1991).

U.S. Peacekeeping Endeavors. Hearings before the House Comm. on International Relations (April 9, 1997).

TABLE OF CASES

U.S. Supreme Court Cases

Adarand Constructors, Inc. v. Pena, 515 U.S. 200 (1995).

Boy Scouts of America v. Dale, 530 U.S. 640 (2000).

Board of Trustees of University of Alabama v. Garrett, 531 U.S. 356 (2001).

Brown v. Legal Foundation of Washington, 123 S. Ct. 1406 (2003).

Dept. of Commerce v. U.S. House of Representatives, 525 U.S. 316 (1999).

Dickerson v. United States, 530 U.S. 428 (2000).

Food and Drug Admin. v. Brown & Williamson Tobacco Co., 529 U.S. 120 (2000).

Grutter v. Bollinger, 123 S. Ct. 2325 (2003).

Lawrence v. Texas, 123 S. Ct. 2472 (2003).

Morrison v. Olson, 487 U.S. 654 (1988).

Printz v. United States, 518 U.S. 1003 (1996).

State Farm Mut. Auto. Ins. Co. v. Campbell, 2003 WL 1791206 (2003).

Tahoe-Sierra Preservation Council, Inc. v. Tahoe Regional Planning Agency, 535 U.S. 301 (2002).

United States v. Lopez, 514 U.S. 549 (1995).

United States v. Morrison, 529 U.S. 598 (2000).

Zelman v. Simmons-Harris, 536 U.S. 639 (2002).

U.S. Courts of Appeal Cases

Bragg v. West Virginia Coal Association, 248 F.3d 275 (4th Cir. 2001).
In re: Sealed Case, 310 F.3d 7817 (Foreign Int. Surv. Ct. Rev. 2002).
National Rifle Association v. Reno, 216 F.2d 122 (D.C. Cir. 2000).
United States v. Emerson, 270 F.3d 203 (5th Cir. 2001).

U.S. District Court Cases

In re: All Matters Submitted to the Foreign Intelligence Surveillance Court, 18 F. Supp. 2d 611 (Foreign Intel. Surv. Ct. 2002).
Old Town Neighborhood Ass'n v. Kauffman, 2002 WL 31741477 (S.D. Ind. Nov. 15, 2002).
State of Oregon v. Ashcroft, 192 F. Supp. 2d 1077 (D. Or. 2002).
Walker v. Cheney, 230 F. Supp. 2d 51 (D.D.C. 2002).
Wilderness Society v. Rey, 180 F. Supp. 2d 1141 (D. Mont. 2002).
Women's Medical Profession Corp. v. Taft, 162 F. Supp. 2d 929 (S.D. Ohio 2001).
Women's Medical Professional Corp. v. Baird, 2003 Lexis 15623 (S.D. Ohio Aug. 15, 2003).

Miscellaneous Case

Wyoming Outdoor Council v. U.S. Forest Service, 157 IBLA 259 (2002).

Index

Compositor: Michael Bass Associates
Indexer: Herr's Indexing Service
Text: 10/13 Aldus Roman
Display: Franklin Gothic
Printer and binder: Maple-Vail Book Manufacturing Group